ISBN 978-1-333-66671-2
PIBN 10533093

This book is a reproduction of an important historical work. Forgotten Books uses
state-of-the-art technology to digitally reconstruct the work, preserving the original format
whilst repairing imperfections present in the aged copy. In rare cases, an imperfection in
the original, such as a blemish or missing page, may be replicated in our edition. We do,
however, repair the vast majority of imperfections successfully; any imperfections that
remain are intentionally left to preserve the state of such historical works.

1 MONTH OF
FREE
READING

at

www.ForgottenBooks.com

By purchasing this book you are
eligible for one month membership to
ForgottenBooks.com, giving you
unlimited access to our entire
collection of over 1,000,000 titles via
our web site and mobile apps.

To claim your free month visit:

www.forgottenbooks.com/free533093

English
Français
Deutsche
Italiano
Español
Português

www.forgottenbooks.com

Mythology Photography **Fiction**
Fishing Christianity **Art** Cooking
Essays Buddhism Freemasonry
Medicine **Biology** Music **Ancient
Egypt** Evolution Carpentry Physics
Dance Geology **Mathematics** Fitness
Shakespeare **Folklore** Yoga Marketing
Confidence Immortality Biographies
Poetry **Psychology** Witchcraft
Electronics Chemistry History **Law**
Accounting **Philosophy** Anthropology
Alchemy Drama Quantum Mechanics
Atheism Sexual Health **Ancient History**
Entrepreneurship Languages Sport
Paleontology Needlework Islam
Metaphysics Investment Archaeology
Parenting Statistics Criminology
Motivational

EDWARD SMALL
AND
HIS DESCENDANTS

VOLUME II.

FROM 1647 UNTIL 1659
THIS GROUND WAS OCCUPIED
BY THE
WAREHOUSE AND RESIDENCE OF

— ISAAC ALLERTON —

A PASSENGER ON THE SHIP MAYFLOWER
IN 1620
ASSISTANT GOVERNOR OF PLYMOUTH COLONY
THE FATHER OF NEW ENGLAND COMMERCE
ONE OF THE EIGHT MEN OF NEW NETHERLANDS
IN 1643
FOR TWENTY YEARS A LEADING MERCHANT
OF NEW AMSTERDAM

IN GRATEFUL MEMORY OF THE
MAYFLOWER PILGRIMS
WHO FIRST ESTABLISHED
CIVIL AND RELIGIOUS LIBERTY
IN OUR LAND
THIS TABLET IS ERECTED BY
THE SOCIETY OF MAYFLOWER
DESCENDANTS IN THE
STATE OF NEW YORK

erected to the memory of Isaac Allerton, by the Society of Mayflower Descendants n the State of New York, at No. 8 Peck Slip, New York City, June 1, 1904.

DESCENDANTS OF EDWARD SMALL
OF NEW ENGLAND
AND THE ALLIED FAMILIES
WITH TRACINGS OF ENGLISH
ANCESTRY ❧ ❧ ❧ BY LORA
ALTINE WOODBURY UNDERHILL

CAMBRIDGE

Privately Printed at The Riverside Press

1910

CONTENTS

VOL. II

ILLUSTRATIONS

VOL. II

EDWARD[6] SMALL, SR.

MARRIED

SARAH[5] MITCHELL

(Continued)

THE CUSHMAN FAMILY

ROBERT[1] CUSHMAN

It is greatly to be regretted that so little is known of the youth or parentage of one who bore such an active part in the early struggles of the Pilgrims as Robert Cushman. Beyond the statement in the Leyden records that he was from Canterbury, England, nothing has been learned. His name first appeared on the Leyden registers November 4, 1611, when "Robert Cushman, from Canterbury, a wool-comber," purchased from Cornelis Ghysberts van Groenendael a house on the west side of the *Nonnensteeg*, a short street continuing the *Kloksteeg* beyond the *Rapenburg* southerly to the *Achtergracht* (Back Street). "Although in a good neighborhood, being close to the university, it must have been quite small, for its price was but eighty gilders down, with annual payments thereafter, bringing up the whole sum to about one hundred and eighty gilders." The next year, April 19, Cushman bought another house near by in a place on the south side of the *Nonnensteeg*, from van Groenendael, for seven hundred and eighty gilders, Richard Masterson becoming surety for him. The terms were two hundred gilders down, one hundred to be paid in a year, and the balance later; with five gilders annually as ground-rent to the city.* This was in the heart of the city, and adjacent to the house of William Bradford on the *Achtergracht*, upon which house Bradford raised money in 1617.

About this time John Robinson, their pastor, took possession of the large house fronting on the *Kloksteeg*, which he had purchased, subject to a year's lease, on May 5, 1611. The

---

* Dexter's *England and Holland of the Pilgrims*, 1905: 534, 540, 541.

price paid for the house and lot of land, including a garden, was "8000 gilders — $3200, equal in modern money to about $16,000." This estate was situated on the south side of the *Pieterskerkhof;* and there, "within the shadow of the *Pieterskerk* [St. Peter's], or within five minutes walk of that spot," lived at least one hundred and fifty of Robinson's company.

The wife of Robert Cushman was Sarah ——, whom he married as early as 1606. She was the mother of several children, the eldest probably being Thomas[2], b. 1607. While living on the *Nonnensteeg,* they buried a child in St. Peter's, on March 11, 1616. In October, Cushman was called upon to part with two more of his stricken family : his wife, Sarah, who was buried on the 11th in St. Peter's, and another child, who, on the 24th, was buried in the same church. Between March and October, he had removed from the *Nonnensteeg* to the *Boisstraat,* where his wife died; and, at the time of the death of the second child on the 24th, he was living on the *Hontmarckt.** These repeated removals certainly suggest an effort to get away from some infection.

On May 19, 1617, Robert Cushman was betrothed, at Leyden, to Mary Singleton, widow of Thomas Singleton, from Sandwich, County Kent, England; with John Keble and Catherine Carver (wife of John Carver, afterward the first Governor of Plymouth), as witnesses. They were married on June 5. John Keble, "his friend," also was a woolcomber, and from Canterbury, England. In the Leyden records, Cushman's name appeared variously — *Coetsman, Kousman, Koutzman,* etc.; while that of his wife was written *Chingleton.* Although a resident so many years, he was not admitted to citizenship. September 19, 1619, Robert Cushman sold to John de Later the first house which he had purchased on the *Nonnensteeg* for the price paid for it — one hundred and eighty gilders.†

---

* Dexter's *England and Holland of the Pilgrims,* 1905 : 559, 611.

† Dexter's *England and Holland of the Pilgrims,* 1905 : 564-565, 611, 633, 622, 577.

When it became evident to the Pilgrims that Holland did not, and could not, afford the sort of refuge and opportunity they desired; or, in the words of Winslow, "how like wee were to lose our Language, and our name of English; how little good wee did; . . . how unable there to give such education to our children, as wee ourselves had received;" * they resolved to emigrate rather than succumb to the inevitable results of a long sojourn in that place. They feared absorption into the Dutch nation; and they still clung to the hope of "propagating & advancing y⁰ gospell of y⁰ kingdom of Christ" according to their own belief, and in a way that was impossible in Holland.

Unaided they could accomplish nothing. They had little money and less influence. Their ties to the mother country were greatly weakened. Yet they decided to send over to England two of their most active and reliable men, "Mr. Robert Cushman and Deacon John Carver," with instructions to make an application to the Virginia Company, which had been formed in England under the royal sanction, for liberty to settle within the territory of that company in North America, and "to live as a distincte body by them selves, under y⁰ generall Government of Virginia." This was in September, 1617; and their agents returned to Leyden without accomplishing anything. In December, they were again sent over "to end with y⁰ Virginia Company as well as they could;" † but as that company could not promise them religious freedom, and they had no confidence in the honesty or toleration of the king, they hesitated.

For two years, 1618 and 1619, Cushman, Carver, and William Brewster, or two of them, were active at London; but the King's tyrannical interference had so confused the affairs of the Virginia Company that it was difficult to conclude anything. At length, on June 9, 1619, a patent

---

* Winslow's *Hypocrisie unmasked*, London, 1646 : 88–89.
† Bradford's *History of Plimoth Plantation*, 1898 : 37, 39.

was granted to them, under the Virginia Company's seal, and "connived at" by the King. By the advice of friends, as they were non-residents, the patent was taken out in the name of John Wincob (or Wencop), a "religious gentleman then belonging to yᵉ Countess of Lincoln," who intended to go with them. "But God so disposed as he never went, nor they ever made use of this patente, which had cost them so much labour and charge." *

Then they began to "look other ways" to accomplish their object. The Dutch traders to Manhattan (New York), where there was as yet no settlement, offered to transport the entire congregation to their trading-post, providing cattle and supplies, and furnishing protection as long as needed; but leaving them to manage their own internal affairs. While this proposition was still under consideration, Thomas Weston, a merchant of London, suggested terms for their transmigration to the New World. He formed a company, about seventy in number, called the Merchant Adventurers, "which raised the stocke to begin and supply this Plantation." Captain John Smith described them in 1624, as "some Gentlemen, some Merchants, some handy-crafts men, some aduenturing great summes, some small, as their estates and affection serued. The generall stocke already imploied is about 7000. P. by reason of which charge and many crosses, many of [them] would aduenture no more. . . . They dwell most about *London*, they are not a corporation, but knit together by voluntary combination in a society without constraint or penalty, aiming to doe good & to plant religion." †

"The Wincob patent had been superseded, on February 12, 1620, by one running to John Pierce, one of the Adventurers, which conveyed, with self-governing powers, a tract of land to be selected by the planters near the mouth of the

---

* Bradford's *History of Plimoth Plantation*, 1898 : 51–52.
† Smith's *Generall Historie of Virginia, New England, and the Summer Isles*, 1584–1626; London, 1627 : 247.

Hudson. So little did the body of Adventurers know of the Pilgrims that they termed them ' Mr. Pierce's Company.' " *
About this time they heard, through Mr. Weston and others, of the projected settlement of the more northerly part of the country derived from the Virginia patent, to be called by another name, NEW ENGLAND, "unto which Mʳ. Weston, and yᵉ cheefe of them, begane to incline it was best for them to goe . . . chiefly for yᵉ hope of present profite to be made by yᵉ fishing." †

The contract between the Adventurers and those who were to emigrate consisted of ten articles, "which were drawne & agreed unto, and were showne unto him [Weston] and approved by him," ‡ in Leyden. Brewster, who had been active in this matter, remained in Leyden ; while Cushman was sent to London, and Carver to Southampton, to prepare for the voyage. Christopher Martin, who later sailed on the *Mayflower,* was " joined with them."

The unavoidable delays and disappointments of large undertakings occurred. In June, there was complaint that Mr. Weston was negligent in the matter of providing shipping. However, the *Speedwell* was finally purchased in Holland, and the *Mayflower* hired at London by Cushman, who sent her round to Southampton, there to meet the other ship.

Special stress has been laid on the account of these preparations for the voyage because of the adverse criticism of Cushman's share in them. Less than a month before the sailing of the ships, Mr. Weston and his associates insisted that some of the conditions that were first agreed on at Leyden should be altered ; "to which yᵉ 2. agents sent from Leyden (or at least one of them who is most charged with it) did consente ; seeing els yᵗ all was like to be dashte,

---

* Goodwin's *Pilgrim Republic,* 1888 : 44.
† Bradford's *History of Plimoth·Plantation,* 1898 : 55.
‡ Bradford's *History of Plimoth Plantation,* 1898 : 54.

& yᵉ opportunitie lost." The principal difference between
these and former conditions, continues Bradford, "stood in
those 2. points; that yᵉ houses, & lands improved, espetialy
gardens & home lotts should remaine undevided wholy to
yᵉ planters at yᵉ 7. years end. 2ˡʸ, yᵗ they should have had
2. days in a weeke for their owne private imploymente, for
yᵉ more comforte of them selves and their families, espetialy such as had families." These changes were embodied
chiefly in the fifth and ninth articles.* Weston's altera-
tions, accepted by Cushman, had injured their prospects
gravely, said Fuller, Bradford, Allerton, Winslow, and some
others; while "Cushman declared that but for àgreement
to them he could not have drawn a penny from the Adventurers," and he could not wait to hear from Leyden. On
the other side it was alleged that not one quarter of the
Adventurers desired the changes.

About this time the pastor, John Robinson, wrote to Carver that but two mistakes had been made: "yᵉ one, that we
imployed Robart Cushman, who is known (though a good
man, & of spetiall abilities in his kind, yet) most unfitt to
deale for other men, by reason of his singularitie, and too
great indifferancie for any conditions, and for (to speak
truly) that we have had nothing from him but termes and
presumptions. The other, yᵗ we have so much relyed, by
implicite faith as it were, upon generalities, without seeing
yᵉ perticuler course & means for so waghtie an affaire set
down unto us." †

These dissensions led to their telling Weston at Southampton that the original agreement, as made in Leyden,
must stand, or they would not sign it. Upon this Weston
left the Pilgrims in anger, saying that they must "looke to
stand upon their owne leggs." He refused to pay the port
charges of £100; and the poor emigrants were forced to

---

* Bradford's *History of Plimoth Plantation*, 1898 : 56, 75.
† Bradford's *History of Plimoth Plantation*, 1898 : 60.

sell some eighty firkins of butter to raise the £60 required to "clear the port," and were obliged to dispense with many things still lacking. In truth, their entire outfit was inadequate. In a letter to Carver, dated June 10, Cushman wrote: " We have reckoned, it would seeme, without our host ; and, counting upon a 150. persons, ther cannot be founde above 1200 ᶫⁱ & odd moneys of all yᵉ venturs you can reckone, besids some cloath, stockings, & shoes, which are not counted ; so we shall come shorte at leaste 3. or 400 ᶫⁱ . . . You fear we have begune to build & shall not be able to make an end ; indeed, our courses were never established by counsell, we may therfore justly fear their standing. . . . Thinke yᵉ best of all, and bear with patience what is wanting, and yᵉ Lord guid us all.

Your loving friend,
ROBART CUSHMAN." *

LONDON, June 10.
Anᵒⁱ 1620.

When the *Speedwell* reached Southampton, the passengers were divided, ninety to the *Mayflower* and thirty to the *Speedwell.* John Carver was assigned to the *Mayflower*, as " governor," while Christopher Martin and Robert Cushman were respectively "governor " and "assistant" on the *Speedwell,* says Goodwin ; † but Bradford states that Martin "was governour in yᵉ biger ship, & Mʳ. Cushman assistante," ‡ which seems more probable.

After various distresses had caused them to put back twice, first to Dartmouth and then to Plymouth, the *Speedwell* having been judged unfit to proceed, " Mʳ. Cushman & his familie, whose hart & courage was gone from them before," desired to be among those left behind. It appears to have been a voluntary movement on his part, judging from

---

* Bradford's *History of Plimoth Plantation,* 1898 : 69–71.
† Goodwin's *Pilgrim Republic,* 1888 : 51.
‡ Bradford's *History of Plimoth Plantation,* 1898 : 87.

the " passionate letter he write to a friend in London from Dartmouth, whilst yᵉ ship lay ther a mending." Owing to its length, a few extracts must suffice : —

" To his loving friend Ed: S. [Edward Southworth] at Henige House in yᵉ Duks Place, these, etc.

DARTMOUTH, Aug. 17.

" Loving friend, my most kind remembrance to you & your wife, with loving E. M. &c. whom in this world I never looke to see againe. For besids yᵉ eminente dangers of this viage, which are no less than deadly, an infirmitie of body hath ceased [seized] me, which will not in all licᵉlyhoode leave me till death. What to call it I know not, but it is a bundle of lead, as it were, crushing my harte more & more these 14. days, as that allthough I doe yᵉ acctions of a liveing man, yet I am but as dead ; but yᵉ will of God be done. Our pinass will not cease leaking, els I thinke we had been halfe way at Virginia. . . . Our victualls will be halfe eaten up, I thinke, before we goe from the coaste of England, and if our viage last longe, we shall not have a months victialls when we come in yᵉ countrie. Neare 700 ˡⁱ hath bene bestowed at Hampton, upon what I know not. Mʳ Martin saith he neither can nor will give any accounte of it. . . . As for Mʳ Weston, excepte grace doe greatly swaye with him, he will hate us ten times more than he ever loved us, for not confirming yᵉ conditions. . . . I am sure as they were resolved not to seale those conditions, I was not so resolute at Hampton to have left yᶜ whole bussiness, excepte they would seale them, & better yᵉ vioage to have bene broken of [off] then, then to have brought such misirie to our selves, dishonour to God, & detrimente to our loving freinds, as now it is like to doe. 4. or 5. of yᵉ cheefe of them which came from Leyden, came resolved never to goe on those conditions. And Mʳ Martine, he said he never received no money on those conditions, he was not beholden to yᵉ marchants for a pine [penny] they were bloudsuckers, & I know not what. Simple man, he indeed never made any conditions wᵗʰ the marchants, nor ever spake with them. . . . Friend, if ever we make a plantation, God works a mirakle ; especially considering how scante we shall be of victualls; and most of all ununited amongst our selves,

& devoyd of good tutors & regimente. . . . If I should write to you of all things which promiscuously forerune our ruine, I should over charge my weake head and greeve your tender hart ; only this, I pray you prepare for evill tidings of us every day. But pray for us instantly, it may be y⁰ Lord will be yet entreated one way or other to make for us. I see not in reason how we shall escape even y⁰ gasping of hunger starved persons ; but God can doe much, & his will be done. . . . The Lord give us that true comforte which none can take from us. I had a desire to make a breefe relation of our estate to some freind. I doubte not but your wisdome will teach you seasonably to utter things as here after you shall be called to it. That which I have writen is treue, & many things more which I have forborne. I write it as upon my life, and last confession in England. What is of use to be spoken of presently, you may speake of it, and what is fitt to conceile, conceall. Pass by my weake maner, for my head is weake, & my body feeble, y⁰ Lord make me strong in him, & keepe both you & yours.

Your loving freind

Robart Cushman.

Dartmouth, Aug. 17, 1620."

Below the copy of this letter in his History, Bradford adds : "These being his conceptions & fears at Dartmouth, they must needs be much stronger now at Plimoth." He also says of the letter : " the which, besids y⁰ expressions of his owne fears, it shows much of y⁰ providence of God working for their good beyonde man's expectation, & other things concerning their condition in these streats. . . . And though it discover some infirmities in him, . . . yet after this he continued to be a spetiall instrumente for their good, and to doe y⁰ offices of a loving freind & faithfull brother unto them, and pertaker of much comforte with them."[*]

When it was decided to reduce the expedition to one shipload, the twenty or more passengers who were left behind, including Robert Cushman and his family, returned

---

[*] Bradford's *History of Plimoth Plantation*, 1898 : 86–90.

to London. How many persons constituted this "familie"
is unknown; his wife probably was with him, and the son
Thomas who afterward came over, and there may have been
younger children by this second wife; they, however, remained in England. Cushman endeavored to placate the
wrath of Weston and his associates, and to bring them to
the point of further assisting the Plantation in New England. He must have succeeded in a measure, since the
Adventurers sent him over in the *Fortune*, a year later, to
examine affairs and return to them with a report; and with
him forwarded some thirty-five new colonists. Thomas
Cushman, then a lad of fourteen years, sailed with them;
on his father's return, the son was left at Plymouth in the
care of William Bradford.

On November 10, 1621, just one year from the day the
Mayflower sighted the hills of Cape Cod, the *Fortune* reached
the shores of New Plymouth; * her unexpected arrival occa-
sioned great rejoicing. Robert Cushman had come primarily
to persuade the Planters to accept the "two articles" which
they had rejected at Southampton. They were in such
straits that they chose to do so rather than to allow the
Adventurers to abandon the enterprise. Yet it is interest-
ing to know that Cushman labored long and earnestly with
them before the matter was satisfactorily concluded. He
preached a sermon, in the "common-house," where religious
services were held, on Sunday, December 9, 1621, on "The
Sin and Danger of Self-love," taking for his text 1 Cor. x:
24: "Let no man seek his own, but every man another's
wealth." † It is said to have been "in truth rather a dull

---

* "She came yͤ 9. to yͤ Cap [Cape Cod]." (Bradford's *History of Plimoth
Plantation*, 1898 : 127.)

† On his return to England, this discourse, often alluded to as "the first
sermon in New England," was printed; and it has appeared since in several
editions. Goodwin says that the "so-called sermon is mainly the censorious
plea of an attorney for the Adventurers. If any reply was made, Cushman
naturally omitted to print it."

OLD FORT AND CHURCH OF PLYMOUTH, 1622.

affai
theii
cons

A
1.
that
ten

2
witl
hav
sha

the
(e)
co
be
or
cc

fi
y
a

affair" of more than two hours' duration; but it resulted in their signing the ten articles, as amended by Weston and consented to by Cushman in the summer of 1620.

ARTICLES OF AGREEMENT

An°: 1620. July 1.

1. The adventurers & planters doe agree, that every person that goeth being aged 16. years & upward, be rated at 10 ^{li}., and ten pounds to be accounted a single share.

2. That he that goeth in person, and furnisheth him selfe out with 10 ^{li}. either in money or other provissions, be accounted as haveing 20 ^{li}. in stock, and in ye divission shall receive a double share.

3. The persons transported & ye adventurers shall continue their joynt stock & partnership togeather, ye space of 7. years, (excepte some unexpected impedimente doe cause ye whole company to agree otherwise,) during which time, all profits & benifits that are gott by trade, traffick, trucking, working, fishing, or any other means of any person or persons,-remaine still in ye comone stock untill ye division.

4. That at their coming ther, they chose out such a number of fitt persons, as may furnish their ships and boats for fishing upon ye sea; imploying the rest in their severall faculties upon ye land; as building houses, tilling, and planting ye ground, & makeing shuch comodities as shall be most usefull for ye collonie.

5. That at ye end of ye 7. years, ye capitall & profits, viz. the houses, lands, goods and chatles, be equally divided betwixte ye adventurers, and planters; wch done, every man shall be free from other of them of any debt or detrimente concerning this adventure.

6. Whosoever cometh to ye colonie herafter, or putteth any into ye stock, shall at the ende of ye 7 years be alowed proportionably to ye time of his so doing.

7. He that shall carie his wife & children, or servants, shall be alowed for everie person now aged 16. years & upward, a single share in ye devision, or if he provid them necessaries, a duble share, or if they be between 10. year old and 16., then 2. of them to be reconed for a person, both in trasportation and devision.

8. That such children as now goe, & are under ye age of ten

years, have noe other shar in yᵉ devision, but 50. acers of unma-
nured land.

9. That such persons as die before yᵉ 7. years be expired, their
executors to have their parte or sharr at yᵉ devision, proportionably to yᵉ time of their life in yᵉ collonie.

10. That all such persons as are of this collonie, are to have
their meate, drink, apparell, and all provissions out of yᵉ comͦon
stock & goods of yᵉ said collonie.*

The *Fortune* soon was loaded with a valuable cargo of
beaver-skins, clapboards and other prepared lumber, and the
"profitable sassafras;" the total value being about £500.
The ship had brought a letter from Weston, severely cen-
suring the colonists for not sending a cargo by the *Mayflower* on her return the previous spring. He also promised
that he would "never quit the business, though all the other
Adventurers should," if they would give the *Fortune* a good
lading, and consent to the disputed articles. "Strange to
say, without even waiting for a reply to his letter or for the
return of the *Fortune*, he withdrew from the enterprise, the
first and only one to leave it thus early." †

Robert Cushman returned, as he intended, on the *Fortune*,
which sailed on December 23, for England. They had spent
four months on the passage westward, owing to baffling
winds and other causes; but the voyage back was without
incident until they drew near the English coast, when their
little ship of only fifty-five tons was captured by a French
craft and carried into Isle Dieu. Her cargo, of which they
were justly proud, and which they felt would be a surprise
to their English partners, was kept by their captors; but
after fourteen days the ship and her company were released.
Cushman preserved his papers, among which were the signed
agreement, and valuable letters from Bradford, Winslow,
and William Hilton; also Bradford's and Winslow's Jour-

---

* Bradford's *History of Plimoth Plantation*, 1898 : 56–58.
† Goodwin's *Pilgrim Republic*, 1888 : 194, 195.

nals, which were published as *Mourt's Relation*, in 1622, at London.

Cushman still remained the Planters' agent in England; and by the *Anne*, in 1623, sent another letter saying that he was "right sorie yᵗ no supplie hath been made to you all this while [the *Mayflower* had taken over the only supply of food-stuffs], . . . Naitheir indeed have we now sent you many things, which we should & would, for want of money." January 24, 1623–24, he wrote again, in a little more hopeful vein, informing them that "We have now sent you, we hope, men & means, to setle these 3. things, viz. fishing, salt making, and boat making; if you can bring them to pass to some perfection, your wants may be supplyed. . . . I am sorie we have not sent you more and other things, but in truth we have rune into so much charge, to victaile yᵉ ship, provide salte & other fishing implements, &c. as we could not provide other comfortable things, as buter, suger, &c. I hope the returne of this ship, and the James, will put us in cash againe." *

In this letter, dated " Jan: 24, 1623[-24]," Cushman wrote: " We have tooke a patente for Cap Anne, etc," and some of the planters at Plymouth were sent there soon after, to build fishing stages; but, the next year (1625), "some of Lyfords & Oldoms [Oldham's] freinds, and their adherents, set out a shipe on fishing, on their owne accounte, and getting yᵉ starte of yᵉ ships that came to the plantation, they tooke away their stage, & other necessary provisions that they had made for fishing at Cap-Anne yᵉ year before, at their great charge, and would not restore yᵉ same, excepte they would fight for it." † The Governor at Plymouth sent some of the planters to rebuild the stages; but the fishing proved of little value to them, "so as, after this year, they never looked more after them."

---

* Bradford's *History of Plimoth Plantation*, 1898 : 172, 191–192.
† Bradford's *History of Plimoth Plantation*, 1898 : 192, 202, 237.

Captain John Smith said of this period (1624) : "There hath beene a fishing this yeere vpon the Coast about 50. English ships : and by Cape Anne, there is a Plantation a beginning by the Dorchester men, which they hold of those of *New-Plimoth,* who also by them haue set vp a fishing worke." He explains, too, in detail, the charge of setting forth a ship of 100 tons for fishing at the Plantation, which amounted to £420 : 11 : 0.[*]

In the summer of 1625, Captain Standish went to England in the *Little James.* Besides arranging with James Sherley for more satisfactory charges, he was to ask the Council for New England to assist in buying off the Adventurers ; but, owing to the prevalence of the plague, and consequent disorders in the business world, little could be done. He was commissioned to hire a considerable sum of money ; yet he obtained only £150, at fifty per cent interest, to pay his own expenses and procure goods for home. It was at this time that Bradford wrote Cushman to aid Standish in purchasing the return cargo of trading-goods, "for therein he hath the least skill."

The joy at Standish's safe return was quickly followed by sorrow at the news he brought. Many of their friends had suffered losses which prevented them "from doing any further help, and some dead of yᵉ plague." Their pastor at Leyden, John Robinson, had died on the " 1 of March" of that year (1625), and was buried on March 4, in the Pieterskerk. "He further brought them notice of yᵉ death of their anciente freind, Mʳ Cush-man, whom yᵉ Lord tooke allso this year, & aboute this time, who was as their right hand with their freinds yᵉ adventurers, and for diverce years had done & agitated all their business with them to ther great advantage." It was "allso his owne purposs this year to come over, and spend his days" at New Plymouth.[†]

---

[*] Smith's *Generall Historie of Virginia, New England, and the Summer Isles,* 1584–1626; London, 1627 : 247, 245.

[†] Bradford's *History of Plimoth Plantation,* 1898 : 247, 249.

At their first division or "Falles of their grounds which came first ouer in the *May-Floure* according as thier lotes were cast. 1623," the *first* lot, consisting of one acre, lying "on the South side of the brooke to the baywards," had been assigned by the Planters to "Robart Cochman." * As he did not continue on the *Mayflower*, and consequently was not entitled to be considered one of the "First Comers," this grant was a delicate recognition of his services, and one which he had long been planning to enjoy.

Robert Cushman died in England, at the early age of about forty-five years. The exact date of his death is not known. His last letter was written "From London, December 22, A. D. 1624," and he died before Pastor Robinson; we therefore may conclude that his death occurred in January or February, 1625. The last paragraph of this letter is notable in several respects : —

"I hope the failings of your friends here, will make you the more friendly one to another, that so all our hopes may not be dashed. Labour to settle things, both in your civil, and religious courses, as firm, and as full as you can. Lastly, I must intreat you still, to have a care of my son as of your own ; and I shall rest bound unto you, I pray you let him sometime practice writing. I hope the next ships to come to you ; in the mean space and ever, the Lord be all your direction and turn all our crosses and troubles to his own glory, and our comforts, and give you to walk so wisely, and holily, as none may justly say, but they have always found you honestly minded, though never so poor. Salute our friends, and supply, I pray you, what is failing in my letters." †

It is easy to understand, at this distance of time, some of the difficulties with which Cushman had to contend. The Pilgrims ‡ at Leyden were of a high order, intellectual and

---

* *Plymouth Colony Deeds*, vol. 1 : 4. Vide also Francis [1] Cooke.

† *Massachusetts Historical Society Collections*, First Series, vol. 3 : 35.

‡ The term "Pilgrims" is applied properly only to the Plymouth Colonists. It originated with Bradford, who wrote of their departure from Leyden: "So they lefte y[t] goodly & pleasante citie, which had been ther resting place near

somewhat visionary. Their principal reason for seeking a new home was to enjoy " Freedom to worship God," and to establish a church of their own belief. But when it came to the practical part of the business, they were all at sea, — " ununited," Cushman called it, — and his continued reiteration of "terms" and "conditions" only irritated them. That they actually should sail for the New World without adequate provision, and deliberately cut off all hope of supplies from their friends, the Merchant Adventurers, was the height of imprudence, to say the least. Cushman appreciated their position fully, and his heart sank within him. He could see nothing in the venture but despair and death. It was most fortunate for them that he remained in England ; for Bradford himself, who at first had little patience with Cushman, admitted later that there was a Providence in it.

The Patent, or Charter, of the territory about Cape Anne, negotiated through the agency of Robert Cushman and Edward Winslow (the latter having been sent over more directly to represent the Plymouth Colony), is further evidence of the industry and ability of Cushman. This charter, dated January 1, 1623, granted by Edward, Lord Sheffield, as a representative of the Council for New England, to " Robert Cushman and Edward Winslowe for themselves, and theire Associats and Planters at Plymouth in New England in America," conveyed to them " a certaine Tract of Ground . . . in a knowne place there comonly called Cape Anne, Together with the free vse and benefitt as well of the Bay comonly called the Bay of Cape Anne, as also of the Islands within the said Bay And free liberty, to ffish, fowle, hawke, and hunt, truck, and trade in the Lands therabout, and in all other places in New England aforesaid, . . . Together also with ffyve hundred Acres of free Land adiojning to the

12. years ; but they knew they were pilgrimes [Heb. xi : 13] & looked not much on those things, but lift up their eyes to yᵉ heavens, their dearest cuntrie, and quieted their spirits." (Bradford's *History of Plimoth Plantation*, 1898 : 72.)

said Bay to be ymployed for publig vses, as for the building of a Towne, Scholes, Churches, Hospitals, and for the mayntenance of such Ministers, Officers, and Magistrats, as by the said vndertakers, and theire Associats are there already appointed, or which hereafter shall (with theire good liking reside, and inhabitt there And also Thirty Acres of Land, over and beside the ffyve hundred Acres before mencõned, To be allotted, and appointed for every perticuler person, young, or old (being the Associats, or servants of the said vndertakers or their successoᵣₛ that shall come, and dwell at the aforesaid Cape Anne within Seaven yeares next after the Date hereof, which Thirty Acres of Lande soe appointed to every person, as aforesaid, shall be taken as the same doth lye together vpon the said Bay in one entire place, and not stragling in dyvers, or remote parcells not exceeding an English Mile, and a halfe in length on the Waters side of the said Bay."

The consideration for this grant was an annual payment to "Lord Sheffeild, his heires, successoᵣₛ, Rent gatherer, or assignes, for every Thirty Acres . . . Twelve Pence of lawfull English money At the ffeast of St. Michaell. . . . The first payment thereof To begynne ymmediately" after the expiration of "seaven yeares next after the date hereof." *

Throughout this document the name of Cushman precedes that of Winslow, an undoubted proof of his conventional position. To Robert Cushman, then, largely belongs the credit of having procured for the Plymouth Colony a charter, which also embraced the first permanent settlement of the Massachusetts Colony at Cape Anne.† "The two first

---

* Thornton's *Landing at Cape Anne*, 1854 : 31–35.

† It is not generally known that the *Mayflower*, besides carrying the Pilgrims safely to their destination, was one of the five vessels which, in 1629, conveyed Higginson's company to Salem ; and also was one of the fleet which brought over, in 1630, Governor Winthrop and his Colony to Massachusetts Bay. (Winthrop's *History of New England*, 1630–49, Savage's Edition, 1853 : I, 2, 25, 30.)

settlements in Massachusetts were, therefore, to a considerable extent the result of his zeal and perseverance in the Puritan cause." We may reasonably conclude also that "he was one of the first movers and main instruments of the Puritan dissent of England, their pilgrimage to Holland, and their final settlement in America." Together with "those from Leyden," he is the acknowledged founder of Congregationalism in the New World.*

ISSUE

I. Thomas², b. 1607, in Leyden. (Vide infra.)
II. A child, buried March 11, 1616, in St. Peter's, Leyden.
III. A child, buried Oct. 24, 1616, in St. Peter's, Leyden.
IV. Sara². Sara² Cushman has been accepted by the best authorities as presumably the daughter of Robert¹ Cushman, of Leyden; † but whether she was the child of his first wife, Sarah, who died October 11, 1616, or of his second wife, Mary, whom he married June 5, 1617, probably never will be determined. Her marriage in Plymouth is thus recorded: "William Hodgekins & Sara Cushman married Nov. 2ᵈ 1636." ‡ The name Hodgekins, after passing through the variations of Hoggkins, Hodgskins, Hoskine, Hoskin, etc., finally settled as Hoskins or Haskins. Sara Hoskins did not long survive the birth of a daughter, on September 16, 1637, and her husband married again, December 21, 1638, in Plymouth, Ann Hynes.§

William Hoskins was of Scituate in 1634, and was made freeman that year. In 1640 and 1646, his name appeared in lists of the townsmen of Plymouth. In 1642, Mr. Holmes, William Hoskins, and Francis Billington, for the use of their families, were assigned "The browne Cowe and Mʳ Holmes to keepe her." "William Hoskins and ffrancis Billington" were appointed, in 1651, to "goodman Winters Teame,"

---

* Dexter's *Story of the Pilgrims*, 1894 : 30–35.
† Savage's *Genealogical Dictionary*, vol. 2 : 439.
‡ *Plymouth Colony Records*, Court Orders, vol. 1 : 45.
§ *Plymouth Colony Records*, Court Orders, vol. 1 : 107.

on work for the town. From 1640 to 1681, Hoskins served repeatedly on juries and on the "Grand Inquest." February 2, 1672, he was chosen, at a town-meeting, "to see that the towns orders were carried out." * August 22, 1681, he was chosen one of the raters, "to make the Rates both for Mʳ Cotton and the Countrey Rate for this yeer."

The first grant of land to William Hoskins from the town of Plymouth, on December 31, 1646, consisted of "6 or 7 acres at the head of James Hurst land or neare his land, and a garden place by the brooke side, or by his house," which was to be laid out for him by Governor Prince and Joshua Pratt. June 13, 1660, he had another grant of two acres of meadow at "Lakenham." Two years later, June 3, 1662, William Hoskins, with Mr. Prince, Mr. Bradford, Mr. Brewster, Major Winslow, George Soule, Francis Cooke, and others (thirty-two, in all), received a share of land granted for their "first borne children of this goûment." † Hoskins, himself, did not arrive in one of the early ships; he did not settle in Plymouth until after 1634; yet he was gratuitously made the recipient of land apportioned to the fathers of the "first borne children." This surely indicates that it was on account of Sara, his first wife, and that she was daughter to Robert[1] Cushman.

William Hoskins appears to have suffered even more severely than most of his neighbors from the devastation of King Philip's war, since on March 2, 1679–80, the Plymouth Colony Court voted: " The Court haue ordered four pound vnto Wilłam Hoskins, to be payed to him by the Treasurer, in regard of his low condition, haueing lost all hee had in the late warr, and beinge growne old and vnable to labour." ‡ He probably died poor and in obscurity, for there is no record of his death nor settlement of his estate.

The matrimonial ventures of Hoskins were unfortunate. His first wife did not long survive, and his second wife, Ann,

---

* *Town Records of Plymouth*, vol. 1 : 108, 22, 9, 33, 119.

† *Plymouth Colony Records*, Court Orders, vol. 2 : 29; vol. 3 : 194; vol. 4 : 19.

‡ *Plymouth Colony Records*, Court Orders, vol. 6 : 32.

must have been rather an unpleasant person. Not long after their marriage, he and his wife Ann brought suit against "John Danford, . . . in an action for slander," i. e. circulating unsavory stories against Ann; the jury found for the plaintiffs in the sum of "£20 damage and the charges of the Court." This was in June, 1639.* Ann was afterward before the Court a number of times; on March 1, 1663–64, for using "filthy language to Hester Rickard." The Court at the hearing treated them impartially, — for both women were sentenced "to sit in the stockes during the pleasure of the Court," or to pay a fine of twenty shillings, each. They chose the latter.†

These home conditions probably were responsible for the daughter Sarah being "bound out" until she was twenty years of age : —

"Jan. 28, 1643[-44]: William Hoskine of Plymouth, hath put Sarah his daughter, to Thomas Whitney [Thomas Hinckley, in index] and Winefreide, his wyfe, to dwell wᵗʰ them vntill shee shall accomplish the age of twenty yeares, the said Thomas, and Winyfride, his wyfe, vseing her as their child, and being vnto her as father and mother, and to instruct her in learneing and soweing in reasonable manner, fynding vnto her meate, drink, and apparell & lodging during the said terme; and if it shall happen the said Sarah to marry before she shall haue accomplished the said age of twenty yeares, (she being six yeares of age, the xvjᵗʰ of September last past,) that then the sayd Thomas shall haue such satisfaction for her tyme then remayning as shalbe adjudged reasonable & equall by two indifferent men." ‡

Issue by first wife: 1. Sarah² Hoskins, b. Sept. 16, 1637, in Plymouth. At the age of six years she was apprenticed to Thomas Whitney and Winifred his wife for the term of fourteen years, or until she was twenty. Three years after attaining that age she married, Dec. 4, 1660, in Plymouth, Benjamin² Eaton, son to Francis¹ Eaton. §

---

* *Plymouth Colony Judicial Acts:* 12.
† *Plymouth Colony Records*, Court Orders, vol. 4 : 50.
‡ *Plymouth Colony Records*, Court Orders, vol. 2 : 67.
§ Francis¹ Eaton joined the Pilgrims at Southampton, and came over in

Christian Eaton, mother of Benjamin [2], the third wife and widow of Francis [1] Eaton, married, in 1634, Francis [2] Billington, son to John [1] Billington, of Plymouth, by whom she had nine children, besides the three children of her first marriage. The family was so large and the means of support so limited that the town authorities took the matter in hand, and had a voice in the " disposeing of ffrancis Billingtons children." Jan. 14, 1642, Benjamin Eaton, mentioned as " his [Billington's] eldest Boy," was apprenticed to John Winslow until he should reach the age of twenty-one, — " being about xv yeares in March next." Joseph Billington, " now about vi or vii yeares old," was apprenticed to John Cooke upon the same terms. Gyles Rickett (Rickard) took " a gerle about five years of age ; " and Gabriel Fallowell gave a home to another " gerle about [   ] years of age." [*]

On May 24, 1662, less than two years after his marriage, Benjamin Eaton " desired " of the town " a small pcell of meddow about half an acre lying neere ffrancis Billingtons meddow and some upland to it." Jan. 2, 1666, " ten acrees of land was graunted unto Benjamin Eaton lying above ffrancis Billingtons † house neare Rockey nooke," which was

---

the *Mayflower*, 1620, with wife Sarah, and a son Samuel then an infant in arms. Francis Eaton was the twenty-third signer of the Compact. (Vide Appendix LXXXV.) His wife Sarah " dyed in the generall sicknes; and he maried again " before Aug. 14, 1623. Before the division of cattle in 1627, he mar., third, Christian Penn, who came in the *Anne*, 1623. Francis Eaton died of the epidemic of 1633; his inventory was taken Nov. 8. His widow, Christian, in 1634, mar. Francis [2] Billington.

> Issue by first wife : 1. Samuel [2] Eaton, who was apprenticed in 1636 to John Cooke. By 1650, he was married, and had a child. He mar., second, Jan. 10, 1661, Martha [2], daughter to Francis [2] Billington. He early removed to Duxbury, and afterward to Middleborough, where he d. in 1684.
>
> Issue by second wife : 2. Rachael [2] Eaton, mar. March 7, 1646, Joseph Ramsden.
>
> Issue by third wife : 3. Benjamin [2] Eaton, b. 1627. Two other children were living in 1650, but one was an idiot, says Bradford.

[*] *Town Records of Plymouth*, vol. 1 : 12.

† I. " John [1] Billington, and Elen [Eleanor], his wife ; and 2. sones, John & Francis," arrived in the *Mayflower*, 1620. They were of the com-

laid out for him, April 11, 1667, by William Crow. A few years later, " In Reference unto a small psell of Land & a smale Cottage theron formerly possessed by Thomas Dunham deceased : Now desired by Benjamin Eaton the Towne have ordered that the said Benjamin Eaton enter upon the same and possess and Improve it."* This was probably the land that was laid out, in 1668, for Thomas Dunham by Elder Cushman, Jacob Cooke, and Stephen Bryant.

pany from London that joined the Leyden people at Southampton. John Billington was the twenty-sixth signer of the Compact. (Vide Appendix LXXXV.) In 1630, " he way-laid a yong-man, one John New-comin, (about a former quarell,) and shote him with a gune, wherof he dyed." Billington "was arrained, and both by grand & petie jurie found guilty of willful murder, by plaine & notorious evidence. And was for the same accordingly executed." The execution took place "about September." (Bradford's *History of Plimoth Plantation* : 532, 329, 330.) This first serious crime was a great shock to the Pilgrim settlement; had it occurred later, the result might have been different. In 1638, his widow married George Armstrong.

Issue: 1. John [2] Billington, who died before his father.

2. Francis [2] Billington.

II. Francis [2] Billington, b. about 1606, came with his parents in the *Mayflower*. He was then about fourteen years of age. In 1634, he married Christian, widow of Francis [1] Eaton, who at that time had three children. In 1650, Bradford wrote that Billington "hath 8. children." He removed to Yarmouth before 1648, where he died Dec. 3, 1684. Owing to lack of dates, the children are not arranged in their proper order.

Issue: 1. Francis [3] Billington ; mar. Abigail Churchill, and had seven children.

2. Joseph [3] Billington, b. 1635 or 1636, was apprenticed in 1642 to John [3] Cooke.

3. Martha [3] Billington ; mar. Jan. 10, 1661, Samuel [2] Eaton, as his second wife.

4. Elizabeth [3] Billington ; mar. —— Patte, of Providence, R. I.

5. Isaac [3] Billington ; mar. Hannah Glass. Issue : I. Seth Billington.

6. Mercy [3] Billington ; mar. John Martin.

7. Rebecca [3] Billington ; b. 1647, in Plymouth.

8. Mary [3] Billington ; mar. Samuel Sabin, of Rehoboth.

9. Desire [3] Billington.

Vide Davis's *Landmarks of Plymouth*, 1899: 28.

* *Town Records of Plymouth*, vol. 1 : 46, 47, 86, 152.

Benjamin Eaton remained at Rocky Nook, where his children settled about him. The date of his death, or that of his wife, Sarah, has not been learned.

Issue :* I. William [3] Eaton ; d. before 1691, in Plymouth.

II. Benjamin [3] Eaton, b. 1664, in Plymouth ; mar., first, Mary Coombs ; mar., second, Susanna ——. By his first wife he had a family of six children. It is also stated that there were five more, making eleven in all.

III. Rebecca [3] Eaton ; mar. Josiah Rickard.

IV. Ebenezer [3] Eaton; mar. in 1707, Hannah Rickard. In 1721, he was living at Rocky Nook, near the bridge over Jones's River on the " Road Way y[t] goeth To Boston." Issue : six.

Issue by second wife : 2. Mary [2] Hoskins ; mar. Nov. 28, 1660, in Plymouth, Edward Cobb.

3. Rebecca [2] Hoskins, who was called in her marriage record " of Lakenham," and may have been a daughter to William [1]; mar. Aug. 15, 1662, in Taunton, Richard Briggs.

4. Elizabeth [2] Hoskins; mar. July 7, 1666, in Plymouth, Ephraim Tilson.

5. " A son," b. Nov. 30, 1647, in Plymouth. This undoubtedly was the William [2] Hoskins who mar. July 3, 1677, in Taunton, Sarah, daughter to Thomas Caswell.

Issue: I. Ann [3] Hoskins, b. Feb. 14, 1678, in Taunton.

II. Sarah [3] Hoskins, b. Aug. 31, 1679, in Taunton.

III. William [3] Hoskins, b. June 30, 1681. His birth is recorded on this date in both Taunton and Plymouth.

IV. Henry [3] Hoskins, b. March 13, 1683, in Taunton.

6. Samuel [2] Hoskins, b. Aug. 8, 1654, in Plymouth. Samuel and William Hoskins were on the " Grand Inquest," Aug. 2, 1678.

---

* Davis's *Landmarks of Plymouth*, 1899 : 99.

THOMAS ² CUSHMAN

Thomas ² Cushman, son to Robert ¹ and Sarah (———)
Cushman, was born in February, 1608, at Leyden. His
mother, Sarah, whose maiden name is not known, died at
Leyden, October 11, 1616, leaving him, her only surviving
son, motherless at the age of nine years. Thomas Cushman
was undoubtedly with the Cushman family when they sailed
from Southampton in the *Mayflower*, and returned to London with those who could not continue because of the un-
seaworthiness of the *Speedwell*. A year later, he sailed with
his father on the *Fortune*, and arrived November 10, 1621,
at New Plymouth. Robert Cushman returned to England
in the same ship, "which stayed not above 14 days," leaving his son Thomas in the care of William Bradford, then
Governor, who gave him a home, educated him, and treated
him as a son. The last letter written by Cushman to Bradford, dated "London, *December 22*, A. D. 1624," concluded:
"Lastly, I must intreat you still, to have a care of my son,
as of your own; and I shall rest bound unto you, I pray you
let him sometime practice writing. I hope the next ships to
come to you." Bradford replied: "Your son and all of us,
are in good health (blessed be God) he received the things
you sent him. I hope God will make him a good man." But
Cushman had passed away before the comforting message
reached him.

Bradford, in some degree a self-taught scholar, was familiar with the Dutch and French languages, and "had attained
a considerable intimacy with Latin and Greek." Throughout his whole life he was much devoted to literary pursuits.
His *History of Plimoth Plantation* and other writings are
a rich legacy to the American people. As Governor of the
Plymouth Colony, he served continuously from 1621 until
his death, in 1657, except the five years that he begged

to be relieved by others. Nothing more fully demonstrates the hardships endured at Leyden than the fact that such a man was compelled by the exigencies of the situation to support his family by his labor as a fustian-weaver.* "As a leading man of the Plymouth Colony, he displayed a worthy dignity, much tact, no little shrewdness and worldly wisdom, mingled with a becoming piety and sound business judgment."

Under this influence Thomas Cushman grew to manhood. He also may have been indebted not a little to the instructions of the Ruling Elder, William Brewster. Brewster had been educated at Cambridge, England, though he did not remain long enough to obtain a degree. In Leyden, he was engaged as a teacher of English to the students who were attracted to that University city; he acquired a reputation as a printer, too, more especially of religious works not allowed in England.† After the death of Elder Brewster, in April, 1644, Thomas Cushman was chosen his successor. He was ordained as Ruling Elder on Friday, April 6, 1649, by appropriate religious services; he retained the office until his death, — a period of more than forty-two years.

At Plymouth, previous to 1623, "the company had worked together on the companys lands, each sharing the fruits of another's labors;" but for this community it "was found to breed much confusion & discontent, and retard much imploymēt that would have been to their benefite and comforte." For their encouragement, and to "obtaine a beter crope than they had done . . . after much debate of things, the Govʳ (with yᵉ advise of yᵉ cheefest amongst them) gave way that they should set corne every man for his owne perticular, and in that regard trust to them selves; in all other things to goe on in yᵉ generall way as before. And so

---

* Dexter's *England and Holland of the Pilgrims*, 1905 : 604.
† Dexter's *England and Holland of the Pilgrims*, 1905 : 604–607.

assigned to every family a parcell of land, according to the proportion of their number for that end, only for present use (but made no devision for inheritance), and ranged all boys & youth under some familie. This had very good success ; for it made all hands very industrious, so as much more corne was planted then other waise would have bene by any means y⁰ Govʳ or any other could use, . . . and gave farr better contente." * This was in direct violation of their contract with the Merchant Adventurers, yet the Governor assigned to every person an acre of land, "as neere the town as might be, and they had no more till the 7 years was expired." Some of these lots later became their homesteads.

When the drawing took place, in 1623, in accordance with their plan for division of land among those "which came first ouer in the May-Floure," the first acre was assigned to "Robart Cochman." † It was "on the South side of the brooke to the baywards," now between Sandwich Street and the harbor. Giving him the first lot was a delicate acknowledgment of his services as their agent in England, for he not only had not arrived in the *Mayflower*, but he "was not yet come over," though planning to come at the earliest opportunity. As it was not "for inheritance," his son never possessed the land. But in the assignment "of their grounds [to those] which came in the Fortune according as their Lots were cast, 1623," William Beale and Thomas Cushman were given two acres that "lye beyonde the 2. brooke." This land was situated on the north of the present Woolen Mill Brook, which runs through the land of Benjamin Hathaway (1899), and finds its way into the harbor north of the railroad station.

In the division of cattle, May 22, 1627, "The eleuenth

---

* Bradford's *History of Plimoth Plantation*, 1898 : 163, 162.
† Vide page 451.

lott ffell to the Gouerno^r Mr William Bradford and those with him, to wit, his wife Alles Bradford and

3 William Bradford, Junior

4 Mercy Bradford	To this lott fell An heyfer
5 Joseph Rogers	of the last yeare wch was
6 Thomas Cushman	of the Greate white back
7 William Latham	cow that was brought
8 Manases Kempton	ouer in the Ann, & two
9 Julian Kempton	shee goats." *

10 Nathaniel Morton

11 John Morton

12 Ephraim Morton

13 Patience Morton

Thomas Cushman married, about 1636, in Plymouth, Mary², daughter to Isaac¹ and Mary (Norris) Allerton. Isaac Allerton was married November 4, 1611, in Leyden, to Mary Norris. It was his first marriage, for if he had been a widower, it would have been so stated in the marriage record. The date of birth of the daughter Mary has not been found in Leyden, but she was the youngest of the three children who came with their parents on the *Mayflower*. A daughter Sarah was brought over in the *Anne*, 1623; while a fifth child was buried, in February, 1620, at Leyden, and a sixth was born and died in Provincetown harbor. Hence it is probable that Mary Allerton was born about 1616.†

In the first list of men "admitted into freedom" at Plymouth, January 1, 1633–34, appeared the name of Thomas Cushman. He was also among the men "able to beare

---

* *Plymouth Colony Deeds*, vol. 1 : 12.

This constant repetition in the division of cattle that they were brought over "in the Ann," is an error of early date. The first cattle were brought over by Winslow, in March, 1624, on the *Charity*. Bradford himself states that these were the "first begining of any catle of that kind in ye land . . . 3. heifers and a bull." The heifers were "two black" and one "white-backed." (Bradford's *History of Plimoth Plantation*, 1898 : 189.)

† Vide The Allerton Family.

armes," in 1643. As "The Elder Mr Thomas Cushman," he
was third in the list of freemen in 1683–84.

He shared in nearly every grant of land by the Plymouth
Colony Court to the "old comers," and acquired so much
other land by purchase that the division of his estate among
his heirs, after his decease, placed them all in more than
comfortable circumstances. As early as March 14, 1635–36,
it was ordered by the Court in the assignment of the
hay-ground, " That Mr Prence Joseph Rogers Tho: Cushman & Edw: Dowty haue the ground vpon Jones his
riuer, where Mr Prence and Mr Allerton mowed last yeare."
The following year (March 20, 1636–37), the hay-ground
allotted to Cushman was " the remaynder of the marsh before the house he liueth in (wch M^ris Fuller doth not vse) and
the little p̄cell at the wading place on thother side Joanes
Riuer." * From this it appears probable that he had commenced housekeeping in Mistress Fuller's house at the time
of his marriage, a few months before.

There is no further record showing his residence until
October 20, 1653, when he purchased the former homestead
of his father-in-law, Isaac Allerton, adjoining the land of
Mistress Fuller where he made his first home. The transaction is recorded in part as follows: —

"BRADFORD GOV^r

The 20th of October 1653

" Memorand : That Captaine Thomas Willett of the Towne of
Plymouth . . . and Mr William Paddy of the Towne of Boston
. . . marchant Doe both acknowlidg that for and in consideration of the summe of seaventy and five pounds to them in hand
paied by Mr Thomas Cushman of the Towne of Plymouth in
the Jurisdiction of Plymouth aforsaid yeoman wherwith they Doe
acknowlidge themselves satisfyed . . . Doe bargaine sell enfeofe
and confeirme from them the said capt: Willett and William
Paddy and theire heires to him the said Thomas Cushman and

---

* *Plymouth Colony Records*, Court Orders, vol. 1 : 40, 56.

his heires and assignes forever All that theire house and land lying and being Scittuate att Joaneses River in the Towneshipp of Plymouth aforsaid which they the said capt: Willett and William Paddy bought of M͏ʳ Edmond ffreeman of Sandwidge as appeers in the court records; which was formerly the house and land of M͏ʳ Thomas Prence somtimes of Plymouth aforsaid; and Originally was the house and land of M͏ʳ Isaak Allerton; being bounded with the lands of M͏ⁱˢ ffuller on the one side and of Clement Briggs and Christopher Winter on the other side; the nether end abutting upon the river aforsaid and soe extending itselfe in the length up into the woods with all the meddow land either mersh or upland adioyneing and belonging therunto with all the out-houses barnes stables fences and all other appurtenances belonging therunto with all the additions and enlargements either of vpland or meddow land nearer hand or further of att any time added graunted or any way apperrtaining unto the said house and land with all the said capt: Willett and William Paddy their right title and enterest of and into the said p͏ʳmises or any pte or prcell therof." *

This deed was followed by another of the same date, to which "m͏ⁱˢ Mary Cushman the wife of the said m͏ʳ Thomas Cushman gave her free and full consent." It conveyed, for "seaventy and seaven pounds," to Captain Willett and William Paddy, "All that his [Cushman's] prte portion or share of land both upland and meddow belonging unto him as purchased lying and being at Sowamsett Secunke and place or places adiacent." † Cushman's land at Sowamsett, or "Assowamsett Necke," consisted of a "whole pte" of a purchase by William Bradford, Thomas Prince, Edward Winslow, Captain Standish, "M͏ʳ Cushman," Experience Mitchell, and five others, "att Sowamsett and Matpoisett," for the division of which a meeting had been held on March 7, 1652, at Plymouth.‡ Twenty years later, March 5, 1671–72, the Court confirmed to Thomas Cushman, Sr., "one

---

* *Plymouth Colony Deeds*, Book 2 : pt. 1 : 81, 82.
† *Plymouth Colony Deeds*, Book 2 : pt. 1 : 83.
‡ *Plymouth Colony Deeds*, Book 2 : 39.

half of the last purchase of land made by the Treasurer
[Constant Southworth] of Phillip, sachem of Punkanawkett
. . . lying and being att Assowamsett Ponds, the other half
belonging vnto Thomas Little." With this tract he should
also have "any meadow . . . neare or conuenient vnto the
aforsaid land." * In 1680, Assowamsett Neck was joined
to Middleborough, and Mattapoisett later became the town
of Rochester. Cushman also had an interest in the town's
land at Punkateesett (Little Compton, R. I.) granted to
him in 1651.

When sundry proportions of meadow at Jones's River
were laid out, in 1653, the first six acres were given to Mr.
Hanbury. The second lot is described as "Mr Thomas
Cushmans from M^r hanberryes outter stake along to the
upland to a rock upon the Island containing within it the
cove of mersh which lyeth between the Island and the upland; and from that rock on the Island to run upon a west
norwest line ; and east south east buting upon M^r hanberries
Meddow." The third lot was granted to John Howland, the
fourth to John Cooke, and the fifth to Jacob Cooke.

On May 24, 1660, John Howland was granted by the town
of Plymouth, land "lying att a brook within two miles or
thereabouts of Winnatuxett meddow," and at the same time
the Elder Cushman was granted fifty acres adjacent. These
fifty acres were laid out in 1665, beside the "brook by John
Bosworths." Nine years afterward (May 18, 1674), Cushman received a further grant of fifty acres at Winnatuxet
meadow, "neare a place called Colchester in the Town of
Plymouth." He also had a tract of twelve acres at this
place, which was laid out in 1693 (after the Elder's death),
and divided, March 28, 1700, by his three sons, Thomas,
Isaac, and Elkanah Cushman.†

" Elder Thomas Cushman for his children " was granted,

---

* *Plymouth Colony Records*, Court Orders, vol. 5: 86.
† *Town Records of Plymouth*, vol. 1: 39, 81, 139, 140, 206, 278.

June 7, 1665, one share of thirty acres "on the westerly Side of Namasskett Riuer . . . with all the appurtenances belonging thereunto." Namassakett was incorporated June 1, 1669, as the town of Middleborough.

It was an established principle with these Pilgrim Fathers that any land taken from the Indians should be conveyed to them by deed, and due compensation given therefor. One of the earliest Indian deeds, dated March 29, 1653, from the "Sachem Ousamequin" (Massasoit) and "Wamsitto his eldest son," conveyed "severall prcells and neckes of upland Swamps and meddowes lying and beinge on the southerly side of Sincunke allis Rehoboth bounds." The consideration was £35. The grantees included the more prominent men of the Colony: "Thomas Prence Thomas Willett Myles Standish Josiah Winslow agents for themselves and William Bradford senior gen^t: Thomas Clarke John Winslow Thomas Cushman William White John Addams and Experience Michell." *

In the ordering of town affairs, the Elder Thomas Cushman bore a prominent part. In 1640 and 1646, with "William hoskins" and others, he appeared in lists of townsmen of Plymouth. When it was decided in town-meeting, September 28, 1643, to appoint a watch to guard against the Indians, it was "agreed upon that there shalbe a watch house forthwith built of brick," on Burial Hill; it was also appointed that "Nathaniell Sowther Thomas Southwood [Southworth] John Dunhame and Thomas Cushman shall divide the number of the Inhabitants into sevrall watches according to the form[er] order." Cushman also was chosen, October 9, one of the "Raters to rate and assesse the charges of this yeare for this Towne for the fortyfycation work donn about the ordinance, for the building of the watchhouse and the officers wages." In 1644, he was one of five who were chosen "to make a Rate for the payment

---

* *Plymouth Colony Deeds*, Book 2 : pt. 1 : 78.

of the publicke officers;" in 1648, one of five "Raters for comman charges." In 1672 and 1674, the Elder Cushman was on committees "to make rates for Plymouth."*

That his services as a surveyor often were required is evident. With Nicholas Snow, Richard Sparrow, and Josiah Cooke, he was chosen March 3, 1639–40, a surveyor of highways. They were reappointed the next year; but were presented at Court December 1, 1640, "for not mending the heigh wayes at the Second Brooke, Smylt Riuer, New Bridge, and other places." Upon condition that they should make the needed repairs "this year," they were discharged.†In 1667, the fifty acres of Richard Wright at Winnatuxet were laid out by "Captaine Bradford and the Elder Cushman." The Elder, Jacob Cooke, and Stephen Bryant, in 1668, laid out land at Jones's River for Thomas Dunham.

Thomas Cushman served on the "Grand Enquest" a number of sessions from 1635 to 1676. Between 1636 and 1666, he served twenty-two terms on juries. The actions in Court were for debt, trespass, slander, land damages, the accidental burning of a house, trespass upon "an ould way," "Tryall of Yssues [issues] betwixt p̄ty & p̄ty," and one case of "assault & battery." ‡ His last service as juryman was on July 9, 1686, when he was seventy-eight years of age.§

In recognition of his valuable public services, on August 5, 1672, "Att this meeting it was voated by the Towne that the Elder Cushman be ffreed from paying any Rate to the Minnestry for the future in Regard of his many emergent occasions and expence of time ; therein Improved for the publicke good." ‖ The individual assessment for the support of gospel preaching was most rigorously collected in every

---

* *Town Records of Plymouth*, vol. 1 : 108, 20, 22, 15, 16, 19, 28, 125, 139.
† *Plymouth Colony Records*, Court Orders, vol. 1 : 141, 155 ; vol. 2 : 5.
‡ *Plymouth Colony Judicial Acts* : 5, 6, 7, 8, 12, 14, 15, 17, 20, 22, 23, 25, 26, 28, 31, 32, 37, 38, 41, 45, 129, 285.
§ *Plymouth Colony Records*, Court Orders, vol. 6 : 195, 196.
‖ *Town Records of Plymouth*, vol. 1 : 118.

town, and the Elder Cushman's exemption from this tax, "for the future," carried with it a value little realized at the present day. It was a unique honor generously bestowed by his townsmen.

The importance of Thomas Cushman's position as Ruling Elder of the church at Plymouth, the "First Congregational Church in America," cannot be overestimated. The society was formed in 1606, at Amsterdam. Three years later, the pastor, John Robinson, who exercised a patriarchal care over his flock, removed them in a body to Leyden. When they decided to emigrate to the New World, it was planned at first that the Pastor also should go. Later, in view of the numbers necessarily left behind, it was arranged that Robinson should remain in Leyden, while his Ruling Elder, William Brewster, should "depart into the new country" and abide there until such time as Robinson should be able to join them. Brewster was a power for good in the infant settlement; but John Robinson, though in Leyden, still was regarded as the pastor of the church at New Plymouth, and continued to exercise not only a moral, but a pastoral, influence over his people. After the death of Robinson, in 1625, it was the universal wish that Brewster should succeed him. Brewster, however, steadily refused an ordination as pastor, though, in fact, he performed the duties of both offices.

As the Colony increased in numbers, a minister, John Lyford, was sent over from England, in March, 1623-24, to assist Brewster. Proving unworthy of the office, he soon was dismissed and banished. In 1628, "Mʳ Rogers" was brought over to minister to them; but "because of a disordered brain" they sent him back to England the next year. In 1629, Ralph Smith, another minister, was chosen their pastor, continuing in that office about five or six years. "Thinking it too heavie a burthen," he voluntarily resigned. Roger Williams, though not ordained, officiated for a time as assistant pastor and as pastor. Bradford called him "a man godly & zealous, having many precious parts, but very unsettled in judgmente." He finally was banished to Rhode Island for his " Baptist beliefs." John Norton preached one winter for the people at Plymouth, but refused to be settled permanently. Later, he went to Ipswich. The distinguished Charles Chauncey also preached for a short time. In January, 1636–37, Mr. John Rayner, "an able and a godly man," was sent to them; "whom after some time of tryall, they chose for their teacher, the fruits of whose labours they injoyed many years." *

It was during Mr. Rayner's pastorate that Thomas Cushman, in 1649, was ordained Ruling Elder. The office of the Pastor, or Teaching Elder, was to preach, to teach, and to administer the sacraments. The Ruling Elder was "to help the Pastor in ruling and overseeing." The Rev. Philemon Robbins, pastor of the First Church in Branford, Connecticut, in a sermon preached January 30, 1760, at the ordination of his son, Rev. Chandler Robbins, "to the pastoral office over the First Church and Congregation in Plymouth," referred to the labors of Thomas Cushman in that church, as follows : —

" After Mr. *Brewster's* decease, the Church Chose Mr. *Thomas Cushman* as his successor in the Office of Ruling Elder, . . . Son of that faithful Servant of Christ Mr. *Robert Cushman* . . . and this his Son inheriting the same Spirit, and being competently qualified with Gifts and Graces, proved a great Blessing to this Church, assisting Mr. *Reyner*, not only in ruling, catechising, visiting, but also in public Teaching, as Mr. *Brewster* had done before him. . . . It being the professed Principle of this Church in their first Formation, to choose none for governing Elders but such as are able to teach : — which Ability (as Mr. *Robinson* observes in one of his Letters) other reformed Churches did not require in their Ruling Elder."

The Rev. John Rayner remained eighteen years, closing his pastorate in November, 1654. He died at Dover, New

* Bradford's *History of Plimoth Plantation*, 1898 : 314, 369, 318, 319.

Hampshire, in April, 1669. After his departure, the Plymouth Church was without a pastor for some years, the Elder Cushman "being assisted by some of the brethren; insomuch that not one Sabbath passed without two public meetings in which the word of God was dispensed." "At length it pleased the Lord to send among us Mr. *John Cotton, Jun*, son to the Rev. Mr. *John Cotton*, that famous gospel preacher in Boston." He was first called in September, 1666. Although he arrived with his family at Plymouth November 30, 1667, he was not ordained until June 30, 1669. The churches at Barnstable, Marshfield, Weymouth, and Duxbury were represented by their pastors at his ordination. "Elder Thomas Cushman gave the charge, and the aged Mr. John Howland was appointed by the church to join in the imposition of hands. The Ruling Elder [Cushman] with the new Pastor, made it their first special work to pass through the whole town, from family to family to enquire into the state of souls." The following is a facsimile of their signatures in 1681–82 : —

March, 16 $\frac{81}{82}$
Plimouth

John Cotten Pastour

Thomas Cushman Elder *

"In November began the Catechising of the Children by the Pastor (constantly attended by the Ruling Elder) once a Fortnight; the Males at one time and the Females at the other. The Catechism then used was composed by the Rev. Mr. *William Perkins;* . . . Some years after the Assemblies Catechism was introduced." Together they regularly

* Cushman's *Genealogy of the Cushmans*, 1855: 89.
These autographs, unlike the others in this volume, probably are reduced in size.

held meetings on week days at the Pastor's house, or with
the brethren in their homes, "the Elder always present,
and making the concluding prayer."

During the many years that Thomas Cushman ministered
to the people as Ruling Elder, and for long periods acted
as pastor, the church went through many trials. Between
1640 and 1650, it was greatly weakened by the removal of
many of its members to remote settlements on Cape Cod
and elsewhere. The troubles arising from the Quakers who
"infested the country . . . much endangered the Church
of Plymouth; several were wavering and hesitating." But
"the Lord was pleased to bless the endeavours of their faithful elder, Mr. Cushman, in concurrence with several of the
brethren, to prevent the efficacy of errour and delusion ; and
(though destitute of a pastor) the body of the Church was
upheld in its integrity, and in a constant opposition to their
pernicious tenets." While the "provocations of the Quakers
were as great here as elsewhere," the Plymouth Colony did
not make "any sanguinary or capital laws against that sect,
as some of the colonies did."

The united labors of the Rev. John Cotton and the Elder
Cushman placed the church at Plymouth on a firm founda-
tion. In the nearly thirty years of Mr. Cotton's ministry the
membership increased from "47 members in full communion" to two hundred and twenty-five. Mr. Cotton resigned
his pastorate at Plymouth on October 3, 1697, "to the grief
of a number of the church and Town who desired his Continuance."

Six years before, on December 11 (10th, in the Town
Records),* 1691, after a lingering illness, the Elder Thomas
Cushman had been gathered to his fathers. The first volume of records of the First Church of Plymouth contains
this notice of his death : —

---

* "On the 10th day of december 1691 That precious and Eminant servant
of god deceased The Elder Thomas Cushman being Entered into the 84 yeare
of his age." (*Town Records of Plymouth*, vol. 1 : 202.)

" 1691. It pleased God to seize upon our good Elder, M^r. Thomas Cushman, by sicknesse & in this yeare to take him from us. He was chosen & ordained Elder of this Chh April 6: 1649: he was neere 43 yeares in his office, his sicknesse lasted about 11 weekes; he had bin a rich blessing to this chh scores of yeares, he was grave holy & temperate very studious & solicitous for the peace & prosperity of the chh & to prevent & heale all breaches; He dyed December 11: neare the end of the 84 yeare of his life; December 16: was kept as a day of Humiliation for his death, the Pastor prayed & preached. Mr Arnold & the Pastors 2 sons assisted in prayer; much of Gods presence went away from this chh when this blessed Pillar was removed. . . . A liberal contribution was made that fast day for the Elders widow, as an acknowledgment of his great services to the chh whilst living." *

In the same book these items are found : —

" 1691. Elder Thomas Cushman dyed December 11: having within two moneths finished the 84th yeare of his life; He was ordained Ruling Elder of this Church April 6 1649: he was neere 43 yeares in his office." †

"August 7, 1715. A Contribution was moved & made both by the church & Congregation To defray The Expense of Grave Stones sett upon ye grave of that worthy & useful Servant of God Eld^r Thomas Cushman the whole congregation were very forward in it." ‡

He was buried on the southerly brow of Burial Hill, in a beautiful spot overlooking the meeting-house in which he so long had prayed and worshipped. The gravestone erected by the Plymouth Church twenty-four years after his death was removed when the Cushman family erected the large monument upon the lot in 1858; but it is now restored as

---

* *Records of the First Church of Plymouth* (copy): 27, 28.
The original records of the First Church of Plymouth, beginning in 1667, are kept in the safe of Pilgrim Hall, at Plymouth. They are so frail that reference to them is allowed only by special permit. An excellent copy, however, is always accessible to visitors.

† *Records of the First Church of Plymouth* (copy): 152.

‡ *Records of the First Church of Plymouth* (copy): 83.

near as possible to its original position. The stone, of "purple Welsh slate," was brought from England; it stands about three and a half feet high, and is in a good state of preservation. The inscription is yet distinct and legible, the letters being about three-fourths of an inch in height: —

> HERE LYETH BURIED Y^s BODY
> OF THAT PRECIOUS SERVANT OF
> GOD Mr THOMAS CUSHMAN, WHO
> AFTER HE HAD SERVED HIS
> GENERATION ACCORDING TO
> THE WILL OF GOD, AND
> PARTICULARLY THE CHURCH OF
> PLYMOUTH FOR MANY YEARS IN
> THE OFFICE OF A RULEING ELDER,
> FELL ASLEEP IN JESUS DECEM^r
> Y^e 10 1691, & IN Y^e
> 84 YEAR OF HIS AGE.

It will be noticed that the date of his death is given upon this stone as December 10, while that in the church records is December 11. The latter more probably is correct.

About a year before his death, Elder Thomas Cushman made his will. Judging from the amount of real estate that he left to his widow and children, and from the fact that his personal property amounted to £49 : 19, — of which £4 was in books, — the Elder possessed more than ordinary wealth for his time.

"To All People to Whome these presents shall Come etc. Know Ye that I Thomas Cushman sen^r of the Town of Plimouth in New England being through Gods Mercy and Goodness unto me at this present in Some Measure of Good Health of Body and of Sound understanding and Strength of memory Yet Considering my frailty and uncertainty of my abiding in this Vale of tears Do make this to be my last Will and Testament * And by these presents I do make this to be my last Will and Testament to Remaine firme and Inviolable for ever as followeth. Imprimis I Give and bequeath my Soul to God that Gave it and my Body to ye Dust & to be decently Buried in hopes of ye Grace of God through Jesus Christ to Enter into a joyfull Resurrection — And

---

* *Plymouth County Probate*, Book 1 : 129–132.

for my outward Estate I dispose of as followeth vizt I Will and bequeath Unto my Dear and Loving wife Mary Cushman All my house and housing together with all my uplands and meadow lands I am now possessed of in this Township of New Plimouth to be for her use and support during ye time of her naturall life Excepting such parcels as I do in this my Will Give to my children : Item I Give unto my Son Thomas Cushman two twenty acre lots lying upon the Southerly side of Mr Joseph Bradfords land as also ye enlargements at ye head of those lots And also twenty acres of upland more or less lying upon the Easterly Side of Jones River by the Bridge with a Skirt of meadow lying by said River And also one third of my meadow at Winnatuxet And also a parcell of Salt Marsh Meadow from our Spring unto a Creek Westerly of a Salt hole and So down to ye River which said parcel of meadow is to be his after our decease All ye above said parcels of upland and meadows I do by these presents Give and Bequeath unto my son Tho? Cushman to him and his heirs for Ever. Item I Give unto my son Isaac Cushman one twenty acre lot with ye addition at ye head lying on the northerly side of Samuel ffullers land in ye Township of Plimouth and also the one half of my land lying at Namasket Pond in ye Township of Middleborough as Also ye one half of my Right in the Sixteen shilling Purchase so Called in the Township abovesaid and also one third part of my meadow at Winnatuxet in Plimouth All which parcels of Uplands and meadows last above expressed I do by these presents Give & bequeath unto my Son Isaac Cushman and to him & his heirs for ever together with all the priviledges thereunto belonging. Item I do Give unto my Son Elkanah Cushman one twenty acre lot with the addition at the head lying on the Northerly side of ye land I now Improve But in Case my Son Thomas's now Dwelling house be upon part of this lot my Will is my Son Thomas enjoy ye land his house now Standeth on without molestation. as also I Give to my Son Elkanah Cushman the one half of my land lying at Namasket Pond as also ye one half of the Sixteen shilling Purchase above Expressed as also one third of my meadow at Winnatuxet All the abovesaid Parcels of lands and meadows last above Expressed With all the priviledges thereunto belonging I do by these presents Give unto my Son Elkanah Cushman and to his heires for ever Item I do Give unto my Son Eleazer Cushman The Rest of my lands both uplands and meadow lands not above Disposed of in Plimouth and Duxborough as also my now Dwelling house and out housing Which house and Lands I do by these Presents Give and bequeath unto my Son Eleazer Cushman to him and his heires for ever to enjoy after I and my Wife are deceased And my Will is that my four Sons Thomas Isaac Elkanah & Eleazer Shall Each of them allow twenty shillings to their Sisters that is to say Sarah Hoaks and Lidiah Harlow As also my Will is that if any of my Sons Se cause to make sale of their land I have Given them in Plimouth that they do let their Brothers that do Reside in Plimouth have the said Lands as they shall be valued by indifferent men as also my Will is and I do by these presents Give and bequeath unto my three Grandchildren in Lin the Children of my daughter Mary Hutchinson Deceased to Each of them twenty shillings to be paid unto them out of my Estate Soone after my Decease And I do Constitute and appoint my Dear and Loving Wife Mary Cushman to be the sole Executrix of this my last Will and Testament My debts legacies & funerall charges being first paid my Will is That what ever other Estate is found of mine in Goods Chattels or debts Either in Plimouth or Else Where shall be for y⁰ Support of my Wife During her naturall life And my Will is that what Remains of my s^d Estate at my Wifes Decease the one half I do Give to my Son Eliaz Cushman and the other half unto my two daughters to Sarah Hoaks and Lidiah Harlow to be equally Divided between them And my Will is And I do by these presents appoint my two sons Thomas Cushman & Isaac Cushman and Thomas ffaunce to be y⁰ Supervisors of this my last Will and Testament Much Confiding in their Love and faithfullness to be helpfull to my S^d Executrix in the acting and Disposing of Particulars according to the tenour thereof thus hoping that this my last Will and Testament will be performed and Kept Revoaking all other Wills Either written or verball I have in Witness thereof Signed Sealed and Declared to be his last Will and Testament Set to my hand and Seal on the 22^d of October 1690.

In presence of us   THOMAS CUSHMAN SEN^R

Witnesses   and a (seal)

  JAMES WARREN

  THOMAS FFAUNCE

"James Warren and Thomas ffaunce the Witnesses here named made oath before the County Court at Plimouth March ye 16th 1691/2 that they were present and Saw the above named Mr Thomas Cushman Signe and Seal and heard him Declare the above Written to be his Last Will and Testament And that to ye best of their judgment he was of Sound mind and memory when he so did

Attest SAM^L SPRAGUE Clerk.

"An addition to ye last Will of Thomas Cushman sen^r which is as followeth Whereas in my last Will which was in sixteene hundred & ninety That I then left out a Certain peece of land Undisposed of Which was one hundred acres of Land Lying in the Township of Plimouth Upon a Brooke Comonly Called Colchester Brooke on both sides of ye s^d Brooke which I Reserved to sell for my Support or my Wifes after my decease My Will is therefore That my Son Thomas Cushman and my Son Isaac Cushman shall have the aboves^d hundred acres of Land to be divided Equally between them to them and their heirs and Assigns for Ever Provided that they equally Shall pay or cause to be paid ten pounds in Currant Silver money to me above said Thomas Cushman sen^r or my Wife Mary Cushman after my Decease or after [her] decease to be paid Equally to my to Daughters Sarah Hauks and Lidia Harlow Also I the abovesaid Thomas Cushman Do Will and bequeath to my four Sons Thomas Cushman and Isaac Cushman and Elkanah Cushman and Eleazer Cushman all my Books equally to be Divided among them onely two Small Books to my Daughter Lidiah Harlow And my best Bible to my Loving wife Mary Cushman Likewise also I do Give and bequeath unto my Son Elkanah Cushman one acre of meadow which was Granted unto me lying at Doteis Meadows This Addition is to the Last Will of me Elder Thomas Cushman of Plimouth being now in perfect understanding — Aprill : 1 : 1691.

Signed Sealed and delivered   THOMAS CUSHMAN sen^r (seal)
in presence of us witnesses
   JONATHAN SHAW sen^r
   PERSIS SHAW her P Mark.

"Jonathan Shaw one of yᵉ Witnesses here named made oath before yᵉ County Court at Plimouth march 16ᵗʰ 1691/2 that he was Present and saw Elder Thomas Cushman above named signe seal & heard him Declare the above written Codicil to be his Will — and an Addition to his former Will And that he yᵉ sd Shaw Subscribed to it as a Witness and that he saw Persis his Wife Subscribe with him as a Witness alsoe

Attest Sᴀᴍᴸ Sᴘʀᴀɢᴜᴇ Clerk

"March 16ᵗʰ 1691/2 Mʳˢ Mary Cushman Relict Widdow of Elder Thomas Cushman late of Plimouth Deceased Coming personally before yᵉ County Court then held at Plimouth Did freely acknowledge yᵗ she hath Received fifty two shillings and six pence of Isaac Cushman her son in part of yᵉ five pounds which yᵉ sd Isaac is to pay for his part of yᵉ 100 acres of Land at Colchester abovesaid:

Attest Sᴀᴍᴸ Sᴘʀᴀɢᴜᴇ Clerk

"Memorandum that

Persis Shaw yᵉ other Witness made oath Before Wm Bradford Esqʳ Judge of Probate that She also was present and saw and heard yᵉ within named Elder Cushman Sign Seal & declare this within Codicill as an Addition to his Will And that he was of Sound mind and memory when he did yᵉ same to yᵉ best of her judgment.

Attest Sᴀᴍᴸ Sᴘʀᴀɢᴜᴇ Register

Sepᵗ 25ᵗʰ 1701

"An inventory of the estate of mʳ Thomas Cushman senʳ late of Plimouth Deceased taken and apprised by us whose names are hereunto Subscribed on yᵉ 17ᵗʰ Day of Decembʳ 1691: —

	£	s	d
Imprimis his wearing Apparell both linnen and woollen . .	04	02	00
Item in books at	04	00	00
Item in Cash	01	02	00
Item in two Beds and Bedding to them	10	00	00
Item in Pewter and Brass	02	15	00
Item in Jron pots & Kettles hakes & other jron vessels . .	01	12	00
Item in Tables and Chests and chaires	01	16	00
Item In cotton & sheeps wooll & linnen yarn & flax . . .	01	03	00
Item in Saddle Bridle and Pillion	01	05	00
Item in Linnen wheel and old lumber	00	15	00
Item in Iron wedges and Glass Bottels	00	05	00

	£	s	d
Item in cart tacklen	oo	10	oo
Item in Indian and English corne	04	01	oo
Item in Neat Cattell	13	10	oo
Item in sheep	01	oo	oo
Item in Swine	oo	18	oo
Item in a Loome	01	05	oo
Item in Debts due from yᵉ estate	oo	o8	oo

THOMAS CUSHMAN
ISAAC CUSHMAN
THOMAS FFAUNCE

"Mⁿ Mary Cushman relict widdow of Elder Thomas Cushman late of Plimouth Deceased made oath before yᵉ County Court at Plimouth March 16ᵗʰ 1691/2 that yᵉ above written is a true Inventory of the Goods and Chattels of her sᵈ late husband so far as she yet Knoweth and that if more shall be Discovered to her she will make it known.

Attest SAMᴸ SPRAGUE clericus

"The Aged Widow Mary Cushman deceassed November The 28ᵗʰ day 1699," * say the Town Records of Plymouth, but make no mention of her age. Although ninety years †

---

* *Town Records of Plymouth*, vol. 1 : 203.

† On September 16, 1858, the Cushman Monument Association dedicated, with appropriate ceremonies, a beautiful shaft on the Cushman lot in the old graveyard on Burial Hill. It is built of Quincy granite ; its form is that of an obelisk, having a Grecian base standing upon an ornamented pedestal. The extreme height is about twenty-seven and one half feet; the square of the lowest plinth is about eight feet. Each of the four bronze panels of the pedestal measures about thirty-six by twenty-two inches. The east tablet is in memory of Robert ¹ Cushman : —

ERECTED BY
THE DESCENDANTS OF
ROBERT CUSHMAN,
IN MEMORY OF THEIR PILGRIM ANCESTOR,
XVI SEPTEMBER, MDCCCLVIII.

This is continued on the north and west tablets, closing with a quotation from his " Sermon." The south tablet bears the following inscription : —

usually is given as her span of life, she could not have been much above eighty. She lived to see her sons and grandsons occupying positions of honor and trust; and the Plymouth Colony, united with that of Massachusetts Bay, secure in strength and prosperity.

ISSUE

I. Thomas[8], b. Sept., 1637; mar., first, Nov. 17, 1664, at Plymouth, Ruth[3], daughter to John[1] Howland, "one of the old comers" of the *Mayflower*, 1620. She was living when her father made his will, May 29, 1672, but died before 1679. Thomas Cushman mar. Oct. 16, 1679, in Rehoboth, as his second wife, Abigail[2] Fuller, b. about 1653, daughter to Robert[1] and Sarah (——) Fuller, of Salem and Rehoboth.

Thomas Cushman's name appears in several lists of freemen; he was a surveyor of highways a number of years for the town of Plymouth. The homestead where he lived and died consisted of a large farm, with numerous buildings, lying on both sides of Colchester Brook at the west of the highway running northward from the meeting-house at Plympton. This site originally was in Plymouth, but when Plympton was set off, in 1707, the division brought it within the limits of the new town. Thomas Cushman and his wife Abigail were members of the Congregational Church at Plympton, of which his brother Isaac was pastor. He died Aug. 23, 1726, at Plympton, aged eighty-nine years. The

---

THOMAS CUSHMAN,
SON OF ROBERT, DIED X DECEMBER, MDCXCI,
AGED NEARLY LXXXIV YEARS.
FOR MORE THAN XLII YEARS HE WAS
RULING ELDER
OF THE FIRST CHURCH IN PLYMOUTH,
BY WHOM A TABLET WAS PLACED, TO MARK HIS GRAVE
ON THIS SPOT,
NOW CONSECRATED ANEW BY A MORE ENDURING MEMORIAL.

MARY,
WIDOW OF ELDER CUSHMAN AND DAUGHTER OF ISAAC ALLERTON,
DIED XXVIII NOVEMBER MDCXCIX, AGED ABOUT XC YEARS,
THE LAST SURVIVOR OF THE FIRST COMERS IN THE MAYFLOWER.

stone which marks his grave in the Centre Burying-Ground at Plympton is inscribed : —

HERE LYES Y^E
BODY OF M^R. THOMAS
CUSHMAN WHO DEC^D
AUGST Y^E 23^D
1726 IN
Y^E 89TH YEAR
OF HIS AGE.

Issue by first wife: 1. Robert⁴, b. Oct. 4, 1664, in Plymouth ; mar., first, Persis ——, who died at Kingston, Jan. 14, 1743–44. When he was eighty years of age, he mar. Feb. 1744–45, Prudence Sherman, of Marshfield, "a maiden turned of seventy." He died Sept. 7, 1757, at Kingston, aged ninety-two years, eleven months, and three days. Issue by first wife : I. Robert⁵. II. Ruth⁵. III. Abigail⁵. IV. Hannah⁵. V. Thomas⁵. VI. Joshua⁵. VII. Jonathan⁵.

Issue by second wife : 2. Job⁴, b. probably about 1680, in Plymouth ; mar. Lydia Arnold. His widow, Lydia, and her brother, Edward Arnold, were appointed administrators to his estate, May 21, 1740. The inventory amounted to £322 : 3 : 10. Lydia Cushman's will was proved Sept. 27, 1746. Issue : I. Maria⁵. II. Job⁵. III. Lydia⁵.

3. Bartholomew⁴, bap. March 13, 1684, in Plymouth ; died without issue, Dec. 21, 1721, at Plympton, aged thirty-eight years.

4. Samuel⁴, b. July 16, 1687, in Plymouth ; mar. Dec. 8, 1709, Fear Corser, or Courser (now usually written Corse). In 1727, they removed from Plympton to Attleborough, where all their children were born. Issue : I. Desire⁵. II. Mercy⁵. III. Samuel⁵. IV. Joseph⁵. V. Jacob⁵. VI. Jemima⁵.

5. Benjamin⁴, bap. March 1, 1691, in Plymouth ; mar., first, Jan. 8, 1712, Sarah⁴ Eaton, daughter to Benjamin³ and Mary (Coombs) Eaton. Sarah⁴ Eaton, b. 1695, in Plymouth, was granddaughter to Benjamin² and Sarah²

(Hoskins) Eaton.* The second wife of Benjamin Cushman, whom he mar. March 14, 1738–39, was the widow
Sarah Bell. He lived on a part of his father's farm at
Colchester Brook in Plympton, and died there Oct. 17,
1770, at the age of seventy-nine.

    Issue by first wife: I. Jabez⁵. II. Caleb⁵. III. Solo-
    mon⁵. IV. Jerusha⁵. V. Benjamin⁵. VI. Sarah⁵.
    VII. Abigail⁵. VIII. Thomas⁵. IX. Jerusha⁵ (again).
    X. Huldah⁵.

II. Sarah³, b. in Plymouth; mar. April 11, 1661, as his second
wife, John³ Hawkes, of Lynn. The first wife of John³
Hawkes was Rebecca³, daughter to Moses¹ Maverick, of
Marblehead. They were married June 3, 1658; she died
Nov. 4, 1659, leaving a son, Moses, a day or two old.

John Hawkes, b. 1633,† was second son to Adam¹
Hawkes, of Lynn, who came in the fleet with Winthrop and
landed in June, 1630, at Salem. In 1634, Adam Hawkes
was admitted freeman; he was then of Charlestown. His
wife, Anne, who is supposed to have been the mother of all
his children except Sarah, was the widow of —— Hutchinson. As the wife of Adam Hawkes, she was admitted Nov.
21, 1634, to the First Church of Charlestown.‡ She died
Dec. 4, 1699, in Lynn; and her husband married, second,
in June, 1670, Sarah Hooper.

The four acres of planting-ground which Adam Hawkes
possessed Jan. 10, 1635–36, in Charlestown, he sold not long
after to N. Eaton and J. Sibley. Before 1638, he had removed to Lynn, for in that year he received, as "an inhabitant of the Town," a grant of one hundred acres. The farm
was on the banks of the Saugus River,§ and there he built
a house. This house soon afterward was burned; the only
persons in it at the time were a servant girl and twin in-
fants, who escaped unharmed through the snow. The second house which he built was in part constructed from the

---

* Vide issue of Robert¹ Cushman.
† *Essex County Court Records*, Book 11 : 85.
‡ Budington's *History of the First Church, Charlestown*, 1845: 247.
§ "Saugust is called Lin, Nov. 20, 1637." (*Massachusetts Bay Records*,
vol. 1 : 211.)

material of the first, — bricks brought from England. When the house was demolished, in 1872, a brick was found bearing the date *1611*. There was found also an ancient fireback, about two feet square and weighing nearly a hundred pounds, on which was moulded what was supposed to be the British arms; later, this has been thought to be a coat-of-arms, possibly that of the Hawkes family. It is said that Adam Hawkes owned the land where iron ore was found, and that he believed that one of the mines contained silver.

In September, 1653, Adam Hawkes (Sr. or Jr.), of Lynn, appeared on John Gifford's "bill for work diet provisions &c for Iron works at Hammersmith & Braintree." "Mʳ. Adam hawks" was chosen as one of the "gentlemen of the grand jury," by order dated "23 oct. 1660."* He died April 13, 1671–72, in Lynn, aged sixty-four years,† leaving a

---

* *Essex County Court Records*, Book 2 : 59; Book 6 : 62.

† Although much has been printed about the Hutchinson family, this line never before has been published. It is compiled from the original records.

ISSUE OF ——¹ AND ANNE HUTCHINSON

I. Samuel² Hutchinson, b. 1617 or 1618, was of Lynn and Reading. He was a farmer. In 1638, the town of Lynn granted him ten acres near the hundred-acre farm of Adam Hawkes, which he sold in 1648, with the dwelling-house upon it, for £30. With wife, Hannah, he sold for £300, May 14, 1670, his homestead in Reading, "on the side of Great Pond," to Richard Sutton, of Roxbury. Samuel probably removed to Andover, where his will, dated April 23, 1740, was proved, Aug. 24, 1741.

II. Elizabeth² Hutchinson, b. 1622; mar. about 1650, Isaac¹ Hart. He was b. about 1614 or 1615, at "Scratby" (Scratly, a part of Ormsby), England; he sailed from London, April 11, 1637, in the ship *Rose*. Isaac Hart was first at Watertown, but soon drifted to Lynn. Aug. 1, 1656, Thomas Hutchinson conveyed for £120 to Isaac Hart, his house and barn, with two hundred acres of upland and nineteen acres of meadow, adjoining land of Edward Hutchinson, but as he could not meet the payments, Hart made over sixty acres to Francis Hutchinson. In 1673, Hart purchased five hundred acres in what is now Lynnfield, on which he resided until his death.

At the time of the witchcraft persecution, Mrs. Elizabeth Hart was imprisoned for six months; but finally was allowed by the Court to return to her home. She d. Nov. 28, 1700, her husband having d. Feb. 10, 1699–1700. His will, dated Feb. 6, 1697, mentioned wife, Eliza-

widow, Sarah. His son, John Hawkes, was appointed administrator; and, with the consent of the Court, was "to paye unto the Seuerall persons conserned, as are hereafter named:"—

"Viz: to giue vnto his mother wid Sarah Hauks a parcell of upland containeing nine skoare acres more or lesse lying in Lyn bounds, not joyneing to the farme," eight acres of meadow in "The great medow," and "one third part of all the moueable things contained in the Inventory."

"2: John Hauks is to paye vnto Sarah Hauks Daughter vnto the said widow, fower Skoare & ten pounds;" the last fifty "at eighteen years of age or at her marige daye ... to be payd in corne or cattell."

"3: John Hauks is to Deliuer and sett out vnto Moses Hauks his sonn which he had by rebeckah Hauks, daughter to mr Moses Mauericke ... one haulfe part of that fearme which the said

---

beth, sons, Thomas, John, Samuel, and Adam Hart, and daughters, "Elizabeth Wenborne and Dabra Procter."

III. Edward² Hutchinson was of Lynn. He d. Dec. 8, 1694, leaving a widow, Mary, who probably was a second wife. Issue: 1. Hananiah³, "the eldest son;" mar. Martha ——. 2. Benjamin³, d. unmar. in 1716. 3. Nathaniel³, "youngest son," d. unmar. in 1744. 4. Mary³, b. "7mo: 1656;" mar. John Chaplin; had children. 5. Anna³, mar. intention, Aug. 29, 1695, to John Perkins. Issue: five. 6. Sarah³, b. "24: 7mo: 1671;" mar. John Harnden. 7. Mary³ or Mercy.

IV. Thomas² Hutchinson was of Lynn, but later removed to Long Island. Sold his farm, 1656, to Isaac Hart.

V. Francis² Hutchinson, b. 1630; mar., second, about 1679, Mary³, daughter to Elder Thomas³ Cushman.

ISSUE OF ADAM¹ AND ANNE (HUTCHINSON) HAWKES

VI. Adam² Hawkes, d. before his father.

VII. John² Hawkes (twin), b. 1633, probably in Charlestown; mar. Sarah³, daughter to Elder Thomas³ Cushman.

VIII. Susanna² Hawkes (twin), b. 1633, probably in Charlestown; mar., 1649, William³ Cogswell, son to John¹ and Elizabeth (Thompson) Cogswell. William³, b. 1619, in Westbury Leigh, County Wilts, England; came over, in 1635, on the *Angel Gabriel*, with his father.

IX. Moses² Hawkes; d. before his father.

X. Benjamin² Hawkes; d. before his father.

XI. Thomas² Hawkes; d. before his father.

ISSUE OF ADAM¹ AND SARAH (HOOPER) HAWKES

XII. Sarah² Hawkes, b. June 1, 1671, in Reading.

Hauks liued & died vpon . . . being in Lyn . . . when the aforesaid Moses comes to twenty & one years of age . . . this aforesaid giuft is the legacy of m^r Adam Hauks to his grandchil Moses Haukes."

"4: John Hauks is to pay vnto m^r William Cogswell for the use of his wife the some of fower Skoare & ten pounds . . . in corne & cattell or goods."

"5: John Hauks is to paye vnto ffrances Huchisson twenty pounds to be payd in corne cattell or goods."

"6: John Hauks is to pay vnto Samuell Huchisson fiue pounds to be payd in a twelf months time in corne or cattell at the now Dwelling house of John Hauks."

"7: John Hauks is to [pay] Thomas Huchisson fiue pounds in corne or cattell."

"8: John Hauks is to paye vnto Edward Huchisson fiue pounds in corne or cattell."

"9: John Hauks is to paye vnto Elizabeth Hart fiue pounds in corn or cattell."

"lastly all the rest of the estate of Adam Hauks deceased, contained in the said Inventory, boath of houseing lands & other goods, not in this writeing giuen awaye is herby confeirmed vnto the aforesaid John Hauks & his heirs for euer as witnes all ye hands this 27: March: 1672

"This aproued alowed & confirmed by the Court to all the ptyes in court

Ipswich the 2 of March 1672
ROBERT LORD cl"†

---

* In the original, the signature of Francis Hutchinson is at the right of that of Sarah Hawkes, — making him the third signer.

† *Essex County Probate* (Original), Docket: 12899.

The inventory, taken March 18, 1671–72, amounted to £817 : 11 : 00.

Throughout his life, Adam Hawkes was truly a father to the Hutchinson children; they shared in all things with his own. Francis, who could not have been much above a year old when his mother married Hawkes, seems to have been an especial favorite with his stepfather, though they all settled near him.

John[3] Hawkes was made freeman in 1690; he was then called "Senior." During King Philip's War he belonged to the "Lynn Troopers" as a private. Early in 1675, he was reported by Lieut. John Floyd as one of the seven delinquents "at the rendevew at Concord;" but on April 2, 1676, he appeared in an account of Nathaniel Bissell "for ferriage of himself and Samuel Patrick, with three horses . . . 0 : 2 : 4."*

Upon the death of his father, John Hawkes received one half of the farm in Lynn, bordering upon the town of Reading. It consisted of a dwelling-house and barn, valued at £120, and five hundred and fifty acres of land and meadow, estimated at £550. This was well stocked with cattle, bees, and farming-tools. John Hawkes died, without making a will, Aug. 15, 1694, leaving a widow, Sarah, and five children. The following month his heirs signed an amicable agreement for the division of his estate : —

"This Indenture Covenant and Agreement † made Between The Widdow and the Surviving children of m^r John Hauks deceased one with Another Respectively with Reference to The setlement of The Estate of Lands and moveables That The said m^r John Hauks Dye Seized off which Setlement According To This Indenture we whose names Are Subscribed Doe Bind ourselves our heirs Executors for ever by these These presents to Rest satissfyed And Contented and Contented with, never for The future to Molest or disturb each other farther Then what Is here Agreed upon but

---

* *Massachusetts Archives*, Military, 1675–1676, vol. 2 : 244–245; vol. 3 : 128, 228.

† *Essex County Probate* (Original), Docket : 12920.

That Reall And harty Love and peace may be maintained between vs suitable to The neer Relation we Stand In one to Another The principle Motive In This Covenant and Indenture.

" Impr   Agreed, and consented unto That Sarah Hauks our Honourd Mother Have for her Annuall Maintainance six pounds In Money, or what ever else she may have occasion for to her satissfaction to be paid by John & Thomas Hawks and Ebenezer Hawks when s^d Ebenezer he comes to The Age of Twenty one years, and In The mean Time s^d John to pay his proportion for him; The Said Bretheren to Bear an Equall proportion In The s^d payment: Allsoe The s^d widdow Sarah Hauks to have The bigest of The Lower Rooms In The Dwelling house wheir She now Resides together with The Bed and Bedsted and furniture In S^d Room and Improvement of the Household Stuff and provision for Meat and Drink comfortable Dyet During her Abode with her sons In Said House to be provided By John Hauks The Consideration of The S^d six pounds to gether with The premises The said widdow Sarah Hauks Doth Accept of and rest satifyed & Contented with.

" Jt.   Agreed and Consente unto, That Moses Hauks (In Consideration of The Lands willed To him By his Grandfather Adam Hauks and out of The Love that he Beareth to his Bretheren and Relations) The said Moses Doth Accept off and for ever to Rest Satisfyed with The Said Lands willed to him, and which he now enjoyeth viz as m^r John Hauks deceas^d and Said Moses Agreed Said Tract of Land or Lands to be Bounded, all and every The Sd Bounds to Stand firm and good without any molestation of any of his Bretheren : As Allsoe The S^d Moses Hauks to have a certain parcell of Land which his father John Hauks Dyed Seized off, six Acres be Jt more or Less Adjoining to the Lands of Moses Hauks Neer his Dwelling house Bounded Norwardly by a Brook and Soe on to his own Lands called by The name of The horse pastor; The S^d Moses Is hereby Allsoe discharged from paying any debts due from The Estate of his father John Hauks deceas^d or any Legacies what Soever. and the South Bounds of Said Six Acres by a white oak tree, & y^n e & west to a Rock And soe on to a Red oak Tre And soe To The Brook

" Jt   Agreed and Consented That John Hauks son to John Hauks deceas^d Is to have The Dwelling house of his father deceas^d to gether with one hundred Acres of Land And meddow Adjoining be Jt more or Less Butted and Bounded Westerly upon the Land of m^r Gefford's Norwardly upon The Land of Adam Hauks deceas^d, southwardly upon the Brook Adjoining to the Land of Moses Hauks Eastwardly upon The Land of Moses Hawks & Lyn comon.

"Jt   Agreed And Consented That Thomas Hauks have his divisionall part of Land one Hundred Acres be Jt more or Less Butted and Bounded Southward upon The Land of Moses Hauks by a Brook which Runs Through Dexters Marsh Soe Called, Westerly upon the Land of S^d Moses and Said Brook Es^tward upon The Marsh Called Dexters Marsh, Norward upon The Land of s^d Moses Hauks

Turn over

"Agreed And Consented unto By Ebenezer Hauks and his Guardian Francis Huchinson That The S^d Ebenezer doe Accept of his Divisionall part of Land for his portion out of his fathers estate One hundred Acres within The Bounds of his fathers farm deceas^d. Be Jt more or Less Butted and Bounded Eastwardly at a great Rock with an heap of Stones and from Thence by a line to The Bridge neer The Old orchard, westward by The side of Thomas Hauks his orchard and from the Corner of the orchard Westward to a stake by The Brook which Adjoins to Moses Hauks his Land Southward upon the Town Comon; Allsoe a certain percell of Land to be The Sd Ebenezers which John Hauks deces^d exchanged with The Town of Lyn Lying on Saugust River Adjoining to The Land of Moses Hauks.

"Agreed and Consented to That Mercy Hauks Have for her portion forty pounds Jn or as Silver Mony to Be paid By John Thomas and Ebenezer Each to pay an Equall proportion Ebenezer his proportion when he Arives at The year of Twenty and one and John and Thomas To pay Their proportions to S^d Mercy within The Complement of fower years next Ensuing The date of These presents, The Sd Bretheren paying The S^d sum of monys to their Sister Mercy, She doth discharg The state of her father deceas^d. Jn reference to her Claim as her portion.

"And for The Tru performance of The premises according to all Tru Intents and purposes We The Above mentioned persons Respectively Concerned have hereto Set our hands and Affixed our Seals This fourth Day of September Anno Domini. one Thousand Six hundred ninety and fower.

"Furthermore it is agreed before ye Signing Sealing & Acknowledgment hereof That John Hawkes & Thomas Hawkes & ffrancis Huchison Guardian to Ebenezer Hawkes shall Pay all ye Just Debts

of y⁰ Said John Hawkes Deceased, Out of their part & portion &
y⁰ rest to be no wayes Chargeable for y⁰ Same.

Sign'd Seald	her SARAH ✕ HAUKS Mark	(Seal)
and deliverd	MOSES HAWKS	(Seal)
	JOHN HAUKES	(Seal)
Jn The presents	THOMAS HAWKES	(Seal)
of vs	FFRANCIS HUTCHINSON	(Seal)
HANANIAH HUTCHISSON	Guardian & in behalfe of	
BENIAMEN LARRABE	EBENEZER HAWKES	
BENJAMIN HUTCHISSON	MARCY HAWKS	
	marke of ELIZABETH ✕ HAWKS Guardian to her Son JN⁰: HAWKES	

"Sarah Hawkes Moses Hawkes John Hawkes Thomas Hawkes
ffrancis Huchison Guardian & in behalfe of Ebenezer Hawkes, &
Marcy Hawkes all personally appeared before me y⁰ Subscriber
Judge of y⁰ probate of Wills &c in y⁰ County of Essex & ac-
knowledged this Instrument together wᵗʰ what is anexed relating
to y⁰ payment of y⁰ debts to be their act & Deed
This 3ᵈ Day of December 1694.
BARTH⁰ GEDNEY

"Elizabeth Hawkes as Guardian to her Son John Hawkes Acc-
knowledged the Above Written to be her act and Deed In Consideration that all the other persons above Subscribed quit claime
to Land Sett out & delivered her Jn Right of her Husband Addam
Hawks deceased this 8ᵗʰ of Aprill 1695
before me   BARTH⁰ GEDNEY J P "

On April 8, 1695, Sarah Hawkes, the widow of John
Hawkes, Sr., "Removed her right of administration" upon
her husband's estate in favor of her sons, John and Thomas.
At the same time, John Hawkes quitclaimed * to Elizabeth,
widow of Adam Hawkes, his brother, who had died before
their father, and to "John Hawks only son of the Said Adam
Hawkes . . . four Score acres . . . Sittuate in y⁰ town
Ship of linn . . . with Sawgust riuer to y⁰ west [and bounded]
northward with the land of Danˡˡ Eaton." This land was to

* *Essex County Probate*, Book 303 : 116.

be held by the widow and her son John " as a clear & absolute Estate of Inheritance in fee Simple without any Incum-
brance w'soever." All the heirs who signed the agreement
affixed their signatures to this release.

Sarah, widow of John Hawkes, survived him several years,
but the exact date of her death is not known. By the will
of their father, Elder Cushman, she and her sister, Lydia
Harlow, received twenty shillings; but to this was added one
half of the residue of his estate after the decease of their
mother, "to be equally Divided between them." This Hawkes
family evidently occupied a good position in the town, and
possessed more than ordinary wealth for the times. Some
of their descendants are now residing in Lynn.

> Issue by first wife: 1. Moses [8] Hawkes, b. Nov. [before
> the 4th], 1659, in Lynn. In the division of his grand-
> father's estate, made March 27, 1672, John [8] Hawkes,
> as executor, was "to deliver and sett out unto Moses
> Hawks his sonn, which he had by rebeckah Hawks,
> daughter of M[r] Moses Mavericke," certain tracts of
> land. Moses Hawkes mar. May 10, 1698, Margaret [8]
> Cogswell, daughter to John [2] and Margaret (Gifford)
> Cogswell, of Ipswich. Moses [8] Hawkes d. Jan. 1,
> 1708–9. His son Moses [4], of Lynn, "being come to
> y[e] age of one & Twenty years," March 5, 1719–20,
> accepted his portion of the estate as set forth in his
> father's will.[*]

> Issue by second wife: 2. Susanna [8] Hawkes, b. Nov. 29,
> 1662, in Lynn. With two of her sisters, she died " the
> last of November 1675," a few days after their younger
> sister, Mary, was born.

> 3. Adam [8] Hawkes, b. May 12, 1664, in Lynn. He mar.
> Elizabeth ——, and had a son John. He died before
> his father.

> 4. Ann [8] Hawkes, b. May 3, 1666, in Lynn; d. the last of
> Nov., 1675.

> 5. John [8] Hawkes, b. April 25, 1668, in Lynn. His auto-
> graph signature appears in the agreement of 1694.

---

* *Essex County Deeds*, Book 38 : 3.

6. Rebecca[3] Hawkes, b. Oct. 18, 1670, in Lynn; d. the last of Nov., 1675.

7. Thomas[3] Hawkes, b. May 18, 1673, in Lynn; signed the agreement as "thomas hawkes."

8. Mary[3] Hawkes, b. Nov. 14, 1675, in Lynn. She appears in the agreement as Marcy.

9. Ebenezer[3] Hawkes, was a minor at the time of his father's death, and both the agreement and quitclaim were signed in his behalf by his guardian, Francis Hutchinson. The latter was the husband of his mother's sister, Mary[3] (Cushman) Hutchinson.

III. Lydia[2], b. in Plymouth; mar. about 1682, William[2] Harlow, b. 1650, eldest son to William[1] and Rebecca (Bartlett) Harlow.

William[1] Harlow, a young man, appeared in Lynn in 1637. He removed to Sandwich, then to Plymouth, where he mar., first, in 1649, Rebecca, daughter to Robert Bartlett. After her death he mar., second, in 1658, Mary, daughter to John Faunce.

William[2] Harlow, Jr., and wife, Lydia, had issue as follows:

1. Elizabeth[3] Harlow, b. "3d Weke of february 1683," in Plymouth; mar. Thomas Doty.

2. Thomas[3] Harlow, b. March 17, 1686, in Plymouth; mar. Jedidah Churchill.

3. A dau., b. Feb. 5, 1687; d. March 5, 1687–88, in Plymouth.

4. Isaac[3] Harlow.

5. Lydia[3] Harlow; mar. Barnabas Churchill.

6. Mary[3] Harlow.

7. Rebecca[3] Harlow; mar. Jabez Holmes.

8. William[3] Harlow; mar. Joanna Jackson.

IV. Isaac[2], b. Feb. 8, 1647–48, at Plymouth. (Vide infra.)

V. Elkanah[2], b. June 1, 1651, in Plymouth; mar., first, Feb. 16, 1676–77, Elizabeth Cole, daughter to James[2] Cole, Jr., by his second wife, Abigail (Davenport) Cole. Elizabeth d. Jan. 4, 1681–82, and he mar., second, March 2, 1682–83, Martha[3] Cooke, daughter to Jacob[2] and Damaris[2] (Hopkins) Cooke, of Plymouth. Martha Cooke was b. March

16, 1659–60, at Plymouth, and d. Sept. 17, 1722, at Plympton, aged sixty-two.

Elkanah Cushman was admitted freeman June 7, 1681. He served on the jury 1682–86, and many other years. On Oct. 31, 1682, he was one of the twelve men at the trial of two Indians — one of whom had been arrested "for his incorrageble theft the second time, in robing of a bark and other theft." Elkanah Cushman was deacon of the church at Plympton, of which his brother Isaac was pastor, for about nine years; he also was an Ensign. The Plympton church records say: "At a chh. meeting in Plympton, Dec. y⁰ 26. 1718, Ensign Elcanah Cushman [and two others] were chosen Deacons." "Memorandum that on Sabbath day some time in March in y⁰ year 1718–19 Samuel Sturtevant, Elcanah Cushman and Daniel Bosworth were ordained Deacons by the imposision of hands."

Elkanah Cushman served as Representative to the General Court of Massachusetts three sessions, beginning May 29, August 7, and October 23, in the year 1723.* His house stood on the highway leading eastward from Plympton Green to Kingston, and was the first dwelling-house north of the bridge over Colchester Brook. He died Sept. 4, 1727, in Plympton. His will, dated Oct. 14, 1725, was proved Sept. 26, 1727.†

The following is the inscription on his gravestone in the Plympton Cemetery: —

> HERE LYES BURIED
> Yᴱ BODY OF
> DEACON ELKANAH
> CUSHMAN WHO DECᴰ
> SEPT. Yᴱ 4ᵀᴴ
> 1727 IN
> Yᴱ 77ᵀᴴ YEAR
> OF HIS AGE.

Issue by first wife: 1. Elkanah⁴, b. Sept. 15, 1678, in Plymouth; mar. Feb. 23, 1702–03, Hester³ Barnes, b.

---

* *Massachusetts Archives*, Acts and Resolves, vol. 10: 284.
† *Plymouth County Probate* (Original), Docket: 5813.

Feb. 18, 1682, in Plymouth, daughter to Jonathan[3] and Elizabeth (Hedge) Barnes. He d. Jan. 9, 1714–15, and she mar., second, Oct. 25, 1716, Captain Benjamin Warren. Elkanah Cushman was interred at Burial Hill, Plymouth. Issue by first husband: I. Elizabeth[5], b. Dec. 5, 1703. II. Elkanah[5], b. July 10, 1706. III. James[5], b. Aug. 29, 1709. IV. Hannah[5]. Issue by second husband: V. Joseph Warren, b. Sept. 4, 1717. VI. Mercy Warren, b. May 15, 1721.

2. James[4], b. Oct. 20, 1679, in Plymouth; d. young.
3. Jabez[4], b. Dec. 28, 1681, in Plymouth; d. May, 1682.
Issue by second wife: 4. Allerton[4], b. Nov. 21, 1683, in Plymouth; mar., first, Jan. 11, 1710–11, Mary Buck. She d. Oct. 15, 1725, and he mar., second, Sept. 15, 1726, Elizabeth, daughter to George Sampson. Allerton Cushman d. Jan. 9, 1730–31, in Plympton; his widow, Elizabeth, d. April 17, 1744. Issue: I. Allerton[5]. II. James[5]. III. Mary[5]. IV. Ephraim[5]. V. Alice[5]. VI. Joseph[5].

5. Elizabeth[4], b. Jan. 17, 1685–86, in Plymouth; mar. Dec. 5, 1723, Robert[3] Waterman, b. Feb. 9, 1681, as his second wife.* She d. March, 1724–25, without issue.
6. Josiah[4], b. March 21, 1687–88; mar. Dec. 29, 1709, by the Rev. Isaac Cushman, to Susanna, daughter to Captain William Shurtleff. She was b. 1691, at Plymouth; d. July 27, 1763. Josiah Cushman was Lieutenant in the Militia, and lived in that part of Plymouth now Carver. He d. April 13, 1750. Issue: I. Susanna[5]; d. young. II. Martha[5]. III. Susanna[5]. IV. Anna[5]. V. Josiah[5].

7. Martha[4]; mar. June 6, 1717, Nathaniel Holmes.
8. Mehitable[4], b. Oct. 8, 1693; never married.
VI. Fear[3], b. June 20, 1653; d. before her father made his will.
VII. Eleazer[3], b. Feb. 20, 1656–57; mar. Jan. 12, 1687–88, Elizabeth Combes. He lived in Plympton, and was received into the church in that town during the ministry of his brother, Rev. Isaac Cushman.

---

* Vide issue of Isaac[3] Cushman.

In November, 1733, a petition was presented by "divers inhabitants of Plympton" to the General Court that a new precinct or township be set off. A committee from both Houses repaired to the town, "perambulated & carefully viewed the Lands," and concluded "upon the whole [that they] are of the Opinion, that the prayer of the petition be Granted, the petitioners paying one third part of the aged & Revd Mr Cushman's Salary during his Life as it appears to us they are one third part of the rateable Estate of the said Town." Eleazer Cushman and four others were allowed to remain in the "old precinct, with their Ministerial Lands . . . & the new precinct to have none of the Issues & profits thereof." The new precinct was incorporated in July, 1734, as the town of Halifax. This shows that Eleazer's farm was on the northwesterly side of the town, bordering on Halifax. Little is known of his later years ; he probably removed to a distance with some of his children.

Issue : * 1. Lydia⁴, b. Dec. 13, 1687,† in Plymouth ; mar. Dec. 29, 1709, by the Rev. Isaac Cushman, to John³ Waterman, of Halifax, son to Deacon John² Waterman, one of the first deacons of the church at Plympton.

2. John⁴, b. Aug. 13, 1690, in Plymouth ; mar. Jan. 19, 1715, by the Rev. Isaac Cushman, to Joanna Pratt. Issue : three sons.

3. Moses⁴, b. about 1693, in Plymouth ; mar. Aug. 22, 1721, Mary Jackson. He was chosen deacon May 2, 1757. He was a blacksmith. He d. Aug. 12, 1766, in Plympton. Issue : three sons and seven daughters.

4. James⁴, b. in Plymouth. He settled in that part of Dartmouth now Fair Haven, and the house that he built was standing in 1850. Issue : five sons and six daughters.

5. William⁴, b. Oct. 27, 1710, in Plympton (set off in 1707 from Plymouth) ; mar. Abigail Lee, and removed to Mansfield, Connecticut. Abigail Lee was b. April 9, 1713 ; d. April, 1803. William Cushman d. Dec. 27,

---

* Deacon Lewis Bradford, of Plympton, says : "There were, doubtless, other children of this family."

† *Town Records of Plymouth*, vol. 1 : 20.

1777, at Willington, Connecticut. Issue: seven sons and four daughters.

VIII. Mary[8], b. about 1659, in Plymouth, mar. Francis Hutchinson, of Lynn and Reading.

In a deposition, dated March 1, 1665–66, he gave his age as thirty-six years,* from which it appears that he was born about 1630. His first wife, Sarah Leighton, whom he married "11: 10mo: 1634" (Dec. 11, 1634), in Lynn, died twelve days later — "23: 10mo: 1634." † He probably married Mary Cushman in 1679, when she was twenty years of age, since Francis, the eldest of their three sons, was born about 1680. She was not living when her father made his will, on October 22, 1690, bequeathing "unto my three Grandchildren in Lin the Children of my daughter Mary Hutchinson deceased to each of them twenty shillings to be paid unto them out of my Estate Soone after my decease." From the absence of any mention of his son-in-law's name, or transaction between them, it is apparent that Elder Cushman did not approve of his daughter Mary's marriage. This may have been due to the difference of twenty-nine years in their ages.

Francis[2] Hutchinson was youngest son to ——[1] Hutchinson, whose widow, Anne, married, about 1631, Adam[1] Hawkes, of Charlestown. She had, at that time, five young children: Samuel[2], Elizabeth[2], Edward[2], Thomas[2], and Francis[2] Hutchinson. Whether the father of these children died before they left England, on the voyage coming over, or soon after their arrival, cannot be ascertained.

For a time all the Hutchinson children remained in the neighborhood of their stepfather, Adam Hawkes; and the loss of a colt valued at £11:9:2, given to John Hawkes by his father Adam, was the cause of various depositions ‡ that show the relationship. Isaac Hart, who had married Elizabeth Hutchinson, called John Hawkes "his Bro: [bro-

---

* *Essex County Court Records*, Book 11 : 85.

† *City Records of Lynn.* In these early records this name, written Sara Layghton, has been wrongly copied as Sara Luggston.

‡ *Essex County Court Records*, Book 4 : 11–122.

ther]," and Thomas Hutchinson testified "that my father in law [stepfather] Addam: Hakes did giue to his sone John Hakes such a colt & hee did put it to Jsaake Hartes to keepe." "ffrancis Hutchinson" also testified "that J did see Isack Hart and sammell Hutchinson to mark John hawkes coult and J was one of the compeny that did fetch up the Coult to the Marrking and that that this Coult that is now in Contrievarcy J doe verrlie be leeue that it is John hawcks Coult." Sworn to in Court, "2 : 10 : [16]58."

When Adam Hawkes, on June 18, 1660, brought suit against the Iron Works "ffor Damning their waters so high as it is cause of flotting his Lands well and Bridge to his great Damage for several years," Francis Hutchinson testified, with others, "that Mr Adam Hawkes sufer[ed] much Damage by the waters of the Irne worrkes . . . sume time thay fallen in Danger for to breacke thar leggs." * Evidently there no attempt was made to draw off the water, and in the face of tardy justice the Hawkes family probably had taken down a part of the dam, since, in 1663, suit was brought against John Hawkes, Sr., and his brother Moses, by Samuel Appleton and his son Samuel, in an action of appeal from the County Court at Salem to the Court of Assistants in Boston. Judgment was given in favor of the plaintiffs for £30 damages, and "the defendants shall make vp the great dam as Good as before in twelue months time next ensuing or pay £250" and costs. John Hawkes appealed; and on March 4, 1663, "the Jury brought in their verdict they found for the plaintiff [Hawkes] Reuersion of the former Judgment & costs of Court nine pounds." †

Edward Hutchinson, too, lived near, — for in 1661, the estate of William Lampson, of Ipswich, included four acres of meadow "in the great meddow in the bounds of Lynn bounded by meddow of Edward Hutcheson towards the North the meddow of Jsaac Harte towards the South . . . and Jsaac Hart his farme east." ‡

---

* *Essex County Court Records*, Book 5 : 106, 109.
† *Records of the Court of Assistants*, Boston, 1630–1692, vol. 1 : 236, 243.
‡ *Essex County Court Records*, Book 7 : 33.

Francis Hutchinson settled in the North Precinct of Lynn, which in 1644 was established as the town of Reading. His farm was a part of the land sold by his brother Thomas to Isaac Hart, Aug. 21, 1656. The original tract consisted of two hundred and eighty-nine acres. In 1715, when the title of the sixty acres which Hart had given to Francis Hutchinson was questioned, Shubael Stearns, an old friend and neighbor, seventy-four years of age, deposed: That about fifty years before (in 1665) he had bought a lot next adjoining the sixty acre lot where "Francis Hutchinson then dwelt on partly in Reading & partly in Lynn;" and that his sons, Francis and Thomas, had been in "quiet possession ever since." At the house of Isaac Hart in Lynn, Stearns heard Mrs. Hart often say that her brother, Francis Hutchinson, had paid her brother, Thomas Hutchinson, for "s^d lot of 60 acres," and "particularly once when she was discoursing of the matter her husband m^r Isaac Hart coming in she said to him I wonder you dont give Francis a Deed of his land you know he has paid for it he answered he dont ask me for one . . . he paid an horse and something else." Adam Hart, above sixty years of age (1715), had heard his mother, Elizabeth Hart, say when her brother Thomas "was about to go to Long Island they being not ready to make payment for the whole," the sixty acre lot was given to Francis Hutchinson to make payment for the same.*

In 1685, the town of Reading voted, "that all those persons that inhabit on the north side of Ipswich River, in our town bounds, viz. . . . Francis Hutchinson and [eight others] . . . shall have those two pieces of land, namely: the towne's land in Sadler's Neck, so called [and] that piece of Common land, that lyeth at the upper end of Mr. Bellingham's farme and belongs to the towne."† This land Francis Hutchinson bequeathed to his youngest son, John.

Living in a section which since has been divided into several townships, it has been difficult to learn much about his life. On May 17, 1662, when the "Troopers of Essex County"

* *Middlesex County Deeds*, Book 14: 263; Book 32: 499.
† Eaton's *History of Reading*, 1874: 30.

were to be newly arranged, the towns that had not already organized companies were to "haue Libertie to nominate a compleate number of officers according to Law." Under this order, Francis Hutchinson was chosen Captain of the Lynn company in 1663.* Although the inventory of his estate mentions two guns, also a "Repure [rapier] & belt," he was not recorded in the service of the later wars.

Francis Hutchinson "owned yᵉ Covenant" in the First Church of Reading (now Wakefield), Sept. 6, 1687.† This is conjectured to be soon after the death of his second wife, Mary, the mother of his three sons. In 1688, he subscribed £3 toward the new meeting-house of the First Church; among other subscribers living at "Lynn End" (now Lynnfield) were Edward Hutchinson, £2:10, and Isaac Hart, £10:01. The date of the death of Francis is given in the inventory of the estate of "mʳ ffrancis Hucheson of Reading whoe deperted This life the 12ᵗʰ of November 1702." His will, dated Feb. 18, 1698–99, is as follows:—

"In the name of God Amen. ᛋᛋ ʝ ffrances Huchinson of Redding in the County of Middˣ Jn his Majᵗˢ Province of the Massatusets Bay in New-England, Yeoman being Aged and also attended with many Weaknesses and Jnfermetyes of body, but thro ᴖ gods Goodness of sound vnderstanding and perfect Memory, and knowing it to be a Christian duty for A man to sett his hous in Order, do therefore make and publish this wrighting to be my last Will and testament,‡ — & first ʝ giue my Soule to god that gaue it me, and my body to the Earth to be decently buryed, Jn hopes of A gloryous Resurection to life againe thro yᵉ death and merritts of Christ Jesus my lord and only Saviour, and as to that portion of this Worlds goods, yᵗ god of his bounty hath bestowed on me, ʝ do giue and bequeath as falloweth, after my Just debts & funerall Charg is payᵈ

"Jmprˢ my Will is and ʝ do hereby giue and bequeath vnto my beloued Wife Martha Huchinson one third part of all my personall Estate (that J haue not giuen away before my death) both Within doars

---

* Lewis and Newhall's *Annals of Lynn*, 1865: 255.

† "Earliest Records of the Congregational Church at Wakefield," from the *Citizen and Banner*, Nov. 21, 1902.

‡ *Middlesex County Probate* (Original), Docket: 8704¼.

and ⌒ Without doars, to be sett out to her by my Executers
herein after ⌒ named, that is one full third part quantety for qual-
ety, and my will is that Jf my said Wife do desire it, she shall haue
those things in perticuler as part of her thirds, y^t J received with
her vpon Marriage, and that the other part of her thirds of my personall Estate be made vp to her as afor s^d, all Which thirds J
do freely giue it her for her own Vse to her and her heirs for Ever,
⌒ ⌒ only here it is Jntended and to be Vnderstood, as J have
hinted before that J haue giuen away alredy to my three sons : viz :
ffrances Thomas and John Huchinsons, namely three small things
y^t are not to be mentioned nor Aprised in my Jnventory, they being
in posession therof alredy before my death, which are, first my
Son ffrances A silver Cup marked with y^e. two first letters of his
name, and to my son Thomas J haue giuen my gold-ring, and J
haue giuen my son John my largest peuter platter marked with
thess three things are not to be Aprised in my Jven-
tory becauss giuen away alredy, ⌒ also my Will is
and J do giue vnto my said Wife one third part of
my housing and lands situate in Redding afor s^d to be sett out to
her by my Exec^r quantety for quallety both of housing orchards
plowland pasterland and Meadows to be for her Vse and Jmproue-
ment for her Comfort and for her Vse only, dureing her Naturall
life, and after her decease y^n. to returne to my sons to Whome J
haue herein after bequeathed the same,

"2ly my Will is and J do hereby guie and bequeath vnto my two Eldest
sons namely ffrances and Thomas all my homstedd, both housing, orchards, plowlands, pasterlands, and Meadows, it being by Estema-
tion seventy-four acres more or less, to be Equaly devided betweene
them, and when it is devided my Eldest son ffrances shall haue
the liberty of Choyce which halfe he will take, only they shall not
distirbe their mother afore named in the quiet possession of her
third part thereof dureing her Naturall life as afor s^d and further
my Will is and J do hereby giue vnto these my two Eldest sons,
afer my Just debts and funerall Charges is fully pay^d the other two
thirds of my personall Estate that is as Yett Vndisposed of, to be
Equaly devided betweene them, and when they are devided then
my Will is that my son ffrancis shall haue his Choyce which halfe
he will haue

Turne over

"3ly my Will is and J do giue and bequeath vnto my Son John Huchinson my timber lott adjoyning to Stephen ffishes land it being
twenty fiue acrs more or less as also one lott of swamp it being
fiue acres more or less all Which thirty acres more or less J do

giue to my said son John Huchinson to him his heirs and assignes for Ever, and my will is that he the said John Huchinson shall be bound out to A trade by ord^r. of my Exec^rs. ᴗ

" 4ly   my Will is that Jf any of these my Children aforenamed shall dy before they Come at age, that then such portion as J haue giuen them shall be Equaly devided among my surviueing Children

" Lastly   my Will is and j do hereby Nominate and appoint my Eldest son ffrances Huchinson Exec^r. to this my Will, and for asmuch as he is not yett of the age of twenty one years J do Nominate and apoint my loueing Cousen [nephew] Hannaniah Huchinson of Linn in y^e. County of Essex in New England afor s^d to be my Executer to this my Will Vntill my son ffrances aforsᵈ. be twenty one Years of age and then he to take ye Executership vpon him as afor s^d.

   " Jn wittness whereof J the said ffrances Huchinson sen^r. haue herevnto sett my hand and affixed my seale this Eighteenth day of ffebruary Anno: Domini Sixteene hundred ninty Eight nine, and in the Eleventh Yeare of his Maj^st Reigne, W^m the third over England &c: King &c:

ffranris ffutshinfon { SEAL* }

" Signed sealed and published by ffrances Huchinson sen^r. this ⎱
Wrighting on this and y^e. other side the leafe ᴗ his last Will ⎰
and testament before Vs ᴗ ᴗ ᴗ

SHUBAEL STARNS
BENJAMIN HUTCHISSON
JAM^S CONVERSE ᴗ "

   This will was sworn to by the witnesses, Shubael Stearns, Benjamin Hutchinson, and James Converse, at "Cambridge: Decr 7° 1702." The inventory, taken by Jeremiah Swain and John Brown, Nov. 26, 1702, included among other items: "To Milletiry Arms: 2 guns one Repure & belt . . . £03: 06: 00;" also about fourteen acres of meadow in "Lyn bounds att . . . £28;" and about twenty-five acres at "Sadler's Nook . . . £15." Administration was granted, Dec. 7, 1702, to Francis Hutchinson, the eldest son, who had reached his majority since the will was made.

---

   * This seal has been stamped with some impression ; but, as the document is covered with silk tissue to preserve it, the design is indistinct.

The gift of three articles by Francis Hutchinson to his sons, which were not to be considered a part of his estate, carries with it a peculiar significance. It suggests the legacy of Elder Cushman to the three children of his daughter, Mary Hutchinson, in Lynn ; but, being of greater value than the twenty shillings he gave to each, it probably represented their share in the estate of their mother.

The widow, Martha, was the third wife of Francis Hutchinson, and probably at the time of her marriage to him, a widow. In his will he desired that "she shall haue those things in perticuler as part of her thirds, y^t I received with her vpon Marriage, and that the other part of her thirds . . . be made vp to her." Martha, widow of Francis Hutchinson, died Aug. 15, 1708, in Reading. Her husband's death, Nov. 12, 1702, also is recorded there.*

Issue by second wife : 1. Francis³ Hutchinson, b. about 1680, in Lynn or Reading ; mar. May 18, 1708, in Reading, Mary, daughter to John and Joanna Jefferds, of Lynn.†
In the settlement of the estate of her father, "m^r John Jefferds," Mary Hutchinson gave a receipt, June 19, 1734, for the sum of £8 : 04 : 07, in full for her share.‡

Francis³ Hutchinson was a resident of Lynn, that part later called Lynnfield. He died intestate, in Lynn, about Jan., 1755, as his inventory was ordered by the Court Feb. 10, and taken March 21, of that year. In March, 1752, he had given to his daughter, Anne Sheldon, wife of Amos Sheldon, of Lynn, for £200, a deed of one half of his homestead, including the house, barn, and thirty acres of land in Lynn and Reading, bounded north by the highway, east by land of Nathaniel Sherman, south by Bare Meadow, and west by the land of Thomas Hutchinson ; also eighteen acres in Lynn, adjoining the land of Samuel Stearns and "Willises Meadow." This deed was acknowledged by witnesses, Jan. 21, 1755, to be the "deed of Francis Hutchinson now deceased." §

* *Town Records of Reading* (copy), vol. I : 13, 11.
† *Town Records of Reading* (copy), vol. I : 193.
‡ *Essex County Probate*, Book 316: 505.
§ *Essex County Deeds*, Book 122 : 106.

The inventory of his estate includes: one half of the house, half of the barn, half of the homestead, half of thirteen acres at " Willises Meadow," and half of eight acres at Bare Meadow, £139: 09: 04; household furniture, live-stock, "half a cyder mill & the whole Press," farming-tools, warming-pan, etc., £50 : 15 : 06; "His Plate viz One Silver Cup . . . £3:04: 10." This cup was evidently his most cherished possession, as it was second in the list, his wearing apparel, valued at £3 : 11, being mentioned first. This doubtless was the cup representing his share in his mother's estate.

Upon the petition of Mary, the widow, "she being very infirm of body," her son-in-law, Amos Sheldon, was appointed administrator. The widow was given her thirds ; and the remainder was settled upon Anne (Anna) Sheldon, wife of Amos, who was to pay to the heirs of Thomas Hutchinson, deceased, the only son, " his double share," and to Mary Newhall and Elizabeth Hutchinson the money equivalent to their shares : — these "being All yᵉ children & heirs of yᵉ sᵈ Deceᵈ "*

Issue: I. Anne⁴ Hutchinson ; mar. Amos Sheldon, of Lynn. II. Thomas⁴ Hutchinson ; mar. about 1749, Anna, daughter to William and Anna (———) Bryant, of Reading. Anna Bryant was b. July 19, 1733, in Reading. Her husband, Thomas⁴ Hutchinson, d. in Jan., 1749–50 ; the next month, Feb. 9, the widow Anna petitioned that her father, William Bryant, Jr., "may administer upon the estate of my late husbund," she being under age and unable to attend to it. Dec. 31, 1750, her father was appointed guardian to her posthumous son Thomas, then about six months old. July 19, 1762, Brown Emerson was appointed guardian in place of Mr. Bryant, the son "now being about twelve years old." † Issue : 1. Thomas⁵ Hutchinson, b. June, 1750, in Reading. III. Mary⁴ Hutchinson ; mar. Samuel Newhall, of Lynn. IV. Elizabeth⁴ Hutchinson.

2. Thomas³ Hutchinson, b. about 1681 or 1682 ; mar. Mary

* *Essex County Probate*, Book 332 : 542 ; Book 333 : 12, 464, 466 ; Book 346: 183.

† *Middlesex County Probate* (Original), Docket : 14441.

———. He lived on a part of his father's farm on the border of Lynn and Reading, but was better known as a resident of Reading. In 1732, he was chosen one of the deacons of the First Church of North Reading; he was also selectman that year.* April 23, 1754, Thomas Hutchinson, of Reading, yeoman, and his wife, Mary, conveyed to Benjamin Flint, of Reading, for £133 : 06 : 08, thirty acres, "partly in Reading and partly in Lynn," with the buildings thereon, together with three acres in "Willisses" meadow adjoining land of his brother Francis and Samuel Stearns. This deed was acknowledged by Thomas Hutchinson, March 21, 1755 ;† as his wife did not join with him, she may have died. He probably removed soon after this sale of his homestead, for there is no probate of his estate in Middlesex or Essex counties.

Issue: ‡ I. Adam⁴ Hutchinson (twin), b. Nov. 25, 1712, in Reading. II. Thomas⁴ Hutchinson (twin), b. Nov. 25, 1712, in Reading, d. aged ten days. III. Lydia⁴ Hutchinson, b. May 7, 1721, in Reading. Perhaps she was the Lydia who mar. Nathan Flint, b. 1716, son to Ebenezer and Gertrude (Pope) Flint, of the North Precinct of Reading.

3. John³ Hutchinson, b. 1683 or 1684, was "bound out" and learned the trade of a blacksmith, as stipulated in his father's will. Soon after reaching his majority, " John Huchason of Lynn blacksmith," for £87 in silver, purchased of Mrs. Sibyl Wigglesworth, widow of the Rev. Mr. Michael Wigglesworth, of Malden, her dwelling-house, barn, and the six and a half acres upon which the buildings stood, near the meeting-house, in Malden ; with several other small tracts of land. The transfer, dated Feb. 28, 1705–06, was witnessed by his brother, Thomas Hutchinson, and John Hawkes.§

---

* Eaton's *History of Reading*, 1874 : 213, 283.
† *Middlesex County Deeds*, Book 57 : 219.
‡ *Town Records of Reading* (copy), vol. 1 : 21, 34, 14, 69.
§ *Middlesex County Deeds*, Book 14 : 151.

The name of the wife of John Hutchinson was Mary; together they sold, Dec. 21, 1715, to his brother, Thomas Hutchinson, of Reading, for £6, twelve and a half acres of the land given to him by the will of his father, at Sadler's Neck, near Bare Meadow.* He previously had conveyed the other half of this land to his brother Francis. The will of John Hutchinson, of Malden, dated April 4, 1760, was proved Sept. 6, 1762. He bequeathed to his daughter, Mehitable Hutchinson, "the one half part of my Real Estate except my shop," and all the personal estate "except my smith tools and Military arms;" to his "beloved granson John Turfs [Tufts] the other half part of my Real Estate with my Shop and smith tools and my Miletary arms," he to pay to his brothers and sisters, within one year, £2 : 13 : 04, "to be equally divided between them;" to daughter, Phebe Sprague, besides what he already had given her, £13 : 06 : 08. His daughter Mehitable was to be executrix.†

Issue : I. Mehitable⁴ Hutchinson. II. Daughter, who mar. —— Tufts, and had a son John and other children. III. Phebe⁴ Hutchinson ; mar. —— Sprague.

ISAAC³ CUSHMAN

Isaac³ Cushman, second son to Elder Thomas² and Mary (Allerton) Cushman, was born February 8, 1647–48, in Plymouth. He married, about 1675, Rebecca Rickard, who was born in 1654, at Plymouth.

Isaac Cushman appears to have been an early example of the self-made man. Without special advantages, he obtained a better education than was common in his time, and excelled in widely diverging attainments. At the age of twenty-eight he commenced surveying, following in the footsteps of his father ; he served on many committees for the town ; was Deputy to the General Court ; and the last thirty-seven years of his life he was the beloved pastor of the First Church of Plympton.

---

* *Middlesex County Deeds*, Book 32 : 499.
† *Middlesex County Probate*, Docket : 8707.

He lived in that part of Plymouth which was set off June 4, 1707, as Plympton. His large farm, partly inherited from his father and partly acquired in 1703 by a grant from the town, extended from the burying-ground northwardly, on the east of the present highway. The grant of May 24, 1703, was of a tract of eighteen acres, to be equally divided between Isaac Cushman and Benjamin Soule, adjoining land they already possessed, "on Condition that they allow a sufficient road to be laid out by the select men of the town through their other lands for the use of the Neighbors & Travellers." *

As surveyor of highways for the town of Plymouth, Isaac Cushman was first chosen on May 4, 1676; he also served as surveyor of highways and "to lay out land," in 1684 and 1694–98. He was selectman 1687, 1688, 1692, and 1694; "Rater" for the town, "for a year," from July 27, 1685. In 1695, he was on a committee to make a rate of £85 for the support of the minister, Rev. John Cotton.† He took the freeman's oath June 6, 1683,‡ and served many terms on juries and the "Grand Enquest."

On November 24, 1684, he was one of the "agents" to "defend the Northerly line of the Towne." Eleven years later, March 29, 1695, "Major Bradford, Left John Bradford, Isaac Cushman," and three others, were "A Comitty to Consider of and draw up such agrements as may be of use to defend the Towns Right on the North sid of the Towne." Isaac Cushman was chosen, Jan., 1687–88, on a committee to defend the "towns Rite In Clarks Iland." In 1697, he was elected "to settle any difference that might Arise in the Rainges of Land, . . . & to see that the Towns Comons be not Intruded on." §

When the people of New England took advantage of a

---

* *Town Records of Plymouth*, vol. 1 : 313.

† *Town Records of Plymouth*, vol. 1 : 147, 231, 238, 239, 250, 252, 176, 189, 195, 205, 232, 233, 235, 183, 240.

‡ *Plymouth Colony Records*, Court Orders, vol. 6 : 110.

§ *Town Records of Plymouth*, vol. 1 : 176, 236, 193, 249.

revolution in England, forcing James II. to flee the country, and seized and imprisoned Andros in the spring of 1689, the citizens of Plymouth chose their two ablest men to represent them in the legislature. The deputies chosen at town-meeting, May 28, 1689, were John Bradford and Isaac Cushman. At the first session of the General Court of that year, which opened June 4, at Plymouth, the Court "appointed John Walley, Esqr, Lieu^t Ephraim Morton, John Bradford, Isaac Cushman, and John Barker, or any three of them, to make enquiry concerning any goods or estate of the colonies that may be in the hands of any person . . . and give accompt thereof to the Court; also to accompt with the Treasurer and the late county sheriffs, or county treasurers, with respect to rates or fines, money or other estate, in any ways belonging to the King, or countrey, or county. And s^d countrey Treasurer, county sheriffs, and county Treasurers are ordered and required to accompt with s^d comĩtee accordingly." At the second session, beginning August 4, 1689, it was written of Cushman: "He appeared & attended at s^d Court;" he also was present at the third session, which opened December 25.*

John Bradford and Isaac Cushman again were elected as Deputies on June 3, 1690, and June 2, 1691. The last session of the Plymouth Colony Court was held on July 7, 1691. "The Deputies y^t appeared & served at s^d Court [were] these following, vizt:—[No. 1] John Bradford, [No. 2] Isaac Cushman, [No. 6] Benjamin Stetson," and twenty-one others. The closing record was as follows: "Ordered by this Court, y^t ye last Wednesday of this instant be kept & observed by all ye inhabitants of this Colony as a day of publique fasting and prayer, &c." † In 1692, a new charter was sent over which converted the Colonies of Massachusetts Bay, Plym-

---

* *Town Records of Plymouth*, vol. 1 : 195, 201, 203; also *Plymouth Colony Records*, Court Orders, vol. 6 : 205, 210, 211, 222.

† *Plymouth Colony Records*, Court Orders, vol. 6: 240, 263, 268, 269.

outh, and Maine into one Province; but the people had no power to make any laws except such as the king approved. The Deputies thereafter met at Boston.

After the death of Elder Thomas Cushman, in December, 1691, the church at Plymouth for some months remained without a Ruling Elder. To provide assistance for the pastor, Rev. John Cotton, on September 11, 1692, "divers Brethren were nominated as sutable to read the Psalmes: viz Jonathan Shaw Thomas Cushman Isaac Cushman Elkanan Cushman John Morton Ephraim Morton Junr Eleizer Churchel William Shurtliffe John Bradford & Baruch Jordan: & it was concluded that any of these might be called forth by the Pastor to this service." Later, Mr. Samuel Fuller succeeded Thomas Cushman in the position of Ruling Elder, but was dismissed early in 1694 to be "the Teacher of the chh at Middlebury." March 7, 1694–95, action was taken by the church again to fill the office of Ruling Elder, notice having been given the Sabbath before "to prepare their thoughts to nominate some brethren to serve in the office of Deacons and Elders. The chh spoke man by man, and all but two or three of the brethren nominated Deacon Faunce and Bro. Isaac Cushman for Elders." At the same time Messrs. George Morton, Nathaniel Wood, and Thomas Clark were chosen Deacons.*

On June 16, 1695, the "Elders being desired to give their answers; Bro. Faunce declined a present acceptance of the call from sense of his own unfitness. Bro. Isaac Cushman desired further time for consideration." Cushman's indecision arose from the fact that he was at that time preaching to the people of the Western Precinct, later known as Plympton, who desired him to become their settled pastor; and he also had received a call from Middleborough "to be their Teacher," in place of Rev. Samuel Fuller, who had died a few months after accepting that office. The church

---

record so quaintly describes the matter that it is here copied
in full : —

"The chh was called to meet on September 1 : which they did,
and the Pastor acquainted them with those 2. calls our brother
had. The chh manifested generally their good respect to him
and desires not to part with him, but that he should be an Elder
here in his blessed Father's room, and desired him now to give
his answer to that call, which accordingly he did : That the Providence of God was mysterious, but he apprehended he should
rather accept the call of this chh to be Elder here, because it was
first given before the other two calls ; the chh acted no further
in that matter at that time, only voted that it would be noe offence
but acceptable to them if Bro. Cushman did improve his gifts in
teaching at Middlebury or any other place where the orderly
providence of God should call him. God soe disposed that he
harkened to the call of our Brethren and neighbours of the new
society where he now lives and constantly attends the work of
Preaching amongst them and is well accepted and acknowledged
by them."

The Western Precinct of Plymouth was incorporated November 25, 1695, though its first meeting of record was not
held until January, 1701. This incorporation made it possible for the inhabitants to settle a pastor and contribute to his
support, and relieved them from any further tax for the par-
ent church at Plymouth. The uniform traditional testimony
of aged people in Plympton is that, before the Rev. Isaac
Cushman preached to them, both men and women generally
walked to Plymouth to attend "meeting" on Sunday. His
church probably was the outgrowth of neighborhood prayer-
meetings held in their homes, because they were so far from
the regular church services.

It appears from the Plympton church records that the
Rev. Isaac Cushman was ordained October 27, 1698, and
that he had been preaching in the Western Precinct for
three years before his ordination. The delay was caused by
the diversity of opinion as to the fitness of installing as Pas-

tor one who had not been ordained, and who had not served as Ruling Elder. The Rev. Mr. Cotton and a minority of the members of the Plymouth Church took the negative side of the question; Mr. Cotton probably felt that the power and influence of the clergy were at stake. Cushman was then about forty-seven years of age, and was resolved to enter the ministry, for which he undoubtedly had peculiar "gifts and graces." He and a majority of the church opposed Mr. Cotton, and approved of the ordination. In the mean time, Mr. Cushman commenced preaching at Plympton, without being ordained. That increased the flame; and "many ill reports were propogated." At length it became apparent that Mr. Cushman and his supporters "would prevail, for he *would* preach and the people at Plympton *would* hear him — ordained or not." Thereupon the Rev. Mr. Cotton sent in his resignation, October 3, 1697, "to the great grief of a number of the Church and Town who desired his continuance." The following account of his ordination is from the first page of records of the Plympton Church :—

"Whereas the Inhabitance of the western part of Plimouth in y⁰ year 1695 obtained liberty of being a distinct Society by themselves from the generall Court, having before sought to God for help and direction, did, on the first daye of Janewary in said year set apart a daye for thanksgiuin — after which upon their desire Mr. Isaac Cushman preached the gospell there untill the 27ᵗʰ daye of October, in y⁰ year 1698, upon which daye after a confession of faith and a church couenant was made, he was chosen and ordained to the pastorell office amongst them by the Elders and messengers of thre of the neighbouring churches, viz : Plimouth Duxborough and Marsfeeld being those present and assisting."

The Plymouth church records bear these notes :—

"This second Church in Town had been formed about a Twelvemonth before, and Mᵣ *Isaac Cushman* was ordained their pastor, who afterwards proved a useful Instrument of building up Christ's Kingdom : This was the 4ᵗʰ Church derived from us, seated at a Place since called *Plympton*." "In April 1699, they [the Plymouth Church] chose Deacon Thomas Faunce their Ruling Elder to be helpful to Mr Little in church affairs. He was ordained to that office by Messrs. *Little* and *Cushman*, Oct. 25, 1699."[*]

In the peaceful settlement of the heated controversy between the two churches, which to-day appears so small but at that time was a matter of great moment, was founded the principle of the Congregational body of believers, — "that each church was entirely independent in its organization from all others," and that the vote of the majority should rule. The "Creed and Confession of Faith," written in the church records by the Rev. Isaac Cushman himself, "are *precisely* the same that are now [1855] used by the Congregational Church at Plympton. In the year 1793, under the ministry of Rev. Ezra Sampson, it was changed, and its ultra-calvinism somewhat modified. But in the year 1808, the original, as prepared by our ancestor, was again adopted and has since remained unchanged."[†] To this "Creed and Covenant" were attached the names of fourteen males, the first being "Mr Isaac Cushman;" and twenty females, the first — "Mrs Rebeckah Cushman," his wife. The following had been dismissed from the church in Plymouth:

"Mr Isaac Cushman   Rebecca Cushman
   Stephen Bryant   Persis Shaw
   Jonathan Shaw   Anna Waterman
   Joseph Dunham   Abigail bryant
   John Waterman   Elizabeth Cooke
   John Rickard   Stirtevant
   Samuel Stirtevant   Elizabeth King
                             Mary Rickard
                             Rebecca Rickard
                             Susanna Rausom
                             Elizabeth Cannady."[‡]

[*] *Records of the First Church of Plymouth*, vol. 1: 22, 23.
[†] Cushman's *Genealogy of the Cushmans*, 1855: 104, 110, 109.
[‡] *Records of the First Church of Plymouth*, vol. 1: 51.

It should be remembered that Plympton, for many years after its incorporation in 1707, included besides its present limits, all the town of Carver, the greater part of the town of Halifax, and a strip of Kingston. Many of Mr. Cushman's parishioners went long distances to hear him. Deacon Lewis Bradford * wrote of him: "He was a pious and godly man. He had not a college education. He used to preach without notes, but studied his sermons beforehand and committed them to memory. It is said that those who worked with him could generally tell what his text would be the Sabbath following. I have heard my grandfather, Gideon Bradford, Esq., say that when the Rev. Mr. Cushman met with children or youth, he always had something to say to them of a religious nature, and at parting, gave them his blessing; that he himself had received many a blessing from him." On Sundays, when he preached, the Rev. Mr. Cushman is said to have worn a black velvet cap, instead of the customary wig.

His dwelling-house stood "on the high ground near the easterly end of a small piece of fresh meadow, the water from which, when it runs, crosses the road about forty rods northward of the burying-ground at Plympton." The first meeting-house, which probably was built before Mr. Cushman was ordained, "stood on the Green opposite to the old Lane which led eastward from the Green down to the house of the first Benjamin Soule in Plympton." This meeting-house, which was a small building, was so constructed that each side of the house had a gable end, allowing the rain to run off at the four corners of the roof. The roof of Mr. Cushman's house was "such a one as this meeting-house had."

The number of church people increased so that the old meeting-house could not accommodate them; and the Town

* Deacon Lewis Bradford was Town Clerk of Plympton for nearly forty years; and, for a long period, Clerk of the Congregational Church. "He was a most laborious and persevering genealogist and antiquarian." He died, suddenly, from an accident, Aug. 10, 1851, in Plympton, æt. eighty three years.

voted, September 16, 1714, to build a new and larger structure. The second meeting-house was first used in 1716;
and, about that time, the old one was sold to Mr. Benjamin
Soule, who moved it off and made it into a barn. The new
building is described as facing the south, and having its
interior walls plastered. Overhead, it had no "garret-floor"
nor plastering. There were no broad aisles, there was no
middle aisle, and no porch. "The Liberty Pole which was
erected about the commencement of the Revolutionary
war, or rather in 1774, stood in the centre of the Site of
this Second Meeting-house, from north to south."

The salary received by the Rev. Isaac Cushman, in 1701,
was £35; one half in money, the other half in "marchant-
able produce." This fortunately was supplemented by the
profits from his large farm. From time to time his salary
was increased until, in 1728, it had reached £85, as money
was then reckoned. Previous to his eighty-fourth year,
he had borne the weight of parish work unaided; but, September 3, 1731, the Rev. Jonathan Parker was ordained as
"Colleague Pastor." After the death of Mr. Cushman,
Mr. Parker continued in the ministry at Plympton to the
end of his life — a period of about forty-five years.

The Rev. Isaac Cushman died October 21, 1732, in Plympton, aged eighty-four years, eight months, and thirteen days.
He was buried in the old Burying-Ground at Plympton
"next to the road, about middle way between the north and
south ends of the yard." "His memory has been much
respected." The plain slate headstone bears the following
inscription : —

> HERE LYES ENTEAR[D] Y[E]
> BODY OF Y[E] REV[D]
> M[R] ISAAC CUSHMAN Y[E]
> 1ST MINISTER OF Y[E] CHURCH
> OF CHRIST IN PLYMPTON
> DEC[D] OCT[BR] Y[E] 21ST
> 1 7 3 2 IN Y[E]
> 84TH YEAR OF HIS
> AGE & IN Y[E] 37TH
> YEAR OF HIS MINISTRY.

At the foot of the grave : —

Yᴱ REVᴰ Mᴿ
ISAAC CUSHMAN
1 7 3 2

His will, dated October 25, 1727, was proved October 30, 1732, nine days after his decease : —

" Know all Men by these Presents that I, Isaac Cushman Senʳ of Plimton in the County of Plymouth in the Province of yᵉ Massachusetts Bay in New-England being at this present time in Health & of sound Mind & Memory Thanks be to God for the Same Yet calling to Mind the Mortality of my Body and knowing that it is Appointed for all Men once to dy do Make & ordain this my last Will & Testament * That is to Say principally & first of all I Recommend my Soul into the Hand of God that gave it & my Body I recommend [to] the Earth to be buried in decent Christian Burial at the Discretion of my Execut ʳ nothing Doubting but at yᵉ General Resurrection I shall recieve the Same by the mighty Power of God And as touching Such worldly Estate wherewith it hath pleased God to bless Me in this Life Having given to my Son Isaac Cushman Decᵈ his full Portion in land to his full Satisfaction And as concerning my Son Ichabod Cushman he has had his Portion already to his full Satisfaction — Yet notwithstanding for the Love & fatherly affection which I bear towards him I Give to him the fift Part of my Books & twenty Shilling to be paid to him out of my moveable Estate — Imprim I Give to my Grandson Nathaniel Cushman my Share of Cedar Swamp lying in Colchester Swamp : And also concerning yᵉ Rest of my moveable Estate besides what is Above Expressed I Give in Manner following Imprim I Give to my Daughter Rebekah Mitchel one quarter Part of my moveable Estate besides what is Above Expressed — Item I Give to yᵉ Children of my Daughter Mary Waterman deceased One quarter Part of my Moveable Estate besides what is above Expressed — Item I Give to the Children of my Daughter Sarah Briant deceasd One quarter Part of my Moveable Estate besides what is Above Expressed — Item I Give to my Daughter Fear Sturtevant One quarter Part of my

---

* *Plymouth County Probate*, Book 6 : 248.

moveable Estate besides what is Above Expressed And if it should please God to take away by Death Either or Both my Daughters wch are now Surviving before my Self then what I have given to them shall belong to their Children : And my Will is that my Son in Law Robert Waterman shall be my Executor to this my last Will & Testament to Recieve all Debts due to the Estate & also to pay all Debts due from the Estate & Funeral Charges before any Division be made of ye Above said Particulars amongst my Children & Grand Children — And I do hereby Request my loving ffriends Capt. Benoni Lucas & Deacon David Bozworth to be Overseers of this my last Will & Testament And to be Assistant unto my afores^d Execut^r in the Performance of ye Same. In Witness Whereof I have hereunto Set my hand and Seal this twenty fift day of October One thousand Seven hundred twenty & Seven

Isaac Cushman [Seal]

" Signed Sealed & Declared by ye Aboves^d Isaac Cushman Senr̤
to be his Will and Testament in ye Presence of Us.

IGNATIUS CUSHING
DAVID BOZWORTH
BENONI LUCAS

"Octob^r the 30, 1732. The Within Named Ignatius Cushing & David Bozworth Made Oath that they Saw the within named Isaac Cushman Sign Seal & heard him Declare the within written to be his last Will & Testament & that they at ye Same time In ye Presence of ye s^d Testator Together wth Benoni Lucas Set to their hands as Witnesses and that according to the best of y^r Observation he then was of a Sound & Disposing Mind & Memory Before ISAAC WINSLOW Judge of Probate "

"An inventory * of the personal Estate of the Revd Mr Isaac Cushman late of Plimton Deceasd taken by Us ye Subscribers Novr 2^d 1732

To Books	£12- 0- 0
To Bonds	220-12-10
To Province Bills of Credit	03- 5- 0
To Wearing Apparel	23- 2- 0

* *Plymouth County Probate*, Book 6 : 267, 365.

To Bedding & ffurniture	63–15– 6
To Peuter	09–17– 9
To Brass	04–07– 0
To tin	00–09– 0
To Iron Pots & Kettles	03– 1– 0
To Knives & Forks	00–13– 0
To fire tackling & Iron Hatchet	05–13– 0
To old Iron	03–00– 0
To glass Ware	00–10– 6
To Earthen Ware	00– 4– 6
To Chairs	02–11– 0
To Chests & Tables	03–12– 0
To trays & dishes & barrels & other House lumber . .	03–14– 0
To Yarn & Wooll & Tow	04– 9– 7
To tobacco	00– 7– 0
To Cart & Wheels	01–10– 0
Saddle & Bridle	00–10– 0
To Provision	50– 2– 5
To Cattle & Horse	48–15– 0
To Hay	34–14– 0
Debts due to the Estate	134–16– 2
Debts due from ye Estate	42–16–11

£635. 12–3.   DAVID BOSWORTH
                BENJAMIN WESTON
[Sworn to Dec. 19, 1732.]   IGNATIUS CUSHING

"An acct of Debts due & charges brought in against the Estate of ye Revᵈ Mʳ Isaac Cushman since the Inventory was given in Plimton June 28th 1733 —

To funeral Charges & others	£8–8
To due from the Estate	0–6–7
To Prizing Estate Proving Will & Register	7–7–0
Exᵈ = Total	16–1–7 "

Rebecca Cushman, of whom little is known, died September 3, 1727, — five years before her husband, the Rev. Isaac Cushman. Her monument stands beside his : —

HERE LIES BURIED Yᴱ
BODY OF MRˢ REBEKAH
CUSHMAN WIFE TO Yᴱ
REVᴰ Mᴿ ISAAC CUSH
MAN DECᴰ SEPᴮᴿ
Yᴱ 3ᴰ 1 7 2 7
IN Yᴱ 73ᴰ YEAR
OF HER AGE

ISSUE

I. Isaac[4], b. Nov. 15, 1676, in Plymouth; mar., first, Jan. 28, 1700–01, widow Sarah Gibbs, daughter to Nathaniel Warner. She d. Oct. 28, 1716, at the age of thirty-three years, and he mar., second, Oct. 10, 1717, widow Mercy Freeman, daughter to Major John[3] and Mary (Warren) Bradford, of Kingston. Mercy[4] Bradford, b. Dec. 23, 1681, in Kingston, was mar. in 1708 to Jonathan[5] Freeman, who d. April 27, 1714, in Harwich, aged thirty-six years.[*]

The will of John Bradford, Gent., of Kingston, dated Oct. 2, 1732, proved Dec. 21, 1736, gave to his wife, Mary, an interest in his grist-mill and fulling-mill, in Kingston. He also bequeathed "unto my Daughter Mercy y[e] Widow of Isaac Cushman jun[r] late of Plimton Deceas[d] the Sum of fffty Pounds to be paid w[th]in one Year after y[e] Decease of my Self & Wife." [†]

Isaac Cushman was Lieutenant of the Militia Company of the town of Plympton, where his life was spent; he also held the office of Town Clerk from 1711 to the time of his death, in 1727. He served as selectman and assessor almost continuously; and was well known as a surveyor. He was chosen Representative to the General Court, where he served from May 26, 1725, to April 14, 1726, — two sessions. He was twice reëlected, 1726 and 1727, serving three sessions each year.[‡]

He and both of his wives were active members of the church in Plympton. He died intestate, Sept. 18, 1727, and administration of his estate was granted Nov. 6, following, to his widow Mercy. In the division of his estate, March 27, 1734, the homestead, valued at £560, was set off to

---

[*] Issue : 1. Jonathan[6] Freeman, b. March 26, 1709–10, in Harwich.
    2. Mercy[6] Freeman, b. April 24, 1711; mar. 1728, Thomas[4] Waterman.
    3. Bradford[6] Freeman, b. Aug. 15, 1713.
    4. Ichabod[6] Freeman, b. Aug. 2, 1714, — "born four months after his father's decease."
(Freeman's *Genealogy of the Freeman Family*, Second Edition, 1875 : 57.)

[†] *Plymouth County Probate*, Book 7 : 260.

[‡] *Massachusetts Archives*, Acts and Resolves, vol. 10 : 574, 649; vol. 11 : 4, 57, 68, 132, 186, 205.

the widow for her "only son," Nathaniel Cushman; and the remainder was divided into four shares for the surviving daughters, Abigail Cushman, Priscilla Cushman, Fear Cushman, and Phebe Spooner, who "was wife of Nath'l Spooner late of Dartmouth, Bristol Co., dec'd." * The tombstone of " Lft^nt Isaac Cushman " still is standing in the old Burying-Ground at Plympton. His widow, Mercy, d. June 27, 1738, aged 56 years. She was buried beside him, and her stone also is standing.

Issue by first wife: 1. Phebe⁵, b. March 14, 1702-03, in Plymouth; mar. Nathaniel Spooner, of Dartmouth.

2. "Alles"⁵ (Alice), b. June 26, 1705, in Plymouth; mar. Jonathan Bosworth.

3. Rebecca⁵, b. Oct. 14, 1707, in Plymouth; mar. Dec. 8, 1726, Jabez Newland, of Plympton. No issue.

4. Sarah⁵, b. Dec. 2, 1709, in Plympton; mar. Benjamin Spooner.

5. Nathaniel⁵, b. May 28, 1712, in Plympton; married twice, and had fourteen children. He was Captain in the Militia; lived in Lebanon, Connecticut, and in Bernardston and Montague, Massachusetts. He d. Oct. 25, 1793, at the home of one of his sons, in Montague. From his grandfather he received a legacy of his share of land in "Cedar Swamp lying in Colchester Swamp."

Issue by second wife: 6. Fear⁵, b. July 10, 1718, in Plympton; mar. Nehemiah Sturtevant.

7. Priscilla⁵, b. Dec. 12, 1719, in Plympton; mar. Israel Holmes.

8. Isaac⁵, b. Sept. 29, 1721, in Plympton; d. Oct., 1721.

9. Abigail⁵, b. Dec. 31, 1722, in Plympton; mar. Gideon Sampson. No issue.

II. Rebecca⁴, b. Nov. 30, 1678, in Plymouth; mar. Nov. 18, 1701, Jacob Mitchell, of Plymouth.† Her father remembered her in his will, as follows: "I Give to my Daughter

---

* *Plymouth County Probate*, Book 5: 317, 580; Book 7: 20-24; Book 8: 301.

† Vide page 384.

Rebekah Mitchel one Quarter Part of my moveable Estate," after the payment of certain legacies.

III. Mary [4], b. Oct. 12, 1682, in Plymouth ; mar. March 19, 1702, Robert [3] Waterman, of Halifax. Mary Waterman d. in Plympton, March 13, 1722–23. Her husband mar., second, Dec. 5, 1723, Elizabeth [4] Cushman, daughter to Elkanah [3] and Martha [3] (Cooke) Cushman, of Plympton. She d., without issue, March 13, 1724–25 ; and Robert mar., third, Abigail ——.

Robert [3] Waterman, b. Feb. 9, 1681, in Marshfield, son to Deacon John [2] and Anne (Sturtevant) Waterman, was grandson to Robert [1] Waterman, of Salem, 1636 ; Plymouth, 1638 ; and Marshfield, 1639. He was identified, in his later years, with the interests of the town of Halifax, which was set off in 1734 from Plympton, Middleborough, and Pembroke. The births of all of his children were recorded in Plympton.[*] "M[r] Robert Waterman Sen[r]" d. Jan. 10, 1749–50, in Halifax.[†]

Issue by first wife : 1. Isaac [4] Waterman, b. May 11, 1703, in Plymouth.

2. Josiah [4] Waterman, b. March 5, 1704–05, in Plymouth.

3. Thomas [4] Waterman, b. Oct., 1707, in Plympton ; mar. by Rev. Isaac Cushman, June 23, 1728, to Mercy Freeman.

4. Rebecca [4] Waterman, b. Oct. 9, 1710, in Plympton ; mar., first, May 20, 1731, in Plympton, Joseph Holmes ; mar., second, William Rand.

5. Robert [4] Waterman, b. March 2, 1712–13, in Plympton ; mar. April 8, 1734, Martha [5], daughter to Lt. Josiah [4] Cushman.

6. Mary [4] Waterman, b. Feb. 25, 1715–16, in Plympton ; mar. Jonathan Holmes, of Kingston ; d. Jan. 26, 1749–50.

7. Samuel [4] Waterman, b. Aug. 11, 1718, in Plympton.

8. Anna [4] Waterman, b. March 6, 1720–21, in Plympton.

Issue by third wife : 9. Abigail [4] Waterman, b. March 5, 1728–29 ; d. April 9, 1729, aged one month.

---

[*] *Town Records of Plympton*, vol. 1 : 146.
[†] *Town Records of Halifax*, vol. 1 : 18.

IV. Sarah[4], b. April 17, 1684, in Plymouth ; mar. July 8, 1708, in Plympton, by Rev. Isaac Cushman, to James[3] Bryant, of Plympton, later Halifax. He was b. July 26, 1682, son to John[3] and Sarah (——) Bryant, and grandson to Stephen[1] Bryant (of Duxbury, 1643; Plymouth, 1650) by Sarah, his first wife. Sarah[4] Bryant d. Feb. 2, 1724–25, in Plympton, and her husband mar., second, May 12, 1725, Dorcas Whipple.[*]

Issue by first wife: 1. Barnabas[4] Bryant, b. March 7, 1710–11, in Plympton; d. young.

2. Rebecca[4] Bryant, d. April 26, 1711, in Plympton.

3. Hopestill[4] Bryant, b. June 23, 1713, in Plympton.

4. Barnabas[4] Bryant, b. Nov. 18, 1715, in Plympton.

5. Seth[4] Bryant, b. July 16, 1718, in Plympton.

6. Rebecca[4] Bryant, b. Feb. 4, 1720–21, in Plympton.

Issue by second wife: 7. Sarah[4] Bryant, b. Sept. 14, 1726, in Plympton.

8. Matthew[4] Bryant, b. Dec. 15, 1727, in Plympton; d. March 22, 1727–28.

9. Abishai[4] Bryant, b. Jan. 3, 1728–29, in Plympton; d. Feb. 22, 1728–29.

10. Jemima[4] Bryant, b. 1732, in Plympton.

V. Ichabod[4], b. Oct. 30, 1686, in Plymouth ; mar., first, Esther[3], daughter to Jonathan[2] and Elizabeth[2] (Hedge) Barnes. Esther[3] Barnes was b. Feb. 18, 1682 ; her mother, Elizabeth[2] Hedge, was daughter to William[1] Hedge, of Yarmouth ; her father, Jonathan[2] Barnes, was son to John[1] Barnes, of Plymouth, 1632, Yarmouth, 1639. The second wife of Ichabod Cushman, whom he mar. Nov. 27, 1712, was Patience[4], b. 1690, daughter to John[3] and Patience (Faunce) Holmes, of Middleborough (John[2], John[1] Holmes). She was the mother of all his children.

Ichabod Cushman was of Plympton and Middleborough. He died, intestate, in the latter town, in 1732, and Patience, his widow, was appointed administratrix of his estate, Nov. 2, of that year. "M: Seth Tinkom M: Jacob Tomson & M: Jabez Vaughn all of Middleborough," were appointed on

---

* *Town Records of Plympton*, vol. 1 : 117, 152, 122.

the same day "to take a view & make a just and equal appriesement." The inventory, which was taken on Dec. 20, 1732, included among other items : "Weareing apparrell & books, £07 : 07 : 10 ; Spining Wheele Woosted Combs Hatchel & cards, £02 : 10 : 06 ; Taylors Goose Box Jron & Heater, £00 : 08 : 06 ; Tools & Tackling for Carpentry & Husbandry, £18 : 18 : 08 ; Neat Cattel Jades Sheep & lean Swine with the Hay, £83 : 08 : 00 ; Boards & Board logs, £02 : 17 : 06 ;" land "whereon yᵉ Housing standeth" and several other tracts, £690 : 00 : 00, and land in " Great Cedar Swamp, £20 : 00 : 00. Total valuation, £903 : 13 : 02.*

Widow Patience Cushman mar., second, before June 13, 1737, Elanathan Wood. On that date she appeared as "his now wife " in the final settlement of her first husband's estate. Elnathan Wood previously had been appointed guardian to her six minor children : Experience, Patience, Mary, Ichabod, Rebecca, and Isaac Cushman. The inventory of the estate of Elnathan Wood, taken May 15, 1752, shows a total valuation of " £2305 : 11 : 6 : Old Tenour . . . Reduced to Lawfull Money is [£]307 : 08 : 02½."†

Issue by second wife : 1. Joanna⁵, b. Dec. 17, 1713, in Plympton ; mar. Ichabod Bosworth. Issue : a son and a daughter.

2. William⁵, b. Oct. 13, 1715, in Plympton ; mar. twice ; d. Aug. 27, 1768. Issue : twelve.

3. Sarah⁵, b. Nov. 8, 1717, in Plympton ; mar. Aug. 12, 1735, Daniel Vaughan. Issue : four.

4. Experience⁵, b. July 12, 1719, in Middleborough ; mar. Sept. 6, 1737, Jonathan Smith. Issue : nine.

5. Patience⁵, b. April 8, 1721, in Middleborough ; mar. July 23, 1739, Caleb Sturtevant. Issue : I. Joanna. II. Betsey. III. Susan. IV. Fear. V. Sarah ‡. VI. Patience. VII. Jabez Sturtevant.

---

* *Plymouth County Probate*, Book 6: 245, 263, 264; Book 7 : 313, 317, 262–264.
† *Plymouth County Probate*, Book 12 : 474.
‡ Sarah Sturtevant mar. Josiah Whitman, of Bridgewater, Mass. Their son, Hon. Ezekiel Whitman, was of New Gloucester and Portland, Maine. He was a distinguished counselor-at-law, Chief Justice of the Court of Common Pleas, also Chief justice of the Supreme Court of the State of Maine.

6. Mary⁵, b. Dec. 22, 1723, in Middleborough; mar. Nov. 24, 1743, Jedediah Lyon. Issue: eight.

7. Ichabod⁵, b. May 12, 1725, in Middleborough; mar., first, Patience Mackfern; mar., second, Hope White.

8. Rebecca⁵, b. July 11, 1727, in Middleborough; mar. Jan. 14, 1744–45, Manassah Clapp.

9. Isaac⁵, b. Aug. 12, 1730, in Middleborough; mar., about 1756, Sarah — (probably Sarah Miller). He d. Aug. 1, 1820, aged ninety years; she d. Aug. 11, 1806.

VI. Fear⁴, b. March 10, 1689, in Plymouth; mar. Feb. 12, 1707–08, William Sturtevant, of Halifax. She d. July 13, 1746, aged fifty-seven years; his second wife was Joanna ——.

The will of William Sturtevant, of Halifax, dated Aug. 7, 1753, was proved Sept. 3, following. The inventory, taken Sept. 8, includes one sixth of one saw-mill and one fourth of another. Total valuation, £378 : 11 : 08. To his wife, Joanna, he left £3 : 06 : 08, annually, "during widowhood." To his daughters, Hannah Ripley and Fear Waterman, he bequeathed the one sixth of a saw-mill.*

Issue by first wife : † 1. Isaac Sturtevant, b. Aug. 10, 1708, in Plympton. His father mentioned in his will "grandchildren," the "children of my late son Isaac Stertevant vizt William Isaac Simeon Samuel Jesse Nathl Deborah & Martha."

2. Hannah Sturtevant, b. Aug. 20, 1711, in Plympton; mar. Jonathan Ripley.

3. Rebecca Sturtevant, " born July y^e (deceas^t) 1715," in Plympton.

4. Fear Sturtevant (twin), b. April 7, 1719, in Plympton; mar. Capt. John Waterman, Jr., of Halifax, whom her father appointed executor of his will.

5. Elizabeth Sturtevant (twin), b. April 7, 1719, in Plympton.

---

* *Plymouth County Probate*, Book 13 : 130, 369.
† *Town Records of Plympton*, vol. 1 : 149.

THE ALLERTON FAMILY

ISAAC [1] ALLERTON

No one of the Pilgrim Fathers is more widely known to-day than Isaac Allerton, fifth signer of the Compact; yet the praise accorded to him is modified by insinuations that greatly mar his memory. Bradford, failing to understand him, wrote with an unwarrantable prejudice, unmindful of the fact that Allerton, as agent for the Colonists, was endeavoring to solve an almost impossible financial problem. Some of our later historians, following Bradford, represent him as a shrewd schemer, who trampled upon the rights of others regardless of everything except his own aggrandizement.[*] That this estimate is unjust is shown by a study of the original records of the Colonies of Plymouth, Massachusetts Bay, and New Haven, as well as those of Maine and New Amsterdam.

The date of birth of Isaac Allerton usually is assumed to be 1583 or 1585; but a deposition, later given in full, dated Plymouth, September 26, 1639, in which he states his age as "about 53 yeares," indicates that he was born about 1586. His birthplace is unknown. Prior to his removal to Holland about 1609, he was of London. He belonged to an old and honorable family of mixed Saxon and Danish ancestry, some of whose representatives still are to be found in England. There is a fine coat-of-arms of the Allerton family at the Heraldic College in London, but it is not known that Isaac was of the knighted branch.

He may have been with the Pilgrims in Amsterdam, but probably joined them with the others from London, at Ley-

---

[*] Goodwin's *Pilgrim Republic*, 1888 : 322, 330, 346, 347; also Drake's *Pine Tree Coast* : 236.

den. His name first appeared in the Leyden records with that of a widowed sister, Sarah (Allerton) Vincent, whose marriage to Degory Priest occurred on the same day as his own. Degory Priest and Sarah, widow of John Vincent, also were from London. The record of the double marriage has been photographed expressly for " The Mayflower Descendant," and is as follows : —

[The Dutch Record]

tje de 8. 10. 1611	Diggorie Preest Jongman van Londe In
tije de 15. 10. 1611	Engelant Vergeselschapt vergeselchapt
tiije de 22. 10. 1611	met William Leesle & Samuel Fuller
zyn getrout voor Willem	zyn bekende
Corsn Tybault & Jacob	met
Paedts Schepene	Sarah Vincent mede van Londe in
Dezen iiije Novembris 1611	Engelant wedue van Jan Vincent
	Versegelschapt met Jannetge Diggens
	& Rasemyn Gipsyn haer bekende

tje de 8. 10. 1611	Isaack Allerton Jongman van Londe
tije de 15. 10. 1611	In Engelant vergeselchapt met Ed-
tiije de 22. 10. 1611	ward Southward Richard Masterson &
zyn getrout voor Willem	Ranulphe Thickins zyn bekende
Cornelison Tybault &	met
Jacob Paedts Schepene	Marie Norris Jonge dochter van Nu-
Dese iiije Novembris	bere In Engelant Vergeselchapt met
xvie elfte	Anne Fuller & Dille Carpenter haer
	bekenden

[The English Translation]

Degorie Priest, unmarried man, from London, in England, accompanied by William Lisle and Samuel Fuller, his acquaintances, with

Sarah Vincent, also from London, in England, widow of John Vincent, accompanied by Jane Thickins and Rosamond Jepson, her acquaintances.

Isaac Allerton, unmarried man, from London, in England, accompanied by Edward Southworth, Richard Masterson and Randall Thickins, his acquaintances,

with

Mary Norris, single woman, from Newbury, in England, accompanied by Anne [Susanna] Fuller and Dille [Priscilla] Carpenter her acquaintances.

The entries "tj^e de 8. 10. 1611," etc., refer to the first,
second, and third dates of publication of the banns ; beneath
is added :—

[English Translation]

They were married before William Cornelison Tybault and
Jacob Paedts, sheriffs, this 4th of November, 1611.*

While in Leyden, Isaac Allerton was a tailor.   He was
admitted to citizenship February 7, 1614, upon the guaranty
of Roger Wilson and Henry Wood; November 16, 1615,
he "guaranteed" his brother-in-law Priest.   With his wife,
Mary, he witnessed the betrothal, April 27, 1618, of Edward
Winslow (who arrived in the *Mayflower,* 1620, and afterward was Governor) to Elizabeth Barker, of Chester, England; he also witnessed the betrothal of Roger Wilkins to
his second wife, Margaret Barrow, on September 16, 1619.
Allerton buried a child, February 5, 1620, at St. Peter's.
He was then living in *Pieterskerkhof.*   Dexter states that
"apparently the *Pieterskerkhof* was similar in appearance
to the 'hofs' in a modern Dutch town and evidently
was the little colony of houses built upon the grounds of
the Robinson estate.   Sometimes it was called the *Groene-
poort."* †

The few records of 1620, in Leyden, do not throw much
light on the last few months of the Pilgrims' sojourn there.
That Allerton was actively engaged in the preparations for
removal is evident from the letter written by Samuel Fuller,
Edward Winslow, William Bradford, and himself, on June
10, to Robert Cushman and John Carver, then in England.
It criticised "ye new conditions . . . which all men are

---

* *The Mayflower Descendant,* vol. 7 : 129, 130.
† Dexter's *England and Holland of the Pilgrims,* 1905: 601, 639, 649, 640,
639, 601, 600.

against;" and added, "whereas Robart Cushman desires reasons for our dislike, promising therupon to alter ye same, or els saing we should think he hath no brains, we desire him to exercise them therin, refering him to our pastors former reasons, and them to ye censure of ye godly wise. But our desires are that you will not entangle your selvs and us in any such unreasonable courses as those are, viz. y^t the marchants should have ye halfe of mens houses and lands at ye dividente; and that persons should be deprived of ye 2. days in a weeke agreed upon, yea every momente of time for their owne perticuler; by reason wherof we cannot conceive why any should carie servants for their own help and comfort; for that we can require no more of them then all men one of another.* . . . We hope you have not proceeded far in so great a thing without us." †

But Robert Cushman already had acceded to the demands of the Merchant Adventurers, for he wrote on the same date (June 10), that no one of the Adventurers except Mr. Weston had seen the disputed articles before they were agreed upon at Leyden; but when they did learn of them, there was widespread dissatisfaction, and a threat of withdrawing the promised financial assistance. In the three letters of about the same date, "to them at Leyden," Cushman wrote: "Now whilst we at Leyden conclude[d] upon points, as we did, we reckoned without our host, which was not my falte. . . . If you had beaten this bussines so throuly [thoroughly] a month agoe, and write to us as now you doe, we could thus have done much more conveniently. But it is as it is." He also told them that if they would only agree upon the present terms, "your money which you ther must have, we will get provided for you instantly," otherwise "we may goe scratch for it." ‡ In the face of

---

* Vide page 516.
† Bradford's *History of Plimoth Plantation*, 1898 : 61, 62.
‡ Bradford's *History of Plimoth Plantation*, 1898 : 63–71.

all this, the Pilgrims, of whom Bradford, Allerton, Winslow, and Fuller, upheld by the counsels of Pastor Robinson, were certainly the leaders, sailed from Southampton without signing those articles. History shows how dearly they paid for this mismanagement.

The *Speedwell* left Delfshaven with Isaac Allerton and his family on board ; when the passengers were readjusted at Plymouth, England, and some were sent back to London, the Allertons continued with the *Mayflower* on its eventful voyage. Bradford, in enumerating "those which came over first, in yᵉ year 1620," mentions "Mʳ Isaack Allerton, and Mary, his wife ; with 3. children, Bartholomew, Remember, & Mary ; and a servant boy, John Hooke." * The youngest daughter, Sarah, followed soon after in the care of her aunt Sarah, widow of Degory Priest, who had married Mr. Cuthbert Cuthbertson.†

While on the *Mayflower* in the harbor of Cape Cod (Provincetown harbor), a second son was born to Isaac and Mary Allerton, who did not live. The mother, enfeebled with the hardships and privations of that terrible winter, "dyed with the first," February 25, 1620–21. She was buried at Cole's Hill, near the foot of the present Middle Street. John Hooke, the servant boy, died about the same time. In 1626, Isaac Allerton married Fear², daughter to Elder William¹ and Mary (——) Brewster. Elder¹ Brewster, with his wife,

---

* Bradford's *History of Plimoth Plantation*, 1898 : 531.

† Degory¹ Priest, a hat-maker from London, mar. Nov. 4, 1611, Sarah¹ (Allerton) Vincent, sister to Isaac ¹ Allerton. Priest arrived, without his family, in the *Mayflower*, 1620; but died "in the first sickness," Jan. 1, 1620–21. Widow Sarah Priest was betrothed in Leyden to Cuthbert Cuthbertson, Oct. 25, and mar. Nov. 13, 1621. Cuthbertson first mar. May 27, 1617, in Leyden, Elizabeth Kendall, by whom he had a son Samuel.

Issue of Degory¹ and Sarah Priest : I. Mary² Priest, who came in the *Anne*, 1623, with her mother and sister Sarah ; mar. between 1627 and 1633, Phineas Pratt, of Plymouth and Charlestown. II. Sarah² Priest, mar. John Coombs, of Plymouth. "Mʳ John Combes" possessed land lying upon the south side of Phineas Pratt's homestead in Plymouth. (*Plymouth Colony Deeds*, Book 1 : 81.)

Mary, and sons, Love[2] and Wrestling[2], came over in the *Mayflower;* another son, Jonathan[2], came in the *Fortune,* 1621; and the daughters, Patience[2] and Fear[2], in the *Anne,* 1623. Fear Allerton died December 12, 1634, of "the pestilent fever," then prevailing in Plymouth.[*]

About a year before her death, a maid-servant, named Alice Grinder, was brought to Plymouth by Mr. John Grant, a ship-master. In the absence of her master, Isaac Allerton, she was apprenticed to him, November 24, 1633, by the Court for five years.[†] The only child of Fear, Isaac, Jr., was then about three years old. After the death of the mother, it does not appear what disposition was made of Allerton's elder children by his first wife, but the young Isaac was cared for by his grandfather Brewster's family. The settlement of Elder Brewster's estate, August 20, 1645, demanded that Jonathan, the elder son, should pay £4 to his brother Love, in consideration of his wintering some cattle, "and for the dyett of Isaack Allerton a grandchild of the said Willm wᶜʰ he had placed wᵗʰ his sonn Love to table."[‡] As Love Brewster and his wife, Sarah, occupied the homestead where the father dwelt also, Isaac, Jr., then fifteen years of age, evidently was being brought up by the Elder. The third wife of Allerton, by whom he had no children, was Johanna ——, whom he married before 1644.

Isaac Allerton invariably was mentioned by others as "Mʳ" or "Gentleman," an indication of his high position; he styled himself "merchant." During his later years in Connecticut, he bore the title of "Captain" or "Master." In the assignment of the seven "Garden plotes of [those] which came first layd out 1620 . . . Mʳ Isaack Allerton" was to build his house next to Francis Cooke on the south;[§]

---

[*] Winthrop's *History of New England,* Savage's Edition, 1853, vol. 1: 463.

[†] *Plymouth Colony Records,* Court Orders, vol. 1: 20.

[‡] *Plymouth Colony Deeds,* Book 1: 198.

[§] Vide pages 447, 448.

there is no doubt that much of the labor was done with his own hands. In 1623, when the land was distributed by the casting of lots, " m^r Isaack Allerton " was given seven acres " on the south side of the brooke to the baywards," * between the present Sandwich Street and the harbor.

The name of every member of his family appears in the list of cattle distributed by order of the Court, dated May 22, 1627 : —

" 2 The second lot fel to Mr Isaac Allerton & his companie ioyned to him his wife ffeare Allerton

 3 Bartholomew Allerton
 4 Remember Allerton
 5 Mary Allerton
 6 Sarah Allerton To this lot fell the Greate Black cow
 7 Godber Godberson came in the Ann to which they must
 8 Sarah Godberson keepe the lesser of the two steers and
 9 Samuel Godberson two shee goats
10 Marra Priest
11 Sarah Priest
12 Edward Bumpasse
13 John Crackstone " †

Soon after the death in April, 1621, of John Carver, their first Governor, William Bradford was chosen Governor " in his stead, and being not yet recovered of his ilnes, in which he had been near ye point of death, Isaak Allerton was chosen to be an Assistante unto him, who, by renewed election every year, continued sundry years togeather." ‡ Allerton was Bradford's sole Assistant until 1624, when the number of Assistants was raised to five ; but he probably continued as one of them for several years longer.§ When the Colonists had bought out the Merchant Adven-

---

* Vide page 451.

† *Plymouth Colony Deeds*, vol. 1 : 9.

‡ Bradford's *History of Plimoth Plantation*, 1898 : 121, 122.

§ Whitmore's *Civil List*, 1870 : 37 ; also Bradford's *History of Plimoth Plantation*, 1898 : 187.

turers and had established an independent government, Isaac Allerton again was chosen Governor's Assistant, January 1, 1633–34.* On the same date, the name "Mʳ Isaac Allerton" headed the first complete list of freemen of Plymouth Colony; as " Isaack Allerton gen [gentleman]," he appeared, March 7, 1636–37, in the second list. March 25, 1633, he was assessed the largest tax in the Colony, — £3 : 11 : 00.†

At what period Isaac Allerton became a resident of Rocky Nook, at Jones's River, is not known. He was assigned mowing-ground there in 1633, and had built a house before 1635 near " the Old Wading Place." This property later passed into the possession of his son-in-law, Elder Thomas Cushman; the spring upon it is called Elder's Spring to this day.

In December, 1633, Bradford was appointed by the Court to settle the estate of Godbert Godbertson and Sarah his wife, both deceased ; and to discharge the debts of the same " so far as his estate will make good." " Mʳ Isaac Allerton, of Plym, merchᵗ, late brother of the said Zarah," the largest creditor, to whom £75 : 10 : 03 was due, gave " free leaue " that all others should be paid before himself, "desiring rather to lose all rather then other men should lose any." ‡

On October 27, 1646, Allerton gave to " his son-in-law, Mʳ Thomas Cushman," power of attorney (signed " Isaacke Allerton ") to collect the debts from John Coombs and others to the estate of Godbert Godbertson. The Court ordered, August 1, 1648, that Thomas Cushman, for that year, should have certain proportions of corn, rye, fruit, and hemp "due vnto Mis Coombe ; " also "a p̃te of the encrease thereof [i. e. of land at Rocky Nook] for some time should bee payed to Mʳ Cushman afoʳsaid, to whom the monyes was due." The last payment was made in

* *Plymouth Colony Records*, Court Orders, vol. 1 : 21.
† *Plymouth Colony Records*, Court Orders, vol. 1 : 3, 52, 9.
‡ *Plymouth Colony Deeds*, Book 1 : 12, 13.

1654, and acknowledged May 6, 1656, by "Thomas Cushman as the agent for Isaacke Allerton, for the profits of land at Rocky Nooke . . . as followeth : —

If, in corn receiued . . . . 19 : 01 : 00¾

If, in fruite receiued, one hundred ninety one bushells and a halfe of aples." *

After the death of Robert Cushman, in 1625, Isaac Allerton was sent over to England repeatedly as the agent of the Colony. An account of his doings for the several succeeding years would be about as "intermixte" as the cargo he brought over in 1628, when "they knew not which was theirs, & wᶜʰ was his . . . for ther was no distinction." Allerton's strongest ally was James Sherley, of London, one of the Merchant Adventurers, who still had faith in the struggling Colony; and who, after the disaffection of Weston, was largely instrumental in holding the weak organization of Adventurers together. January 25, 1623, Sherley wrote a letter to New Plymouth informing the Colonists of a meeting held on Thursday, January 8, preceding, to discuss the "artickls betweene you and us." The meeting was anything but harmonious, and broke up in confusion. "But on yᵉ 12. of Jan: we had another meting, but in the interime divers of us had talked with most of them privatly, and had great combats & reasoning, pro & con." The result was the friendliest meeting they ever knew, ending with "a potle of wine . . . which we dranke freindly together." "Our greatest enemise offered to lend us 50 ˡⁱ," wrote Sherley. Shortly afterward, Winslow, who was already in England for the purpose of obtaining supplies, returned in the *Charity* with the "first catle" and "a prety good supply" of general merchandise.†

The next year, December 18, 1624, four of the Adventurers, "wᶜʰ stuck to them," as Bradford puts it, sent over a

---

* *Plymouth Colony Records*, Court Orders, vol. 1 : 20; vol. 2 : 131–133; vol. 3 : 98; vol. 4 : 81.

† Bradford's *History of Plimoth Plantation*, 1898 : 189–191.

statement of their affairs, praying that "you will doe your best to free our ingagements, &c." They represented that owing to factions among the Adventurers, lack of money, and other excuses, principally "that you are Brownists, &c ... the former course for the generalitie here is wholly dissolved from what it was; and wheras you & we were formerly sharers and partners, in all viages & deallings, this way is no more, but you and we are left to be thinke our sellves what course to take in ye future, that your lives & our monies be not lost." They also suggested that those now at Plymouth gather together such commodities as the country yielded, and send them over to pay their debts and "ingagements hear, which are not less then 1400^{li}." At the same time, they sent over "catle, cloath, hose, shoes, leather, &c.," and committed them to the "custody of Mr Allerton and Mr Winslow, as our factours, at whose discretion they are to be sould, and comodities to be taken for them, as is fitting." This letter was signed only with initials, " J. S. W. C. T. F. R. H. &c.," * which undoubtedly represented the names of James Sherley, William Collier, Thomas Fletcher, and Robert Holland. The money advanced to purchase these supplies was at a ruinous rate of interest, "thought unreasonable by some, and too great an oppression upon ye poore people, as their case stood."

To meet these heavy financial obligations, the Colonists had two main sources of revenue, trading and fishing. Fishing along the coast of Maine had been a prominent industry from the time of the earliest settlement. Ships were sent over from every part of England, with Pemaquid and the Isles of Shoals as their objective points; and the Merchant Adventurers began to clamor for returns from the fisheries before the Plymouth Colonists were fairly housed. Yet Bradford, in 1624, wrote that fishing was "a thing fatall to this plantation," for every attempt ended in disaster.

Allerton himself had begun the Plymouth Colony trade

---

* Bradford's *History of Plimoth Plantation*, 1898: 239–243.

with the Eastern Indians. By a little barter from year
to year at Monhegan and in that vicinity, he became acquainted with the fur trade and fishing, and recognized
the possibilities of both. After the harvest was gathered in
1625, a shallop-load of corn was sent from Plymouth to
Kennebec, and exchanged for "700 ͥ of beaver besids some
other furrs."

In the summer of 1626, the Governor "and such as were
designed to manage the trade," hearing that the plantation
at Monhegan "was to break up, and diverse usefull goods
were ther to be sould," took a boat and went up there.
They purchased goods, goats, and other things, to the value
of £400, sterling. There was also a French ship cast away
at Sagadahock, about this time, whose cargo they purchased
for above £500, and paid for in " beaver & comodities they
had gott yͤ winter before . . . and yͭ somer." The profits
from these expeditions enabled them to repay "the money
taken up by Captaine Standish,* and yͤ remains of former
debts."

It was at this juncture that Allerton again was sent over
to England "to make a composition" with the Merchant
Adventurers, which Captain Standish had attempted the
year before (1625), but abandoned. He was instructed to
make the best terms he could, and "not to conclud absolutly till they knew yͤ termes, and had well considered of
them." They also gave him "a comission under their hands
& seals " to borrow money not exceeding a specified sum,
which he was to expend for the "use of the plantation."

"At yͤ usuall season of yͤ coming of ships," that is, in
the early spring of 1627, "Mͬ Allerton returned," bringing
goods, and "£200 ͥ which he now gott at 30. per cent."
After "much adoe and no small trouble," he had succeeded
in bringing back the draft of an agreement with the Merchant Adventurers, "drawne by the best counsell of law
they could get, to make it firme." By this contract, dated

---

* Vide page 524.

London, November 15, 1626, the Adventurers sold their entire interest to the Plymouth Colony for £1800; the sum of £200 to be paid annually, beginning in 1628, at the feast of St. Michael, on the west side of the Royal Exchange in London. "Least any forfeiture should fall on ye whole for none paimente at any of ye days," they were to forfeit "30^s a weeke if they missed ye time." This agreement gave general satisfaction; and though they hardly knew how to raise the money, besides discharging their other debts and supplying their own needs, "yet they undertooke it," wrote Bradford. He also added that "they rane a great adventure" in so doing; but "it was absolutly confirmed on both sids . . . and ingrossed in partchmente." * Four of the Merchant Adventurers retained their interest in the affairs of the Plymouth Colony; they were known later as the English partners of the Purchasers.

Before sending Mr. Allerton back to England, the Governor and "some of their cheefe freinds had serious consideration, not only how they might discharge those great ingagments which lay so heavily upon them, . . . but also how they might devise means to help some of their freinds

---

* The list of Merchant Adventurers (originally seventy in number) who signed the agreement is given below. "John White" undoubtedly was the celebrated clergyman of Dorchester, England, the reputed author of the *Planter's Plea.*

John White,	Samuel Sharpe,	Thomas Hudson,
John Pocock,	Robert Holland,	Thomas Andrews,
Robert Kean,	James Sherley,	Thomas Ward,
Edward Bass,	Thomas Mott,	Fria. Newbald,
William Hobson,	Thomas Fletcher,	Thomas Heath,
William Penington,	Timothy Hatherly,	Joseph Tilden,
William Quarles,	Thomas Brewer,	William Perrin,
Daniel Poynton,	John Thorned,	Eliza Knight,
Richard Andrews,	Myles Knowles,	Thomas Coventry,
Newman Rookes,	William Collier,	Robert Allden,
Henry Browning,	John Revell,	Lawrence Anthony,
Richard Wright,	Peter Gudburn,	John Knight,
John Ling,	Emnu. Alltham,	Matthew Thornhill,
Thomas Goffe,	John Beauchamp,	Thomas Millsop.

(*Massachusetts Historical Society Collections*, First Series, vol. 3 : 48.)

and breethren of Leyden over unto them, who desired so
much to come to them." To effect this, "they resolved to
rune a high course, and of great adventure, not knowing
otherwise how to bring it aboute." After some agitation
an agreement of the "joint purchasers" was made upon the
following conditions : *—

"Articles of agreemente betweene y⁰ collony of New-Plimoth
of y⁰ one partie, and William Bradford, Captein Myles Standish,
Isaack Allerton, &c. one y⁰ other partie ; and such shuch others
as they shall thinke good to take as partners and undertakers
with them, concerning the trade for beaver & other furrs & comodities, &c. ; made July, 1627."

The first of the seven articles "covenanted" that the Undertakers, as they were termed, should discharge every debt due for
the purchase (£1800), "or any other belonging to them." By the
terms of the second article the new company was to enjoy the
free use of their "pinass latly built, the boat at Manamett, and
y⁰ shalop, called y⁰ Bass-boat," with all their implements ; also
their stock of "furrs, fells, beads, corne, wampampeak, hatchets,
knives, &c. . . . now in y⁰ storre." The third article gave them
the whole trade of the Colony "for 6. full years, to begine y⁰ last
of September next insuing." The fourth article stipulated that
"every severall purchaser" should annually pay to the Undertakers, for the term of six years, "3. bushells of corne, or 6 ᴸⁱ of
tobaco, at y⁰ undertakers choyse." The Undertakers agreed, in
the fifth article, that they should "bestowe 50 ᴸⁱ per annum in
hose and shoese, . . . to be sould unto them [the joint Purchasers]
for corne at 6ˢ per bushell ; " and, in the sixth article, that the
whole trade at the end of six years should "returne to y⁰ use and
benefite of y⁰ said collonie, as before." Lastly, it was provided
that the Undertakers should obtain the consent of their English
partners to these articles, "to stand in full force," or to abandon
them and "remaine as formerly they were."

This agreement was signed by the representative men of
the Colony, though "some would not subscribe, and some

---

* Bradford's *History of Plimoth Plantation*, 1898 : 271, 272.

were from home." * Bradford's Letter Book states that the first three signers "made choice of these other," who joined with them; the names of the Undertakers who were to manage the trade of the Colony were as follows: —

"William Bradford	John Howland	*And these of London*
Captain Standish	John Alden	James Shirley
Isaac Allerton	Thomas Prince	John Beauchamp
Edward Winslow		Richard Andrews
William Brewster		Timothy Hatherly " †

---

* " The Names of the Purchasers.

Mᵣ Wᵐ Bradford	Abraham Pearse
Mᵣ Thom̄ Prence	Steeven Tracy
Mᵣ Wᵐ Brewster	Joseph Rogers
Mᵣ Edw̄ Winslow	John Faunce
Mᵣ John Alden	Steeven Deane
Mᵣ John Jenney	Thom̄ Cushman
Mᵣ Isaack Allerton	Robte Hicks
Capt̄ Miles Standish	Thom̄ Morton
Mᵣ Wᵐ Collyer	Anthony Annable
Mᵣ John Howland	Samuell Fuller
Mannasseth Kempton	Franc̄ Eaton
Francis Cooke	Wiltm Basset
Jonathan Brewster	Francis Sprague
Edward Banges	The Heirs of John Crackstone
Nicholas Snow	Edward Bumpas
Steven Hopkins	Wiltm Palmer
Thomas Clarke	Peter Browne
Ralph Wallen	Henry Sampson
Wiltm Wright	Experience Michell
Elizabeth Warren, widdow	Phillip Delanoy
Edward Dotey	Moyses Symonson
Cuthbert Cuthbertson	Georg Soule
John Winslow	Edward Holman
John Shaw	
Joshua Pratt	Mᵣ James Sherley
John Adams	Mᵣ Beauchampe
Λ Billington	Mᵣ Andrewes
Phineas Pratt	Mᵣ Hatherly
Samuell Fuller	Mᵣ Wᵐ Thomas
Clement Briggs	

53.

In all 58."

(*Plymouth Colony Records*, Court Orders, vol. 2: 177.)
† *The Mayflower Descendant*, vol. 6 : 147.

With the return of the ships they sent Mr. Allerton again
to England. This was early in the fall of 1627. He carried
a copy of the agreement for their English friends to sign.
James Sherley hesitated to set his "hand to yᵉ sale, being
yᵉ receiver of most part of yᵉ adventurs, and a second causer
of much of yᵉ ingagments," but rather than that the bargain "should faile, Mͬ Alerton having taken so much pains,"
Sherley wrote, December 27, 1627, "I have sealed wᵗʰ yᵉ rest,
with this proviso & promise of his, yᵗ if any trouble arise
hear, you are to bear halfe yᵉ charge." Another letter from
James Sherley, dated November 17, 1628, acknowledged
the receipt of a barrel of otter skins, which he had sold for
£78 : 12, sterling, giving the money to Mr. Allerton. He
added : * —

" It is true (as you write) that your ingagments are great, not
only the purchass, but you are yet necissitated to take up yᵉ stock
you work upon ; and yᵗ not at 6. or 8. ℔ʳ cent, as it is here let out,
but at 30. 40. yea, & some at 50. ℔ʳ cent. which, were not your gaines
great, and God's blessing on your honest indeaours more than
ordinarie, it could not be yᵗ you should longe subsiste yᵉ maintaining of, & upholding of your worldly affaires. And this your honest & discreete agente, Mͬ Allerton, hath seriously considered,
& deeply laid to mind, how to ease you of it. He tould me you
were contented to accepte of me & some few others, to joyne with
you in yᵉ purchass, as partners ; for which I kindly thanke you
and all yᵉ rest, and doe willingly accepte of it. And though absente,
shall willingly be at shuch charge as you & yᵉ rest shall thinke
meete." Sherley also was "contented to forbear" his part of the
interest about to become due, and persuaded " Mͬ Andrews and
Mͬ Beauchamp to doe yᵉ like." †

Isaac Allerton carried with the agreement a power of
attorney from the Undertakers, "William Bradford Govͬ of
Plimoth, in N. E. in America, Isaac Allerton, Myles Standish, William Brewster, & Ed: Winslow, of Plimoth afore-

---

* Bradford's *History of Plimoth Plantation*, 1898 : 272–277.
† Bradford's *History of Plimoth Plantation*, 1898 : 275.

said, merchants," by which " James Sherley, Goldsmith, & John Beachamp, Salter, citizens of London," were appointed their "true & lawful agents, factors, substitutes, & assignes " to receive all goods or merchandise sent to London or any part of England; "allso to vend, sell, barter," or exchange their wares according to the judgment of these agents, jointly or severally. They were to purchase supplies for New England ; and to "demand for us & in our names all such debtes & sumes of money, as now are or hereafter shall be due . . . by any wayes or means ; and to acquite, discharge, or compound " with any or all of the creditors. The bond was signed, November 28, 1628. This sweeping power of attorney was their undoing ; or, as Bradford has it, — " some inconvenience grue therby afterward." Isaac Allerton retained his "authoritie under their hands & seals for ye transacting of ye former bussines, and taking up of moneys," etc.*

During his stay in London, Allerton obtained "a reasonable supply of goods for the plantation," at a less interest than before ; he brought home an account of the beaver sold and how the money was disbursed for goods and the payment of debts; and, above all, he had made the first payment of £200 for the purchase, and " brought them ye bond for ye same canselled ; so as they now had no more foreine debtes but ye abovesaid 400 ᶦᶦ and odde pounds, and ye rest of ye yearly purchass monie."

Following instructions received before leaving Plymouth, he also brought (1628) a patent for a trading-place at Kennebeck. This was greatly desired at Plymouth, in order that they might control the trade at that point, and " shutte out " the planters from Piscataqua and " to the eastward," for the Pilgrims held that they "them selves had first begune and discovered the same [and] brought it to so good effecte." But the patent "was so straite and ill bounded, as they were faine to renew & inlarge it the next year." Yet they lost no time in taking possession of the land thus granted, and

* Bradford's *History of Plimoth Plantation*, 1898: 277-279.

at once erected a fortified trading-house well up the river at the most convenient place for trade (now Augusta). This was provided with such commodities as the fishermen and Indians needed : coats, shirts, rugs, blankets, biscuit, pease, prunes, knives, hatchets, and wampum ; and a brisk trade for beaver was opened with the natives.

For several preceding years Isaac Allerton occasionally had brought over small quantities of goods, " upon his owne perticuler," to supply the pressing needs of the community. But this year (1628) he fetched a larger and more varied assortment than ever before, and this was construed as a direct interference with the trade of the Colony. It was claimed that Allerton's goods were " most vendible, and would yeeld present pay" before their own. He now commenced "to sell abroad to others of forine places, which . . . they began to dislike," says Bradford. Complaint also was made about the stowing of Allerton's latest cargo ; that their goods and his were so intermixed that "if any casualty had beefalne at sea, he might have laid y° whole [loss] on them, if he would ; for ther was no distinction. . . . Yet because love thinkes no evill . . . they tooke his faire words for excuse, and resolved to send him againe this year for England; considering how well he had done y° former bussines, and what good acceptation he had with their freinds ther ; as also seeing sundry of their freinds from Leyden were sente for, which would or might be much furthered by his means." *

In August, 1629, the first company of the Pilgrims who had been left in Leyden reached Salem. They came on the *Mayflower*, William Peirce, Master, having left Holland in May. Bradford says there were " 35. persons," but Prince construes it thirty-five *families*. The second and last detachment left Holland the following March with the same master (Peirce), then in the *Lion*, who landed them near the end of May, 1630, at Charlestown. At the great charge of

---

* Bradford's *History of Plimoth Plantation*, 1898 : 293.

£550, "besids ther fetching hither from Salem & yᵉ Bay" in a shallop, they had been shipped from Holland to England, and then to New England. When it is considered tha. those passengers were lacking clothing to the extent that it required " 125. yeards of karsey, 127. ellons of linen cloath, shoes, 66. pᵣ, with many other perticulers," to make them comfortable for the voyage, the charge does not appear so excessive.*

Allerton had been for three months, with Mr. Sherley, in Holland, making arrangements to convey these Pilgrims to New England. When they reached England, Allerton did his best to obtain the two patents that he had been commissioned to procure: a patent or charter for the Plymouth Colony, and a more satisfactory adjustment of the Kennebeck patent which they already held. Sherley afterwards wrote of this period: —

" But till our maine bussines, yᵉ patent, was granted, I could not setle my mind nor pen to writing. Mᵣ Allerton was so turrmoyled about it, as verily I would not nor could not have undergone it, if I might have had a thousand pounds; but yᵉ Lord so blessed his labours . . . as he obtained yᵉ love & favore of great men in repute & place. He got granted from yᵉ Earle of Warwick & Sᵗ Ferdinando Gorge all that Mᵣ Winslow desired in his letters to me, & more also, which I leave him to relate. Then he sued to yᵉ king to confirme their grant, and to make you a corporation, and so to inable you to make & execute lawes, in such large & ample maner as yᵉ Massachusett plantation hath it; which yᵉ king graciously granted, refferring it to yᵉ Lord Keeper to give order to yᵉ solisiter to draw it up." The Lord Keeper furthered it all he could, also the solicitor, but when it reached the Lord Treasurer, "to have his warrante for freeing yᵉ custume for a certaine time . . . he would not doe it, but reffered it to yᵉ Counsell table. And ther Mᵣ Allerton atended day by day, when they sate, but could not gett his petition read."

---

* Bradford's *History of Plimoth Plantation*, 1898 : 295-299; also *New Haven Historical Papers*, vol. 3 : 102, 103.

Allerton finally was forced temporarily to abandon the whole matter, for Mr. Peirce was waiting with his passengers at Bristol. He left "yᵉ further prosecuting of it to a solissiter," and sailed in the *Lion* with the last of the Pilgrims. Sherley concluded his letter with an attempt to pour oil upon the troubled waters; said there was no doubt that the patent would be granted, "but such things must work by degrees; men cannot hasten it as they would," and requested the return of Allerton by the first ship. This letter was dated March 19, 1629–30.

In 1630, Allerton again was despatched to England,—"though it was with some fear & jeolocie"—to complete negotiations for the patent. After months of patient endeavor, hampered by lack of adequate financial support, he was forced to abandon the effort, and this patent never was granted. But Allerton and the London partners, with the coöperation of Captain William Peirce, did obtain a patent of land on the Penobscot, now Castine.* After Allerton returned to Plymouth, in the summer of 1630, the Council for New England sent over a new patent, antedated January 13, 1629[–30]. This "Warwick patent" was from the Earl of Warwick to William Bradford, his "heirs, associates and assignes;" it fixed the bounds of the tract on the Kennebec; it also defined the boundary lines of the Plymouth Colony. Though it granted certain rights, it was not so favorable as the one abandoned, and complaint was made that it was not so liberal as the patent of Massachusetts Bay.† By securing these two patents (Kennebec and Penobscot), Allerton provided the desired opportunity for the Plymouth Colony to control trade and fishing along the coast of Maine. He also sent Edward Ashley from England as agent to manage the trade at Penobscot. This the Colonists resented; but later were

---

* Bradford's *History of Plimoth Plantation*, 1898: 313, 307, 308.
† Goodwin's *Pilgrim Republic*, 1888: 337, 338.

induced to further the enterprise, and to send supplies to Ashley.*

To drive off all competitors in that region with the small boats then at Plymouth was impossible. Their little fleet consisted of "2. very good & strong shalops," built at Plymouth in 1624, one of which had been enlarged two years later by a "house carpenter," who "sawed her in yᵉ midle" and added some five or six feet to her length, "and laid a deck on her." The third ship was a small pinnace built at Manamet (Sandwich), in 1627. No one of these was fit to cross the ocean, and Bradford mentions no other.† To carry on the work of the Colony, Allerton and the English partners, acting by their power of attorney, purchased the *White Angel* and hired the *Friendship*. The two ships were fitted out for the double purpose of trading with the Indians and "bass-fishing." Sherley and the others saw in these ships a means of being repaid for the losses they already had sustained, and, at the same time, of building up the interests of the Purchasers. The Colonists were preparing to trade on a scale for which such vessels would appear to be the first requisite. Although previously determined "to runne a high course and of great adventure," yet the knowledge that ships had been obtained without their consent brought "grief and astonishment" to William Bradford and his associates.‡

The *Friendship* was "sett out on fishing," but after eleven weeks' beating at sea, from foul weather, she was forced to turn back with her provisions "spente and spoyled." As the season was too far advanced for a renewal of the fishing venture, they sent her over at midsummer with goods to Massachusetts Bay. Timothy Hatherly, one of the London partners, had come over in her, but that did not prevent the general dissatisfaction "that this fishing ship should

---

* Bradford's *History of Plimoth Plantation*, 1898 : 307–311.
† Bradford's *History of Plimoth Plantation*, 1898 : 267, 203, 253, 266.
‡ Bradford's *History of Plimoth Plantation*, 1898 : 320, 321, 307, 272.

be set out, and fraight with other men's goods, & scarce any of theirs." As for bass-fishing with the other ship, the *White Angel*, it was prophesied it "would certainly turn to loss. And for M: Allerton to follow any trade for them, it was never in their thoughts." *

Besides all these querulous complaints, their debts had reached such large proportions that they were "strucken with some sadness aboute these things." Allerton had expended about £500 in his vain endeavor to obtain a more satisfactory patent for the Colony; they had "been to great charge" for the *White Angel* and *Friendship ;* and, in all, the Purchasers found themselves owing £4770 : 19 : 02, besides £1000 still due for the purchase. Mr. Hatherly, who lately had been much associated with Allerton, did not escape censure. When it was demanded of him "how he should make this good . . . he tould them he was sent over as their agente, and had this order from them, that whatsoever he and M: Allerton did togeather, they would stand to it; but they would not alow of what M: Allerton did alone, except they liked it; but if he did it alone, they would not gain say it. Upon which they sould to him & M: Allerton all yᵉ rest of yᵉ goods, and gave them present possession of them," and a writing to that effect.†

Meanwhile, Mr. Winslow had been sent to England with instructions "to see how yᵉ squars wente," and if he found things unsatisfactory, "to discharge M: Allerton for being any longer agent for them, or to deal any more in yᵉ bussines." There is no record of such discharge; but Bradford rather spitefully wrote, in 1630, that "M: Allerton followed his affaires, & returned [to England] with his White Angell, being no more imployed by yᵉ plantation." ‡ A pronoun rarely is used with so great effect — <u>his</u> *White Angel.*

---

* Bradford's *History of Plimoth Plantation*, 1898 : 321, 189, 322, 323.
† Bradford's *History of Plimoth Plantation*, 1898 : 324, 325. 346.
‡ Bradford's *History of Plimoth Plantation*, 1898 : 319, 328.

Therein lay the gist of the trouble. When the storm of protest arose about the two new ships, "M.ʳ Allerton tould them that yᵉ ship Whit-Angele did not belong to them, nor their accounte, neither neede they have anything to doe with her, excepte they would. And M.ʳ Hatherly confirmed yᵉ same." Mr. Sherley and the other London partners disclaimed any responsibility for the purchase, from which Bradford and others deduced that from the first she "was not intended for yᵉ plantation," but for Allerton's private gain. *

Mr. Winslow could not prevent Mr. Sherley and the other English partners "from putting both yᵉ Friendship and Whit-Angell on yᵉ generall accounte; which caused continuall contention betweene them." This was explained in a letter from Mr. Sherley to Bradford and others, dated January 2, 1631[-32], in which he stated that the purpose of himself and friends was to keep the accounts of the two ships "for yᵉ last year viages, on the generall accounte;" but that they had now let the *White Angel* to Mr. Allerton "at 30 ᴵᴵ pᵉ month, by charter-partie," and "bound him in a bond of a 1000 ᴵᴵ to performe covenants, and bring her back to London." Sherley also promised to send over Allerton's three books of accounts, or copies of them, — "one for yᵉ company, another for Ashley's bussines, and yᵉ third for yᵉ Whit-Angell and Freïdship. . . . The totall sume, as he hath put it, is 7103.17.1. Of this he hath expended, and given to M.ʳ Vines & others, aboute 543 ᴵᴵ ode money." The sum of £7103 : 17 : 01 evidently was the full amount which had passed through the hands of Allerton, as agent. Bradford says : " Concerning M.ʳ Allerton's accounts, they were so larg and entrecate, as they could not well understand them, much less examine & correcte them, without a great deale of time & help, and his owne presence, which was now hard to gett amongst them ; and it was 2. or 3.

---

years before they could bring them to any good pass, but never make them perfecte." *

Again, Bradford writing, it must be remembered, long afterwards, says under date of 1632, that Allerton had paid no hire for the *White Angel;* "he broke his bonds, kepte no covenante . . . nor was ever like to keep covenants," and their only redress was "a few catle & a litle land & some small maters he had here at Plimoth." † Bradford's memory was prejudiced; the Plymouth Colony Court records show that in January, 1633-34, Allerton's tax was the third largest in the Colony, and at the same time he again was chosen Assistant.

Early in the year 1631, Bradford wrote that, Mr. Allerton having been discharged, "their bussines began againe to rune in one chanell, and them selves better able to guide the same, Penobscote being wholy now at their disposing." Ashley had been sent back to England as a prisoner, for violating the terms of his bond; and Captain William Peirce, who "had a parte ther . . . was glad to have his money repaid him, and stand out." But their troubles did not cease.

At the beginning of their differences in 1629, the Purchasers had demanded of Sherley, and the other London partners, the return of their "comission," or power of attorney, which they refused to give up while "shuch great sumes" were owing them. Allerton was then appealed to, but he put them off from time to time, and never returned it. He considered that he had been unfairly used, and that his good name had been tarnished. He felt justified in withdrawing from the Colony. Yet, Bradford, under date of 1631, fretfully wrote that "Mr Allerton doth in a sorte wholy now deserte them ; having brought them into ye briars, he leaves them to gett out as they can." ‡

---

* Bradford's *History of Plimoth Plantation*, 1898 : 333, 338, 344.
† Bradford's *History of Plimoth Plantation*, 1898 : 358.
‡ Bradford's *History of Plimoth Plantation*, 1898 : 278, 334, 335, 348.

Not only the partners criticised Allerton sharply, but the church censured him. In 1631, when he returned to Plymouth from one of his many voyages, "y° church caled him to account for . . . his grosse miscarriages; he confessed his faulte, and promised better walking, and that he would wind him selfe out of these courses as soone as he could, &c."*

Mr. Sherley, too, joined in the disaffection toward Allerton, whom he had at first praised so warmly. In 1631, he wrote: "Verily had he [Allerton] run on in that desperate and chargable course one year more, we had not been able to support him; nay, both he and we must have lyen in y° ditch, and sunck under y° burden." Two years later: "Oh the greefe & trouble y* man, M° Allerton, hath brought upon you and us! I cannot forgett it, and to thinke on it draws many a sigh from my harte, and teares from my eyes; . . . verily, at this time greefe hinders me to write, and tears will not suffer me to see." Still, Sherley himself did not escape censure from the Plymouth Colonists (1636–1641); and, in 1637, Mr. Beauchamp "sued him in y° Chancerie" for an accounting of money and goods sent over to Mr. Sherley, Mr. Andrews, and himself, in partnership.†

Although they found fault with Allerton, Plymouth Colony could not spare him. For several years he had been engaged in commercial pursuits at Marblehead, New Amsterdam, and elsewhere; but when an independent government was set up in January, 1633–34, the Colonists elected him Assistant, evidently as an inducement for his return. Still, the matter of the *White Angel* and *Friendship* was tossed to and fro with the regularity of a shuttlecock, "to y° great loss & vexation of y° plantation." ‡ Three depositions taken in 1639 are of special interest because of their bearing in this matter: —

---

* Bradford's *History of Plimoth Plantation*, 1898 : 349.

† Bradford's *History of Plimoth Plantation*, 1898 : 339, 368, 413, 415, 436, 448, 450, 431.

‡ Bradford's *History of Plimoth Plantation*, 1898 : 329.

Timothy Hatherly, of Scituate, within the jurisdiction of Massachusetts Bay, " affirmed upon othe, taken before yᵉ Govʳ & Dep: Govʳ of yᵉ Massachusetts, Mᴿ Winthrop & Mᴿ Dudley : That this ship — Frindship was not sett out nor intended for yᵉ joynt partnership of yᵉ plantation, but for yᵉ perticuler accounte of Mʳ James Sherley, Mᴿ Beachampe, Mᴿ Andrews, Mᴿ Allerton, & him selfe. This deposition was taken at Boston yᵉ 29. of Aug: 1639." *

" Isaacke Allerton of New Plimmouth in New England merchant aged about 53 yeares sworne saith that the ship White Angell was heretofore in the yeare of our Lord 1631 bought at Bristoll of Alderman Aldworth by this deponent to the use of Mᴿ James Sherley, Mᴿ Richard Andrewes, Mᴿ John Beauchamp of London merchants Mᴿ Timothy Hatherly then of London feltmaker & this deponent, but this deponent saith that the said Timothy Hatherly did afterward refuse to accept of the said bargaine. And this deponent saith that the ship Frendship was heretofore hired & victualled by this deponent in the yeare aforesaid for the use of the said Mᴿ Sherley Mᴿ Andrews Mᴿ Beauchampe Mᴿ Hatherly and all the partners & purchasers of the plantation of Plimmouth aforesaid. And further this deponent saith that afterwards divers losses falling out upon the said ship Friendship the said Mᴿ Hatherly and this deponent did in the behalf of themselves & the said Mᴿ Sherley Mᴿ Andrews & Mᴿ Beauchampe agree & undertake to discharge & save harmlesse all the rest of the said partners & purchasers of & from the said losses for two hundred pounds."

Sworn to before " yᵉ Govʳ & Deputie, the 7. of Sep: 1639." †

" Mʳ Winslow deposed, yᵉ same time, before yᵉ Govʳ afore said [Winthrop], &c. that when he came into England, and yᵉ partners inquired of yᵉ success of yᵉ Whit Angell, which should have been laden wᵗʰ bass and so sent for Port, of Porting-gall [Oporto, in Portugal], and their ship & goods to be sould ; having informed them that they were like to faile in their lading of bass, that then Mᴿ James Sherley used these termes : Feck, we must make one

---

* Bradford's *History of Plimoth Plantation*, 1898 : 342.

† *Thomas Lechford's Note-Book*, 1885 : 189–90 ; also Bradford's *History of Plimoth Plantation*, 1898 : 343.

accounte of all; and ther upon pressed him, as agente for yᵉ partners in Neu-England, to accepte yᵉ said ship Whit-Angell, and her accounte, into yᵉ joynte partner-ship; which he refused, for many reasons, and after received instructions from New-Engl: to refuse her if she should be offered, which instructions he shewed them; and wheras he was often pressed to accept her, he ever refused, &c." *

Why there should have been such strong, unreasoning opposition to the *White Angel* and *Friendship*, on the part of the Pymouth people, is incomprehensible. To paralyze all operations for a time, as they did while indulging in their undignified quarrel, was most disastrous to their finances and to their credit abroad.

An agreement finally was concluded, on October 15, 1641, between James Sherley, John Beauchamp, and Richard Andrews, who were represented through power of attorney by Mr. John Atwood, of Plymouth, "with yᵉ advice & consente of William Collier, of Duxborrow," and "William Bradford, Edward Winslow, &c., in yᵉ presence of Edmond Freeman, William Thomas, William Pady, [and] Nathaniel Souther." The agreement stipulated first, that there should be "an absolute end " to the former partnership. With the aid of their present book-keeper, Josias Winslow, they estimated their assets, including housing, boats, bark, implements, and commodities, as " 1400 ˡⁱ. or ther aboute." Upon this basis, " William Bradford, Edward Winslow, &c.," were " bound in the sum of 2400 ˡⁱ. for paymente of 1200 ˡⁱ. in full satisfaction of all demands;" the " bond of 2400 ˡⁱ. to be deposited into yᵉ hands of yᵉ said John Attwode." The agreement was given into the care of the Rev. Mr. Reyner, teacher of the Plymouth Church.†

The individual claims of the three English partners were: Sherley, £150; Andrews, £544; and Beauchamp,

---

* Bradford's *History of Plimoth Plantation*, 1898 : 344.
† Bradford's *History of Plimoth Plantation*, 1898 : 451–456.

£400. Andrews charged the two others with defrauding Plymouth; "he believed nothing due Sherley, nor more than £150 to Beauchamp." To protect himself, Andrews returned the land which had been granted him by the Plymouth Colony, and gave his claim of £544 to Massachusetts Bay, "which very promptly exacted the last penny from Plymouth." This claim was paid at once. Sherley, "the chief Shylock," as Goodwin calls him, also received his money and signed a release, June 2, 1642;* but with Beauchamp "matters dragged provokingly." In 1645, he received £210 : 10, in sundry houses and lands from Bradford, Prence, Standish, Alden, and Winslow; finally, in March, 1646, a settlement was completed, and "the Pilgrim Republic for the first time enjoyed the luxury of owing no man anything." †

Winslow and the others, having voluntarily surrendered their property to free the Colony from indebtedness, tried in vain to get Allerton to adjust his accounts. Had Allerton forced his private claims in Plymouth, he would have been better prepared to meet his obligations to the Colony. The probate files of Plymouth County show that many estates were indebted to him. Of those who died in the epidemic of 1633, Godbert Godbertson, Richard Lanckford, John Thorp, and Francis Eaton owed him respectively, £75 : 10 : 03, [   ], £9 : 04 : 04, £105 : 00 : 00. In 1643, there was due to Allerton from the estate of John Atwood, £14 : 17 : 08. ‡

At length, being pressed by the Plymouth Colony Court for a settlement, upon a motion made by his son-in-law, Thomas Cushman, March 3, 1645, Mr. Allerton was "allowed a years tyme for recoûing his debts in this goûment, vpon books and papers." § Two weeks later (March 16), it is re-

---

* Bradford's *History of Plimoth Plantation*, 1898 : 483, 481.
† Goodwin's *Pilgrim Republic*, 1888 : 410, 411.
‡ *Plymouth Colony Probate*, Book I : 11, 15, 17, 48.
§ *Plymouth Colony Probate*, Book I : 11, 15, 17, 48.

corded: "That whereas Mr Isaac Allerton formly sold vnto Mr Willm Bradford Mr Edward Winslow Mr Thomas Prence &c̃ one house and garden place scituate on the South side of the heigh streete in Plymouth in pt payment of certain accounts betwixte them," they now, jointly and severally, conveyed the said house and garden place with all appurtenances to Mr. Edmond Freeman, and agreed to give him a deed within the space of twelve months. The "house and land at Joaneses Riuer sometime apertaineing vnto Mr Isaack Allerton" was sold February 3, 1648, for £75, to Captain Willett and Mr. Paddy.* These transfers were authorized by the following order:—

" 1646 Isaac Allerton for himself his heires execut & administr: did Ratifie whatsoever Mr Wm Bradford Edw winslow^e & Capt Miles Standish Agents for Mr Sherley Mr Andrews & Mr Beecham have done or hereafter shalbe done about the sale of any lands or goods & Cattle formerly his in propriety: provided they do cleerly acquitt him frō all debts & demands due from the said Isaac Allerton to the said Mr Sherley, Andrewes & Beecham & this was by him done the XIIth (3) 1646," at Boston.†

On March 10, 1652, Mr. Edmond Freeman, of Sandwich, brother-in-law of John Beauchamp, together with William Paddy, whom Beauchamp in a letter called "Loveing Cozen," requested of Governor Bradford that they might have the estate of Mr. Beauchamp "recorded in the courte booke," as they held "Letters of Attorney," and were about "to make Return to England [of] all the estate of Mr Beachampe." This list embraced "Mr Bradfords land at Secunke . . . Mr Winslows house at Plymouth . . . Mr Prences house at Plymouth and five acres of land at second brooke . . . Mr Alden and captaine Standish land att South river," etc., together with certain "moneyes Received," to which these items were added:—

---

* *Plymouth Colony Deeds*, Book 1 : 130, 133.
† *Aspinwall Notarial Records*, 1903: 21.

"Sold to Mr Willett Mr Allertons house   £   s   d
at Plymouth att the Rate of 07:00:00
Mr Prences ffarme att Joaneses River
sold to Mr Willett and William Paddy for
Thomas Coachman . . . . 75:00:00" *

This farm at Jones's River was conveyed by Captain Willett and Mr. Paddy to Elder Thomas Cushman, October 20, 1653; it was then described as "Originally . . . the house and land of Mr Isaak Allerton." †

From the time the Purchasers began to find fault with Allerton, Plymouth had little of his presence. Bradford says : "so in ye end removed, as he had allready his person, all his from hence." ‡ It is uncertain when he left Plymouth. His deposition concerning the two ships proves that he retained his citizenship as late as 1639, though most of his time was spent at sea, or looking after his varied interests. As all matters of trust had been taken from him, and he was no longer their agent, he naturally turned to his own affairs and made the most of every opportunity.

It was when he went to England in the fall of 1630, in the *White Angel*, that he hired the same ship from Mr. Sherley for £30 a month, and fitted her out for commercial purposes of his own. Early in the spring of 1631, he set forth. His passage was perilous in the extreme, from the fact that the ship was overladen and her cargo badly stowed, and that the crew was a roistering set of fellows, who proved troublesome. Allerton was forced to put into Milford Haven, where the cargo was "new-stowed;" thence he proceeded to the coast of Maine. By reason of the delay, he was late for the fishing season, so he "sells [his] trading comodities to any y^t will buy, to ye great prejudice of ye plantation here," says Bradford; "but that which is worse, what he

---

* *Plymouth Colony Deeds*, Book 1 : 128; Book 2: pt. 1 : 34, 32, 33.
† Vide pages 538, 539.
‡ Bradford's *History of Plimoth Plantation*, 1898 : 358.

could not sell, he trusts." He ran "into every hole, & into ye river of Kenebeck, to gleane away ye trade from ye house ther," continues the same author, "and sets up a trading house beyoned Penobscote, to cute of [cut off] ye trade from thence also." *

Whether this new trading-post at Machias (Indian name Mechisses) was opened at the "instigation" of the English partners, as claimed, or by Sir Richard Vines and Allerton, certainly no one was better fitted to carry it on than the latter. The result of this venture is concisely given by Governor John Winthrop : —

"[November, 1633] News of the taking of Machias by the French. Mr. Allerton of Plimoth, and some others, had set up a trading wigwam there, and left in it five men and store of commodities. La Tour, governor of the French in those parts, making claim to the place, came to displant them, and, finding resistance, killed two of the men, and carried away the other three, and the goods." The trading-house was burned.

La Tour, at that time Governor of Nova Scotia, was but protecting his own, for the French then claimed all the land east of the Penobscot River, and not until 1782 were the eastern boundaries of what is now the State of Maine fully defined. Early in the spring of 1634–35, "Mr. Allerton" went in his pinnace to Port Royal to fetch the men who had been taken from his trading-camp at Machias, and to demand his goods or their equivalent. La Tour told him that "he took them as lawful prize," and that if Allerton or any other English "traded to the east of Pemaquid, he would make prize of them. Being desired to show his commission, he answered that his sword was commission sufficient." Nine years later (1643), in a review of this matter before the Governor, it was stated that goods to the value of £500 had been taken at Machias, and that the seizure had been due to the violation of a tacit agreement between "Mr. Vines,

---

* Bradford's *History of Plimoth Plantation*, 1898 : 348, 349.

of Saco, who was part owner of the goods and principal trader," and La Tour.*

The summer after La Tour's occupation of Machias, that is, in 1635, the French, by a ruse, surprised and took possession of the Pilgrims' trading-post which had been established by Ashley at "Biguyduce" (called by the Indians Matchebiguatus, and later by the whites Majorbagaduce), now Castine. While all the trading commodities were kept by the French, the men were allowed to "have their shalop and some victualls to bring them home." †

The records of Maine give proof of Allerton's association with Sir Ferdinando Gorges, and with Sir Richard Vines, other than at Machias. June 25, 1630, "Mr Isaacke Allerton, Capt. Thomas Wiggin, Mr Thomas Purchase," and three others, were witnesses to possession taken by "John Ouldham and Richard Vines Gentlemen," of land at "Swackadock," between Cape Elizabeth and Cape Porpus, now Biddeford, Maine. Their patent from "Ro: Warwicke Ed: Gorges fferd: Gorges & Tho: Smith," who constituted the "Councell for New England," was dated February 12, 1629.‡ Allerton also witnessed, July 21, 1632, a memorandum that John Winter, attorney for "Robert Trelawny and Moses Goodyeare," accepted for them of Richard Vines a tract of land extending from Cammock's patent at Black Poynt "along the sea-coast eastward." July 30, following, Allerton witnessed that possession was given to John Winter of the same land, by Vines.§

On January 27, 1636–37, "Sir Fardinando Gorges," for £100, granted to George Cleeves and Richard Tucker, of Casco Bay, a patent of that portion of the land at "Machegonne . . . to the Falls of Pesumpsca [Pesumpscott] . . .

---

* Winthrop's *History of New England*, Savage's Edition, 1853, vol. 1 : 139, 184; vol. 2 : 151, 152.
† Bradford's *History of Plimoth Plantation*, 1898 : 395–400.
‡ *York County Deeds*, vol. 1 : pt. 2 : 9.
§ *Maine Historical Society Collections*, Second Series, vol. 3 : 15.

that yᵉ sᵈ Geo: Cleeves & the sᵈ Richᵈ Tucker, haue planted, for diverse yeares already expired . . . estimated in the whoole to bee fiveteen hundred acres . . . for the full Tearme of Two Thousand years. . . . The sᵈ Ferdinando Gorges doth appoynt his trusty and well beloved Isaacke Allerton & Arthur Mackeworth, gentle: his true & lawful attorneys, jointly or seuerally, for him and in his name, to enter into the sᵈ Landˢ . . . in the name of the whoole: And . . . to take full and peaceable possession." They were then to deliver the same "vnto the sayᵈ Geo: Cleeve, and Richard Tucker, theyʳᵉ heyres and assigns, according to yᵉ . . . true meaning of these P'sents." *

That Allerton also was well known in other parts of Maine is shown by a letter from William Hilton, dated Piscataqua, April 18, 1633, which says, "one Richard Foxwell . . . bringeth nuse . . . he heard from Mr. Alerton whoe was making ready at Bristol for to come to this cuntery." †

Another venture of Allerton's was located at Marblehead, in the Massachusetts Bay Colony. About 1631 or 1632, with Moses Maverick, afterwards his son-in-law, he established the headquarters of his fishing-fleet at Marble Harbor, set off from Salem in 1649 as the town of Marblehead. Here he built a warehouse, with stages for curing fish. In the spring of 1633-34, Winthrop says that Allerton, that season, "fished [here] with eight boats," while "seventeen fishing ships were come to Richman's Isle and the Isles of Shoals," off the coast of Maine. It probably was with reference to this business of Allerton's that in April, 1633, the Massachusetts Bay Court ordered: "That if any swine shall in fishing time, come within a quarter of a myle of the stage at Marble-Harbor, they shalbe forfeited to the owners of sd stadge, & soe for all other stadges within their lymitts."

---

* *York County Deeds*, vol. 1 : 96; also vide pages 27, 81, 83.
† *Maine Historical Society Collections*, First Series, vol. 3 : 21.

On February 1, 1634, Matthew Cradock's * house at
Marblehead was "burnt down about midnight . . . there
being then in it Mr. Allerton, and many fisherman, whom
he employed that season." The fire was discovered by a
"tailor who sate up that night at work in the house, and,
hearing a noise, looked out and saw the house on fire above
the oven in the thatch." No one was injured, and "most of
his goods therein " were saved.†

The period of Allerton's residence at Marblehead was a
time of misfortune. Every undertaking resulted in loss. In
Bradford's opinion it was a direct judgment upon him for
his "evil courses," and "God crost him mightily." Besides
the failure of his trading-camp at Machias and the burning
of the house at Marblehead, a pinnace which he had sent on
a trading voyage to France was lost with its entire cargo.
To add to his troubles, on March 4, 1634–35, the Court of
Massachusetts Bay "agreed, that Mʳ Allerton shalbe sent
for, by pcess, to the nexte Court of Assistants, to the intent
that hee may vnderstand the desire of the country for his
removall from Marble Harbor, & soe to be enioyned to be
att the ñexte Genall Court, or otherwise to be dealt withall,
as the p̃ticular Courte shall thinke meete." The steps taken
to accomplish Allerton's removal must have been summary,
for on May 6 (1635) it is recorded in a "Memorand :" of the
Court, "that Mʳ Ollerton hath giuen to Moses Maûacke, his
soñe in lawe, all his howses, buildings, & stages, that hee hath
att Marble Head, to enioy to him & his heires for euer." ‡

---

* " Mʳ Allerton of New Plymouth " had been entrusted, in November, 1628,
with a letter from Matthew Cradock (first Governor of Massachusetts Bay,
though he never came over) to John Endicott, at Salem, stating that he proposed sending over two or three hundred persons and one hundred head of
cattle, and requesting that "convenient howsinge " be speedily prepared for
them. This anticipated the coming of Winthrop's fleet. (*Massachusetts Bay
Colony Records*, vol. 1 : 383.)

† Winthrop's *History of New England*, Savage's Edition, 1853, vol. 1 :
148, 147.

‡ *Massachusetts Bay Colony Records*, vol. 1 : 140, 147.

Allerton is said to have departed then ; but he evidently retained some interest at that place, as at Plymouth, since, in June, 1642, his "servant" or clerk, Thomas Bryant, who had been "imprisoned neare 2. months, was discharged from prison wthout whipping, and sent to Mr Moses Mavericke to be imployed for his master." * Isaac Allerton shared in the division of pasturage to the forty-four families of Marblehead, December 22, 1648; he was allowed shares for two cows and Moses Maverick for three.† Allerton joined the First Church of Salem, of which Marblehead was then a part, in 1647. Felt's list of members ‡ gives his name thus : "1647 — Isaac Allerton, + 1639," — the mark before the second year denoting that he was a resident that year or prior to it. A later hand has added "1634," which probably is correct.

On August 16, 1635, "a mighty storm of wind and rain" visited the New England coast, demolishing houses, uprooting trees, and causing great damage to shipping. Bradford adds that "the moone suffered a great eclips the 2. night after it." In the same tempest a bark, sailing from Ipswich to Marblehead, "was cast away upon Cape Ann, and twenty-one persons drowned." Among the lost were the Rev. Mr. Avery, his wife, and six small children, who were emigrating to Marblehead. The only ones saved were Mr. Thacher (cousin to Mr. Avery) and his wife, who were cast on shore ; he, after "a quarter of an hour beaten up and down by the waves, not being able to swim one stroke ; and his wife sitting in the scuttle of the bark, the deck was broke off, and brought on shore, as she stuck in it." A powder-horn and a bag of flint, a goat, a cheese, some bedding, and other necessaries, also were washed ashore ; which enabled them to subsist until they were taken off the island, three days later.§

* *Massachusetts Bay Colony Records*, vol. 2 : 6.

† Roads's *History and Traditions of Marblehead*, 1880 : 8, 20.

‡ Felt's *Annals of Salem, Massachusetts*, 1827 : 552.

§ Winthrop's *History of New England*, Savage's Edition, 1853, vol. 1 : 195-197.

The reef upon which they struck has since been known as Avery's Woe, and the spot upon which they landed, as Thacher's Island. It was Allerton who sent for Parson Avery to minister to them at Marblehead, since the Salem church was so far away that the large group of fishermen employed, described as "something loose and remiss in their behavior," rarely attended those services.* It also was Allerton's ill-fated bark which was dashed against the rocks, and was lost. The impulse which he gave to the fishing-trade at that point, of which he may justly be called the founder, has extended from generation to generation to this day. At this moment, the finest building for business purposes in the ancient town is called "Allerton Block."

The following March, 1635–36, while returning from a trading-voyage to Penobscot, Allerton came near losing another bark. She "was cast upon an island, and beat out her keel, and so lay ten days; yet he gate help from Pemaquid, and mended her, and brought her home." In the winter of 1644–45, he was shipwrecked at Scituate, with his third wife, Joanna, and some others, in a northeast storm of great violence "with much snow;" but all were saved.†

The differences between the Massachusetts Bay Colony and Isaac Allerton, at the time of his residence in Marblehead, are vaguely suspected to have been the outgrowth of Allerton's championship of Roger Williams and his peculiar religious belief ; however that may be, his earlier relations with the Bay Colony were pleasant. Allerton was enabled to assist the new settlement at Boston very materially. He and Captain Peirce were the first to greet John Winthrop, on the *Arbella*, as she neared the port of "Nahumkeck," now Salem, June 12, 1630. Sailing by on a voyage to Pemaquid in his shallop, Allerton met the *Arbella*, and went aboard to welcome Winthrop and his company to the New World.

---

* Mather's *Remarkable Providences*, Offer's Edition, 1856: 2.
† Winthrop's *History of New England*, Savage's Edition, 1853, vol. 1 : 466; vol. 2 : 258.

The first letter of Winthrop to his son in England, dated "Charlton [Charlestown] July 23, 1630," says : "We are forced to send to Bristowe for supply of provisions, by Mr. Peirce and Mr. Allerton, for which I have given them a bill of exchange. You must needs take order, the money may be provided presently for them, for they can't stay." * November 18, following, Captain Peirce wrote to John Winthrop, Jr., still in England : "my ship is so full y^t I cannot take in what I would & should; but Mr Allertown hath a ship to depart from Barnstable very shortly, vnto ye wch we can send away what I cannot take in." † Winthrop, in June, 1631, mentions letters from Barnstable brought "out of the White Angel (which was lately arrived at Sauco). She brought [   ] cows, goats, and hogs, and many provisions for the bay and for Plimoth." When the *White Angel* sailed into the Bay, July 22, following, she landed twenty-one heifers and a store of supplies at Boston. On her way to Plymouth she ran aground "near Gurnett's Nose," but got off and proceeded on her way. Winthrop adds that "Mr. Allerton returned in this ship" to England. From another letter of Winthrop's it appears that the trading venture in March, 1635-36, when Allerton's bark was cast upon the rocks near Pemaquid and "beat out her keel," brought misfortune to him also. Owing to the disaster, "Mr. Mayhew and he [Allerton] could get but little provisions, and at extreme rates, but six hogsheads of bread, and a few peas. . . . Some pork they brought, but so lean as I have not seen the like salted." ‡

The following petition and bill, presented by Isaac Allerton to Governor Dudley, for the payment of goods brought from England to Boston in the years 1630, 1631, and 1632,

---

* Winthrop's *History of New England,* Savage's Edition, 1853, vol. 1 : 29, 448.

† *Massachusetts Historical Society Collections,* Fifth Series, vol. 1 : 196.

‡ Winthrop's *History of New England,* Savage's Edition, 1853 : 69, 70, 71, 466.

never before have been published. Their special value lies in the fact that they bear the autograph signature of the Rev. John White, of Dorchester, England, prove his active assistance to the Massachusetts Bay Colony, and cite Isaac Allerton's ships as the means used by Mr. White to transport his supplies:—

" To thee Right Worship¹ Thomas Dudley Esqʳ Gouernoʳ and thee rest of the magistrates herein Boston and to the deputyes now assembled in generall Court in boston

" The humble petition of Shweth your worshipˢ that wereas your petitioner — being bound for England wth Mr Peirce from these partes in the yeares 1630 : 3i : 32 : was desired by the magistrates and othere gentˡ here to take care for thee buying and transportation of pvisions thither for the releife of thee countrys then necessities as is well knowen to some of your worships, The care and Charge a whereof your petitioner was willing to vndertake whereby he mought bee serviceable to this country to thee vtmost, Did (by Gods goodnesse) vpon his safe arriuall in england prosecute that desseigne with his best endeavors, which through Gods blessing took effect, though with great trouble to your petitioner at Cancell board and elsewhere as is knowen : And further whereas mr white did then out of his good affections to this country pcure diuers pvisions for its supply in its then necessities hee the sd mr white Did alsoe imploy your petitioner for the transportation of them heither and did imbarke them in your petitioners sd ship, all which sd pvisions were by Gods goodnesse saffley landed here at boston and deliuered vnto the then Gouernor and magistrates to bee disposed of to the countrys vse which was done accordingly : But soe it is, may it please your worships, that your petitioner having layed out diuers sumes of monye for the charges of the sd pvisions and is yet out of purse for the fraight and Charge of the sd pvisions and soe hath bine a longe tyme ase

---

* *Massachusetts Archives*, vol. 100 : 8. This petition of Isaac Allerton undoubtedly was written by himself. His autograph shows the same characteristics as the one given in the latter part of this sketch.

To the Right Honoble Gover[nor] & Thomas Dudley Esqr
Gouernor and they ar[e] of the magnifforth... Deputy Gover[nor]
bound to the saftyes goe to accompes of principle... in Before

The humble petition of [   ] Morton

Sheweth Your mo[st] [   ] that wheras [   ] Your petitio
being bound for England... his Pisars from high [   ] in this yeares
1630. 31. 32: was desired by the magistrats and other princible to take into
this buyeing and transportation of greious sattisffor for ... on behalf of the towne
them neggissios as is will ... to some of your wor[shi]ps, The same also being
... of Your petitioner was nothing to answer ... to me soe ... the Greivance
that to many to doe ... of Desiers By Your gen[er]ous soe ... By ... arrived [   ]
Englands prefonoty that Disfferes will ... ... upon through God
... for effect though ... ... great trouble to Your petitioner at ... gr[eat]
... ... as is knowen: And further so... as much Did them out of ...
... to his country Even divers greivons for its supply ... the more
... to me w[i]th Big ... imployd Your petitioner for his... pition of ...
... the to ... Begin in Your... ...
Petitioner Did... ...
... By Your worshi...

AUTOGRAPH PETITION OF ISAAC ALLERTON TO GOVERNOR DUDLEY, 1640

by an accompt of the foresd mr white vnder his hand herewith
pduced may more fully appeare the ballance whereof remaines
vnsatisfied as yet vnto your petitioner to his great detriment and
lose. mr white having not payed it neither will he pay it, as
appeares vnder his hand vpon accompt,

> " May it therefore please your Worship⁵ to take the equitie of
> the premises into consideration And to take order that your
> petitioner may be forthwith satisfied the ballance of the sd
> accompt amounting vnto the sume of 49ˡ : 12ˢ : as by the sd
> accompt appeares, And your petitioner shall euer acknow-
> ledge your righteous fauor herein and shall pray to thee God
> of wisdom and grace to fill you with his Spiritt for the guid-
> ing of you in all your wayes to his glory and thee good of
> this his people/

[Endorsed on the margin in a different hand]

"we Conceiue it Requisite yᵗ enquirie should be made whether such
Goods were dd. to yᵉ Gouno.ʳ & assistants as are brought in vppon
accounts: & if so to whom they haue ben Distributed: & as
many as can be found to haue Recᵈ. any of yᵉ sd goods & are able
should giue satisfaction to yᵉ petitioner if it appeare to be Due &
in case yᵉ psons are not able or cannot be found that then yᵉ
seũall Townes where they Dwelt at yᵗ time are liable to giue satisfaction

[The following autograph endorsements are on the back]

" The howse of Depᵗˢ. haue made choyce of Majoʳ. Gibbons &
wiſlm Parks to speake wth oʳ honoʳed magˢᵗˢ. to. know wᵗ became
of yᵉ goods. yᵗ mʳ Allerton brought ouʳ for yᵉ Country, & to make
returne thereof to yᵉ howse.

ROB : BRIDGES.

" The howse of Depᵗˢ, conceive it meet, yᵗ mʳ Allerton. shall be
Allowed by. yᵉ Tresurer, yᵉ some of forty nyne pounds & twelve
shillings; acording to his petition; for yᵉ Cause therein men-
coned, so as yᵉ said mʳ Allerton depose; yᵗ it is now Dew vnto
him, & vnpaid: & Desires oʳ honnoʳed magisᵗˢ to concuere wᵗʰ
them herein

EDWARD RAWSON.

" If m^r Allerton can prove, that hee Delivered goods to the then Gov^{r}n^r or any other appointed by authority to receive them to the valewe of 179^t. 12^s for the use of the Country, & will take his oath, that there is yet due to him 49. 12th to ballance his accoumpt let it be paid out of the Country.

" The magistrates doe concure wth the Deptȳs in   Aller^s
Petition so far as is here aboue expressed.

Jo. winthp: ⚡: G:

" ye Dep^{ts}. consent to y^r magis^{ts} retourne

                                    EDWARD RAWSON "

" Vera Copia   The coppy of an accoumpt * delivered me by Mr Allerton
7 Septemb.   to [sho]w vnto Mr White to write to the Governour of the
1632.   bay that it is due vnto Mr Allerton, & that he hath not payd
it, but they of the Bay ou[ght] to pay it, M^r white haviinge noe
monyes in his hands for that busines. & to desier his note to that
effect they will pay it, noe reason M^r w[hite] should, Jt is sufficient
he pcured the yings [things]

    " An accoumpt of charges of a barke of goods sent by Mr George
Way [of] Dorchester for the accoumpt of M^r Jno: white minister
or preacher of Gods worde at dorchester from Padstow in Cornȩ-
we[ll] followeth.

" 1631.   Inpr. payd a barks fraight Loaden with Corne to
Decemb. 18   Bristoll . . . . o8 : [   ]o:
                 for M^r wayes mans diet aboard the barke . . . . oo : [   ] oo
    for the barks Companies supper . . . . oo : [   ] o6
    for the returne of the warrants . . . . oo : [   ] 19
    for a certificate to Barnestaple ℘ major . . . . o[   ] oo
    pd the Corne measurer for his fee . . . . [   ] oo
    pd the barks fraight from Bristoll to Barnestaple . . o[   ] oo
    pd boats & porters to land the [   ] . . . . [   ]o
    pd for storehouse to put the meale in 2/8 . . . . . [   ] 14 : oo
    pd for an other storehouse to put the remaynder of the
      meale in . . . . oo : o5 : oo
    pd for a man to goe downe with the Barke . . . . . o1 : oo : oo
    the goods beinge steyed to cleare them, these goods part
      amounteth but to . . . . o5 : 13 : o6
    pd for a barke from Barnestaple to Bristoll back againe o5 : oo : oo

                    * *Massachusetts Archives*, vol. 100 : 9.

for 2 boats & porters to land the goods . . . . 00 : 10 : 00

for a mans charges that came with the goods . . . . . 00 : 17 : 00

pd demeurradge vntill a storehouse was pvided ȷ being
not there myselfe . . . . 00 : 13 : 11

pd for a warrant, & officers fees in custome house . . . 00 : 15 : 00

for fraight of 6 butts : 49 ỉỉ. 30 barr: of meale from Padstow
WW by Mr way marked as in the margent. And 2 ỉỉ of meale
TS.RS & pease sent from Padsto by Mr way from Mr Southcott.
And 25 tearses of pease & oatmeale sent by M william
Vassell by Mr whites order wch he payd for. And Mr
way sent 1 ỉỉ of wheate marked W W W W all [ ] ½ at
4 b pton : Mr wayes was for Mr Purchas' accoumpt . 97 : 00 : 00

for hawlinge craindge litridge & wharfidge at 3/8 pton . . 03 : 12 : 09

windage to the ships company . . . . 02 : 08 : 06
                                                  _____
                                                  134 : 04 : 10

For charges on these goods being 24 tons & ¼ accordinge
to the pportion on the whole about 35/8 4d ¼ ptonn is . 42 : 09 : 02
                                                  _____
                                                  176 : 14 : 00

Mr way demaundeth mony for 8 bushells of meale beinge
one ỉỉ marked W W W W wch beinge heare put
ashore & vsed it must be allowed at 7/8 3d pbushell . 2 : 18 : 0[
                                                  _____
                                                  179 : 12 :[

Mr White is Creditor

decemb. 1630 : p 50 b res p his order of Mr Arthur Kinge
of Bristoll . . . . 50 : 00 : 00

May 20. res of Mr way p bill of Exch : p Mr whits order &
accoumpt . . . . 40 : 00 : 00

Aprill 15. 1632. res of him by exch : by Mr whits order . 40 : 00 : 00
                                                  _____
                                                  130 : 00 : 00

due to Mr Allerton to ballance this accoumpt . . 49 : 12 :[
                                                  _____
                                                  179 : 12 :[

ffor the article of 42ʷ — 9ˢ — or for the charges vppon the
goods sent for the releiving of the poore people in New-
England ȷ payd to Mr Allerton as having Disbursed before
more money then ȷ received as appears by the account wᶜʰ
ȷ gave in to the Contributors wᶜʰ ȷ testify this September
17. 1640.

John White.

---

* The above autograph of the Rev. John White, of Dorchester, England, is pronounced genuine by Mrs. Frances Rose-Troup, of Ottery St. Mary, Devon, England, who has been engaged for nearly twenty years in writing the life of that reverend gentleman.

" Thomas Bushroade merchant aged thirtie six or thereabou[t] being sworne maketh oath that this abouewritten was subscribed as the act & deede of the abouesaid m^r: John White of the said Thomas.

THO: BUSHRODE

" Jurat : Coram me
[Signature undecipherable]   Gus: N : B.
    2. die Sept^m, "

This bill, accompanying the petition of Isaac Allerton for its payment, evidently is a copy of an account originally presented to Governor Winthrop, who ordered the supplies. From the petition to Governor Dudley, which is without date, and the endorsement of the Rev. John White, in 1640, it is apparent that at that late date the amount of £49 : 12 remained unpaid.

While yet a citizen of Plymouth, Allerton had extended his operations eastward along the entire coast. He had a residence and warehouse at Marblehead, and was well known in Boston. At the same time he established business relations in New Amsterdam (the present city of New York) and New Haven, with a home in each place. He also acquired large interests at Delaware Bay and Virginia. In proof that the confidence reposed in Allerton by his business associates in Massachusetts Bay and elsewhere still continued, the following abstracts of " powers of attorney " are given from the records of Thomas Lechford and William Aspinwall, notaries of Boston, and other sources : —

March 29, 1639 : " Thomas Beech now remayning att the Dutch Plantation " was indebted to " Peter Garland of New England Mariner " the sum of £33 : 04 : 06, and other debts which he had been intrusted " to take up " amounting to £6 : 03 : 09. By letter of attorney Peter Garland appointed " my trusty ffriend Isaacke Allerton of New England mariner my lawful Attorney " to collect these amounts.*

March, 1645 : " A ftre [of] Atturney from Mr Tho : ffowle to

---

* *Lechford's Note-Book*, 1855: 60, 61.

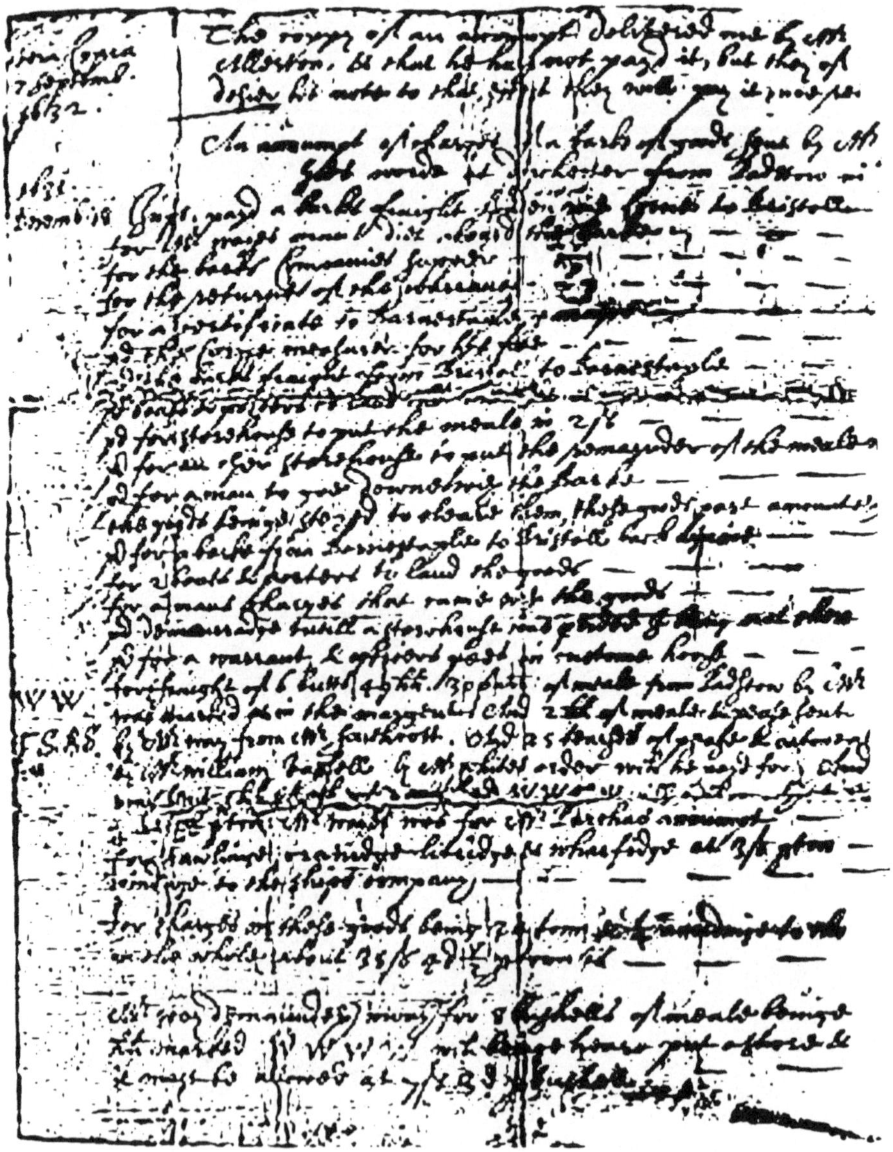

A COPY OF AN ACCOUNT OF MR. ISAAC ALLERTO
APPROVED BY THE REV. JOHN WHI

Isaac Allerton to Account with peter Johnson," and to sue him for £200.

October 13, 1646: "A ttre [of] Atturney from John Manning of Boston Merch^t unto Isaac Allerton of New Haven Merch^t to aske leavie recover & receive of Thomas Bushrode in Virginia merch^t . . . goods effects actions creditts where ever they may be found the valew of 16804 pounds tobacco due to him uppon Accounts & certaine other moneys pd for him uppō his Bills of Exchange & to compound agree &c : & to substitute other under hi^m wth like or limited power : &c : "

August 6, 1647: Isaac Walker constituted Isaac Allerton his attorney to collect ("& to compound &c: & to appeare in any Court") the sum of £7 from "Cloyse Cornelius & Peter Cloise . . . payable the 3 (4) 1647 in Bev^e [beaver], Otter skins or money."

August 23, 1647: "Mr Adam Winthrop constituted Isaac Allerton of New haven" his attorney to collect a debt of £12, sterling, "payable in Bever to himself & Benjamin Gillom, . . . also to compound &c & to appeare in any Court or Courts, in New Netherland or elsewhere to sue implead . . . attach imprison & condemne &c : "

August 25, 1647: Articles of agreement by which Captain Jelmer Thompson, commander of the ship *Great Garret*, and Captain Jan (John) Clawson Smale, commander of the *Beaver*, said ships "now rideing at Anchor in Charles river nigh unto Boston," contract with "Mr Raph Woory of Charlestown Merch^t . . . to transport & lade what merchantable goods or Cattle he please from this place to the Barbados," provided they retained command of their ships. Mr. Richard Smith, who had an interest in the venture, was placed under bond to pay £100 to Governor Stuyvesant. Smith failing to meet the obligation, it was to be paid by "Mr Isaac Allerton upon Certificate of the Arrivall & delivery of the s^d freight at Barbados." March 4, 1649, William Aspinwall recorded: "I attested a Copie of Mr Isaac Allertons oath touching the freightm^t of yelmer Thomson in the great Garrat."

September 9, 1647: Valentine Hill of Boston, merchant, constituted Isaac Allerton of New Haven, merchant, his lawful attorney, "granting him full power . . . to aske &c : of Thomas

Bushrode of Kikatm * in Virginia Merchᵗ 24 C of Porke & 60 barrˡˡˢ Indian Corne due by bill, & 1850ˡᵇ wᵗ of Tobacco uppon Account under hand of sᵈ Bushrode, & of the receit to give acquittance &c: also to compound . . . arrest &c."

May 24, 1649: "Capt (Theo:) Cromwell of Boston gent." gave "Isaac Allerton of Newhaven merchᵗ," £200, "to purchase the frigot that was taken out of the Harboʳ of Newhaven when she shall arrive at the manhatas." June 4, following, Captain Cromwell advised Allerton: "Yoᵘ are to doe nothing concerning the purchaseing of the ffrigot that was taken from Newhaven but what Nicholas Shapley [of Kittery, Maine] shall advise wᵗʰ yoᵘ, & if yoᵘ buy not the ffrigott then yoᵘ to Deliver unto the sᵈ Nicholas Shaply the two hundred pounds sterl yoᵘ received of mee . . . in so doing this shalbe yoʳ discharge."

June 11, 1649: "Mʳ John Treworgie [of Kittery] did acknowledge to have received foure thousand wᵗ of Tobacco by Isaac Allerto[n] for the Account of Mʳ Georg Ludlow of Virginia."

August 23, 1649: Edmund Leach, of New Haven, delivered to Isaac Allerton, wampum and trading-cloth to the value of £180" sterling, to be exchanged at Boston for "Merchantable bever at price current," before the first day of June next.

June 28, 1650: Isaac Allerton, William Phillips, and six others signed a contract with Richard Thurston, of Boston, mariner, to build a ship "for ouʳ uses not exceeding the burden of eight score Tonns or thereabouts;" Allerton and Phillips, each, to own one eighth.†

---

* Kikatan, also written Kiquotan, Kiccoutan, Kecoughtan, etc., now Hampton, Virginia. In 1608, Captain Smith "was very hospitably entertained by the Kecoughtans," a small tribe of Indian warriors. The English settlement upon this peculiarly healthful spot, known as Kecoughtan, was one of the eleven boroughs entitled, in 1619, to two Representatives in the House of Burgesses; the name was soon changed to Hampton.

Col. Thomas Bushrod, b. 1604; d. 1661, in the adjoining county of York, Virginia. In March, 1658–59, he was a Burgess of York County. His wife was Elizabeth, widow of Captain Thomas Hill. Descendants of this family married into the Washingtons and Allertons, of Virginia.

(Fiske's *Old Virginia and Her Neighbours*, 1900, vol. I: 131, 178, 199; also Hayden's *Virginia Genealogies*, 1891: 636, 81.)

† *Aspinwall Notarial Records*, 1903: 5, 31, 81, 82, 83, 84, 215, 103, 216–220, 218, 239, 324.

November 28, 1653: "Michall Tainter master of m^r Alertons Catch & now bownd to verginea haue Recd of Euan Thomas Vintner of Boston one hhd two barrels of mackrill . . . to aduenture a^t halfe proffitt . . . allso Two hhds of Stronge beere . . . to aduenture in like manner." The next day (November 29), Allerton gave a receipt to Evan Thomas for "one hhd & fower barrels of mackryll to aduenture for halfe proffytt," which he signed

"ISACH ALLERTON SENIOR" *

Little has been known of the last years of Isaac Allerton in New Amsterdam and New Haven. It has been "lamented that the later years of Allerton are not illustrated by public services;" † yet he was quite as prominent in New Amsterdam as in Plymouth. He "could talk Dutch as well as English," ‡ besides undoubtedly possessing considerable knowledge of the Indian tongues. These continuing pages show that he occupied positions of unusual trust no less than before, and that his activities ceased only with his life.

The earliest references to Allerton in New Amsterdam are contained in the Registers of the Provincial Secretary. These books give abstracts only of the original papers, but they are sufficient to show Allerton's many transactions and his high standing in the community. The first record is a declaration of Director Kieft, dated February 17, 1639, that he had offered to receive tobacco from Mr. Allerton in exchange for corn or money.§ This appears to have been the beginning of those business relations at New Amsterdam, which later assumed such large proportions. Wilson mentions Thomas Hall and Isaac Allerton as "the English

---

* *Suffolk County Deeds*, vol. 2: 191, 192.

† Winthrop's *History of New England*, Savage's Edition, 1853, vol. 1 : 29; also *Massachusetts Historical Society Collections*, Third Series, vol. 7 : 243.

‡ *New York Biographical and Genealogical Recorder*, 1876, vol. 7 : 99.

§ *Calendar of Historical Manuscripts* in the Office of the Secretary of State, Albany, New York, Edited by E. B. O'Callaghan, 1865, vol. 1 : 5.

tobacco-planters."* There is hardly sufficient evidence to show that he actually raised tobacco there, but he may have done so; he certainly was a large dealer in it. Much of the arable land at Manhattan was devoted to the raising of that crop, which was considered "not much inferior" to the tobacco exported from Virginia. Allerton early saw that dealing in tobacco was remunerative, and he built a warehouse on the shore of the East River for its storage.

On May 19, 1643, Albert Cuyn conveyed by deed "a house and two lots," at New Amsterdam, to Isaac Allerton and Govert Loockerman; † and within a month (June 2), Allerton and Loockerman received a grant of land in New Amsterdam from the West India Company, of Amsterdam, Holland. The later grant consisted of "two lots on the east side of the Great Highway [Broadway] on the island of Manhattan, containing 160 rods, 9 ft., 2 in.," running back to the marshes. ‡ It may have been intended as a site for a warehouse, but probably was not used for that purpose, since it was sold later by the above grantees. The land upon which Isaac Allerton built his warehouse, "a capacious two-story building," included in "Allerton's Buildings," he purchased, April 10, 1647, from Philip de Truy. It was a triangular lot, a few feet in width at the southern end, but broadening to the width of more than five hundred feet of water frontage on East River. The little haven upon which it abutted, long ago filled in, forms the modern Peck Slip; the site of the warehouse very nearly corresponds to numbers "8 and 10 Peck Slip," of to-day. § The "Duke's Plan" of New York, 1661, represents "Allerton's Buildings" on

---

* Wilson's *Memorial History of the City of New York*, vol. 1 : 207, 231.

† Govert Loockerman, then a youth, arrived at New Amsterdam in 1633, as a ship's cook. For years he was closely associated with Allerton in various business ventures; and, after the death of Allerton, was the leading merchant of New Amsterdam.

‡ *Calendar of Historical Manuscripts*, etc., of New York, Edited by E. B. O'Callaghan, 1865, vol. 1 : 22, 336.

§ Innes's *New Amsterdam and Its People*, 1902 : 335, 336.

Warehouse and residence of Isaac Allerton at New Amsterdam.

the East River, outside of the city limits, just south of the " Passage Place " to Long Island ; and the same is given on " Nicoll's Map," 1664–1668.*

There is good reason to believe that a picture of the old warehouse and residence of Isaac Allerton is shown in one of a series of sketches made, in 1679, by the Labbadist missionaries, Danker and Sluyter, taken from a boat upon the waters of the rivers and bay. The sketch shows a little bay or cove that has been filled in to make the present Peck Slip. On the lower side is a wharf, on which stands two large, two-story buildings, connected by a shed. There is little doubt that they represent " Allerton's Buildings " as shown on the various maps.†

An ordinance passed by the Director-General of the Council of New Amsterdam, in 1650, also indicates Allerton's location. Fort Amsterdam was being repaired, for " this decayed fortress, formerly in fair condition, has mostly been trodden down " by cattle ; the inhabitants were warned " not to allow hogs, sheep, goats, horses or cows to run free between the Fort, the Company's Bouwery at the end of the Heeren Way [Broadway] now tenanted by Thomas Hall, and the [ware]house of Master Isaac Allerton, without herder or driver," under penalty of a " fine of 6 fl [florins]." ‡

In 1654, Allerton's Building was hired by the burgomasters for the temporary reception of fifty boys and girls who had been brought over from the almshouse in Amsterdam, to be " bound out." When the Indians surprised the settlement on Manhattan Island, September 15, 1655, in the absence of the Director-General Stuyvesant and his soldiers, they commenced their work of violence at this warehouse. They numbered five or six hundred, but fortunately the

---

* *New England Historical and Genealogical Register*, July, 1890.
† *Bulletin of the Society of Mayflower Descendants in the State of New York*, June, 1904: 5, 8.
‡ *Records of New Amsterdam*, 1653–1674, vol. 1 : 16.

guns of a Dutch ship in the East River were brought to bear upon them, which frightened them off before any serious damage was done. In 1656, George Woolsey,* who then lived in the house, obtained permission "to keep tavern;" at the same time he requested "to be allowed to tap" there, but was refused. Later, a license to "sell beer and wine" was granted. This old warehouse, which, during Allerton's life, was the resort of most of the English doing business in New Amsterdam, towards the close of the seventeenth century passed into the possession of the Beekman family, who owned property on the opposite side of the street. It has since been demolished.

In the summer of 1643, an Indian uprising began at New Amsterdam. The exciting cause was the killing of "an old Dutchman" by a drunken Indian. The people called upon Director Kieft to apprehend the murderer, but he "thought it not just, or not safe," so put them off. While the matter was pending, the Mohawks, "either upon their own quarrel, or rather, as report went, being set on by the Dutch," surprised some of the friendly Indians near the Dutch and killed about thirty of them. A Dutch captain, with the consent of Kieft, retaliated by slaying "about 70 or 80 men, women and children." Upon this the Indians burned the settlers' farmhouses, slew or carried off their cattle, and "killed all they could meet with." The trouble extended from the mainland to Long Island, until the Dutch were "pressed so hard" that they were forced to call the English to their aid.†

At the request of Director Kieft, the "Commonality of

---

* As early as 1646, George Woolsey was called servant to Isaac Allerton, that term then being synonymous with clerk or agent. He continued his relations with Allerton probably until the death of the latter in 1659. In December, 1647, Woolsey married Rebecca Cornell. Among his many distinguished descendants was Theodore D. Woolsey, president of Yale College from 1846 to 1871.

† Winthrop's *History of New England*, Savage's Edition, 1853, vol. 2: 116, 117.

the Manhattas" elected, September 13, 1643, eight select-men as Council in the emergency. These "Men of Eight," as they were termed, consisted of : —

"Joachim Pietersen [Kuyter]   Isaac Allerton
Jan Damen   Thomas Hal [Hall]
Barent Dirksen   Gerrit Wolphertsen
Abraham Pietersen   Cornlius Melyn " *

As it was stipulated that any person then chosen could be rejected, Jan Damen was excluded, and Jan Evertsen Bout was put in his place.

"The Eight Men" immediately drew up a letter of complaint to the "Assembly . . . of the General Incorporated West India Company at the Chamber in Amsterdam," stating the details of the Indian uprising which had devastated the country so that the "few settlers remaining were defenceless and starving." Then followed an urgent appeal for help, signed by : —

"Cornelius Melyn   Gerrit Wolphersen
Abraham Pietersen   Isaac Allerton
Thomas Hal [Hall]   Jan Evertse Bout
Barent Dirksen   Jochem Pietersen [Kuyter]

Done Manahatas this 24ᵗʰ October
in New Netherland, Anno 1643." †

"Captaine John Underhill and Mr. Allerton" were despatched immediately to New Haven for assistance. Their "proposition," presented to the General Court held at New Haven, October 27, 1643, was a request for one hundred soldiers, "armed and victualled, to be led forth by Captaine Underhill against the Indians now in hostility." The Court decided that the soldiers could not be sent without the consent of the United Commissioners, for fear of involving the Colonies in a general Indian war; nevertheless, if corn and

---

* *Documents Relating to the Colonial History of New York*, 1856, vol. I: 191, 192.

† *Documents Relating to the Colonial History of New York*, 1856, vol. I: 191.

provisions were needed, the Court resolved to give the Dutch all the assistance in its power.*

In November following, the "Eight Men" sent an elaborate "Memorial" to the "Noble, High and Mighty Lords . . . of the United Netherland Provinces," praying for speedy assistance or they would be obliged to betake themselves and families "to the English at the East, who would like nothing better than to possess this place." This was signed : —

"Cornelius Melyn	Jan Evertse Boudt
Tomas Hal [Hall]	Gerrit Wolphertse
Isak Allerton	Barent Dirckse
Abraham Peiterse	Jochem Pieterse Kuyter

Dated Manhatan, in New Netherland, this 3ᵈ November, 1643; Stil: Rom*e* "†

On October 28, 1644, the "Eight Men" sent a letter to Amsterdam, charging Director Kieft with malfeasance in office and inciting the recent Indian war, and requesting his removal. Isaac Allerton's signature was second in the eight. Their efforts eventually were rewarded by the arrival, in May, 1647, of Peter Stuyvesant, who was sent over as Director-General to supplant Kieft. Within a few days after Kieft had been removed from his office, Cornelius Melyn and Jochem Pietersen Kuyter, as representatives of the "Eight Men," brought a formal complaint of ten charges against the former Director Kieft, which had been circulated for signatures by Isaac Allerton and Jacob Stoffelse. In a letter, dated June 18, 1647, Kieft says that the charges are lies, and that Allerton and Stoffelse have cheated the people and abused the "Lords Patroons." Yet Allerton and Stoffelse escaped punishment, though the "Eight Men" were prosecuted by the Fiscal, while Kuyter and Melyn were banished.‡

---

* *Records of the Colony of New Haven*, 1638–1649: 112, 116.
† *Documents Relating to the Colonial History of New York*, 1856, vol. I : 139.
‡ *Documents Relating to the Colonial History of New York*, 1856, vol. I : 204, 250.

Isaac Allerton was a burgher or freeman in New Amsterdam, though his name does not appear in the first list, dated April, 1657. The "Burgher Right" was not established until January 23, 1657. On March 9, following, in a statement of taxes, assessed by the "Burgomaster and Schepens" in October, 1655, but now overdue, and ordered to be collected by the Court Messenger, Allerton's tax was sixty florins. Of the sixty or more persons named in the list, but five were taxed a larger amount. In November, 1656, he said of himself that he "is a Burgher here." *

The miscellaneous services of Allerton in New Amsterdam extended over a long period, and, as recorded in the Registers of the Provincial Secretary, were notable. The first group of extracts refers chiefly to business entrusted to him by others : —

1639 (entered before May 18): Note from George Homs (Holmes) to John Jenney, for "sixty carolus guilders," with receipt of Isaac Allerton for the same, dated December 29 (1638 ?). September 7, 1642, John Jenney gave Isaac Allerton a power of attorney to collect other money due him. In December, 1639, John "Celes" gave to Allerton power of attorney to collect money due him from George Spencer. In 1645, Jan Evertson Bout and Jan Jansen Damen empowered Allerton to sell the ship *St. Peter* in New England. June 6, 1647, certain men gave Allerton power of attorney "to sell horses on their account in Virginia." In September of that year, Allerton himself gave power of attorney to John Ogden and Richard "Cloff" to collect his debts ; in March, 1648, he gave the same to Johannes Verbrugge to collect money from Captain Francis Aerly, Jr., of Virginia.

April 27, 1641: Note of Nanne Beets to Isaac Allerton "for 755 guilders 13 stivers ; " May 29, following, a bond from Allerton as guardian of Eva, daughter to Nanne Beets. July 25, 1644, a mortgage was recorded from Jannitje, wife of Thomas Broen, to Isaac Allerton of a house on the island of Manhattan, near

* *New York Historical Society Collections,* 1885: 5; also *Records of New Amsterdam,* 1653–1674, vol. 7 : 143; vol. 2 : 225.

Fort Amsterdam. Isaac Allerton registered in Court as referee, December 12, 1642. In November, 1644, he was referee with Captain John Underhill in a case of difference between "Mr Moor" and Mr. Wedderly respecting a bark. In Court Proceedings, January 22, 1643, the case of John Brint, cooper, *vs.* Mr. Heyl was referred to Mr. Allerton and Thomas Baxter for settlement. In 1645, Allerton was a referee in a case of violation of contract in trading.*

August 14, 1647, Isaac Allerton signed a bond as security for a debt due from John Wilcox; September 23, 1648, he was security for Nicholas Hart. Thomas Adams and Isaac Allerton gave a bond, June 8, 1654, for the delivery of 3000 pounds of tobacco to Director Stuyvesant. Thomas Adams and Edward Bushell, of "Haccomacco," Virginia, gave a bond to Isaac Allerton June 9, 1654, to indemnify him for any loss he might suffer as their security. Thomas "More," of New Haven, and Isaac Allerton, Sr., gave bond to Jan Jansen, of St. Obyn, to restore a certain bark stolen by Thomas Baxter, and sold to said "More." Declaration was made by Isaac Allerton, of Suffolk, October, 1655, that he had paid the amount of a bond that he had given for "Ralph Whory," a leather-dresser, of Charlestown.† December 6, 1655, Isaac Allerton, "the elder," gave a bond for "Grinfil Lerben," captain of the ship *Charles*, about to sail for Curaçao. Clearance was given, on the same date, to Isaac Allerton for the ship *Charles*, "Greenfield Lerben," commander, to sail to the "Curaçao islands" for salt and horses.‡

The second group of extracts gives his dealings in connection with ships and cargoes:—

---

* *Calendar of Historical Manuscripts*, etc., of New York, Edited by E. B. O'Callaghan, 1865 : 8, 20, 12, 31, 37, 41, 51, 15, 29, 21, 31, 84, 93.

† At several different periods, Isaac Allerton is mentioned as "of Suffolk;" yet in 1639, and again in 1640, Governor Winthrop certifies "that Isaacke Allerton merchant hath no visible estate reall or personall heere in this Jurisdiction or Country for the present to my knowledge and yet I am well acquainted wth him & his trade & dealings in this Country." (*Lechford's Note-Book* : 189, 378.)

‡ *Calendar of Historical Manuscripts*, etc., of New York, Edited by E. B. O'Callaghan, 1865 : 40, 44, 57, 60, 63, 156.

Isaac Allerton, in January, 1642, sold the yacht *Hope* to Govert Loockerman. November 17, 1644, he gave a note in favor of the owners of *La Garce* for "500 guilders," a balance due for sugar. January 18, 1644, he gave another note to the owners of *La Garce* "for 3773 guilders," also for sugar. May 31, 1647, Isaac Allerton, of New Amsterdam, and Thomas Willett, of New Plymouth, were securities on a bill of sale of the ship *Amandare*, from Peter Stuyvesant, to go to Boston. A transfer was made, September 21, 1647, by Thomas Baxter to Isaac Allerton, of his share of a certain sloop. The certified copy of a receipt given by Isaac Allerton and others, agents of "Augustyn Herrmann," dated December 14, 1650, was for sundries delivered to them by Governor John "Prins" (Governor Prince, of Delaware Bay) on said Herrmann's account. Power of attorney was given, May 12, 1651, by Augustyn Herrmann to Isaac Allerton, to collect beavers from Governor "Prins." In September, 1652, "Carel Gabry" sued George Woolsey for payment of cordage sold to Governor "Printz," in the South River (Delaware), by Augustyn Herrmann, for which Isaac Allerton was security. March 29, 1656, intelligence was brought by Isaac Allerton's ketch that a Swedish ship, called the *Mercury*, had arrived at the South River, and order was given not to allow the Swedes to land.*

On August 16, 1646, Captain John Underhill † brought suit, in New Amsterdam, against Isaac Allerton; alleging that, before the plaintiff came there, Allerton had promised him that the commonalty (of New Amsterdam) would pay him higher wages than he could get from the New Haven company. The defendant denied ever having made such a

---

* *Calendar of Historical Manuscripts*, etc., of New York, Edited by E. B. O'Callaghan, 1865: 18, 30, 31, 37, 41, 52, 127, 164.

† In July, 1642, Captain Underhill, whose early training had been wholly military, finding no employment in Boston "that would maintain him and his family," resolved to go to the Dutch, — "he speaking the Dutch tongue and his wife a Dutch woman." The church in Boston gave him leave to depart to Stamford, Conn., and provided a pinnace to transport him; but "when he came there he changed his mind, or at least his course, and went to the Dutch." (Winthrop, vol. 2 : 76.) From the above it appears that Allerton was instrumental in Underhill's removal to New Amsterdam. His last years were spent at Oyster Bay, Long Island.

promise, and demanded proof. Underhill promised in Court that the defendant should not be troubled again by himself or his heirs on this subject.*

The Court Minutes of New Amsterdam abound in references to Isaac Allerton, his house, his servants, and his affairs. He seems to have been in great demand as security or bail for others; and, in a suit brought by "Robbert Passele" against "Skipper Igsiter," in 1658, for wages earned as seaman, the skipper requested the services of "Mr Allerton as interpreter," who appeared in Court.†

In November, 1656, William Beekman, of New Amsterdam, brought suit against Isaac Allerton, Sr., for the payment of the balance of a note due thirty days after the arrival of the ships from *Patria*, the amount being "fl. 952," with costs and damages. Allerton acknowledged the debt, but requested a delay of "3 months as he is a Burgher here," on paying interest. At the end of that time he paid. In 1658, the Court declared an attachment of Thomas Hall's tobacco by Allerton invalid, "inasmuch as his [Hall's] goods are not liable to arrest, according to the privilege of the city of Amsterdam, [he] having a house & lot here & keeping *fixum domicilium*." ‡

About this time (1658), Allerton was somewhat embarrassed financially. He had reached the age of seventy-two years, and was beginning to feel the effects of his strenuous life. In July, he appeared before D. Van Schelluyne, notary at "Breuckelen" (Brooklyn), acknowledging that he owed Cornelis Schutt a balance of purchase-money for Virginia tobacco, "amounting to 1757 guilders." To meet this obligation, he mortgaged two mares with their foals, four cows, and, further, his house and farm on the South River near

---

* *Calendar of Historical Manuscripts*, etc., of New York, Edited by E. B. O'Callaghan, 1865: 104.

† *Records of New Amsterdam*, 1653–1674, vol. 2: 381.

‡ *Records of New Amsterdam*, 1653–1674, vol. 2: 225, 307, 346, 377, 382, 405.

"fort Neuwer Amstel" (Delaware Bay), occupied by Jan Jansz Van Cranenburgh. In September, following, he mort. gaged his ketch called "Willem en Jan" (*William and John*), to meet a note of "1392 guilders, 12 stivers," dated November 14, 1656, which he had given Joannes Pietersz Verbrugge.[*]

Though at that time a resident of New Amsterdam, Allerton probably was one of the earliest promoters of the settlement at Delaware Bay. George Lamberton, of New Haven, a friend of Allerton's, while on a trading voyage to Virginia in his bark *The Cock*, discovered that there was a brisk fur trade with the Indians along the Delaware. This was in the fall and winter of 1638–39.[†] A company was at once formed, comprising, among others, Governor Theophilus Eaton, the Rev. John Davenport, pastor of the church, Deacon Robert Newman, and Captain Nathaniel Turner. August 30, 1641, a town-meeting was held at New Haven "which voted to itself authority over the region of Delaware Bay," and the acts of the Delaware Company were approved. Some fifty families already had removed to the Bay and settled in a plantation on Varkin's Kill, now Salem, New Jersey. A fortified trading-house was built or occupied at Passayunk (Philadelphia). The Swedes also had established themselves nearby on the same territory, calling it New Sweden, and the fort which they had erected, Fort Christina. John Printz, or Prince, was their governor.[‡]

The next year, 1642, the Dutch, fearing further encroachments upon what they considered their territory, "resolved to drive the insolent English away." They burned their trading-houses, imprisoned Lamberton and several other Englishmen, seized goods and did damage to the extent of £1000, sterling. The Swedes made common cause with the Dutch against the English. Lamberton was tried at Fort

---

[*] *Year Book of the Holland Society of New York*, 1900 : 165, 173.
[†] *New Haven Historical Society Papers*, vol. 3 : 93, 94.
[‡] Levermore's *Republic of New Haven*, 1886 : 91, 92.

Christina, July 10, 1643, by a "court of ten persons, among whom no English name appears." He showed that the English had purchased the land at Varkin's Kill, two years before, from a chief representing the sachem of all that country. Governor Printz produced testimony to prove that Peter Hollander, their agent, had bought all the country thereabouts from the head sachem himself, three days before Lamberton's bargain. "The court concluded that the English were trespassers, and that Lamberton must pay double duty on his beaver."

The difficulties arising from this triple occupation of the same territory led the United Colonies to open a commission to examine their claims, and if possible secure a peaceful solution of present disagreements. The members of this body, probably the first " Mixed Commission " ever convened on this continent, were selected from the Swedish, Dutch, and English nations. The examination is supposed to have taken place in the Swedish fort, and a degree of harmony resulted from it which was fairly satisfactory to the United Colonies. The questions and answers were long and tedious. A translation of the Dutch copy, dated " Anno 1644 Jan 16," certifies that : " The vnderwritten examination was vpon the letters of the governor of New-england to the governor of New Sweden. it was taken vpon oath in the p^sence of

Capitaine Christian Boy	The Governo^r John Printz
Comis Hendrick Huggen	Capitaine Turner
Capitaine Mons Clinge	Mr Isaac Alerton
Wachtmeister Gregory Von Dyck	Secretary Carl Janssen "*

The English settlers remaining at Delaware Bay, when their cup of misery seemed full from loss of homes, stores, vessels, and trade, were further reduced by "a sickness which fell upon them." But the poverty and distress were not con-

* Kidder's *Swedes on the Delaware and their Intercourse with New England,* 1874 : 46, 45.

fined to those who had risked their persons in the enterprise. The leading families in New Haven suffered severely, and the town's financial strength was crippled. But they did not despair. In 1650, the matter of colonization at Delaware Bay was reopened, at a town-meeting, with the result that another party set sail for the Delaware; this time, armed with a commission from Governor Eaton. The expedition was intercepted at Manhattan by Governor Stuyvesant, who confiscated the commission, imprisoned many of the colonists, and released them only under condition of an immediate return to New Haven. At this juncture, New Haven asked assistance from Plymouth "to plant a united colony at Delaware;" but Plymouth refused. The United Colonies were appealed to with a like result; and the Dutch remained masters of the situation.*

In July, 1651, a military force under Stuyvesant was stationed on the Delaware River, at Raccoon Creek, near Fort Christina, for the purpose of opposing the Swedish settlement. A conference was held with the Indians, who pretended they had sold no lands to the Swedes except the site of Fort Christina. This was reduced to writing; and, upon requisition of Director-General "Petrus Stuyvesant," was certified to, July 9 (new style), by "Wilhelmus Grasmeer, V. D. M. Cornelis de Potter, merchant, Isaack Allerton of Suffolk, merchant, Brian Newton, Captain-lieutenant, George Baxter, Ensign, Isaac de foreest, Selectman." These witnesses also testified to the formal gift to the Dutch of land "on the west side of the river," by the sachems Mattehoorn, Pemenatta, and Sinquesz, through "Sander [Alexander] Boyer," interpreter. This land was now occupied by the Swedes; "to wit — the land from the west point of the Minquaas Kil, where Fort Christina stands, called in their language Supeskongh, unto Boompgens hook, in their language called Neuwsings. And Pemenatta, the present and ceding proprietor," stipulated that whenever anything was

---

* Levermore's *Republic of New Haven*, 1886 : 96, 97.

the matter with his gun, it should be repaired for nothing; also that he should be given maize, "when he come empty among our people." The conference was closed and "confirmed" by the Indians, with "solemn shaking of the hands of the General and of us the undersigned."

"Thus done at Fort Nassau, on the South river of New Netherland, this 9 July, 1651.

[Signed]

Wilhelemus Grasmeer, clergyman
Cornelius de Potter, Isaac Alderton,
Bryan Neuton, George Baxter,
A. Hudde [witness], Alexander Boyer, as Interpreter,
R[oeloff] de Haes [witness], the ✗ mark of Jan Andriesen [witness], made by himself."

The "four witnesses" (Pieter Harmensen, for some reason, did not sign), all of whom were "well versed in the language of the Indians on this river," were vouched for, as "of competant age and credible," by "Marten Cregier, Captain Lieutenant of New Amsterdam burghess company," and "Abraham Staats, Surgeon and elder of Renslaers Wyck."[*] By virtue of this transaction, the region north of Fort Christina remained under the jurisdiction of the West India Company, and the name of the fort was changed to "Altona."

"During the next three years the New England Confederation trembled on the verge of a war with Stuyvesant." War was declared between England and Holland. In the spring of 1654, Oliver Cromwell sent out an expedition to seize New Netherland, and several men-of-war arrived at Boston. Intelligence of the projected expedition being carried to Director Stuyvesant by Allerton, the Council was instantly summoned (May 30) at Fort Amsterdam. Money was borrowed and plans made for defence; but before hos-

---

[*] *Documents Relating to the Colonial History of the State of New York,* 1856, vol. I : 597–599.

tilities began, word arrived of a treaty between the English and the Dutch, and the whole matter dropped.*

Notwithstanding all the intervening tribulations, the colonists at New Haven did not lose hope. In July, 1654, on the day when peace was publicly proclaimed, the General Court despatched a letter to the authorities at New Sweden, asserting their right to large tracts of land on both sides of Delaware Bay and River; the Court also desired "a neighbourly correspondency with them both in trading and planting there." Allerton appears to have anticipated this movement, since on June 22, preceding, Schepen Poulus Leedertsz Van de Grift made a declaration in New Amsterdam, "at the request of Isaac Allerton, merchant at New Amsterdam," concerning merchandise held for "said Isaac Allerton, Senior," in the warehouse of the Crown of Sweden on the South River.† From this it appears that Allerton sustained friendly business relations with the Swedes at Delaware Bay, as well as the English, — for he certainly was in good favor at New Haven. As for the Dutch: it was upon the protest of Isaac Allerton, Sr., dated April 6, 1657, that Jan Paul Jacquet was removed, fourteen days later, from his office as commander on the South River.‡ Governor Stuyvesant ordered Jacquet to transfer the company's effects to "Andries Hudde." This was done, and Jacquet, upon his return to Manhattan, was arrested and prosecuted. Allerton, in his so-called will, mentions debts due from Delaware Bay, showing that he retained interests there throughout his life.

The traffic of the New Amsterdam and New Haven merchants with Virginia was directly with the English planters,

---

* Brodhead's *History of the State of New York*, 1853 : 583; also *Calendar of Historical Manuscripts*, etc., of New York, Edited by E. B. O'Callaghan, 1865, vol. 1 : 137.

† *Year Book of the Holland Society of New York*, 1900 : 173.

‡ *Calendar of Historical Manuscripts*, etc., of New York, Edited by E. B. O'Callaghan, 1865 : 184.

and not with the aborigines as at Delaware Bay. Tobacco,
the staple export, and beaver, purchased from the Indians,
were exchanged by the planters for supplies from England,
Barbadoes, and northern Colonial ports. Yet Allerton, assisted by his familiarity with their ways, appears to have
obtained his land in Virginia directly from the Indians.   In
Northumberland County (then including Westmoreland), it
is recorded, under date of February 6, 1650, that "according
to an order of the Governor and Council, inquiry had been
made concerning the complaint of the Machoatick Indians
about Mr. Allerton's intending a plantation upon them ; . . .
but due inquisition being made, the said Indians, and the
werowance Peckatoan (also the name of a well-known plantation in Westmoreland) declared they were well content
with Mr. Allerton staying there, so long as the land, 'wherever hee hath already cleared,' be useful." But they desired
"that no more houseing be there built than is now upon it,
and to keep his cattle and hogs on the other side of Machoatick river," a small tributary of the Potomac.   Allerton's plantation is laid down on Herrmann's map of Virginia
and Maryland, made in 1670. In 1657, William Nutt deposed
"that about February preceding, he and the other commissioners of Northumberland County, being appointed by the
Governor and Council to inquire concerning the seating of
M.ʳ Isaac Allerton's land at Machoatic, M.ʳ W.ᵐ Cooke being
requested to be interpreter, the deponent heard Captain
Peter Lefebeer promise to pay, on the said Allerton's behalf,
to the said Cooke, 1,000 lbs. of tobacco in case Allerton
seated further." *

After the death of his father, in 1659, Isaac Allerton,
Jr., removed to this tract of land on the Machoatick River,
where he built a stately mansion, and spent the remainder
of his life. His descendants are prominent among the
"many Virginia families of distinction . . . descended from
ancestors of gentle lineage," who "intermarried with the

families of Lee, Travers, Cooke, Colston, Corbin, Willoughby, Newton," etc., of Virginia.*

At what date Isaac Allerton, Sr., removed his family to New Haven is uncertain. In a deed of October 27, 1646, and repeatedly afterward, he called himself a merchant of New Amsterdam, in the Province of New Netherlands,† where he maintained his trading-house on Manhattan Island for many years. Yet, at a General Court held in New Haven, March 10, 1646–47, " when the names of people as they were seated in the meeting-house were read in Court, and it was ordered that they should be recorded," Isaac Allerton and his wife were assigned seats of honor. In the first seat were the Governor and Deputy-Governor; in the second seat, Mr. Malbon, magistrate. " In the cross seats at the end," second seat, "Thom. Nash, M. Allerton, Bro. Perry." "Secondly for the Women's seats . . . Sister Fowler, Sister Ling, Sister Allerton." This was under the pastorate of the Rev. John Davenport. After Mr. Hooke [Hooker?] became the colleague of the Rev. Mr. Davenport, new seats were assigned to the congregation, February 11, 1655–56; " M.ʳ Allerton, sen.," was placed in the first seat "in the cross seats at the upper end," and " M.ʳˢ Allerton, the elder," in the first seat "in the cross seats for women." In the third plan of the seating, by authority of the Court, on February 20, 1661–62, " M.ʳˢ Allerton" was given the first seat "in the short seats at the upper end," the most prominent position for women in the church.‡ The cross seats of the brethren were always at the preacher's right; those for the sisters, at his left.

The town of New Haven was laid out in "squares," the central square being what is now the Common, or "Green;"

---

* Hayden's *Virginia Genealogies*, 1891 : xvi.

† *Plymouth Colony Deeds*, Book 2 : 16.

‡ The three plans for seating in the First Church of New Haven are shown in Atwater's *History of the Colony of New Haven*, 1902 : 542, 543, 546, 547, 550, 552.

about this were eight other squares. The town plan of 1641 does not show Allerton's location; but he was granted later a lot on the east side of the present Union Street near Fair Street. The lot, consisting of about two acres, is now thickly covered with houses; "yet it is obvious, that when Allerton built his house there, it was just such a spot as would strike the fancy of a 'sea-captain.' There was a gradual but very considerable slope towards the harbor, on the south, and towards the creek, on the west. He must have had, from his upper windows, a fair view of a great part of the town, in one direction, and the harbor and sound even to Long Island, on the other, while, on the north, the fine bluff of East Rock, and very likely that of West Rock, the refuge of the Regicides, were in full view." The house itself, a "grand house with four porticoes," must have fronted upon Union Street, between Cherry Street on the north and Fair Street on the south, near the present residence (1882) of Mr. Edward Buddington. President Styles records the tradition that Thomas Gregson's house "was one of the four which excelled in stateliness all other houses erected in New Haven by the first generation of its inhabitants;" the other three were those of Governor Theophilus Eaton, Rev. John Davenport, and Mr. Isaac Allerton.* The house of Allerton was taken down about 1742. His warehouse, without doubt, was opposite his residence; standing on the bank of the creek, which was accessible to small vessels until after the Revolution, but which is now the bed of the railroad.†

The Colonial Records of New Haven contain but few references to Allerton or his affairs. In 1647, "John Bishopp, serv^t to M^r. Allerton" was complained of for want of arms. November 12, 1649, the General Court taxed Allerton "20^s for a single rate." In December, 1647, and sub-

---

* *Massachusetts Historical Society Collections*, Third Series, vol. 7 : 301.

† *New Haven Historical Society Papers*, vol. 3 : 104-105.

sequently, he was the bearer of important letters passing between Governor Stuyvesant and the Governor and Deputy-Governor of New Haven, which showed that his advice was sought by both parties.*

At a Court of Magistrates, held in New Haven, January 26, 1654, one "Lawranc Corneliusson, a Dutchman," was before the Court "charged with seuerall great miscarriages" at Milford, principally a quarrel with "another Dutchman, who had bine scandalously, and for himselfe, dangerously, drunke." Mr. Allerton, whom Lawrence "desired might be p'sent to speake for him," said "he did beleeve they [the charges] were all true . . . but thinks the man was in such a passion as he knows not what he did." However, the Court fined Lawrence £40, which, at Allerton's request, was reduced to £30, "with three months time in which to pay" it.†

In 1655, Mr. Allerton, Ensign Bryan, and Mr. Auger appeared before the Court with the complaint that, by reason of bad biscuit and flour that they had from the baker of Milford, they had suffered much damage, "and likewise the place lies under reproach at Virginia and Barbadoes, so as when other men from other places can have a ready market for their goods, that from hence lies by and will not sell, or if it do, it is for little above half so much as others sell for." May 25, 1657 : "Some difference betwixt James Mills, M̅r̅ Goodyeare, M̅r̅ Allerton and M̅r̅ Larebee, was presented to the court, but after, by consent [it was] wᵗhdrawne and referred to a private determination." ‡

That there are so few references to Isaac Allerton in the New Haven Colony Records would seem strange if it were not for his great interests elsewhere. It may be that he purposely refrained from becoming closely identified with the affairs of his "home town," choosing rather to keep it as a retreat from governmental affairs.

---

* Hoadly's *Records of the Colony of New Haven*, vol. 1 : 309, 499, 520–533.
† Hoadly's *Records of the Colony of New Haven*, vol. 2 : 124–126.
‡ Hoadly's *Records of the Colony of New Haven*, vol. 2 : 142–143, 204.

In the spring of 1659, Winthrop says: "The winter hath been extraordinarily long and sharp and sickly among us." The "common sickness of the town," at that time, Mr. Davenport describes as accompanied with such symptoms as "gripings . . . agues and fevers, giddiness, much sleepiness, and burning. It comes by fits every other day;" worse than all else, "the supply of medicine . . . is spent." * Isaac Allerton died at New Haven between February 1, 1658–59, when he appeared in Court as defendant in a suit brought to compel the payment of an old debt, and February 12 (the same month), the date on which his inventory was taken.† His will, informal and without date, but duly sworn to by subscribing witnesses, was allowed by the Court.‡

" At a Court ⎫ A writeing presented as the last will & Testa-
of Magistrates ⎬ ment of Isaac Alerton, late of Newhaven de-
Octob. 29. 59 ⎭ ceased, wth an account of certaine debts, dew
                  to him; & from him;
       An account of debts at the Duch/

first. 700. & gilders frõ. Tho. Hall by Arbitration of Captaine Willet, & Augustine Harman — about Captaine Scarlet wch I paid out,

And there is 900 gilders owing by John Peterson the Bond, as by Georg woolseyes booke will appeare; & severall obligations thereto,

ffrom Richard Cloufe owed as Georg woolseyes Booke will make appear; I thinke 900 gilders, but his Estate being broken. I Desire that what may be gotten may be layd hold on for mee,

Due frõ. william Goulder 270, od gilders, by his Bill appears;

Due frõ./John Snedecare a shoomaker 150, od gilders as by his acc°. appears,

frõ. the widdow of the Hanc Hancson due as by severall Bills & accounts;

Peter Corneliusson 120. od guilders as by ye account will appeare.

---

* Atwater's *History of the Colony of New Haven*, 1902 : 369.
† *The Mayflower Descendant*, vol. 2 : 155-157.
‡ *Probate Court Records, New Haven, Connecticut*, vol. 1 : pt. 1 : 82, 83.

Due frō. Henry Brasser for rent for 18 moneths, frō. the first October 1656. to the last of May 58 : for three roomes at 3 gilders a week. I am in his debt for worke of the old acc° wch must be deducted.

there is 20 ^{li} in George woolseyes hand, that came frō. m^r Tho Mayhue for mee

There is 400. od. gilders that I owe to Nicholas, the ffrenchman, & a Cooper I owe something to, wch I would have that 20 ^{li} in George woolseyes hand, & the rest of that in Henry Brassers hand to them two ;

> And now I leave my Son Isaac Allerton and my wife, as Trustees to receive in my debts, & to pay what I owe, as farr as it will goe & what is ouerpluss I leave to my wife & my Sonne Isaac, as far as they receive the Debts to pay what I owe./

In Captaine Willetts hand, a pcell of booke/ lace 1300 & odd guilders wch I have received some of the pay. wch I left in trust with him, & Shipper Low about ye vessell I left in trust with Captaine willett to take care of : [seal]

My brother Breuster owes mee foure score pounds & odd. as the obligations will appeare.

Besides all my Debts in Delloware Bay & in virgenia wch in my booke will appeare : & in Barbadoe[s] what can be gott./

Witnesses   Isaac Allerton Senio^r
John Harriman
Edward Preston

"An Inuentory of the estate of Isaac Allerton late of Newhaven deceased taken ffeb 12 : 1658

	li	sh	d
Imp^r — the Dwelling house Orchard & Barne wth two acres of meadow	75	00	00
a pcell of Tubbs & other cask, & 2 bush apples	01	12	06
8 Jarrs, a case of bottles, & 2 cases w^{th}out bottles	01	03	00
1 pr. of small stilleyards 1 old sieve, 6 stooles & 3 old chaires	01	02	00
1 chest of Drawers, 1 bedstead wth cord, & one small chest, & 1 old booke	01	17	00
1 pr. of Ondirons, & 4 pott hangers, & other irō	00	08	00
1 rugg. 2 blankitts. 1 old feather bed & bolster & pillow	04	13	00
1 Drawtable, 2 chaires, & a forme & a carpet	02	06	00
a pr. of blankitts of cotton & sheeps wooll	01	16	00

	li	sh	d
1 Sea chest, small box, & 2 warming pans	00	17	06
4 old skellitts. & 2 small old bottles	00	15	00
3 Iron potts, 2 frying panns, & a pcell of Tinware	01	17	04
5 brase candlesticks, & a brass chaffing dish	00	09	06
1 bolster, 1 blankitt, a remn! trading cloath	01	10	00
a pcell of wearing cloaths	06	17	06
curtaines & vallens for a bed, & a sm: turky carpet	02	06	00
2 old blankitts, a pcell of carpeting & a small old Table . . .	01	08	00
a pcell of pewter	02	17	10
8. ounces of plate at 5! p.	02 : 00 : 00		
a pcell of old linnen wth threed	02 : 07 : 04		
2 sowes & 4 piggs	02 : 10 : 00		
a bedstead, old curtaines, & a mortar & peshell			
a chest case, & two old tubbs, & a pr. spectacles, old hat, & capp	01 : 05 : 06		
5 cushions, some old bands, wth some other old linnen . . .	00 : 11 : 06		
brimston, & sheeps wooll	00 : 14 : 06		
	118 : 05 : 02		

Prisers
Will: Andrews }
Will: Russel }

Debts Due to the Estate in Newhaven.

M! Goodenhouse p_r Order of m^r Malbō 50! frō. wch he Deducts 20. that he saith m! Allerton owed him, and 8! paid m^r mills, Rests	01 . 12 . 00
m! Tuttle by the Rest of 40! ord^red by m! Malbon	00 : 10 : 00
Goodm : Hull is Dr	00 : 16 : 00
m^r Gilberts man Isaac Hall	01 : 00 : 00

Humphry Spinigh
m! w^m. Trowbridg for his
    p^rdessesso^r Daniell Sillivan "

    This will, which is little more than memoranda of debts due to him, and amounts that he wished to have collected and used to pay his creditors, gives but a vague idea of Mr. Allerton's many possessions. His homestead in New Haven, valued at £75, had greatly depreciated with other estates in the town ; but his interests in New Amsterdam, Virginia, Delaware Bay, and Barbadoes, as developed by his son Isaac, gave to his immediate descendants a position which wealth only could confer. The judicial account of the settlement of the estate, in which Isaac Allerton, Jr., prayed to be dismissed from his trust as executor, "vnlesse he might be left free to act in it as he saw conuenient," is as follows : * —

"Whereas at a court held at Newhaven Aprill the 5th 1659, an inventory & an account takē & prsented to the court, of an estate left by Mr Isaac Allerton sen. deceased here, at wch time the court was informed that there was a will left by the deceased, wch was supposed to be in the hands of M^r. Isaac Allerton, who was now gone from home, vpon wch ground the court proceeded not further in that business at that time, onely they signified there desire that the will spoken of might be brought forth at his returne ; accordingly at a court held at Newhaven the 5th of July 1659, M^r. Allerton appeared, & prsented the said writeing as the will of his deceased father, but the court findeing that neither M^r. Allerton nor any other was willing at that time to administer vpon the said estate, it was ordered that ye bookes of accounts, wth all bills & speciallties appertaining to the said estate, should be deliured to the secretary, and that by a writeing sett vpon the door post of the meeting house, intimation should be given to such as were creditors to that estate, that if they made their appearance at the court of magistrates in October next, their demands should be considered ; at wch court sundry creditors appeareing, to make clayme of considerable somes due from the said estate, M^r. Isaac Allerton prsented a writeing, as the last will of the deceased, now witnessed vpon oath by John Harriman & Edward Preston, that it was sealed & subscribed by M^r. Allerton deceased, whilest he had the vse of his vnderstanding & memory in a competant measure, by wch writeing it appeared y^t M^r. Allerton himself & his mother, the widdow of the deceased, were made ioynt trustees to gather in & dispose of the estate for paym^t of the said iust debts due from the same. The said widdow renouncing her part of that trust & nō els appeaing who were willing to administer, the court vpon request of the M^r. Isaac Allerton, established the sole trust of that business vpon him, to collect & dispose of the estate for the ends aforesaid, within any of the English jurisdictions in these parts of America."

---

* Hoadly's *Records of the Colony of New Haven*, vol. 2 : 307–309.

The Court instructed Mr. Allerton to make "p^{r}sent payment proportionally" to each and all of the creditors according to the value of the estate as apprised in the inventory; and to gather in the debts elsewhere with all "conuenient speed" and make payments "yearly, in proportion to all the creditors . . . vntill all iust debts be sattisfied. . . . But Mr Isaac Allerton junior, in his more serious thoughts about ye business, came the next day vnto the court & pfessed his discouragment to proceed in that trust, vnlesse he might be left free to act in it as he saw conuenient, & might be dismissed therefrom vpon account, wheneuer he desired." The Court refused to discharge him until it "saw a satisfying or iust account given of the faithful discharge of that trust, wch he was the rather to be obliged to because he was the deceaseds eldest or onely sonne, who had conferred that trust vpon him for attendance vnto righteousness on his fathers behalf." Allerton persisted in his "renouncing & refusing to vntertake the matter, vpon the tearmes aforesd; wherevpon . . . the court vpon request of the creditors, who had long waited for an issue . . . did, with the consent of the creditors," appoint Mr. Richard Miles and Gervase Boykin "commissioners in trust, for collection & conservation of the said estate."

At a Court of Magistrates held in New Haven, May 28, 1660, at the request of Ensign Bryan, Deacon Miles and Gervase Boykin gave in their account, "viz. that they had sould the time of service dew frō John Little, servant to Mr Allerton deceased, for 3 ." The Court also was informed "that there is in Mr Ogdens hand a mare & 2 colts belonging to this estate, onely an account wth Mr Ogden is to be considered, wch is not yet come to hand; also a debt dew frō Captaine Morris of Road Island; also that there came frō Barbadoes, (since Mr Clarke came thence) to Mr Lake, 4 hogsheads of sugar, part of which belongs to this estate." It was ordered by the Court, at this time, that no claims would be considered after October next. Still, one more account was allowed at a session of the Court of Magistrates, May 27, 1661, — a debt from "Isaacke Allerton sen^r vnto Edward Batter of Salem . . . which being attested was by this court accepted to come in with other debts " upon his estate.*

Several matters connected with the settlement of Isaac Allerton's estate are found in the Court Minutes of New Amsterdam : —

August 23, 1659, in the Writs of Appeal, appears a summons to "Peter le Feber," to pay and discharge, upon pain of fore-closure, "a certain mortgage on his bouwery and cattle at the Walebocht on Long Island, passed to the late Isaac Allerton, and by him assigned to Wallewyn van der Veen." †

"Tues 9 Dec 1659: M! Isaack Allarton the younger appears in Court requesting that the Court may appoint curators to the residuary estate in this country, of his father dec!, and regarding the papers remaining at New Haven in the hands of the Court there, requests that they be written to, to send them here. The Court appoint as curators Paulus Leenderzen van der Grift, Govert Loockermans, M! Jan Lauwerens, and M! George Wolsy." A week later, obeying a summons to the Court "to know if they will be pleased to accept " the trust, "Paulus Leenderzen van der Grift says, that there are a great many bad debts here and that those of New Haven might take the best debts to themselves, sending the creditors to them." Whereupon the Court agreed to request the magistrates at New Haven "to send the books, papers and a/cs concerning this place and to communicate with each other; arranging also together for any trouble that may attend it." They were told "to draw their fees of office; " and finally, "after much conversation," they accepted.

March 29, 1661–62 : "Abraham Van Nas, attorney for Isaaq Allerton, Senior, dec!," asked to be relieved of papers and docu-ments relating to deceased's estate, and to receive 65 fl. (florins) "commission money." He also wanted to know whom "to deal with." The Court referred him to the above named curators, who as yet had received no "Acte of Authorization," but now were supplied promptly therewith.

---

* Hoadly's *Records of the Colony of New Haven*, vol. 2 : 347, 354, 355, 417.
† *Calendar of Historical Manuscripts*, etc., of New York, Edited by E. B. O'Callaghan, 1865, vol. 1 : 326.

Two months before, January 29, one Joannes Withart brought a suit in which he insisted "on being preferred in the proceeds of the sold ketch, *William and John*, formerly belonging to Isaack Allerton, the Elder." His claim for furnishing " sails and rigging " for that vessel in January, 1658, was dismissed by the Court. *

The final statement of "the estate of M.ʳ Allerton deceased," in New Haven, "according to the inventory was 118ˡⁱ, 05ˢ, 02ᵈ, wᶜʰ (Mʳˢ Allertons thirds of the houses and lands being deducted,) falling into the hands of yᵉ creditors, they sould vnto M.ʳ Isaac Allerton the dwelling house, orchard & barne, wᵗʰ 2 acres of meadow for 120ˡⁱ." † By deed of October 4, 1660, he "alienated" to his stepmother, Johanna, for life, the homestead in New Haven, with reversion to his eldest daughter, Elizabeth. Mrs. Johanna Allerton occupied the house until her death, early in 1682. On March 10, 1682–83, the deed was confirmed, and the property passed into the possession of Mrs. Elizabeth Eyres. Soon after her death, which occurred November 17, 1740, the ancient house was demolished.

The early Colonial records of New England and New Amsterdam pertaining to Isaac Allerton, so fully quoted but by no means exhausted, prove the high estimation of Allerton's abilities held by his contemporaries. It has, however, remained for the present generation, nearly three centuries later, fully to realize his worth.‡ No injustice is done to

---

* *Records of New Amsterdam*, vol. 3 : 90, 92, 288, 254.

† Hoadly's *Records of the Colony of New Haven*, vol. 2 : 309.

‡ Mr. Walter S. Allerton, of the New York Society of Mayflower Descendants, has published a *History of the Allerton Family*, which describes the life of his ancestor, Isaac Allerton, in merited terms of praise. He depicts him as "superior to all of them [the Pilgrims] in knowledge of the world and familiarity with business, . . . his mental horizon was far wider and his views more liberal and more tolerant of the opinion of others." Of his accomplishments in London, "it is not too much to say that the very existence of the Plymouth Colony depended for a time upon the success of his negotiations there." Vide Allerton's *History of the Allerton Family*, 1888 : 45, 46.

Mr. Isaac J. Greenwood, a resident of New York city, has written an article upon the *Allertons of New England and Virginia* (reprinted in pamphlet

the memory of other Pilgrims by claiming for him a broad spirit of enterprise, exceeding in its results that of any other of the *Mayflower* passengers. With his far-reaching activities, he certainly was a strong factor in welding together the Colonies. His mission was ever one of conciliation and peace. It also is not too much to assert that, were he alive to-day, he would exercise a strong and successful influence in our commercial (and possibly political) world; but, hampered as he was by circumstances due to his environment and the narrow spirit of the age, many of his undertakings were unsuccessful.

The records show him to have been one of the mainstays in Holland, and no other was deemed fitted to bring the last of the Pilgrims from Leyden to New Plymouth. He was one of the "first five signers of the Compact" in Provincetown harbor, who, Dr. Fowler * claims, "should be placed on the same high level in the annals of the world as the immortal five who drafted the Declaration of Independence." At Plymouth, when Massasoit, accompanied by his warriors, made friendly overtures, March 22, 1620–21, it was Captain Standish and "Isaac Alderton" who were sent out "to the brooke" to meet him and escort him in; the treaty of peace so ruthlessly broken more than fifty years later by his son Philip was then signed.† The next day, to cement the friendship, Standish and Allerton "went venterously" into the woods to Massasoit, who gave them "three or foure ground nuts, and some Tobacco." ‡ Allerton also was Bradford's first Assistant; he served in that office many years, the last term being 1633–34.§

---

form from the *New England Historical and Genealogical Register*, July, 1890), which deals appreciatively with the public life of Isaac Allerton after leaving the Massachusetts Bay Colony.

   * Mr. William Chauncey Fowler, LL. D., of Durham, Conn. Vide *New England Historical and Genealogical Register*, vol. 25: 278.

   † Vide page 377.

   ‡ *Mourt's Relation*, Dexter's Edition, 1863: 90–95.

   § Vide pages 602, 618.

After the death of Robert Cushman, their agent in England, early in 1625, Isaac Allerton was chosen immediately to fill his place. He voyaged untiringly between the old country and the new on errands of doubtful expediency that brought him little else than unfriendly criticism ; yet the supplies that he brought over during the period of disaffection of the Merchant Adventurers, though so strongly condemned by Bradford as "on his owne perticuler," saved much distress. The sums due to him from the estates of those who died in 1633 show not only that he had supplied the present necessities of their families, but that he had "trusted" a much larger amount than would have saved his home.* Later, when free to follow his own inclinations, he visited, in his bark, every known port on the Atlantic coast, besides Barbadoes, the Dutch West Indies, Spain, Portugal, and England. Carrying valuable cargoes of his own, or those entrusted to him by others, he bartered or purchased fish, grain, tobacco, and other staple commodities. He also was the bearer of many important messages and letters between the Colonies and England, as well as home ports. Mr. Trowbridge,† in a paper read, February 10, 1877, before the New Haven Historical Society, said that Isaac Allerton "well merited the title that had been given him: 'The Father of New England Commerce.'" He was more than that. He was *The Father of American Commerce.*

Isaac Allerton has the unique distinction of having been the only one of the Pilgrim Fathers who became a resident of New York, a fact which has been recognized by the New York State Society of Mayflower Descendants. On June 1, 1904, a tablet to his memory was placed at No. 8 Peck Slip, the site of his warehouse.‡ He was not the first Englishman to take up his abode in New Amsterdam, — Thomas Hall and George Holm (Holmes ?) preceded him (in 1638) by a

---

* Vide page 622.

† Mr. Thomas Rutherford Trowbridge, Jr. Vide *New Haven Historical Society Papers*, vol. 3: 101.

‡ Vide frontispiece, volume II.

few months; but the part he bore in public affairs clearly shows him to have been the most prominent, in that frequently he was the only Englishman present among the Swedes, Dutch, and Indians. His presence was requested, and his suggestions and decisions uniformly were adopted.

Allerton's practical expression of sympathy was one of his strongest characteristics, so far little recognized. He was a friend in need to many an unfortunate, giving his bond in all the courts, and acting again and again, "by request," as interpreter, referee, or arbitrator. It is suspected that his censure from the Plymouth Church and Colony was due quite as much to the liberality of his religious sentiment and toleration of Quakers as to his business methods; and that his unceremonious invitation to leave Marblehead was the result of kindness shown to Roger Williams, who had been long under the ban, and who, in the winter of 1634–35, was ordered to leave the Massachusetts Bay Colony.

It was Isaac Allerton who succored the three ministers, Mr. Tompson, Mr. Knolles, and Mr. James, who came near foundering in the vicinity of Hell Gate, in the "dead of winter," 1642–43, while sailing from New Haven to Virginia. They barely escaped with their lives. "The Dutch governor gave them slender entertainment," says Winthrop, "but Mr. Allerton of New Haven, being there, took great pains and care for them, and procured for them a very good pinnace and all things necessary, . . . so as with difficulty & danger they arrived safe in Virginia." *

There is a well-founded tradition that the regicide Judges, Colonel Whalley and Colonel Goffe, found temporary shelter and concealment in the New Haven residence of Mr. Allerton, in the summer of 1661. He had died two years before, but his widow, Johanna, was living there; and, notwithstanding a proclamation had gone out from Massachusetts Bay "that whosoever shall be found to have a hand in concealing

---

* Winthrop's *History of New England*, Savage's Edition, 1853, vol. 2 : 96.

the said colnels, or either of them, shall answer for the same as an offence of the highest nature," she is thought to have surreptitiously harbored them from June 11 to June 22, if not longer.* Probably she was sustained by the thought that her husband, in her place, would have done the same. Her burial-place is unknown; but the beautiful "Green" in New Haven is supposed to be the last resting-place of our Forefather, Isaac Allerton. \ No monument marks his place of burial; but the site of his house, on Fair Street, has been indicated by the New Haven Colony Historical Society by a suitably inscribed tablet : —

ISAAC ALLERTON
A PILGRIM OF THE
MAYFLOWER
AND THE FATHER OF
NEW ENGLAND COMMERCE
LIVED ON THIS GROUND
1646 TILL 1659

The house on which the tablet was placed was recently demolished, as it stood in the direct path of railroad improvements; the tablet itself is now in the rooms of the Historical Society, awaiting the time when it can be reset near its former position.

But his most enduring monuments are the localities which bear his name: Allerton Street, in Plymouth; Allerton's Hill, so called in the early settlement of Duxbury ; and Point Allerton in Boston harbor (known in 1634 as Point Alderton), nine and a half miles from the city of Boston.

Physically, Isaac Allerton is described by a descendant as "slightly above the average height, of a spare but muscular frame, with dark hair and beard, a clear complexion and strongly marked features, a good looking rather than a handsome man. In the great majority of his descendants there can be noticed a great similarity of development in the upper portion of the head and face, more especially notice-

---

* Atwater's *History of the Colony of New Haven*, 1902 : 419-444.

able in the forehead, eyes and nose, and there can be no doubt that these physical marks, together with certain well-defined traits of character, have descended to us from our common ancestor." *

A number of autograph signatures of Isaac Allerton have appeared, without reference to their source; but the following is vouched for as genuine by Justin Winsor, who includes it in a group of autographs of "Mayflower Pilgrims." †

The name of Allerton "will be forever cherished by the entire people of that mighty nation, the corner-stone of whose foundations was so deeply and so enduringly laid by the Pilgrims of Plymouth."

ISSUE BY FIRST WIFE

I. Bartholomew [2], b. about 1612, at Leyden. He came with his parents in the *Mayflower*, and was in Plymouth at the division of cattle in 1627. He returned to England and remained there. Bradford, writing in 1650 of Mr. Allerton's family, says: "His soné Bartle is maried in England, but I know not how many children he hath." ‡

II. Remember [2], b. about 1614, at Leyden, came in the *Mayflower*. She was mar. before May 6, 1635, to Moses [2] Maverick, of Marblehead. Bradford's account of 1650 says: "His [Allerton's] daughter Remember is maried at Salem, & hath 3. or 4. children living." She died in Marblehead between Sept. 12, 1652, and Oct. 22, 1656. On the latter

---

* Allerton's *History of the Allerton Family*, 1888: 45, 46.
† Winsor's *Narrative and Critical History of America*, 1884, vol. 3: 277.
‡ Bradford's *History of Plimoth Plantation*, 1898: 535.

date, Moses Maverick married, second, at Boston, Eunice, widow of Thomas² Roberts, of Boston;* they were married by Governor John Endicott.

"The Maverick family was one of prominence in Colonial days, noted for hospitality, religious tolerance, and active philanthropy." Moses² was the fourth and youngest son of the Rev. John¹ Maverick, of Dorchester, in New England; Samuel², Elias², and Antipas² were his brothers. The Rev. John¹ Maverick, born in 1577, in County Devon, England, was ordained deacon at Exeter, England, July 26, 1597; and, later, by a bishop of the Episcopal Church, as a minister of the Church of England. In 1615, he was rector of Beaworthy, County Devon. He made the acquaintance of the Rev. John Warham, also a minister of the Church of England, who was established at Exeter.† These "West Country ministers" became imbued with the spirit of the Reformation, and joined a company of Puritans of Devonshire, Dorsetshire, and Somersetshire, who were about to embark for the New World.‡

On March 20, 1629-30, this company gathered in the "new hospital" at Plymouth, England, and there the Rev. John White, of Dorchester, preached to them in the forenoon. In the afternoon, under his direction, they formed themselves into a church, of which "the godly Mʳ Maverick" and "the gratious servant of Christ," Mr. John Warham, were chosen associate pastors. The company, numbering one hundred and ten, "set sail on the 30ᵗʰ of March following," in the *Mary and John*, a vessel of four hundred tons, Captain Squeb, master; and "on Lord's day, May 30th [20th], arrived at Nantasket, where the captain put them ashore, notwithstanding his engagement was to bring them up Charles river." Through

---

* Thomas² Roberts, of Boston, may have been son to John¹ Roberts, of Roxbury, where he previously had lived and was a church member. The maiden name of his wife, Eunice, is not known. Thomas Roberts, in 1644, was a member of the Ancient and Honorable Artillery Company; freeman in 1645. He d., probably, in July, 1654. Issue: I. Timothy³. II. Elizabeth³. III. Lydia³. IV. Eunice³, b. Aug. 18, 1653.

† Clapp's *History of Dorchester, Massachusetts*, 1859: 64, 404.

‡ Morton's *New England's Memorial*, 1669: 162.

the wilderness they made their way inland to a place which they soon named Dorchester, in honor of the home town of the Rev. John White, from which some of the settlers also had come. This settlement was formed a month before the arrival of Governor Winthrop and his company at Charlestown.[*]

The names of "Mr John Maûacke" and "M[r] Jo: Warham" appear at the beginning of the first list of freemen in the Massachusetts Bay Colony, dated May 18, 1631.[†] These two men, with William Gaylard and William Rockwell, deacons of the church at Dorchester, assigned lots to the inhabitants, issued town orders, and had full control of affairs temporal, as well as spiritual, until Oct. 28, 1634, when a form of town government was established by the election of "Tenn men chosen to order all the affayres of the Plantation." Two years after this, Mr. Warham joined the swarming colony that removed to Windsor, Connecticut; Mr. Maverick remained at Dorchester. His death occurred Feb. 3, 1636–37, probably in Boston, at the age of about sixty years; he was buried in the "Old Burying-Ground" at Dorchester.[‡] On Oct. 9, 1668, his widow was still living, when Samuel Maverick wrote to Secretary Sir William Morice that his mother "presents her humble service."[§]

The relationship of these early members of the Maverick family has been questioned; but Sumner states that "all the known circumstances connected with the births, lives, business relations, and residences of Samuel, Elias, Moses and Antipas, lead to the conclusion that they were brothers."[‖] John Josselyn, writing in 1674, refers to "Mr. Maverick" (whom he couples with "Mr. Wareham," calling them "Ministers"), as "the Father of Mr. Samuel Maverick, one of his Majesties Commissioners."[¶] If further proof is needed, it

---

[*] *Massachusetts Historical Society Collections*, First Series, vol. 9: 148, 149; also *Young's Chronicles*, 1846: 347, 348.

[†] *Massachusetts Bay Colony Records*, vol. 1 : 79, 366.

[‡] *Massachusetts Historical Society Collections*, First Series, vol. 9: 170; also Clapp's *History of Dorchester, Massachusetts*, 1859: XI, 404.

[§] *New England Historical and Genealogical Register*, vol. 48 : 207.

[‖] Sumner's *History of East Boston*, 1858 : 168.

[¶] Josselyn's *Chronological Observations of America*, London, 1674 : 253.

is found in the statement of Colonel Cartwright, who, in 1665, says in his Memorial: "M^r [Samuel] Maverick hath his mother, wife, children & brothers living there . . . in the Massachusets."*

---

* *New England Historical and Genealogical Register*, vol. 48: 207.

A brief sketch of the Maverick brothers will show how thoroughly they were identified with others mentioned in this volume: —

I. Samuel², b. about 1602, in England. He wrote of himself, in 1660, that he had spent his time "in America, even from the year 1624 till within these two years last past." It is now known that he came in Sir Ferdinando Gorges' first company to Wessagusset (Weymouth) in 1623, with Blackstone and Walford. From there he went to Winnisimet (Chelsea); and, later, to Noddle's Island (East Boston), where, "with the helpe of one Mr. David Tompson," he built a small Fort, "placing therein foure Murtherers [pieces of ordnance] to protect him from the Indians." He had no sympathy with his father's dissent, and early in life was an avowed Episcopalian. This probably was the reason why he was not made freeman until Oct. 2, 1632, though his name was first on the list of "such as desire[d] to be made Freemen," Oct. 19, 1630. Yet he was popular, — "a man of a very loving and curteous behavior, very ready to entertaine strangers." He was appointed April 2, 1664, by Charles II, to be one of four Royal Commissioners; a year later, they were recalled. There is no doubt that he knew Isaac Allerton well, for he eventually retired to New Amsterdam, where he is supposed to have died before 1676. His wife was Amias, widow of David Tompson, who assisted in building his Fort. Her maiden name was Cole, or Colle. "David Thomson and Amyes Colle" were mar. July 13, 1613, in Plymouth, England.

Issue: 1. Nathaniel³ Maverick.

2. Mary³ Maverick, was mar., first, Feb. 8, 1655, to John Palsgrave; mar., second, Sept. 20, 1660, to Hon. Francis Hooke, of Kittery Point, Maine.

3. Samuel³ Maverick, mar. Dec., 1660, Rebecca, daughter to Rev. John Wheelwright. He d. March 10, 1664, at Boston. His widow was mar. March 12, 1671-72, at Boston, to William Bradbury.

II. Elias² Maverick, b. about 1604, in England, was of Charlestown and Chelsea. He was made freeman June 11, 1633; was a member of the Charlestown church, and of the Ancient and Honorable Artillery Company. He married Ann Harris, and d. Sept. 8, 1681. Issue: Five sons and six daughters.

III. Antipas² Maverick, b. ——, in England, is recorded as "belonging to ye Ile of Shoals." June 23, 1646, "Edward Smale" sold his entire property at Kittery, Maine, to Antipas Maverick, who remained there until his death, July 2, 1678. (Vide page 4.) Antipas Maverick mortgaged

Moses [2] Maverick, the youngest of the brothers, who married Remember Allerton, was born about 1610, in County Devon, England. He was, without doubt, a member of the First Church of Dorchester, of which his father was pastor, before its reconstruction in 1636 ; for he was admitted freeman of the Massachusetts Bay Colony on Sept. 3, 1634, being then accounted a citizen of Dorchester,[*] and no one was then made a freeman who was not already a church member. While there is no record of a grant of land to Moses Maverick, in Dorchester, it is evident that he had a grant, from the mention in the Town Books, Jan. 2, 1637–38, that Goodman Greenway should have all the land at Pine Neck "for his great lott except 4 acres belonging to Good[man] Bingham and 6 Acres bought of Moses Mauericke."[†] This lot is alluded to again in a deed of Greenway to his son-in-law, Robert Pearce, and Ann, his wife, dated Feb. 5, 1650, when he conveyed to them all his land at Pine Neck in Dorchester, adding that "six acres was purchased of moses mauericke together with the meadow in the said necke belonging to the same together with the Comõns appertayning to the six acres afore mentioned."[‡]

Roads says that Moses Maverick arrived at Marblehead with Isaac Allerton, in 1631, in the *White Angel*. They probably were directed to that point by Samuel Maverick, who later described Marblehead as the best place for fishing on

---

this "house & land that is scittuate & being in Kittrie," Dec. 16, 1663, to Moses Maverick, of Marblehead, for £90. He also became involved in transactions with Thomas Booth ; but appears to have met his obligations, at least in part, since his heirs conveyed, in 1682, forty acres of the original hundred to one Dennett. (*Essex County Deeds*, Book 3 : 389–390; also Appendix I, II.)

Issue: 1. Catherine [3] Maverick, mar. Stephen Paul, of Kittery.
2. Abigail [3] Maverick, mar. Edward Gilman, of Exeter, N. H.
IV. Moses [2] Maverick, b. about 1610, in England.
V. Abigail [2] Maverick (probably), who was admitted, Feb. 18, 1637–38, to the First Church of Charlestown.

[*] *Massachusetts Bay Colony Records*, vol. 1 : 369; also *Records of the First Church of Dorchester, 1636–1734*, 1891 : XV.
[†] *Town Records of Dorchester*, 1880 : 26.
[‡] *Suffolk County Deeds*, vol. 1 : 201.

the coast. "Here be good harbour for boates, and safe riding for shippes," wrote Wood, in 1633.* The first settlement was at Peach Point, near Little Harbor, and here Moses Maverick lived as early as 1634. He and Allerton, with their servants, were engaged in fishing.

There is no record of early land-grants in Marblehead to Moses Maverick. On May 6, 1635, he came into possession of all the houses and stages of his father-in-law, Isaac Allerton, "to enioy to him & his heires for euer." † In 1650, Sarah Webber, widow of John Webber, of Lynn, made over to Maverick a small parcel of land at Marblehead, "being in the possession of the sd moses mavericke." ‡ He also acquired, in 1653, a dwelling house and half an acre of land near Mr. Walton's orchard, and with William Pitt, eighty-five acres bordering on the northeast on the town of Manchester. Two years later, 1655, Thomas Chubb, of Manchester, and "Anis his wife," conveyed to Maverick and Pitt a dwelling-house, and fifty acres upon which the house stood.§

His fishing-stages, house, etc., on "his island or poynt of land comonly caled Maverick's Island," containing two acres, "Moses Maverick of Marblehead, marchant," and Eunice his wife, conveyed, Aug. 20, 1672, to William Browne, "for a valuable consideration." The island is described as "being scittuate in Marblehead aforesaid & is surrounded with the sea at high water;" by the same deed he also conveyed "one halfe of a warehouse, standing neere the orchard of Mr. Walton deceased." ‖

Mr. Moses Maverick became a member of the First Church of Salem in 1638; and thereafter was active in all the enterprises of the church and town. He usually appears on the records with the title of "M^r^." In 1638, he was active in assisting Mr. William Walton, minister of the Salem church, to build the first meeting-house; in 1659, he was one of

* William Wood's *New-England's Prospect*, 1865: 48.

† Vide page 629.

‡ *Suffolk County Deeds*, vol. 1: 134.

§ *Essex County Deeds*, Book 1: 70, 69.

‖ *Essex County Deeds*, Book 3: 530–533.

a committee to have the meeting-house "sealed" (ceiled). He was chosen, April 6, 1672, chairman of a committee to settle a serious quarrel as to seating the congregation in the new "lean-to" of the meeting-house.* On May 24, 1684, the First Congregational Church of Marblehead was formed, with Samuel Cheever, Ruth Cheever, Moses Maverick, and Eunice Maverick first in the list of its fifty-four members.†

On June 7, 1636, "Mʳ Moses Maverick paid the Govʳnoʳ [of Massachusetts Bay] 40ˢ rent for Nodles Iland." ‡ It is supposed that he hired the island during the absence of his brother Samuel in Virginia, in order "to hold it during his [Samuel's] Southern excursion." After this, Moses was wholly identified with the interests of Marblehead, where his tax, Jan. 1, 1637–38, was next to the largest in the town. Sept. 6, 1638, he was "pmitted to sell a tuñ of wine at Marble Head, & not to exceede this yeare." § Dec. 23, 1638, he and the Rev. Mr. Walton were chosen to lay out certain lots of land. In 1648, when there was a shortage of common pasture land, Moses Maverick was allowed a share for three cows, and Isaac Allerton for two.‖

The record of the first town-meeting, held at Marblehead in 1649, names Mr. Moses Maverick and six others, who were chosen selectmen. In 1662, he was the first to sign an agreement as to a public landing-place or wharf in the town. Again, he was the first of a hundred and forty signers of a petition against imposts at Marblehead.¶ The Samuel Maverick who also signed is thought to have been Samuel ², son to Moses, who was of age on Dec. 19, 1668. The petition, though undated, probably was presented to the General Court about February, 1668–69. In May, 1669, a reduction of duties throughout the Colony was ordered.**

---

* Roads's *History and Traditions of Marblehead*, 1897 : 14, 21, 26.
† *Manual of the First Congregational Church of Marblehead*, 1876: 15.
‡ *Massachusetts Bay Colony Records*, vol. 1 : 176.
§ *Massachusetts Bay Colony Records*, vol. 1 : 236.
‖ Roads's *History and Traditions of Marblehead*, 1897 : 15, 20.
¶ *New England Historical and Genealogical Register*, vol. 9 : 82.
** *Massachusetts Bay Colony Records*, vol. 4: pt. 2 : 418.

On June 1, 1677, "M.͏ͬ Moses Mauericke" and two others were empowered by the Court "as coṁissioners to end smale causes at Marblehead according to law; and also that M.͏ͬ Mauericke haue power to joyne persons in marriage w.͏ᵗʰin the sajd toune . . . , and also to administer oathes both in civil & criminal cases."* It is probable that Mr. Maverick already had served as magistrate for a number of years, though this was the first record of his formal appointment to that office, since he is mentioned as having been "the founder and for many years the only magistrate in Marblehead." Mr. Roads, in his "History of Marblehead," gives a photograph of an affidavit, dated Nov. 28, 1677, in the handwriting of Moses Maverick, "Commissioner."† The three commissioners asked the Court, March 29, 1681, to remit a fine of £10, for not having sent the town's quota of soldiers in time of war; one half of the fine was remitted. On July 4, 1684, Mr. Maverick was appointed chairman of a committee of three to investigate the claims of certain Indians, heirs to the Squaw Sachem of Saugus, to land in Marblehead.

The last of Moses Maverick's many and valuable public services, which extended over a period of fifty years, were those rendered as Town Clerk. There is no entry to show when he began to serve; it is probable that he had done the clerical work of the settlement before the town was established. He died at Marblehead, Jan. 28, 1685–86, aged seventy-six years. The town record of his death states that he "solemnized the preceding marriages and being Clerke registered y.͏ᵉ births and deaths preceding."‡ His widow, Eunice, survived him, and was living on Dec. 5, 1698.

The will of Moses Maverick, dated "this [   ] day of January: Anno Dom: 1685," lacked not only the day of the month but the signature. For that reason, when it was presented to the County Court, held at Ipswich, March 30, 1686,

---

* *Massachusetts Bay Colony Records*, vol. 5: 148.
† Roads's *History and Traditions of Marblehead*, 1897: 486.
‡ *Vital Statistics of Marblehead*, 1900, vol. 2: 614.

some of the children objected to its allowance.* Samuel Cheever, minister of the church at Marblehead, who drew the will, delivered it to the Court; yet the depositions of Ambrose Gale, of Marblehead, a "loving freind" of Maverick, and Archibald Ferguson and John Norman, his sons-in-law, were taken, in 1685 and 1686, at the County Court in Salem, to attest to the circumstances attending the making of the will. These depositions and the will, which was allowed, are filed in the Registry of Probate at Boston.† After making ample provision for his widow, Eunice, during her lifetime, he provided that, at her decease, "Moses Hawks yᵉ onely surviving child of my daughter Rebecca deceased," should be paid £5; and the same should be paid to each of the four children of his "daughter Abigail deceased, vizᵗ Samᵘ: Ward, Abigail Hinds, Mary Dallaber & Martha Ward." The remainder of the estate was to be divided equally between his "four daughters, vizᵗ Eliz: Skinner, Rememᵇ Woodman, Mary ffergoson & Sarah Norman."

The inventory of the estate, taken Feb. 26, 1685–86, amounted to £342 : 19 : 00. "His house & Land with one Cow-commonage: with the outhousing," was estimated at £150; a small pasture behind yᵉ meeting house, £8; meddow ground before the house, £60; his part in the ffarme, £60; and one Cow lease, £5." The remainder consisted of "two old swords & gun, 15ˢ," household furniture, a few books, cattle, farming implements, etc. The widow gave a bond, July 15, 1686, as administratrix of the estate, but neglected to fulfil her duties, and several times was called upon by the heirs for an accounting. Finally, "the house [being] much decayed, and in a ruinous condition," the widow and heirs signed an agreement,‡ Nov. 29, 1698, for the sale of the entire estate, with stipulations for the "creditable and comfortable maintenance" of the widow, out of her thirds, and the division of the remaining two thirds

---

* *Essex County Court*, 1682–1692, Ipswich, Case No. 35.
† *Suffolk County Probate*, Docket : 1472.
‡ *Essex County Probate*, Docket : 18029.

among the heirs. This agreement, which gave general satisfaction, was signed in the presence of the Rev. Samuel
Cheever, by

> "Eunice Maverick   [Seal]
> Archibald fferguson [Seal]
> Moses Hawks   [Seal]
> John Norman ⎱
> Sarah norman ⎰
> Samuel Ward   [Seal]
> elizebeth hewes   [Seal]
> Tho: Jackson   [Seal]
> Thomas Perkins   [Seal]"

The above parties acknowledged the above "within y^e
County of Essex . . . Decemb^r 5th 1698 " before Jonathan
Corwin.*

Issue by first wife: 1. Rebecca³ Maverick, bap. Aug. 7,
1639; mar. June 3, 1658, John² Hawkes, of Lynn; d.
Nov. 4, 1659, soon after the birth of a son Moses³.
The second wife of John² Hawkes was Sarah³, daughter to Elder Thomas² Cushman.†

2. Mary³ Maverick, bap. Feb. 14, 1640–41; d. Feb. 24,
1655, in Boston, aged fifteen years.

3. Abigail³ Maverick, bap. Jan. 12, 1645; mar. ——
Ward. Issue: I. Samuel Ward. II. Abigail Ward;
mar. about 1681, to William Hinds or Hines; d.
1688. Issue: three children b. in Marblehead, and
perhaps others. III. Mary Ward; mar. —— Dol-
liber, or Doliver. Issue, bap. at Marblehead: 1.
Joseph. 2. Abigail. 3. Peter Doliver. IV. Martha
Ward; mar. —— Wood.

4. Elizabeth³ Maverick, bap. Dec. 3, 1646; d. before
Sept., 1649.

5. Samuel³ Maverick, bap. Dec. 19, 1647. He signed a
protest, about Jan., 1668–69, with his father and
others, against imposts at Marblehead, but probably

---

* All the papers in connection with the settlement of this estate, including
the will, are given in *The Mayflower Descendant*, vol. 5: 129–141.

† Vide pages 556, 564.

was not living in 1685, as he was not mentioned in the will or settlement of the estate of his father.

6. Elizabeth[3] Maverick, bap. Sept. 30, 1649; was mar., first, April 6, 1665, to Nathaniel[2] Grafton, son to Joseph[1] and Mary Grafton. He d. Feb. 11, 1671–72, at Barbadoes, and she was mar., second, to Thomas Skinner,* of Boston. The first wife of Thomas Skinner was Mary ——; their daughter Mary was b. Oct. 4, 1670, in Boston. He d. Dec. 28 [1690], in Boston.

Issue by first husband: I. Elizabeth Grafton, b. Dec. 18, 1667; mar. Nov. 25, 168[?], at Boston, to William Hughes.

II. Remember Grafton, b. Sept. 29, 1669.

III. Priscilla Grafton, b. March 12, 1671; mar. Oct. 15, 1690, in Boston, by Isaac Addington, Esq., Assistant, to Thomas Jackson.

Issue by second husband: IV. Rebecca Skinner, b. Jan. 22, 1677–78, in Boston.

V. Sarah Skinner, b. Sept. 18, 1687, in Boston.

7. Remember[3] Maverick, bap. Sept. 12, 1652; mar., first, to Edward Woodman, Sr., of Boston, later called a mariner of Marblehead. She was mar., second, July 26, 1694, in Boston, by the Rev. Cotton Mather, to Thomas Perkins. Remember Perkins d. before Nov. 29, 1698. Issue by first husband: I. Remember Woodman, b. 1673. II. John Woodman, b. 1676; and five others.

Issue by second wife: 8. Mary[3] Maverick, bap. Sept. 6, 1657; mar. to Archibald Ferguson, b. about 1649. She d. about 1695, at Marblehead.

Issue: I. Archibald Ferguson, b. Oct. 19, 1684, in Marblehead; d. young.

II. James Ferguson, b. Jan. 3, 1685–86, in Marblehead.

III. David Ferguson, b. Feb. 26, 1687–88, in Marblehead.

---

* Not before published. Miss M. B. Fairbanks, Boston.

IV. Archibald Ferguson, b. May 11, 1690, in Marblehead.

V. Mary Ferguson, b. July 22, 1694, in Marblehead.

9. Moses[3] Maverick, bap. " 4 day 1ᵐᵒ 1660," in the First
Church of Boston ; d. young.

10. A son[3], b. March 20, 1663 ; d. 1698.

11. Sarah[3] Maverick ; the only child living Nov. 29, 1698,
at the division of the estate of Moses[2] Maverick.
She was mar. Nov. 10, 1683, to John Norman, of
Marblehead, b. about 1660.

   Issue : I. Richard Norman, b. Sept. 4, 1684, in Marblehead.

  II. Margaret Norman, b. 1685, in Marblehead.

  III. Eunice Norman, b. March 14, 1686, in Marblehead.

  IV. Moses Norman, b. Feb. 23, 1687, in Marblehead.

  V. John Norman, b. March 2, 1690, in Marblehead ; d.
young.

  VI. Sarah Norman, b. Jan. 26, 1693, in Marblehead ;
mar., 1718, John Broughton.

  VII. Benjamin Norman, b. Aug. 18, 1694, in Marblehead ;
d. young.

  VIII. John Norman, bap. April 26, 1696, in Marblehead.

  IX. Benjamin Norman, bap. Oct. 8, 1699, in Marblehead.

  X. Jonathan Norman, bap. March 9, 1700–01, in Marblehead.

  XI. Elizabeth Norman, b. Aug. 30, 1706, in Marblehead.

III. Mary[2] Allerton, b. about 1616, at Leyden ; mar., about 1636,
in Plymouth, to Thomas[2] Cushman ; d. Nov. 28, 1699, in
Plymouth, aged about eighty-three years. She was the last
survivor of those who came, 1620, in the *Mayflower*.[*]

IV. Sarah[2] Allerton, b. about 1618, at Leyden. Sarah came to
New England in the *Anne*, 1623, with her aunt, Sarah
Cuthbertson.[†] It has been stated by many that she
became the wife of Moses Maverick ; but his first wife
is proved to have been her sister Remember, his second
wife was Eunice (Cole) Roberts, and he never, at any
time, had a wife Sarah. It is probable that Sarah Aller-

---

      * Vide pages 537, 553, 554.   † Vide page 600.

ton died before 1651, as Bradford makes no mention of her at that time with the others.

V. A child,[2] buried Feb. 5, 1620, in the *Pieterskerk*, at Leyden.*

VI. A son[3], born and died in Provincetown harbor.

ISSUE BY SECOND WIFE

VII. Isaac[2], b. about 1630, in Plymouth. His mother died when he was four years of age. On his father's removal to New Amsterdam, about 1639, the young Isaac remained at Plymouth with his grandfather Brewster, who prepared him for college. In 1650, when he was twenty years of age, "Isaacus Allertonus" was named in the catalogue of "Harvard College, Cambridge, New-England," as having received a degree.† Upon returning to his father's home, then in New Haven, Isaac, Jr., was closely associated in commercial and maritime pursuits with his father, for whom, in the later years of Isaac, Sr., he frequently acted in the courts.

At the time of his father's death, in 1659, Isaac, Jr., was "gone from home," but, upon his return, produced the will by which he and his stepmother were made joint trustees or executors under the will. The widow "renounced" her part of that trust, and Isaac declined to proceed "vnlesse he might be left free to act as he saw conuenient." Two others were chosen trustees; yet it is apparent that Isaac was consulted with regard to the settlement of the estate, both in New Haven and New York, and through his endeavors the homestead was saved for the widow during her lifetime. In New York, "Mr Isaack Allarton the younger" appeared in court, Dec. 9, 1659, with the request that curators of the estate be appointed there.‡ The following year he removed to the land in Virginia which his father had received ten

---

* Dexter's *England and Holland of the Pilgrims*, 1905 : 601.

† Mather's *Magnalia*, vol. 2 : 30; *Catalogue of Harvard College*, vol. 2 ; also Langdon's *Biographical Sketches of Graduates of Harvard University*, 1873, vol. 1 : 253–256.

‡ *Records of New Amsterdam*, 1653–1674, vol. 3 : 90.

years before from the Indians; here he remained until his death.

Isaac[2] Allerton married, about 1652, in New Haven. Nothing is known of this first wife except that her name was Elizabeth, and that she was the mother of two children, who survived her. His second wife, whom he married in Virginia about 1663, was Elizabeth, widow of Major George Colclough, and daughter to Captain Thomas Willoughby, of Virginia. Colonel Thomas Willoughby was her brother.

Elizabeth Willoughby was mar., first, as his second wife, to Simon Overzee, a Hollander, who was prominent as a merchant in Maryland and Virginia. Overzee's first wife was Sarah, daughter to Captain Adam and Sarah Thoroughgood; she was buried Oct. 9, 1658. Administration was granted, Dec. 18, 1660, to Elizabeth, widow of Simon Overzee; and soon after she was mar. to Major George Colclough, as his second wife. Ursula, the first wife of Major Colclough, mar., first, Richard Thompson; second, Colonel John Mottrom; and third, Colclough. The death of Major Colclough occurred about 1662, and, in 1663, his widow was the wife of Isaac[2] Allerton.* By this it appears that Elizabeth (Willoughby) (Overzee) (Colclough) Allerton was married three times within five years. She died before October, 1702.

Though no mention is found of Allerton's homestead, it is evident from contemporaneous history that he became a large and successful planter, and enjoyed the friendship and confidence of his neighbors. On March 10, 1670, he entered into a compact with John Lee, Henry Corbin, and Thomas Gerrard to build a Banqueting House " at or near the corner of their respective lands, where they joined." The agreement, as recorded, states that Corbin and Lee should build the house " where Mr. Allerton & Mr. Gerard shall think fit, for the continuance of good Neighborhood." It was stipulated that every person " bear an Equal charge to the building thereof . . . and each man or his heirs, yearly, according to his due course [turn] to make an Honorable treatment [entertainment] fit to entertain the undertakers

* *The Virginia Magazine of History and Biography*, vol. 3: 323, 324.

thereof, their wives, mistress [sweetheart or fiancée] & friends, yearly & every year, & to be begin upon the 29th of May [1671]."* Thus was inaugurated "that kind of dissipation which proved so destructive to Virginia."

Gerrard, professedly a Roman Catholic, died on his plantation on Machoatick Creek, and, by his will, dated Feb. 5, 1672, appointed " Major Isaac Allerton," John Lee, and John Cooper to settle his estate. In September, 1675, Major Allerton was second in command of forces under Colonel John Washington (great-grandfather of George Washington) which were sent out to dislodge the Susquehannock Indians from an old blockhouse on the Maryland side of the river.† In 1676, Major Allerton, Colonel St. Leger Codd, and Colonel George Mason were appointed to superintend the building of a garrison or storehouse, "60 × 22, and a magazine 10 feet square, at Neapsico, near Occaquan, on the Potomac River."‡ Later, he was mentioned as Colonel Allerton.§

Isaac Allerton was appointed April 22, 1663, Justice of the Peace for Northumberland County. On November 1, 1667, he was a member of the "Committee of Association of Northumberland, Westmoreland and Stafford Counties;" member of the House of Burgesses, February 16, 1676–77; "2[d] in the commission of the peace for Westmoreland, and of the quorum, Nov. 5, 1677;" member of the Council, 1683. Governor Nicholson, in a letter dated June 10, 1691, reported to the English government that Richard Lee (the younger), Isaac Allerton, and John Armistead, out of scruples of conscience, refused to take the oath of allegiance to William and Mary, and "so were left out of the Council;"‖ it was alleged that they were papists. But Isaac Allerton again appeared on the "Roll of Burgesses at an Assembly beginning the 24th day of Sept., 1696."¶ In 1699, he was

* *Virginia Magazine of History and Biography*, vol. 8 : 171, 172.
† Fiske's *Old Virginia and Her Neighbours*, 1900 : vol. 2 : 52, 60.
‡ *New England Historical and Genealogical Register*, July, 1890.
§ *Virginia Magazine of History and Biography*, vol. 1 : 199.
‖ *Virginia Magazine of History and Biography*, vol. 1 : 199–200.
¶ *Virginia Magazine of History and Biography*, vol. 3 : 425.

"Naval Officer and Receiver of the Virginia duties in West-moreland County, including Yeocomico River." *

The exact date of the death of Isaac[2] Allerton is un-known; his will,† dated October 25, 1702, was proved Decem-ber 30, following; his age was seventy-two years. As no mention was made of his wife, she was not then living.

His will, which was witnessed by Humphrey Morriss, John Gerrard, and Daniel Oceany, bequeathed, first, to the "church of Cople parish," in the lower or eastern part of Westmoreland County, "the sum of ten pounds sterling." To "my dear daughter Sarah Lee & my grandson Allerton Newton," two large tracts of land in Stafford County, "to be equally divided between them;" and to the latter "one thousand pounds of tobacco to be pd at the yrs of one & twenty." To "my dear Daughter Elizabeth Starr als. Heirs who lives in New England," six hundred acres of land on the south side of Rappahannock River; also "two thousand pounds of tobacco to be pd upon demand." "And forasmuch as my daughter Traverse has had a sufficient part or proportion of my estate given her in consideration of marriage I do therefore for memorial sake give unto her three daughters Elizabeth, Rebecca & Winifred Travers the sum of one thousand pounds of tobacco ‡ apeice to be pd them at the yrs of seventeen or the day of mar-riage which shall first happen."

"Item — I give bequeath and devise all the remaining part of my land & tenements not above bequeathed how and wheresoever situ-ate & being to my well beloved son Willoughby Allerton and to his heirs forever." His son Willoughby was appointed sole executor.

Issue by first wife: I. Elizabeth[3], b. Sept. 27, 1653, at New Haven; mar. Dec. 23, 1675, to Benjamin Starr, of New Haven, who d. in 1678, aged thirty-one years. She was mar., second, July 22, 1679, to Simon Eyres, or Heyres, a sea captain, and cousin to her first husband. He was b. Aug. 6, 1652 in Boston; d. 1695.

On March 10, 1682–83, her father confirmed to her the homestead, which she enjoyed before and after the death of

---

* *The Mayflower Descendant*, vol. 7 : 173.

† *The Mayflower Descendant*, vol. 7 : 174-176.

‡ English money, at that time, was scarce in Virginia, and tobacco was the "common currency and measure of value," as beaver skins had been in some of the northern Colonies.

her grandmother, Johanna Allerton, until her own death on Nov. 17, 1740. The house was torn down soon after. She also was generously remembered in the will of her father.

> Issue by first husband: I. Allerton Starr, b. Jan. 6, 1677, in New Haven.

> Issue by second husband: II. Simon Eyres, b. Sept., 1682, in New Haven. III. Isaac Eyres, b. Feb. 23, 1683-84, in New Haven; and perhaps others.

2. Isaac², b. June 11, 1655, in New Haven. He was about five years of age when his father removed to Virginia. In 1683, he returned to New Haven, and resided there and at Norwich in that State. He was a farmer, taking little part in public affairs, "but serving with credit in the Indian wars."* The date of death of Isaac² Allerton is unknown; he is said to have passed away at the home of his son John⁴, in Coventry, Rhode Island. Nothing is known of his wife, nor with certainty how many children he had.

> Issue: I. John⁴, b. about 1685, in New Haven; was a farmer at Coventry, Rhode Island; married and had a large family.

> II. Jesse⁴, b. about 1686 or 1687, in New Haven; married and had a son Zachariah, and other children.

> III. Isaac⁴, b. about 1690, in New Haven; d. young and unmarried. There probably were other children.

> Issue by second wife: 3. Willoughby², b. in Virginia; mar., about 1719 or 1720, Hannah, widow of Captain John Bushrod, of Nominy Plantation,† and daughter to William Keene, of North County.

Willoughby Allerton, like his father, was prominent in civil and military life; he also was a large landed proprietor, living on the west side of Machoatick Creek, and owning slaves. In 1711, he was Deputy Collector of Customs for York River. His will, which was drawn up January 16 and

---

* Allerton's *History of the Allerton Family*, 1888: 55.

† John Bushrod, b. Jan. 30, 1663, in Gloucester County, Virginia; d. Feb. 6, 1719. Issue: I. Hannah Bushrod. II. Sarah Bushrod.

17, 1723–24, was proved March 25, following. He called himself "Willoughbby Allerton, Gent.," and directed his executors that he "be interred in silence, without any show of funebrious rites and solemnities, and that my grave be impall^d with a brick wall, together with all the rest of my friends & ancestors, a year's time after my death, . . . and further I desire that none of my friends may wear anything of mourning-cloathing in representacon of grief and sorrow for my death." His homestead, "some 500 acres," and his sword, he willed to his son Isaac — upon attaining his majority. To his daughter, Elizabeth Allerton, he left land and personal estate; and to his widow, Hannah, he gave back all the negroes, cattle, horses, sheep, etc., which she brought to him at her marriage.*

> Issue: I. Elizabeth[4]; mar. —— Quills, and had children, Sarah and Margaret, living in 1639.
> II. Isaac[4]; mar. Ann ——; d. 1639. In the probate of his will he was mentioned as "gentleman of Cople parish, co. Westm: [Westmoreland]." Issue: 1. Garwin[5]. 2. Isaac[5]. 3. Willoughby[5].

4. Sarah Elizabeth[3], b. about 1670, in Virginia; probably mar., first, —— Newton, and had a son, Allerton Newton. Her second husband was Hancock[2] Lee, son to Colonel Richard[1] Lee, of Virginia. The first wife of Hancock Lee was Mary, daughter to Colonel William Kendall, of Newport House, by whom he had children. Hancock Lee was Justice of Northampton County, in 1677; in 1688, he removed to Wycomico Parish in Northumberland County, where he was Justice, 1689, 1699, 1702; burgess, 1688; naval officer, 1699. In 1729, he was buried on his estate; his widow, Sarah, died two years later. The inscription on the tomb of Hancock Lee says: "and Sarah his last wife, daughter of Isaac Allerton Esq., who departed this life the 17th May, Anno Domo 1731, Aeta 60 years."

Issue by first wife: I. William[3] Lee. II. Richard[3] Lee.

---

* *New England Historical and Genealogical Register*, July, 1890.

III. Anne [8] Lee; mar. to William Armistead. IV.
John [8] Lee. Issue, probably by second wife: V.
Isaac [8] Lee, b. 1707; d. 1727, in England. VI. Han-
cock [8] Lee (twin). VII. Elizabeth [8] Lee (twin).

5. Frances [8]; mar., about 1685 or 1686, to Captain Samuel [8]
Travers, b. 1660, son to William [1] Travers, of Vir-
ginia. They lived in Richmond County, at Fairham
Creek, North Fairham Parish. In 1693, he was
Justice of Richmond County.

Issue: I. Elizabeth [8] Travers. II. Rebecca [8] Travers;
in 1721, the wife of Charles Colston. III. Winifred [8]
Travers.

THE ANDREWS FAMILY

THOMAS[1] ANDREWS

THOMAS ANDREWS and his son Joseph came from County Devon, England, and settled in Hingham, Massachusetts, prior to the arrival of the Rev. Peter Hobart and his company in 1635.* At the drawing of the house-lots, on September 18, 1635, Thomas Andrews drew five acres, including back land on Town Street, now North Street. His lot was the one upon which stood, in 1899, the dwelling owned by the heirs of the late Perez Lincoln. He was aged at the time of his arrival, and did not long survive. The Rev. Peter Hobart wrote in his diary, under date of August 21, 1643: "Old Thomas Andrews dyed."

ISSUE

I. Joseph[2]. (Vide infra.)

II. Thomas[2];† who has been mentioned as probably son to Thomas[1] Andrews, of Hingham, though no evidence has

---

* The Rev. Peter Hobart and his twin brother, Edmund, were sons of Edmund Hobart, of Hingham, England. They were baptized Oct. 13, 1604, in that town. The diary of the Rev. Peter Hobart contained many valuable records, among them the following: "I with my wife and four children came safely to New England June ye 8 : 1635." He arrived at Charlestown, but in September following removed his family to Hingham, where, after a pastorate of forty-four years, he died Jan. 20. 1679. To him the town probably owes its name.

† This Thomas Andrews was not one of the Merchant Adventurers. (Vide page 607.) It is probable that Thomas and Richard Andrews, of London, who signed the agreement, were brothers. Both men assisted the Massachusetts Bay Colony with liberal contributions of money, and with their services. Thomas Andrews served as Deputy in England before Winthrop's colony came over in 1630; he also was chosen, June 17, 1629, in England, as auditor of the Bay Company's "accompts." In 1651, "The Right Hon. Thomas Andrews esq." was Lord Mayor of London. Vide Young's *Chronicles*, 1846 : 81 ; also *Massachusetts Historical Society's Collections*, vol. 10 : 27.

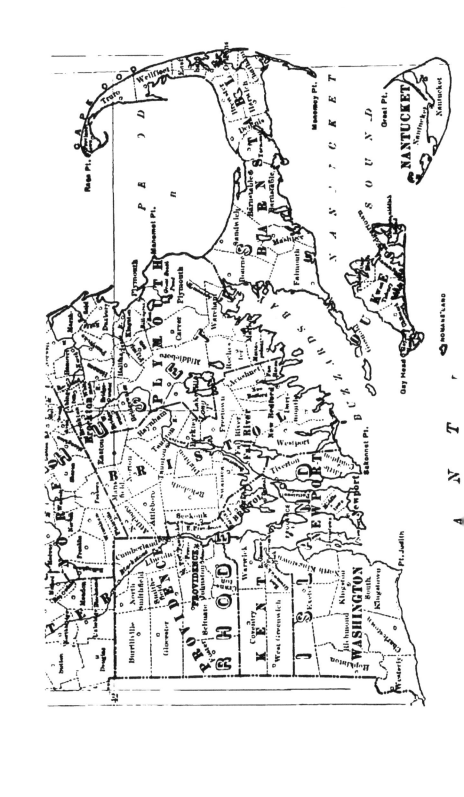

been found to establish that relationship beyond the similarity of names, and the fact that this Thomas does not belong to any other Andrews family at that time in New England. He settled in Dorchester. "Mattapan" became the town of Dorchester Sept. 7, 1630, and the bounds were established six years later.

On Dec. 17, 1634, three acres of land were granted Thomas Andrews next the house which he already had built. Before 1636, he and his wife "Ann" were members of the First Church; but the date of their admission was on the early missing records. On March 6, 1637–38, the sale of Mr. Gurling's land was confirmed, and it was appointed to be laid out "by Mr Benjamin & Mr Joseph Weld to Mr Andrews."[*] In 1637, Thomas Andrews was one of the ninety-five inhabitants among whom Dorchester Neck was divided. He was bailiff in 1660.[†] "Thomas Andrews Departed this life the 20th (Mon: 3^d) May 1673." His will, dated two weeks before his death, is found in the Suffolk County Probate. "Anne Andrewes widow died January: 13th: [16]84."

Issue: 1. Thomas^3, bap. June 23, 1639, in Dorchester; mar. Dec. 31, 1667, Phebe, daughter to Richard Gourd (Goard). He was then "Thomas Andrews Junr," and of Dorchester.

Issue: I. Thomas^4, b. Dec. 31, 1668, in Dorchester.

II. Joseph^4, b. Dec. 25, 1675, in Dorchester; mar. Elizabeth ——, and had, in Dorchester, issue: 1. Phebe^5, b. March 25, 1706. 2. Elizabeth^5, b. Feb. 19, 1707–08. 3. Hannah^5, b. Nov. 1, 1709. 4. Mary^5, b. Nov. 5, 1712. 5. Thankful^5, b. May 19, 1715. 6. Ebenezer^5, b. April 13, 1721. 7. Joseph^5, b. July 15, 1724.

III. Thankful^4, b. May 1, 1680, in Dorchester.

IV. John^4, b. "the last weeke in July: 1686," in Dorchester; mar. April 8, 1708, in Dorchester, Mar-

---

[*] *Massachusetts Bay Colony Records*, vol. 1: 219.

[†] Drake's *Materials for Early History of Dorchester*, 1851: 9.

[‡] *Dorchester Births, Marriages, and Deaths*, 1891: 28, 120.

garet Lord. Issue: 1. Thomas[5], b. Jan. 28, 1708–
09; d. young. 2. Margaret[5] b. June 11, 1710.
3. Mary[5], b. April 9, 1712; d. young. 4. Mary[5],
b. March 28, 1714. 5. John[5], b. March 10, 1715.
6. Thomas[5], b. Feb. 14, 1717–18. 7. Sarah[5], b.
Feb. 14, 1720–21. 8. Samuel[5], b. Oct. 19, 1722.
9. William[5], b. July 15, 1725.

2. Susanna[8]; mar. to William Hopkins. They removed
to Roxbury. She and her children were mentioned
in her father's will.

JOSEPH[2] ANDREWS

Joseph Andrews, born about 1597, in County Devon,
England, went with his father to Hingham, Massachusetts,
before 1635. His house-lot granted by the town, September
18, 1635, was "next west" of that of his father, and contained
five acres, including back land.

He was the first Town Constable, being "sworne constable of Barecove" (afterward incorporated as Hingham) July
8, 1635.* At this unsettled period the office was of the
utmost importance, since the law and order of the community were under the control of the Constable. Besides this,
if the Captain of the Train Band were not present on training days, the Constable took his place. Joseph Andrews was
sent as Deputy from the town of Hingham to the General
Court of the "Bay Colony" six sessions, commencing May
25, 1636; September 8, 1636; April 18, 1637; May 11, 1637;
September 11, 1637, and May 2, 1638.† He was also the
first Town Clerk of Hingham.

September 8, 1636, Joseph Andrews was one of twelve
"gentlemen . . . deputed as comittes to inqu[r] after y[e]
townes true valuation," in all the towns of the Colony, "so
as to make an equall rate for the first 600[l] now graunted to

---

* *Massachusetts Bay Colony Records*, vol. 1: 149.
† *Massachusetts Bay Colony Records*, vol. 1: 174, 178, 192, 194, 204, 227.

be levyed . . . the meeting to bee at Boston, the returne to bee made to the Treasurer/." He was also one of a committee of eleven, chosen August 1, 1637, "for the raising of a rate of £400." * May 17, 1637, "the commissioners, M^r. Wm Aspinwall and Mr Joseph Andrews," on the part of Massachusetts Bay, together with "Mr Timothy Hatherly and Mr Nathaniel Tilden," on the part of the Plymouth Colony, were appointed to "settle the line between the two colonies," † although the bounds were not fixed until some years afterwards.

Joseph Andrews later became a resident of Duxbury in Plymouth County, where he was " empannelled vpon a pettye jury and sworne, at Generall Court holden att New Plymouth the sixt Day of March 1654." ‡ William Bradford was then governor. Joseph Andrews also was appointed upon the "jury before Generall Court," October 3, 1654; March 2, 1657–58; October 2, 1660; and October 3, 1665. § He was chairman of "The Grand Enquest" in 1655 and 1661; ‖ a surveyor of highways 1654 and 1655, and was chosen Constable of Duxbury, June 8, 1664, under Governor Thomas Prince.¶

In 1757, Joseph Andrews, who described himself as "of Duxbury . . . in New England . . . Planter," conveyed to William Huser, Jr., of Hingham, for £12, "all that parcell of Vpland & Meadow lying in Hingham aforesaid neere Captaines Tent . . . conteining fiue acres."

(Signed)

JOSEPH ANDREWS ** [seal].

"Joseph Andrewes and Elizabeth Andrewes the wife of s^d Joseph Andrewes," of Duxbury, conveyed on October 16, 1665, to

---

* *Massachusetts Bay Colony Records*, vol. 1 : 180, 201.
† *Massachusetts Bay Colony Records*, vol. 1 : 96.
‡ *Plymouth Colony Records*, Court Orders, vol. 3 : 73.
§ *Plymouth Colony Judicial Acts*: 72, 87, 98, 100, 126.
‖ *Plymouth Colony Records*, Court Orders, vol. 3 : 78; vol. 4 : 12.
¶ *Plymouth Colony Records*, Court Orders, vol. 3 : 82; vol. 4 : 61.
** *Suffolk County Deeds*, Book 6 : 300–301.

Thomas Andrews, of Hingham, "our naturall* Sonne . . . all that our house Lotts Containeing tenn † acres of Land with all the houses Orchards & fences Standing & being vpon the S^d house Lotts bounded with the Towne Street Southward & with broad Coave Northward . . . & also our Salt Meadow . . . wch Salt Meadow Lyeth in a place Called the home Meadow and Containeth eight acres . . . & also y^t peece of Land Lying at a place Called Pyne Hill . . . & also the Northpart of a piece of Land Called Rocky necke . . . all Lying & being Within the Township of Hingham.

(Signed)

JOSEPH ANDREWES   [seal]

the m^rke of

ELIZABETH E A ANDREWES " ‡ [seal]

Late in life Joseph Andrews returned to Hingham, where he conveyed to his son Thomas, September 10, 1679, "all that my Shares of Land in all the four divisions of Connihassett [Cohassett] upland and also all the right of Com̄ons belonging to the s^d two shares . . . lately given and granted unto me the s^d Joseph Andrews by the towne of s^d Hingham." §   He evidently was very feeble, since this deed was signed with his mark; as was also his will, dated ten days later. His death occurred in Hingham, January 1, 1679–80, at the age of eighty-three years, and his will was proved in the same month : —

" I Joseph Andrewes of hingham of the County of suffolk in Neweingland being weak in body but of pfect memory, doe make & ordayne this my last will | and Testament in manner & forme as followeth Revoaking & herby making voyd all other will or wills

---

* At that time the term "natural" was used to distinguish one's own child from a stepchild, a child-in-law, or an adopted child. Vide Goodwin's *Pilgrim Republic*, 1888 : 344.

† The ten acres represented the grants to himself and his father, five acres each, in 1635.

‡ *Suffolk County Deeds*, Book 6 : 209–210.

§ *Suffolk County Deeds*, Book 11 : 354–355.

| *Suffolk County Probate*, Docket : 1128 ; also Book 6, pt. 2 : 318–320 ; Book 12 : 336.

formerly made by me the said Joseph andrews either by word or wrighting Impmis I giue & bequeath my soule into the hands of Jesus Christ my Redemer and my body to be buryed with Decent buriall, Item I giue & bequeath vnto Elizabeth andrewes my well beloued wife all that my estate of mouable goods nowe in possession for her to vse & Improue during her naturall life, Item I giue and bequeath un to my Daughter Elizabeth emes that featherbed and bedstead with all the furnytur therevnto belonging whereon I now ly, Item I giue and bequeath vnto my Daughter hannah ganitt one peauter platter Item I giue vnto my Daughter mary beard one peauter platter and one Candlestick Item I giue vnto my Son Joseph andrewes my Sword and my goold Ringe and a bible and also tenn pounds to be paid him by my executor if he come to Demand it, Item I giue vnto Ephraim Andrewes my Son all that estate of mine that is in his hands which he had of me when he went to newe Jazsy [New Jersey] Item I giue vnto Hipsebeth maning my Daughter three pounds of that bill of eight pouuds that I had of her husband Jeffery maning, and my mind and will is that the Remaynder of the said bill which is fiue pounds shall bee equally Deuided between Rehobath gannitt and Israell thorne fifty shillings a peece, Item I giue and bequeath vnto all my grand Sons that beare my name Joseph each of them & euery one of them a peauter platter Item I giue & bequaeth vnto Ruth andrewes my Daughter in law my newest Chist Item I giue vnto Ruth andrewes my grand Daughter my ould Chist and my frame table & forme Item I giue to my grand Son Thomas andrewes a Cowe, Item I giue to my grand Son Steaven Andrewes and Jededyah each of them an Iron pott Item I giue to benjamine andrewes my grand Son my Desk Item I giue vnto Elizabeth andrewes my grand daughter my warming pann Ite I giue vnto my grand Daughter Abygall andrewes my frying pann, Item I giue and bequeath vnto Thomas Andrewes my Son all the Rest & Remaynder of my goods and houshould Stuffe, and doe hereby make and apoynt him the said Thomas Andrewes my Soel executer of this my last will and testament And my minde and will is that whatsoeuer I haue giuen & bequeath of my goods & estat in this my will abouesaid Shall not be Claymed by any of the persons abouesaid vntill after the decease of my said wife but shall be for her vse as abouesaid in witns whereof I the abouesaid Joseph Andrewes haue herevnto Set my hand and Seale this Seauen & twenty day of September Annoq3 Doᵐ 1679.

The marke of

JOSEPH ℱ𝒜 ANDREWS [seal]

Signed & Sealed in the
presence of us — witnesses —

JOSIAH LORING   Josiah Loring & Edmᵈ Pitts
EDM PITTS —   the two witnesses to this
Instrumᵗ made oath before Simon Bradstreet Esqʳ Govoʳ & Humphry Davie Esqʳ assist 21ᵉ January 1679 [–80] that they were present & did see Joseph Andrews Signe & Seale and heard him publish it to be his last will and that then he was of a disposing minde to their best knowlidge.

as attests Isᵃ̣ ADDINGTON Cler "

"The 12ᵗʰ Day of January Annᵒ Dom 1679[–80]
An Inventory of yᵉ goods of Joseph Andrews of Hingham Deccᵈ apprized by us whose names are under subscribed

	£	s	d
Impˢ. his wearing Apparrell — — — — — — — — — — —	10.	9.	6
It. one gold ring 10. one Silver cup and Silver tooth picker 14ˢ	1.	4	—
It. one Sword — — — — — — — — — — — — — —	—	5	—
It. In Bookes — — — — — — — — — — — — — —	3.	10	—
It. three Cowes — — — — — — — — — — — —	7.	10	—
It. one Bedstead with matt and cord and ffeather bed one pair of blankets and one pair of Sheets one coverlid one bolster and one pillow and curtains and vallents	10.	—	—
It. one Bedstead and cord and small old ffeather bed with one old overworne bedding	2.	13	—
It. one Buriall Cloth — — — — — — — — — — —	1	—	—
It. one frame Table and frame forme — — — — — — —	—	15	—
It. two old Chests and one old Deske — — — — — —	—	12	—
It. one pair of Taylors Shiers pressing Iron — one small hammer and two Button hole Cheezels	—	5	—
It. ten pewter platters- — — — — — — — — — —	1.	10	—
It. one small pewter dish, one plate one bason two porringers, two pewter candlesticks one vinegar one Salt one dram cup and one old Razor	—	13	—
It. one glass bottle and Earthen ware — — — — — —	—	4	—
It. one small brewing tub one washing Keeler and payle	.	4	—

It. one warming pan, one brass Skillet and one Ladle one Scummer and meate fforke	—	8 . 6
It. one wainscoat box - - - - - - - - - - - - - -	—	5 —
It. one small Swine - - - - - - - - - - - - - -	—	7 —
It. ffour pillowbeers - - - - - - - - - - - - - -	—	7 . 6
It. three tablecloths Six towels and one Napkin - - - -	—	12 —
It. two pairs of Sheets - - - - - - - - - - - - -	1	5 —
It. Lumber - - - - - - - - - - - - - - - - -	—	5 —

Totall £45 07 6

Edm : pitts. Josiah Loring

Tho : Andrews Executor made Oath before Simon Bradstreet Esq: Gov: and Humphry Davie Esq: Assist 21° Janur? 1679[-80] to the truth of this Inventory and w? more appears to adde it

Attests. j : Addington Cler' "

The mention of " one pair of Taylors Shiers pressing Iron — one small hammer and two Button hole Cheezels " suggests that he was a tailor. Elizabeth, widow of Joseph Andrews, died August 12, 1688, in Hingham, probably at the home of her son Thomas.

ISSUE

I. Thomas[2], b. Nov., 1632, probably in England. (Vide infra.)

II. Joseph[2], b. about 1634-35. His father willed to him " my Sword and my gold ringe & a bible ; " also £10 " if hee comes to demand it."

III. Elizabeth[2], bap. March, 1637-38, in Hingham, by the Rev. Peter Hobart; mar. —— " Emes."

IV. Ephraim[2], bap. Aug., 1639, in Hingham, by the Rev. Peter Hobart. Before 1679, he had removed to New Jersey.

V. Hannah[2]; probably was married to Matthew Gannett, Sr., of Scituate, who died at Scituate in 1695, leaving sons, Matthew, Joseph, Rehoboth, and three daughters.

VI. Mary[2]; mar. to —— Beard (probably Thomas Beard).

VII. Hepzibah[2]; mar. to Jeffrey Manning.

VIII. Abigail[2], b. 1647 ; mar. July 25, 1667, to John[2] Wadsworth, son to Christopher[1] Wadsworth, of Duxbury. Deacon John Wadsworth died May 15, 1700, in Duxbury. His widow, Abigail, died Nov. 25, 1723, in the same town, aged seventy-six years. She was the only child not mentioned in her father's will. Issue: eleven.

THOMAS[3] ANDREWS

Thomas, eldest son to Joseph and Elizabeth Andrews, was born in November, 1632, probably in England. He lived in Hingham on the home lot, which had been conveyed to him by his parents in 1665; the original house formed part of the dwelling owned by the heirs of the late Perez Lincoln in 1889, and possibly is still standing.

Thomas Andrews served the town as Constable in 1654 and 1661; selectman, 1670, 1672, 1676, 1679, 1685, 1687, and 1688.[*] He was sent from Hingham, as Representative to the General Court, May 8, 1678.[†]

In the uprising of the people against the tyranny of Sir Edmund Andros, "Cap: Tho[s] Andrews" was chosen to represent the town "At the Council for the Safety of the People and Conservation of the Peace," in the sessions of May 22, June 5, October 24, and December 3, 1689.[‡]

On the 18th of April, 1689, Edmund Andros was arrested by the inhabitants of Boston.[§] The next day, the conduct of public affairs was assumed by the Council of Safety, of which Simon Bradstreet was chosen President.[||] On May

---

[*] *History of Hingham, Massachusetts,* 1889: 11.

[†] *Massachusetts Bay Colony Records,* vol. 5: 184.

[‡] *Massachusetts Archives,* Court Records, 1689–1698, vol. 6: 25, 30.

[§] "In 1686 when Sir Edmond Andros came to New England as Governor . . . the rights of property were so invaded, according to Increase Mather, that no man could call anything his own. Danforth wrote, 'Our condition is little inferior to absolute slavery.' When the people pleaded for *habeas corpus* and the simple rights of Magna Charta, Andros answered with a gibe.

"With Dudley censor of the press, the General Court abolished, the assembling of a town meeting made an act of sedition, it is certain that to those then living the times seemed big with dangers." Vide *The Social Unrest,* by John Graham Brooks, 1903: 73–74.

[||] *Massachusetts Archives,* Court Orders, 1689–1698, vol. 6: 1.

8th, acting doubtless under the orders of this extraordinary body, the Train Band of Hingham went to Boston, where the next day were gathered the sixty-six Representatives of forty-four towns. Cushing's diary tells us that a town-meeting was held in Hingham, on the 17th of the same month, to choose a member of the Council; and the choice fell upon Captain Thomas Andrews, already distinguished in town affairs. "It was an honor wisely bestowed."

In 1684, Thomas Andrews had been appointed Sergeant of the Train Band; but soon after he was elected their Captain. On the 6th of August, 1690, he and a number of his company joined the ill-fated expedition under Sir William Phips for the reduction of Canada, Sir William having chosen Captain Thomas Andrews as one of the twenty-one captains that he desired should go with him. Three days later (August 9), they set sail from Hull, "near Boston," with a fleet of thirty-two ships and tenders, and more than two thousand men on board the whole fleet.

Adverse winds up the St. Lawrence River delayed them so that it was the 5th of October when they dropped anchor near Quebec. The castle was commanded by Frontenac, an old and distinguished French officer, who repulsed the attacks of the Colonial troops for two days. After suffering great loss, appalled at the severity of the wintry weather which had set in, Sir William Phips started on his return to Boston with the remnant of his army and fleet. On the way home, the fleet was scattered by "cross-winds;" one vessel never was heard from, a second was wrecked, and a third was lost on an uninhabited shore, so that all the men either were starved or drowned. In addition, the small-pox broke out among the troops, and many were stricken with "a kind of Camp-Fever."

The few survivors reached the harbor of Boston on November 9; but some died, even then, before they could be taken to their homes. Most of the Hingham men died

on this expedition; and on November 25, 1690,* Captain
Thomas Andrews succumbed to the hardships he had endured. His age was fifty-eight years. There evidently was
an error in the town records as to the time of his death, as
his will was dated November 26, 1690. Captain Andrews
was in very comfortable circumstances, wealthy for those
times. His will was as follows : —

"I Thomas Andrewes S^{nr} of Hingham † in ye County of Suf-
folke within their Maj^{ties} Territory & Dominion of New-England ; being very weake of body but (through mercy) of perfect Understanding & Memory, do thus dispose of y^t part of
ye World which it hath pleased God to bestowe upon me ;
declareing this to be my Last Will & Testament:

"Imp^{rs} I give unto my Son Thomas Andrewes, that Dwelling-
house wch I built for him with ye Land about it y^t was Edmond Pitts's y^t I bought of his Son & Daughter Eastman ;
and also my great Lott ; & this to have now :

"Item   As for all my other estate my Will is y^t all my Four Sons
Shall be equal ; & my three Daughters all alike halfe as
much apiece as one of my Sons ; & also my wife to have
for her Livelihood out of ye whole of my Estate as she shall
have need off, as long as shee shall bear my Name, & if she
shall marry, then she to have Sixty pounds of my Estate
at her own disposing ; And if any of Children shall dye
without any Children, then what Land they had of mine to
return unto ye rest of their Brothers & Sisters according as
ye rest is ordered ; Only what I give unto my Son Thomas
I mean his House & Land it stands upon & my great Lott
to be att his own disposing :

"Item   I give unto my Son Thomas now two Oxen two Cows, &
three young Cattle for his own besides a single Portion
equal with his Brothers :

"Item   My desire is y^t Jedediah may be brought up to Learning
if it can be : or if it be, then I do desire ye Revrd Mr Jo^n Nor-

---

* *Town Records of Hingham, Massachusetts.*
† *Suffolk County Probate*, Docket : 1801 ; also Book 8 : 24-25, 198.

ton wth my Wife to order it & what they think is Reason, to take out of his Portion for y^t use ; so y^t his Brothers & Sisters be not too much wronged :

" Item   As for ye Sixty pounds which I give to my wife my Will is y^t it be taken not out of my Land, but out of ye moveable part of my Estate :

" Item   it is to be understood y^t all which I have given unto my Son Thomas (except his Single Share equal with ye rest of his Brothers) & what he hath gained upon it ; is clear unto him-selfe, & at his own disposal :

" Item   I do constitute & appoint my trusty & well beloved Son Thomas Andrewes ; & my Dearly beloved Wife Ruth Andrews to be ye Executor, & ye Executrix of this my Last Will & Testament : In Witness whereof I have hereunto Sett my Hand & Seal this Twentie-sixth day of Novem-ber An^o Domⁱ One thousand, Six hundred and Ninety ; Annoq3 Regni R^s & Regina, Gulielmij & Maria Anglia &c^a Secundo :

"Read Signed & Sealed in y^e
Heareing, Presence of
Thomas Thaxter
Sam^{ll} Shepard "

The Mark & Seal of

[seal]

Thomas Andrewes

" Boston February 5th 1690/1

"Thomas Andrews Executo^r of this will presented this will for probate the Ex^{xr} could not come up.

" Thomas Thaxter & Samuel Shepard the two subscribing Wit-nesses made oath before the worshipfull Samuel Sewall & John Smith Esq^{rs} assis^{ts} y^t they were present & did see Capt Thomas Andrews Signe Seale & heard him publish this Instrument to be his last will and testam^t and y^t when he did so was of dispos-ing minde to their best understanding."

That Captain Thomas Andrews signed this document with his mark was due to weakness, for he was a man of more than ordinary education. The inventory of his estate, which amounted to £724 : 7 : 6, is especially inter-esting : —

"An Inventory of the Estate of Cap.ⁿ Thomas. Andrews. late of Hingham deceased taken and Apprized this 10th Day of december 1690. by us under written./

Imprimis, his wearing Apparel ..	09 : 19 : 00
# In silver	01 : 19 : 00
# 2 Gold Rings	00 : 15 : 00
# Arms & Ammunition } 2 : 17 : 00 Bookes. 30! }	04 : 07 : 00
# Pewter and brass	06 : 00 : 00
# Iron potts. & other Iron things	02 : 04 : 00
# Earthen ware 7! working tools & old iron 37! }	02 : 04 : 06
# cart Plow & chaines	02 : 10 : 00
# butter cheese & tallow	02 : 00 : 00
# corne and meat	13 : 00 : 00
# to beds & bedding	21 : 18 : 00
# sheets table cloths napkins & towels }	07 : 15 : 00
# Cotton & linnen yarne	01 : 07 : 00
# New Cotton & linnen cloth	03 : 10 : 00
# Sheeps wool 20! a sadle 5!	01 : 05 : 00
# Tables chairs & cushions 35! a chest 12! }	02 : 07 : 00
# Tubs for meat brewing & washing }	02 : 04 : 00
# Spinning wheels	00 : 10 : 00
# Glass bottles & trenchers & spoons }	00 : 06 : 00
# a looking glass	00 : 05 : 00
# One house & home lott barne & other buildings }	60 : 00 : 00
# 4 Oxen 5 Cowes	21 : 00 : 00
# 3 cattle of 2 years old	06 : 00 : 00
# 5 young cattle	06 : 00 : 00
# 1 young Bull year old & upwards }	00 : 10 : 00
# in horse kind	04 : 00 : 00

# twelve swine	08 : 00 : 00
# 27 Sheep	07 : 00 : 00
# a piece of land at Pine Hill	46 : 10 : 00
# to a piece of land at Planters hill	10 : 00 : 00
# a piece of land at Rocky neck	60 : 00 : 00
# the first division of at } Cohasatt	22 : 00 : 00
# 2.ᵈ division goeing to } Cohaset	18 : 00 : 00
# 3.ᵈ division at James Hill wᵗʰ a lot that was Thomas Joyes. & some land that belong to that division that lyeth by scittuate pond wᵗʰ land that was John Ripley lying neer said pond }	20 : 00 : 00
# To the 4.ᵗʰ division	07 : 00 : 00
# Twelve Shares of Comon	24 : 00 : 00
# A piece of Saltmarsh neer y.ᵉ Towne }	100 : 00 : 00
# A piece of Salt Marsh at Cohaset }	36 : 00 : 00
# A piece of fresh meadow at Turkey hill }	04 : 00 : 00
# To halfe a share of land called y.ᵉ small shares }	06 : 00 : 00
# To interest in scittuate comon }	02 : 00 : 00
# A lott at straights pond	00 : 10 : 00
# a piece of land lying wᵗʰ Josiah Lorings land in Plimouth colony }	02 : 00 : 00
# to wages due from Y.ᵉ country }	28 : 00 : 00
# to a load of Cedar bolts	00 : 12 : 00
# housing and lands and cattle given to his son Thomas in present possession }	150 : 00 : 00

John Jacob Thom.ᵉ Thaxter

Funeral charges.   10 : 00 : 00

"Boston April 28, 1691.

"Ruth Andrews. & Thomas Andrews. the Execut.ʳˢ of the last Will & Testam.ᵗ of Cap.ᵗ Thomas Andrews. made Oath in County Court that this is a true Inventory of the Estate of s.ᵈ Thomas. Andrews. dec.ᵈ so far as is come to their knowledge & that when they know more will cause it to be added. ∫∫ Attest.ʳ Joseph Webb cler

"Ex.ʳ Joseph Webb cler."

Ruth, widow of Thomas Andrews, and the mother of all his children, was mentioned in the will of Joseph Andrews (1679) as "Ruth Andrews my daughter in law," with the gift of "my newest chest." She survived her husband many years, and passed away at Hingham, October 23, 1732, in her ninety-seventh year.

ISSUE

I. Joseph[4], b. Sept. 22, 1656, in Hingham; died, unmarried, Nov. 24, 1724, in Hingham.

II. John[4], b. Sept. 30, 1658, in Hingham; mar. Dec. 21, 1685, in Hingham, Patience Nichols; he died July 3, 1695, in the same town, aged thirty-six years. Patience (Nichols) Andrews was b. Dec. 25, 1660, in Hingham. She was mar., second, Feb. 12, 1695–96, to Joseph Beal. Issue by first husband: 1. Patience[5]. 2. John[5]. 3. Abigail[5].

III. Ruth[4], b. Aug. 6, 1660, in Hingham; mar. Feb. 22, 1687–88, to Ambrose Low.

IV. Thomas[4], b. June 26, 1663, in Hingham; mar., first, April 12, 1693, Abigail Lincoln, daughter to Stephen and Elizabeth (Hawke) Lincoln. She was b. in Hingham, April 7, 1673; d. Aug. 18, 1713, aged forty years. He mar., second (published Nov. 19, 1714), Susanna Stutson (Stetson), of Boston, who survived him.

Thomas Andrews, known as "Lieut. Thomas," was a tailor by trade. "L! Tho⁵ Andrews," of Hingham, was Representative, Feb. 12, 1689–90, and throughout the year, at the "Council for Safety of the People and Conservation of the Peace." *

He resided at the homestead of his father and grandfather until his death, Aug. 5, 1727, at the age of sixty-four years. The homestead is said to have remained in the possession of this family down to the seventh generation (Joseph[2], Thomas[3], Thomas[4], Thomas[5], Thomas[6], Thomas[7]). The seventh Thomas Andrews, styled "Gentleman," died on the old home place on North Street, formerly Town Street, oppo-

---

* *Massachusetts Archives*, Court Orders, vol. 6, 1689–1698: 113.

site Thaxter's Bridge, on March 27, 1821, aged sixty-one
years.

    Issue of Lieut. Thomas [4] Andrews, all by wife Abigail
Lincoln: 1. Abigail [5]. 2. Ruth [5]. 3. Thomas [5]. 4.
Elizabeth [5]. 5. Joseph [5]. 6. Ephraim [5]. 7. David [5].

V. Elizabeth [4], b. Sept. 22, 1665, in Hingham; mar. May 22,
    1690, to Joseph Joy.

VI. Ephraim [4], b. Oct. 27, 1667, in Hingham; d. Sept. 7, 1669.

VII. Abigail [4], b. Jan. 6, 1669, in Hingham; mar. Jan. 16,
    1693–94, to Joseph Blany.

VIII. Stephen [4], b. March 6, 1672, in Hingham; mar. Bethia
    Stetson. (Vide infra.)

IX. Jedediah [4], b. July 3, 1674, in Hingham; married, and
    had a son Ephraim [5], who was a physician in Baltimore,
    Maryland, and died there about 1781.

    Jedediah Andrews was graduated from Harvard College
in 1695. During the following two years he taught Latin,
Arithmetic, etc., in his native town. Subsequently, he settled as a minister at Philadelphia.

X. Benjamin [4], b. March 11, 1677, in Hingham; mar. Mary
    Sweetzer, and had issue: 1. Benjamin [5]. 2. John [5]. 3.
    Ephraim [5]. He resided in Boston.

STEPHEN [4] ANDREWS

    Stephen Andrews, b. March 6, 1672, in Hingham; mar.,
first, June 23, 1697, Bethia [8], * daughter to Benjamin [2] and
Bethia [2] (Hawke) Stetson, of Scituate, Mass. †

---

* Matthew Hawke, from Cambridge, England, embarked with his wife,
Margaret, and servant, John Fearing, in the ship *Diligent*, of Ipswich, for
New England, and arrived August 10, 1638. The following year they were
residents of Hingham, and lived on Main Street at the centre of the town.

    Matthew Hawke was made freeman May 18, 1642; was the third Town
Clerk of Hingham; Selectman, 1663; also schoolmaster, 1679–83.

    Margaret Hawke died in Hingham, March 18, 1683–84; her husband fol-
lowing, Dec. 11, 1684, aged seventy-four years (gravestone inscription). He
made his will Sept. 24, 1684.

---

† Vide The Stetson Family.

Bethia[3] Hawke was first cousin to Deborah[3] Hawke, born January 14, 1691–92 (daughter to James[2] and Sarah (Jacob) Hawke), who was married May 2, 1716, to John[4] Lewis, of Hingham. John[4] and Deborah[3] (Hawke) Lewis were the parents of Judge John[5] Lewis,[*] of North Yarmouth, who married, in 1746, Mary[5] Mitchell, eldest daughter to Jacob[4] Mitchell, Jr., of North Yarmouth, half-brother to Seth[4] Mitchell.

By the will of his grandfather, Joseph[2], Stephen[4] Andrews was to become the possessor of "an Iron pott," after the death of his grandmother. His father, Thomas[3] Andrews, first giving to his eldest son, Thomas[4], the homestead and other property, provided that the remaining portion of "all my four sons shall be equall."

Stephen Andrews, by trade a weaver, removed from Hingham soon after the birth of his third child, Benjamin, in 1706; but there is no record that shows his place of residence during the intervening years between that date and 1734, when he is mentioned as of Duxbury : —

"Stephen Andrews, Jonathan Peterson and Reuben Peterson, all of Duxborrough in the County of Plymouth . . . do jointly own, and are possessed of a certain peice of salt meadow lying

---

ISSUE

1. Elizabeth[2], b. July 14, 1639, in Hingham; mar. Feb., 1660, Stephen Lincoln, of Hingham.
2. Sarah[2], b. Aug. 1, 1641, in Hingham; mar. 1657, John Cushing, of Scituate.
3. Bethia[2], b. Jan. 21, 1643–44, in Hingham; mar. Aug. 15, 1665, Benjamin[2] Stetson, of Scituate. Their daughter Bethia[3] mar. June 23, 1697, Stephen[4] Andrews, of Hingham.
4. Mary[2], b. Aug. 2, 1646, in Hingham; mar. Benjamin Loring, of Hingham.
5. James[2], b. May 27, 1649, in Hingham; mar. Sarah Jacob, of Hingham.
6. Deborah[2], b. March 22, 1651–52, in Hingham; mar. John Briggs, of Duxbury.
7. Hannah[2], b. July 22, 1655, in Hingham; mar. June 4, 1685, Peter Cushing, of Hingham.

[*] Vide pages 408–412.

and being in Duxbury aforesaid, the meadow lyeth adjacent to the beach called the salt house beach, and the hummock called Rouses hummock, and is the meadow that Mr Jonathan Peterson purchased of Mr John Wadsworth of Duxborough afore said, and as yet no deeds of partition being signed by us, Now Know all men by these presents, that we . . . do divide the same as followeth, viz. . . .

(Signed)

Dated, Dec. 5, 1734.	STEPHEN ANDREWS	[seal]
"Signed Sealed and	JONATHAN PETERSON	[seal]
delivered in presence of	REUBEN PETERSON " *	[seal]
MICAH SOULE		
ELIZABETH ANDREWS "		

A few years later, Stephen Andrews appeared as a resident of Pembroke when he purchased, for £39, of Joshua Hopkins, of Taunton, a homestead in Taunton consisting of twenty acres in the home-lot and twenty acres additional. This was on March 28, 1738. In 1747, Stephen Andrews purchased, for £50, of James Andrews, of Taunton, one sixth of James's land.†

As both the Town and Church records of Taunton, previous to 1820, were burned, very little can be learned of Stephen Andrews in that town. A compilation of Taunton records, made up from every available source, bears this item : "Old Stephen Andrews died 4th March 1770."‡ His age was ninety-eight years. His will, dated October 20, 1762, when he was ninety years of age, was proved April 30, 1770. There is no record of the death of his wife Bethia, but a second "wife Mary" is named in his will : § —

"In the Name of God Amen I Stephen Andrews of Taunton in the County of Bristol Husbandman this Twentyeth day of october and in the second year of his Majesty's Reign annoque

---

* *Duxbury Town Records*, 1893, 1642–1770 : 13.
† *Bristol County, Massachusetts, Deeds*, Book 27 : 462 ; Book 35 : 132.
‡ *Town Records of Taunton, Massachusetts* (Compilation), vol. 1 : 142.
§ *Bristol County, Massachusetts, Probate*, Book 21 : 234–237.

Domini 1762 being in Good health of Body and of a sound & disposing mind & memory thanks be Given to God therefore & Calling to mind the uncernty of Life do Make and ordain this my Last will & testament in manner and form following that is to say Principally and first of all: I Give & Recommend my soul into the hands of God, that Give it to me & my body to the Earth to be Decently buried in a Christian Manner at the discretion of my Executors hereafter named Nothing Doubting but at the Generall Resurrection I Shall again Receive the Same by the Mighty power of God and as touching such worldly Estate as God in his providence have bestowed on me I Give and Bequeath and dispose y^t in the following Manner & form

" Imp^s My will is that all my Just debts and funerall Charges be paid first out of my Estate by my Executor hereafter named within Convenient time after my decéase

" Item I Give to my well beloved wife Mary Andrews one Good Cow for Ever and all my Indoor Moveables that I had before my Inter marrige with my wife mary as well all she brought with her at sd time to be for Improvement and not to dispose of the same nor no part thereof) for and dureing her widow hood and my Indoor moveables after my sd wifes decease or marriage to be disposed of as hereafter mentioned and if my sd wife Mary should see Cause to marry after my decease then my will is that she to have no more than that part of my Indoor Movabls that was hers before our Inter marriage —

" Item I Give to my Grandson Stephen Andrews and to his heirs and assigns for Ever one Great bible & my book Called Concordance & ye Book Called the Secatarys Gide and one Book more Called Gospell Church and all the Rest of my books to be Equally Divided between him sd Stephen and my Grandson Thomas Andrews I allso Give to him my sd Grandson Stephen Andrews one pair of worsted Combs ye best Iron doggs and all my wareing Apparell as also all my Husbandry tools and my Gun sword and walking Cane and I also Give him the fifth part of all my money that shall be found Due to me after the payments made as aforesd for funeral Charges and Just Debts and What I shall Give my Grandson Thomas Andrews

"Item   I Give to my Daughter mary Doty the wife of Edward Doty the one half of all my weaveing Tackling and also the fifth part of all the Money that shall be found due at my decease Excepting that first payment be made for Just Debts & funerall Charges as aforesd and What I Shall Give my Grandson Thomas Andrews —

"Item   I Give to my Daughter Hannah Coombs the wif of Ashemar Coombs the other half of all my weaveing Tackling and the fifth part of all my Money that shall be found due at my Decease Excepting the payments being first made as aforesd — and after my wifs death or day of Marriage all my Indoor Moveables that was not my wifs mary before our Inter Marriage nor Given to my Daughter Deborah Mitchel hereafter mentioned Neither plainly Given away in this my Last will my will is that they be Equally divided between my four Daughters viz Mary Doty Hannah Coombs Bethia winslow and Deborah Mitchel —

"Item   I Give to my Daughter Bethiah winslow the one fifth part of all the Money that shall be found Due after my decease debts & funerall Charges being first paid out as aforesd —

"Item   I Give to my Daughter Deborah Mitchel the fifth part of all the Money that shall be found due after Just Debts and funerall Charges being first paid out as aforesd I also Give my Daughter Deborah the Best-bed with the furniture thereto belonging which bed I had before my Inter marriage with my wife Mary Andrews —

"Item   I Give to my Grand Son Thomas Andrews and to his heirs for Ever three pounds Lawfull Money & to be paid to him by my Exector hereafter named in one year after my decease and to be paid out of my money that shall be found due after debts & funerall Charges being first paid and also the other half of my Books as made Mention of in my Legacy to my Grandson Stephen I hereby nominate and Appoint Edward Doty & John Winslow both of Rochester in the County of Plimouth sole Executors of this my Last will & testament whom I order to Receive in all my Just Deues and pay all my Debts and Legacys and all and Every part of my Estate not before Given away in this my Last will &

testament I Give to my Executors aforesd to them and their heirs and Assigns for Ever they paying out the severall Donations as aforesd. Utterly Revokeing and Dis allowing all other wills by me made Ratifying and Confirming this and only this to be my Last will and Testament.

"In Witness Whereof I the Sd Stephen Andrews have hereunto set my hand and seal the day and year first Mentioned — four places Interlined before Signeing

"Signed Sealed Published and Pronounced & Declared by the sd Stephen Andrews to be his Last will & Testament in Presence of us the Subscribers Seth Knap

ABIGAIL ╳ PRATT

ZILPAH PRATT

GEORGE GODFREY"

STEPHEN ANDREWS

[seal]

His ownership of the "Great bible . . . Concordance . . . Secatarys Gide . . . Gospell Church, and all the Rest of my books to be Equally Divided between" his grandsons, Stephen and Thomas Andrews, proves him to have been much more scholarly than the average person of that period. When his will was allowed, April 30, 1770, Edward Doty and John Winslow were appointed executors. The inventory, submitted May 1, 1770, mentions clothing, "great Bible," looms, farm tools, beds and bedding, household goods, dishes of iron, pewter, "earthen," and wood ; linen, a black cow, red cow, red heifer, and a "mair." Total valuation, £169 : 14 : 10.*

ISSUE

I. Bethia[5], b. May 26, 1699, in Hingham; mar. to —— Winslow ; probably was a widow at the time her father made his will. She had a son John, who resided at Rochester, Mass.

---

* *Bristol County, Massachusetts, Probate*, Book 21 : 237, 410.

II. Mary⁵, b. Sept. 15, 1703, in Hingham; mar. to Edward
   Doty, and was living in Rochester, Mass., in 1762.

III. Benjamin⁵, b. Jan. 25, 1705–06, in Hingham. No record of
   his death appears in Taunton, nor in the Bristol County
   Probate. His sons, Stephen and Thomas Andrews, were
   mentioned in their grandfather's will.

IV. Hannah⁵; was the wife of Ashemar Coombs at the time her
   father's will was made.

V. Deborah⁵; mar. about 1730, to Seth⁴ Mitchell, of North
   Yarmouth, son to Jacob³ and Rebecca⁴ (Cushman) Mitch-
   ell. Seth⁴ Mitchell, b. March 16, 1705–06, in Plymouth,
   Mass.; d. Aug. 26, 1760, in North Yarmouth, Maine.*
   His widow, Deborah, was living there in 1785.

By the will of her father she was to receive one fifth of
the money that remained after all just debts and funeral
charges were paid, "the Best-bed with the furniture thereto
belonging," that probably had belonged to her own mother,
and one fourth of all the "Indoor Moveables" that he had
before his marriage to his second wife, Mary.

---

* Vide pages 429–442.

THE STETSON FAMILY

ROBERT[1] STETSON

ROBERT[1] STETSON, b. 1612, tradition says, came from
County Kent, England. A Stetson coat-of-arms, found
among ancient papers once belonging to him, has been reproduced in a small pamphlet written, in 1847, by Mr. John
Stetson Barry, and is considered authentic. The spelling of
this family name in New England was somewhat erratic, as
was common at that period ; but during Robert's later years
it usually was "Studson." Some of his sons retained that
form, though most of them changed it to Stetson.

Early in 1634, Robert Stetson appeared as a resident of
Scituate, Massachusetts. The name of his first wife is nowhere recorded, and is unknown. She is supposed to have
been the mother of all his children, the first of whom was
born in June, 1639. His second wife, the widow Mary Bryant, survived him. After many years of usefulness in the
affairs of the town and of Plymouth Colony, Robert Stetson
died where he had spent his life, in Scituate, on February
1, 1702–03, at the advanced age of ninety years, — "having
lived long and left a good name."

His farm was situated on the banks of the North River,
his house being located on a beautiful plain nearly opposite
"Cornet's Rocks." These rocks, jutting out of the river
east of the farm, are well known to this day. An unfailing
and valuable spring of water, from which eight generations *

---

* The children of Charles[7] Stetson, in 1830, were the eighth generation
who had lived on the old homestead, which had descended from Cornet
Robert[1] Stetson through Joseph[2], Robert[3], William[4], William[5], Stephen[6],
to Charles[7] Stetson. Vide Dean's *History of Scituate, Massachusetts*, 1831 :
341–342.

of the family have been supplied, marks the spot upon which the house stood. July 3, 1653, this farm was further enlarged, as follows : " Fifty acres of land is graunted [by the General Court] to Robert Studson, aded to twenty acres which he hath bought, which was James Dauis his land, for which said Robert Studson shewed a deed in Court; the said fifty acars of land to lye to the seaward of Plymouth Path, towards the Indian Head Riuer, incase it has been found not to intrench on any former graunts ; and incase it shalbee soe found to doe, then to haue it in soɱ other conuenient place where hee shall find it." *

About 1653, Robert Studson, who was a carpenter,† Timothy Hatherly, and Joseph Tilden erected a saw-mill on the "Third Herring Brook," in Scituate, where remains of the dam still are to be seen. For this mill a very extensive tract was overflowed, now called "The Old Pond." In 1676, the mill was burned by the Indians, and never was rebuilt. Later, for valuable services rendered the struggling Colony, there was "graunted by the Court vnto Cornett Studson, two hundred acrees of land . . . on the southerly side of the three mile square of land formerly graunted vnto Mr Hatherly . . . to be layed out for him by Leiftenant James Torrey." This order was dated June 7, 1665; but Lieutenant Torrey having deceased, "The major and Treasurer [were] appointed by the Court to lay out the two hundred acrees of land graunted vnto Cornett Studson," the bounds of which were fixed March 5, 1666–67, "on the north side by those lands that were graunted att Accord Pond." ‡

In 1668, Cornet Stetson was commissioned to purchase from the Sachem Josias Chickatabutt, for the use of the Colony, a tract of land mainly included in the present towns of Hanover and Abington. It was near Accord Pond, south of land formerly granted to Mr. Timothy Hatherly. It was

---

* *Plymouth Colony Records*, Court Orders, vol. 3 : 106.

† *Plymouth Colony Deeds*, vol. 3, pt. 1 : 323.

‡ *Plymouth Colony Records*, Court Orders, vol. 4 : 95, 127, 142 ; vol. 5 : 130.

called by the Indians "Nanumackeuitt." The deed was made out April 13, 1668, and recorded in 1674; the witnesses were Josias Winslow and John Browne. On July 10, 1669, this land was conveyed to the Cornet, "for £7.5ˢ of Currant New England pay," by "Thos. Prence, Governor . . . to the proper use and behoof of him the sd. Robert Stetson, hee his heires and assignes forever." *

"Robte Steedson" was chosen Constable of Scituate, March 7, 1642–43; he also appeared that year in the list of males "able to beare Armes." June 3, 1652, "Robert Studson" was made freeman.† He was on the "Grand Enquest," June 7, 1652; "on pettye jury or jury of life and death," March 6, 1654–55, March 5, 1660–61; and, as "Cornett Studson," on jury, March 3, 1662–63, and March 3, 1665–66.‡ "Cornett Robert Studson" was "approved by the Court as a selectman of Scittuate, June 5, 1666," June 2, 1667, June 22, 1674, and other years.§ He was sent as Deputy from Scituate to the General Court of Plymouth twenty-two sessions, which began on these dates: —

"Robert Studson"		— March 7, 1653–54.
"	"	June 6, 1654.
"	"	Aug. 1, 1654.
		June 8, 1655.
		June 2, 1656.
		June 1, 1658.
		June 7, 1659.
		Oct. 3, 1659.
"Cornett	"	June 6, 1660.
"		Aug. 7, 1660.
"		June 4, 1661.
		June 3, 1662.
"	"	"	June 5, 1666.

* *Plymouth Colony Deeds*, vol. 4: 1–3.
† *Plymouth Colony Records*, Court Orders, vol. 2: 53; vol. 3: 8.
‡ *Plymouth Colony Records*, vol. 3: 73, 205; vol. 4: 30, 115.
§ *Plymouth Colony Records*, vol. 4: 124, 149; vol. 5: 149.

"Cornett Robert Studson" — June 5, 1667.
"   "   "   June 1, 1669.
"   "   "   June 7, 1670.
                          June 5, 1671.
                          June 3, 1673.
                          Sept. 15, 1673.
                          June 3, 1674.
                          June 5, 1677.
"   "   "   June 5, 1678." *

The military title of Cornet had been bestowed upon him October 6, 1659; at which time "Captaine Wiłłam Bradford, Leiftenant John Freeman, and Cornett Robert Studson [were] confeirmed by the Court to bee comission officers of the troop of horse." † This was the first "Light Horse Corps" raised in the Colony. He previously had been on a committee "For the cecuring of the countreyes powder [and] to hier workmen to make a place to cecure it in." June 10, 1662, when "the Major," Captain Southworth, and Captain Bradford were appointed by the Court "to draw vp a forme of comission for military officers [there were] aded vnto these . . . for advice and councell . . . Cornett Studson" and three lieutenants.‡ Early in the year 1667, this "Troop of Horse" was sent on a "journey to the sachem Phillip in behalfe of the countrey," for which "the Major" received £5, as his due. At the same time (June 5, 1667), "the Treasurer" received £3, Captain Southworth 40ˢ, and "Cornett Robert Studson, his horse, time and paines 40ˢ;" while "two shillings and sixpence a day [was] alowed vnto the troopers . . . on the abouesaid expedition." §

In 1675, when it was suspected that neither King Philip nor the Narragansett Indians would be faithful to their

---

* *Plymouth Colony Records*, vol. 3 : 44, 49, 63, 79, 99, 135, 162, 170, 187, 198, 214; vol. 4: 14, 122, 148; vol. 5 : 17, 34, 55, 114, 135, 144, 231, 256.
† *Plymouth Colony Records*, vol. 3 : 174.
‡ *Plymouth Colony Records*, vol. 4 : 21.
§ *Plymouth Colony Records*, Court Orders, vol. 4 : 151.

treaties of amity, the town fathers of Scituate ordered additional garrisons for defence; and also ordered that the "twenty three men from Scituate ... pressed for this war" be "raised." General Cudworth, Cornet Stetson, Isaac Chittenden, and Joseph White were chosen a committee "to procure clothing &c., for the soldiers." After the "Narragansett fight" of December 25, 1675, the Indians became still more troublesome, committing ravages in every direction. In May, 1676, following an attack on Hingham, where they burned five houses, they went into Scituate by the "Indian path," which led from Scituate to the Matakeeset settlements at Indian Head Ponds, by the Cornet's mill on the Third Herring Brook. This saw-mill they burned, on May 30. The losses in the town of Scituate were given: * "13 dwelling houses burnt with their barns — one saw mill — six heads of families and many others killed and made cripples." †

The veteran Cornet Stetson during this period was constantly on horseback, either in making voluntary excursions, as tradition asserts, with General Cudworth, also "waxing old," or in returning to encourage the garrisons at home, or in guiding the directions of the Council of War. In consideration of these services and losses by the destruction of the Indians, "Major Cudworth" ‡ and "Cornett Studson" were awarded by the authorities of Plymouth Colony £12 out of the £124 : 10, which was their allotment of the £450 sent over in 1676 from Ireland, termed the "Irish Donation." §

On April 2, 1667, Cornet Stetson was appointed "to be

---

* Deane's *History of Scituate, Massachusetts*, 1831 : 128, 401–402.

† Goodwin says that twenty-two houses were burned. Vide Goodwin's *Pilgrim Republic*, 1888 : 558.

‡ Early in 1675, Major James Cudworth was advanced to the rank of General (at 6s a day), a title then bestowed for the first time in the Colony. After six months' service in command of the troops, he retired to civil life; but the title of Major still clung to him.

§ Vide *Plymouth Colony Records*, Court Orders, vol. 5: 222; also pages 466, 467.

of [the] Councell [of War] with the Comission Officers in each towne;" he also appeared June 5, 1671, with "such as are aded to the Magistrates to be off the Councill of Warr." His last election to this council was on July 7, 1681, when he was sixty-nine years of age.*

Cornet Robert Stetson also was something of a surveyor, his earliest appointment by the Court dating June 7, 1659, when he was one of a committee of three chosen "to run the line betwixt the Bay goũrment and vs." † Not, however, until five years later — May 29, 1664 — did the commissioners of the two Colonies report to the General Court of Massachusetts Bay, the "bound ljne betwixt the colonjes of the Massachusetts Bay and New Pljmouth." This report was signed by three commissioners from each government, as follows : —

[Plymouth]   "Robert Studson
                              Constant Southworth
                              Jos : Winslow
[Massachusetts Bay]   Joshua Fisher
                              Rogʳ Clap
                              & Elea : Lusher"

May 15, 1672, when it was determined to "run over the line from Accord Pond to Bound Brook," as that boundary did not give general satisfaction, "Cornet Studson" of the "Pljmouth comissioners . . . told vs [the Massachusetts commissioners] they should concurr wᵗʰ what wee did, but [they] were not willing to be at charge for it.

                              Joshua Hubbard
                              & Joshua Fisher" ‡

Cornet Stetson frequently was chosen to "lay out land," to "view the land," to "view a fence;" and, June 3, 1668, he was chosen surveyor of highways for the town of Scitu-

---

* *Plymouth Colony Records*, Court Orders, vol. 4 : 145; vol. 5 : 64; vol. 6 : 67.
† *Plymouth Colony Records*, Court Orders, vol. 3 : 166.
‡ *Massachusetts Bay Colony Records*, vol. 4, pt. 2 : 114–116, 531.

ate. When Thomas Andrews made petition to the Court in behalf of two "ancient servants of the town . . . that a supply of land be settled vpon them," the Court ordered "the Treasurer and Cornett Studson to lay out to each of them sixty acres of land." This was on July 7, 1668. The Cornet was appointed June 3, 1679, surveyor of highways by the General Court of Plymouth Colony. In 1678 and 1679, Cornet Stetson and Mr. Nathaniel Thomas were appointed by the Court "collectors of the rents for the proffitts of the Cape fishing," for bass and mackerel.*

Yet, with all these positions of trust filled so acceptably by Cornet Stetson, nothing exceeds in interest or importance his connection with the Kennebec trade. The Plymouth Colonists early had established, at the mouth of the Kennebec River, a trading-post with the Indians, which was a constant source of trouble and disappointment. They hoped much from it, but it never had been profitable. On July 2, 1655, "Mr Josias Winslow, Senr, Mr Josias Winslow, Junr, Mr Hinckley, Th^o Clarke and Robert Studson," were appointed by the General Court "as a comittee to meett with the majestrates att the next Court of Assistants, to treat with them about letting of the trade att Kennebecke, and about regulateing the disorders of the goûment there." October 6, 1659, this committee had "covenanted and agreed together with the farmers of the said traid, viz: Mr Thomas Prence, Mistris Allice Bradford, Seni^r, Captaine Thomas Willet, and Major Josias Winslow;" and the paper was signed by both parties, the only ones making their marks being Mrs. Alice Bradford (widow of the Governor, who had died two years before) and Robert Studson: —

"The marke of ℳ Robert Studson."†

---

* *Plymouth Colony Records*, Court Orders, vol. 4: 181, 189; vol. 6: 12, 18.

† *Plymouth Colony Records*, vol. 3: 87, 170. It is not quite clear why he should have made his mark here, as his autograph signature appeared several times afterward — notably May 29, 1664.

June 13, of the following year, "Leiftenant Southworth, Mʳ Constant Southworth and Cornett Studson, and Mʳ Josias Winslow Seniʳ., or any three of them [were authorized] either to sell or otherwise dispose of the said trad[e] in the countreyes behalfe." The measures taken evidently were successful, since at a meeting of the General Court, June 1, 1663, "Cornett Studson was appointed by the Court to accompany the Treasurer in demanding and receiueing the moneyes due to the countrey from the purchasers of Kenebecke;" and at the same meeting it was ordered by the Court "that a convenient, handsome rome [room] be aded to the Goûnor's house, and that the charḡ of the building therof bee defrayed out of the pay for Kenebecke, if that kind of pay will doe it . . . the major, the Treasurer, and Cornett Studson are impowered to take course for the procureing of the thinge done." * For this Kennebec service, Cornet Stetson received the grant previously mentioned of two hundred acres of land adjoining that of Mr. Timothy Hatherly.

During the "Inter-Charter" period, shortly before Andros was appointed Governor, "The Town being met together [May 27, 1686], and the New Book of Laws being read, and being sensible of our inability to undergo the Change which this new form will occasion, and what consequences thereby may accrue, if changes shall come, and being desirous to prevent what may be hurtful, chose Mʳ John Cushing, Samuel Clap, Capt. John Williams, Cornet Robert Stetson, Jeremiah Hatch, Elder Thomas King, and Isaac Buck, to draw up our grievances and impart their apprehensions to the Town before the next Court." The committee reported at the next town-meeting an elaborately extended protest against existing conditions and the "expected changes" of government. † This action of the town of Scituate, in which Cornet Stetson bore a leading part, is

---

* *Plymouth Colony Records*, vol. 4: 38, 44.
† Deane's *History of Scituate, Massachusetts*, 1831: 103–105.

more noticeable from the fact that the general uprising of the people did not occur until three years later — 1689.

Throughout these years of hardship and danger, no citizen of Scituate bore a stronger part in the affairs of the town and Colony than Cornet Robert Stetson. His advice and assistance were sought, both in public and private capacities, and to no one did he turn a deaf ear. The last few years of retirement at his home were well earned. His will, dated Scituate, September 4, 1702, when he had reached the age of ninety years, shows that he had retained his mental faculties to a remarkable degree, although through physical infirmities it is signed with a mark. On February 1, 1702–03, he passed away. Ten days later, the inventory of his property was taken; it was presented on March 5, at the time his will was proved : —

"Scituate the fourth day of September Anno Domini one thousand seven hundred and two I Robert Stetson of Scituate in yᵉ County of Plimouth in New England being Aged and weak of Body but of Sound disposing mind and memory praises be rendered to God for yᵉ same —

" And being in dayly Expectation of my last & Great Change & desirous to settle things in order before my decease Do therefore hereby make & declare this my last Will * and Testament in manner following Imprimis I Humbly Commit my Spirit to yᵉ father of Spirits and my body to decent Burial when it Shall please God to call me hence And Touching Such outward Estate as it hath pleased God so to Bless me withall, my will is that yᵉ same shall be Imployed & bestowed according as herein is Expressed. Item I Give and Bequeath to Mary my welbeloved Wife vpon yᵉ prouiso and condition herein after Set down the Sum of Twelve pounds in money And ten pounds worth of my houshold Goods Such as She Shall Choose with the sole use and Benifit of yᵉ South End of my now Dwelling house & one half of my Celler And two Cows with Sumer pasture & wintering of them with

---

* *Plymouth County Probate*, Book 2: 15–17. This is a copy from the original — one of the few ancient wills remaining in the probate files of Plymouth County.

fifteene bushels of Good merchantable bread Corne, Annually paid & delivered to her and Sufficient and Convenient fire wood Cut and layd at her doore as she shall need yᵉ same The sd The said Ten pounds worth of Goods and two Cows with yᵉ twelve pounds in money to be at her own dispose as to her shall Seeme meet The other particulars to be for her Support & Comfort during her Remaining my widdow & no longer The sd ten pounds worth of Goods & Cows to be paid & Delivered to her by my Executors within two months after my decease The sd twelve pounds in money and other particulars to be paid & Delivered to her by my Eldest Son Joseph Stetson as follows that is to say yᵉ sd money at three Severall payments vizt four pounds to be paid within one year after my decease & other four pounds within two years after my decease & yᵉ Residue at yᵉ Expiration of three years after my decease the sd Bread Corne Summering & wintering sd Cows & fire wood provided to be annually delivered paid & performed by my sd Son as yᵉ same is above Expressed Always provided and it is yᵉ true Intent & meaning of this my will and yᵉ Condition of yᵉ bequests & Divice abovesd & Every particular of yᵉ same, That my sd wife shall & do within two months after my decease In writing under her hand & seale Absolutely Quit Claime to & Release her Right of Dower and power of thirds in and unto all my lands & housing in Scituate aforesd that she may thenceforth have or pretend to have in or unto yᵉ same or any part thereof * except what is above given to her unto my sd Eldest Son & his heirs &c Item I Give & bequeath to my Sd Eldest son Joseph Studson All that my Dwelling house out houses upland & meadows being yᵉ farm on which I now live & dwell to hold to him & his heirs for Ever according to yᵉ Known & accustomed boundaries of yᵉ same Excepting out of it onely one acre of meadow which I have formerly promised to Give to my son Samuel Lying next unto his other meadow which sd Excepted Acre of meadow I hereby Give & bequeath to yᵉ sd Samuel & his heirs for Ever Hereby Enjoyning my sd Eldest Son Joseph to

---

* As his wife Mary had children by her former husband, whom he considered spendthrifts, this provision was made in order that the homestead should be enjoyed by his eldest son, Joseph. Vide Barry's *Genealogy of the Stetson Family*, 1847 : 13.

pay deliver & perform unto my sd wife as abovesaid upon her Release of dower as above sd & acceptance of what is by this my will Given & bequeathed unto her which if She shall neglect deny or Refuse to do then I hereby declare that what I have above bequeathed unto her & Every particular of the same Shall thenceforth be null & void. further it is my will that my Sd Eldest Son Shall not alien or sell any of yͤ lands above Given him unless to his Children or one of them.

" Item I Give & bequeath to my son Benjamin Ten pounds out of my moveable estate.

" Item I Give & bequeath to my son Thomas five pounds to be paid to him out of my movables.

" Item I Give to my Son Samuel yͤ suᵐ of Eight pounds out of my movable Estate.

" Item I Give to my Daughter Eunice Rogers yͤ Suᵐ of ten pounds out of my movable Estate

" Item I Give to my son Robert my wearing Cloaths which with wt I have formerly Given him I Judge convenient for him. Item I Give to my Daughter in Law Abigail yͤ Relict & widdow of my son John deceased yͤ suᵐ of ten pounds to be paid to her out of my movables Estate.

" Item I Give unto my Grand children that are now Surviving to Each of them six shillings. Item my debts legacies & funerall Expences being paid I hereby order yͤ Residue of movables to be Equally divided betweene my three Children vizt Benjamin Samuel and Eunice Lastly I nominate & appoint my two sons namely Benjamin & Samuel Joynt Executors of this my last will & testament & hereby Revoak & make voyd any former will or wils by me made & declare this onely to be my last will & Testament

" In Testimony whereof I have hereunto sealed and Subscribed yͤ day & year first above written

The mark of Cornet

Robert  Stetson [seal]

" In presence of these witnesses
Joseph Bearstow
William Bearstow
Samˡ Sprague.

" on the fift day of march 1702–3 before Nathaniel Thomas Esq : the s^d Jòseph Bearstow William Bearstow & Samuell Sprague made oath y^t they did see & hear the aboves^d Robert Studson sign Seale & declare the above written to be his last will & testament & that he then was of a disposeing minde to the best of their knowledge & Judgments.

as attests Nathaniel Thomas Register."

" Scituate the 10 of february 1702–3
"An Inventory* of all the goods & Chattels of Cornet Robert Stedson Deceased as followeth taken by us whose names are hereunto Subscribed

Item in apparrill both linen & wooling – – – – – – – – –	5	10	..
Item in money & plate & books – – – – – – – – – –	2	8	..
Item four fether beds & furniture – – – – – – – – – –	27	..	..
one Couerled – – – – – – – – – – – – – – –	1	10	..
Item twenty fiue pair of Sheets – – – – – – – – –	20	1	..
in houshold linen pillow coats & table clothes napkins & Towels	5	15	..
in new linning & wolling cloth & leather – – – – – – – –	3	8	..
in pewter new & old – – – – – – – – – – – –	5	7	..
in Brass new & old – – – – – – – – – – – – –	6	..	..
more in Iron – – – – – – – – – – – – – – –	4	8	..
Iron old & new – – – – – – – – – – – – – –	2	16	.6
one old bed a flock bed & beding & baskets – – – – – –	2	..	..
in woll threed cooper ware & trays – – – – – – – –	1	8	..
in wooden dishes glass bottles Earthenware & Spoons – – –		8	..
in Prouition beefe Porke butter Cheese & Corn – – – – –	4	15	..
armes & amunition – – – – – – – – – – – – –	1	16	..
Chairs & Cushings & other small things – – – – – – –	..	15	..
in Chests boxes & table & forme – – – – – – – – –	.1	.8	..
in Sheep Cattle & horse – – – – – – – – – – –	16	.5	..
in lumber – – – – – – – – – – – – – – – –	..	18	..
two piggs – – – – – – – – – – – – – – – –	..	10	..

four pound of bullets one Shilling sence discouered
one bill of Seventeen pounds
as a desparate debt   Samuel Clap
Debts due from the Estate   Thomas King
                                                              Richard Dwelly "

[Sworn to by the executors, March 5, 1702–03.]

ISSUE BY FIRST WIFE

I. Joseph², b. June, 1639, bap. Oct. 6, 1645, in Scituate. His father bequeathed to him the homestead and "farm on

---

* *Plymouth County Probate*, Book 2 : 17.

which I now live & dwell;" and, like his father, he lived and died in Scituate. His will * was dated April 4, 1722, and his inventory May 8, 1724. The maiden name of his wife, Prudence, does not appear. Issue: 1. Joseph³, bap. June, 1667. 2. Robert³, b. Dec. 9, 1670. 3. Lois³, b. March, 1672; mar. —— Ford. 4. William³, b. Dec., 1673; d. Aug. 14, 1699. 5. Desire³, bap. Sept., 1676; mar. Aug. 16, 1703, to Richard Sylvester, of Scituate. 6. Prudence³, b. Sept., 1678; mar. Dec. 17, 1707, to Ebenezer Leach, of Bridgewater. 7. Samuel³, b. Dec., 1679. 8. Hannah³, b. June, 1682. In her father's will she was called Hannah Lincoln; it is probable that it was she who was mar. April 25, 1705, to Solomon Lincoln.

II. Benjamin², b. Aug., 1641, bap. Oct. 6, 1645, in Scituate. (Vide infra.)

III. Thomas², b. Dec. 11, 1643, bap. Oct. 6, 1645, in Scituate. His wife, whom he mar. in 1671, was Sarah, daughter to Anthony Dodson. As his will,† dated July 2, 1729, does not mention her, she probably had died previously. Issue: 1. Hannah³. 2. Thomas³. 3. Gershom³. 4. Sarah³. 5. Joshua³. 6. Caleb³. 7. Elisha³. 8. Elijah³. 9. Mary³. 10. Ebenezer³. 11. Ruth³. 12. Margaret³.

IV. Samuel², b. June, 1646, bap. July 12, 1646, in Scituate. He was prominent in town affairs, had the military title of sergeant, and was one of the executors of his father's will. His first wife, Lydia ——, was the mother of all his children. His second wife, Mercy or Mary ——, survived him. He died in 1687. Issue: 1. Samuel³. 2. Elizabeth³. 3. Lydia³. 4. Patience³. 5. Jonah³. 6. Mary³. 7. John³. 8. Silas³. 9. Seth³. 10. Nathaniel³. 11. Deborah³. 12. Rachael³.

V. John², b. April, 1648, bap. May 7, 1648, in Scituate. During the "Revolution of 1689," it was recorded, Dec. 25, "That John Stetson have 15ˢ pʳ weeke for his service, & being helpful to yᵉ comisary." ‡ For the Canada expe-

---

* *Plymouth County Probate*, Book 4: 417.
† *Plymouth County Probate*, Book 6: 296.
‡ *Plymouth Colony Records*, Court Orders, vol. 6: 229.

dition of 1690, under Sir William Phips, Scituate furnished sixteen men. Joseph Sylvester was Captain;
Israel Chittenden, Lieutenant; and John Stetson, Ensign. Ensign John Stetson served at the taking of Port
Royal and the attempt to take Quebec, and died during the expedition. In the settlement of his estate, the
Court ordered "that the oldest son John shall have and
enjoy the house and land which his father died seized
of," when said son shall attain to the age of twenty-
one years, he paying to his sister Honour and to Barnabas his brother, each of them, fifty shillings, when
they are twenty-one or are married, "which shall first
happen." The widow was to have the use of all goods
and chattels until the heir should come of age, for bringing up her children; she was to pay to Abigail, the eldest
daughter, and to Anne, the youngest, each fifty shillings upon marriage or at the age of twenty-one years.
The widow of Ensign John Stetson, in 1703, received
£10 from the estate of her father-in-law, Cornet Robert Stetson. Deane says that the name of this widow
was Mary, but the will clearly gives it Abigail. Issue:
1. Abigail³. 2. John³. 3. Honour³. 4. Barnabas³. 5.
Anne³.

VI. Eunice², b. April 28, bap. May 19, 1650, in Scituate; was
mar. to John² Rogers, son to John¹ Rogers. "Eunice
Rogers" was remembered by her father with a legacy
of £10.

VII. Lois², b. Feb., 1652, in Scituate; probably died before
her father, as he did not mention her in his will.

VIII. Robert², b. Jan. 19, bap. Feb. 26, 1653, in Scituate. The
year that he was married, 1676, his house was burned
by Indians. On June 3, 1684, he was chosen Constable
of Scituate,* but there is no record of his family in that
town. In 1711, he was of Pembroke, and in 1712, he
and his son Isaac were named in a list of the heads
of families there. His descendants have been noted for
mechanical ingenuity, and some have owned rolling-

---

* *Plymouth Colony Records*, Court Orders, vol. 6: 128.

mills. The wife of Robert Stetson was Joanna Brooks. Issue: 1. Isaac². 2. Timothy². 3. Resolved². 4. Sarah². 5. Nathaniel².

IX. Timothy², bap. Oct. 11, 1657, in Scituate; probably died before his father.

BENJAMIN² STETSON

Benjamin², second son to Cornet Robert¹ Stetson, was b. August, 1641, bap. October 6, 1645, in the Second Church of Scituate. At the age of twenty-four years, he married, August 15, 1665, Bethia², third daughter to Matthew¹ and Margaret Hawke, of Hingham.*

"Benjamin Studson" was chosen Constable for the town of Scituate, June 3, 1668; and again, June 2, 1685.† In 1684, he was on a committee to make the rate; June 2, 1685, he served on a jury at the General Court. As Benjamin "Stetson," he appeared as Deputy from his native town to the General Court, two sessions in the year 1691, commencing June 2 and July 7. ‡

When the Massachusetts Bay Colony lost her charter in 1684, and her civil rights under the rule of Sir Edmund Andros in 1686, the Plymouth Colony fared no better. "If the stronger colony fell prostrate, what could the weaker do?" The power of Andros terminated with his arrest, April 8, 1689, as a result of the insurrection spreading over the country, which he termed "a general buzzing among the people." Every effort was put forth to reunite the scattered forces of the two colonies in their respective governments, and the strongest men were sent to represent the several towns. These colonies gradually had been tending toward each other, and Benjamin Stetson's services in 1691, as Deputy, were in the last sessions of the Plymouth Colony

---

* Vide pages 702, 703.
† *Plymouth Colony Records*, Court Orders, vol. 4: 180; vol. 6: 166.
‡ *Plymouth Colony Records*, Court Orders, vol. 6: 263, 268.

Court.* On October 7, 1691, the two colonies were united under a new charter, as the Royal Province of Massachusetts Bay. The Governor was to be appointed by the Crown.

" Mr Benj^a Stutson " was Representative from the town of Scituate to the legislature of Massachusetts Bay in the sessions commencing May 31 and November 8, 1693. He also served in the same capacity, as "Capt Benj^a Stutson," May 9, 1700, and throughout that year.† "His Ex^cy Richard [Coote], Earl of Bellomont, &c," was then the Royal Governor.

A second company of militia was established at Scituate in 1695, and the town records state "that the Commands of Capt. Chittenden on the north, and Capt. Stetson on the south were to be limited by the first Herring brook." ‡ This year, probably, was the date of Benjamin Stetson's commission as Captain.

Captain Stetson was prominent in the church, as well as in civil and military affairs. In 1698, he was chosen with Deacon Thomas King " to go to the neighboring elders and acquaint them with our present state and condition and intreat their advice what sd. church may and ought to do." At a subsequent meeting they were appointed "to look out and get a minister for us." In 1702, he was chosen on a committee to settle Mr. Eels. In 1708, he was chosen with Mr. Collamore to make application to the town to rectify a mistake in laying out some of the parsonage land.§

He died May 4, 1711. His widow, "Bethya Stetson Relict of Capt Benj. Stetson late of Scituate deceased," was appointed administratrix of his estate, June 11, 1711; and, at the same time, a committee was appointed to appraise the land. The inventory, taken June 1, mentions books, arms and ammunition, beds and bedding, wool, linen, pewter and earthen ware, glass and iron, carpenter's tools,

---

* Vide page 580.
† *Massachusetts Archives*, Court Orders, vol. 6: 279, 300; vol. 7: 70.
‡ Deane's *History of Scituate, Massachusetts*, 1831: 131.
§ Barry's *Genealogy of the Stetson Family*, 1847: 49.

farming-tools, household furniture, corn and provisions, stock, wood, land in the woods, etc.[*]

The division of the estate, according to the account of Mrs. Bethia Stetson, "exhibeted June 27, 1715, and allowed," gave to the widow her thirds. "The Whole Sum to be divided amongst the Children, whereof the Eldest Son Benjamin hath a double Portion, is £164 : 2 : 10; Each Nineth Part or Single Share is the Sum of £18 : 4 : 9."

"Each of the childrean have had of their father's Estate in his Life time as their mother affirms

viz To Benjamin the Vallue of	1 : 17 : —	
To Samuel Nothing	— — —	
To James the Value of	1 : 17 : —	
To Bethia Andrews	15 : — —	66 : 3 : 6
To Hannah Tileston	8 : 9 : —	
To Deborah Fisher	20 : 10 : —	
To Eunice James	15 : 6 : —	
To Mary Partridge	3 : 4 : 6	

"The Eldest Son Benj[a] double portion is — 36 : 9 : 6, whereof he hath already had from his father 1 : 17 : — ; There remains due to him the Sum of 34 : 12 : 6.

And to Samuel remains the Sum of	18 : 4 : 9
And to James (deceased) his two children remains y[e] Sum of	16 : 7 : 9
And to Bethia Andrews remains the Sum of	3 : 4 : 9
And to Hannah Tileston remains the Sum of	9 : 15 : 9
And Deborah Fisher hath had more than her Portion	2 : 5 : 3
And to Unice James remains the Sum of	2 : 18 : 9
And to Mary Partridge remains the Sum of	15 : — : 3[†]"

It is not known when or where Mrs. Bethia Stetson died.

ISSUE

I. Benjamin[2], b. Feb. 16, bap. May 19, 1668, in Scituate, where he lived and died. He mar. Jan. 22, 1690, Grace Turner;

---

[*] *Plymouth County Probate*, Book 3 : 66, 67, 97.
[†] *Plymouth County Probate*, Book 3 : 381.

died about 1740.* Issue: 1. Matthew⁴. 2. Grace⁴. 3. Margaret⁴. 4. Benjamin⁴. 5. Bethia⁴, b. May 4, 1699; mar. Sept. 5, 1728, to Nicholas Powers. 6. Leah⁴. 7. Abijah⁴.

II. Matthew³, b. June 12, 1669, in Scituate; d. Nov., 1690, in the expedition of Sir William Phips to Canada. Matthew's father was appointed administrator of his estate.†

III. James³, b. March 1, 1670, in Scituate; mar. Nov. 26, 1696, Susanna Townsend, of Boston, and lived in Boston, where all his children were born. Issue: 1. Susanna⁴. 2. James⁴. 3. Lydia⁴. 4. William⁴. 5. John⁴.

IV. Samuel³, b. Oct., 1673, in Scituate. There is no record of his having any wife or family.

V. Bethia³, b. May 14, 1675, in Scituate; mar. June 23, 1697, to Stephen⁴ Andrews, son to Thomas³ and Ruth (——) Andrews, of Hingham.‡

VI. Mary³, b. April 21, 1678, in Scituate; mar. to —— Partridge.

VII. Hannah³, b. June 1, 1679, in Scituate; mar. to —— Tileston.

VIII. Deborah³, b. Dec. 3, 1681, in Scituate; mar. to Samuel [?] Fisher.

IX. Eunice³, b. March, 1683, in Scituate; mar. March 18, 1700, in Scituate, to Deacon John James, only son to John and Lydia (Turner) James. Deacon James was born in 1676, at about the time of the death of his father, who had been "wounded by the Indians." He was a prominent man in Scituate. Eunice, his first wife, died, leaving eight children; and he mar. in 1719, Lydia, daughter to Nathaniel Turner.§

X. Margaret³, b. Sept., 1684; d. Feb., 1685, in Scituate.

---

* *Plymouth County Probate*, Book 8 : 190.
† *Plymouth County Probate*, Book 1 : 74.
‡ Vide page 702.
§ Deane's *History of Scituate, Massachusetts*, 1831 : 293.

EDWARD⁷ SMALL, JR.

MARRIED

REBECCA⁶ PRATT

THE PRATT FAMILY

MATTHEW[1] PRATT

MATTHEW PRATT, the Weymouth Planter, is supposed to have come to New England with the Gorges Company that began the first permanent settlement at Weymouth, in August, 1623. He may have been a relative of Phineas and Joshua Pratt, who were at Plymouth in 1627,[*] but there is no record that establishes any connection. They all came from England, where the name of Pratt, which occurs among the earliest English surnames, is spelled variously in ancient writings. Some of its forms are: Prat, Prate, Pratt, Pratte; and, still earlier, Du Pre, De Preaux, de Pratellis, etc.; all supposed to have been derived from the Latin *pratum*, a meadow.

The Pratt family undoubtedly went to England from Normandy, where, in 1096, a number of that name joined the crusaders. In 1173, Hamelin and Matthew de Pratellis were of the party of the Earl of Chester and Ralph de Fouguers, who joined Louis of France in the revolt of Normandy against Henry II, in which all the sons of the King were engaged against their father. The Pratts appear in many counties of the British Isle, notably Suffolk, York, and Leicester, as Knights of the Shire and as members of Parliament. They also married into titled families, and one Matthew Pratt was the younger son of a British Lord. Another Matthew Pratt was the second son of John Pratt, of Appleby, County Leicester, whose will, dated July 7, 1611, was proved December 10, 1612.[†] It is known that Matthew Pratt, of Weymouth, was of a knighted branch, but the writer

---

[*] Vide page 356.   [†] Chapman's *Pratt Family*, 1864: 13, 15, 29.

has been unable to obtain copies of the papers sent over from England that prove it.

Little can be learned of the earlier years of Matthew Pratt in Weymouth, though the settlement there, called Wessaguscus, was second to that of Plymouth. It was the scene of the failure of Weston's Colony, upon the site now locally known as "Old Spain," in 1622, and of the more permanent settlement by Captain Robert Gorges, son to Sir Ferdinando Gorges, in 1623. On July 8, 1635, it was recorded : "There is leave graunted to 21 ffamilyes to sitt downe at Wessaguscus." On September 2, 1635, the name of Wessaguscus is "hereafter to be called Waymothe;" and, at the same session of Court, it was "Ordered that Waymothe shall have a Deputy." On May 13, 1640, "Mathewe Prat" was made a freeman of Massachusetts Bay Colony."* That year, a large body of new settlers arrived ; but it was not until December, 1641, that the dated town records were begun.† A few earlier items were incorporated, particularly of possessions of land. The First Church of Weymouth names 1623 as its date of organization, but all its records prior to 1724 were destroyed by fire.

Land was granted to Matthew Pratt at "A General Court holden at Boston the 7th day of 10th month, December, A. D. 1636;" it was recorded, with grants to other old settlers, on the earliest existing records of Weymouth : —

"THE LAND OF MATTHEW PRATT

"Twenty acres in the mill field twelue of them first giuen to Edward Bates and eyght acres to him selfe all ofit bounded on the East with the land of John Gill on the west with the land of Richard Wealing on the north with Rocky hill on the south with the land of Richard Addames and Thomas Baly also Eighteen ackers of vpland first giuen to Edward Bennet now in the possession of mathew pratt bounded on yᵉ east with the mill Riuer

---

on the west with John whittmans lot on the north with y⁰ mill ground on y⁰ south with y⁰ pond." *

Mill River flows from South Weymouth, in a northeasterly direction through Weymouth, into Whitman's Pond. Land that was bounded with Mill River on the east and "y⁰ pond" (not Whitman's, but a smaller pond) on the south, must have been a mile southeast of the present centre of Weymouth. There are several families of Pratt descent still living in the neighborhood, but their houses are of comparatively recent date.

The name "Macut Prat" appears among the names of "townsmen," or selectmen, signed to a report of their meeting, "the Last Day of the Last Month 1648." † In 1649 and 1650, he continued as townsman; but in the town-meeting of March, 1650–51, his name is not seen. His autograph again appears in "The names of the Townsmen . . . The first Day of the 12 moᵗʰ 1657."

" *macuth Pratt* " ‡

The same name, "macuth Pratt," is number two in a list, dated February 3, 1651, of those entitled to great lots, — "which great lots are to but on Hingham line on the East." §

As in other places, the early Planters of Weymouth were greatly troubled by the depredations of wild animals and birds; so much so that, in 1657, a bounty was offered by the town authorities for killing them :—

"[The] Town is Debitoʳ to seuerall [per]sons for Service done & vpon account as followtʰ: 1657 : 11moᵗʰ . . . To Macuth Pratt for a wolfe & woodp[ecker]: [£]1–6–8 payed in boards." ‖

---

* *Town Records of Weymouth*, vol. 1 : 18.
† *Town Records of Weymouth*, vol. 1 : 17.
‡ *Town Records of Weymouth*, vol. 1 : 39.
§ *Town Records of Weymouth*, vol. 1 : 281.
‖ *Town Records of Weymouth*, vol. 1 : 4.

In January, of that year, " it did appeare Then vpon account That Macuth Prat & his son Thomas had entred 22000 of boards the father 15000 & son 700, dew to the Town 1ˢ 9ˢ : 6ᵈ payd : 22: 10: 58."*

In the distribution of land by the selectmen, Matthew Pratt received grants, as follows : " 1658. The 17ᵗʰ Day of the 10 moᵗʰ" . . . it was "ordered also that Mar. Pratt should have a Swamp lot at the same place [the Great Swamp] to be layd out by Sergeant Whitmarsh." He also was to have four acres of upland, to be laid out in some convenient place "neere the head of the pond above the mill & Joyning to the Great lotts." On December 19, 1659, he was given "an Iland in the fresh pond above the mill as an addition to the fower acrees formerly graunted him ; " to which was added a lot in "guppies Swamp." † In the first division, Dec. 14, 1663, of "great Lotts" beginning on the Braintree line, " Micaeth Pratt " was granted ten acres in lot fifty-one; his sons Thomas, Matthew, and John, [   ] "Acres 4, Lot 62," "Acres 5, Lot 73," respectively. In the second division, that year, "Miceth Pratt" was assigned "Acres 30, Lot 52 ;" while his son Thomas received "Acres 21, Lot 20," and Matthew, "Acres 12, Lot 44." The son John was not mentioned in the second division.‡

The wife of Matthew [1] Pratt was Elizabeth Bate or Bates. She is said to have been daughter to an older brother of Elder Edward [1] Bates, of Weymouth, whom Matthew names in his will as "kinsman," but there is no evidence that the older men of the name in the town or state were related to Edward. It is more probable that Elizabeth was sister to Edward Bates. She was generously provided for by the will of her husband, of which she was made sole executrix. Very little of the property was to go to the children until after her death, which occurred in 1676.

---

* *Town Records of Weymouth*, vol. 1 : 38.
† *Town Records of Weymouth*, vol. 1 : 43, 47.
‡ *Weymouth Historical Society Collections*, 1885 : 282-283.

Matthew Pratt died October ("8$\underline{mo}$") 29, 1672, in Weymouth. His will, dated March 25, 1672, was proved April 30, 1673, as follows : —

"Macute Pratt of Waymoth being in health of bodie and having A Competet Use of his understanding and memory doe make this to be his Last Will * and Testament as folloe and saith

"first I doe and bequeath my soule to God that gave it and after my decease my Body to be deacently Buried and all my debts Honestly payd and then all my Worldly goods I disspose of thus

"I doe give to my Loving Wife Elisabeth Pratt all my Whole Estate reall and personall except that which is hearafter Exprest that is for her naturall Life

"I doe give to my sonn Thomas Pratt after my wives decease, these parsells of Land as folloe four Acres of Land that did belong to Shaws house And my share of Land that I bought of James Nash And that fiftene Acres I bought of Deacon John Roggers: And I doe give him that Little I Land in the fresh Pond: it I doe give him ten acres in the Ceder swamp Plaine which was a part of my great Lott: Ad I doe give him my share in the two acres and halfe of salt marsh at Hoclie (?) upon the condition he shall pay to my daughter Chard at my wives decease four pounds

"I I doe Give to my Sonn Mathew Pratt at my wives decease these parsells of House and Land as folloe my now dwelling House with all my Housing and all my orChards and my Land Ajoyning twenty acres be it more or Less: It I doe give him ten Acres in the Ceder Swomp Plaine which is alsoe a part of my gret Lott puided he pay to my daughter Chard or her Assignes three pounds at my wives Decease

"I doe give to my sonn John Pratt one ewe and Lamb.

"I doe give to my sonn Samuell Pratt twelve acres of Land neare his House four acres of it was William Brandems and eight acres of it was John Gurneyes and when he hath fenct it out as

---

* *Suffolk County Probate* (original) Docket: 645; also Book 7 (copy): 299–300.

far as it is Pasture he shall have it and not before And I doe give him one acre of salt marsh by John Pratts House at my decease: And I doe give him that pt of my Com̅on Lott Laid out to me at Smelt Brook It I doe give him my two aCres of Swomp Lott it is in the woods: It he shall have one Cow in stead of that spot I thought he should have in my orChard. I doe give to my sonn Joseph Pratt that Lott that was first Edward Bennetts at the pond twenty acres be it more or Less.

"I doe give to my daughter Chard seaven pound stirling in good pay at my wives decease which is to be paid by Thomas Pratt and Mathew Pratt as Above is expressed: it I doe give to her daughter Johanah Chard my best bed and Coverliad at my wives decease.

"I doe give to my daughter White after my wives decease all that parsell of Land that I have in wearieland which is of Marsh and upland about three or four acres which is all except that which is above given to my sonn Thomas Pratt: And I doe give her two ewes at my decease.

"I doe give to Thomas Pratts sonn William Pratt that halfe mare with her increase that is between Thomas Pratt and myselfe to be devided at my decease

"I doe give to my sonn Thomas Pratts Daughter Sarah five pounds at my wives decease.

"I doe Apoint my Loving wife to be my sole Exequitrix to fullfill all this my Last will and to have full power to improve my whole estate for her Life and at her decease to give what she Leafs to my Children and thire Children as she shall then please

"I doe desier the Reverent Pastor mr Samuell Torrey and my Kinsman Elder Edward Bate and my sonn Thomas Pratt to be the overseers to se that this my Last will be in all points fulfiled I doe alsoe commit full Power into the hands of these overseers to sell or dispose of Any thing that I have Left to my wife if she shall have need of it for her Comfortable Livelihood but not otherwise to despose of Any Land but as above expressed and heareunto I have Set my hand and Seale the twenty fifte of march 1672 "the Word Real in the fourth Line was entred before Sealing And the twenty sixt Line was blotted out before Sealing

Signed Sealed in the   MACUTH ⁑ PRATT   [seal]
presents of us
EDWARD BATE
THOMAS DYER

"At a County Court held at Boston Aprill 30th 1673 Elder Edward Bate & Thomas Dyer made Oath that having Subscribed theire Names as Witnesses to this will did see & hear Macute Pratt Signe Seal & publish it as his last will & Testament & wn hee soe did hee was of a sound disposing minde.

As Attests ISAAC ADDINGTON Cler./

Recorded May 20th 1673 p I. A. Cler.

"An Inventory * of the Estate of Macaieth Pratt who deceased the 29 . 8mo 1672 & apprized by us who were called thereunto the the 12th of the 10th month 1672 who have hereunto Subscribed o⁚ hands /

	£	s	d
Impr Dwelling House out housing & Orchard	30	0	0
6 acres of broken upland at 4£/6/8 p acre	26	0	0
15 acres of Woodland & unbroken is	25	0	0
30 acres of the second division of Town Comons	06	0	0
18 acres neere the dwelling house pasture land & some medow . .	45	0	0
one acres & halfe of broke upland neere ye dwelling house . . .	06	0	0
one acre of Salt Marsh lying by Jno Pratt his house	15	0	0
one acre & halfe of Salt Marsh neere hokely	15	0	0
20 acres at Cedar Swamp plaine	20	0	0
a little Island at the head of the great pond	02	0	0
wearing Cloathes	05	0	0
a ffeather bed	02	10	0
a boulster	01	0	0
two feather pillows	0	10	0
two pillow beers	0	05	0
two paire of Sheets	01	10	0
a flock boulster	00	05	0
a bed Rug	01	10	0
four brass kettles	01	10	0
one brass Skellet	00	03	0
two Candlestick & a brass pan	00	05	0

* *Suffolk County Probate*, Book 7 (copy) : 301-303.

	£	s	d
4 pewter platters	00	11	0
a pewter quart pot & a pewter pinte pot	00	04	0
two peeces of old pewter	00	01	6
two pot hangers & a paire of pot hookes & tongs	00	07	0
Earthen ware	0	01	6
Spoons 6ˢ & other house lumber	3	09	0
Sheeps Wool	01	03	0
Six Cows & a two year old bullock	20	0	0
Sixteen Sheep	06	0	0
5 Swine	03	0	0
horses in partner ship	06	5	0
of all sorts of Corn	06	0	0
In hay & Straw	06	0	0

The marke of the Tomas Done

"Memorandn

"Twelve acres neere Sam Pratts house in the possesion of Samˡˡ
Pratt before the decease of his father Micaeth Pratt ten yeer
or upward given in marriage . . . . 24 . 00 . 00
more ten acres of woodland at Smelt brook . . . . 05 . 00 . 0
& two acres of Swamp purchased by Samuell Pratt of his ffather
Micath pratt about 5 year before the sᵈ Micaths death . . . 01 . 0 . 0
20 acres above mentioned was halfe of it paide for before the
decease of the sᵈ Micath Pratt by Joseph Pratt his Sonne & the
whole 20 acres was possett by the said Joseph Pratt about seven
yeare before the saide Micath's decease   28 . 10 . 0
"the reason why the said Micath Pratt mentioned these lands
in his will was because hee gave them noe deede of gift of the
aforesaid lands

(Signed) EDWARD BATE
the marke of The Tmas Done

"Elizabeth Pratt made Oath in Court Aprill 30ᵗʰ 1673 that this paper con-
teines a just & true, Inventory of the Estate of her late husband Macute Pratt
to her best knowledge & that when shee knows more shee will discover the
same

As Attests Isaac Addington Cler
"Recorded May 20ᵗʰ 1673   p. I. A. Cler "

The amount of the inventory, £257 : 09 : 12, with the
value of the land which Matthew Pratt already had given to
his sons, Samuel and Joseph, £58 : 10 : 00, makes the estimated worth of the estate £315 : 19 : 12. In these papers
the name of the testator is spelled Macute, Macuth, Macaieth, Micath, and Micaeth, yet it appears in the list of

freemen as "Mathewe," and Matthew is generally conceded to have been his name. The date of death of Elizabeth, widow of Matthew Pratt, is not known.

ISSUE

I. John [2], b. about 1622, probably in England. He was made freeman of the Massachusetts Bay Colony, May 10, 1643,[*] which is proof that he was then of age. On Nov. 22, 1656, he mar. Mary [2], daughter to John [1] Whitman, of Weymouth ; she d. July 10, 1716, three months before her husband, aged eighty-two years.

John Pratt, lovingly called "uncle John" by his numerous nephews and nieces, exercised a fatherly care over the whole town. His house was a landmark ; and, in the affairs of his family and friends, he was sought as a witness, appraiser, or executor, again and again, particularly in the later part of his life. In 1684, and probably other years, he was Constable ;[†] he also held other town offices. He accumulated a considerable estate. By trade, he was a cooper; late in life, he was called a husbandman. No children are recorded, and he probably never had any, which would account for the small bequest of his father in his will of "one ewe and lamb."

John Pratt d. Oct. 3, 1716, in Weymouth, aged not less than ninety-four years. His will, signed with his autograph, "John Pratt," and dated July 12, 1714, was proved Nov. 19, 1716, at Boston,[‡] by William Dyer and Mary Dyer, executors. It said that he was "aged and weake in body but of Perfect mind & Memory;" provided that his wife Mary (who passed away before him) should enjoy the "whole estate," both real and personal, "for her Support and Comfortable Maintenance during her Natural life;" and set "at perfect liberty and freedom" his two "servants," or slaves, Ruth Pratt and Silence Critchfield, with presents of goods and money, and "Liberty to dwell in my house until

---

* *Massachusetts Bay Colony Records*, vol. 2: 293.
† *Weymouth Historical Society Collections*, 1885: 49.
‡ *Suffolk County Probate*, Book 19: 215-216.

they See Cause to Dispose of themselves otherways." John Pratt also gave to his "kinsman John Gurney Twenty and five pound when he Shall arive at the age of Twenty one years if he live with me so long as I live or to the age aforesaid;" to his "nephew Lieu' John Pratt [son to Samuel ⁹] of Weymouth," £10; and to his "nephew Deacon Thomas Pratt of North Purchase [Easton]," £10. To his nephew, Ebenezer ⁸ Pratt, youngest son to Samuel ², he gave the sum of "fourty pound if he Do bring up a Son of his at the Colledge and when he dose put his Son to the Grammar School, in Order there unto to have five pound paid to him and so five pounds ℟ year until the forty pound be paid." Lastly, he gave the "residue of my whole Estate," after his wife's decease, to Mary Dyer, daughter to Samuel ² Pratt, who had lived in his family before her marriage, and "now near two years Since She was married together with her husband William Dyer . . . provided they Continue with us and be faithful to and careful of us." By this arrangement he secured for himself and his wife the attention they needed in their extreme old age.

II. Thomas ², b. in Weymouth as early as 1626, since, on May 26, 1647, he became a freeman of Massachusetts Bay Colony.* His first wife was Mary ——— ; his second wife, who survived him, was the widow Lydia ———. In the first division of land in Weymouth, Dec. 14, 1663, Thomas Pratt is named with the grantees, but the amount of land is not given ; in the second division, 1663, he received twenty-one acres in lot number twenty, on the Braintree line. By the will of his father, dated 1672, he was to become the possessor of more than thirty acres of land, after the decease of his mother ; but he probably died before her, in the same year.

Sergeant Thomas Pratt, of the Weymouth Militia, was killed by the Indians not far from his home in Weymouth. The date is shown by the "Diary" of his eldest son, William, who wrote : "My father was slaine by the Indians the 19ᵗʰ day of April, in the year 1676." This encounter was the

---

* *Massachusetts Bay Colony Records*, vol. 2 : 295.

occasion of a petition from the Town to the General Court representing "the danger to the terror-stricken town and asking for protection, and at least that six men impressed for general service may be discharged and returned to the distressed town." William Torrey, Captain of the Weymouth Militia, also petitioned the Court that more "men should remain at home and defend their own firesides," for we "have the enemy appearing daily at our very doors, four killed already, all in danger wheresouer we go; in expectation euery day and hour of being assaulted, stand continually on our guard, whereby planting is obstructed and all things turning into confusion and destruction." * The losses which the town sustained in this war were sufficiently severe to induce the General Court to allow the abatement of a portion of its tax.†

Thomas Pratt left no will; but the inventory of the estate of "Serg.ᵗ Thomas Pratt of Weymoth, who was Slain by the Indians the 19ᵗʰ day of April 1676," ‡ was "apprized by Elder Edward Bate and John Kingman." Besides household goods, a variety of farming-tools, produce, and a few cattle, it mentions: "a dwelling house barne & part of the Orchard adjoining," £45; "13 acres ½ neere the house 4 acres by Richᵈ Fosters and 2 acres in weary land," £66; "¾ of Salt Marsh by bound brooke and 1 acre ¾ at Hockley," £20; marsh and land at "Drakes lott," £11.10; "18 acres at the old cedar Swamp plain" and "21 acres in the 1ˢᵗ and 2ᵈ division," £7; "13 acres of Land neare the house that was the widdow Pools house," £10; "a Sword," £6; "The Estate the widdow brought with her apprised — in pewter," £1 : 05 : 05; and "an Iland in the fresh pond about two acres," £2. Total value of the estate, £278 : 11 : 01.

Lydia Pratt, widow of Thomas, who had been appointed one of the administrators, "appearing in Court July 27, 1676," declared that she had agreed with John Pratt, the other administrator, as follows: "to bee paid . . . twenty

---

* *Massachusetts Archives*, vol. 68 : 79.
† *Weymouth Historical Society Collections*, 1905 : 50.
‡ *Suffolk County Probate*, Book 12 (copy) : 49–50.

pounds in money . . . and to have all the Estate Shee brought with her . . . in full of her Dower." "Brother John Pratt and brother-in-law White" were appointed guardians to the four children under age. In the division of the estate, Jan. 27, 1679–80, it was set forth that John Pratt, administrator and guardian, with Thomas White, the other guardian, and Ephraim Frost, husband of the eldest daughter, Hepzibah, agreed as to the division.*

Issue : 1. Hepzibah⁸, b. about 1653; since she is mentioned in the settlement of her father's estate, in 1676, as "about twenty-three years" of age. Before Jan. 27, 1679–80, she was mar. to Ephraim Frost.

2. Sarah⁸; called "helpless and incapable" in the settlement of the estate of her father. Her grandfather, in his will, left £5 to Sarah, daughter to his son Thomas, "at my wives decease."

3. William⁸. During his life he kept a little "Pocket Almanac, or Diary;" a few extracts from it best tell his history: "I was borne on the 6ᵗʰ of March in the year 1659. I was married the 26ᵗʰ day of Oct. in the year 1680. I removed from Waymouth to bridgewater the 19ᵗʰ day of December in the year 1705. — removed from Waymouth to dorchester about the middle of April in the year 1690. I was taken sick with the smal pox the 26ᵗʰ day of March in the year 1691. In the year 1697, the 16ᵗʰ day of December I was ordained Ruling elder of the Church of Christ. Swearing in a religious manner is a duty when called unto it."

This perhaps needs a little explanation. His wife was Elizabeth Baker, of Dorchester, in New England, who was b. 1655; d. Aug. 20, 1728, aged seventy-three years. In 1690, they removed from Weymouth to Dorchester, where he became interested in an organization "for Carrying the Gospel Ordinances" to South Carolina. In the "Brigantine *Friendship*," of Boston, he sailed with the expedition to Ashley River, above Charleston, where a town was planted named

* *Suffolk County Probate*, Book 6: 321–324.

Dorchester. It was there that he was ordained Ruling Elder over this small "religious colony." The climate did not agree with him, and he soon returned to Weymouth. In 1705, he removed to Bridgewater, Mass.; and subsequently (about 1711) to Easton, where he died Jan. 13, 1713. His grave and that of his wife are in the Old Burying-Ground at Easton.

The inventory of his estate, valued at £429 : 11 : 06, includes "two young negroes, £50 ;" their names were Heber and Hagar. They became the property of the widow Elizabeth, and lived with her until she gave them their freedom and a portion of land, in 1722. Heber was called "Heber Honesty," and "was held in good esteem by all." The widow Elizabeth was mentioned as "a person of excelling Piety and uncommon prudence . . . one of a Charitable spirit."

Issue: 1. Thankful⁴, b. Oct. 4, 1683, in Weymouth; mar. May 13, 1702, to Daniel Axtell, whose first wife was Lady Axtell. Daniel Axtell came to New England and settled in Taunton (now Berkley), where he died. The descendants of their ten children, the Cranes, Marshes, and others, of Berkley and Bridgewater, have been distinguished in many walks of life.*
Issue by second wife : I. Elizabeth Axtell, b. 1703. II. Daniel Axtell, b. 1704–05. III. Rebecca Axtell, b. 1706. IV. Hannah Axtell, b. 1710. V. William Axtell, b. 1713. VI. Henry Axtell, b. 1715. VII. Samuel Axtell, b. 1717. VIII. Ebenezer Axtell, b. 1724. IX. Thankful Axtell, b. 1725. X. Thomas Axtell, b. 1727.

4. Thomas³, b. in Weymouth. He was still under guardianship when his father's estate was divided, in 1679–80. His first wife was Deborah ——, who d. Jan. 12, 1727. He mar., second, March 5, 1729, Desire Bonney. About 1695, he removed to Middleborough ; was selectman, 1704, town treasurer, 1705. Soon after 1710, he went to Easton, Mass., where his children married and remained. At Easton, he was a deacon of the church ; also selectman. His uncle, John Pratt,

* Pratt's *Genealogy of the Pratt Family*, 1889 : 31.

who was his guardian after the death of his father, referred to him in his will as "Deacon Thomas." He d. Dec. 1, 1744, in Easton. The house which he built was standing, in 1889, at South Easton, and had "never passed out of the possession of the family." Issue by first wife : I. Thomas⁴. II. Mary⁴. III. Jane ⁴. IV. James⁴. V. Abigail⁴. VI. Hepzibah⁴.

5. Abigail ⁸, b. May 15, 1662, in Weymouth ; mar. to William Tirrell, son to William and Rebecca Tirrell.

III. Matthew², b. 1628, in Weymouth. He mar. Aug. 1, 1661, at the age of thirty-three years, Sarah, daughter to Enoch and Sarah Hunt. She was b. July 4, 1640; d. Aug. 3, 1729, in Weymouth.

Matthew Pratt received various grants of land from the town of Weymouth. After the decease of his mother, by the terms of his father's will he came into full possession of the homestead, "with all my Housing and all my orChards and my Land ajoyning."

Matthew Pratt and his wife were totally deaf; yet their large family of three sons and six daughters were carefully and intelligently reared, their infirmities not appearing in any of their descendants. The name of Matthew more frequently appears in this line than in any other.

Cotton Mather, in his " Magnalia," in connection with the ministry of the Rev. Thomas Thatcher, thus refers to the worthy couple : * —

"One Matthew Prat, whose religious parents had well instructed him in his minority, when he was twelve years of age became totally *deaf* through sickness, and so hath ever since continued. He was taught after this to *write*, as he had before to *read*; and both his reading and his writing he retaineth perfectly; but he has almost forgotten to speak; speaking but *imperfectly*, and scarce *intelligibly*, and very *seldom*. He is yet a very judicious Christian, and being admitted into the communion of the church, he has therein for many years behaved himself unto the extream satisfaction of good people in the neighbourhood. Sarah Prat, the wife of this man, is one also who was altogether deprived of her *hearing* by sickness when she was about the third year of her age; but having

---

* Mather's *Magnalia*, 1620-1698, vol. 1 : 494-495.

utterly lost her hearing, she utterly lost her *speech* also, and no doubt all remembrance of everything that refers to *language*. Mr. Thatcher made an essay to teach her the use of *letters*, but it succeeded not; however, she discourses by signs, whereat some of her friends are so expert as to maintain a conversation with her upon any point whatever, with as much *freedom* and *fulness* as if she wanted neither *tongue* nor *ear* for conference. Her children do learn her *signs* from the breast, and speak sooner by her *eyes* and *hands* than by their lips. From her infancy she was very sober and modest, but she had no knowledge of a Deity, nor of anything that concerns another life and world. Nevertheless, God of his infinite mercy has *revealed* the Lord Jesus Christ and the great *mysteries* of salvation by him unto her, by a more *extraordinary* and *immediate* operation of his own spirit upon her. An account of her *experiences* was written from her by her husband; and the elders of the church employing her husband, with two of her sisters, who are notably skilled in her way of conversation, examined her strictly hereabout: and they found that she understood the *unity* of the divine essence, the *trinity* of persons in the Godhead, the *personal* union in our Lord, the *mystical union* between our Lord and his church, and that she was acquainted with the impressions of *grace* upon a *regenerate soul*. . . . Yea, she *once* in her exercise, wrote with a pin upon a trencher, three times over, 'Ah, poor soul!' and therewith, before divers persons, burst into tears. . . . She was admitted into the church with the general approbation of the faithful, . . . and her carriage is that of a grave, gracious, holy woman."

This sketch of Matthew Pratt and his wife by Mather conveys to the thoughtful reader much of interest. It appears that they had some sort of a sign code, in which the sisters of Sarah Pratt also were skilled, that they used with considerable facility. Her writing " with a pin upon a trencher " is evidence that the endeavors of her pastor (the Rev. Mr. Thatcher) to teach her " the use of letters," were more successful than he thought; or that her husband had taught her later. The travail of soul through which she evidently passed, and catechising by the Elders of the church, were in accordance with religious methods of that time; and this " gracious, holy woman " was thus enabled to enjoy the privileges of church fellowship, which meant so much more to her than to others.

Matthew[2] Pratt d. Jan. 12, 1712–13, in Weymouth, aged eighty-five years. His will, dated July 30, 1711, was proved June 4, 1713, at Boston.* His three sons, Matthew, William, and Samuel, were named executors. He gave to his "Beloved wife Sarah Pratt" his dwelling-house and barn, with land adjoining, on "the way that leadeth to my Brother John Pratts house," together with all the personal estate, for life. The sons, Matthew and William, were to pay annually to their mother fifty and forty shillings, respectively. To his son Matthew he gave "All that my housing and Lands I bought of my cousin William Pratt," and other land; to his son William, various tracts of land; and to his son Samuel the homestead, after "my wifes decease." To his daughter, Susanna Porter, he bequeathed £10; to Mary Allen, £15; to Dorothy Whitman, £15; to Sarah Ford, £10; to Anne White, £13; and to his daughter, Hannah Whitmarsh, a lot of land "near the late Dwelling house of Samuel Whitmarsh in Weymouth." Stephen French, Sr., and Capt. John Hunt, "my loving Friends," he appointed to be "overseers." The will was signed with his autograph : —

"MATTHEW PRATT"

Nearly all the legacies were to be paid after the decease of his wife; in consideration of her infirmity, no inventory was taken of the estate until after her death, which occurred August 3, 1729, at the age of eighty-nine years. The inventory of the estate of "M.[r] Matthew Pratt of Weymouth" was taken Dec. 6, 1731, as follows : —

	£ s
"Imp.[rs] I or [?] Womans aparrell and a chest	18: 9
To one Feather Bed and one Straw Bed Cloathes belonging to said beds	7: 7
To Real Estate Housing and Lands	1301: 0
	[£] 1326: 16

Ezra Whitmarsh
Ebenezer Porter
Sam.[l] Badlam "†

---

* *Suffolk County Probate*, Book 18 (copy) : 109.
† *Suffolk County Probate*, Book 29 (copy) : 323–324.

Matthew Pratt, the eldest son, had long been a resident of Abington, William, the second son, died a year after his father, and Samuel, "one of the Surviving Executors," and the only son remaining in Weymouth, made oath that it was a true inventory of the estate of his father, at Boston, Dec. 13, 1731, before the "Honble Josiah Willard Esqr," Judge of Probate. Of all the sons of Matthew[1] Pratt, Matthew[2], Jr., despite his infirmity, became the wealthiest.

His widow, Sarah, conveyed, June 12, 1720, to her children, "land which descended to [the said] Sarah Pratt from her father Hunt." * She was at that time eighty years of age.

Issue: 1. Matthew[3], b. Sept. 18, 1665, in Weymouth; mar. Mary ——. She was b. Jan. 2, 1665; d. 1761, in Abington, aged ninety-six years. Matthew Pratt removed about 1713 from Weymouth to Abington, and died there July 1, 1746, aged eighty-one years. Issue: I. John[4]. II. Micah[4]. III. Samuel[4]. IV. Mary[4]; mar. to Rev. Samuel Brown, of Abington.

2. Mary[3], b. Nov. 27, 1669, in Weymouth; mar. to —— Allen.

3. Hannah[3], b. Nov. 3, 1670, in Weymouth; mar. to Samuel Whitmarsh.

4. Sarah[3], b. 1672; mar. to Isaac Ford; d. Sept. 16, 1788.

5. William[3], b. May 5, 1673, in Weymouth; mar. Hannah ——. He d. Sept. 18, 1714, and his widow, Hannah Pratt, mar. Dec. 23, 1719, Thomas Randall, of Easton. Issue: I. Sarah[4]. II. William[4]. III. Joshua[4]. IV. James[4]; d. young. V. James[4]. VI. Matthew[4]. VII. Ann[4]. VIII. Betty[4]. IX. Mary[4]. X. Hannah[4].

6. Samuel[3], b. April 3, 1676, in Weymouth; mar. Hannah ——; d. Oct. 16, 1715. Issue: I. Samuel[4]. II. Daniel[4]. III. Hannah[4]. IV. John[4]; d. young.

7. Dorothy[3], b. in Weymouth; mar. Aug. 13, 1700, to John Whitman.

8. Ann (Anne), b. Sept. 14, 1682, in Weymouth; mar. to Samuel White.

---

* *Suffolk County Deeds*, Book 34: 221.

9. Susanna⁸, b. Sept., 1684, in Weymouth; mar. to Thomas Porter.

IV. Samuel², b. in Weymouth; mar. Hannah Rogers. (Vide infra.)

V. Joseph², b. Aug. 10, 1639, in Weymouth; mar. May 7, 1662, Sarah Judkins. She was b. 1638; d. Jan. 14, 1726, aged eighty-eight years.

On March 11, 1673–74, "Joseph Pratt Wejm" was made freeman of Massachusetts Bay Colony.* That he was of "Wejm [Weymouth]" was recorded to distinguish him from another Joseph Pratt, who was made freeman the previous year.

Joseph² Pratt was the youngest son, and lived with his parents until about the time of his marriage. In the town records, where his birth, marriage, and death appear, he is shown to have been prominent not only in town affairs, but in the church. In 1666 and 1673, he was a fence-viewer; in 1667, he cut five hundred shingles for his house. He was appointed, in 1681, to cut five cords of wood a year for the pastor; in 1682, was on a committee to rebuild the meeting-house. In 1685, he was a "way-warden;" 1686, a surveyor; 1693, named a "freeholder;" 1706, surveyor of highways; 1709, chosen to lay off land adjoining his own. In 1710, eighty-seven rods of land were laid out for Joseph Pratt, senior, bounded by land owned by himself and Samuel Whitmarsh, who had married his niece. His occupation was that of a "husbandman."

The death of Joseph Pratt occurred Dec. 24, 1720, in Weymouth, at the age of eighty-one years; his will, dated March 5, 1718–19, was presented for probate, at Boston, on Feb. 10, 1720–21,† by his son Samuel, executor. To his aged wife, Sarah, he bequeathed all the "moveables and Household goods and a good convenient maintenance so that she may live comfortably upon the Income of my Estate to be brought in unto her by my Executor." To his son Joseph he left ten shillings beside what he already had given

---

* *Massachusetts Bay Colony Records*, vol. 4 : pt. 2 : 587.
† *Suffolk County Probate*, Book 22 (copy) : 80–81.

him; to his "Son John Pratt, Ten Shillings if he should ever
come hither again;" to his son William, five shillings "besides what he hath had of my Estate already." He gave
ten shillings to Aaron Pratt, his son-in-law, to be equally
divided between the children of "his late wife Sarah Pratt;"
to his daughter, Experience Battle, £8, "beside what she
has had;" and to his daughter, Hannah Hines (?), £5,
"beside what she has had." His son Samuel was appointed
the "only & sole executor," with the gift of all the "Housing
Lands Messuages and Tenements in Weymouth and all my
Meadow Land." This will was signed with the mark of
Joseph Pratt, probably from illness, as he mentioned himself, at that time, "through . . . Old Age weak in Body;"
it was witnessed by Edward Bate, John Reed, and Joshua
Torrey.

    Issue: 1. Sarah[8], b. May 31, 1664, in Weymouth; mar.
to Aaron Pratt, of Hingham, son to Phineas Pratt. She
d. July 22, 1706; her husband mar., second, Sept. 4,
1707, Sarah (Cummings) Wright, a widow, who d. Dec.
25, 1752. Aaron Pratt d. in 1735, aged eighty-one years.
As the dates of births of the children are not known,
they cannot be arranged in proper order, neither can
the children be separated as belonging to the first or
second wife.

    Issue : I. Henry Pratt. II. Daniel Pratt. III. Aaron
Pratt. IV. John Pratt. V. Jonathan Pratt. VI. Moses
Pratt. VII. Sarah Pratt. VIII. Mercy Pratt. IX.
Elizabeth Pratt. X. Hannah Pratt. XI. Nathaniel
Pratt. . XII. Phineas Pratt. XIII. Benjamin Pratt.

    2. Joseph[8], b. Feb. 2, 1665, in Weymouth; mar., first,
Sarah Benson, of Hull, by whom he had twenty children. He lived to a great age, and his will, dated
March 13, 1755, when he was ninety years of age,
mentions but seven of them.

In 1704, he sold a mill at Abington, and soon after removed to Bridgewater. As Joseph Pratt, Jr., he was a
fence-viewer, surveyor of highways, etc., in Weymouth. In
Bridgewater he served on the grand jury, Feb. 17, 1720, and

as selectman in 1739. He was called "Little-leg Joe," on account of one leg being a trifle short.

The wife of his old age, whom he mar. Dec. 14, 1721, in Bridgewater, was Ann Richards; she d. March 21, 1766, aged ninety-two years. "The Boston News-Letter" of January 31, 1765, gives the following account of his death: "On the fourteenth of this month died at Bridgewater Joseph Pratt, aged 100 years. A man of good character and religious profession. He had twenty children by his first wife, but none by his second, who still survives him, about 90 years of age."

> Issue by first wife: I. Joseph⁴. II. Nathaniel⁴. III. Benjamin⁴. IV. Solomon⁴. V. David⁴. VI. Samuel⁴. VII. Sarah⁴; mar., 1728, to Ebenezer Snow; d. before 1655.

3. John³, b. May 17, 1668, in Weymouth; mar. Mercy Newcomb. He was mentioned in his father's will; the date of his death is not known.

> Issue: I. John⁴, b. May 8, 1692; d. young. II. John⁴, b. May 26, 1696; married and had nine children.

4. William³, b. in Weymouth; mar. Experience King.

> Issue: I. Joanna⁴. II. William⁴. III. Isaac⁴. IV. Experience⁴. V. Ann⁴.

5. Ephraim³, b. in Weymouth; mar. Phœbe ——; d. about 1745. His widow, Phœbe Pratt, d. Dec. 2, 1736. The will of Ephraim Pratt, dated Feb. 9, 1740–41, was proved Feb. 7, 1748, at Boston; the inventory of his estate amounted to £191 : 08.*

> Issue: I. Ephraim⁴. II. Phœbe⁴. III. Joseph⁴. IV. John⁴. V. Mary⁴.

6. Experience³, b. in Weymouth; mar. to —— Battle.

7. Hannah³, b. in Weymouth; mar. to —— Hines (?).

8. Samuel³, b. in Weymouth; was the executor of his father's estate. In 1710, land was granted by the town of Weymouth to Samuel Pratt, son to Joseph Pratt. Little is known of him, probably because of his removal elsewhere.

---

* *Suffolk County Probate*, Book 42 (copy): 164–168.

VI. Elizabeth[2], b. in Weymouth; mar., as his second wife, William Chard, of Weymouth. They were married by Capt. John Torrey, Nov. 22, 1656, at the same time that her brother, John[2] Pratt, married Mary[2] Whitman. The first wife of William Chard was Grace ——, who d. Jan. 23, 1655.

On Nov. 26, 1651, William Chard was granted lot number fifteen, in the "great lots on the East side of Fresh Pond, next to Mrs. Richard's mill." In the first division of the grant of 1663, he received "Acres 6, Lot 12," and in the second division, "Acres 18, Lot 53,"* on the west side of the town near the Braintree line. He was the schoolmaster of Weymouth almost continuously from April 10, 1667, to 1696; he also was chosen the first Town Clerk, and continued in that office many years. As the "Town Scrivener" he wrote many wills, as well as conveyances of land and public documents. On June 24, 1689, in a town-meeting, he was reëlected Clerk; and, at the same time, was appointed "to Ring the Bell & Sweep the Meeting house," his services to begin July 6, 1689. The pay for the latter was to be "forty shillings a year in money, or three pounds in town pay."

William Chard removed about 1696 to Abington, where he probably died. Elizabeth Chard d. Feb. 26, 1726, in Weymouth.

    Issue by second wife: 1. Thomas Chard, b. Sept. 27, 1657. 2. A child, b. March 22, 1659. 3. Caleb Chard, b. Oct. 19, 1660. 4. Mary Chard, b. April 8, 1663. 5. Samuel Chard, b. Oct. 1, 1665. 6. Joanna Chard, b. Aug. 17, 1667. 7. Patience Chard, b. April 20, 1671. 8. Hugh Chard, b. Jan. 4, 1674.

VII. Mary[2], b. in Weymouth; mar. to Thomas[2] White, of Braintree, son to Thomas[1] White, of Weymouth. Thomas[2] White was made freeman in 1681; d. April 11, 1706.

    Issue: 1. Thomas[3] White; mar., first, Mehitable Addams; mar., second, Mary Bowditch. 2. Mary[3] White; mar. to Thomas Holbrook. 3. Samuel[3] White, b.

---

* *Weymouth Historical Society Collections,* 1885: 281, 282, 283.

Sept. 19, 1676; mar., first, Deborah Penniman; mar., second, Sarah Torrey. 4. Joseph[3] White; mar. Sarah Bayley. 5. Ebenezer[3] White, b. 1683; mar. Lydia ——.

VIII. Sarah[2], b. in Weymouth; mar. about 1671, to John[2] Richards,* son to William[1] and Grace (Shaw?) Richards. William Richards was at Plymouth, March 25, 1633, but removed about 1635 or 1636 to Scituate. In 1645, he was at Weymouth, where he served in 1659 as Constable. His will, dated Jan. 18, 1680, was proved July 25, 1682;† it mentioned wife Grace and sons John, Joseph, James, William, and Benjamin.

John[2] Richards purchased land in Weymouth, in 1678, of John and Jane Lovell; took the freeman's oath Oct. 12, 1681. He died intestate; the inventory of his estate, taken Dec. 23, 1695, amounted to £202 : 13. His widow survived him.

Issue: 1. Sarah[3] Richards, b. June 20, 1672. 2. Bathsheba[3] Richards, b. Nov. 16, 1674. 3. John[3] Richards, b. Feb. 20, 1679; d. May 15, 1712. 4. William[3] Richards, b. April 12, 1685; d. May 25, 1712. 5. Ephraim[3] Richards, b. April 30, 1687; mar. 1715, Mary Vining. 6. Grace[3] Richards, b. March 16, 1689. 7. Lydia[3] Richards, b. Nov. 8, 1691.

SAMUEL[2] PRATT

Samuel Pratt, fourth son to Matthew[1] and Elizabeth (Bate) Pratt, was born about 1637 in Weymouth, but the date of his birth is not upon the records. He married September 19, 1660, Hannah[2], daughter to Deacon John[1] Rogers, of Weymouth.

Deacon John Rogers was in Weymouth before 1643, and probably was the John Rogers who was admitted freeman with Edward Bate, March 13, 1638–39.‡ He often has been

---

* Mr. Quincy L. Reed, who is well known in Weymouth as an antiquarian, is authority for this statement.

† *Suffolk County Probate*, Book 6 : pt. 2 : 388–389.

‡ *Massachusetts Bay Colony Records*, vol. 1 : 375.

confounded with others of the name who were early residents of Plymouth, Duxbury, Marshfield, and Scituate. Mr. Drummond, in his exhaustive researches to separate these men, believes that John Rogers of Weymouth "must have lived there for some years previous" to 1643; and that Judith, his widow, was probably a second wife.* He was selectman in " 1645, 1646, 1652, when, as such, he witnessed the addition to the Indian deed of Weymouth, 1654, 1655, 1657, 1659," and other years; in 1651, he was chosen "town recorder." He died in Weymouth, February 1, 1661. The will of "Deacon John Rodgers [dated] this 8 12mo 1660" (written in the third person), bequeathed to his wife Judith the life use of her thirds; gave legacies to his son John, "without wife or child," to his daughter Mary Kane, wife of John Kane, to his daughter Lydia White, wife of Joseph White, and to his daughter Sarah Pratt; to his daughter "Hannah Pratt five pound." Samuel Pratt (not called son-in-law) was to have the son John's portion in case the latter died unmarried;† John, however, married January 29, 1662–63, Mary[2], daughter to Elder Edward[1] Bate, of Weymouth, by whom he had several children.

Samuel Pratt was made freeman of the Massachusetts Bay Colony, May 23, 1666.‡ He was a large land-owner in Weymouth, and frequently filled town offices. On July 16, 1673, Samuel Pratt, of Weymouth, carpenter, and Hannah his wife, conveyed, for a valuable consideration, to his brother, John Pratt, one acre of salt marsh near John's house.§ By the terms of his father's will, Samuel Pratt was to receive "twelve acres of Land neare his House . . . and when he hath fenct it out as far as it is Pasture he shall have it and not before;" also an acre of salt marsh by John Pratt's house, which he conveyed to John, as above, soon

* *Maine Historical Society Collections*, 1896: 275–300.
† *Suffolk County Probate*, Book 1: 364.
‡ *Massachusetts Bay Colony Records*, vol. 4: pt. 2: 582.
§ *Suffolk County Deeds*, Book 10: 172.

after it came into his possession. To this was added a part of the "Com̄on lot . . . at Smelt Brook," two acres of swamp land in the woods, and "one Cow in stead of that spot I thought he should have in my orChard."

The exact date of the death of Samuel Pratt is not known; but he died between April 12, 1679, the date of his will, and September 5 of that year, when his inventory was taken. His age is supposed to have been about forty-two years. The seven children were all minors; John, the eldest, being sixteen. His will, written by another in a small hand very difficult to decipher, is signed with his mark, probably because of illness: —

"Samuel Pratt of waymoth being Sicke and werke and minding his mortallety Though at the psent of rationall vnderstanding and of a desposing minde doth make this to be his Last will and Testament * ffirst I doth giue my Soull and body vnto god that gaue it and after my decese doe apoint my body to be desently buryed and my funerall Exspenses discharged and my just debts honestly paid and for all the rest of my worly Estate I despose of as foloeth

"I doe apointe my Loueing wife and my brother John Roggers to be my Executores and to do in all things as becometh Executores and my will is that they shall haue honest Satisfextion for there paines and charge about it and forder I doe Leue my my holle estate in my wifes hands vntill my children are of age as Long as She conteniou my wedow and what I doe giue to my children thay shall haue it eury one of them as Sone as he or She is twenty and one years ould and whene euer my wife hanah Pratt doth mary that then She Shall haue twenty pounds starling paid to her and after that She Shall not improue any of my estat but as an Executore to the fullfilling of this my will

"fforder I doe giue vn to my Son John Pratte one halfe that Land as Lyeth between John Prattes Land and Elder bates Land that the west end of that Land

---

* *Suffolk County Probate* (original), Docket: 1117; also Book 6 (copy): pt. 2: 476–479.

"fforder I doe giue vnto my Son Samuel Pratte half that Lotte at pen^e plaine *

"fforder I doe giue vnto my Son Ebenezear Pratt one halfe of all my housing and Land ajoyening to it one halfe of it

"fforder I doe giue vnto all the rest of my children Seuen poundes Sterling apese euery one of them Seuen pound and all this as I haue apointed for my children it is my will that it Shall all be paid and deleuord vnto them as Sone as thay ar of the age aboue Said

"fforder my Will is that my Sone John Pratt Shall haue the other halfe of that Lott as he is to haue one half when he is of age when my wife is desesed and he is of age or when my wife is maryed and also that then he Shall haue one acor of fresh medow which is in my forty acor Lott ner pen plain and also one acor of my Salt medow vpon hingham fresh reuer if it be not Spent in my wife wedohod or in bringing vp of my children

"and my Will is that my Son Samuel Pratt Shall haue after my wifes desese and he is of age the remainders of my Lott at plen plaine as he is to haue eighteen acores when he is of age if it be not Spent in my wifes wedouhod or in bringing vp of the children also with one acor of Salt medow at hingham fresh reuer

"and fforder my will is that my Son Ebenesar Pratt Shall haue the other part or halfe of my houseing and and Land with

---

* A river that flows from the Rockland line through the swamps to the Fair Grounds at South Weymouth was anciently called Pen River, because near the river was a "pen" in which sheep were enclosed before shearing. The plain near by was known as Pen Plain, later Dyer's Plain.

Another plot of land in Weymouth, "wearieland," mentioned in the will of Matthew[1] Pratt, is said by Mr. Quincy L. Reed to have probably taken its name from "Weary All Hill," now called Otis Hill, in Hingham. The land between the hill and the Weymouth line, including part of Weymouth, may have been known as Weary Land. In that vicinity the United States government has secured a site for a naval magazine.

"Hoclie," also mentioned in the will of Matthew[1] Pratt, was a familiar landmark for years. In 1752, it is described in a deed as "Hockley's Meadow," lying partly on land owned by "the heirs of William Dyer . . . partly on Joshua Lovet . . . and Northerly on the Dam including the Dam." (*Suffolk County Deeds*, Book 89: 243.) To-day it is known as a tract on the banks of Back River, at East Weymouth. Vide pages 734, 1733.

one acor of Salt medow at hingham fresh reuer that Land is a joyning to my house as he was to haue the other halfe when he was of age this halfe he Shall haue after my wife is desesed or mayed and he is of age if it be not Spent in my wifes wedowhod or in bringing up of my children

"and fforder my Will is that my wife hanah Pratt Shall despose of all the rest of my Estat as She pleseth with that prouser that She giue it to my children

"and fforder it is my will that my daughters Legasyes Shall be equaly tacen out of my three Sones portiones if my Sones doth not paiy them other wise and that my Executores Shall Se it don

"fforder my will is that my brother Joseph Pratt and John Richards and Samull white Shall be ouerSeuers to this my Last will and testament to Se it be don acording to what is here writen

"and by this my Last will I doe make void and null all my former wills and Testementes of this nature and that this is my Last will and Testement I doe for the rateficatyon and Conformatyon here of Set to my hand and Sele and doe publish this to be my Last will and Testement this twelvth Day of Aprill in the year of our Lord god one thosand Six hundred Seuenty and nin

Signed Seled and deleuord
in the presentes of vs
  John Rogers
  Jonas Humfrye
  Joseph Lyan

fforder it is my will that my Son John prat shall haue nin acors of Land more which Lieth in part of to Lotes of tow Lowr deuesones [divisions] this is besides what my wife is to despose of

the marke of

Samull   Pratt   (seal)

"John Rogers and Jonas Humfrys made oath. before the Worpp.ll Tho: Danforth Esq.r Deputy Gov.r and Humphry Davie Esq.r Assis.t 16. octob.r 1679. that they were present and did see Sam: Pratt Signe and Seale and heard him publish this Instrum⁸ to bee his Last will and that then hee was of a disposing minde to their understanding

attests. J. Addington Cler

Examin.⁴ p.ʳ Jsaac Addington Cler "

" A true Inventory of the Estate of Samuel Pratt late of Weymouth . Dece⁴ apprized . 5. 7ᵐᵒ 1679. by us whose names are Subscribed.*

	[£]	[s]	[d]
Imp.ʳ To Wearing Apparrell	6	"	"
To a Dwelling House, Barn and 13 Acres of Land adjoneing	65	"	"
To. 3 Acres of Salt meadow at fresh River	30	"	
To. a Lot of Land 12 Acres neere Hezekiah Kings house	24	"	
To. 40 Acres of Land neere the Pen plaine	40	"	
To. the Wood and timber. of 15 Acres in the 2.º Division	2	"	
To. about 15 Acres of Land in the 2.ᵈ Division	3	"	
To. 3 Acres of Cedar Swamp at the head of the pond	6	"	
To. one small Lot neer the great Marshes	3	"	
To. a part of two Lots in the first Division	2	"	
To. 2 Oxen £7. three Cows, 2. heifers 15ˡⁱ is	22	"	"
To. 1 yearling bullock 30ˢ thirty Sheepe 6ˡⁱ is	7	10	"
To. 6 Swine 5ˡⁱ one more and 1 horse 4ˡⁱ 10.ˢ is	9	10	"
To. 1 Cart and Wheeles and plough and tacklin	7	10	"
To. 1 ffeather bed and bolster. 3ˡⁱ Six p.ʳ of Sheets 3ˡⁱ	6	"	"
To. 1 Table cloth and napkins 1ˡⁱ one Rugg 6.ˢ 3 coverlits 3ˡⁱ	4	"	"
To. 4 pillowbeers 10.ˢ three ffeather pillows 12.ˢ	1	2	"
To. 5 blankets 30.ˢ one p.ʳ of Curtains and valents 12.ˢ	2	2	"
To. 1 bed ticking and fflock bed	1	10	"
To. Bed steeds bed cords and Bed matts	"	8	"
To. 28ˡⁱ of cotton Woole 21.ˢ twenty pound of Sheeps Woole 12.ˢ	1	13	"
To. 14ᵈˢ of Woolen Cloth 2ˡⁱ — 25 y.ᵈˢ cotton Cloth 2ˡⁱ	4	"	"
To. a Remn.ᵗ of Red Cotton 5.ˢ blew Linnen 3.ˢ	"	8	"
To. a Long Table 15.ˢ two Chests 4 Boxes 12.ˢ	1	7	"
To. 4 Chaires one Cushin	"	5	"
To. 1 musket Sword Cutleasce Bandileers	1	10	"
To. 1 Saddle 10.ˢ Brass and pewter 30.ˢ is	2	"	"
To. 1 Jron pot; Jron kettle 6.ˢ ffrying pan tongs 6.ˢ tramel	1	10	"
To. Bookes 10.ˢ Wooden ware 30.ˢ	2	"	"
To Spinning Wheele Cards and Reele	"	8	"
To. 1 Table and forme 10.ˢ 22ˡⁱ of Woolen yarn 33.ˢ	2	3	"
To. Carpenters Tooles and other Jron tooles	1	10	"
To. a Remn.ᵗ of Searge 26.ˢ English grain in the Barn 7.ˡⁱ	8	6	"
To. 2 Acres of Indian Corne 2.ˡⁱ Hay 3ˡⁱ	5	"	"
To. Lumber and things y.ᵗ may bee forgotten	1	"	"
Sume totall	275	12	"

Edward Bate ·/ Stephen ffrench.

"John Rogers and Hannah Pratt Exec.ᵣˢ made oath before Tho: Danforth Esqᵗ. Depᵗ. Govᵣ. and Humpᵗ. Davie Esqᵗ. Assist. 16ᵗ. October. 1679. to the truth of this Jnventory being so they at present know and wᵗ more appears to cause it to bee added./

attests. Jsᵉ: Addington Cler."

The town records of Weymouth * state that Hannah, widow of Samuel Pratt, died October 16, 1715.†

ISSUE

I. "Judah [ᵉ], son of Samuell & Hanna pratt Born June 25 — 1661," ‡ in Weymouth; died before his father made his will.

II. John ⁸, b. Aug. 17, 1663, in Weymouth; mar., first, Mary —— ; mar., second, Elizabeth, daughter to Thomas Swift, of Milton. She d. Dec. 25, 1736, aged seventy-five years; and he mar., third, Dec. 8, 1737, Sarah Gardner, or Garner, a widow, of Hingham.

John Pratt early in life attained the rank of Lieutenant, and as "Lieut. John," his name frequently appears on the town records in positions of trust and honor. He was a man of great energy, not only in the affairs of the town and military matters, but also in the church. His pew was near that of his brother Ebenezer, "on the west side of the great dore " of the meeting-house, for which he paid £3. Lieutenant John ⁸ Pratt was mentioned in the will of his uncle, John ² Pratt; he d. Feb. 8, 1743-44, in Weymouth, aged eighty-one years.

Issue by first wife : 1. Samuel ⁴, b. Oct. 15, 1683, in Weymouth.

Issue by second wife : 2. Nathaniel ⁴, b. Oct. 26, 1702, in Weymouth. 3. Thomas ⁴, b. Jan. 3, 1705, in Weymouth.

III. Hannah ⁸, b. Dec. 21, 1665, in Weymouth; mar. in 1699, to Ebenezer Shaw, of Hingham.

---

* *Town Records of Weymouth*, vol. 1 : 20.

† It also is said that the widow, Hannah (Rogers) Pratt, mar. Thomas Bailey, Jr., after the death of his first wife, Ruth, daughter to Richard ¹ Porter; and that Hannah Bailey had a son, Thomas Bailey, b. April 24, 1687, and that her death occurred May 29, 1721, at the age of seventy-seven years. Vide Porter's *Genealogy of the Porter Family*, 1878: 13-14.

‡ *Town Records of Weymouth*, vol. 1 : 102.

IV. Mary[2], b. March 3, 1668, in Weymouth; mar. about 1712 to William Dyer. She lived with her uncle, John[3] Pratt, for many years, and received by his will a valuable property.[*]

V. Samuel[3], b. Nov. 15, 1670, in Weymouth; mar. Patience ——, b. 1675; d. Jan. 8, 1735, in Taunton. They removed soon after the birth of their first child, in 1695, to Taunton, that part of the town later set off as Norton. He was a man of considerable prominence, owning a large estate. His will was dated July 31, 1728, and his death occurred in Taunton, Aug. 11, following. Inventory, £300.

Issue: 1. Judith[4], b. Nov. 23, 1695, in Weymouth; mar. to William Caswell. 2. Samuel[4]. 3. Josiah[4]. 4. Jonathan[4]. 5. Benjamin[4], b. 1705; d. June 29, 1785. 6. Peter[4], b. 1711; d. Feb. 16, 1760. 7. Paul[4]. 8. Hannah[4]. 9. Patience[4]; mar. Jan. 2, 1734, to Moses Knapp, Jr.

VI. Experience[3], b. Jan. 8, 1672, in Weymouth.

VII. Ebenezer[3], b. 1674, in Weymouth. (Vide infra.)

EBENEZER[3] PRATT

Ebenezer[3] Pratt, youngest child to Samuel[2] and Hannah (Rogers) Pratt, was born in 1674, at Weymouth. He mar., first, about 1700 or 1701, Martha ——, who was the mother of all his children; she d. May, 1720. He mar., second, Dec. 25, 1720, the widow Waitstill Washburn, of Bridgewater; mar., third., Hannah ——, who survived him. He paid £4 5[s] for a pew in the meeting-house, on the "west side of the great dore," near that of his eldest brother, John; and was active in matters pertaining to the welfare of the church. He also held a number of town offices.

On March 6, 1699–1700, Ebenezer Pratt and Martha, his wife, conveyed, for £85, to Robert Waterman, of Hingham, "a dwelling house & Barn & about Thirty acres of Land," in Weymouth, near the Elder's Mill-Pond, which he inherited from his father. It was bounded on the north by land of

---

[*] Vide page 737.

John Pratt, of Bridgewater, late of Weymouth ; on the west
"by yᵉ said Fresh pond." They also gave a deed, on the
same day, for £20, of an acre of salt marsh to Nathaniel
Nichols.* It is probable that, after this sale of the homestead near the centre of the town, Ebenezer removed to
North Weymouth, and built the house afterward occupied
by his son Samuel. To enlarge his estate in that section of
the town, " Ebenezer Pratt Senʳ of Weymouth, Weaver," purchased of John Pratt, Sr., and Elizabeth, his wife, for £450,
on January 18, 1724-25, sixteen acres ; described as bounded
" Northerly partly by land belonging to Humphreys & partly
by land lately sold to Philip Torrey westerly by the Towns
Common Southerly and Easterly by the Land of Ebenezer
Pratt aforesaid." † By will, Ebenezer Pratt divided all his
real estate between his two sons, Ebenezer and Samuel,
the latter to have "the North end of my dwelling house he
now lives in, and also My Barn ; " and by the above boundary
lines his land can be traced for several generations.

Ebenezer Pratt was identified with the establishment of
the fishing trade between Weymouth and Cape Sable. At
a town-meeting held March 7, 1715, "John Torrey, James
Humphrey, Joseph Torrey, Ezra Whitmarsh, Enoch Lovell,
Ebenezer Pratt & divers others their partners who had
agreed to begin a fishing trade to Cape-sables, requested of
the town that they might have that piece or parcel of land
at the mouth of the fore river in the northerly part of Weymouth called and known by the name of Hunts Hill and the
low land and Beach adjoining thereunto, that is so much as
they shall need for the management of said trade. The
Town after consideration thereof Voted that they should
have the said land and Beach to manage their fishing
trade." ‡

---

* *Suffolk County Deeds*, Book 20 : 13-17.
† *Suffolk County Deeds*, Book 40 : 211-212.
‡ *Proceedings on the 250th Anniversary of the Permanent Settlement of Wey-
mouth*, July 4, 1674 : pub. 1874 : 61.

By the will of his uncle, John[2] Pratt, Ebenezer was to have £40, "if he Do bring up a Son of his at the Colledge." It does not appear, however, that either of his sons enjoyed an extended education.

The death of Ebenezer Pratt occurred about January, 1751–52, at the age of seventy-four years; he was buried in the "Old Burying-Ground" opposite the Pratt Schoolhouse, in North Weymouth. His will, dated Dec. 5, 1744, was proved Feb. 11, 1752; it is unique in that every line but three, except the seven interlined before signing, begins with a capital letter. The will was written in a large, clerkly hand by another, but the signature is his own autograph : —

" In the name of God Amen :
 I Ebenezer Prat of Weymouth, within the County of
ᛁ Suffolk, in his majesties province, of the Massechusetts bay
 In New England, being of a Sound, disposing mind and
 Memory, but calling to mind, the mortality of the Body and
 That it is appointed, for all men once, to die, do make, and
 Ordain, this my last will, & testament : * Committing my body
 To Earth, to christian decent burial, at the discretion
 Of my Executors, & recommending my Soul to God, through
 Jesus Christ, in hopes of a Joyful union, at the resurrection
 Of the Iust, as touching Such worldly goods, that God my
 Bountifull benefactor, hath graciously, bestowed upon me
 I do will, and bequeath, them as follows : ∿ ∿ ∿ ∿ ∿
Imprimis I do give and bequeath, Unto Hannah my well beloved wife,
 The South end of my dwelling house, four barrells of cydar
 Yearly what Apples She wants out of my orchards for her
 Family use, and all within door moveables except what I
 Hereafter, otherwise dispose of, during her remaining my
 Widow, said Cydar, and Apples to be found her by my
 Executors hereafter named ; I further give unto her, a bed
 And bedding, a cow, & Six Sheep, to be at her dispose ; Said
 Cow and Sheep, to be well kept & provided for by my
 Executors during her remaining my Widow, I also give
 Unto my Said wife, twelve pounds old tenor, to be
 Paid Yearly by my Executors during her natural life : ∿
 And lastly I give unto my Said wife four Cords of good wood
 To be found her Yearly, by my Executors during her rema-
 -ining my Widow ; ∿ ∿ ∿ ∿ ∿ ∿ ∿ ∿ ∿ ∿ ∿

* *Suffolk County Probate* (original), Docket: 9950; also Book (copy) 46: 23–24.

Item I give and bequeath Unto my Son Ebenezer & to his
Assigns for ever, My Cedar Swamp in the Birch Swamp
And also another piece of Cedar Swamp lying near the Second
Bridge leading to paper bridge ; ∾ ∾ ∾ ∾ ∾ ∾

Item I give Unto My Son, Samuel & to his Assigns for ever the
North end of my dwelling house he now lives in, and also
My Barn, and all my Interest in the old Swamp ∾ ∾ ∾

And

And I allso give unto my Sons Ebenezer & Samuel and
To their assigns for ever, All my real estate and housing
Not yet disposed of to be divided equally between them
And also all my out door moveables and wearing appa-
-rrell ; but my will is ; that whereas I have given deeds of
Gift to each of My Sons of Some parcels of my lands
That those Several deeds Shou'd be look't upon and
Deemed by my Sons as Null and void, and if either of
My Sons, look upon and esteem Said deeds of any
Manner of force or Virtue after my decease, he that
So does and pretends to hold any lands by virtue of sd
Deed, my will is that this my Said Son, Shall have no more
Of my lands than is Supposed to be conveyed to him in
Said deed under which he claims and all the rest or
Remaining part of my lands I will and bequeath to
The other Son, that does not pretend to hold any of
My lands by any deed of Gift whatever :

Item I will and bequeath Unto My daughter Ann Allen one
Bed and bedding & fifteen pounds old tenor to be paid
Within three years after my decease and whereas I have
Given my sᵈ Daughter Ann, while her first husband
Was Living, a bond of thirty pounds old tenor, to be
Paid at my decease in Consideration of her part of
Her Mothers lands and said Bond at present cannot be
Found and if it be utterly lost and cannot be found within
Three years after my decease then my will is that my
Executors pay or cause to be paid, said thirty pounds unto
The children of my sᵈ Daughter An born of her body
In Equal proportion as they come of Age ∾ ∾ ∾

Item I give and bequeath unto my Daughter Mary Pool one
Bed and bedding & fifteen pounds old tenor to be paid by
My Executor within three years after My decease ∾ ∾

Lastly. I Give and bequeath Unto my Daughter Sara Pratt
The Bed and bedding she now Improves and five pound
Yearly during her natural life, to be paid her Equally by
My Executors, in old tenor, in Such things as She may ∾

want

Want, for the Support & comfort of life, and if Said

Five pounds with her Labour is thought not Sufficient
For her necessary Support; than my will is that my
Executors, make up the deficiency, during her natural
Life from year to Year: ∽ ∽ ∽ ∽ ∽ ∽ ∽ ∽
And further My will is that My Executors hereafter
Named, Pay my Iust debts, Legacies and funeral charge
And finally I constitute ordain and Appoint, My Sons
Ebenezer, and Samuel, Executors, of this my last will
And Testament, hereby revoking, all other former wills
or testaments, or Executors Made or named by me In
Witness whereof I have hereunto Set my hand & Seal
On this fifth day of December Anno Domini 1744

Before signing I woud further Express my will about what I have given to my
wife, namly that, if my wife deems the Contract made between my Selfe and her
before Marriage of any force after my decease, than my will is what I have
in my will above within given her be of no force or virtue: and
and will is that my daughters Ann & mary have my in door moveables
not yet disposed of after my decease, who is to have them during her
natural life:

    Signed, Sealed, published
    Pronounced and declared
    By the said Ebenezer
    Prat as his last will &
    — Testament —
    In presence of us the
      Subscribers
    Ezra Whitmarsh Junr
    James Humphrey
    Philip Torrey Junr

Ebenezer pratt

" The within written Will being presented for Probate by the
Executors therein Named James Humphrey & Philip Torrey made
oath that they saw Ebenezer Pratt the Subscriber to this Instrument Sign & Seale & heard him publish & declare the same to
be his Last Will & Testament and that when he so did he was of
Sound disposing Mind & Memory according to these Deponts best
                             discerning
Discerning and that they, together with Ezra Whitmarsh Junr
no[w] absent / set to their hands as Witnesses thereof in the Said
Testators presence

    Boston Feby. 11, 1752

                                Edwd Hutchinson

N. B. The Testator's Widow at ye Same Time Signified to Me

in Writing that she would not accept y.ᵉ bequest of the said Testator 〜 "

There is no record of the marriage contract which evidently was broken by the terms of the will. The small, separate paper preserved with the original will, signed with the autograph of Hannah Pratt, was as follows: —

" To his Honour Edward Hutchinson Esq.ʳ Judge for y.ᵉ Probate of Wills for y.ᵉ County of Suffolk — Ss: These May Jn form Your Honour that I do non except the Bequest of My Husband Ebenezer Prat late of Weymouth deceased in his last Will and testament.

as Witness my hand
Weymouth February 6
  1752 "

Hannah Pratt

The sons, Ebenezer and Samuel, were sworn February 11, 1752, by Edward Hutchinson, executors of their father's estate, and agreed to bring in an inventory " at or before the 11ᵗʰ Day of May next Ensuing ; " there is, however, no record of its return. As no deeds were at any time recorded from Ebenezer to these sons, they appear to have made the amicable division desired by their father.

ISSUE BY FIRST WIFE

I. Ebenezer⁴, b. Aug. 6, 1702, in Weymouth ; mar. Dec. 11, 1726, " Tabatha " Crane, of Weymouth. She d. 1756, in Weymouth ; and her husband d. Oct. 9, 1760, in the same town.
  Issue: 1. Silas⁵, b. Sept. 9, 1729, in Weymouth; d. 1776. He had a son Silas⁶, who went to New York.
  2. Tabitha⁵, b. April 8, 1732, in Weymouth ; mar., in 1754, to Ebenezer⁵ Porter, b. Dec. 7, 1733, son to Ebenezer⁴ and Mary (Lovell) Porter, of Weymouth. Ebenezer⁵ Porter d. in 1763, and his widow was mar., second, to Deacon Jonathan Collier, from Hull. There were children by both marriages.*
  3. Ebenezer⁵, b. May 9, 1734, in Weymouth ; mar., first,

---

* Porter's *Genealogy of the Porter Family*, 1878 : 31, 59.

April 14, 1757, Hannah, daughter to John and Mary (Torrey) Reed; mar., second, Nov. 28, 1761, Molly, daughter to Samuel and Mary (Lovell) Kingman. He was a blacksmith; he d. Jan. 10, 1760. Issue: four sons and three daughters.

4. Abner[5], b. Jan. 14, 1736, in Weymouth; mar., first, June 19, 1756, Mary, daughter to Ebenezer and Melea (——) Porter, b. Dec. 15, 1739; d. 1758. He mar., second, Dec. 19, 1758, Margaret, daughter to James and Ann (——) Humphrey, b. Feb. 8, 1739; d. Jan. 29, 1832. Abner Pratt, a cordwainer, was the executor of his father's will.[*] Issue: four sons and five daughters.

5. Hannah[5], b. Aug. 7, 1738, in Weymouth; mar. in 1754, to Samuel Bate.

6. Stephen[5], b. March 27, 1740, in Weymouth; mar., first, Betsey ——, who d. July 20, 1788; mar., second, Mary Whitman. She d. Aug. 29, 1801; her husband d. Jan. 16, 1806. Issue: three sons.

7. Rebecca[5], b. July 16, 1741, in Weymouth; mar. Oct. 26, 1760, to Stephen Paine, Jr.

8. Sherebiah[5], b. April 5, 1745, in Weymouth. He probably removed to Maine before or soon after reaching his majority, since he is not mentioned in the Suffolk County records. In North Yarmouth, June 15, 1805, Seth Mitchell and Sherebiah Pratt were on a committee of the First Baptist Church. In 1815, Pratt was taxed for a farm of one hundred and thirty acres, with the buildings thereon, situated on the "post road" near the Freeport line; at the same time a Benjamin Pratt was taxed for sixty acres, with buildings, in "lot 43, of the 120 acre division."[†]

9. Reliance[5], b. Nov. 16, 1749, in Weymouth; mar. in 1766, to Ebenezer Hovey.

10. Molly[5], b. in Weymouth; mar. in 1777, to Zachariah Bicknell, Jr.

---

[*] *Suffolk County Deeds*, Book 96: 120.
[†] *Old Times in North Yarmouth*: 432, 68.

II. Ann[4], b. April 24, 1704, in Weymouth. The name of her
first husband is not known; her second husband, mentioned in her father's will, was —— Allen.

III. Mary[4], b. Aug. 23, 1706, in Weymouth; mar. Jan. 4, 1732–
33, to John Pool, of Weymouth. She d. May 30, 1798, in
Weymouth; age not given.

IV. Joseph[4], b. 1707, in Weymouth; d. before his father.

V. Sarah[4], b. Oct. 3, 1708, in Weymouth. She was unmarried
in 1744, when her father made his will.

VI. Samuel[4], b. Dec. 19, 1712, in Weymouth. (Vide infra.)

VII. A son[4], b. April, 1715; d. June 2, 1715, in Weymouth.

SAMUEL[4] PRATT

Samuel[4] Pratt, youngest surviving son to Ebenezer[3] and
Martha (——) Pratt, was born December 19, 1712, in Weymouth. His first wife, whom he married February 17, 1736–
37, in Weymouth, was Betty[5], daughter to Benjamin[4] and
Susanna (Humphrey) Bicknell.* Betty Bicknell was born

---

* The ship "Assurance de Lo" (*Assurance*, of London) sailed for America in the spring of 1635, from Gravesend, County Kent, England, with one
hundred and six emigrants. Among them were "Zachary Bicknell aged 45
yeare . . . Agnis Bicknell his wife aged 37 yeare . . . John Bicknell his sonne
aged 11 yeare . . . John Kitchin his servant 23 yeare." They arrived at Wessaguscus, now Weymouth, in the following summer, where they were soon
enjoying the house built by Zachary on land granted him by the town. There
is a tradition that he was a Captain in the English Navy, retired on half pay,
and that his English home was near Weymouth, in Dorsetshire. Unaccus-
tomed to the hardships of a new settlement and a still harder climate, he died
two years after his arrival, in 1637, æt. forty-seven. His widow, Agnis, mar.
Richard Rocket, or Rockwood, of Braintree, by whom she had a son John,
b. Dec. 1, 1641. She d. July 9, 1643, in Braintree, æt. forty-five.

JOHN[2] BICKNELL

John[2] Bicknell, only child of Zachary[1] and Agnis Bicknell, b. 1624, in England, received a comfortable fortune from his father, and became an influential
citizen of Weymouth. He was selectman many years; in 1661, he was one of
a committee to repair the meeting-house. The record of this service reads:
"Bro Bicknell for making the meeting house title: 3 pounds." He was chosen
Deputy to the General Court, a short time before his death.

About 1650, he mar. Mary ——, who d. March 25, 1658. His second wife,

July 16, 1720, in Weymouth; the date of her death is unknown, but she was the mother of all his children. The second wife of Samuel Pratt was Mary ——, who survived him.

He was one of the executors of his father's will, by which he came into possession of the north end of the house, and the barn, and half of the land. He enlarged this farm by purchasing additional land, and followed the occupation of a farmer throughout his life. He lived in what is now North

whom he mar. Dec. 2, 1659, was Mary [2], daughter to Richard [1] and Ruth (——) Porter, of Weymouth, who survived him. His will, dated Nov. 6, 1678, was proved Jan. 20, 1679, at Boston.

Issue by first wife: I. John [3], b. 1653-54. II. Mary [3]; mar. to John Dyer. III. Naomi [3], b. June 21, 1657.

Issue by second wife: IV. Ruth [3], b. Oct. 26, 1660; mar. to James [2] Richards, son to William Richards. V. Joanna [3], b. March 2, 1663. VI. Experience [3], b. Oct. 20, 1665. VII. "Zechary" [3], b. Feb. 7, 1668. VIII. Thomas [3], b. Aug. 12, 1670. IX. Elizabeth [3], b. April 29, 1673. X. Hannah [3], b. Nov. 15, 1675. XI. Mary [3], b. March 16, 1678; mar. Maurice Truphant, or Trufant.

JOHN [3] BICKNELL

John [3] Bicknell, eldest son to John [2] and Mary (——) Bicknell, b. 1653-54, in Weymouth; mar. Sarah ——. Little is known of him or his wife; he d. Aug. 4, 1737, æt. about eighty-three.

Issue: I. John [4], b. Nov. 24, 1688. II. "Zecharia" [4], b. Oct. 8, 1691. III. Benjamin [4], b. June 8, 1694. IV. Joseph [4], b. Feb. 28, 1698-99. V. Ebenezer [4], b. Jan. 22, 1700.

BENJAMIN [4] BICKNELL

Benjamin [4] Bicknell, third son to John [3] and Sarah (——) Bicknell, b. June 8, 1694, in Weymouth; was published July 6, 1717, in Weymouth to Susannah [4] Humphrey, daughter to Nathaniel [3] and Elizabeth (——) Humphrey. She was b. April 6, 1695, in Weymouth; d. there Jan. 13, 1767, æt. seventy-one.

Issue: I. Susannah [5], b. Aug. 13, 1718, in Weymouth; pub. Aug. 13, 1738, to William, son to William and Sarah (Derby) Dyer, b. Sept. 29, 1717, in Weymouth.

II. Betty [5], b. July 16, 1720, in Weymouth; mar. Samuel [4] Pratt.

III. Hannah [5], b. Nov. 25, 1723, in Weymouth; mar. Jan. 17, 1745, to Joseph, son to John and Mary (Humphrey) Burrill, b. Sept. 24, 1719, in Weymouth.

IV. Benjamin [5], b. June 24, 1727, in Weymouth; mar. Jan. 29, 1747, Mary, daughter to Thomas and Mary (Green) Kingman, b. April 17, 1729, in Weymouth.

Weymouth, on Green Street. The street lies north of the village, and curves toward the northeast and north in a gentle ascent around a grassy hill. The house, which probably was built by his father, Ebenezer[3] Pratt, about 1700, stood a short half-mile from the present (1905) North Weymouth post-office, on the northwest side of the street, facing the village. After this ancient house was burned in 1789, Jonathan[5], one of the twin sons of Samuel[4], rebuilt upon the same spot. Like the houses erected later by his brothers, it is a substantial two-and-a-half story frame house, in good repair, and is now (1905) occupied by Miss Clara Bell[8] Pratt, youngest daughter to Washington[7] and Narissa (Baker) Pratt. Washington[7] Pratt was son to William[6], youngest son to Jonathan[5] Pratt, who rebuilt on the homestead site. Miss Pratt was for many years a teacher in the public schools of Weymouth.

Three other sons of Samuel[4] built and settled near their father, on the same side of the street. Samuel's land extended along both sides of the road, in which a bridge was made near each house for convenience in passing under the roadway down to the fields beyond. The four houses still are standing and are occupied, but all except Jonathan's have passed long since out of possession of the Pratt family. Peter[5] was the second to build; then, beyond him to the south, Benjamin[5] and Sylvanus[5] put up a house together; later, they sawed it in halves, moved one half farther up the street, put an ell on each, and reared their families independently.

In 1807, Jonathan[5] moved a shop which he owned at Fore River to Green Street, and set it on the corner of Shaw Street, almost opposite his own dwelling. The shop was converted into a house, an ell was added, and this became the home of William[6] Pratt until the death of his father, Jonathan[5], in 1732. William[6] then moved into the larger house, while the smaller one was occupied by his son Charles[7], whose widow, Mrs. Maria C. (Totman) Pratt, aged seventy-eight years, with her son Charles[8] and a grandson, still lives there. Mrs. Sarah Louisa[7] (Pratt) Cleverly, also seventy-eight, daughter to William[6] Pratt and widow of Thomas F. Cleverly, is living at the head of Shaw Street by the schoolhouse. Her notebook furnished the date of the burning of Samuel[4] Pratt's old house and the rebuilding by his son Jonathan[5] upon the same spot.

Many descendants of Samuel[4] Pratt are now living in North Weymouth, with a goodly number of the old-fashioned names repeated in the younger generation. Recently, as a bevy of small boys were rushing out of the Pratt schoolhouse, one shouted to another : "Sam Pratt's coming out to play with us this afternoon."

There is no doubt that Samuel[4] Pratt served as private in the early part of the Revolutionary War. Mr. Nash, in his *Historical Sketches of Weymouth*, mentions David, Benjamin, Sylvanus, Matthew, and Samuel Pratt, Jr., among the men in that service.[*] For a time the "Jr." was puzzling, until it became evident that this Samuel was called "Jr." as the younger man of the same name in the town, a practice common at that period. In 1759, Ebenezer[4] Pratt, for "love and good will," gave to his son Abner[5], cordwainer, twelve acres "belonging to my homestead bounded northerly on my Brother Samuel Prat and Philip and William Torrey;" in 1761, Abner Pratt, cordwainer, as executor of his father's estate, conveyed land, it "being the Easterly part of said deceased's Homestead, and is butted & bounded as follows viz! Northwesterly on the land of Samuel Pratt jun! North on the saltmarsh of Philip and William Torrey," etc. The use of the Jr. is further confirmed by the deed of "Samuel Pratt Jr." to his son Jonathan[5], May 5, 1766.[†]

The ancestors of Samuel Pratt from the first had been prosperous farmers of good standing in the community, who

---

[*] *Weymouth Historical Society Collections*, 1885 : 301.
[†] *Suffolk County Deeds*, Book 95 : 166 ; Book 96 : 120 ; Book 164 : 80.

staid by their own firesides. But when those firesides were threatened with British invasion, Samuel prepared to resist to the uttermost. He joined the company of Minute Men of Weymouth who, for months, had been quietly drilling for any emergency that might arise. Furnished with ammunition by the town of Weymouth, these Minute Men, commanded by Captain Jacob Goold, upon the alarm from Lexington marched, on the run, to Roxbury, arriving too late to participate in the fight. Still, the record says that the company served eight days in Colonel Benjamin Lincoln's regiment.* On the last day of that service, April 27, Samuel Pratt enlisted for the " Eight Months Service," signing the form of enlistment adopted on April 21, at a meeting of the Committee of Safety, which was as follows

" I, A. B., do hereby solemnly engage and enlist myself as a Soldier in the *Massachusetts* service, from the day of my enlistment to the last day of *December* next, unless the service should admit of a discharge of a part or the whole sooner, which shall be at the discretion of the Committee of Safety ; and I hereby promise to submit myself to all the orders and regulations of the Army, and faithfully to observe and obey all such orders as I shall receive from any superior officer." †

The pay of each private was to be £2 per month, and " besides the above a Coat for a uniform to be given to each of the Noncommissioned Officers and Privates, as soon as the state of the Province will admit of it." Each town was expected "to furnish good Blankets " for its men. Such was their equipment. On April 29, 1775, the defence of Cambridge consisted of " six three-pounders complete, with ammunition, and one six-pounder." That same day, one half of the militia was ordered to go to Roxbury and Cambridge. Samuel Pratt was stationed at " Fort No. 2," in the latter town. The Committee of Safety, on May 16, sent out no-

---

* Vide Appendix LXXXVII, A.
† Force's *American Archives*, Fourth Series, vol. 2: 744.

tices to the effect that the "female friends of *America*, in the neighboring Counties, are hereby desired to send such quantities of Rags as they can spare, to the Selectmen of their respective Towns, the latter to send them to Comisary *Craigie*," at the hospital in Cambridge.*

Samuel Pratt was discharged September 14, 1775, after a service of five months and thirteen days. His autograph appears on an order for a "Bounty Coat or its equivalent in money," signed by forty-six men (two making their marks), his name being number eleven.

"CAMBRIDGE CAMP Dec:12. 1775

"SIR

Pleas to Pay to Capt Jacob Goold the Money Dew to us for the Cots Promist us By the Province Colo Gratons Regt "

There is nothing that shows any participation in the Battle of Bunker Hill. Men of his age (sixty-three), and even older, formed a large part of the Regiment of Guards at Cambridge. The records of the town of Weymouth, under date of May 7, 1778, state that orders were drawn by the selectmen "To several Persons who served as soldiers at Cambridge last winter' (in addition to the Wages allowed by the Continent) four months and 22 days . . . to each nine pounds & ten shillings." Among these thirteen men was "Saml Pratt 2d," † who is thought to have been the same person who was at Cambridge in 1775.

The difficulties encountered in attempting to determine whether this record of Revolutionary service belongs to this particular Samuel Pratt have been discouraging. But, by a process of elimination in several directions, the conclusion

---

* Force's *American Archives*, Fourth Series, vol. 2 : 766, 775, 747, 761.
† Vide Appendix LXXXVII, B.

seems to be justified that he is the one entitled to the credit
of it. There was in Weymouth a Samuel[5] Pratt (son to
Samuel[4] who died in 1774), born in 1722, died May 12,
1792; there was another Samuel[4] (son to Matthew[8]), born
in 1705, living in 1756, and date of death unknown. He
may have been the Samuel Pratt, Sr. A third Samuel[5] (son
to Daniel[4]), born in 1751, died May 22, 1830.* Not one of
these had a brother Ebenezer, nor a son Jonathan. Hence
it is quite safe to assume from all the evidence that Samuel[4]
Pratt, born December 19, 1712, served in the Revolution.
He died December 28, 1793, in Weymouth, aged eighty-
one years and nine days. He left no will, having previously
divided, by deed, all his property among his children.

ISSUE BY FIRST WIFE

I. Betty[5], b. April 15, 1738, in Weymouth; mar. Dec. 31, 1758,
to James[5] Humphrey, Jr., b. April 12, 1737, in Weymouth,
son to Major James[4] and Ann (Torrey) Humphrey. (James[3],
Jonas[2], Jonas[1] Humphrey, of Dorchester, Mass.)

James[5] Humphrey was a farmer, of Weymouth, whose
land is mentioned in a number of deeds as joining that of
Samuel[4] Pratt and his sons. His house in the north part
of the town was situated "on the Old Plymouth Road,
opposite Meeting-House Lane." He d. Aug. 20, 1811, in
Weymouth, aged seventy-four; his widow, Betty, d. Oct. 24,
1831, in Weymouth, at the great age of ninety-three.

Issue: † 1. Hannah[6] Humphrey, b. May 8, 1759; mar.
April 1, 1784, to Thaddeus, son to Abraham and
Sarah (Tower) Bates. Issue: seven.

2. Mary[6] Humphrey, b. Nov. 21, 1761; mar. July 11,
1782, to David Blanchard. Issue: fourteen.

3. James[6] Humphrey, b. Feb. 17, 1764; mar. Nov. 7,
1811, Molly, daughter to Urban and Hannah (Holbrook) Bates. Issue: three.

4. Joseph[6] Humphrey, b. March 2, 1766; mar. Jan. 7,

---

* Pratt's *Genealogy of the Pratt Family*, 1889 : 40, 67, 68.
† Humphreys's *Genealogy of the Humphrey Family*, 1883 : 866, 876, 878.

1790, Rebecca, daughter to Moses and Rebecca (Tirrell) Nash. Issue : eight.

5. William [6] Humphry, bap. June 30, 1770; mar. Nov. 4, 1792, Jane, daughter to Thomas and Jane (Reed) Webb. Issue : eight.

6. David [6] Humphrey, bap. June 6, 1779; d. Nov. 10, 1801.

7. Charles [6] Humphrey, b. April 4, 1783; d. Oct. 2, 1800.

II. Asa [5], b. July 8, 1742, in Weymouth; probably died before reaching his majority, as he was not mentioned by his father or brothers.

III. David [5] (twin), b. Feb. 12, 1745, in Weymouth; removed before his marriage to North Yarmouth (afterward set off as Freeport), Maine. (Vide infra.)

IV. Jonathan [5] (twin), b. Feb. 12, 1745, in Weymouth; was published March 1, 1766, to Sarah, daughter to William and Susanna (——) Dyer, Jr. Sarah Dyer, b. Dec. 19, 1748; d. a widow, Dec. 25, 1833, aged eighty-five years.

"Samuel Pratt Jr.," yeoman, of Weymouth, conveyed to "his son Jonathan Pratt, house carpenter," on May 5, 1766, for the consideration of £2 : 13 : 04, ten acres of "swamp land lying near the Dwelling house of said Samuel Pratt Jun[r];" bounded southerly by land of widow Hannah Torrey, westerly by land of Joshua Torrey, northerly and easterly by land of " Samuel Pratt Jr.," the grantor. This deed was not recorded until Jan. 6, 1789. On May 5, 1791, not long after the old house was burned, " Samuel Pratt," for £15 paid by his son Jonathan, then called a housewright, gave him a deed of " a House lot as follows viz. ten Rods in front five to y[e] Northward of the middle of y[e] house lately burnt and five to y[e] southward & extending so far back as to make one third of an Acre, with all the Appurtenances (except y[e] buildings now standing)." It was here that Jonathan built the house now occupied by Miss Clara Bell [8] Pratt. Three months later, Aug. 1, 1791, his father conveyed to Jonathan, for £30, three acres more of the choicest part of his farm. It is described as situated " in the North part of the first Precinct in said Town; being apart of Homestead of said Samuel," and bounded "Northwardly partly on the land of James Humphrey, partly on the land of Philip Torrey; Easterly on Rocky bottom fence; Southwardly on the Grantor; Westerly on the Road partly, & partly on the Grantees House." Both deeds were recorded Sept. 13, 1791.[*]

These three deeds, so accurately describing the situation of the homestead of Samuel [4] Pratt, might be called the key to the whole estate; the lands of the other brothers are traced from them. After the death of his father, Jonathan was looked to as the head of the family. His immediate descendants are found in Weymouth, Braintree, Quincy, and Windsor, Mass., and Wilson, New York. His death occurred July 6, 1832, in Weymouth, at the age of eighty-seven years. He left no will.

Issue : 1. Josiah [6], b. Jan. 21, 1768, in Weymouth; mar. Deborah Tower.

2. Susa [6], b. Jan. 8, 1770, in Weymouth; mar. (probably) to Thomas Cook.

3. Jonathan [6], b. April 18, 1772, in Weymouth; mar. in 1793, Sarah Cook. He removed to Braintree, where he had a large family.

4. Betsey [6], b. May 3, 1774, in Weymouth; mar. to William Everson.

5. Sarah [6], b. Aug. 20, 1776, in Weymouth; is said to have married.

6. Mary [6], b. March 15, 1779, in Weymouth; mar. to Samuel Bent.

7. Nathaniel [6], b. Nov. 8, 1780, in Weymouth; mar. June 12, 1803, Lydia, daughter to Asa and Silence (Orcutt) Hunt, b. Jan. 11, 1786. Nathaniel Pratt d. May 27, 1852, aged seventy-two years. Issue: three daughters and one son.

8. William [6], b. June 3, 1785, in Weymouth; mar. Nov. 8, 1804, Martha, daughter to Daniel and Philippi (Damon) Dunbar, of Hingham, b. Feb. 28, 1788. William [6] Pratt took possession of the homestead after the death of his father, and died there, May 16, 1858, at the age of seventy-three.

---

[*] *Suffolk County Deeds*, Book 164 : 80; Book 170 : 164, 165.

Issue: I. William[7], b. Jan. 29, 1805, mar. and had a family of seven children.

. II. A son, b. July 15, 1806; d. aged two days.

III. David Matthew[7], b. July 13, 1807 ; mar. and had one son, David Jackson[8] Pratt.

IV. Hosea D.[7], b. June 13, 1809; mar. and had six children.

V. Washington[7], b. April 5, 1812 ; mar. and had five children.

VI. Alvin[7], b. July 9, 1814; mar. and had five children.

VII. Martha S.[7], b. Oct. 6, 1816; d. unmar. Dec. 31, 1833.

VIII. Mary[7], b. Dec. 27, 1818; mar. to Edwin Everson ; d. Sept. 21, 1847.

IX. Daniel[7], b. Dec. 27, 1820; d. unmar. May 17, 1864.

X. Charles[7], b. March 10, 1821; mar. May 23, 1847, Maria Collyer Totman, b. Oct. 27, 1828, in Hingham, daughter to Stephen and Leah B. (Remington) Totman. Charles Pratt d. March 3, 1892, in Weymouth. His widow lives in the small house remodelled by Jonathan[5] for his son William[6].

Issue: 1. Charles Morris[8], b. April 23, 1849.

2. Elizabeth Harrison[8], b. July 31, 1853; mar. Nov. 29, 1883, to George B. Mitchell, of Brockton.

3. William Austin[8], b. May 9, 1855 ; mar. June 16, 1881, Dora A. Roberts, of Ludlow, Vt. In 1887, the Rev. William A. Pratt was pastor of the Universalist Church in Cedar Rapids, Iowa.

4. Ella Maria[8], b. March 14, 1857; mar. in July, 1890, to Edwin H. French, of Hingham. She d. March 10, 1892. Issue: I. Harold Pratt French.

XI. Seth[7], b. Sept. 23, 1823 ; mar. Sarah Jane Dodge.

Issue: 1. Seth Arthur[8]. In 1889, he was the American consul at Zanzibar, East Africa.

XII. Sarah Louisa[7], b. Feb. 16, 1828 ; mar. Sept. 9, 1852, to Thomas Francis Cleverly, of North Weymouth, b. June 21, 1828, son to Thomas and Elizabeth (Lincoln) Cleverly.

Mr. Thomas F. Cleverly, who d. Aug. 11, 1894, was much interested in historical and genealogical research, particularly in "Old Spain," North Weymouth, his home. To his widow the writer is much indebted.

> Issue: 1. Mary Louisa Cleverly, b. Nov. 10, 1853, in Weymouth; mar. May 1, 1906, to Howard Wilbur Swan, of Norwell.

XIII. Jonathan [7], b. June 14, 1830; d. unmar., Feb. 5, 1859.

XIV. A son [7]; d. in infancy.

XV. A daughter [7]; d. in infancy.

V. Thomas [5], b. in Weymouth, probably about 1748; mar. Mary ———. He removed to Braintree. His father conveyed, for thirty shillings, to "David Pratt of Yarmouth" (Maine), and "Thomas Pratt of Braintree in the County of Suffolk, Housewright," ten acres in the "east Parish" of Weymouth, adjoining land of Jonathan Pratt, "partly on the Road . . . reserving to myself the improvement of the aforesaid premises during my natural life." This deed was dated Sept. 12, 1791, and recorded the same day.[*]

Little is known of Thomas Pratt except that he had a daughter, Polly [6], b. Aug. 6, 1770.

VI. Peter [5], b. 1750, in Weymouth; was published Dec. 26, 1772, to Amy or Amity Porter, who d. Sept. 12, 1838, aged eighty-three years. He d. Dec. 5, 1833, in Weymouth.

Peter Pratt, though mentioned in the deeds as a "Labourer," was a farmer of North Weymouth. He received a share of his father's estate equal to that of his brothers, upon which he lived all his days. The first deed from his father conveyed to him, April 13, 1783, for £3, a third of an acre of land "and the House standing thereon with all the Privileges," etc., bounded easterly, northerly, and southerly by land of his father, and "westerly on the Road." On May 5, 1791, his father sold to him, for £19, an acre in Cedar Swamp and four acres in "another piece of swamp;" and on Aug. 3, following, for £30, three acres "precisely," adjoining his house lot and reaching to the road, between him-

---

self, the grantor, on the north, and Benjamin Pratt, "Southwardly." *

Issue: 1. Samuel⁶, b. Dec. 8, 1774, in Weymouth; d.
young.

2. Samuel⁶, b. Dec. 7, 1775, in Weymouth; mar. March
8, 1798, widow Nabby Cushing (?), b. Sept. 27, 1778.
The date of death of Samuel Pratt is not known;
his widow was mar., second, Nov. 9, 1817, to Capt.
Robert Bates.

Issue: I. Peter⁷, b. Sept. 13, 1799. II. Harriet⁷, b.
April 22, 1803. III. Samuel P.⁷, b. Sept. 16, 1806.

3. Rebecca⁶, b. May 17, 1777, in Weymouth.

4. Molly⁶, b. Sept. 22, 1779, in Weymouth; mar. Jan. 25,
1800, to Jonathan Cleverly. Issue: six sons and one
daughter.

5. Jenny⁶, b. Nov. 2, 1782, in Weymouth; mar. Dec. 1,
1803, to Isaac Damon. They removed to Northampton, Mass.

6. Asa⁶, b. 1786, in Weymouth; mar. Feb. 21, 1809, to
Betsey Leavitt; d. 1821.

VII. Chloe⁵, b. June 8, 1754, in Weymouth; mar. March 19,
1775, to Matthew⁶ Pratt, b. May 20, 1752, son to Matthew⁵ and Mary (Lovell) Pratt (Samuel⁴, Matthew³,
Matthew², Matthew¹ Pratt). Matthew⁶ Pratt d. Oct. 16,
1835, in Weymouth; his widow, Chloe, d. May 19, 1838.
Issue: 1. Matthew⁷. 2. Polly⁷. 3. Abigail⁷. 4. Anna⁷
(or Nancy). 5. Warren⁷. 6. Royal⁷. 7. Deborah⁷. 8.
Betsey⁷. 9. Chloe⁷. 10. Josiah⁷. 11. Sylvanus⁷.

VIII. Benjamin⁵, b. May 29, 1757, in Weymouth; was published Jan. 18, 1783, to Betty Dyer, daughter to Joseph
and Hannah (Bate) Dyer, Jr., b. Aug. 6, 1757.

Benjamin Pratt and his brother Sylvanus occupied, for a
time, a large double house, which appears to have been built
for them by their father. For reasons not now apparent,
they decided to cut the house in two and separate. On
May 7, 1783, their father, Samuel Pratt, conveyed to Benja-

---

* *Suffolk County Deeds*, Book 170: 164; Book 171: 228-229; Book 170:
165-166.

min Pratt, "yeoman," for £3, one third of an acre of land, "And one half of the House Standing thereon, with all the Appurtenances," bounded "West on the Road, Northerly on the Land of Peter Pratt." Samuel also conveyed to his son Benjamin, on Aug. 1, 1791, for £30, three acres "precisely," bounded partly on the westerly side by the "House lot of the Grantee & partly on the Road" and "Southwardly on Sylvanus Pratt." His father had previously (May 5, 1791), for £19, sold to Benjamin one acre in Cedar Swamp, and "a third part of another piece of Swamp and upland," consisting of four acres ; which made his estate equal to that of his brothers, Peter and Sylvanus.*

The dates of death of Benjamin Pratt and his wife are unknown.

Issue : 1. Luther⁶, b. Oct. 27, 1783, in Weymouth ; married and had seven children.

2. Betsey⁶, b. July 1, 1788, in Weymouth ; mar. Dec. 5, 1809, to Ebenezer Humphrey.

3. Abigail⁶, b. Sept. 6, 1794, in Weymouth ; mar. Sept. 22, 1816, to James Thomas.

IX. Sylvanus⁵, b. June 8, 1758, in Weymouth ; was published June 22, 1782, to Hannah, daughter to Urban and Hannah (Holbrook) Bates, b. Aug. 16, 1765.

He is mentioned in the deeds as a "Labourer." His father, who evidently had built and at that time owned the double house in which he lived with his brother Benjamin, conveyed to him, "Silvanus," on May 16, 1783, for £3, a third of an acre of land with "one half of the Dwelling House Standing thereon ; together with All the Privileges & Appurtenances thereunto belonging," bounded "East on the land of sᵈ Samuel Pratt ; West on the highway ; North on the land of Benjamin Pratt ; South on the land of Samuel Pratt aforesᵈ." For £30, his father sold Sylvanus, Aug. 1, 1791, "Three Acres precisely . . . to the Southward of the Dwelling House of the said Silvanus," bounded "Westerly on the Road partly, & partly on the House lot of the said Silvanus Pratt ; Southwardly on the Grantor ; Northwardly

---

* *Suffolk County Deeds*, Book 170: 161, 162; Book 171: 230.

on Benj: Pratt." Sylvanus Pratt also paid his father, May 5, 1791, the sum of £19 for an acre in Cedar Swamp and four acres in "another piece of Swamp and Upland." *

Sylvanus Pratt d. Nov. 26, 1836, in Weymouth, aged seventy-eight years ; his widow, Hannah, d. Sept. 1844, aged seventy-nine.

    Issue: 1. Hannah⁶, b. 1784; mar. to Stephen Richards; d. Sept. 27, 1812. Their only child, Mary Richards, b. Dec. 27, 1804; d. March 29, 1816.

DAVID⁵ PRATT

David Pratt, twin to Jonathan, was born February 12, 1745, in Weymouth. He was the second son born to Samuel and Betty (Bicknell) Pratt, but the first to reach majority. Imbued with the pioneer spirit that already had taken many of his townsmen to North Yarmouth, Maine, he resolved to follow them. The date of his arrival there is not known ; the first record is his marriage, March 28, 1771, at the age of twenty-six years, to Rebecca, daughter to Edmund and Mercy (Fogg) Chandler, of North Yarmouth. Rebecca Chandler was born April 30, 1753, and baptized June 17, following, in the old First Church of North Yarmouth.

On March 2, 1774, David Pratt, "yeoman," of North Yarmouth, purchased of Samuel Grant a lot consisting of thirteen acres, three quarters, and thirty rods, it being part of "lot No. 37, drawn in Right of home lot No. 3 . . . Original, Samuel Smith." † Other acres were added from time to time, until he became the possessor of a large farm. To-day, he is best remembered as a prosperous farmer, although he had learned the trade of a mason ; a trade followed by several of his sons.

The house which he built, "on the Neck," was demolished years ago, but the lines of the cellar are easily traced. It

---

* *Suffolk County Deeds*, Book 170 : 163; Book 171 : 229.
† *Cumberland County Deeds*, Book 10 : 200.

stood on the top of Mitchell's Hill in North Yarmouth, that part of the town that became South Freeport after the division of 1789; the site is easily found by its proximity to a gaunt old pine that has been struck by lightning. The pine stands, maimed and alone, towering above every other tree in its vicinity. Efforts made in town-meetings by some of the citizens to have it removed invariably have been voted down, because of its value as a landmark to the seafaring men of Casco Bay. Mitchell's Hill rises with an abrupt slope on the easterly side of the eastern branch of Cousins's River. The most northerly of the three early settlers on the hill was David[5] Pratt, with Ira Mitchell to the south, and Barnabas[6] Soule still further south. Pratt's house was reached by a lane from the road upon which Mitchell's and Soule's houses stood; the latter winding around the hill to what was then called the Neck Road, the only road leading to Freeport village. Within the remembrance of some of the older people, the present Marsh Road has been built at the foot of Mitchell's Hill, on the westerly side, over which the trolley runs from Portland to Brunswick. The landing beside the bridge over the eastern branch of Cousins's River is called Bailey's wharf.

The site of the house is indicated by a few scattered stones and two doorsteps of split stone, the one near the middle much larger than the other. A depression at the easterly end in which a juniper bush is growing marks the cellar. All that is left of the chimney that probably was built in the middle of the house is a heap of stones. The green spot at the northwesterly corner, of which the outlines are uncertain, is without doubt where the barn once stood. Though the ancient well has been filled to the brim with stones, the water still unceasingly bubbles up and trickles through the rank growth of grass down the hillside; and mounds of spongy moss show where corn was once planted.

The view is picturesque, and extensive on all sides except the north. From the front doorstep, southeasterly, it com-

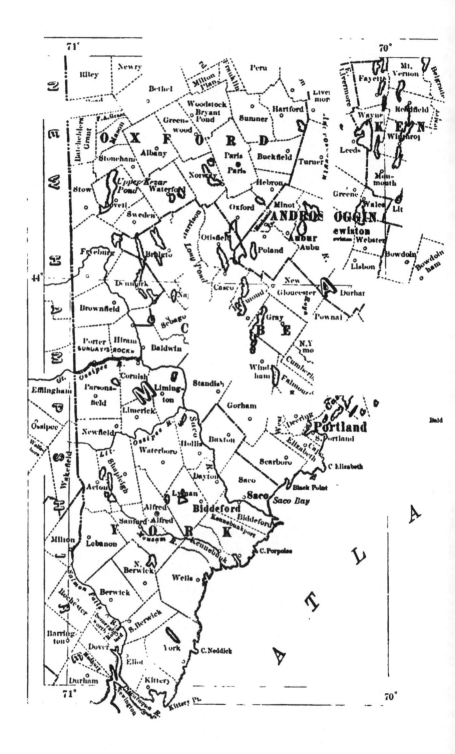

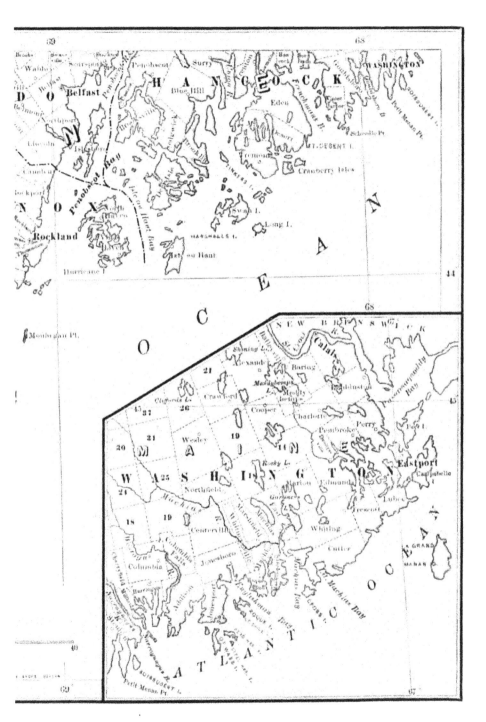

mands the shore and islands of Casco Bay to Portland harbor; to the south and west, the small streams meandering through fertile fields, dotted here and there with farm-build-

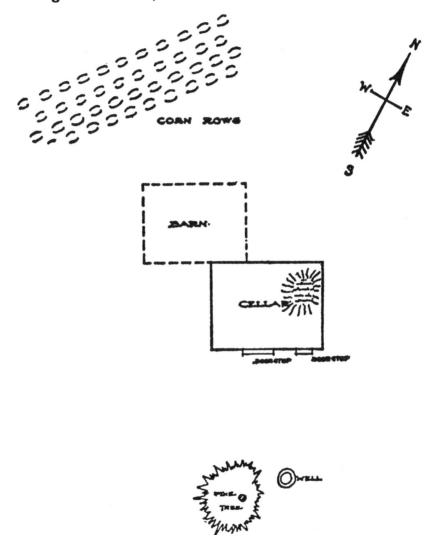

ings, can be followed to their source in the high hills beyond. Late in life, David Pratt left this home "on the Neck" and removed to Pownal. No one remembers the date; but Mrs. Rebecca Pierce said that his daughter Sally, who married

Captain Enos Soule in 1817, was the first child married in the new home. David Pratt and his wife were among the earliest members of the First Baptist Church of North Yarmouth, and they retained that church connection after their removal to Pownal. It was through the marriage of their daughter Rebecca to Edward[7] Small that this branch of the Small family became adherents of the same faith.

David Pratt and his wife spent their last years in the home of their eldest son, Deacon Edmund. He lived to be eighty-two years old, and died, June 10, 1827, "down in the field west of the house owned about 1860 by James and Peter Tuttle;" his widow, Rebecca, survived him. A letter written by their grandson, Captain Enos C. Soule, to his cousin, Robert H. Pratt, dated Newton, February 10, 1893, stated that, as he was but seven years old when his grandfather died, his recollections of him were slight; but he "remembered grandmother well." He added: "It has always been a matter of curiosity to know something about the Pratt family; all I ever heard was that grandfather came from Weymouth (Mass.), and grandmother never saw any of his relatives but once, when she was first married. He took her up there in a carriage to visit his family and she anticipated a good time, but grandfather only consented to stay two days. I never heard he was a twin before I read the [Pratt] Genealogy, and never saw one of our [Massachusetts] relatives until I came up here. . . . She was a woman with a tenacious memory ; imbued strongly with the superstitions of her younger days, she believed in witchcraft thoroughly. Moll Day was the famous witch of the neighborhood, and the family Bible was kept in the baby's cradle to shield the child when left there alone. . . . When General [Edward] Russell delivered the address in the old church at North Yarmouth Foreside, at the Centennial of the first town-meeting ever held at North Yarmouth,* he made the statement

---

* Vide page 396.

that grandmother Pratt related correctly all the old history of the town as she had heard it from her forebears." Her deposition taken at this time, to which Captain Soule referred, appears in the form of a series of answers to questions. From the fact that the paper has been preserved,* it is judged that her information then was considered of great value : —

"June, 1833. Rebecca Pratt, aged 80 last April, daughter of Edmund and Mercy (Fogg) Chandler, born where Reuben Chandler now lives, says : Edmund Chandler, the original owner of lot 81, came from Duxbury, and was my grandfather, and was also grandfather of the first Peleg Chandler of New Gloucester. Joseph Chandler, the boy who was taken by Indians, was my brother. My brother Joseph died in Hispaniola in 1763.

" I suppose Perez Bradford belonged to Duxbury. I have heard that Samuel Fisher came from that town, also Cornelius Soule, also Southworth. Heard my father speak of Dr. Wadsworth of Duxbury. I think Samuel [John ?] White came from Weymouth ; he married Parson Loring's sister. Have heard my uncle Judah say that Dea. White told him where he lived in Weymouth.

"The Fogg family came from Hampton [N. H.]. My mother was a Fogg, daughter of Benoni Fogg by his first wife. My grandmother Fogg's maiden name was Abigail Cass of Hampton.

" I think I have heard that old Mr. Drinkwater came from Stonington. His wife was a Latham, and had relatives in Carolina.

" Mrs. Cutter was Dorothy Bradbury, sister of Moses. Colonel [Jonathan] Mitchell's wife was a Loring, but not a sister to Parson Loring.

" Issacher Winslow, brother of Gilbert, was killed by the stone between Loring's and Powell's. He was the father of 'Chiz Gilbert,' so called. They were making a stone sluiceway.

" I remember that Master Wiswell kept a shop at Mrs. Cutter's. He was the first person that I remember who kept goods to sell.

"Capt. Sykes was an Englishman and an army officer. He came before I was ten years old.

---

* *Old Times in North Yarmouth* : 1171-1172.

"Dr. Russell used to preach in New Gloucester, and sometimes exchanged with Mr. Brooks. I have heard him preach a number of times.

"I have heard that there was a Dr. Raynes in town about fifteen years before I was born.

"My mother and my aunts [Abigail] Bradbury and [Sarah] Thoits [wife of Jonathan] had ten children each.

"Capt. Joseph Drinkwater, b. Aug. —, 1736. John Hamilton, aged eighty-six in 1819.

"Joseph Chandler, son of Edmund and Mercy, born in North Yarmouth, Feb. 11, 1739. Solomon Mitchell, born in Kittery, Sept. 5, 1739; Daniel Mitchell, born in North Yarmouth, June 11, 1744; sons of Benjamin and Mehitable [Bragdon] Mitchell. These three boys were captured by the Indians, in May, 1751, while driving cows; Chandler soon returned. Solomon was sold to a Frenchman, and afterwards returned home. Daniel was with the Indians ten years and ten months." *

It was said that she remembered the date of birth of every child in town. She stated that whiteweed, the bane of New England farmers, was first brought into the neighborhood by some visitors who came from a distance, provided with hay to feed their horse.

Rebecca Pratt died in Freeport, at the home of her eldest son, Deacon Edmund Pratt, April 1, 1837 † (March 31, in family records), aged eighty-four years.

ISSUE ‡

I. Edmund Chandler[6], b. Jan. 11, 1772, in North Yarmouth; was married Jan. 20, 1797, in Freeport, by Mr. Alfred Johnson, to Sarah, daughter to Bailey Talbot, of South Freeport. "Master" Bailey Talbot lived on the "curved road" to South Freeport. The musical talent of this branch of the Pratt family is said to have been inherited largely from the mother.

---

* Vide The Chandler Family.
† *Town Records of Freeport*, vol. 1: 158.
‡ *Town Records of Freeport*, vol. 1: 40.

Deacon Edmund Pratt lived near Hedgehog Mountain in the north part of the town. He was a mason by trade ; and by the thoroughness of his work and sterling integrity he accumulated a comfortable property. He is remembered as a person of very few words, yet observant and of good judg- ment, a man often called upon for aid or advice. A grand- son describes him as possessing a profound mind, with a taste for literature of a high order ; and, as far as his oppor- tunities afforded, he kept in touch with the best writers. His mental grasp was remarkable ; he could "analyze the propositions of Butler's Analogy and Watson's Apology, was thoroughly read in ancient and modern history, was well versed in chemistry, made a study of astronomy and could calculate the declension of the sun." After sixty years of age, never before having had the leisure, he mastered lower and higher algebra. His familiarity with the Bible was equally remarkable.

When he was twenty years of age, he resolved never again to touch alcoholic beverages, and kept his self-made pledge to the end. He was opposed to slavery, "but not ultra." About 1793, he joined the First Congregational Church of Freeport. Later, "through much spiritual exercise and deep reading . . . an entire change of religious view overtook him," which resulted in his early becoming identified with the First Baptist Church of North Yarmouth, of which he became a member July 7, 1799. Upon the formation of a church of that denomination in Freeport, on April 11, 1807, he was dismissed from the church of North Yarmouth, No- vember 15, and received into the Baptist Church of Free- port, November 20, 1807. Four days later (Nov. 24), he was appointed Deacon. Through all these changes his name re- mained on the list of members of the Congregational Church until June 22, 1815, when he was "dismissed . . . to join a Baptist church." * Evidently there was a period when he did not serve as Deacon, since the church records show that on "July 12, 1817 : — At a monthly conference held at the meeting-house voted that Brother Edmund Pratt be restored

* *Manual of the First Congregational Church in Freeport*, 1889: 21.

to his former office as Deacon of the Baptist Church in Freeport." * This office he retained until his death, though unable for the last few years to perform its duties.

His wife, Sarah, was received June 12, 1808, into the same church. She d. April 2, 1865, in Freeport; he d. Sept. 27, following, aged ninety-three years and eight months. Their married life, extending over a period of sixty-eight years, was ideal; after the children had left home, they lived alone for many years, declining either assistance or company. They were nearly of an age, and both retained their physical strength and mental faculties in a remarkable degree to the end.

The Rev. Edgar H. Gray, who was ordained pastor of the Baptist Church of Freeport in October, 1839, wrote to a friend of the death of Deacon Edmund Pratt, as follows: —

" Good old Dea. Pratt has reached home! Truly he will rest and his works will follow him! He is the only man I ever knew in whom I saw no guile. If ever man lived and sinned not, that man was Dea. Pratt. He was a man of few words, yet his influence was great in the Church; a man of no pretensions, still he possessed the best balanced mind of any man I ever knew. He was always regular at all the meetings of the Church, and always in season; a man of great natural diffidence, yet always at his post. Possessed of small pecuniary means, yet always liberal — indeed, any good thing and every good thing can truthfully be said of Dea. Pratt. I regarded him with veneration when I first knew him — my reverence increased with acquaintance; truly he was a model Christian man."

Issue: 1. Simeon [7], b. Nov. 14, 1797, in Freeport; was mar. Oct. 30, 1823, by Enos Merrill (Town Clerk of Freeport, and Justice of the Peace) to Philendia Lincoln,† b. Nov. 5, 1801, daughter to Jacob and Bethia (Talbot) Lincoln, of Freeport.

At the time of their marriage, he and his wife were considered "an exceedingly handsome couple; both tall, he a blonde and his wife with black hair and eyes, and both with

---

* *Records of the First Baptist Church of Freeport*, vol. I : 13.
† *Town Records of Freeport*, vol. I : 122, 263.

high color in their cheeks." Philendia Pratt became a member of the First Congregational Church of Freeport, Aug. 3, 1828, and retained her membership until her death, which occurred July 16, 1835, in Freeport.* The second wife of Simeon Pratt, whom he married in March, 1838, was Mary[4] Dennison, b. July 23, 1807, daughter to Joseph[8] and Dorcas (Lufkin) Dennison. Her stepson George had the greatest love and veneration for this mother; late in life, he told of her kneeling down with him to pray. She died Oct. 1, 1840, aged thirty-three years. Simeon Pratt mar., third, May 14, 1844, Joanna Emerson[4] Dennison, b. Oct. 9, 1814, in Freeport, daughter to David[8] Dennison by his second wife, Susan (Haraden) Griffin,† widow of Captain Benjamin Griffin. This wife also "was greatly loved by all the children;" she died Dec. 27, 1891, in California, aged seventy-seven, having survived her husband sixteen years.

Simeon Pratt, when four years of age, fell into a spring behind the barn at his home; his mother, missing him, rushed for the most dangerous place, and found him there. It was with great difficulty that he was restored to consciousness. Because a fever, from which he suffered in his youth, left one side of his body somewhat weakened, "his father sent him to school more than the other boys;" later, he became a merchant, and in middle life enjoyed perfect health. He received the title of Colonel from his rank in the state militia. He kept store first at the "Old Tavern" at Freeport Corner, and afterwards on the old wharf at South Freeport. In those days he also kept books for the ship-builders, and prospered. During the years when he was a merchant at South Freeport, he lived in the house afterward owned by Captain Enos Soule. It was beautifully situated, commanding a view of the river where it flows into Casco Bay, and overlooking a group of small islands called Crab Islands, and beyond, Little Bustin's Island. The latter is still in possession of the Soule family. Colonel Pratt removed from there to the "old Weatherspoon farm," where he remained for a time.

---

* *Manual of the First Congregational Church in Freeport*, 1889: 28.
† *Dennison's Genealogy of the Dennison Family*, 1906: 108, 71.

When his father became too feeble to manage his farm, he gave it to Simeon as compensation for the care and support of himself and his wife for the remainder of their lives. The aged couple retained two or three rooms, where they lived independently, while Simeon's family occupied the remainder of the house.

Colonel Pratt invested in mackerel-fishing at a time when the waters of Casco Bay and vicinity swarmed with schools of this fish, and great quantities were caught. But there came a day when the fish, though plentiful as before, refused to take the bait. Simeon Pratt, "who had a good many irons in the fire," failed. He was an "indulgent creditor;" had he been able to collect his debts, the result might have been different. This was about the time of his second marriage, in 1838. He then commenced school-teaching, and was teaching at the time of his third marriage.

The town of Freeport manifested its confidence by electing Colonel Simeon Pratt selectman in 1826, 1829, 1830, 1831, 1832, 1834, 1835, and several times afterward. He was Town Clerk several years, was Justice of the Peace, and frequently was appointed administrator of estates. He also surveyed land; his sons have vivid remembrances of tramping through wet underbrush on dewy mornings as they carried the chain.

For many years he was the teacher of singing-schools for the whole country side. The winter singing-schools are a thing of the past, but their memory lingers with those who are so fortunate as to have attended them. One of Colonel Simeon's former pupils, an elderly lady, says that they were the joy of her life; she could sing alone at home, but "the part-singing was so inspiring." She describes her teacher as "at least six feet tall, handsome, cultivated, a fine singer, and withal a great ladies' man." It is said that his voice was the best tenor of that neighborhood, — a voice which developed to the age of forty-five, held its own for ten years, and never wholly left him. His children still remember the evenings when their father "sat by the hearthstone and poured out a stream of song, as he loved to do when all was quiet and the day was done."

The brothers, Colonel Simeon, Rufus, Enoch, Thomas,

Ambrose, and Edmund, Jr., are remembered as "large men of broad ideas," Simeon and Thomas six feet tall, the others somewhat shorter, but all with "strong frames." Parmenas, the youngest and seventh son, with his pranks and jokes, was a constant source of worry to his father, who expected nothing less than that "Parmenas will end up some day in state's prison." Simeon, on the contrary, was a courtly man of the olden type, whose strongest trait was "reverence and respect for both God and man."

In 1871, Colonel Pratt and his wife spent six months in California with his sons Robert, George, and William, who had gone there in 1849. The circumstances of his death, in 1875, were peculiarly sad. He had broken up his home in Freeport, and was on his way to join his sons in California. In Boston, while attempting to board the East Boston ferry-boat, — a little tardy, — he miscalculated, and fell into the dock as the boat was moving out. Assistance was rendered, but it was too late. The First Baptist Church of Freeport records the following: "Col. Simeon Pratt was baptized July 28, 1839, and was received into the church on the same date. April 13, 1848, he was chosen Deacon. Drowned in Boston, Aug. 26, 1875, on his way to California." * He was in his seventy-eighth year. The night before he was drowned he spent at the home of his nephew, Josiah N. Pratt, in Lawrence. His brothers, Enoch, Thomas, and Edmund, also were there, and the four passed the larger part of the evening about the piano, singing the old-time songs and hymns they so often had sung together in Freeport. Those who were present never will forget that singing, especially the beauty of Simeon's voice, which even then, at the age of seventy-seven, was strong and full. In the course of the evening he remarked that in going to California he had but one regret, — that he should not be buried in Freeport. After the accident, he was taken to Freeport and buried in his own lot; his last desire was fulfilled.

Issue by first wife : I. Robert Henry [8], b. Aug. 2, 1824, in Freeport; mar. Louisa Merrill, of Pownal.

* *Records of the First Baptist Church of Freeport*, vol. 2 : 132.

In 1847 and 1848, he was in Lawrence, Mass., working as a mason on buildings with his uncle Enoch. During the excitement caused by the discovery of gold, in 1849, he joined a number of his friends, who chartered a brig to take them to California. At first he engaged in mining; later, with his brothers, he purchased an extensive tract of land which took their name — Pratt Valley. It lies in Napa County, in which the town of St. Helena sprang up. St. Helena became his home. Having acquired a competency, he leased his house and went to Europe for two years. Upon his return, he was engaged by the Southern Pacific Railway, and filled several offices, ending as assistant general manager. He now (1905) is president of the Yosemite Stage Company.

> Issue: 1. Sarah[9], mar. to Colonel B. O. Carr. They reside in Seattle, Washington. She is an ordained Unitarian minister and an author. Her only child, Mary Carr, who is a musician of note, is married to Dr. J. C. Moore, and also lives in Seattle. Issue: I. Torrey Moore, drowned at the age of eighteen years. II. Mary Carr Moore.
>
> 2. Harriet[9]; mar., first, to —— Pierce; mar., second, to General Moses H. Sherman; resides in San Francisco.
>
> Issue by first husband: I. Robert Pierce, who married, and lives in Phœnix, Arizona.
>
> Issue by second husband: II. Hazeltine Sherman. III. Lucy Sherman.
>
> 3. B. Newcomb[9]; he is married; is (1905) superintendent of electric railways in Phœnix, Arizona. Issue: I, II. Twin sons. III. A daughter.
>
> 4. Carlin[9]; mar. to Orlo Eastwood. She is a regular contributor to various magazines.
>
> Issue: I. Merrill Eastwood.

II. George Lincoln[9], b. Dec. 16, 1825, in Freeport.

In 1849, he and his brother William went to California by way of the Isthmus of Panama; for about two years they engaged in gold mining on the American River, near Auburn. In the mean time, their brother Robert arrived, and the three purchased a large cattle ranch in the Sacramento Valley.

After operating it for a time together, they sold it to Dr. Glenn, a large land-owner of that neighborhood. George Pratt then turned his attention to a ranch of his own, about a mile from Pratt Valley toward the city, upon which he has remained. He has been successful in business, and retained his position as director in a local bank until past eighty years. He never married; is now (1906) rather feeble from a shock of paralysis.

III. William Augustus[8], b. April 29, 1827, in Freeport.

He went, by way of the Isthmus, to California, in 1849, with his brother George, where they were joined by Robert, who had taken the longer course in a brig "round the Horn." Together they engaged in mining and ranching. In 1852, William Pratt returned to his old home, expecting to stay; but after two years, he decided that California afforded larger opportunities for a young man, and again went west. For ten years he was associated with his brothers in the cattle business. In 1864, he removed to Napa City; while there he married Miss Mary Ellen Findley, b. April 8, 1849; in 1871, he became a resident of St. Helena. With his brothers, Robert and George, he purchased, in equal shares, five hundred acres of land, comprising what is now known as Pratt Valley, and the southern slope of Howell Mountain where the buildings of the St. Helena Sanitarium now stand. He was one of the few men who organized the association that began, in a small way, what is widely known as the St. Helena Sanitarium, now of such vast proportions; he was ever one of its most liberal friends and supporters.

His farm, situated about two miles north of St. Helena, was very productive, and devoted largely to the cultivation of fruit. He took pride in it, and was constantly improving it. At first he had vineyards; but from religious scruples, because the grapes he sold were made into wine, he uprooted all the vines and set out prune orchards — the first in that section. When the scourge of phylloxera destroyed his neighbors' vines, to their great loss, he was made still more prosperous by the demand for prunes, at a high price.

Though the early religious teaching of William Pratt was strongly of the Baptist belief, his views in later years became somewhat modified. He was a devoted member of the Adventist Church of St. Helena to the end of his days. Dearly loved by all his family, — particularly his half-sisters, — he was equally liked and respected by all who knew him. For nine years he was in failing health, but the failure was so gradual that he was able to attend to business until a few months before his death, Feb. 29, 1896, in St. Helena. His widow survived him.

> Issue: 1. Minerva Alice⁹ (Minnie), b. Nov. 11, 1867; mar. May 30, 1887, to Dr. Thomas Coolidge. Issue: I. Homer Hurlbutt Coolidge, b. March 16, 1889. II. Ethel Myrle Coolidge, b. Dec. 4, 1892. III. Edna Low Coolidge, b. April 14, 1895. IV. Elmer Raymond Coolidge, b. Aug. 2, 1897. V. Carol May Coolidge, b. Oct. 30, 1899.
>
> 2. Robert Madison⁹, b. Nov. 9, 1869; mar. July 5, 1892, Luena Robbins. Issue: I. Lester Leland¹⁰, b. March 30, 1894; d. June 28, 1896. II. Erwin Douglas¹⁰, b. April 12, 1897. III. Orlyn Bernard¹⁰, b. May 23, 1899. IV. Dorothy May¹⁰, b. June 29, 1901. V. William Asa¹⁰, b. Feb. 19, 1903.
>
> 3. Clara Jane⁹, b. Nov. 6, 1871; mar. July 20, 1897, to Henry Parrott. Issue: I. Clara Lois Parrott, b. March 28, 1900.
>
> 4. Amelia Constance⁹, b. March 6, 1874; mar. June 28, 1896, to Arthur Myers. Issue: I. Wilda Bernice Myers, b. May 3, 1897. II. Arthurite Myers, b. Sept., 1898; d. aged twelve weeks. III. Everett Lowell Myers, b. July 2, 1901.
>
> 5. William Edward⁹, b. Dec. 28, 1876; d. Nov. 26, 1897.
>
> 6. Homer Clarence⁹, b. Oct. 1, 1881; mar. Feb. 22, 1904, Ethel Amy Renfro.
>
> 7. George Ernest⁹, b. March 30, 1886.
>
> IV. Amelia⁸, b. Feb. 19, 1829, in Freeport; mar., first, to —— Newcomb; mar., second, to Dr. —— Edwards. She d. Jan. 14, 1877. No issue.
>
> V. Sarah Bethia⁸, b. April 17, 1831, in Freeport; d. Jan. 15, 1850, aged eighteen years.

VI. Edward Lincoln[6], b. Jan. 7, 1833, in Freeport; d. March 18, 1847, aged fourteen years. He was returning home from a voyage in the ship *Arthur;* while nearing port, he fell from the mast into the sea, and never rose. It was supposed that while falling he became unconscious from striking some part of the vessel.

VII. Abba Frances[6], b. July 15, 1834; d. Sept. 18, 1834, in Freeport, aged two months.

Issue by third wife : VIII. Lucy Ellen[6], b. Oct. 9, 1845, in Freeport; mar. Nov. 26, 1878, in St. Helena, California, to Sinon Clare Lillis, a banker. They reside (1905) in San Francisco.

Issue : 1. Helen Clare Lillis, b. Jan. 21, 1880.

IX. Mary Philendia[6], b. Aug. 19, 1847, in Freeport; mar. Dec. 30, 1875, in St. Helena, California, to James Madison Findley, b. Dec. 17, 1829. He is by trade a carpenter and finisher.

Mrs. Findley was dismissed, Dec. 2, 1877, from the Baptist Church of Freeport to a church of that denomination in Oakland, California. She lived for thirteen years at New Era, Oregon; at present (1905), she resides in Ventura, California.

Issue : 1. Lucy Mae Findley, b. May 18, 1877, in Oakland ; mar. June 17, 1897, in Ventura, to Jesse Bert Shaw, b. June 10, 1876. He is a carpenter and finisher; resides in Ventura. Issue : I. Lawrence Maine Shaw, b. April 3, 1889, in Ventura. II. Ernest Findley Shaw, b. June 6, 1899, in Ventura.

2. Alice Emerson Findley, b. April 19, 1881, in New Era, Oregon.

X. John Haraden[6], b. Nov. 20, 1848, in Freeport; was mar. Aug. 23, 1890, in San Francisco, by the Rev. Dr. Edgar H. Gray,* to Sophie Adelheid Christian, b. Dec. 21, 1862.

---

* The first pastorate of the Rev. Dr. Edgar H. Gray was at Freeport, Maine. " Dea. Edmund Pratt, Dea. Reuben Harvey, Brethren Simeon Pratt & Samuel Soule " were the committee chosen to make arrangements for his ordination,

For some years they have resided in San Francisco. Their house was scarcely affected by the earthquake of the spring of 1906, though at the time they "seemed to be travelling over huge rocks;" neither was it reached by the fire, which fortunately was stayed two blocks away. They considered themselves "greatly blessed," in retaining their home.

Mr. Pratt in his younger days served an apprenticeship with the firm of Small, Knight and Company, builders of parlor-organs in Portland, Maine;* at the same time he lived in Mr. Daniel Small's family for a year and a half. He now is a professional musician.

> Issue: 1. Haraden⁹, b. July 18, 1891, in San Francisco.

> XI. Emily Chubbuck Judson⁸, b. Oct. 3, 1854, in Freeport; resides at St. Helena, California.

> XII. Alice Edwards⁸, b. Jan. 9, 1860, in Freeport. On Dec. 2, 1877, she was dismissed with her sisters, Mary and Emily, from the Baptist Church of Freeport to the Baptist Church of Oakland, California.†

She received the degree of Ph. D. from the University of Chicago, where for excellence she won a scholarship entitling her to two years of study and travel in Europe. She has taught in California; also several years at Vassar College, New York.

> 2. Joseph⁷, son to Edmund⁶, b. Aug. 17, 1799, in Freeport; d. Nov. 19, 1803, aged four years.

> 3. Rufus⁷, son to Edmund⁶, b. Aug. 21, 1801, in Freeport; mar. Joanna Harvey. Their marriage intention was dated Oct. 31, 1824, certificate given Nov. 15, following, in Freeport.‡ On June 2, 1839, he was received

---

Oct. 6, 1839, in the Baptist Church. For several years, including 1874, Dr. Gray was Chaplain to the United States Senate. Later, he removed to Oakland, California, and "went across the bay one beautiful Saturday in August" to perform this marriage ceremony.

* Vide page 237.

† *Records of the First Baptist Church of Freeport*, vol. 2:136.

‡ *Town Records of Freeport*, vol. 1:124; also copy:7.

by baptism into the First Baptist Church of Freeport.
Their home was next to that of his brother Enoch,
and was afterwards occupied by Ambrose Pratt and
his family.

Rufus Pratt followed the sea, and became master of some
of the best ships sailing from Freeport and vicinity. He
was so much away from home that no one now living in
Freeport remembers much about him. He was in prosperous circumstances, which enabled his four sons to acquire
good educations. They all served in the United States
Army throughout the Civil War, though the youngest, Lu-
cius, was but twenty years of age when he enlisted. Two of
them were seriously wounded, but all survived and returned
home.

Joanna Pratt d. before 1856; Captain Rufus Pratt d. about
1867.

> Issue: I. Diantha⁸, b. July 8, 1829, in Freeport; d.
> unmar., in Freeport, when a young woman.
>
> II. Algernon Harvey⁸, b. May 29, 1831, in Freeport;
> is married, and lives (1906) in Oklahoma, very
> much crippled with rheumatism. No issue.
>
> III. Samuel A.⁸, b. Feb. 15, 1834, in Freeport. He is a
> farmer, and resides at Glenwood, Iowa; he is
> married, but has no children.
>
> IV. Rufus H.⁸, b. March 2, 1836, in Freeport. He stud-
> ied medicine and practised as a physician many
> years. Dr. Pratt married, but had no children.
> An adopted son, to whom he gave the name of
> Samuel A. Pratt, is a college graduate.
>
> V. Henry T.⁸, b. Sept. 17, 1838, in Freeport; d. before
> he was five years old.
>
> VI. Lucius E.⁸, b. Feb. 28, 1841, in Freeport. He is a
> druggist at Tecumseh, Nebraska; also has a farm.
> He is known as a mathematician and a chess-
> player; he is a Mason, and often preaches in the
> Baptist Church. At last accounts he was still
> unmarried.

4. Enoch⁷, son to Edmund⁶, b. Aug. 13, 1803, in Freeport; mar. Eliza⁷, daughter to Benjamin⁶ and Han-

nah (Sylvester) Porter, of Freeport, b. Feb. 2, 1807, in Freeport. Their marriage intention was dated Nov. 11, and certificate given Nov. 28, 1827, in Freeport.* She was a noted housewife, taking many local prizes for butter and bread of her own manufacture. Her charities were numerous. She d. Aug. 17, 1883, in Lawrence, Mass.

In 1838 and 1839, Enoch Pratt was selectman of Freeport. June 9, 1839, he and his wife, Eliza, were received into the Baptist Church of Freeport; they were dismissed Aug. 10, 1845, to the Baptist Church of Saco.† In 1848, they removed to Lawrence, Mass., where they became identified with the Baptist Church of Lawrence. He was musical; he played the bass-viol, sang bass, and early joined the choir, with which one or more of his children or grandchildren have been connected ever since.

He taught school in his younger days, excelling in mathematics; later, he followed the trade of a mason, like his father. In Lawrence, he was one of the principal builders in brick, constructing the old High School, the former Post-Office, Saunders Hall, the police building, the larger part of Essex Street, etc. During his last years, he was associated with a partner, under the name of Littlefield and Pratt. Though not aspiring to office, he was elected a member of the Massachusetts legislature and served one year. He was not so tall as some of his brothers, about five feet, eight inches, but of sturdy build. His death occurred in Lawrence, Sept. 26, 1877, at the age of seventy-four years; he was buried in Bellevue Cemetery, where, six years later, his widow was placed beside him.

Issue : I. Melissa[8], b. Sept. 29, 1828, in Freeport; resides in Lawrence, Mass.

II. Ellen[8], b. March 3, 1830, in Freeport; mar. April 15, 1849, in Lawrence, to Oliver Hazard Perry Norcross, b. July 24, 1824, in Dixfield, Maine. They removed to Weaverville, Trinity County,

* *Town Records of Freeport*, vol. 1 : 226; also copy: 2.
† *Records of the First Baptist Church of Freeport*, vol. 1 : 34.

California, where Mr. Norcross d. April 19, 1871. His widow survived him.

Issue: 1. Nellie Zelita Norcross, b. May 22, 1850, in Lawrence, Mass.; mar. Oct. 10, 1868, in Weaverville, to Champion W. Smith. They reside at Pacific Grove, Monterey County, California. No issue.

2. Benn Norcross; died young.

3. Frank Gilman Norcross; mar. Isabel Mary Nichols; resides in San Francisco. No issue.

4. Encie May Norcross; mar. April 4, 1885, in Weaverville, to Selden Lafayette Blake. Issue: I. Selden Maurice Blake; d. young. II. Encie Zelita Blake. III. Elinor Blake.

III. Emma Hobbs[6], b. Jan. 7, 1832, in Freeport; d. June 26, 1856, in Lawrence, Mass., aged twenty-four years.

IV. Joseph Porter[6], b. Jan. 12, 1834, in Freeport. He was graduated from Brown University, A. B., in 1860; d. unmar. in 1863.

V. Isabella Hobbs[6], b. Oct. 11, 1835, in Freeport. She was for many years a teacher; resides in Lawrence, Mass.

VI. Enoch[6], b. Feb. 10, 1842, in Freeport. He entered Boston University in 1858, and died Nov. 6, 1859, in Lawrence, aged eighteen years.

VII. Edgar Gray[6], b. Nov. 24, 1843, in Freeport; mar. April 30, 1874, in Lawrence, Mass., Adeline Cecilia Richards, b. Aug. 17, 1849, in Kennebunk, Maine, daughter to John Madison and Adeline (Watson) Richards, of Lawrence.

After finishing her school life in the east, Mrs. Richards spent some time with relatives, Dr. and Mrs. S. W. Jones, in Leavenworth, Kansas. "She at once became the centre of a musical circle, where her voice was always heard with pleasure; and for about two years she was the soprano of a quartette in St. Pauls church." Returning east, she was married to Mr. Pratt. Her home was in Lawrence, Mass., until October, 1897, when she again went west in hope of restoring her health by a change of climate. For a time she seemed to be benefited, and had made plans to return home, when she was stricken with paralysis, and passed away on Aug. 3, 1898, in Leavenworth, Kansas. She was buried on Sunday afternoon, Aug. 7, in Lawrence, Mass.

Mr. Edgar G. Pratt was educated in the Lawrence High School. He was proficient in mathematics, discovering, with his brother Enoch, certain processes for shortening mathematical problems, which he has demonstrated in a chalk-talk before some of the professors of Berkeley University, California. In August, 1862, he enlisted as private in Co. B., 4th Mass. Infantry, and was in active service in Louisiana for about a year, under General N. P. Banks. About the middle of April, 1863, Mr. Pratt was in action at Bayou Teche (Camp Bisland); John Bartol, of Freeport, was with him. At the siege of Port Hudson, under Captain George S. Merrill and Colonel Walker (later Commander of the Ancient and Honorable Artillery Company, Boston), he participated in the unfortunate assault on Port Hudson, June 14, 1863,* and was wounded in both legs by the same bullet. This was fourteen days after his term of enlistment had expired. Ten weeks spent in the hospital enabled him to recover sufficiently to be sent home. In 1864, he entered the firm of Littlefield and Pratt, of Lawrence, retaining this connection a number of years after his father's death, in 1877. He now is retired. Such leisure as has come to him has been spent mainly in travelling to the Pacific coast and other parts of the United States. Probably no other member of the Pratt family has so extensive personal acquaintance with his kin as he. Mr. Pratt is a member of the Grand Army of the Republic. Except in church he has held no office, but for years was prominent in the choir of the Baptist Church, where his children, as they grew up, followed him. Since the death of his wife, Mr. Pratt has lived in Lawrence with his sisters.

Issue: 1. Charlotte Isabel*, b. Feb. 1, 1875, in Lawrence ; mar. Nov. 22, 1893, in Lawrence, to Seth

---

* *The Great Contest*, by Willis C. Humphrey, 1886: 505, 508.

Raymond Kitchin, b. Sept. 29, 1870, in China,
Maine, son to Alonzo McCready and Ellen
(Wentworth) Kitchin. They reside in Maynard,
Mass., where Mr. Kitchin is cashier of the As-
sabet Mills. Issue: I. Doris Richards Kitchin,
b. Aug. 30, 1894, in Lawrence. II. Rachel
Wentworth Kitchin, b. March 16, 1896, in
Lawrence.

2. Edgar Richards[6], b. April 20, 1876; d. Aug. 6,
1878, in Lawrence.

3. Henry Selden[6], b. May 20, 1877, in Lawrence;
mar. Dec. 29, 1902, in Lawrence, Mabel Ellen
Kitchin, b. 1876, daughter to Alonzo McCready
and Ellen (Wentworth) Kitchin.

Mr. Pratt was graduated from Brown University, 1900;
in his senior year, he was captain of the football team. He
resides (1906) at North Easton, Mass., where he is a teacher
in the Oliver Ames High School, and manager and instructor
of the Oliver Ames Gymnasium.

4. Eleanor Richards[6], b. Aug. 7, 1885, in Lawrence;
resides in Fitchburg, Mass.

5. Thomas[7], son to Edmund[6], b. July 7, 1805, in Freeport; mar. March 25, 1834, in Lowell, Mass., " Lydia
Ann R. Robinson," of Lowell.[*]

Thomas Pratt, six feet in height, "was called the best looking and most popular of all the brothers. He was quiet, even
retiring; a Christian gentleman of the highest type. His wife
was one of the kindest, most genial, hospitable souls I ever
knew," writes a relative; "in her earlier years she was considered a beauty." Thomas Pratt had a fine bass voice; he
was a skilled mechanic, and noted as a stair-builder. He was
industrious, and prospered. His residence during the earlier
years of his married life is not known, but about 1846 or
1847, he came into possession of the homestead of his father-
in-law on Rock Street, Lowell, and remained there. Of his
four children, one only is living, and she has lost her mind.
There were no grandchildren, so the family is practically

---

[*] *City Records of Lowell, Massachusetts,* vol. A : 141.

extinct. The date of his death cannot be learned, it does not appear in the Lowell records. His widow, Lydia Ann, died about 1902.

Issue: I. Ann Maria⁸ (Annie), b. about 1835; mar. Nov. 13, 1867, to Lawrence Kidder Stanwood, b. Aug. 31, 1835, in Lowell, Mass., son to Samuel and Hannah (Loring) Stanwood, of Lowell. Lawrence K. Stanwood was a mechanic; their home for many years was St. Albans, Vermont, where they built for themselves a house.

Before his marriage, he enlisted for service in the Civil War. He was mustered Feb. 1, 1865, from Andover, Mass., as private in Co. F., First Battalion, Heavy Artillery; he was discharged June 24, 1865, at the expiration of his term of service. Mr. Stanwood died about 1892; his widow removed to Lynn, Mass., where she now resides. No issue.

II. Mary Ellen⁸, b. about 1837; died, a young lady. She is said to have inherited her mother's good looks, and to have been the most promising of all the children.

III. Thomas Franklin⁸, b. about 1842. He enlisted from Lowell, Mass., and served throughout the Civil War, 1861–65. After his return, he mar. Augusta ——, a widow. He died suddenly, about 1893 or 1894, in Lowell, where his widow was living in 1906. No issue.

IV. Albert F.⁸, b. Aug. 7, 1847, in Lowell, was the only child whose birth is recorded there. He mar. Aug. 26, 1871, in Lowell, Alice A. Sothard, b. 1852, in Waterville, Maine, daughter to Theodore and Abbie F. Sothard. His occupation, as given in the marriage record, was "actor."* He d. about 1901, "a year before his mother." No issue.

6. Mary⁷, daughter to Edmund⁶, b. Oct. 7, 1807; d. Jan. 7, 1808, in Freeport, aged three months.

---

* *City Records of Lowell, Massachusetts,* vol. C: 51; vol. H: 131.

7. Rebecca[7], daughter to Edmund[6], b. Feb. 19, 1809, in
   Freeport.

When a little child, she received an injury to the left side
of her face from the kick of a horse, which left a conspicuous
scar. At maturity, she was about medium height, with dark
brown eyes and hair, rather slight, and, even in her old age,
she was surprisingly agile. She was educated at South Freeport and at the Old North Yarmouth Academy,* the latter a
famous school in its day ; she taught school in South Freeport and vicinity until her marriage. Lacking the opportunity in her earlier years, she studied music and French after
she was forty. Throughout her long life she was a great
reader, until nearly ninety years of age, when blindness threatened her. With complete rest, she partially recovered her
sight.

On May 28, 1848, she was married to the Rev. Hosea
Pierce, son to Ephraim and Hannah Pierce, of Freeport, b.
Aug. 7, 1823, in that town. She was then thirty-nine and her
husband under twenty-five years of age, but the union was
particularly happy ; it was saddened only by the death of
their only child, a daughter, at the age of fifteen years. At
the time of their marriage, Hosea Pierce was about complet-
ing his studies for the ministry ; not long after, he accepted
a call from the Baptist Church of West Gardiner, Maine.
He had been a member of the Baptist Church in Freeport
since Aug. 6, 1843 ; his wife, Rebecca, had united with it
on May 30, 1840. She was dismissed Feb. 17, 1850, to the
church in West Gardiner. The Rev. Hosea Pierce later was
settled over churches in Hallowell and one or two other
Maine towns, and completed thirty years of ministry at
Skowhegan. The quick wit and cheerfulness, kind heart and
every ready sympathy of his wife must have been especially
helpful to him and his parish. Throughout her life she was
blessed with the most perfect health, and with a large store of
self-reliance ; those who knew her best recognized a character in which were blended the noblest qualities of mind
and heart.

* Vide pages 283, 434.

Her husband died March 10, 1879, in Skowhegan, aged fifty-six years; she soon returned to Freeport, where she resumed her old church relations. She purchased a small cottage near the main road at South Freeport, and lived very comfortably for a time upon the small sum remaining from the scanty savings of a country minister's wife. But her years were many, and she was obliged to accept remittances that came regularly from her nieces and nephews in California. Finally, in the fall of 1900, she sold her house with the proviso that she should remain in it as long as she lived, without paying rent. The money so obtained was used for necessary expenses, and was not all gone when she died.

The companion of Mrs. Pierce's old age was a widowed sister of her husband, less than a month older than herself, Mrs. Joanna (Pierce) Bean, widow of Andrew Bean, Jr. Together they lived in the little house, with only the assistance of a relative, who occasionally came in "to tidy them up a bit;" their mutual helpfulness was very beautiful. In the summer of 1902, when the trolley-line from Portland to Brunswick was opened beside her home, she and her sister-in-law, Joanna, were taken to Brunswick; it was the first trolley-ride in their lives, and the last. Early in January following, Mrs. Pierce was stricken with the grip, and passed away a few days later, — January 7, 1903, — aged "93 years, 10 months, 18 days." Her sister-in-law, Mrs. Bean, died February 17, following, at the age of "93 years, 11 months, 14 days."

It is given to few to retain all their powers, both physical and mental, as did Mrs. Pierce. Each birthday her friends called to offer congratulations, with the hope that she might see many more years. The townspeople were proud of her, and frequently appealed to her to elucidate some long-forgotten matter of years before, with her clear memory of facts and often of dates. The writer also acknowledges great obligations to her.

Issue: I. Sarah Boardman Pierce, b. March 23, 1849; d. Jan. 7, 1865, in Hallowell, Maine, aged "15 years, 9 months, 15 days."

MRS. JOANNA (PIERCE) BEAN AND MRS. REBECCA (PRATT) PIERCE

8. Ambrose⁷, son to Edmund⁶, b. April 25, 1811, in Freeport; mar. about 1837,* Lydia Ann Nelson, b. Nov.
14, 1815, at Exeter, N. H., daughter to John and
Susan (West) Nelson, of Freeport.

Ambrose Pratt was by trade a mason. About four years
after his marriage, he went to Lawrence and Methuen, Mass.,
with his brother Parmenas, where they commenced the erec-
tion of brick houses. This took him away from home for
long periods, for his family still remained on the farm that
he owned in Freeport. This farm, which had acquired the
name of "the Todd place" from a previous occupant, was
near the "old Wetherspoon place," where Simeon Pratt was
then living. Because of failing health, Ambrose returned to
Freeport about 1850. He sold his farm and built a house at
"the Corner," now Freeport village, in order that his children might have better school privileges.

Ambrose Pratt possessed the same love of music as his
brothers; he sang tenor, played the violin, and taught music.
He and his wife were worthy members of the First Baptist
Church of Freeport. He d. Oct. 2, 1853, in Freeport, aged
forty-two years. The church records state that "Lydia Ann
Pratt" was received into the church June 17, 1840, and
"died Jan. 23, 1889, in Freeport, aged 74 yrs. 2 m. 9 d." †

Issue: I. Josiah Nelson⁸, b. March 14, 1838, in Freeport; mar., first, Feb. 18, 1859, in Freeport, Harriet
Amanda Corliss, daughter to George and Vienna
(Stetson) Corliss, of Freeport. She died Oct., 1868,
at Freeport; he mar., second, March 11, 1871, in
Fairfield, Maine, Delia A. Howe, daughter to Isaac
and Sarah (Ellis) Howe, of Solon, Maine.

Josiah N. Pratt was educated in the schools of Freeport;
at one time he was under the instruction of his aunt Rebecca
(later the wife of Rev. Hosea Pierce), whom he remembers
with great love and veneration. At the age of eighteen years,
he went to Portland, Maine, where he served an apprenticeship as mason. From 1861 to 1864, he was employed as

---

* The family Bible is in storage, and no one remembers the date.
† *Records of the First Baptist Church of Freeport*, vol. 2 : 132.

a skilled mechanic on the fortifications of Portland harbor (principally in the construction of Fort Gorges), and at Fort Knox, on the Penobscot River. On Sept. 2, 1864, he enlisted, in Portland, as landsman, on board the *U. S. S. Enterprise*, though credited to the Freeport quota. Soon afterward, he was transferred to the *U. S. S. Ohio*, at the Charlestown (Mass.) Navy Yard, where he remained until March 1, 1865. At that time, he was drafted to the *U. S. S. Trefoil*, Captain G. C. Wells, which was ordered to the West Gulf Squadron, to report to Admiral Thatcher, who had succeeded Admiral Farragut. The *Trefoil* was engaged with the fleet in the combined movement against the city of Mobile, Alabama, the land forces under General Granger closing in at the same time. The siege lasted from March 26 until April 11, when the remnant of Confederate troops fled to the interior. On the 12th, the Mayor of Mobile surrendered to Admiral Thatcher and General Granger;* Mr. Pratt was one of the first who landed in Mobile after the surrender. The Confederate naval fleet, which fled up the Tombigbee River, also surrendered soon after. At about the beginning of the siege, Mr. Pratt was appointed Yeoman of the ship, and held that office until discharged, on Aug. 31, 1865, at the Charlestown Navy Yard. He returned to his home in Freeport, and was reinstated in his former position at Fort Gorges; but, having contracted fever and ague in the service, he was obliged to resign in order to get away from the seacoast.

Immediately following the great fire in Portland, Maine, in 1866, Mr. Pratt had charge of the construction of some of the most prominent buildings in that city. Two years later, he removed to Lawrence, Mass., where he also engaged in building. In 1882, he became connected with the Jarvis Engineering Company, as superintendent of construction; in 1887, he was appointed treasurer and general manager. His specialty is constructing steam motive power for electrical plants, under the name of "The Pratt Construction Company." Since 1888, he has resided in Somerville, Mass. He served that city as alderman in 1895 and 1896. He is a Free-

---

* Harper's *Pictorial History of the Civil War*, 1866: 744–748.

mason, also a member of the Grand Army of the Republic; in politics he is a republican. He and his wife attend the Perkins Street Baptist Church of Somerville.

> Issue by first wife: 1. Ambrose Everett[9], b. Feb. 5, 1860, in South Freeport, Maine; mar. May 29, 1883, in Sandwich, Mass., Ida Louise Whittemore, b. Aug. 3, 1861, in Sandwich, daughter to Ebenezer Stowell and Mary Louisa (Murray) Whittemore. Ebenezer Stowell Whittemore, b. Sept. 4, 1838, in Rindge, N. H., is not living; his widow, Mary Louisa, b. Aug. 13, 1837, in Charlestown, Mass., resides at Watertown, Mass.

Mr. Ambrose E. Pratt removed with his parents to Lawrence. He learned the drug business, in which he became engaged, in 1881, at Sandwich, Mass. In 1886, he "took up" journalism, representing Boston and New York papers on Cape Cod. During the presidency of Grover Cleveland, he was stationed for four summers at Buzzard's Bay, "covering the movements of the President." From 1895 to 1901, he occupied the position of private secretary, at different intervals, to Senator Henry Cabot Lodge, and Congressmen Simpkins, Greene, and Sprague. Since 1901, he has been confidential secretary to Mrs. Edward D. Brandegee, formerly wife of Congressman Sprague; he also is editor and publisher of the *Brookline Press*. He is a Freemason, Elk, Odd Fellow, and a member of the Episcopal Church; he resides in Brookline, Mass.

> Issue: I. Lora Whittemore[10], b. 1886; is in the class of 1907, Boston University.
>
> II. Everard Stowell[10]; is in the class of 1910, Dartmouth College.
>
> 2. Clara Emma Baker[9], b. Aug. 1, 1862, in South Freeport; mar. Nov. 27, 1879, in Lawrence, to Rev. John B. Gough Pidge, b. Feb. 4, 1844, in Providence, R. I., son to Edwin and Mary Elizabeth (Gough) Pidge, of Providence.*

---

* Mary Elizabeth Gough, now deceased, was sister to John B. Gough, a leading orator in the temperance cause in America, and later in the British

The Rev. Dr. Pidge was graduated from Brown University in June, 1866, and from Newton Theological Seminary in 1869. He was ordained and assumed charge of the First Baptist Church in Lawrence, Mass., in September, 1869, where he remained ten years. In May, 1879, he accepted a call to the Fourth Baptist Church of Philadelphia, Pa., of which he has since been pastor, — a period of twenty-seven years. He received his degree of D. D. from Bucknell University.

Issue : I. Rachel Pidge, b. Sept. 15, 1880, in Philadelphia.

II. Harry Story Pidge, b. June 18, 1882 ; d. Aug. 10, 1882, in Philadelphia.

III. John Gough Pidge, b. May 21, 1884, in Philadelphia.

II. Abby Frances [8], b. Nov. 14, 1839, in Freeport ; was mar., first, to Asa Humphrey, who had a daughter living (by his first wife), now Mrs. Freeman Sanborn, of Chicopee, Mass. After the death of Mr. Humphrey, Abby Frances Pratt became the second wife of Charles Augustus Litchfield, of Freeport.* She had no children of her own ; her death occurred July 2, 1903, in Freeport.

III. Mary Dennison [8], b. Sept. 3, 1841, in Freeport ; mar. Edmund Pratt [7] Soule, son to Joshua [6] and Rachel Chandler [6] (Pratt) Soule, of Freeport.†

IV. Susan Ophelia [8], b. Nov. 18, 1845, in Freeport ; was mar., first, in Freeport, to Montella Evans, and resided in Wakefield, Mass. Her second husband, whom she married at Fort Dodge, Iowa, was Harry P. Walker. He d. June 23, 1895.

Isles. He was b. Aug. 22, 1817, in Sandgate, County Kent, England, where for more than twenty years his mother was the village schoolmistress. His father was a soldier, retired from active service on an annual pension of £20. At the age of twelve years (1829), the son came to America, where in 1833, his mother and sister (also born in Sandgate) joined him. The mother died soon afterward, and the sister became the wife of Edwin Pidge.

* Vide Rachel [7] Soule, b. Oct. 29, 1821, daughter to Joshua [6] and Rachel Chandler [6] (Pratt) Soule, first wife of Charles Augustus Litchfield.

† Vide Rachel Chandler [6] (Pratt) Soule.

Issue by first husband: 1. Frank Herman Evans, b.
Sept. 23, 1866, in Wakefield, Mass.; d. June 17,
1875, aged nine years.

2. Emma Ildefonsa Evans, b. Sept. 24, 1870, in Wakefield; mar. Aug. 12, 1901, to Matthew Charles
Hendrie; resides in Clifton, N. J.

V. Charles Adams⁶, b. 1847, in Freeport. He had risen
to the rank of first mate, on board ship; d. from
illness, unmar., at the age of twenty-five years.

VI. Julius⁶, b. 1849, in Freeport; went to sea very
young, and was drowned off Thatcher's Island,
near Gloucester, Mass., aged about sixteen.

VII. John Edward⁶, b. 1850, in Freeport; mar. Sarah
Cornish, who is not living. Dr. John E. Pratt is
a physician, and resides in Dumont, New Jersey.
Issue: I. Mabel⁹; married. II. Marion⁹; married. III. Eva⁹.

VIII. Sarah Dianthe⁶, b. June 20, 1852, in Freeport; mar.
Nov. 14, 1871, in Freeport, to George Frank
Fogg, b. 1852, in Freeport, son to Azariah Fogg.
George F. Fogg was a ship-carpenter; he d. Aug.
29, 1904, in Freeport, aged forty-two years. His
widow resides in Roslindale.

Issue: 1. Annie Nelson Fogg, b. March 13, 1873, in
Freeport; mar. 1893, to Robert W. Williams;
resides in Portland, Maine. They have two
daughters, and a son, Cedric.

2. Julius Howard Bradford Fogg, b. Dec. 27, 1875,
in Freeport; was graduated, 1902, from Colby
University; is studying law at Harvard University.

9. Samuel⁷, son to Edmund⁶, b. Oct. 9, 1813; d. April 9,
1815, in Freeport, aged one and a half years.

10. Edmund⁷, son to Edmund⁶, b. Sept. 10, 1815, in Free-
port; mar. May 25, 1841, in Freeport, Mary Grant
Alden, daughter to Samuel⁶ and Hannah (Reed)
Alden, of Freeport. Mary G.⁷ Alden, b. Nov. 2, 1816,
in Freeport, was of the seventh generation from
John¹ Alden, who came over in the *Mayflower*, 1620,

and was the last survivor of the forty-one signers of the Compact.* Samuel⁹ Alden, her father, was b. July 19, 1784, in Duxbury, Mass., d. Feb. 21, 1866, in Freeport ; her mother, Hannah Reed, was b. Dec. 9, 1787, in Freeport; d. there, 1849.

Edmund Pratt lived in Freeport, about three miles from the village, in what long has been recognized as the " Pratt neighborhood." He was a carpenter, and followed that trade all his life. Like his brothers, he was a large man, of sturdy physique, strong mentality, and some musical talent; he sang bass, and played the clarinet and violin. At the time of their marriage, his wife was a member of the Congregational Church of Freeport, which her parents had joined in 1824; but when her husband became a member of the Baptist Church, on June 6, 1858, she left her own church and went with him. Ten years later, March 15, 1868, they were dismissed to the Baptist Church of Portland, Maine,† to which city they had removed.

After two of their children had married and removed to Boston, where they built houses and made homes for themselves, Edmund Pratt and his wife followed, about 1872. In 1877, they removed to Roslindale, within the limits of the city of Boston, and lived in a part of the house occupied by their daughter, Mrs. Hudson, until their death. Mr. Pratt never was in perfect sympathy with the Baptist belief, though strongly religious. Late in life, through association with the Rev. Charles F. Dole, of Jamaica Plain, he became a Unitarian. He d. May 25, 1882, in Roslindale ; his widow d. there, March 3, 1887.

Issue: I. Thomas Clarkson⁹, b. May 19, 1843, in Freeport; mar. June 13, 1870, Grace C. Reed, of Portland.

Thomas C. Pratt enlisted, in 1862, in Co. G., 25th Mass. Infantry, for the "nine months' service." Though sent south, he never participated in an engagement; he returned home with impaired health, a disappointed man. He d. Jan. 1, 1879, in Dorchester, Mass.

---

* Vide Appendix LXXXV.
† *Records of the First Baptist Church of Freeport*, vol. 2 : 136.

Issue: 1. Edgar Reed[9], b. Jan. 26, 1871 ; d. May 14, 1871, aged three months.

2. Anna E.[9], b. June 3, 1877 ; mar. June 8, 1897, to Charles Bertram Briggs. They reside in Beachmont, Mass. Issue: I. Chester Haskell Briggs, b. April 2, 1899.

II. Edmund[8], b. May 19, 1844, in Freeport ; d. there Oct. 11, 1860, aged sixteen years.

III. Cassius Marcellus Clay[8], b. Jan. 30, 1846, in Freeport ; mar. Jan. 8, 1874, Esther V. Cole, of Lancaster or Berlin, N. H.

He is in the piano business in Minneapolis, Minn. ; his wife teaches vocal and instrumental music. They both sing in the quartette choir of the Baptist Church of Minneapolis, of which they are members.

Issue: 1. Harold[9], b. Nov. 13, 1875 ; d. July 8, 1881 (?).

2. Robert Henry[9], b. July 8, 1882 ; mar. Aug. 18, 1903, Winnie E. Race. He was graduated at a Minneapolis University ; he is now (1906) at Newton Theological Seminary, studying for the Baptist ministry. Issue: I. Alden Cole[10], b. June 23, 1904. II. Harold[10], b. Dec. 30, 1905.

IV. Florence R.[8] (twin), b. Jan. 13, 1849, in Freeport ; mar. Oct. 13, 1869, to William R. Hudson.

Mr. Hudson enlisted for three years in the regular army, 17th U. S. Infantry, during the Civil War. He was stationed at Fort Preble, Portland Harbor, most of the time. At the end of his term he was discharged, greatly incapacitated from having broken both ankles and their not being properly cared for. He recovered sufficiently to walk with a cane, but used his feet with difficulty as long as he lived. He d. May 10, 1906, in Roslindale, where his widow remains.

Issue: 1. William E. Hudson, b. Dec. 23, 1870 ; d. Sept. 1871.

2. Mary G. Hudson, b. Aug. 28, 1872 ; was graduated from the Boston Normal School, 1895, and teaches in the Robert G. Shaw District, West Roxbury. She resides with her mother in Roslindale.

V. Clara G.[8] (twin), b. Jan. 13, 1849, in Freeport ; re-
sides with her sister in Roslindale.
VI. Henry W.[8], b. Aug. 23, 1847, in Freeport ; mar. Susan
Sewall, of Minneapolis ; was divorced, and has
married again. He resides at Seattle, Washing-
ton.
Issue : 1. Clarence[9]. 2. Edmund[9].
11. Parmenas[7], son to Edmund[6], b. July 12, 1818, in Free-
port ; mar. April 11, 1844, in Hampstead, N. H.,
Tryphena Webster Mooers, b. July 4, 1825, in
Hampstead. She was daughter to Edmund and
Hannah (Brickett) Mooers, of Hampstead.

Parmenas Pratt, the youngest child in this large family,
was full of life and fun, a great favorite with everybody. He
sang, and played on every instrument that belonged to his
brothers. He liked to dance, which was a great trial to
his father, Deacon Edmund. From his father he learned
his trade, and soon became a master-mason. Searching for
larger opportunities than his home town afforded, he made
his way to Massachusetts, with his brother Ambrose, where
he built the first brick house in the city of Lawrence ; it is
now standing. He also constructed other buildings in neighboring towns and cities, and prospered. In 1849, he joined
the expedition to the gold-fields of California that chartered
a brig to take them " round the Horn." As a good business
venture, he carried a quantity of house-frames, ready to be
put together quickly. The voyage was tedious ; six months
were consumed before they entered the Golden Gate at San
Francisco. His nephew, Robert H. Pratt, four years younger
than himself, was of the company. Afterward, in describing
the voyage, Robert said that his uncle Parmenas was much
depressed, and seemed to regret the step he had taken. Parmenas did not long survive ; he died of an acute illness, near
Weaverville, Trinity County, California, on Oct. 4, 1850,
aged thirty-two years. His nephew Robert was with him at
the time.

His widow was married, second, Feb. 17, 1856, in Manchester, N. H., to Nathaniel Marshall Ladd, by whom she
had one son. They reside at Bordentown, N. J.

Issue: I. Rosa Lucretia⁶, b. July 1, 1847, in Methuen, Mass. She was graduated from the Framingham Normal School, and taught before her marriage. On April 2, 1872, she was married in Andover, Mass., to Henry Chapin Sawin, b. Aug. 22, 1843, in Saugus, Mass., son to the Rev. Theophilus Parsons Sawin. That same year, 1872, Mr. Sawin accepted the position of head master of the Bigelow School, in Newton, Mass., a position which he ably filled for thirty-three years, until his death, on April 28, 1905. The services held in Eliot Church, Newton, on May 8, were attended by a large number of people, old and young, who came to pay loving tribute to his memory; and the casket was buried beneath a wealth of rare flowers.

His influence for good in the community cannot be over-estimated. Two generations — for many of his later pupils were children of those who were under his teaching in earlier years — were guided and uplifted by his judicious counsels to a desire for a higher education, not only for their own gratification, but that they might be of use to others. A friend wrote of him as "a man possessed of a quiet, retiring, unostentatious disposition. He was never known to even refer to his long years of public service in behalf of the education of the young; he was never known to shirk a duty; he was always at his post, and was ever alert to acquire new methods and new ideas. He was a great reader, a broad thinker, and a ripe scholar. . . . We mourn the demise of such a valuable public servant and loyal fellow-citizen." His widow resides in Newton.

Issue: 1. Edmund Chapin Sawin, b. Feb. 24, 1873, in Newton; mar. Feb. 24, 1895, in Newton, Isabelle Aston. He is an electrician; resides at Wollaston, Mass.

II. Betsey⁶, daughter to David⁵, b. Oct. 13, 1773, in North Yarmouth; probably d. young.

III. Samuel⁶, son to David⁵, b. May 6, 1776, in North Yarmouth. His marriage certificate was dated Dec. 19, 1801, certificate given March 10, 1802, to Sally Soule, of Freeport.* Little is remembered of him. He left his wife and two young children to go on a voyage, and never returned. It was supposed that he was lost at sea; but, many years afterward, it was reported that an old acquaintance had met him in the south.

Issue: One or two children — names unknown.

IV. David⁶, son to David⁵, b. July 6, 1778, in North Yarmouth; mar., first, Polly Mann, of Freeport, b. 1781.

Their marriage intention was dated Feb. 27, 1801, certificate given April 22, 1801, in Freeport.† Her name at this time was recorded as Polly, and her sisters always called her Polly, though late in life she oftener was called Mary. As "Polly Pratt" she appears in a list of the members of the First Congregational Church of Freeport, who were admitted "between 1806 and 1810;" on Aug. 9, 1818, she was dismissed to the Congregational Church of North Yarmouth.‡ It was about this time that they removed to the latter town, where she d. Jan. 28, 1840, aged fifty-nine years.

The second wife of David Pratt was Margaret (Humphrey) Favor, widow of Timothy Favor, of North Yarmouth; they were married "at the house of the bride," Sept. 11, 1842. Margaret Humphrey, b. June 10, 1796, was mar., first, May 6, 1822, to Timothy Favor, b. 1777; he d. Sept. 16, 1837. They had one daughter, Sarah Favor, b. May 17, 1823; she became the wife of Asa Humphrey, and d. Dec. 31, 1858, leaving one daughter. The second wife of Asa Humphrey was Abby Frances⁸, daughter to Ambrose⁷ and Lydia Ann (Nelson) Pratt.

In his youth, David Pratt learned the trade of a shipwright, and was employed in constructing vessels in the then famous shipyards of Freeport. These yards have long been idle, and, though some of the wharves and buildings remain, they are in a dilapidated condition. At this time he lived in his father's house on Mitchell's Hill, at South Freeport. It was a "roomy" old house, measuring forty feet across the front,

---

* *Town Records of Freeport*, vol. 1: 70, 130.
† *Town Records of Freeport*, vol. 1: 54.
‡ *Manual of the First Congregational Church in Freeport*, 1889: 23.

by thirty feet at the end, with a low, gable roof. Before 1835, it was demolished. On Nov. 3, 1807, Cornelius Soule and Edmund Pratt, both of Freeport, yeomen, together "with David Pratt Ju^r of the same Freeport Shipwright," for $350, paid by Barnabas Soule, conveyed to him "a certain piece of land lying in Freeport aforesaid adjoining the easterly side of the Eastern branch of Couzens's River Containing about fifty acres more or less known by the name of Equivalent Lot, Number^d twenty six, bounded westerly on Couzens's River, Northerly on William Brown's land, Easterly on land of Cornelius Soule, and Southerly on land of David Pratt Junr." [*] This lot was on the westerly side of Mitchell's Hill, and either a part of David Pratt, Sr.'s original land, or adjoining it. The settlers on this hill were few; David Pratt's house near the pine tree was the most northern; [†] to the south, divided by a stone wall still there, was the homestead of Ira Mitchell. A little southeasterly was the house of Captain Enos [6] Soule, whose wife was Sally [6] Pratt; and, about west from the latter, the house of Barnabas [5] Soule, father to Captain Enos [6]. On April 25, 1834, Ira Mitchell and his wife, Sarah, conveyed to "Enos Soule of s^d Freeport mariner," a small strip of land "on the East side of the Town road leading from the County road by said Soules now dwelling house." [‡] These two deeds give a good description of David Pratt's location.

In 1808 and 1809, David Pratt, Jr., was a surveyor of roads in Freeport; he does not appear to have filled other town offices. Before 1818, he removed to North Yarmouth; the house that he owned and occupied there still is standing, in good condition in its exterior. The interior is much out of repair. Originally it was a small house of one story, which he purchased of Dr. David Jones and moved nearer the street.[§] He added to this another room, and built a second story over the whole, with a commodious woodshed

---

[*] *Cumberland County Deeds*, Book 54: 113.
[†] Vide pages 777–779.
[‡] *Cumberland County Deeds*, Book 164.
[§] *Old Times in North Yarmouth*: 607.

in the rear. The steep and narrow stairway, like the com-
panionway of a vessel, the woodwork of the interior and
outside frames of the windows, all suggest the work of a shipwright rather than a carpenter. After the death of " Master
David," as he was familiarly called, the house and all its
furnishings were sold, the house passing into the possession
of Mrs. Susan (Pierce) Pratt, wife of his youngest son, David [6].
Several years later, Susan Dunham, daughter to David [6],
bought the house and lived in it. She sold it to a Mr. Plummer. When occupied by David Pratt, the house was the first
on the right of the road to Freeport, after crossing the bridge
just below the first fall on Royal River. It stands on a slight
elevation that, in his day, sloped to the river with an unob-
structed view of his shipyard. Since then, another house has
been built between it and the river. In recent years, the ancient wooden bridge has been replaced with a substantial
structure of iron.

One of the earliest industries of North Yarmouth was
getting out lumber ; much of it was white oak, of a quality
so superior for shipbuilding that many of the most prominent
men turned their attention that way. For many years an upright saw-mill at Gooch's Falls (the second falls, near the
present Pulp-Mill) was owned and operated by " John Gooch,
David Pratt, John Sargent, Benjamin Gooch, Rufus Gooch,
John Cutter, James Russell, Joseph Russell, Ebenezer Pratt,
and Jeremiah Baker." [*]

David Pratt's shipyard was on the bank of Royal River,
south of his house. How early he launched a ship of his
own construction does not appear. The first on record
was the brig *Cornelia*, of 160 tons, built in 1826. There
were other builders, but few ships were set afloat in North
Yarmouth of more than 500 tons; "Master David" con-
fined himself to the smaller craft in great demand for the
coasting and fishing trade. His "vessels were noted for
their thorough build, graceful models, and superior sailing
qualities." The following is a list of the ships he built, with
their tonnage ; three schooners, not included because their

DAVID PRATT'S SHIPYARD, 1880, NORTH YARMOUTH, AT THE LOWER FALLS ON ROYAL'S RIVER.

DAVID PRATT'S SHIPYARD, 1885, THE LAST SHIP ON THE WAYS, NORTH YARMOUTH, MAINE.

dates are unknown, were the *David Pratt*, *Clio*, and *Oxford* : —

	tons	year		tons	year
Brig *Cornelia*	- 160 -	1826.	Brig *Pallas*	- 160 -	1835.
Brig *Ilsley*	- 135 -	1826.	Schooner *Lucy*	- 115 -	1835.
Sloop *Milo*	- 46 -	1826.	Brig *Trojan*	- 191 -	1836.
Ship *Saratoga*	- 335 -	1827.	Brig *Anna Maria*	- 116 -	1837.
Schooner *Midas*	- 115 -	1827.	Brig *Homer*	- 221 -	1838.
Schooner *Jane*	- 97 -	1827.	Brig *Norman*	- 200 -	1839.
Sloop *Packet*	- 49 -	1828.	Bark *Abby Baker*	- 259 -	1840.
Schooner *Caspian*	- 103 -	1829.	Brig *Levant*	- 167 -	1841.
Schooner *Vesper*	- 106 -	1829.	Schooner *Boston*	- 75 -	1841.
Schooner *Ellen*	- 175 -	1829.	Bark *Pilgrim*	- 326 -	1843.
Brig *Conway*	- 135 -	1830.	Brig *Lucy Ellen*	- 170 -	1844.
Schooner *Native*	- 63 -	1832.	Schooner *Effort*	- 85 -	1844.
Schooner *Catherine*	- 133 -	1833.	Schooner *Advance*	- 85 -	1844.
Brig *Halcyon*	- 150 -	1834.	Bark *J. Baker*	- 787 -	1857.[*]

Several of "Master David's" sons-in-law worked in his shipyard, and afterward became builders on their own account. Why he should have built the *J. Baker*, in 1857, after thirteen years of idleness, is not apparent, unless it was to show that, notwithstanding his seventy-nine years, he could construct a large ship as well as the younger men. The decline of shipbuilding in North Yarmouth was due to various causes, prominently the fact that long voyages of two or three years' duration ceased to be as profitable as formerly. The old shipmasters were passing away, and the younger generation did not care to follow the sea. The last ship launched from the yard, in 1885, was photographed.[†] After years of idleness and decay, the banks of Royal River at this point are being utilized for other purposes; and the trolley line from Portland passes by.

David Pratt was a member of the First Baptist Church of North Yarmouth for many years. The records of the church at this period are so fragmentary that reference to volume and page is impossible, but from them it is gleaned that, in 1823, Edward Small, David Pratt, and Ebenezer Pratt were the standing committee of the church.[‡] In 1824, David Pratt was taxed on an "income of $2,120" the pre-

---

[*] *Old Times in North Yarmouth*: 743-746.
[†] Vide page 224.   [‡] Vide page 244.

vious year. The revenue for support of the church appears
to have been a pro rata tax on the incomes of the members,
and he paid the highest tax; few other incomes exceeded
five hundred dollars a year. He was considered a wealthy
man. The causes that led to his change of faith are unknown, but on March 1, 1829, he and his wife Mary were
received, "by public profession," into the Congregational
Church of North Yarmouth, and the date of her death is
recorded there.* It appears, from her being received a
second time as a member of that church, that she probably
for some years attended the Baptist Church with her husband.

Margaret, the second wife of David Pratt, was a devoted
member of the Baptist Church; she always attended its
services, while her husband went to the Congregational
Church. He died, from what is now called pneumonia, on
May 1, 1861, aged eighty-two years and ten months. His
widow Margaret died in the summer of 1882, aged eighty-six
years.

> Issue by first wife: 1. Timothy[7], son to David[6], b. about
> 1802, in Freeport; mar. Jane Chandler, b. March 6, 1802,
> in Freeport. She had a twin sister, Charlotte; they were
> daughters to Joel[5] and Pamelia (Lincoln) Chandler, of
> that town.†

Timothy Pratt followed the sea from his boyhood, and
early attained the rank of captain. His home was a cottage
situated on the main street of Yarmouth, just above where
the Cumberland road comes down to Main Street,‡ near the
Baptist Church. This cottage was destroyed about 1848, by
fire; the family and such household goods as were saved
were sheltered temporarily in a house near by. The following spring, rumors of the discovery of gold in California
reached the Eastern States. Captain Timothy determined to
go there; and it is thought to-day that the loss of his home
was responsible for his taking so many of his family with
him. He chartered one of his father's ships, the bark *Abby*

---

* *Records of the First Congregational Church of North Yarmouth*, 1848: 34.
† Vide page 905.
‡ *Old Times in North Yarmouth*: 949, 950.

Baker, called his eldest son, Augustus, from his studies at Bowdoin College, and made him first mate; Enos, the next son, was second mate. The only daughter, Jane, was placed in school, and the third son, Franklin, was left with a near neighbor who was very fond of him. The captain's wife and twin sons, William and Henry, completed the family of six that sailed, with a few seamen, on that eventful voyage. The cargo was house-frames.

It was not often that sailing vessels attempted to go through the Strait of Magellan; Captain Timothy, however, tried it, with the result that he was becalmed for eighty days, under the most trying conditions. They were becoming short of provisions and of water, to say nothing of the harassing delay. Favorable winds at last took them out on the open sea, and they sailed up the west coast of South America. One day the captain dropped dead on deck; it was thought his death was caused solely by grief and anxiety. The sailors rowed ashore and buried him on the nearest land, an island near San Luis Obispo, about a hundred miles below San Francisco, on the coast of California. The son Augustus then took command of the ship, and brought her into Sacramento Bay. Shortly after reaching port the cholera broke out; the sailors deserted the ship, and "robbed them of everything they could lay hands on." Augustus commenced a letter to his aunt, Susan Dunham, saying, "Already the ravages of this dread disease are upon us." The unfinished letter finally reached her and was kept for years. After Augustus and Enos, William, one of the twins, aged about eleven, was the next to succumb. The mother died of a broken heart. Captain Talbot, of Freeport, happened to sail into the harbor; he went on board and found Henry Pratt, the other twin, the only survivor on board. He buried William and the mother, and took Henry with him, with such effects as he thought prudent. Captain Talbot's voyage was long, and it was a year or two before Henry reached home. What became of the *Abby Baker* is not known; she probably was taken for salvage. If a bark of only 259 tons should undertake such a voyage to-day, it would be thought suicidal.

Issue: I. Augustus[9], b. in Yarmouth, was a talented young man and something of a poet; he entered Bowdoin College, expecting to graduate. He d. in Sacramento Bay, California.

II. Enos[9], b. in Yarmouth; d. in Sacramento Bay, soon after Augustus.

III. Edward C.[9], b. in Yarmouth; was left at home when his parents sailed for California. His mother is remembered as "a beautiful woman, with black eyes and black curly hair, and Edward looked like her." At the beginning of the Civil War, he enlisted in the navy; after his service expired, it was necessary to confine him in the Insane Asylum at Augusta, Maine. In 1879, he escaped, and is supposed to have drowned himself.

IV. Franklin[9] (twin), b. in Yarmouth. He was adopted by a family of the name of Thomas, who lived in the next house to his Yarmouth home. They gave him their name, and he was known as Franklin Pratt Thomas. In 1876, he was a resident of Reno, Nevada; the following year he was heard from at Benton, California; later, he was at Oakland, that state; he is supposed to have died.

V. A son (twin to Franklin), died in infancy.

VI. Jane A.[9], b. in Yarmouth; mar., first, Waitstill Curtis, better known as "Waite." Her second husband was Frank Yeaton. For many years she resided in Portland and Belfast, Maine, but is not living.

Issue by first husband: 1. Henry Curtis. 2. Jenny Curtis.

Issue by second husband: 3, 4. Twins, one of whom, Inez Yeaton, is living.

VII. William[9] (twin), b. 1838, in Yarmouth; d. in Sacramento Bay, aged eleven years.

VIII. Henry[9] (twin), b. 1838, in Yarmouth, was the only survivor of the voyage. He enlisted in the navy, during the Civil War. When last heard from, he was unmarried.

2. Mary[7], daughter to David[6], b. March 4, 1804, in Freeport, was mar. in 1826, at Yarmouth, to Isaac Allen, Jr., son to Isaac and Elizabeth (Alexander) Allen, of Freeport. The first wife of Isaac Allen, Jr., was Susan Dunham, sister to George Dunham who married Susan[7] Pratt.

Isaac Allen, Jr., b. Oct. 3, 1798, in Harpswell, Maine, was a shipjoiner, and worked more or less at his trade until very aged. About 1848, he bought a farm in Freeport, three miles north of Freeport Corner towards Brunswick. Here he remained until his death, on June 20, 1888, at the age of ninety years, having survived his wife, Mary, nearly twenty years. She d. Dec. 6, 1869, in Freeport, at the age of sixty-five. They both attended the Free Baptist Church of Freeport.

> Issue by first wife: I. Robert Allen, who d. aged six years.

> Issue by second wife: II. Isaac Henry Allen, b. 1827, in Freeport; d. 1848, in Freeport, aged twenty-one years.

III. Susan Maria Allen, b. 1829, in Freeport.

IV. Mary Elizabeth Allen, b. Nov. 6, 1831, in Freeport; mar. Jan. 6, 1854, to Albert A. Byram (or Byron), b. Jan. 22, 1829, in Freeport.

> Issue: 1. Helen Byram; mar. to Walter Milliken Rogers; resides in Chelsea, Mass. Issue: I. Walter Byron Rogers. II. John Albert Rogers.

> 2. Frank Melville Byram, unmar., resides in California.

> 3. Angenette Byram; mar. to John Strahan; resides in Chelsea, Mass. Issue: I. Jean Gordon Strahan. II. Byron Bradstreet Strahan.

> 4. Mary Elizabeth Byram; d. aged two years.

> 5. Lavinia Gertrude Byram, resides in Chelsea. •

> 6. Ethel Marie Byram, resides in Chelsea.

V. Sarah Jane Allen, b. 1833; d. 1847, aged fourteen years.

VI. Enos Pratt Allen, b. 1836; mar. 1864, Mary Jane Carver, daughter to Blaney and Sally Carver, and twin sister to Sarah Ann Carver, wife of Thomas[7] Pratt.

VII. Juliette Allen, b. 1839; mar. 1865, Harlan Knight.

VIII. Albion Seabury Allen, b. 1842; mar. 1866, Arabella Curtis, daughter to Joseph and Susanna Curtis.

IX. Angenette Allen, b. 1845; mar., first, to James Greene, who d. 1870; mar., second, to Isaac Byram, in 1879, son to Rufus and Margaret (Dunham) Byram.

X. Fanny Allen, b. 1849; d. 1864, in Freeport, aged fifteen years.

3. Dorcas[7], daughter to David[6], b. Dec. 7, 1808, in Freeport; mar. June 3, 1826, in North Yarmouth, to Albion Seabury, b. Oct. 27, 1806, in North Yarmouth, son to John and Lucy (Grant) Seabury.

Albion Seabury was one of the most prominent shipbuilders of his native town; his shipyard was on the northeast side of Royal River, at East Yarmouth. The first vessel that he launched probably was the brig *Harry*, in 1831. Other vessels of his construction were the schooners *Union*, *Exchange*, *Albion*, *Hope*, *Kate Aubrey*, brigs *Helen*, *Maria*, *Star*, *Sophia*, *Persia*, *Russia*, *America*, *Union*, *Ann M. Knight*, sloop *Gull*, and the ship *Hudson*. From 1842 to 1847, he was associated with George Dunham, as " Seabury and Dunham," and from 1849 to 1879, with Joseph Seabury, as " J. and A. Seabury." *

The house built and occupied by Albion Seabury, opposite that of his father-in-law, David Pratt, is a large and beautifully constructed building, which is now (1906) the home of his youngest daughter, Mrs. Dresser. Mr. Seabury and his wife, Dorcas, for many years were members of the old First Congregational Church of Yarmouth; on March 30, 1859, they were dismissed to the Central Congregational Church.† He d. in Dec., 1881, in Auburn, Maine; his widow, Dorcas, d. Oct. 13, 1897, in Yarmouth, aged ninety years.

---

* *Old Times in North Yarmouth:* 744–746, 832.
† *Second Manual of the First Congregational Church in Yarmouth,* 1878: 14.

Issue: I. Mary Eliza Seabury, b. Oct. 23, 1828; bap.
Nov. 4, 1832, in the First Church of North Yarmouth;
mar. Sept. 16, 1847, in Yarmouth, to Enoch Chandler
Farrington, b. Dec. 14, 1815, in Fryeburg, Maine, son
to John and Nancy (Royce) Farrington. He was a
teacher of music, and resided in Auburn, Maine,
where he d. Dec. 13, 1870. His widow, Mary Eliza,
d. there, June 6, 1900.

Issue: 1. Jenny Lind Farrington, b. Nov. 18, 1850,
in Auburn; mar. Feb. 26, 1877, in Dansville, Nova
Scotia, to Jacob Jackson Abbott, b. May, 1850, in
Uxbridge, Mass., son to Jacob Jackson and Mar-
garet Fletcher (Whitin) Abbott. They reside in
Denver, Colorado.

Issue: I. Margaret Farrington Abbott, b. Aug. 6,
1878, in Lake City, Colorado; mar. April 21,
1904, in Auburn, Maine, to George W. Blanchard.

II. James Dudley Abbott, b. July 3, 1880, in Lake
City, mar. June 14, 1906, Mary MacLean.

III. Edward Farrington Abbott, b. April 3, 1882, in
Lake City; mar. June 7, 1906, in Auburn,
Maine, Mary Hale Dana.

IV. Jacob Jackson Abbott, b. July 9, 1883, in Lake
City.

V. Catherine Whitin Abbott, b. Nov. 3, 1887, in
Lake City.

VI. Charles Cushman Abbott, b. Sept. 22, 1889, in
Lake City.

VII. Dorothy Abbott, b. May 4, 1894, in Lake City.

2. Lena Annetta Farrington, b. April 11, 1856, in
Auburn, Maine; mar. June 21, 1878, in Boston,
Mass., to Charles Livingston Cushman, b. May
13, 1856, at Minot, Maine, son to Ara and Julia
Woodman (Morse) Cushman. Charles L. Cush-
man is a shoe manufacturer of Auburn, Maine.
No issue.

II. George Albion Seabury, b. Jan. 8, 1831; baptized
Nov. 4, 1832, with his elder sister; mar. April,

1854, Charlotte Fitch. He was a farmer of Yarmouth, but removed some years ago to Oregon. Issue: 1. Charlotte A. Fitch Seabury.

III. Lucy Grant Seabury, b. Nov. 24, 1833, in North Yarmouth; mar. Jan. 1, 1850, to Francis Woodbury Seabury, b. May 6, 1820, in North Yarmouth, son to David and Mary (Low) Seabury, a shipmaster of North Yarmouth. Francis W. Seabury was a ship-joiner in Yarmouth; later, he removed to California, where he was known as a merchant and a builder. He d. May, 1893, in Mancos, Colorado; his widow resides at Los Angeles, California.

Issue: 1. Sarah Grant Seabury, b. Aug. 16, 1856; d. May 16, 1859, in Yarmouth, Maine.

2. Frank Edwin Seabury, b. Aug. 17, 1858, in Yarmouth; mar. Sept. 7, 1885, in Boston, Eliza J. McWhirk. At about sixteen years of age, Frank E. Seabury entered the printing-office of his uncle, Julius A. Dresser. Two years later, he became connected with a wholesale boot and shoe house in Boston. For several years he was with his cousin, W. G. Seabury, in Kansas. About 1884, he returned to Boston, which since has been his home. For six years he has been connected with the Standard Oil Company, of New York. No issue.

3. Arthur Woodbury Seabury, b. Oct. 21, 1864, in Yarmouth, Maine; mar. March 1, 1896, in Durango, Colorado, Hattie Ellen Scott. He is a physician, and resides at Lamar, Colorado. Issue: 1. Doris Gertrude Seabury, b. July 20, 1899, in Buena Vista, Colorado; d. June 8, 1900, at Lamar.

IV. Abby Frances Seabury, b. Sept. 15, 1842, in Yarmouth; mar. May 16, 1860, in Yarmouth, to Ambrose Samuel Dyer, b. 1833, in Brewer, Maine, son to Jesse and Rachel (——) Dyer.
Ambrose Samuel Dyer enlisted, at the beginning of the

Civil War, as 2d Lieutenant of Co. H, 5th Maine Regiment. This company consisted largely of men from Yarmouth, Freeport, and the surrounding towns. Dyer soon was promoted to 1st Lieutenant; in that capacity he served during the company's encampment at Portland, Maine. He was taken ill almost immediately after their arrival in Washington, D. C., and was sent home to Yarmouth, where he d. Sept. 1, 1861.

His widow returned home to her father with her infant son, not yet three months old. She had a thorough musical education and soon began teaching, which she has followed as a profession all her life. In June, 1906, she gave up a large class at Los Angeles, California, and returned east to make her home with her son at Lansdowne, Pennsylvania.

Issue: 1. Samuel Haley Dyer, b. July 2, 1861, in Yarmouth, Maine; mar. Oct. 2, 1885, in Auburn, Maine, Elizabeth Frances Hall, b. Oct. 2, 1864, in Dixfield, Maine. He is a lumber manufacturer; resides at Lansdowne, Pennsylvania.

Issue: I. Ralph Seabury Dyer, b. Feb. 8, 1886, in Portland, Maine; d. May 11, 1886, aged three months.

II. Lena Cushman Dyer, b. Aug. 28, 1888, in Portland, Maine.

III. Jessica May Dyer, b. Feb. 6, 1890, in Portland, Maine.

IV. Dorrance Seabury Dyer, b. Sept. 9, 1894, in Portland, Maine.

V. Elizabeth Jane Dyer, b. Nov. 19, 1897, in Portland, Maine.

VI. Samuel Dyer, b. June 20, 1904, in Lansdowne, Pa.; d. Aug. 17, 1904, aged two months, in Ocean City, N. J.

V. Annetta Seabury, b. May 6, 1844, in Yarmouth; mar. Sept. 2, 1863, in Yarmouth, to Julius Alphonso Dresser, b. Feb. 12, 1838, in Portland, Maine, son to Asa and Nancy (Smart) Dresser, of Portland.

Mr. and Mrs. Dresser, for many years, were engaged in

the work of spiritual healing, in Boston. Even a brief exposition of their philosophy of life is impossible here, but it is embodied in "The Power of Silence," written by their eldest son, Horatio W. Dresser; and a brief account of their work may be found in another of his publications, "Health and the Inner Life," page 121. Mr. Julius A. Dresser d. May 10, 1893, in Boston, Mass. His widow resides in the homestead of her father, at Yarmouth.

> Issue: 1. Horatio Willis Dresser, b. Jan. 15, 1866, in Yarmouth, Maine; mar. March 17, 1898, in Boston, Mass., Alice Mae Reed, daughter to Elliott Gregory and Betsey H. Reed.

Mr. Dresser was educated in Harvard University; A. B., 1895, A. M., 1904. Since 1903, he has been Assistant in Philosophy in the University, and resides at Cambridge. He is, however, chiefly a writer; his publications, previous to 1907, embrace: "The Power of Silence," a study of the values and ideals of the inner life, "Living by the Spirit," "A Book of Secrets," "Methods and Problems of Spiritual Healing," "In Search of a Soul," "Voices of Hope," "The Christ Ideal," "The Perfect Whole," "Voices of Freedom," "The Heart of It," "Education and the Philosophical Ideal," "Health and the Inner Life," and "Man and the Divine Order."

> Issue: I. Dorothea Dresser, b. Dec. 18, 1901. II. Malcolm Dresser, b. Oct. 14, 1905, in Cambridge.

> 2. Ralph Howard Dresser, b. April 21, 1872, in Boston; d. young.

> 3. Jean Paul Dresser, b. July 7, 1877, in Boston; mar. Aug. 2, 1906, to Faith Leah Storer.

> 4. Philip Seabury Dresser, b. Sept. 11, 1885, in Boston.

4. Joseph[7], son to David[6], b. 1810, in Freeport; d. there, aged one and a half years.

5. Enos[7], son to David[6], b. 1812, in Freeport; was lost at sea, aged about twenty-one years.

6. Susan[7], daughter to David[6], b. Jan. 30, 1815, in Freeport; mar. Sept. 30, 1832, in North Yarmouth, to George Dunham, b. July 30, 1811, in Brunswick,

Maine, son to Caleb and Margaret (Morse) Dunham, of Brunswick.

George Dunham was a large shipbuilder, as well as a ship-owner, in Yarmouth. He was associated with Albion Seabury, under the firm name of Seabury and Dunham, from 1842 to 1847. During that time they built the barks *Henry Kelsey*, 200 (tons), *Archimedes*, 291, *J. W. Blodgett*, 250, *Polka*, 165, *Ellen*, 200, schooners *Westogustogo*, 105, *Petrel*, 130, sloop *Empress*, 35, brig *Vancouver*, 180, and ships *Helen Augusta*, 450, *Blanchard*, 598. They also had a large sail-making loft in a storehouse on Union Wharf.* Mr. Dunham, in 1848, formed a partnership with Matthias Allen; during that year they constructed and launched the bark *Sunny-Eye*, 252 tons, and the brig *Harriet*, 173. The following year, 1849, Mr. Dunham removed to Winterport, then called Frankfort, on the Penobscot River, where he built large ships, chiefly by contract. One of his large ships, a clipper called the *Nonpareil*, is said to have crossed the Atlantic in nine days, and "broken the record."

In 1856 and 1857, during a season of great business depression, Mr. Dunham built two large ships with his own capital. He held them for a time, but finally was obliged to sell them at a loss; this caused his failure. He gave his comfortable home and everything to his creditors, and removed to a farm in Strong. But "Sandy River was not navigable," and farm life was not congenial; a few years later, he removed to Bangor, and resumed shipbuilding, which he continued until his death. He is described as "genial, generous, and hospitable." His wife "was essentially a home-maker, devoted to her family, fond of reading, and particularly gifted in the use of her needle." They both were members of the Congregational Church.

George Dunham d. July 18, 1867, in Bangor, Maine; his widow, Susan, d. May 10, 1893, in Malden, Mass., aged seventy-eight years.

Issue : I. Ellen Melinda Dunham, b. June 26, 1833, in North Yarmouth; mar., first, Jan. 17, 1850, in

---

* *Old Times in North Yarmouth* : 744-745, 359.

Winterport, to Eliphalet Greeley, who d. Dec.
9, 1864, in Bangor. She was mar., second, Dec.
13, 1870, in Boston, Mass., to Daniel Copeland, b.
Sept. 6, 1806, in Boston ; he d. about 1895. Mrs.
Copeland resides (1906) in Malden, Mass. Issue
by first husband : 1. George Dunham Greeley,
b. Feb. 5, 1853, in Winterport, Maine ; mar. Oct.
28, 1881, in Boston, Jenny Loring, adopted daughter to Ansil and Lucy Loring. No issue.

II. **Arabella Dunham**, known as Belle, b. Dec. 2, 1836,
in North Yarmouth ; mar. Sept. 17, 1856, in Winterport, to Captain Benjamin Thompson, b. Sept.
10, 1834, in Winterport. Captain Thompson followed the sea, and his wife sailed with him on
long voyages to all parts of the globe. He d.
Oct. 31, 1904, in Winterport. His widow now
(1906) resides in Malden, Mass.

Issue : 1. Louise Thompson, b. Feb. 19, 1858, in
Winterport ; mar. in May, 1879, in Bangor, to
Frank Williams, of Bangor. Issue : I. Hilda
Frances Williams, b. Jan. 13, 1888, in Newton,
Mass.

2. William Thompson, b. Feb. 28, 1875, in Malden,
Mass. ; mar. in Oct., 1902, in Boston, Mary
Arey, of Winterport. No issue.

III. **Abby Estelle Dunham**, b. May 28, 1845, in North
Yarmouth ; mar., first, May, 1866, in Bangor, to
Joseph White. After his death, she mar., second,
George A. Nourse, of Oakland, California.

Issue by first husband : 1. Marion White, b. Dec. 9,
1869, in Bangor ; mar. Nov., 1889, in Fresno, California, to Charles W. Miller, of Fresno. Issue : I.
Helen Dunham Miller. II. Alice Earley Miller.
III. Margaret Elizabeth Miller. IV. Marian Miller.

IV. **Mary Alice Dunham**, b. July 4, 1859, in Strong,
Maine ; mar. June 14, 1877, in Yarmouth, to
George G. Vianello, of Yarmouth. He d. July
17, 1884 ; his widow resides (1906) in Malden,
Mass.

Issue: 1. George Leslie Vianello, b. April 11, 1880,
in Lewiston, Maine; mar. Jan, 21, 1905, in Boston, Reba Squiers, of Boston. Issue: I. Alice
Jeanette Vianello, b. Oct. 17, 1906, in North
Adams, Mass.

2. Ralph Dunham Vianello, b. Nov. 15, 1882, in Yarmouth, Maine; resides in Malden.

7. Eliza⁷, daughter to David⁶, b. May 17, 1818, in Freeport; was mar., about 1839, to Captain Hiram Chesley
Hatch, a seafaring man. He was b. 1812, in Minot,
Maine, son to Chesley and Betsey (Perkins) Hatch,
of Minot.

Chesley Hatch was a blacksmith, who had removed to
Minot from North Yarmouth. His father, Hiram Hatch, of
North Yarmouth, appears to have been the first manufacturer of wagons and carriages in that section; the iron-work
he used came from the blacksmith shop of his son Chesley.
It also is recorded that Hiram Hatch made the first "bel-
lows-topped chaise," and wore the first "long trowsers," in
town. His wife was a Brown, whose "father lived to be over
ninety years old." This Hatch family doubtless was descended from Barnabas Hatch, cooper, sometime of Tolland,
Conn., of Duxbury, 1727, and of North Yarmouth, 1729.*

Hiram Hatch lived in what was called "No. 9," opposite
the schoolhouse. For a time, after his marriage, the family
of Captain Hatch lived in his grandfather's house. Early
in the "gold fever" of 1849, the captain went to California,
where he remained. After the marriage of her eldest daughter, Mrs. Hatch joined her husband in the fall of 1856, taking with her the two younger daughters, Harriet and Mary.
But the climate did not agree with her, she had constant
trouble with her throat while she was there; in about a year
she returned to Portland. In 1861, she moved to Falmouth,
where she lived, with all her children, in the old Buckman
Tavern; later, her sisters induced her to return to Yarmouth,
and she was living there when her husband died, in 1863.

Captain Hatch was very successful in his business enter-

* *Old Times in North Yarmouth:* 609, 276, 282, 684, 682, 1198.

prises on the Pacific coast ; he was interested in mills, and had established a line of vessels that were plying between Humboldt Bay and San Francisco, with passengers and merchandise. Between those two points there was a dangerous shoal, called "The Bar," upon which he was wrecked on Feb. 22, 1863. His vessel was lost, with all on board, but his body was found and buried on the shore. As soon as Mrs. Hatch received the letter informing her of her husband's death, she went to San Francisco, leaving home on April 11. When she reached there, the people were very kind and sympathetic, for her husband was well known as a careful and skilful navigator; but the main object of her long journey was not realized. Captain Hatch's partner, one McLean, was lost with him, as well as valuable papers ; and she was told that there was no estate to settle. On reaching home, July 8, 1863, she removed to Portland, where she lived until her death, Dec. 26, 1883, at the age of sixty-five years.

> Issue: I. Almira Adelaide Hatch, b. Aug. 6, 1840, in Yarmouth ; mar. April 15, 1856, in Portland, to William J. McDonald, who d. July 5, 1890, in Westbrook, a suburb of Portland. She d. March 23, 1886, aged forty-five years.
>
> > Issue: 1. William Herbert McDonald, b. May 11, 1857, in Portland; mar. June 23, 1890, in Randolph, Maine, Caroline L. Yeaton, of Randolph. He is night editor of the "Portland (Maine) Argus."
> >
> > 2. John Percy McDonald, b. April 6, 1859, in Portland ; mar. Oct. 24, 1881, in Augusta, Maine, Cordelia Littlejohn.
> >
> > 3. Hattie May McDonald, b. Sept. 13, 1861, in Falmouth, Maine ; was mar. Sept. 12, 1888, in the Church of the Messiah, Portland, to Charles F. Hamblen, of Boston, formerly of Portland. She d. Jan. 28, 1890, in Boston, aged twenty-eight years.
> >
> > 4. Irving Parker McDonald, b. Dec. 16, 1865, in Portland.

5. Frank Clifford McDonald, b. July 4, 1869, in Portland; mar. Sept. 30, 1891, in Malden, Mass., Sarah S. Keeler.

6. Harry Wadsworth McDonald, b. Aug. 15, 1876, in Portland.

7. Bertie McDonald (son), b. April 9, 1880, in Portland.

II. Lizzie Hatch, b. 1842, in Yarmouth; d. aged about six months.

III. A son, b. 1845, in Yarmouth; d. one day old.

IV. Harriet Elizabeth Hatch, b. Sept. 14, 1847, in Yarmouth, resides (1906) in Portland, Maine. She distinctly remembers the journey she made, with her mother and sister Mary, to California, when she was nine years of age; also the fearful earthquake that occurred while they were there. At several different periods she lived with her aunt, Mrs. Henry Dyer,* in Portland, and her aunt wished to adopt her, as she had no daughter, but her mother would not give her consent.

V. Mary Etta Hatch, b. Sept. 15, 1849, in Yarmouth.

VI. David Chesley Hatch, b. June 15, 1858, in Portland; d. May 6, 1879, of consumption, in Portland. He was a printer in the office of the "Portland Argus."

8. Sarah Jane⁷, daughter to David⁶, b. June 6, 1821; bap. Aug. 2, 1829, in the First Church of North Yarmouth; mar. about 1839, in Yarmouth, to Ebenezer Davis Lane, a shipmaster of Yarmouth. Captain

---

* Issue of Chesley and Betsey Perkins Hatch, of Minot, Maine:—

I. Leonard Hatch.

II. Louisiana Hatch.

III. Betsey Hatch; mar. to Henry Dyer, a boat-builder of Portland, Maine; d. May 23, 1893, in Portland. Henry Dyer d. Jan. 5, 1896, in Portland. Issue: 1. Joseph Dyer.

IV. Lydia Jane Hatch.

V. Harrison Hatch.

VI. Levi Hatch.

VII. Hiram Chesley Hatch, b. 1812, in Minot; mar. Eliza⁷ Pratt.

Lane was b. Feb. 2, 1805, in Gray, Maine; d. April
29, 1880, in Yarmouth. "Mrs. Sarah J. (Pratt) Lane"
was received, July 5, 1840, into the First Congregational Church, of Yarmouth; she d. Oct. 13, 1862.*

Issue: I. Leila Ianthe Lane, b. Nov. 3, 1842, in North
Yarmouth; mar. Sept. 8, 1865, in that town, to
Captain John H. Humphrey, a shipmaster. She d.
May 3, 1900, in Yarmouth.

Captain Humphrey, who retired from a seafaring life some
years ago, resides in Yarmouth beside the Merrill Memorial
Library. As chairman of the Board of Selectmen of the
town of Yarmouth, Captain Humphrey accepted for the
town, on Sept. 15, 1904, the gift of that library and the land
upon which it stands. He also was chosen, in 1904, one of
the eight persons composing the first Board of Trustees of
that library.†

Issue: 1. Elizabeth J. Humphrey, b. April 18, 1867,
in Yarmouth; mar. May 10, 1892, to Dr. A. R.
Smith.

2. Edith Gertrude Humphrey, b. Aug. 12, 1868, in
Yarmouth; mar. June 17, 1896, to John C. Bur-
rowes; they reside in North Carolina.

3. John E. L. Humphrey, b. Aug. 28, 1873, in Yarmouth; resides, unmarried, in Reno, Nevada.

4. Leila May Humphrey, b. Aug. 18, 1877, in Yarmouth.

5. Wilder C. Humphrey, b. Dec. 10, 1880, in Yarmouth; mar. Aug. 1, 1906, Lucy Crockett, of
Rockland, Maine.

6. George Howard Humphrey, b. Feb. 10, 1882, in
Yarmouth.

II. Samuel Bucknam Lane, b. May 2, 1844, in Yarmouth; was lost at sea in 1862.

III. Alfred E. Lane, b. June 6, 1846, in Yarmouth; d.
1865, at Key West, Florida.

---

* *Second Manual of the First Congregational Church in Yarmouth, Maine,*
1878: 15.

† Vide page 412.

IV. Sarah Helena Lane, b. May 10, 1848, in Yarmouth;
mar. June 15, 1869, in Yarmouth, to Benjamin
Franklin Whitcomb, b. May 8, 1846, in Sweden,
Maine, son to Benjamin Franklin and Harriet
Pike (Whitehouse) Whitcomb. Mr. B. F. Whitcomb, Jr., who was a paper manufacturer, d. Nov.
25, 1876, at Turner's Falls, Mass.; his widow resides at Exeter, N. H.

Issue: 1. Gertrude Florence Whitcomb, b. Jan. 8,
1871, in Laurel, Indiana; mar. Sept. 2, 1896, to
Frank Melbourn Bucknam; resides in Skowhegan, Maine. Issue: I. Alvan William Bucknam, b. Jan. 6, 1899.

2. Inez Maud Whitcomb, b. Nov. 2, 1873, in Hard-
wick, Mass.; mar. April 2, 1902, to Dr. William
Beaman Kenniston; resides in Exeter, N. H.
Issue: I. Faith Elizabeth Kenniston, b. July 5,
1905.

V. Mary Gertrude Lane, b. Nov. 30, 1851, in North
Yarmouth; mar. Dec. 24, 1873, to Irving F. True,
a banker. Their home, for a number of years, has
been the mansion in Yarmouth, on the road to
Portland, built about 1810 by Captain Seth
Mitchell.*

Issue: 1. Levi True; d. in infancy.

2. Herbert True; d. in infancy.

3. Marion True, b. Aug. 30, 1878, in Portland, Maine;
mar. Sept. 17, 1902, to Ralph Bissell Redfern,
b. Sept. 9, 1877, in Winchester, Mass., son to
Charles Edward and Harriet (McLellan) Redfern, of Winchester. Ralph B. Redfern was graduated from Amherst College, 1899; his wife was
graduated from North Yarmouth Academy, 1895,
from Smith College, 1900. They reside in Winchester. Issue: I. Katherine True Redfern, b.
Dec. 1, 1904, in Boston, Mass.

VI. Herbert Lane; d. in infancy.

* Vide pages 434, 435.

VII. Levi Lane; d. in infancy.

9. David[7], youngest child to David[6], b. about 1823, in Freeport, Maine; mar., about 1848, Susan Day Pierce, b. Jan., 1827, in the "Gooch neighborhood," at North Yarmouth. She was the thirteenth and last child of John and Sarah (Mitchell) Pierce. Sarah Mitchell's family lived at Falmouth Foreside. Susan Pierce was tall (five feet, seven and a half inches); her usual weight was about one hundred and twenty-two pounds.

David Pratt, Jr., did not attain the height of his father; he was only five feet, nine inches tall, but he was powerfully built. At the age of sixteen years he commenced going to sea, and made his first voyage with his brother, Captain Timothy, "round the Horn," in 1839. After that he sailed as mate on the *Reaper*, a number of years. As captain, he succeeded Captain Benjamin Webster in the *Heloise*, and sailed in her for five years (1862 to 1867), carrying passengers and freight, between San Francisco and Hongkong. During this time he was forced to remain at Hongkong, for six months, by the Confederate cruiser *Alabama*. The *Alabama* had come into Chinese waters, by way of the Cape of Good Hope and the Indian Ocean, and coaled at Singapore, Dec. 23, 1863; not until she was reported to have rounded the Cape of Good Hope, on her return to France in March, 1864, did any American shipping dare venture out.* Captain Pratt and his wife were royally entertained at Hongkong by the American consulate and by Chinese mandarins. A Russian corvette, whose officers were all noblemen, took them up to Tokio, where they spent several weeks. But as soon as the embargo was off, Captain Pratt resumed his regular trips from San Francisco. The intervals between these trips were consumed in coasting from San Francisco along the shore to what now is Alaska,† at

---

* *The Great Contest*, by Willis C. Humphrey, 1886: 601.

† The name Alaska was adopted by the United States at the suggestion of Charles Sumner, after the purchase of this valuable territory from Russia, on March 30, 1867.

his own venture, for ice, furs, and fish. He was the first person to introduce trade in fresh fish at San Francisco.

Early in 1868, Captain Pratt and his wife returned to their home in Yarmouth; from there he made several short voyages, usually without his wife. His last voyage as captain was on the *J. Baker*, built by his father in 1857. He was to take her "round the Horn" to California, for other parties, but the bark was overladen by those who sent her out, and at Callao the crew mutinied because they considered her unsafe. With difficulty he quelled the mutiny, but not before he had received several wounds, one of which permanently injured the sight of one eye. At Acapulco the ship was condemned and sold. Because of defective eyesight he never again took command, but was sailing-master for a number of years on the *Alice Cooper*, of which John H. Humphrey, of Yarmouth, was captain. About 1884, he removed with his family to Atlantic (a village in the town of Quincy, Mass.), where he engaged in stair-building. He d. March 1, 1892, in Atlantic, aged sixty-nine years.

Susan Pratt passed through the experiences common to the wives of seafaring men. In the earlier years of their married life, when her husband was at sea most of the time, she lived with her children in a small cottage between the home of her father-in-law and Daniel L. Mitchell. When "Master David's" house was sold, after his death in 1861, she bought it, and moved in with her little family. But she had not been there much more than a year before her husband returned, obtained command of the *Heloise*, and took her with him to the Pacific coast. Her home was broken up, the daughter was placed in boarding-school, and the son with relatives. Upon her return to Yarmouth, five years later, she resumed housekeeping. The valuable curios, gathered by her and her husband in foreign lands, she left by will to her only grandson, William Frederick Pratt. She d. Jan., 1896, in Atlantic, having just passed her sixty-ninth birthday.

Issue: I. Susan Adelaide⁸, b. June 6, 1850, in Yarmouth, Maine; was mar., first, in Boston, Dec. 10, 1870, by the Rev. Justin Fulton, to John Edward

Robinson. He d. Jan. 16, 1891, in Revere, Mass., their home. She was mar., second, Dec. 16, 1895, in Montgomery, Alabama, to Warren Ralph Dickinson, who was killed in a railroad accident, Sept. 10, 1896. Her third husband, to whom she was married March 2, 1901, at her home in Revere, is Frank Tuthill Sterling.

Mrs. Sterling received her early education in Yarmouth. While her parents were abroad, 1862 to 1867, she attended the old North Yarmouth Academy, and boarded in the family of the principal, Edwin Hoyt. Those five years had changed her from a rosy little girl of twelve to a rather tall and pale young lady of seventeen, whom her father did not recognize when he returned. After her marriage, she lived many years in Revere; but in 1893, she sold her property there, and since has resided in Somerville, Mass.

> Issue by first husband : 1. Grace Adelaide Robinson, b. March 1, 1872, in Boston, Mass.; mar. Sept. 23, 1897, in Somerville, to Andrew Willard Freeman; resides at Arlington Heights, Mass.
>
> Issue : I. Ruth Adelaide Freeman, b. Feb. 7, 1899.
> II. Helen Grace Freeman, b. March 28, 1902.
> III. Priscilla Freeman, b. Feb. 8, 1904.
>
> II. David William[8], b. Dec. 29, 1852, in Yarmouth, Maine; mar., first, about 1873, in Stockton, Maine, Agnes Irene Staples, b. about 1850, in Stockton, daughter to Frederick Staples; she d. in Boston, Mass. He mar., second, about 1878, in Portland, Oregon, Maud Cornelius, of Portland, Oregon. After her death, he mar., third, about 1889, in Norfolk, Virginia, Lily Dozier.

Captain Pratt first went to sea with his father, at about the age of seventeen years. Several years later, he went on a voyage as mate with another captain ; the captain became insane and jumped overboard, and Pratt brought the ship home. The owners of the ship gave him the position of captain on her next voyage; and thereafter he sailed in command of large ships on foreign voyages, until about the time of his third marriage. From 1891 to 1895, he was manager of hotels in Fernandina, Florida, Thomasville, Georgia, and Suwanee, in the same state; then he went to New York City. For some time Captain Pratt has been in command of the yacht *Aquilla*, owned by Mr. Eno, of the New York Yacht Club.

> Issue by first wife: 1. William Frederick[6], b. 1874 (?), in Cardiff, Wales; mar. 1903, Ada Waters; resides at Revere, Mass.
>
> Issue by second wife: 2. Ruth[6], b. in Portland, Oregon; mar. 1906, in Portland, Oregon.
>
> Issue by third wife: 3. Maud[6], b. about 1893, in Thomasville, Ga.

V. Timothy[6], son to David[5], b. July 22 (27), 1780, in North Yarmouth; mar. April 18, 1803, in Freeport, Hannah[6], daughter to Samuel[5] and Mary (Bartol) Winslow.* Hannah Winslow, b. March 11, 1783, in Freeport, was the fourth in a family of eight children. Her father was the fifth generation from Kenelm[1] Winslow, of Plymouth (Gilbert[4], Gilbert[3], Nathaniel[2], Kenelm[1]).†

Early in life, Timothy Pratt followed the sea; but, a few years after his marriage, he engaged in farming on a tract of land which he cleared on the "Merrill Road," bordering on the line between Freeport and Pownal. About 1818, he removed with his wife and three children to Jay, Maine. He lived in Jay and Canton, Maine, until after his daughter, Mary Richardson, went to Concord, Mass. He and his wife spent their declining years with this daughter, or near her. Hannah Pratt d. Sept. 4, 1862, in Concord, aged seventy-nine years; she was buried in the adjoining town of Sudbury. Timothy Pratt d. Feb. 17, 1865, in Concord, aged eighty-four years, and was buried beside his wife.

Issue: 1. Arthur[7], b. in Freeport.

2. David[7], b. in Freeport. This name is mentioned in "Old Times" as David; the "Winslow Memorial" has it Daniel.

3. Annis[7], b. in Freeport; mar., first, to —— Pray. After

---

* *Town Records of Freeport*, vol. 1 : 71, 131.

† Dr. Holton's *Winslow Memorial*, 1888, vol. 2 : 733.

his death she was mar. to Adelbert Jordan. She
lived some years in Lawrence, Mass.

Issue by first husband: I. Martha Pray. II. Medora
Pray.

Issue by second husband : III. A son, —— Jordan.

4. Hannah Winslow[7], b. probably in Jay.

5. Mary Fitts[7], b. in Jay; was mar. by Hewer Dow,
Esq., on May 23, 1839, in Canton, Maine, to Jesse
Cooledge Richardson, b. March 26, 1816, in Jay.

In 1852, Jesse C. Richardson removed his family to Concord, Mass., where he purchased " the Haywood Farm . . .
so called . . . partly in Concord, partly in Sudbury . . .
with the buildings " thereon. It consisted of two hundred
and forty acres. He mortgaged the farm to Aaron and Cyrus
Hunt, of Sudbury, on Nov. 3, 1852, for $4,000 ; the mort-
gage was discharged Dec. 27, 1855.* In 1874, they still were
living at Concord.

Issue : I. Emma Jane Richardson, b. April 25, 1840, in
Jay.

II. Darius Osman Richardson, b. Aug. 1, 1842, in Jay.

III. Willard Sherman Richardson, b. Aug. 24, 1844, in
Jay; d. young.

IV. Deborah Meggs Richardson, b. Dec. 24, 1846, in
Jay ; d. young.

V. Deborah Pratt Richardson, b. Feb. 8, 1848, in Jay.

VI. Willard Laforest Richardson, b. Aug. 2, 1849, in
Jay.

VII. Mary Hannah Richardson, b. Jan. 12, 1851, in Jay ;
in 1874 was living in Concord, Mass.

VIII. Norman Hudson Richardson, b. June 20, 1852, in
Jay.

IX. Lucy Chase Richardson, b. Sept. 2, 1853, in Concord.

X. Annette Lincoln Richardson, b. Oct. 19, 1854, in
Concord.

XI. Jesse Stone Richardson, b. April 11, 1856, in Concord.

---

* *Middlesex County Deeds*, Book 641 : 289.

XII. Hattie Winslow Richardson, b. Aug. 10, 1857, in Concord.

XIII. Ellen Groer Richardson, b. April 10, 1859, in Concord.

6. Timothy Wainwright[7], b. in Jay.

7. Artson Knight[7], b. in Jay.

VI. Joseph[6], son to David[5], b. Sept. 22, 1782, in North Yarmouth; mar. Oct. 22, 1808, in North Yarmouth, Mary[6], daughter to Samuel[5] and Eunice (Davis) Soule. Mary Soule was b. May 13, 1786, in North Yarmouth; d. there, May 15, 1853, aged sixty-seven years.

Joseph Pratt lived about two miles from the village of Yarmouth, on the road leading to Pownal, but only a short distance from the main road to Brunswick. Timothy Davis, whose daughter Eunice married Samuel[5] Soule, lived in the last house in town on that road, with Joseph Pratt beside him.* Mr. Pratt kept a small store, near his home, where he received farm produce and cord-wood in exchange for West India goods, calico, etc. All trade at that day was by barter, very little money being in circulation. After a time he gave up the store and purchased a farm near his house; but he always lived on the same place until a few years before his death, when he purchased a house in the village and moved there. All the children were born in the first house, and remained at home until scattered by marriage. On August 14, 1818, Joseph Pratt and his wife Mary were received, from the First Congregational Church in Freeport, into the First Congregational Church in North Yarmouth.† He died Nov. 21, at the age of seventy-three years, and was buried Nov. 24, 1855, in the Baptist burying-ground. His wife, who had been buried in Davis's family burying-ground on the Davis farm, was removed and placed beside him.

Issue: 1. Darius[7], b. Jan. 5, 1810, in North Yarmouth; mar. Jan. 14, 1835, Margaret Noyes Gooch, bap. Oct. 20, 1822, daughter to Rufus and Dorcas (Noyes) Gooch.‡

---

* *Old Times in North Yarmouth*: 975, 274.
† *Records of the First Congregational Church in North Yarmouth*: 31.
‡ *Old Times in North Yarmouth*: 1124.

Captain Darius Pratt was well known as a man of superior ability. He commanded large ships that sailed to foreign ports, on voyages of two and three years' duration. In 1854, while master of the *Pumgustic*, loaded with railroad iron, from Cardiff, Wales, to New York, he was shipwrecked. His wife and only child were with him. The ship was lost; but Captain Pratt, with his family and a part of the crew, was rescued and taken to Liverpool. They sailed for home on the ill-fated *Arctic*, which was lost in September, 1854. After leaving England the *Arctic* never was heard from, and the supposition was that she encountered an iceberg and foundered in mid-ocean.

> Issue: I. Norman⁸, b. July 7, 1836; was lost in the *Arctic*, Sept., 1854, aged eighteen years. II. Infant⁸, buried Jan., 1838, in North Yarmouth.

> 2. Lydia⁷, b. April 21, 1812, in North Yarmouth; mar. to Samuel A. Lawrence; she d. June, 1865.

> Issue: I. William Lawrence, b. March 31, 1842. He is a dwarf, unmarried, and resides with his aunt, Mrs. Eliza Mitchell, in Yarmouthville, Maine.

> II. and III. Twins, who died April 10, 1844, in infancy, without names.

> IV. Julia Lawrence, b. Aug., 1846; mar. June, 1866, to Dudley Haley, of Bath, Maine.

> V. George Lawrence, who was lost at sea, aged about eighteen years.

> 3. Eunice⁷, b. Feb. 3, 1814, in North Yarmouth; mar. to Captain Benjamin Webster, of Portland.

Captain Benjamin Webster was a man greatly respected, and of considerable wealth accumulated in a seafaring life. Their home for many years was on Spring Street, Portland. Mrs. Eunice Webster d. March 16, 1896, in Portland; her husband d. July 29, 1902, in the same city. They had no children, but adopted, or educated, several young people.

> 4. Joseph⁷, b. Nov. 28, 1815; bap. Sept. 22, 1816, in North Yarmouth; mar. Oct. 28, 1845, Margaret Ann Akerman, b. Oct. 30, 1828. She d. May 12, 1895.

> Issue: I. Anna R.⁸, b. 1846. II. Joseph⁸, b. 1848. III. Walter⁸, b. 1850. IV. Arthur⁸, b. May 6, 1853. V.

Edith[5], b. 1856. VI. Jennie[5], b. 1859. VII. Horace[5], b. Feb., 1867.

5. Catherine[7], b. Sept. 27, 1817, in North Yarmouth; mar. May 26, 1840, Captain David Seabury, Jr. She d. in Oct., 1865, three years and a half after her husband.

Captain Seabury sailed on long voyages to foreign ports, his wife and daughter usually accompanying him. He acquired a considerable fortune, retiring from the sea a few years before his death, which occurred March 4, 1862.

Issue: I. Annie Belle Seabury; d. in infancy.

II. Grace Fletcher Seabury; d. in infancy.

III. Flora Williams Seabury, b. May 12, 1845; mar. Oct. 3, 1866, to Charles Henry Pettengill, b. May 1, 1844. She resides in Auburn or Lewiston, Maine. Issue: 1. Charles Jason Pettengill. 2. Harry Seabury Pettengill.

6. Eliza S.[7], b. Oct. 1, 1819, in North Yarmouth; mar. March 6, 1851, to Daniel Lewis[6] Mitchell, b. Jan. 22, 1819, in North Yarmouth.*

VII. Mercy[6], daughter to David[5], b. April 3, 1785, in North Yarmouth; mar. March 6, 1812, in Freeport, to Daniel Tuck, b. May 2, 1786, in North Yarmouth. He was son to Lemuel and Susanna (Fellows) Tuck, of Farmington, Maine. Susanna Tuck d. April 19, 1828, in Farmington, aged seventy-nine years.† Lemuel Tuck d. in the same town, Feb. 19, 1842, aged ninety-eight years. Daniel Tuck d. Feb. 8, 1869, in Farmington; his widow, Mercy, d. there Dec. 12, 1871, aged eighty-six years.‡

Issue: 1. Joseph Fellows Tuck, b. Feb. 24, 1813. He never married; in 1885, he was living in Temple, Maine.

2. Daniel Corydon Tuck, b. April 11, 1814; mar. April 9, 1855, Elizabeth T. Crane.

For a number of years, Corydon Tuck, as he generally was known, was working as a stair-builder with his cousin,

---

* Vide The Mitchells from Kittery.

† Vide page 425.

‡ Butler's *History of Farmington, Maine*, 1885: 593-595.

Thomas⁷ Pratt, in Lowell. He finally retired to the family homestead, near Porter's Hill, in Farmington, where he continued stair-building, as well as farming.

Issue: I. Sadie Miriam Tuck, b. May 24, 1865, in Farmington.

3. Mary Mitchell Tuck, b. Sept. 28, 1815; mar. Feb. 25, 1838, to George Mosher. Issue: three.

4. Lydia Ann Tuck, b. April 7, 1818; she never was married.

5. Sarah Pratt Tuck, b. Aug. 8, 1823; mar., first, to Crocker W. Sampson; mar., second, May 7, 1849, to William T. Brackley. In 1885, they resided in Avon, Maine. No issue.

VIII. Rebecca⁶, daughter to David⁵, b. March 18, 1788, in North Yarmouth; mar. Dec. 22, 1803, in Freeport, to Edward⁷ Small,* son to Edward⁶ and Sarah⁵ (Mitchell) Small.†

IX. Enos⁶, son to David⁵, b. June 28, 1790, in Freeport (set off Feb. 14, 1789, from North Yarmouth). He was lost at sea, Aug. 2, 1810, aged nearly twenty years.

X. Jonathan⁶, son to David⁵, b. Aug. 25, 1792, in Freeport; he doubtless was named for the twin brother of his father who remained in Weymouth.

Jonathan Pratt was married Sept. 8, 1814, in Freeport, by the Rev. Reuben Nason, to Harriet Loring,‡ who was b. Feb. 26, 1795, four months after the death of her father, Thomas⁶ Loring, of Hingham, Mass. Thomas Loring was b. Nov. 18, 1758, in Hingham; mar. April, 1782, Lydia Lincoln, b. Jan. 30, 1762, daughter to Captain John and Lydia (Jacob) Lincoln, of Hingham.§ Captain John Lincoln served in the Revolutionary War, from the town of Hingham. Thomas⁶ Loring in early life was a schoolmaster in his native town; at the time of his death, he had filled for some years the position of clerk, also weigher and gauger, in the Boston Custom House. He d. Oct. 11, 1794, in Boston; in

---

* *Town Records of Freeport*, vol. 1 : 131.
† Vide pages 240, 442.
‡ *Town Records of Freeport*, vol. 1 : 136.
§ *History of Hingham, Mass.*, 1893, vol. 3 : 37, 38.

1805, his widow removed to Freeport with two or three of her seven children, where she was mar., second, to Silas Holbrook. Her old family Bible is in the possession of her great-grandson, Timothy Pratt, of Freeport.

Jonathan Pratt lived on a farm, and worked a part of the time as ship-carpenter in the shipyards. He was a man of extraordinary strength, and is said to have been in great demand for the heavy work of shipbuilding because he could handle twice the weight attempted by other men. He lived in Wales and Saco, Maine, but returned to Freeport, where his home was "on the Neck," near Cousins's River. He d. Oct. 29, 1864, in Freeport, aged seventy-two years. His widow, Harriet, d. Oct. 3, 1880, in the same town, aged eighty-five. Of her ten children, nine reached maturity; at the time of her death there were forty grandchildren and twelve great-grandchildren.

Issue: 1. Charles⁷, b. Aug. 1, 1815, in Freeport; d. young.

2. Harriet Loring⁷, b. Feb. 14, 1817, in Freeport; mar. to Daniel Patrick Talbot, of Freeport, b. 1813. They lived at Strout's Point, Freeport. In her old age, she became blind.

Issue: I. Josiah Talbot, b. Feb. 25, 1845, in Freeport; d. unmar., Sept. 7, 1879, in Freeport, aged thirty-four years.

II. George Washington Talbot, b. Aug. 11, 1846, in Freeport; resides in Haverhill, Mass.

III. Edgar A. Talbot, b. March 11, 1848, in Freeport; mar. July 22, 1884, Marietta Coffin; he resides in Freeport, and is interested in a saw-mill.

Issue: 1. Hattie Cecilia Talbot, b. Oct. 20, 1889, in Freeport.

IV. Annabelle Talbot, b. Nov. 7, 1850, in Freeport; mar. to —— Brewer, of South Freeport. She d. June 26, 1874, in Freeport.

V. Florilla Barker Talbot, b. Feb. 28, 1855, in Freeport; mar. April 16, 1873, to Captain Joseph Fickett, of Cape Elizabeth, Maine. She was lost at sea, about 1885.

VI. William Eugene Talbot, b. April 20, 1859, in Freeport ; mar. June 5, 1903, in San Francisco, California, Albertena Mathelda Englund, b. April 19, 1863, in Sweden, daughter to Larz and Anna L. (Person) Englund, of Matala, Sweden. Resides (1906) in Sacramento, California. No issue.

3. Charles Loring[7], son to Jonathan[6], b. June 19, 1819, in Freeport; mar., first, May 22, 1842, Alice Jane Curtis, daughter to Benjamin Curtis; she had no children. He mar., second, 1848, Catherine Hersey Allen, daughter to John Allen. The third wife of Charles L. Pratt, whom he mar. in 1869, was Martha[6] Dennison, b. Sept. 5, 1849, daughter to Caleb and Pamelia (Allen) Dennison, of Freeport.

Charles L. Pratt inherited the strength and endurance of his father. At the age of fourteen years he commenced going to sea, and led an active and industrious life until past seventy. Notwithstanding his eighty-seven years, in the summer of 1906 he frequently walked two miles. He has lived in Bath and Baldwin, Maine; now resides in Freeport.

Issue by second wife: I. Charles Loring[8], b. April 24, 1849, in Freeport; d. in infancy.

II. Alice Jane[8], b. July 26, 1850, in Freeport; d. in infancy.

III. Fred[8], b. Nov. 27, 1851, in Freeport ; mar. June 21, 1880, in Pownal, Tillie Perkins Coombs, daughter to Joshua and Mary S. (Davis) Coombs, b. Jan. 10, 1858, in Freeport. On Nov. 6, 1887, Fred Pratt and his wife became members of the First Congregational Church of Freeport. He is a carpenter and mason, and resides in Freeport. His knowledge of the Pratt families of his native town, and those allied to them, has been of great assistance to the writer.

Issue: 1. Osborne Chester[9], b. March 28, 1881, in Freeport. He is a mason by trade, Superintendent of the Sabbath School of the First Congregational Church of Freeport, and a good bass singer. With his two brothers and three sisters, he united with that church, on March 3, 1901.

2. Percy Clifford[9], b. Jan. 21, 1883, in Freeport. He is a mason by trade; he sings baritone.

3. Ethel Mellie[9], b. Jan. 2, 1885, in Freeport. She plays the organ of the First Congregational Church, of which she is a member; she also possesses a good alto voice.

4. Everett Noyes[9], b. Feb. 24, 1887, in Freeport. His trade is that of a machinist; he sings bass. He is six feet, seven inches, in height.

5. Laura Belle[9], b. Jan. 4, 1889, in Freeport. She is engaged in shoe-work; she sings soprano.

6. Clara Louise[9], b. March 21, 1891, in Freeport. She sings alto; she is now in school.

IV. Maria Soule[8], b. Oct. 31, 1853, in Freeport; d. Nov. 3, 1868, aged fifteen years.

Issue by third wife: V. Timothy[8], b. Jan. 7, 1870, in Freeport; mar. Jan. 30, 1897, in Freeport, Hattie Mabel Sampson, b. Dec. 21, 1880, in Buckfield, Maine, daughter to Colby Sampson, b. July 7, 1840, in Quincy, Mass., and his wife, Caroline Britton (Poland) Sampson, b. Jan. 15, 1844, in Durham, Maine.

Timothy Pratt is superintendent of the Freeport Water Company. On June 9, 1899, Mr. Pratt joined the Portland Commandery, No. 2, of Knights Templar; Dec. 31, 1900, he was elected Worshipful Master of Freeport Lodge, No. 23, in which he has held nearly every office, including that of secretary.

Issue: 1. Ruth[9], b. May 20, 1898, in Freeport.

2. Naomi[9], b. Jan. 5, 1901, in Freeport.

3. Eunice[9], b. Oct. 16, 1903, in Freeport.

4. Gladys[9], b. Dec. 11, 1905, in Durham.

VI. Alice J.[8], b. July 4, 1872, in Bath, Maine; mar. to Frank Thompson; went to Massachusetts.

VII. Katie[8], b. Sept. 5, 1873, in Baldwin, Maine; resides in Haverhill, Mass.

VIII. Nellie[8], b. April 13, 1879, in Baldwin, Maine; mar. a son to George Dennison, of Mast Landing, Freeport, and has several children.

IX. David[8], b. Sept., 1884, in East Baldwin, Maine; is married and lives in New Hampshire.

4. Lydia L.[7], daughter to Jonathan[6], b. Sept. 23, 1821, in Freeport; d. unmar., in Freeport, aged about twenty years.

5. Sarah T.[7], daughter to Jonathan[6], b. May 11, 1824, in Freeport; mar. Nov. 27, 1842, to Amos Carver Allen, b. Nov. 18, 1818, in Freeport. He d. Dec. 7, 1897, at Topsham, Maine; his widow d. April 11, 1903, in Freeport.

Issue: I. Ellen F. Allen, b. June 30, 1844, in Freeport; d. May 29, 1861, at Topsham, aged sixteen years and eleven months.

II. Charles W. Allen, b. Sept. 20, 1846, in Freeport; d. June 8, 1874, in Topsham, aged twenty-seven years.

III. Harriet P. Allen, b. Aug. 3, 1848, in Freeport; mar. March 7, 1874, to Frank W. Leonard. She d. Dec. 9, 1875, in Topsham, aged twenty-seven years.

Issue: 1. Abbie E. Leonard, b. Nov. 24, 1875, in Topsham; mar. Dec. 25, 1899, to Milton W. Coombs; resides in Topsham.

IV. Edward Amos Allen, b. Jan. 31, 1851, in Freeport; mar. May 1, 1872, Fannie Dunning. He d. Feb. 20, 1886, in Portland, Maine, aged thirty-five.

Issue: A son who died very young.

V. Jonathan P. Allen, b. April 17, 1853, in Freeport; he is married.

VI. Maria S. Allen, b. July 26, 1855, in Topsham; d. Oct., 1855, aged three months.

VII. Adrian M. Allen, b. Aug. 9, 1856, in Topsham; mar. Fannie Smith; d. March, 1893, aged thirty-six years. Issue: three children, including a son, Frank, who resides at Lisbon Falls, Maine.

VIII. Amelia S. Allen, b. June 21, 1859, in Topsham; mar., first, Oct. 31, 1877, to William H. Harris; mar., second, to E. L. Hunter.

Issue by first husband: 1. Eva M. Harris, b. Aug. 7, 1878.

2. Hattie E. Harris, b. March 5, 1880 ; mar. to Harry Grady; lives in Topsham. Issue: I. Ernest Grady.

3. Flora B. Harris, b. March 4, 1882 ; mar. Dec. 1, 1902, to Harry A. Hall; resides at Freeport.

IX. Howard Leslie Allen, b. May 28, 1862, in Topsham, Maine ; mar. in Lynn, Mass., Ida May Crowell, b. March 10, 1865, in Lynn, daughter to George and Jennette (Smith) Crowell, of Lynn. Howard L. Allen is a shoemaker; resides in Lynn. His wife d. Jan. 10, 1895, in Lynn.

Issue: 1. Ida May Allen, b. Sept. 12, 1886, in Lynn ; d. Sept. 1, 1888, aged two years.

2. Jennette Talbot Allen, b. Sept. 13, 1888, in Lynn.

3. Gertrude Ethel Allen, b. Oct. 10, 1890, in Lynn.

4. Amelia Southworth Allen, b. Oct. 15, 1893, in Lynn.

X. Sarah F. Allen, b. Feb. 12, 1865, in Topsham; mar. Oct. 8, 1904, to Alvah A. Plummer; resides at Auburn, Maine.

XI. Dwinel P. Allen, b. Aug. 25, 1867, in Topsham; mar. May 9, 1900, at Freeport, Edwina Elise Coffin, b. May 26, 1878, in Winthrop, Maine. They reside at Freeport. Issue: 1. Elvira Louise Allen, b. Aug. 19, 1901, in Freeport. 2. Viola Edwina Allen, b. Oct. 15, 1903, in Freeport. 3. Agnes Allen, b. April 17, 1905, in Freeport.

6. John William [7], son to Jonathan [6], b. Aug. 23, 1826, in Freeport ; mar. Caroline Carver ; lived in Bath, Maine, and had several children.

7. Rebecca C.[7], daughter to Jonathan [6], b. Feb. 6, 1829, in Freeport ; mar. to Isaac Allen, 3d, son to John Allen, brother to Isaac Allen, Jr., who mar. Mary [7], daughter to David [6] Pratt, Jr.*

Rebecca C. Allen married at the age of nineteen years, and died when her child was a year and a half or two years old.

* Vide page 817.

8. Amelia A.[7], daughter to Jonathan[6], b. May 10, 1831, in Freeport ; mar. Oct. 12, 1851, in Freeport, to William Southworth, b. Dec. 26, 1826, in Duxbury, Mass., son to Jedidiah and Elizabeth (Thomas) Southworth, of Duxbury. William Southworth is a carver and gilder by occupation ; he lived for a number of years in Newcastle, but now resides in Bath, Maine.

Issue : I. Allston Southworth, b. July 14, 1852, in Newcastle, Lincoln County, Maine.

II. Elizabeth Southworth, b. June 12, 1857, in Newcastle; d. June 2, 1865, in Newcastle.

III. William Southworth, b. Dec. 17, 1862, in Newcastle.

IV. Alice Southworth, b. April 13, 1865, in Newcastle ; d. April 28, 1865, aged fifteen days.

V. Frederick Southworth, b. April 4, 1867, in Newcastle ; mar. Nellie Coby, or Colby.

VI. Jennie E. Southworth, b. Nov. 16, 1869, in Newcastle ; mar. to Fred M. Cook. She d. May 19, 1904, in Bath, Maine.

9. Mary A.[7], daughter to Jonathan[6], b. June 16, 1834, in Freeport ; mar. Benjamin Swett, " a purser on the Boston and Portland boat," from whom she was divorced. She d. Oct. 8, 1897. No issue.

10. Thomas Odiorne[7], youngest child to Jonathan[6], b. Feb. 27, 1838, in Freeport. His wife was Sarah Ann Carver (known as Sally), twin sister to Mary Jane Carver, wife of Enos Pratt Allen.* They were married about 1863.

In his earlier years, Thomas Pratt followed the sea. He never would talk of his experiences, but another sea-captain of Freeport, who was an eyewitness to the affair, tells this story:

Thomas Pratt had risen to the rank of second mate, when a mutiny occurred among the crew of his vessel as they were nearing the Canary Islands. The fourteen men comprising the crew intrenched themselves in the forecastle and refused duty; at the same time they threatened death to any one who tried to enter. Not one of the other officers dared to make a move, but Pratt de-

* Vide pages 817–818.

clared that he would fight it out single-handed, if he could get no help; and he did. With only his hands to aid him, he made a rush for the forecastle; "there was some wild work for a few minutes," but he effectually quelled the mutiny, though he received a stab in the back that nearly ended his life.

During the Civil War, he was in the 30th Maine Regiment of Volunteers. After the war was ended, he returned to Freeport and worked as ship-carpenter. He lived in Brunswick and Bath, Maine; about 1897, he was mysteriously drowned at New Haven, Conn.

> Issue: I. Clara Estelle [8], b. June 16, 1864, in Freeport; resides in Hartford, Conn.
>
> II. A daughter [8], who d. soon after her father.
>
> III. Thomas Stockbridge [8], b. June 28, 1873, in Freeport; resides in Hartford, Conn.

XI. Rispah [6], daughter to David [6], b. Aug. 1, 1794 (1796?), in Freeport; mar. Nov. 5, 1811, in Freeport, to John Toby.*

This family is quite lost sight of, but the story of "Aunt Rispah's" first visit still lingers in Yarmouth. It is said that, after having been away for some years, she went home for a visit, and her first appearance to her sister, "Sally Soule," was in this fashion: unheralded, she made her way around the house to the back, where she found Sally sitting on the doorstep shelling peas. Putting her carpet-bag down on the grass, she seated herself in silence and commenced shelling peas, too. It is not remembered which spoke first, but the end was a real old-time visit, such as is unknown in this generation; the visitor helped with the housework and sewing, "swapped receipts," exchanged family news in detail, and assisted in spinning, weaving, or knitting, whichever was on hand.

Rispah Tobey is said to have lived about three years in Wales, Maine, and then removed to China, Kennebec County, where she died. China is now a small, but picturesque country village, where few records were kept until recent years.

Of ten children, the ninth, Sarah Morton, is the only one living, and she is too feeble to be of assistance. The grand-

---

* *Town Records of Freeport.*

children are widely scattered; few are left in their native towns.

Issue: 1. Edmund Tobey; he lived and died in South China, Maine.

2. Davis (David?) Tobey, lived and died in South China.

3. Bartlett Tobey; he also lived and died in South China.

4. Mercy Tobey, died in Albion, a town adjoining China on the northeast.

5. Harriet Tobey; she died in Albion.

6. Nancy Tobey, lived and died in Vassalboro, a town adjoining China on the west.

7. John Tobey; he went west, and died in Minnesota.

8. Phebe Tobey; nothing is known of her.

9. Sarah Tobey; she was mar. to —— Morton, and is the only child living.

10. Martha Tobey; mar. to —— Danforth; died in Boston, Mass. Her daughter, Helen M. Danforth, was mar. to —— Rich, and resides in Boston.

XII. Sarah[6], daughter to David[5], best known as Sally, b. June 30, 1798, in Freeport, was the first child married from her father's new home in Pownal, after his removal from Mitchell's Hill. The marriage intention of " Enos Soule of Freeport & Sally Pratt of Pownal " was dated Oct. 23, 1817.[*]

Enos[6] Soule, b. Nov. 29, 1792, in Freeport, was the seventh child to Barnabas[5] and Jane[3] (Dennison) Soule, of Freeport.[†]

---

[*] *Town Records of Freeport:* 54.

[†] Barnabas[5] Soule, b. March 25, 1758, in Freeport; mar. May 17, 1781, Jane[3] Dennison, b. Jan. 10, 1764, in Freeport. He lived on Mitchell's Hill at " the Neck," in South Freeport, where he d. Jan. 25, 1823. His widow, Jane, d. March 5, 1825.

ISSUE

I. David[6] Soule, b. 1782; d. Feb. 14, 1784.

II. David[6] Soule, b. Feb. 12, 1783; mar. Cynthia Litchfield; d. Nov. 22, 1846. Issue: ten.

III. Esther[6] Soule, b. Feb. 12, 1785; d. 1862, aged seventy-seven years.

IV. Thomas[6] Soule, b. Oct. 20, 1787; mar., first, Bethia Dunham; mar., second, Sarah Follansbee; he was lost at sea, Feb., 1825. Issue: three.

V. Jane[6] Soule, b. Sept. 5, 1789; d. Aug. 27, 1800, aged eleven years.

Early in life a sailor, he rose by gradual but certain steps to the command of some of the largest vessels that left the harbors of Maine; among these were the ship *Don Juan*, of 645 tons, built in 1841, and the ship *Haidee*, of 655 tons, built in 1843. He was one of the "Soule Brothers" (Enos, Henchman S., and Clement H.), who, for more than a quarter of a century, carried on a large shipyard at Strout's Point. One or another of these brothers at first commanded the vessels built by the firm; eventually they retired from the sea, but continued to build and to manage vessels. Some of the largest, staunchest, and handsomest ships built during that period were constructed and launched in their yard; among the number were ten large ships, five barks, two brigs, and three schooners, besides innumerable smaller craft.

In the war of 1812, Captain Soule, then about twenty, was taken prisoner on the high seas and carried to Dartmoor prison, in England. He was but one of the 2500 sailors captured at sea soon after the breaking out of hostilities against the United States, and imprisoned; their only "crime" was refusing to serve in the British navy, because

---

VI. Eliphaz[6] Soule, b. April 20, 1791; he was lost in the privateer *Dash*, Jan. 23, 1815. (Vide The Roberts Family.)

VII. Enos[6] Soule, b. Nov. 29, 1792; mar. Sally[6], daughter to David[5] Pratt.

VIII. Joanna[6] Soule, b. Jan. 12, 1795; mar. Daniel[7] Small, b. Sept. 1, 1794. (Vide pages 228–239.)

IX. Alfred[6] Soule, b. June 23, 1797; mar. Martha Talbot; he was lost at sea. Issue: two.

X. Henchman[6] Soule, b. Aug. 2, 1799; mar. Pamelia, daughter to Jacob and Bethia (Talbot) Lincoln (sister to Col. Simeon Pratt's wife); he d. March 2, 1860, in New Haven, Conn. Issue: eleven.

XI. Jane Bradbury[6] Soule, b. Nov. 16, 1801; d. June 3, 1839, aged thirty-seven years.

XII. William[6] Soule, b. Oct. 16, 1803; lost at sea, 1827, off Cape Sable.

XIII. Clement Hall[6] Soule, b. July 20, 1808; mar. Mary Jane, daughter to Ambrose, Jr., and Jane (Pickerman) Talbot. She was sister to his brother Alfred's wife, Martha Talbot. He was interested in shipbuilding, with his brothers, Enos and Henchman. Previous to 1869, he removed to Passaic, N. J., where he d. June 10, 1874. Issue: six.

they were American citizens. They were treated with great harshness; and those who were so fortunate as to survive were kept until the end of the war. Enos Soule spent two years within those walls. His record in Freeport as "a model citizen, public-spirited, patriotic, and of unbending integrity," survives him; but the last few years of his life were clouded by hallucinations and fancies, — harmless, though often extravagant, — which made it necessary to place a guardian over his extensive financial interests. His condition then was largely attributed to the sufferings he endured in Dartmoor prison, from which he never fully had recovered.

The homestead of Captain Enos Soule, on the road between Freeport and South Freeport, is said to have been the land once owned and occupied by John Hayes[5] and Hannah (Bowdoin) Mitchell.* Later, he removed "to the old field called the Neck." He d. Nov. 8, 1869, in Freeport. His wife, familiarly known as "Aunt Sally Soule," was a woman of sterling character, a true helpmeet to her husband. She is said to have closely resembled her sister Rebecca, wife of Edward Small,† and to have been much like her. She always had a luxuriant flower garden, and when the making of wax flowers came into vogue, she had great success in reproducing her favorites. The store of linen she laid away in lavender for her daughters, when they should marry, rivalled that of a German hausfrau. She d. Dec. 31, 1881, in Freeport, aged eighty-three years.

Issue: 1. Francis B.[7] Soule, b. July 6, 1818, in Freeport; mar. Nov. 6, 1869, Eliza M. (W?) Wait.

Issue: I. Edgar de Lettre[8] Soule, b. Sept. 20, 1847, in Freeport.

II. Wilhelmina[8] Soule, b. Sept. 26, 1848, in Freeport.

III. Frances E.[8] Soule, b. May 21, 1850, in Freeport.

IV. Sydney S.[8] Soule, b. May 11, 1856, in Freeport.

V. Norman Pratt[8] Soule, b. April, 1857, in Freeport; mar. July 12, 1882, in Freeport, Clara O. Dennison, b. Feb. 8, 1857, daughter to Benjamin Griffin

---

* Vide The Mitchells from Kittery.   † Vide pages 240-258.

and Martha (Soule) Dennison, of South Freeport.
Issue : seven.

2. Enos Corydon[7] Soule, b. June 4, 1820, in Freeport;
   mar. May 13, 1857, Helen Louisa Gore, b. Oct. 11,
   1838, daughter to William and Helen (Nye) Gore.

Captain Enos C. Soule began a seafaring life at the age of
seventeen years ; he became master in 1846, and sailed on
long voyages until 1860. At that time he took charge of the
old shipyard so long controlled by the " Soule Brothers," and
constructed, within the next few years, the ships *Enos Soule*,
of 1518 tons, *Lucille*, 1394 tons, *Tam O'Shanter*, 1602 tons,
Uncle Tobey, 1100 tons, *Superior*, 1240 tons, *Yerick*, 1187 tons,
besides other craft.* Eighteen years later (1878), he stopped
building, " under the conviction that iron would soon replace
wood in naval architecture," and soon after removed to Newton, Mass.† He d. Jan. 20, 1894, in Newton, aged seventy-
three years ; his widow, Helen, d. Aug. 5, following, in Newton, aged fifty-five.

Issue : I. Herman C.[8] Soule, b. Feb. 19, 1858, in Freeport ; resides in Newton.

II. Sarah H.[8] Soule, b. March 23, 1860, in Freeport;
resides in Newton.

III. Clara G.[8] Soule, b. Dec. 3, 1863, in Freeport ; resides
in Newton.

IV. William G.[8] Soule, b. Sept. 24, 1866, in Freeport;
mar. June 10, 1899, Margaret Wallace. Issue: 1.
Wallace[9] Soule, b. Dec. 8, 1901, in Newton.

V. Frank Enos[8] Soule, b. Jan. 14, 1869, in Freeport;
resides in Newton.

VI. Elizabeth N.[8] Soule, known as Bessie, b. March 2,
1871, in Freeport ; resides in Newton.

VII. Leonora N.[8] Soule, b. April 12, 1872, in Freeport;
resides in Newton.

VIII. Walter S.[8] Soule, b. Dec. 14, 1875, in Freeport ; d.
1898, aged twenty-three years.

IX. Laura[8] Soule, b. Feb. 16, 1877, in Freeport ; resides
in Newton.

* Vide page 233.   † Vide pages 780-781.

3. Martha Jane[7] Soule, b. July 6, 1822, in Freeport; d.
   Feb. 12, 1826, aged three years, seven months.
4. Laura Ann[7] Soule, b. Sept. 15, 1824, in Freeport; mar.
   Jan. 19, 1853, to Charles Bliss, of South Freeport.
   No issue.
5. Lydia Lincoln[7] Soule, b. July 23, 1827, in Freeport;
   mar. to Charles Bliss, after the death of her sister
   Laura. She d. Sept. 20, 1894. No issue.
6. Horace B.[7] Soule, b. Feb. 21, 1830, in Freeport; mar.
   Emeline Talbot. He d. Aug. 16, 1898.
   Issue: I. Horace Everett[8] Soule, b. July 27, 1861. II.
   Maud Hamor[8] Soule, b. March 10, 1864. III. Lina
   Frances[8] Soule, b. Aug. 5, 1868. IV. Paul Henchman[8] Soule, b. June 25, 1875. V. Thatcher H.[8] Soule,
   b. June 30, 1877.
7. Barnabas[7] Soule, b. March 16, 1832, in Freeport; d.
   Oct. 23, 1849, aged seventeen years.
8. Emilie Sarah[7] Soule, b. Oct. 2, 1834, in Freeport; mar.
   to Josiah Soule, Jr.
9. Ellen Thompson[7] Soule, b. Dec. 8, 1836, in Freeport;
   d. Dec. 1, 1856, aged twenty years.
10. Margaret Pratt[7] Soule, b. May 25, 1839, in Freeport;
    mar. to James E. Wengren, a banker, of Portland,
    Maine. Issue: 1. Elmer Sanberg Wengren; he was
    graduated from Harvard University in 1889; he re-
    sides in Portland.
11. Julius Seymour[7] Soule, b. Feb. 11, 1842, in Freeport;
    mar. June 6, 1876, in Freeport, Edith M. Creech,
    daughter to William H. and Catharine E. (Means)
    Creech. His first voyage extended over a year, from
    1857 to 1858, and he continued for some time to fol-
    low the sea. As master, Captain Julius Soule sailed
    the *H. S. Soule*, later called the *Suliote*, and the *Tam
    O'Shanter*,* built in 1875 by his brother Enos, and
    other ships. He still resides in Freeport, near the
    centre of the town.

---

* Vide page 236.

Issue: I. Sarah Elizabeth[8] Soule, b. Jan. 19, 1882, in Freeport.

II. Albert Creech[8] Soule, b. Jan. 23, 1885, in Freeport.

III. Helen[8] Soule, b. Feb. 11, 1891, in Freeport.

12. Henrietta C.[7] Soule, b. April 25, 1844, in Freeport; d. unmar., May, 1899, aged fifty-five years.

XIII. Rachel Chandler[6], daughter to David[5], b. July 26, 1800, in Freeport; was married in Freeport, to Joshua[6] Soule, b. July 31, 1796, in Freeport, son to James[5] and Martha (Curtis) Soule. She, also, was married from her father's house in Pownal.

"There is no spot on any of Joshua Soule's descendants; they are honest, moral, temperate men and women," writes a distant relative. During "the great famine in Ireland," 1846–47, Captain Rufus Pratt brought over two Irish girls, Annie and Margaret ——, to save them from starvation. Annie was sickly and did not live long; Margaret was adopted by Joshua Soule. She was "a remarkable girl, the life of the home circle, a sincere Christian, and a member of the Baptist Church." She became a milliner, and went into business at Augusta, Maine, where she made her home with friends of the family of Hon. James G. Blaine. "She did as much for the comfort of Joshua and Rachael Soule in their declining years as any of their children." Afterward, she married an "educated and handsome man, who had the misfortune to have lost a leg." Her son was young at the time of his mother's death.

The homestead of Joshua Soule, at Porter's Landing, Freeport, is occupied (1906) by his youngest son, Edmund Pratt Soule. Joshua Soule d. Oct., 1873, in Freeport, aged seventy-seven years; his widow, Rachel, d. April 16, 1885, in Freeport, aged eighty-four years and nine months. Her grandchildren remember her as "a dear old soul, one of the salt of the earth."

Issue: 1. Joshua Chandler[7] Soule, b. Sept. 12, 1819, in Freeport. He was a ship-carpenter, and spent all his life in his native town. His wife was Mary Staples, b. July 29, 1819, in Freeport, daughter to Reuben and Betsey (Carver) Staples, of Freeport; they were mar. Oct. 15,

1846, in Freeport. She d. March 1, 1890, in Freeport; Joshua C. Soule d. Oct. 15, 1904, in Freeport, aged eighty-five years.

Issue: I. Ella [8] Soule, b. May 9, 1848, in Freeport.

II. Ralph [8] Soule, b. Dec. 28, 1850, in Freeport; mar. Nov. 25, 1880, in Freeport, Luella Stoddard.

III. Victor [8] Soule, b. May 8, 1859, in Freeport; d. April 16, 1880, in Whitinsville, Mass., aged twenty-one years.

2. Rachel Pratt [7] Soule, b. Oct. 29, 1821, in Freeport; mar. Nov. 2, 1846, in Freeport, to Charles Augustus Litchfield, b. Nov. 19, 1821, in Freeport, son to George and Hannah (Anderson) Litchfield.

Charles A. Litchfield was a ship-carpenter and caulker. He is represented by a friend and relative as " a strong man, honest, industrious, and frugal. A man of strong opinions and strong prejudices, a good hater or a good friend." Rachel Litchfield d. Dec. 6, 1884, in Portland, Maine, leaving two daughters. Her husband's second wife was Abby Frances [8] (Pratt) Humphrey, daughter to Ambrose [7] and Lydia Ann (Nelson) Pratt, and widow of Asa Humphrey.* The death of Charles A. Litchfield occurred June 19, 1898, in Freeport.

Issue by first wife: I. Emilie Bennett Litchfield, b. Aug. 12, 1847, in Freeport; mar. Dec. 16, 1874, in Jefferson, Maine, to Samuel Albert Richardson.

Issue: 1. Charles Albert Richardson, b. Dec. 17, 1875. He was graduated from Hebron Academy, and McGill University; he is a physician in King's County Hospital, Brooklyn, N. Y.

2. Mary Emilie Richardson, b. July 17, 1877. She was graduated from Hebron Academy, and is a trained nurse in Bellevue Hospital, Brooklyn, N. Y.

3. Samuel Albert Richardson, b. Sept. 24, 1880; mar. Sept. 27, 1906, in Calais, Maine, to Flora Hines, of Calais. He was graduated from Hebron

* Vide pages 803, 810.

Academy, Maine, and Bryant and Stratton's
Business College, Boston, Mass. He is now of
the firm of Patch and Richardson, at Southern
Pines, North Carolina.

4. Frank Cummings Richardson, b. July 6, 1886. He
was graduated from Hebron Academy; he is now
in the University of Maine, at Orono.

II. Hannah Anderson Litchfield, b. May 26, 1852, in
Freeport ; mar. Nov. 24, 1880, in Jefferson, Maine,
to Marshall Atwood Bond ; resides at Porter's
Landing, Freeport. No issue.

3. Deborah Stover[7] Soule, b. Dec. 10, 1824, in Freeport ;
d. aged about nineteen years.

4. Charles William[7] Soule, b. July 7, 1829, in Freeport ;
mar. Oct. 22, 1854, in Freeport, Margaret Alice
Chase, who d. July 2, 1906, in Freeport. He. d.
Nov. 22, following.

Issue : I. Carrie Estella[8] Soule, b. May 26, 1857, in
Freeport; mar. Dec. 25, 1879, to Herman E.
Brewer; lives at South Freeport. Issue : 1. Stella
Alice Brewer, b. Oct. 2, 1880, in Freeport ; mar.
Jan. 4, 1906, to Henry C. Pritham, of Free-
port.

II. Sumner Chase[8] Soule, b. Oct. 2, 1864, in Freeport ;
mar. Nov. 16, 1887, Grace Soule. He d. Nov. 3,
1892. Issue : 1. Leland Sumner[9] Soule, b. July
19, 1888. 2. Arthur Burnham[9] Soule, b. April 16,
1890.

III. Margaret Flora[8] Soule, b. Jan. 19, 1874, in Freeport ; mar. March 7, 1899, to Howard A. Roberts,
of Turner, Maine.

IV. Helen Cummings[8] Soule, b. March 26, 1876, in
Freeport.

5. Isaac Smith[7] Soule, b. April 27, 1832, in Freeport ;
mar. Harriet Davis. He is a ship-joiner ; resides at
Porter's Landing, Freeport.

6. Edmund Pratt[7] Soule, b. Jan. 25, 1835, in Freeport ;
mar. Nov. 28, 1860, in Freeport, Mary Dennison[8]

Pratt, daughter to Ambrose[7], and Lydia Ann (Nelson) Pratt, of Freeport.*

Edmund P. Soule, a shoemaker by trade, has always lived in Freeport, and now occupies the homestead of his father at Porter's Landing. He and his wife are members of the Baptist Church. Issue: I. Stella Lee[8] Soule, b. April, 1868, in Freeport; lived but a few hours.

---

* Vide page 804.

THE CHANDLER FAMILY

EDMUND[1] CHANDLER

EDMUND CHANDLER, of Duxbury, Massachusetts, in 1633, is supposed to have been the person of that name who was with the Pilgrims in Leyden, though there are no records that positively prove it. Yet the positions of trust to which he was chosen, in the early settlement of the town of Duxbury, show that he was well acquainted with the others who had removed there, and that they had confidence in him. He may have been with the Pilgrim band at Amsterdam, but his name does not appear until after their removal, in the summer of 1609, to Leyden. He was admitted to citizenship in Leyden, November 11, 1613, under the guaranty of Roger Wilson and Henry Wood. This is evidence that he was then of age; consequently the date of his birth may have been as early as 1592, if not earlier. Subsequently, he "guaranteed" others for citizenship; on April 27, 1615, John Keble, on May 5, 1623, Roger White, and on April 17, 1626, Edward Coolidge. Like the others who, as Bradford says, had been "constrained to leave their native soyle and countrie, their lands & livings, and all their freinds & familier acquaintance"[*] in England for the shores of Holland, to escape religious persecution, he was enabled to engage only in the most menial occupations. When he was admitted to citizenship, in 1613, he was called a "say-weaver," — "say" being a coarse woolen cloth, something like a blanket. In 1623, he was mentioned as a "draper," in 1626, as a "pipe-maker." He buried a child March 26, 1619, in St. Peter's ; he then lived in *Nieuwestadt.*[†]

These records, which are all that have been found in Ley-

---

[*] Bradford's *History of Plimoth Plantation*, 1898 : 15.
[†] Dexter's *England and Holland of the Pilgrims*, 1905 : 609, 648, 652.

den concerning him or his family, prove that he belonged to the remnant of the Pilgrim body that remained after the first three ships, the *Mayflower*, the *Fortune*, and the *Anne*, had been sent to New England. Impatiently they awaited the time when they, too, should join their brethren. Their beloved pastor, John Robinson, had sickened and died (March 1, 1625); this added greatly to their discouragement, "and many, being aged, begane to drop away by death." But the little band continued to "hould close togeather, in peace and quietnes; . . . though . . . very weake." * Through the instrumentality of Isaac Allerton, aided by Mr. Sherley, they were brought over in two companies, the first in 1629, the second in 1630.†

In 1633, Edmund Chandler, then a resident of Duxbury, was made freeman, church membership (before 1686) being a necessary qualification. He again appeared in lists of freemen, March 7, 1636–37,‡ and in 1658.§ On January 3, 1636–37, he was chosen Constable for the town of Duxbury, and "sworne" to that office on March 7, following.‖ At that time, and for many years afterward, the Constable was the chief executive officer in the parish or town; he carried a staff, and his duties were surrounded with much formality. "Edmond Chandler and Jonathan Brewster" were sent, June 4, 1639, as the first Deputies from the town of Duxbury to the Plymouth Colony General Court; Bradford was then Governor. Edmund Chandler again served, as Deputy from Duxbury, in sessions beginning August 29, 1643, and March 5, 1643–44.¶ Like most of the early settlers, Edmund Chandler acquired large tracts of land by purchase and by grants: —

At Duxbury, in 1633, his share of the mowing ground

---

* Bradford's *History of Plimoth Plantation*, 1898: 250, 248.
† Vide page 613.
‡ *Plymouth Colony Records*, Court Orders, vol. 1 : 4, 52.
§ *Plymouth Colony Miscellaneous Records*, vol. 8 : 198.
‖ *Plymouth Colony Records*, Court Orders, vol. 1 : 48, 54.
¶ *Plymouth Colony Records*, Court Orders, vol. 1 : 126; vol. 2 : 60, 68.

is not recorded, but in assigning the plots for "mowing of Grasse for the p^{r}sent yeare, 1633 . . . Manasseh Kempton" was given "that at the Iland Creeke abutting vpon Stephen Tracies ground & Edmund Chandlers." On "Oct. 20, 1634, Edmun Chanler came and had recorded that he had sold [for £12] unto John Rogers a lot of land adjoining the land of Robert Hicks, on Duxbery side, the lot which he had bought of John Barnes." * "April 2, 1638: Threescore acres of land are graunted to Edmond Chaundler, lying on Duxborrow side and to be layd forth for him by Captaine Standish & Mr Alden, w^{oh} was accordingly layd forth on the northeast side of the lands graunted to Moyses Symons, & ranging as his doth in length north & by east and south & by west from the marked trees." † This was his homestead which was occupied later by his sons.

"July 19, 1639: Mr Thomas Besbeech [Bixby] of Duxborrow," for twenty shillings paid by Edmund Chandler, conveyed to him one acre of land on the north side of his land, "next to the highway . . . the said Edward is to set up the fence betwixt them before the beginning of the next March." Here Chandler built a house. In 1647, Bixby sold to "Mr John Reiner [Rev. John Reyner] of Plymouth," all "his house and houseing and sixty acars of vpland . . . excepting one acar sould vnto Edmond Chandeler of Duxbery." This acre "Edmond Chandeler" conveyed, June 8, 1650, to "John Browne of Duxborrow, weaver." It was then described as "an house Scittuate in Duxburrow aforesaid, and an acar of land on w^h the said house standeth next aioyning vnto the house and land of Mr John Rener above the path . . . with all the boards shelues dores locks and windows belonging vnto the said house with all the fencing stufe and all other apurtenances now standing vppon the aforesaid acar of land," etc.‡

---

* *Plymouth Colony Records*, Court Orders, vol. 1 : 14, 31.

† *Plymouth Colony Records*, Court Orders, vol. 1 : 82.

‡ *Plymouth Colony Deeds*, vol. 1 : 46, 141, 187.

November 2, 1640, in a grant of land by the General Court, at "North Riuer," the share of "Edmond Chandlor" was "fifty acres, wth some meddow to y^t" This tract of "marsh meddow and vpland" Chandler sold, June 7, 1651, for £10, to "Thomas Byrd of Scittuate."* On May 4, 1653, James Lendall, of Duxbury, tailor, for £3, sold to "Edmond Chandeler of the towne aforesaid . . . planter," two acres of marsh meadow, "sometimes the meddow of Peeter Brownes Children . . . neare unto the Dweling place of the said Edmond Chandeler; being bounded on the one side with other land of the said Edmond Chandelers; and on the other side with a certaine pcell of meddow belonging to John Washburn Junier." This sale was acknowledged before "Mr John Alden asistant." On July 15, 1653, Edmond Chandeler exchanged, "upon equall tearmes," with Edward Bumpas of Marshfield, all his interest "in Duxburrow New plantation commonly called and knowne by the Indian Names of Satuckquett and Nunckatatesett [Bridgewater] and places adiacent; ffor all . . . Right title or enterest the said Edward Bumpas hath . . . as one of the thirty-foure purchasers . . . att the places commonly called and knowne by the Indian names of Cushnet and Coakset [Dartmouth]; and places adiacent." This exchange also was acknowledged before "Mr John Alden asistant."† "Duxburrow New Plantation," later Bridgewater, had been granted, in 1645, to fifty-four persons who were proprietors of the town of Duxbury, including Edmund Chandler. ‡

On July 3, 1656, the General Court granted unto sundry of the ancient freemen of that jurisdiction certain tracts of land from "Assonate Neck to Quaquerchand, alias the Plain" — afterward called Freetown. Three years later (April 2, 1659), a deed was signed by the Indians, conveying this tract to Captain James Cudworth, Josiah Winslow,

---

* *Plymouth Colony Records*, Court Orders, vol. 1: 165; *Plymouth Colony Deeds*, vol. 1: 207.

† *Plymouth Colony Deeds*, vol. 2: pt. 1: 51, 53.   ‡ Vide page 359.

Constant Southworth, Edmund Chandler, Love Brewster, Kenelm Winslow, John Waterman, son to Robert Waterman, and others.* This share of land "by Taunton Riuer" Chandler left, by will, to his son Joseph.

For a few years the services of Edmund Chandler, in the town of Duxbury and in the Colony, were important and varied. As his name does not appear in the list of males able to bear arms, in 1643, it may be inferred that he then was over sixty,† or incapable of performing military service. At a session of the General Court, held October 2, 1637, "Jonathan Brewster & Edmond Chandler for Ducksborrow" were chosen a committee, with the Governor and Assistants, to divide a tract of five hundred acres of "meadow grounds betwixt Eele Riuer and South Riuer." ‡ The First Church of Duxbury "was gathered" in 1632; but steps were not taken to build a meeting-house until March 21, 1635–36, on which date the two factions that could not agree upon a site met together. On one side were "Mr William Collier, Stephen Tracy, Mr Joh. Howland, Edm. Chandler [and] Josuah Pratt," on the other side, "Capt. Myles Standish, Manasseh Kempton, George Kenrick, John Jenney, & Edwards Bangs." All were present but Edward Bangs; seven of the nine held "Jones River to be the fittest place & there to build a meeting howse & towne . . . the other two preferred Morton's Hole." § The "old burial place" is near the site of the meeting-house built during that year, and of the second structure erected in 1706 on the same site. The oldest stone in the graveyard bears the date of 1697.‖

On June 7, 1636, Edmund Chandler was chosen upon a "jewry that serued vpon trials;" ¶ September 1, 1640, he served on jury before the General Court, and October 5, fol-

---

* *Plymouth Colony Records*, Court Orders, vol. 4: 67, 68. † Vide page 361.
‡ *Plymouth Colony Records*, Court Orders, vol. 1: 67.
§ *Plymouth Colony Records*, Court Orders, vol. 1: 41.
‖ *Historic Duxbury*, by Laurence Bradford, 1900: 51, 55.
¶ *Plymouth Colony Records*, Court Orders, vol. 1: 42.

lowing, on jury before the Court of Assistants.* In 1639, he took to himself an apprentice, with the customary bond, as follows : —

" 29 Jan. 1638–9.   Memorand : That John Edwards hath put himself apprentice to Edmond Chaundlor, of Duxborrow, yeom. [yeoman] and after the manner of an apprentice wth him to dwell from the last day of September next ensuing the date hereof vnto the end & terme of fiue yeares thence next ensuing, to serue him in all such lawful labors as the said Edmund shall ymploy him in during the said terme ; the said Edmond Chaundler fynding vnto his said servant meate drinke and apparell during the said terme, and in thend thereof to giue him double apparell throughout, in convenyent manner, wth one suite for Lords days and another for working days." †

The inventory of the estate of Godbert Godbertson (Cuthbert Cuthbertson) and Sarah (Allerton), his wife,‡ which was presented in Court November 11, 1633, mentions £2 : 05 due to " Edm. Chandler."   On November 13, 1637, the inventory of the estate of William Palmer, " the elder," of Duxbury, was taken by " Jonathan Brewster Edmond Chaundler Willia Basset & John Willis," — due to " Edmond Chandler . . . 00 : 05 : 0."§   On page sixty-two of the " wast book," or blank book, now called *The Brewster Book*, which is supposed to have belonged to Elder William [1] Brewster, and is known to have become the property of his eldest son, Jonathan [2] Brewster, is this incomplete memorandum, in the handwriting of Jonathan : —

" [worn] nd Chandeler had of me the [worn] of June. 1644. in bookes."‖

These books may have been the same that were mentioned in the inventory of Edmund Chandler, in 1662, as " a pcell of bookes att . . . 00 : 10 : 00."

---

* *Plymouth Colony Judicial Acts*, 1636–1692 : 17, 18.
† *Plymouth Colony Records*, Court Orders, vol. 1 : 110.
‡ Vide pages 600, 603.   § *Plymouth Colony Probate*, vol. 1 : 13, 28.
‖ *The Mayflower Descendant*, vol. 1 : 6.

The only transaction in which Edmund Chandler appears with a member of his family is where he gave bail, May 30, 1637, for Samuel Chandler, his eldest son. John Jenney brought suit "against Samuel Chaundler, in an action vpon the case to the damnage of XX^l, wherevpon a p̅cell of beauer of the deffen^{ts} was arrested aboard the s^d Mr Jenneys bark. Edmond Chaundler became bayle to the action, and to satis-fye the debt what it should be." Upon the agreement of Edmund Chandler to pay the indebtedness, the action was "wthdrawne." Two years later, June 2, 1639–40, Samuel Chandler brought an action in court against "John Jenney gen̅t . . . to the dam̅. of XL^l ;" the jury found for the plain-tiff.* Possibly it concerned the same matter.

No mention of a wife of Edmund Chandler is made, either in Leyden or in New England, yet it is probable that he married at least twice. His eldest son, Samuel, was of age in 1633, and he lost a child in 1619, at Leyden ; the children of a younger, or second, wife were Benjamin, married about 1671, Joseph, married before 1673, and four daughters, who all appear to have been unmarried when his will was made, in 1662. His death, when he probably was more than eighty years of age, occurred between May 2, 1662, the date of his will, in which he calls himself "old and weake," and the taking of an inventory of his persoṇạl belongings and debts, on June 2, following. His homestead and other real estate in Duxbury, Dartmouth, and Taunton, together with the "three thousand and five hundred [weight] of sugar," at Barbadoes, were not included in his inventory, which is chiefly a list of the effects of an aged man whose wife was not living. His will was as follows : —

" The Last Will and Testament of Edmond Chandeler † late deceased exhibited to the Court held att Plymouth the fourth day of June i662 on the oathes of Mr John Aldin and Mr Con-stant Southworth

---

* *Plymouth Colony Judicial Acts*, 1636–1692 : 6, 15.
† *Plymouth Colony Probate*, Book 2 : pt. 2 : 75, 76.

" These p^rsents witnesseth that I Edmond Chandeler being old
and weake in body; yet in good and pfect memory doe make and
ordaine this to bee my last Will and Testament —

"first my will is that when it shall please god to take mee
out of this world vnto himselfe that my body bee decently buried and that out of my whole estate my funerall charges be defrayed

" 2 My will is that out of the Remainder of my whole estate
all my Just and lawfull debts bee payed

" 3 I giue and beqveath vnto my son Samvell Chandeler my
whole share of land that is att the place or places Called by name
of Akoaksett and Cushenah [Dartmouth] which said land hee
doth and shall presently possesse;

" 4 I giue and beqveath vnto my sone Benjamine Chandeler
to him and his heires for euer all that tract or trackes of land
lying in Duxburrow both vpland and meddow with all the housing belonging thervnto; onely hee is not to enter vpon the possession therof till the tearmes of six yeares be ended,

" 5 I giue and beqveath vnto my son Joseph Chandeler to him
and his heires for euer my whole share of land which now lyeth
by Taunton Riuer neare vnto a place Comonly knowne by the
falls with all my further Interest belonging thervnto

" 6 I giue and beqveath vnto my three daughters Sarah Anna
and Mary three thousand and fiue hundred of sugar which be-
longes to mee att Barbadoes.

" 7 I giue and beqveath vnto my three Children viz Benjamine Josepth and Ruth Chandeler the four last yeares Rent due
to mee from my son Samuell Chandeler for my land and Cattle;
eqvally to bee devided amongst them and for the first two yeares
Rent I Reserue it for my selfe and to dispose of as I shall see
good

" 8 My will is that that stocke of Cattle of mine which is in
my son Samuells hand shall after the tearme of six yeares (which
hee tooke them for) bee eqvally devided between my three Children
Benjamine Josepth and Ruth

"further I doe by this my last Will and Testament make Constitute and appoint my deare and loveing son Joseph Chandeler
to bee sole exeqvitor of this my last Will and Testament;

" In Witness that this is my last Will and Testament I haue

sett to my hand and seale this third day of May one Thousand six hundred sixty and two i662

" In the p^{r}sence   Edmond Chandeler
of John Aldin   and **A**   [seale]
Constant Southworth

"An Jnventory of the goods and Chattles of Edmond Chandeler deceased taken this second of the fourth month [June 2] i662 by those whose names are vnderwritten and exhibited to the Court held att Plymouth the fourth of June i662

	℔	s	d
"Jmp^{rs}: foure Cowes prised att	15	00	00
Jtem two oxen att.	10	00	00
Jtem one feather bolster and two pillowes	01	00	00
Jtem three Canvas sheets	00	17	00
Jtem one old Rugg and one blankett att	01	08	00
Jtem two old Curtaines att	00	04	00
Jtem wearing Clothes att	02	06	00
Jtem 3 paire of old stokens and paire } of spatterlashes * }	00	06	00
Jtem 2 shirts att	00	10	00
Jtem 4 old linnine Capps and one } old knit capp att }	00	02	00
Jtem 3 towells 1 old pillowbeer and 3 } old Neckcothes }	00	03	00
Jtem one old hatt att	00	03	00
Jtem a pcell of bookes att	00	10	00
Jtem 4 old pewter dishes one old pott & } one chamber pott three spoones }	00	10	00
Jtem one frying pan 2 candlestickes one } skillett att }	00	09	00
Jtem one smale Compas 1 looking glase } and severall smale thinges }	00	19	00
Jtem 1 sword shot moulders burning } marke and sheers powder hornes }	00	11	00
Jtem one Darke lanthorne pot hangers } and tonggs pot hookes }	00	12	00
Jtem three Chists	00	14	00
Jtem two old hogsheads 2 beer Caske one } powthering tubb and other old } thinges all att }	00	14	00
Jtem one wheele 1 old horne and old skales	00	03	06

---

* Spatterdash.. ; long gaiters.

Jtem one chaire and two Cushens att	oo o5 oo
Jtem six Jron wedges att . . . , ...	oo o8 oo
Jtem one little Table forme halfe pecke ⎱ and old box ⎰	oo o3 o6
Jtem one bedsteed and sifting trough att	oo o8 oo
Jtem a lamp att	oo o1 o4

suma   38 o7 o4

Debts oweing by the estate as followeth

Jmp⁽ⁿˢ⁾ To Samvell Chandeler	o4 15 oo
Jtem to Moses Simons	oo 10 o6
Jtem to Josepth Chandeler	oo 18 oo
Jtem to makeing of the coffin and grave	oo o3 oo

Debts oweing to the estate

Jmp⁽ⁿˢ⁾ : by John Thomas one bushell of corne	oo o3 oo
Jtem by Abraham Sampson	oo oo 10

John Aldin
Phillip Delano "

ISSUE (PROBABLY) BY FIRST WIFE

I. **Samuel**², b. as early as 1612, in Leyden, since he was of age when he was taxed, March 25, 1633, in Plymouth, "[£]oo : o9 : oo," in corn at six shillings per bushel ; March 27, 1634, he was taxed the same.*

In 1637, John Jenney brought suit against him for £20, and held a " p̄cell of beaver . . . aboard the s^d Mr Jenneys bark," as security ; two years later, Samuel Chandler recovered £41 from John Jenney, which may indicate that the original action was unwarranted.† In 1639, Samuel Chandler was mentioned as a " planter," of Duxbury.‡ In 1657, he took the Oath of Fidelity at Duxbury.§ At the time of his father's death in May, 1662, Samuel had occupied his father's house, and had the use of his father's land and cattle for two years of a " tearme of six yeares (which hee tooke them for)." The next year, Dec. 1, 1663, he made complaint " that the range of the land is not sett betwixt Moses

---

* *Plymouth Colony Records*, vol. 1 : 11, 28.   † Vide page 861.
‡ *Plymouth Colony Records*, Court Orders, vol. 1 : 137.
§ *Plymouth Colony Miscellaneous Records*, vol. 8 : 181.

Simons & himselfe;" the Court ordered three men to "run the line with the best care they can." On May 1, 1666, an error in this line, which was acknowledged by the Court "a mistake," was rectified. That same year, June 5, Samuel Chandler and Joseph Wadsworth were chosen surveyors of highways in Duxbury.* Joseph Chandler and Samuel Chandler served on a jury to lay out a highway for George Soule; their report was dated " 19 — first month — 1678–79." †

Three years after the death of his father, Samuel Chandler received his first grant of land from the town of Duxbury — " Sixty acres of land between Indian head river, and the great Cedar Swamp, with the condition that he shall not sell it except to a townsman." This grant was dated Oct. 21, 1665.‡ In 1678, he sold, for £10, to John Rouse, Jr., all his interest in " those Lands . . . which goe vnder the Name of the servants Lands . . . at a place comonly knowne by the name of Saconett Necke," which he bought of " Thomas Bryant one of the companies servants." This deed was signed with

Witnesses "The marke
"The D marke of of Samuell Chandeler," [seal]
John Rouse seni^r :
John Soule "

It was acknowledged before Constant Southworth, Assistant, Jan. 27, 1678, by " Samvell Chandlerer and his wife." §

Samuel Chandler died, intestate, at Duxbury, in 1683. The only mention of his wife is in the above deed and in the settlement of his estate; in neither, however, is her name given. After his death, the following order was passed by the Court:

" March 5, 1683–84

" In reference to the settlement of the estate of Samuell Chandeler, deceased, in as much as the estate is but smale, the Court thought meet to settle the intire estate on the widdow, which was

---

* *Plymouth Colony Records*, Court Orders, vol. 4: 48, 120, 123.
† *Plymouth Colony Records*, Court Orders, vol. 6: 15.
‡ *Town Records of Duxbury*, vol. A: 214.
§ *Plymouth County Deeds*, Book 3: 16.

his wife, and haue graunted tres of administration to the said widdow and John Soule, to administer on the said estate." *

The inventory of his estate was as follows : † —

" Duxboroug this 17 day of yᵉ 9 month 1683 An Jnventory taken of yᵉ estate
of yᵉ late deceased Samuel Chanler by vs Thomas Delano & John Rouse

	[£ s d]
Jt two Cowes	04 00 0
Jt 4 heifers	06 00 0
Jt one mare	01 00 0
Jt one ox	02 00 0
Jt twelue sheep. 9 dead	02 14 0
Jt two piggs one dead	00 04 0
Jt wearing Clothing & money	02 18 0
Jt Bedding	01 04 0
Jt meat & Sider	01 10 0
Jt new Cloth	00 16 0
Jt 4 brass Kettles one warming pan	01 02 6
Jt one pott & posnett	00 05 0
Jt wedges & plow	01 00 0
Jt pewter	00 12 0
Jt one saddle	00 05 0
Jt Wheat Rye Jndian Corne	04 05 0
Jt Earthen ware	00 10 0
Jt one frying pan	00 01 0
Jt Tobacco	00 15 0
Jt Trammell & Tongs	00 05 0
Jt Hay	03 04 0
Jt The widdows bed & bedding	04 00 0
Jt Posts & Rayles	00 15 0
yᵉ Totall sum	39 08 6

The Debts yᵗ ar Due out of yᵉ estate

To Capt Thomas	06 13 1
to John Delano	00 04 0
to yᵉ Constable	00 04 0
to Edward Southworth	00 02 0
to Joseph chaunler	00 06 0
to good wife Browne	00 05 0
to John Sprague	00 01 0
to Sam Howland	00 01 0
to mʳ Wiswell	00 12 0
to Ruth West	00 03 6

---

* *Plymouth Colony Records*, Court Orders, vol. 6: 124.
† *Plymouth Colony Probate*, Book 4: pt. 2: 145.

```
to John Rouse . . . . . . . . . . . . . . . . . . .    oo 19 0
to John sole . . . . . . . . . . . . . . . . . . . .   oo 03 6
to Moses Simonds . . . . . . . . . . . . . . . . .    01 07 9
to John Simonds . . . . . . . . . . . . . . . . . .   oo 13 9
to William Brewster . . . . . . . . . . . . . . . .   oo 02 0
to William Vobes [Forbes?] . . . . . . . . . . . .    oo 06 3
to Sam¹ West . . . . . . . . . . . . . . . . . . . .  oo 04 0
to Joseph Pryer . . . . . . . . . . . . . . . . . .   oo 02 0
to Thomas Delano . . . . . . . . . . . . . . . . .    oo 01 6
```
$$12\ 12\ 0$$

"Duxburroug y° 17 : 9ᵐ 83
    Thomas Delano
    John Rouse"

While he was treated in the Plymouth Colony with due consideration, Samuel Chandler appears to have been a son quite unworthy of his respected father. It is easy to conjecture that his early surroundings in Holland had bred in him the very evils which the Pilgrims, as a body, feared from a long sojourn there.* He was inclined to be lawless ; he was improvident and illiterate. In support of these statements, on Oct. 2, 1637, he was "warned . . . to appeare at the next Court to answer for shooteing off three guns in the night tyme, as if it were an alarm." A little later, he was warned "to psonally appeare at the next Geñall Court to answere . . . concerneing opprobrious & slanderous words spoken by him against the Gouʳ and goûment." Several times he was presented to the Court "for being drunke ;" the last time on record was in June, 1670, when he was fined five shillings, and John Sprague was fined the same "for sufferring Samuell Chandler to be drunke in his house."† The estate settled by the Court upon his widow amounted to the small sum of £26 : 16 : 06. He signed all papers with his mark, and his son Samuel did the same. There probably were other children, but the only one identified is the son Samuel, Jr.

Issue : 1. Samuel⁸, of Duxbury. He married Margaret Bonney, widow of Joseph³ Bonney, of Pembroke.

---

* Vide page 513.
† *Plymouth Colony Records*, Court Orders, vol. 1 : 68, 137 ; also *Plymouth Colony Miscellaneous Records*, vol. 8 : 31.

Joseph [2] Bonney was a younger son to Thomas [1] Bonney, b. about 1604, who came to New England from Dover, England. His first wife was Mary Terry, his second, Mary Hunt. The children of Thomas [1] Bonney were Thomas [2], who mar. Dorcas Sampson, Mary [2], who mar. John [2] Mitchell, Sarah [2], Hannah [2], John [2], William [2], Joseph [2], who mar. Margaret Phillips, and James [2], who mar. Abigail Bishop.* Joseph [2] and Margaret (Phillips) Bonney lived in Pembroke, where he died before 1719. Samuel Chandler, of Duxbury, was appointed administrator of the estate of " Joseph Bonny late of Pembroke," April 8, 1720. The inventory of his estate was sworn to by John Partridge, Thomas Parris, and John Wadsworth, on April 26, 1721. The next day, April 27, Samuel Chandler brought in an account of £21 : 18, for the board, in Hingham, of "two children of the s[d] deceased two years Since his decease." †

The date of marriage of Samuel Chandler does not appear. He was a respected citizen of Duxbury, and lived on land adjoining that of his cousin, Joseph [2] Chandler. On Feb. 1, 1724, they settled the bounds between their farms on Brewster's Brook,‡ in the centre of the town. Samuel also shared in the several divisions of the common lands of the town, of which mention is made in connection with Joseph [2] Chandler. The date of Samuel Chandler's death is not known. There was no inventory of his estate, nor division. His will, dated July 17, 1742, was proved Aug. 2, 1742. It was signed with his mark.

his

" Samuel 🙡 Chandler." §

mark

He called himself " yeoman," and left to his wife " Margett " all his " indoor moveables " and a " comfortable maintenance." His son, Samuel Chandler, named as sole executor,

---

* *The Bonney Family*, by Charles L. Bonney, Chicago, 1898 : 5, 41, 201–208.
† *Plymouth County Probate*, Book 4 : 267, 269.
‡ *Town Records of Duxbury*, vol. 1 : 118.
§ *Plymouth County Probate*, Book 9 : 6, 7.

was to have his land, homestead, stock of cattle, utensils on the farm, etc. His son Thomas was to have £30, "when he comes of age," and half the "moveables," etc., after his mother's decease; his daughter, Abigail Delano, was to have £10, with the other half of the "moveables," under the same condition. The witnesses to his will were Thomas Phillips, Keturah Samson, who made her mark, and Jonathan Peterson.

The will of Margaret Chandler, widow, of Pembroke, to which town she had returned, was dated Sept. 27, 1754, and proved Aug. 7, 1758.* She mentioned sons, Ezekiel Bonney, Nathaniel Bonney, and Thomas Chandler, daughter Margaret Robinson, "daughter Foster's daughter, . . . daughter Delano's daughter," granddaughter "Margrat Crocker," and granddaughter "Martha Delano." The inventory of her estate was extensive.

> Issue by first husband:† I. Mary[8] Bonney, b. Nov. 14, 1708; mar. to Josiah Foster, Jr. She had a daughter, and probably other children.
>
> II. Ezekiel[8] Bonney, b. Nov. 14, 1711; mar. Dec. 26, 1734, Hannah Bryant, of Pembroke. Issue: eleven.
>
> III. Nathaniel[8] Bonney, b. Sept. 11, 1714; mar. Lydia Bryant, of Plympton. Issue: six.
>
> IV. Margaret[8] Bonney, b. ——; mar. to Increase Robinson. Issue: seven.
>
> Issue by second husband:‡ V. Martha[4] Chandler, b. Sept. 22, 1719, in Duxbury; d. before her father.
>
> VI. Abigail[4] Chandler, b. July 1, 1721, in Duxbury; was mar. May 28, 1740, by the Rev. Samuel Veazie, to David Delano, of Duxbury.§ She died before 1758, in which year he mar., second, Sarah ——. David Delano died of smallpox, in 1760, while

---

* *Plymouth County Probate*, Book 15: 74, 75.
† *The Bonney Family*, by Charles L. Bonney, Chicago, 1898: 75.
‡ *Town Records of Duxbury*, vol. 1: 15.
§ *Delano History and Genealogy*, by Major Joel Andrew Delano, New York, 1899: 267.

serving in the " Army at the westward." His inventory was taken in 1761, and his property was divided among the heirs in 1765. Thomas Chandler, on Dec. 3, 1763, was appointed guardian of Jonathan Delano, son to David, deceased, and "nephew of the said Thomas." * Issue: Jonathan Delano, and other children.

VII. Samuel⁴ Chandler, b. Oct. 3, 1723, in Duxbury. Although not quite of age, his father appointed him executor of his estate, which is shown by the following: " Item, I give to my Well beloved daughter Abigail Dellano the sum of Ten pounds . . . to be paid when my Executor Comes to yᵉ age of One and twenty years by my Executor."

VIII. Thomas⁴ Chandler, b. April 30, 1725, in Duxbury; mar., first, Aug. 24, 1749, Silvia Bisbee (Bixby); mar., second, May 6, 1762, Rhoda Blackmore.†

ISSUE (PROBABLY) BY SECOND WIFE

II. Benjamin², born in Duxbury; mar. about 1671, Elizabeth Buck, b. 1653, daughter to Cornet John Buck, of Scituate.

Cornet John Buck was in Scituate before 1650. He and his brother Isaac are supposed to have been sons to James Buck, who came early to Hingham. John Buck was the first proprietor who settled on Walnut Tree Hill in Scituate; his house was on the west side of that hill. He succeeded the veteran Robert Stetson as " Cornet of the Troopers " before King Philip's war,‡ in which he saw constant service. His first wife was Elizabeth, daughter to Samuel Holbrook, of Weymouth.§ Elizabeth, wife of Benjamin Chandler, was his eldest daughter; there were also five other daughters and four sons.‖ Cornet John Buck's will, dated Sept. 4, 1697,

---

* *Plymouth County Probate*, Book 19.
† Winsor's *History of Duxbury*, 1849: 241.
‡ Vide page 712.
§ Harvey's *History of the Buck Family*, 1889: 24.
‖ Mitchell's *History of Bridgewater*, 1840: 125; also Deane's *History of Scituate*, 1831: 229.

gave legacies " to my Daughter Chandler " and " to all my Grand children living at yarmouth and Sandwich." *

Benjamin Chandler, although he received several grants of land in Duxbury,† was a resident of Scituate as late as 1683, and probably several years after. Immediately following the death of his brother Samuel, that is, on " Jan. 20, 1683 [–84] . . . Benjamin Chandler of Scituate," for £10, paid by Edward Wanton, sold to him " all that my sixty acres of land . . . within the Township of duxborough between the old path called the massachusets path and the great Cedar swamp . . . as it was laid out & bounded by Sam^{ll} Nash and phillip dellano," by order of the town of Duxbury, " after it was granted to samuel Chandler now deceased." These sixty acres he confirmed to Wanton, as " all those my lands at s^d duxborough that were lately in the occupation of the above-named Samuel Chandler." This deed was signed:

" Benjamin Chandler   (seal)

The marke of **X** Elizabeth Chandler "   (seal)

It was acknowledged, March 27, 1685, by Benjamin Chandler, before " John Alden assist : " ‡

Benjamin Chandler removed to Duxbury before 1691; in that year he died intestate. The inventory of his estate, taken by Thomas Delano and Edward Southworth, was as follows : —

" An Jnventory § taken of the estate of the late Deceased Benjamin chandler this 6th Day of Octob^r 1691 By us whose names are under written

	£	s	d
" Jtem the House and lands	090	00	00
Jtem Neat cattel	013	15	00
Jtem sheepe	002	10	00
Jtem swine	002	15	00
Jtem Beds and Bedding besides ye widdows Bedd	013	00	00
Jtem Table Linnen	001	10	00
Jtem cloathing money and Books	005	01	00
Jtem one peece of Cloth	002	00	00
Jtem carpenters tooles and Cart taklen	004	00	00

---

* *Plymouth County Probate*, Book 1 : 276.

† Vide Joseph ^{2} Chandler.

‡ *Plymouth Colony Deeds*, Book 6.

§ *Plymouth County Probate*, Book 1 : 128.

	£	s	d
Jtem Jron Brass and Pewter	004	10	00
Jtem one Gun	001	00	00
Jtem about 25 bushells of corne	001	10	00
Jtem chests and spinning wheels and other household lumber and Tobacco and a little sheeps wool	002	00	00
jtem Woorsted and cloth yarn	001	10	00
	145	01	00

The widows Bed & furniture and a Pillion not apprized
Thomas Delano
Edward Southworth

Debts due out of yᵉ estate

	£	s	d
To Capᵗ Thomas about	02	00	00
To Edward Southworth	01	13	00
To John Siṁons	01	17	05
To Joseph ffoord	00	11	03
To John Rouse	00	08	00
To Anthony Callimer	00	04	09
To Hope Besboy [Bixby]	00	06	03
And by other Particulars Debts due to severall psons :	08	14	00

" Elizabeth Chandler relict widdow of Benjamin chandler late of Duxborough Deceased made oath before yᵉ county court at Plimoth March 16ᵗʰ 169½ that yᵉ above written is a true Inventory of his estate so far as she Knoweth and that when more shall be Discovered to her she will make it known

Attest Samˡ Sprague Clerk "

On the same date, March 16, 1691–92, the widow Elizabeth was appointed administratrix of the estate of her late husband. The date of her death is not known.

Issue : * 1. Benjamin ⁸, b. 1672, in Scituate.

2. Martha⁸, b. 1673, in Scituate.

3. Samuel⁸, b. Nov. 30, 1674, in Scituate. He removed to Bridgewater; his wife was Mercy ——. Issue : † I. Jonathan ⁴, b. 1699; mar. Nov. 27, 1751, Rebecca Packard. II. Mary⁴, b. 1702; mar. Oct. 17, 1729, in Bridgewater, to Joseph Perry, of that town.‡ III. Sarah ⁴, b. 1703. IV. Samuel⁴, b. 1709. V. Abraham ⁴, b. 1711. VI. Susanna⁴, b. 1715.

---

* Deane's *History of Scituate*, 1831 : 231.
† Mitchell's *History of Bridgewater*, 1840 : 136.
‡ *The Genealogical Advertiser*, 1898, vol. I : 37.

4. John [2], b. 1675, in Scituate.
5. Mary [2], b. 1678, in Scituate.
6. Joseph [2], date of birth unknown. That he was a son of Benjamin is proved by the following extract from the town records of a petition * presented by Joseph Chandler to the town of Duxbury, March 1, 1747–48 : —

" Whereas my honoured Father Benjamin Chandler late of Duxbury County of Plymouth, Dec[d] died seized of a considerable real Estate in said Town of Duxbury and after his death to wit on third Tuesday of March 1691–2 the County court then holden at Plymouth settled the whole of the Real Estate aforesaid upon the four Sons which my Father left behind him ½ to the Elddest of the said sons ⅙ part to each of the other said sons " the said Joseph made complaint that although an inhabitant and a freeholder he had not received his share of the common lands divided in January, 1709, and prayed " that I may yet have my right." This petition was not granted.

7. Keturah [2], mentioned in her mother's will.
8. Elizabeth [2], also mentioned in that will.

III. Joseph [2], b. in Duxbury. (Vide infra.)
IV. Sarah [2], b. in Duxbury. She and her sisters probably were unmarried at the time of her father's death, in 1662. Her share of his estate was one third of his sugar " att Barbadoes."

V. Anna [2], b. in Duxbury. To her, also, was bequeathed a third of the sugar.
VI. Mary [2], b. in Duxbury. The remainder of the sugar was given to Mary. At that early period corn, sugar, and beaver-skins were used as currency ; and, later, tobacco.†
VII. Ruth [2], b. in Duxbury. With her brothers, Benjamin and Joseph, she was to receive from her father's estate the " rent " of the homestead due from his son Samuel, and a share of the cattle when they were divided at the expiration of Samuel's lease.

---

* *Town Records of Duxbury* (original), vol. 3 : 26.   † Vide page 684.

JOSEPH[2] CHANDLER

Joseph[2] Chandler, son to Edmund[1] Chandler by his second, or last, wife, was born in Duxbury. His father, in his will, dated May 3, 1662, appointed him executor, which is proof that he then was of age; consequently the date of birth of Joseph may be considered as previous to 1641. There is no record of his marriage, but the name of his wife and proof that Edmund was his father are contained in the following extracts from a deed, acknowledged July 7, 1673, by "Joseph Chandeler and Marcye his wife." This deed was written in the old English form, so rare in Plymouth but more common in the other New England Colonies : —

"Know all men by these p[r]sents That I Joseph Chandeler of the Towne of Duxburrow in the Jurisdiction of Plymouth in New England in America Blacksmith for and in consideration of the sume of thirty pounds in currant pay of New England to me in hand payed by henery Brightman of Portsmouth on Rhode Island in the Jurisdiction of Providence plantations in New England in America yeoman;" convey "To him the said henery Brightman and his heires and assignes for euer; a certaine tracte or psell of land belonging to mee lying and being on the easternsyde of Taunton Riuer in the Jurisdiction aforsaid vnto sundry of the freemen of that corporation; It being in Number the fourth lott bounded on the southsyde with the land of Christopher Wadsworth, and on the Northsyde with the land of Samuel house abuting vpon Taunton Riuer aforsaid as yett vndeuided lying on both sydes Taunton Riuer, from Mattapoisett vpon the said Taunton Riuer on both sydes the said Riuer viz: all that my said lott of land which is the fourth lott bounded as aforsaid being on the eastern syde of Taunton Riuer with the Meddowes therunto appertaineing; excepting my meddowes or Rights of meddowes att Sepecan; To haue and to hold [etc.] . . . The which said land and meddow, and appurtenances, are mine by donation and Gift: willed vnto mee by my honored and deceased father

Mr Edmond Chandeler as appeereth by his last will and Testament bearing date the third day of May Ann°: Dom: one thousand six hundred sixty and two To be holden off our Sou^r: Lord the Kinge as off his Mannor of East Greenwich in the County of Kent in the Realme of England in free and comon soccage, and nott in capite nor by Knight service," etc.

(Signed)

" Joseph Chandeler " [seal]

Witnessed
" in the p^rsence of
Jonathan Alden
David Alden "

" This deed was acknowlidged this 7th of the 5th [July] 1673 by Joseph Chandeler and Marcye his wife, before me

John Alden Assistant." *

This Joseph probably was the " Josepth Chandeler " who, with " Certaine psons of Sandwich," was fined ten shillings by the General Court, May 7, 1661, " for refusing and neglecting to assist marshall Barlow, in the execution of his office." † The death of his father, the following year, doubtless was the cause of his return to Duxbury, where he was a prominent citizen throughout his life.

On June 3, 1679, Joseph Chandler and Samuel Chandler were chosen by the General Court to lay out a highway for George Soule. At the same session of the Court, Joseph Chandler was chosen " Constable for Duxbury." ‡ In a bill of charges of the town of Duxbury for the year 1686, Joseph Chandler was paid "[£]0–2–3 . . . for a cunstables stafe & a small matter dew before." § He was " sworne . . . July 1, 1684," to serve on a jury.‖ March 21, 1700–01, "Joseph Chandler Senr" was chosen Grand Juror. " Joseph

---

* *Plymouth Colony Deeds*, Book 3: 287.
† *Plymouth Colony Records*, Court Orders, vol. 3: 213.
‡ *Plymouth Colony Records*, Court Orders, vol. 6: 15, 10.
§ *Town Records of Duxbury* (original), vol. 5: 106.
‖ *Plymouth Colony Judicial Acts*: 279.

Chandler " and others "desiring to take up their freedom"
were approved by the Town May 28, 1689.[*]

For many years the common lands of the town of Duxbury were let out to proprietors. In 1692, Joseph Chandler
was charged "[£]oo-6-o . . . rent dew" for town land.[†]
March 27, 1694–95, he "subscribed" to pay " £oo-02-o "
for the use of town land, for the term of seven years, "on
little wood neck." [‡] On May 17, 1703, measures were taken
by the town for a division of the commons, but action was
deferred because of the remonstrance of thirty-two citizens,
including "Joseph Chanler Sen. [and] Edmund Chanler."
On September 12, 1707, however, it was voted in town-meeting that every freeholder and housekeeper should have
twenty acres of the commons, and those who had previous
grants should have enough more to make up the twenty
acres. Yet a protest was entered at the town-meeting of
March 7, 1709–10, by "Joseph Chandler, Sen[r], Edmond
Chanler, Samuel Chandler," and others, against acts passed
concerning the division.[§] Their protest availed nothing and
appears not to have operated against them, since the members of the Chandler family recorded, June 5, 1710, in a list
of those having rights in the commons, were Samuel, John,
Benjamin, Joseph Sr., Edmund, and Joseph Jr. With the
exception of Samuel, all of the above shared in the divisions by lot, on July 12, 1712, and December 13, 1713.
On June 29, 1714, Samuel shared with them in the drawing.
As late as May 10, 1748, the list of voters who had rights
in the common meadows, at Duxbury, included : —

"Sam[l] Chanlers heirs /   Cp[t] John Chanler /
John Chanler /   Joseph Chanler Jun[r] heirs /
Benj Chanler (2½ rts)   Joshua Chanler /" [‖]
Joseph Chanler Sen[r] heirs /

---

[*] *Town Records of Duxbury* (original), vol. 5 : 44, 12.
[†] *Town Records of Duxbury* (original), vol. 5 : 16.
[‡] *Town Records of Duxbury* (original), vol. 1 : 29.
[§] *Town Records of Duxbury* (original), vol. 2 : 284, 296.
[‖] *Proprietors' Records of Duxbury* (original), vol. 3 : 16, 4, 9, 13, 14, 29.

The early farm or homestead of Joseph[2] Chandler consisted of twenty acres, at the lower end of the town, bounded by "meeting house path" and the Plymouth road. It is best described by the following extract from the Town Records:

"Whereas formerly a tract of land was granted by the town of Duxburrough to Joseph Chandler, lying between the meeting house path and Plymouth road, and was laid out to him, but now no record to be found of it, We Ensign John Tracy, Thomas Delano and Abram Sampson, being desired by Joseph Chandler, have laid out unto him twenty acres of land, more or less, bounded on the East by the meeting house path to a red oak tree marked on four sides, and from said tree by a west south west line to a pine tree which is the corner mark of the town land, and from said pine tree by the same line, a range of trees marked, until we come to a cart road, where we marked a red oak sapling, and then bounded by said path and Plymouth road, and by said road to the lotted land of said Joseph Chandler, and so by Joseph Chandlers line to the meeting house path. . . . This 17th day of February 1699–700." [*]

That this land remained his homestead is proved by the provisions of his will, dated April 21, 1721. He gave to his son Joseph all his cooper's tools and "half of y.e smiths Tools & y.e anvil that he hath in his Possession;" and to his "Grandson John Chandler . . . y.e other half of my smiths Tools." The death of Joseph Chandler, Sr., at above eighty years of age, probably occurred in November or December, 1721; the inventory of his estate, which does not include his many and valuable tracts of land, was taken on the 28th of the latter month. The date of death of his wife, Mercy, for whom he made ample provision, is unknown. The following is a copy of his will and inventory; the originals have not been preserved: —

"In y.e Name of God amen : y.e twenty first Day of aprill in the year of our Lord one thousand seven Hundred twenty & one I

---

[*] *Town Records of Duxbury*, 1893: 71.

Joseph Chandler of Duxbor? in y? County of Plymouth in New: England Being weak in Body but of perfect mind & memory thanks be given unto God therefore Calling to mind y? mortality of my Body & knowing that it is appointed for all men once to Dye Do make & ordain this my last will & Testament :* that is to say Principally & first of all I give & Recomend my Soul into y? Hands of God that gave it & my Body to a Decent Burial at the descretion of my Executor nothing doubting but at y? General Resurection I Shall Receive y? same again by y? almighty Power of God & as Touching Such worldly Estate wherewith it hath Pleased God to Bless me in this Life I Give Demise & Dispose of y? same. In y? following manner & Forme Imprimis I give & Bequeath unto my son Joseph Chandler to Him and His Heirs all my out Lands in y? Town of Duxbor? & y? one half of my meadow at little wood Island & all my meadow at Gottom [Gotham] So called in Duxbor? afores? & my share in y? Beach & y? one half of my Right in y? Great Cedar Swamp & all my Cooper Tools & y? one half of y? Smiths Tools & y? anvil that he hath in his Possession. Item I give & Bequeath unto my Grandson John Chandler all that Part of my Land at Home on y? westerly side of y? way that Leads to y? meeting House Reserving fire wood for my Wife & my Daughter Sarah Chandler & a Quarter of my meadow at little wood Island in Duxbor? & a Quarter of my Right in y? Great Cedar Swamp & y? other half of my Smith Tools. Item I give & Bequeath unto my Daughter Sarah Chandler my Dwelling House & y? Land it Stands upon after my Wifes Decease & a Bed. Item I give & Bequeath unto my three Daughters Esther Glass, Mary Bradford, & Sarah Chandler to them & their Heirs all y? Land on y? Easterly side of y? way y? leads to y? meeting House after my wifes Decease : Item I give unto my Daughter Esher Glass a Quarter of y? great Cedar Swamp and a Bed — Item I give unto my Daughter in Law Elisabeth Chandler four Pounds to be Paid by my Executor in one year after my Decease & y? House and fire wood as long as she Remains a widdow. Item I give & Bequeath unto my Dear & Loving Wife Mercy all y? Rest & Residue of my Estate. & a Quarter of y? meadow at little wood Island as long as she lives & then to my three Daugh-

---

* *Plymouth County Probate*, Book 4: 309–311.

ters & y⁹ Improvement of y⁹ House & Land on y⁹ Easterly side
of y⁹ way during Her Natural Life. Item by these Presents I Do
Constitute & ordain my above named son Joseph Chandler Executor of this my last Will & Testament & Doe hereby Revoke
& disallow all former Wills by me heretofore made. Confirming
this and no other to be my last Will & Testament. In Witness
whereof I have hereunto Set my hand & seal y⁹ Day & year
above written

" Signed Sealed & Declared   Joseph Chandler   [seal]
to be his last Will & Testa-
ment in y⁹ Presence of

Samuel Sprague, Thomas ⟨his mark⟩ Hunt
   Bethiah Sprague "

" January y⁹ 1ˢᵗ 1721 [1721-22] this will was sworn to by the
above witnesses; it was approved and the inventory was ordered
"ʸ⁹ fifth Day of Feb⁹ 1721 [1721-22] "

" An Inventory of y⁹ Estate of Joseph Chandler Sen⁹ late of Duxbor⁹ Dec⁴
   Taken y⁹ 28ᵗʰ Day of December 1721 by us whose Names are underwritten

Imprimis His Purse & apparrel	£16 : 1 : 2
Item to Books	2 : 8 : 0
Item to Neat Cattle	6 : 10 : 0
Item to Swine	1 : 0 : 0
Item to Husbandry Tools	1 : 5 : 0
Item, to Iron Ware & Brass	5 : 14 : 0
Item, to Earthen Ware & Glass Bottles	6 : 6
Item, to Pewter & Tinn	1 : 10 : 0
Item, to wooden vessels	1 : 10 : 0
Item, to arms & amunition	1 : 11 : 0
Item, to Chests & Boxes	1 : 0 : 0
Item, to Bed & Bedding & Table Linnen	25 : 0 : 0
Item, to Feathers	0 : 8 : 0
Item, to Smith Tools	10 : 0 : 0
Item, to Coopers Tools	1 : 0 : 0
Item, to Carpenters Tools	1 : 0 : 0
Item, to Lumber	0 : 15 : 0

Item, to a Grindstone & two Spinning Wheels
to a Pair of Cards & a Meal Bagg

Philip Delenoe
Samuel Sprague

"January y̲ᵉ 1ˢᵗ 1721 [1721–22] Joseph Chandler Executor to
y̲ᵉ last Will and Testament of His Father Joseph Chandler late
of Duxbor̲ᵒ in y̲ᵉ County of Plymouth Dec̲ᵈ made Oath that y̲ᵉ
Within Written is a true & Just Inventory of y̲ᵉ Estate of y̲ᵉ s̲ᵈ
Joseph Chandler Dec̲ᵈ as far as it is Come to His Knowledge &
when more appears he will also give it in.

Before mee Isaac Winslow, Judge of Probates."

The date of the death of Mercy, wife of Joseph Chandler,
who survived her husband, is not known.

ISSUE

I. Edmund ⁸, son to Joseph ² and Mercy (——) Chandler, was
born in Duxbury. His wife was Elizabeth ⁸, daughter to
Jonathan ³ Alden.

Jonathan ³ Alden, son to John ¹ and Priscilla (Mullins)
Alden, inherited and occupied the home of his father, in
Duxbury. His wife, whom he mar. Dec. 10, 1672, was Abigail, daughter to Benjamin Hallett, Esq., of Barnstable.
Captain Jonathan Alden died Feb., 1697, and was buried,
under arms, on the 17th day of that month. He left no will,
but the division of his estate mentions widow Abigail, eldest
son John, who received a double portion, and the two brothers and three sisters of John.* On July 2, 1711, " Jonathan
Alden, Andrew Alden, Edmond Chandler and Elizabeth his
wife, Thomas Southworth and Sarah his wife," all of Duxbury, signed a deed, acknowledging that they had " Re-
ceiveᵈ of our Brother John Alden of Duxborough . . . full
satisfaction as to our Parts and claims to any Part of the
Lands that was our Fathers Jonathan Alden's in Duxborough aforesᵈ ;" May 20, 1723, the deed was recorded.† The
name of the third sister did not appear.

Edmund Chandler is not mentioned as holding any town
office in Duxbury. Although a remonstrant, with his father
and brother Joseph, against the division of the town's common lands, he shared with them in the divisions of 1710,

---

* *Plymouth County Probate*, Book 1 : 255; Book 2 : 28.
† *Plymouth County Deeds*, Book 16 : 197.

1712, 1713, and 1714.* Several of these lots are mentioned in his inventory. He died intestate, in Duxbury, before Feb. 5, 1721. On this date, Isaac Winslow, Esq., Judge of Probate for the County of Plymouth, ordered " Elizabeth . . . Widow of Edmund Chandler late of Duxborough " to bring in an inventory of her husband's " Goods Chattels Rights & Credits ; " it was presented at Court as follows : † —

" An Inventory taken this 26ᵗʰ Day of Febuary by us the Subscribers of yᵉ Real & Personall Estate of Edmund Chandler late of Duxborᵒ Decᵈ

	£	Sh	d
To one fourty acre Lott in Pembrooke yᵉ 28th in Number .	20 :	00 .	0 .
to yᵉ one half of yᵉ 84ᵗʰ Lott in yᵉ Second Division	10 :	.	.
to yᵉ one half of yᵉ 96ᵗʰ Lott in yᵉ Second Division	10 :	.	.
to meadow att blue Fish-River	10 :	.	.
to a share of meadow in yᵉ Second Division	6 :	.	.
to yᵉ House & Barn with a Small Piece of Land	70 :	.	.
to one Horse	5 :	.	.
to one ox & steer	7 :	.	.
to two Cows & two Calves	7 :	.	.
to sixteen sheep	4 :	.	.
to His armes 20/ to Books 30/	2 : 10	.	
to yᵉ widdows Bed not Prised	[		]
to Beds & Bedding. Table Linnen	11 : 12	.	
to Pewter 27/ to Brass 10/	1 : 17	.	
to andirons 15/ to two Pott Hangers 16/	1 : 11	.	
to Potts & Kettles	1 : 18	.	
to one Pair of Tongs & frying Pan	: 4	.	
To one ax & ads & other Tools	1 : 3	.	
to Glass Bottles	: 1		
to Barrels Tubbs & Spinnen wheels	: 10		
to Chests & Chairs 21/ to Sickel 2/	1 : 3	.	

John Partridge, Thomas Southworth, Edward Arnold "
Sworn to by the above, " March yᵉ 5ᵗʰ 1721/22," before " Isaac Winslow, Judge of Probate."
Sworn to by " Elizabeth Chandler widdow . . . of Edmund Chandler late of Duxborᵒ . . . April yᵉ 20ᵗʰ 1722."

" Here is an accompt of yᵉ Debts Due from yᵉ Estate of my Husband Edmund Chandler Decᵈ & it is as followeth.

	£	Sh	d
" To Nathaniel Thomas Esqʳ	5 :	.	.
to John watson Esqʳ	4 : 12 :	.	
to mʳ Murdoch	2 : 11 :	.	

* Vide page 876. † *Plymouth County Probate*, Book 4: 299, 356, 357.

	£	Sh	d
to m? Charls Little	5 :	4 :	6
to m? Edward? of Boston	9 :	.	.
to m? John Wadsworth	9 :	15 :	.
to m? Samuel Seabury	14 :	.	.
to m? Thomas Loring	3 :	4 :	4
to m? Ruth Silvester	12 :	.	.
to Jonathan Alden	5 :	10 :	.
to Jonathan Delanoe	7 :	.	.
to Thomas Fish	7 :	.	.
to Samuel Fisher	1 :	7 :	6
to William Brewster Jun?	3 :	.	.
to John Sprague	1 :	13 :	.
to m? Burton		10 :	.
to Hamshear		15 :	.
to Joseph Chandler	6 :	.	.

£98 : 2 : 4

" Here is an accompt of what was due to y? e[st]ate and that amounts to y? Sum of 5 : 14 : 10."

The widow Elizabeth was mentioned in the will of Joseph[2] Chandler, dated April 21, 1721, by which he bequeathed "unto my Daughter in Law Elisabeth Chandler four Pounds to be Paid by my Executor in one year after my Decease & y? House and fire wood as long as she Remains a widdow." She died between April 22, 1728, the date of her will, and Dec. 5, 1732, when it was proved : —

"The Last Will * and Testament of the Widow Elizabeth Chandler of Duxboro — I being ill & weak & not knowing the day of my Death & yet of sound understanding & good Memory do thus Will my Estate to be Disposed of after my Death — In the name of God amen. I Give my Soul to God my Body I Commit to the Earth to be decently buried & do will that my Debts & funeral charges be paid before any Legacies — Item I Give to my Daughters Mary Keturah & Elizabeth all my Wearing Cloathes Woollen & Linnen equally between them three Only my best Riding hood & my Scarf to Elizabeth more than the other two — I do Give to my Son Samuel one pair of Sheets and twenty shillings — I do Give to my Son Joseph one pair of Sheets & my Tankard & my Bible — I do Give to my Son John my Chest of Drawers & one pair of Sheets & my Silver Spoon and twenty shillings — I do Give to my Son Benjam^n. Twenty Shillings — I do Give to my Son Joseph Twenty

* *Plymouth County Probate,* Book 6: 259–261.

Shillings more than what is above written — I do Will that after my Debts & funeral Charges are paid if any of my Estate remain after y° first Division Three fourth Parts of it be equally Divided betwixt my Three Daughters & the other fourth Part half of it to Deborah Simons the Daughter of Isaac Simons and the Other half to Isaac Simmons, jun⁣ʳ & for Simons his sister equally betwixt them two — I do Constitute & appoint my Son John Chandler to be my Execut⁣ʳ of this my last Will and Testament — And so desiring to live in peace & that my Children may have peace when I am dead I do here unto Set my hand & Seal this twenty Second day of april in the Year of our Lord one thousand seven hundred & twenty eight

The Mark of ⟍⟋ Elizabeth Chandler

" In Presence of these
Witnesses
The mark of X Ephm Norcott
  Moses Simons
  Philip Delano "
  The will was proved December 5, 1732, by the above witnesses, "Ephraim Norcott, Moses Simons & Philip Delano."

" A true Inventory of the Estate of the Widow Elizabeth Chandler late of Duxborough Deceas⁣ᵗ Taken by us the Subscribers this Sixth Day of Decemb⁣ʳ in y° Year of our Lord.

	[£	s	d]
1732 — Viz : To Wearing Cloaths	33	0	0
To Money	05	0	0
To Sheets & Table Linnen	25	17	0
To Cloths	05	0	0
To Beds Bedstead & Bedding	30	9	0
To Chests Desk & Trunk	04	18	0
To Wooden Ware	02	05	0
To Earthen Ware	01	02	0
To Silver & money Scales	01	13	0
To Brass & Jron Ware	06	11	0
To Glass ware Pewter & Books	3	12	0
To Baskets Bags & Chairs	2	9	0
To Cattel	14	15	0

Philip Delano
Ed⁣ʷ Arnold
Moses Simons "
  " Dec⁣ʳ y° 7. 1732. John Chandler Execut⁣ʳ " made oath that this was a true inventory of the estate " of his mother Elizabeth Chandler . . . Deceas⁣ᵈ "

    Issue : 1. Mary⁣⁴, b. in Duxbury.
     2. Keturah⁣⁴, b. Sept., 1688, in Duxbury; mar., Jan. 19,

1703, to Nathaniel [3] Sampson (Abraham [2], Abraham [1] Sampson). He was b. about 1682, in Duxbury, and d. there in 1749. Keturah Sampson d. Jan. 14, 1777, aged eighty-eight years, four months.*

3. Elizabeth [4], b. in Duxbury.

4. Samuel [4], b. in Duxbury.

5. Joseph [4], b. about 1694, in Duxbury, was of Pembroke. He mar. Sept. 8, 1720, Elizabeth, daughter to Samuel Delano; he was then called "Joseph Chandler 3d." About 1748, he removed to Cornwall, Conn., and d. about 1784, in that State.†

Issue: I. John [5], b. Oct. 25, 1722, in Duxbury.

II. Simeon [5], b. Jan. 24, 1724-25, in Duxbury; and probably others.

6. John [4], b. in Duxbury. He was appointed executor of his mother's estate, and probably was the "Grandson John Chandler" mentioned by his grandfather, Joseph [2] Chandler, in his will.

7. Benjamin [4], b. in Duxbury.

II. Joseph [2]. (Vide infra.)

III. John [2], b. Sept., 1676, in Duxbury; mar. March 4, 1707-08, in Duxbury, Sarah Weston.‡

John Chandler was not remembered in the will of his father, Joseph [2] Chandler. This may be accounted for by his having been married a number of years and having no children; but that John [2] was son to Joseph [2] is evident from the following town record: § —

"At A Town Meeting held in Duxburrough, 2 June 1687. The Town did give unto Joseph Chandlers son John who by Gods Providence has lost his hand 50 Acres of Land Lying on the Easterly side of the South River & Northerly side of the Place Called the Rockes Provided that his Father shall have liberty to sell or other wise improve sd Lands for the benefit of the afore sd child."

---

* *The Sampson Family*, by John Adams Vinton, 1864: 14.

† *Delano History and Genealogy*, by Major Joel Andrew Delano, New York, 1899: 508, 517.

‡ *Town Records of Duxbury* (original), vol. A 1: 112.

§ *Town Records of Duxbury* (original), vol. 5: 6.

The child John at that time was eleven years of age, and there is no record of any other Joseph, or John, Chandler previous to 1687, nor for many years afterward. John Chandler received his share of the common lands in the divisions of 1710, 1712, 1713, and 1714; he also was mentioned among those voters who had rights in the commons in 1748.* John Chandler d. April 7, 1759, in Duxbury, aged eighty-two years and seven months.† His will, dated Sept. 14, 1747, proved July 9, 1759,‡ bequeathed to "my kinsman John Chandler of Duxborough abovesaid, who is the Son of my Brother Joseph Chandler all that farme of Land in Duxborough abovesaid whereon I now Dwell both upland & meadow the whole Containing about an hundred acres together also with all my other lands Contiguous thereunto lying in the town of Marshfield . . . with all yᵉ houseing fencing and orchards . . . "   (Signed)

"John Chandler" [seal]

His wife Sarah was appointed executrix. She was b. Oct., 1688, and d. April 13, 1764, in Duxbury, aged seventy-five and a half years.§ No issue.

IV. Esther⁵, b. in Duxbury; mar. Feb. 14, 1705, to John² Glass, of Duxbury. She was his second wife; the name of his first wife is not known.

John² Glass was son to Roger¹ and Mary (——) Glass, of Duxbury.‖ On May 2, 1726, it was ordered by the Court that "mʳ Joseph Chandler Senʳ mʳ Samuel Sprague & mʳ Moses Soul all of Duxboro" should make an inventory of the estate of John Glass, late of Duxbury. The inventory, sworn to by the above appraisers July 4, 1726, included a house and barn, land in Pembroke, land adjacent to Benjamin Chandler's home lot . . . £50; stock, tools, and household goods.¶

Issue: 1. James³ Glass. On Nov. 12, 1733, James Glass and Mercy Glass, "heirs of our honᵈ father Mʳ John

---

* Vide page 876.

† *Town Records of Duxbury* (copy), vol. A 1 : 6.

‡ *Plymouth County Probate*, Book 15 : 238–240.

§ *Town Records of Duxbury* (original), vol. 1 : 250.

‖ Winsor's *History of Duxbury*, 1849 : 262.

¶ *Plymouth County Probate*, Book 5 : 545.

Glass late of Duxbury dec^d," agreed on a division of their father's estate. James, who signed with a mark, was to receive two thirds, and Mercy, one third.* This indicates that they were the only children.

   2. Mercy³ Glass.

V. Mary³, b. in Duxbury ; was mar. to Hezekiah³ Bradford, son to Major William² Bradford (Gov. William¹ Bradford) by his third wife, Mary, daughter to John Atwood, and widow of Rev. John Holmes.

   Issue : 1. Mary⁴ Bradford, an only child.†

VI. Sarah³,‡ b. in Duxbury, probably was the youngest daughter. She was remembered in the will of her father with the gift of "my Dwelling House & y⁰ Land it Stands upon after my Wifes Decease & a Bed." She also shared, with her two sisters, in another tract of land in Duxbury.

JOSEPH³ CHANDLER

Joseph³ Chandler, son to Joseph² and Mercy (——) Chandler, was born in Duxbury, but the date of his birth, through the loss of the town records of that period, is unknown ; it was probably about 1678 or 1679. His wife was Martha, daughter to Samuel and Mary (——) Hunt, of Dux-

---

* *Plymouth County Probate*, Book 6 : 399.

† *Governor William Bradford and his Son Major William Bradford*, by James Shepard, 1900 : 79–93.

‡ Winsor, in his *History of Duxbury* (page 305), adds to this family, Benjamin, b. 1684, in Duxbury, who d. there, March 26, 1771, aged eighty-seven years. Proof that this Benjamin was not son to Joseph³ Chandler is fully shown in the records of the Probate Court. Joseph³ Chandler, son to Joseph², removed to North Yarmouth, Maine, in 1727, and d. there in 1744. But the Joseph Chandler who petitioned for a guardian for "his brother Benjamin Chandler," who had "become non Compus Mentis and intirely unable of taking Care of himself Family or Estate," is stated to have been "of Duxbury." The petition was brought Feb. 3, 1745; he was appointed guardian, and served until 1750. The guardianship continued until the death of Benjamin, in 1771.

Vide *Town Records of Duxbury* (original), vol. 1 : 252. *Plymouth County Probate*, Book 10 : 128, 296–298, 528 ; Book 11 : 352, 360 ; Book 13 : 80 ; Book 19 : 202 ; Book 20 : 491, 492.

bury,* whom he married, February 12, 1700–01, in Duxbury.†
Like his father, he was a prominent blacksmith of that town,
and all his children were born there.

When the town of Duxbury "sold lands to defray the
charges of building the New Meeting House," September
16, 1706, Joseph Chandler purchased, for £15, "a parcel
of vpland, and a parcel of meadow . . . containing about
twenty-four acres, and began at a white oak stump at the
westerly corner of the said Chandler's shop, and thence it
runneth upward along by the countrey road to his home
lot . . . excepting out of this land the Tar-Kiln Pond," ‡
a marshy spot of some three acres. In the division of the
commons, 1710, salt meadows, 1712, and common meadows,
1748, Joseph Chandler, Jr., was allotted the same quantities
of land as his father. In 1748, however, it was granted to
his heirs,§ for he died in North Yarmouth, Maine, before
February 19, 1745, at which time his son, Zachariah, appeared as administrator of his estate. The homestead of
Joseph Chandler in Duxbury is fully described in the following record of a division of land between him and his cousin,
Samuel Chandler : ‖ —

"upon the 1ˢᵗ day of February Anno Domini 1724–25 — We
the subscribers. to wit. Joseph Chanler senʳ ¶ — and Samuel
Chanler both of Duxborough in yᵉ County of Plymouth in yᵉ Province of yᵉ Massachusetts-Bay in New-England, have run yᵉ Dividing line & settled yᵉ Bounds between yᵉ Farms of land whereon
we each of us do now Dwell as followeth. viz we began at a stone

---

* *The Hunt Genealogy*, by W. L. G. Hunt, 1862–63 : 140.

† *Town Records of Duxbury* (original), vol. A 1 : 125.

‡ *Town Records of Duxbury*, 1893 : 78.   § Vide page 876.

‖ *Town Records of Duxbury* (original), vol. 1 : 118.

¶ Joseph³ Chandler, during the lifetime of his father, was always men-
tioned as Joseph Chandler, Jr. After his father's death, in 1721, he was called
Joseph Chandler, Sr., to distinguish him from others of the name in Duxbury.
The settlement of the estate of David³ Alden, of Duxbury, in 1719, mentions
"Joseph Chanler yᵉ second [and] Joseph Chanler yᵉ third." Vide *Plymouth
County Probate*, Book 4 : 186.

set in ye ground in ye Cone of ye Eastwardly side of ye 149th lot
in ye upland in ye second Division of ye Commons which belonged
to ye towns of Duxborough & Pembroke s^d lot being now in y^e
Possession of Thomas Phillips, and from thence we run East 32
Degrees South to Brewsters Brook, so Called, to a Stump and
from thence we run East 6 Degrees Southerly 7 Rods to a stone
set in ye ground & from thence we run North 41 Degrees and a
half Easterly to a stone pitched in ye ground on the westerly side
of the Country Rhoad, which last-mentioned stone is at ye Easterly end of ye s^d Dividing line. and we do mutually agree ye aboves^d
Dividing line shall stand and remain as a Dividing line or partition Between ye above s^d Farms for us our heirs & Assigns forever.
Jn witness whereòf we have hereunto set our hands the day &
year first above written . . .

" Signed in presence of   Joseph Chandler
Ichabod Sampson   his
Ebenezer Thomas   Samuel A Chanler "
                                        mark

    In 1727, when a number of the citizens of the coast towns
of Massachusetts, between Hingham and Plymouth, united
with several men of Boston in an effort to permanently settle the town of North Yarmouth, on the shore of Casco
Bay,* Joseph Chandler and Jacob Mitchell, two prosperous
blacksmiths, left their shops and began anew in North Yarmouth. It is probable that Joseph Chandler did not take
his family there until some two years later, for his son
Judah, b. Aug. 13, 1720, stated, in 1796, that " when he was
about nine years old " he moved there with his father; but
the homestead, in Duxbury, was not sold until 1735. The
deed describes the same land that was mentioned in the
division of 1724–25 : —

    " Joseph Chandler . . . Blacksmith," of North Yarmouth,†
County of York, for £400, conveyed to his son, " Philip chandler
of Duxborough . . . Blacksmith," all " my Farm or Tract of

---

* Vide Appendix LXXXIV : A–R.
† *Plymouth County Deeds*, Book 30 : 173–174.

Land Together with all my Housings or Buildings & Fencings & Orchard & Appurtenances & Commodities & Priviledges whatsoever lying & being in the Township of Duxborough aforesaid, on the Westerly Side of the Countrey Road & is Bounded as follows, viz : . . . [by] the Farm that Joshua Samson lives on . . . to a Maple Stump by a Brook called Brewsters Brook * . . . by yᵉ Countrey Road . . . only Excepting & Reserving a good & Sufficient Cart Way through Gates or Bars for Samuel Chandler that may be most convenient for sᵈ Samuel Chandler and least prejudicial for sᵈ Philip Chandler through sᵈ Farm above mentioned . . ."

Witnesses : (Signed)
"Zachariah Chandler "Joseph Chandler" [seal]
John Wadsworth junʳ"

This deed was dated Sept. 27, 1735, and acknowledged at North Yarmouth, York County, Massachusetts, "Octobʳ yᵉ 22 : 1735," by Joseph Chandler. It was "Receivᵈ Jun 29 : 1736 & Recordᵈ"

In the drawing of the first division of ten acre lots in North Yarmouth, May 16, 1727,† Joseph Chandler's lot was number 81 ; and by right of this lot he received a pew in the "Old Church by the Ledge" when the seats were apportioned to the lot-holders, in 1739.‡ He also received his part of the " 120 acre division [Gedney's claim] . . . drawn by virtue of his home lot Nº 81 ; " in the division of the islands, he received a third part of "Capᵗ Parker's and Seguin Islands." §

When the first town-meeting was held in North Yarmouth, May 14, 1733, in the "framed and boarded " structure of the old First Church, Joseph Chandler was chosen "to be the Cutter of Timber." At the same time he was

---

* "Brewsters Brook" is so called to-day. It is near the geographical centre of the present town of Duxbury — the village centre is south of that point — and flows northerly through Cranberry Factory Pond into South River. The area of the original town of Duxbury has been much reduced by setting off parts to form the towns of Marshfield, Pembroke, and Kingston.

† This date is given also as June 26, 1727.

‡ Vide pages 390, 395. § Vide pages 400, 401.

chosen one of the three selectmen and assessors, filling the
former office again in 1735 and 1741. He was assessor in
1733, 1734, 1735, and 1738.* In the spring of 1734, he was
appointed on a "committee to treat with persons claiming
undivided lands." When the second town-meeting of the
year was held, October 3, 1734, " Joseph Chandler, Benjamin
Prince and Cornelius Sole [were chosen] to receive pro-
posals to build a mill."

Joseph Chandler was number four in the list of nine
founders of the First Church in North Yarmouth, in 1729;
he was received into that church, November 18, 1730, from
the church in Duxbury. His wife, Martha Chandler, was
received August 21, 1737; she died, his widow, January 31,
1759, in North Yarmouth.† The death of Joseph Chandler
probably occurred late in the year 1744, during the prevalence of the "slow fever" that was fatal to so many.‡ He
left no will, but his son Zachariah appeared as administrator
of his estate, February 19, 1745 [1744-45]. The inventory
of his personal estate was as follows:—

"A true Inventory § of the Goods and Estate both Real and
     personal of Mr Joseph Chandler late of North Yarmouth De-
     ceased, as it was Shewed to and taken by us the Subscribers
     on September ye. 14, 1745.

	£ s d
" To his Arms and Ammunition	£8 5 5
Item, to his Wearing Apparrell	18 10 5
Item, to the best Bed and Bedding	10 5 5
Item, to the Second Bed	5 10 5
Item, to one Coverlid one Blanket, & three Sheets	8 10 5
Item, to Books	1 5 5
Item, to Pewter	1 5 5
Item, to a Brass Skillet	1 5 5
Item, to a frying pan	2 5 5
Item, to Iron Ware, as pot, Kittle & Skillet	3 5 5
Item, to Hand jrons Tongs & Fire Shovel	1 2 5

---

* Vide pages 398, 399.
    † *Records of the First Congregational Church, North Yarmouth, Maine*,
1848: 14.
    ‡ Vide page 403.   § *York County Probate*, Book 6: 181-182.

Item, to a Crane and Tramels belonging to it . . . . 2 ᴠ ᴠ
Item, to Knives and Forks . . . . ᴠ 5 ᴠ
Item, to a pair of Worsted Combs . . . . 1 ᴠ ᴠ
Item, to three old Chests and a Table . . . . 3 2 ᴠ
Item, to Six old Chairs . . . . ᴠ 15 ᴠ
Item, to a Cane . . . . ᴠ 5 ᴠ
Item, to a Loom and Tackling . . . . 2 ᴠ ᴠ
Item, to Linnen and woolin Yarn . . . . 2 5 ᴠ
Item, to Smiths Tools . . . . 8 10 ᴠ
Item, to one pair of Stillyards . . . . 1 5 ᴠ
Item, to Carpenters tools . . . . 4 4 ᴠ
Item, to a Sythe & Tackling £1 To a plough £1 . . . . 2 ᴠ ᴠ
Item, to two Cows . . . . 26 ᴠ ᴠ
Item, to a Pʳ of Steears . . . . 23 ᴠ ᴠ
Item, to one Heifer £5 .. 10 .. 0 .. to a Calf 2 .. 10 ᴠ . . . . . 8 ᴠ ᴠ
Item, to Swine . . . . 5 5 ᴠ
Item, to one Right of out Lands in said Town . . . . 110 ᴠ ᴠ
Item, to one Pᵗ Money Scales 8/ to Cash 1 .. 9 .. 4 . . . . . . 1 17 4

This Inventory taken in old Tenor . . . . . . £282 ᴠ 4

Jacob Mitchell
Andrew Gray
Barnabas Winslow

"York Ss Northyarmouth Febʸ yᵉ 15, 1745.

"Then personally appeared the within named Jacob Mitchell Andrew Gray and Barnabas Winslow, and made Oath to the just Apprizement of the above Inventory ᴠ according to the best of their Judgment.

Before me Samuel Seabury, J peace
" York Ss.

"At a Court of Probate held at York Febʸ 19, 1745.

"Zechariah Chandler Administrator of the Estate of the within named: Joseph Chandler Decᵈ appeared and made Oath that the Several Articles mentioned in the within Inventory is all the Estate he knows of within yᵉ: County of York belonging to the Said Deceased, and that if anything more hereafter appear he will give it into the Registers Office

Jer: Moulton
" Recorded from the Original and compared

℔ Simon Frost Regʳ."

The appraisement of the estate of Joseph Chandler, of North Yarmouth, lying in Plymouth County, Massachusetts, taken by

Samuel Seabury and George Partridge, was dated September 20, 1746. It consisted of —
Salt Meadow near Wood Island,
Salt Meadow at a place called Goatam [Gotham],
Cedar Swamp . . . in Pembroke,
Cedar Swamp . . . in Duxboro,
Two shares in the Beach at Duxboro,
"Total £328 10 ⌣"

On October 7, 1747, Zachariah Chandler presented an account of his father's estate, which was allowed; an additional account was brought in by him, October 4, 1749, which was allowed, and he was discharged.* No heirs were mentioned in the settlement, though they all appeared later in deeds that transferred portions of his estate.

ISSUE †

I. Philip⁴, b. July 21, 1702, in Duxbury; mar. Dec. 16, 1725, in Duxbury, Rebecca Phillips,‡ eldest child to Thomas and Rebecca (Blaney) Phillips, of Duxbury. Rebecca (Phillips) Chandler was b. 1704; d. January, 1782, aged seventy-eight years.

Though Philip Chandler lived and died in Duxbury, he probably, at one time, seriously contemplated following his father to North Yarmouth, since he purchased, on Oct. 22, 1735, for £30, of Stephen Larrabee, of that town, "One whole Quarter . . . of all the Lands Islands meadows," etc., that belonged to a certain ten-acre lot in North Yarmouth.§ July 8, 1753, "Philip Chandler, Blacksmith," of Duxbury, joined other heirs of Joseph Chandler in "relinquishing" to Jonas Mason, Esqʳ, of North Yarmouth, and his wife Mary, "all Right Title & Interest . . . in the one Hundred & Twenty acre Division in Northyarmouth . . . that was Drawn in the Right of our Honᵈ Father Joseph Chandler late of Northyarmouth Decᵈ by virtue of his home Lot Nº 81 as

---

* *York County Probate*, Book 7 : 102, 103, 268.
† *Town Records of Duxbury* (original) vol. 1 : 126.
‡ *Town Records of Duxbury* (original), vol. A 1 : 158.
§ *York County Deeds*, Book 18 : 25.

also the Right in the Pew in the meeting house in said Town." *

Philip Chandler d. in Duxbury, Nov. 15, 1764, aged sixty-two years, four months. His stone in the old graveyard gives his age. His will, dated Oct. 9, 1762, proved Dec. 3, 1764, bequeathed to his wife, Rebecca Chandler, one half of the estate, mentioned six sons, Nathan, Perez, Peleg, Philip, Asa, and Elijah, and four daughters, Martha and Mary un-married, Betty and Esther. His "beloved brother Ebenezer Chandler" to be executor. The inventory of his estate amounted to £1028 : 10 : 0 ; it included "land at Northyar-mouth by Information . . . £27 : 0 : 0." An order for the division of his real estate among his six sons was dated Dec. 3, 1764, and division made May 30, 1765.†

Issue: 1. Nathan⁶, b. Oct. 28, 1726, in Duxbury ; mar. first, Ruth —— ; she d. Aug. 26, 1767, aged forty-two years. He mar., second, Feb. 20, 1770, Esther Glass. Issue by first wife : six. Issue by second wife : two.

2. Esther⁶, b. Oct. 22, 1727, in Duxbury ; d. aged sixteen days.

3. Betty⁶, b. Oct. 21, 1728, in Duxbury.

4. Perez⁶, b. July 10, 1730, in Duxbury ; mar. Dec. 11, 1755, Rhoda Wadsworth, and had several children.‡

5. Martha⁶, b. May 31, 1732, in Duxbury.

6. A child⁶, b. April 27, 1735, in Duxbury.

7. Peleg⁶, b. Oct. 24, 1738, in Duxbury ; mar. Dec. 9, 1762, at North Yarmouth, Maine, Sarah⁵ Winslow, daughter to Barnabas⁴ and Mary (Glass) Winslow, of North Yarmouth. Barnabas⁴ was son to Gilbert³ Winslow, prominent among the early settlers of the town. (Nathaniel², Kenelm¹ Winslow, of Plymouth.) Sarah Winslow, b. July 29, 1739, in North Yarmouth ; d. 1823, in New Gloucester, Maine.

Peleg⁶ Chandler removed soon after his marriage to New Gloucester, a distance of fifteen miles, in an ox-cart,

---

* Vide Appendix LXXXVIII : A.
† *Plymouth County Probate*, Book 19 : 148, 226, 233, 234–239.
‡ *Town Records of Duxbury* (original), vol. 5 : 245.

"the first wheeled vehicle that ever had been used to perform that journey." He and his wife were two of the five
members who founded the first church in that town — Congregational. He d. Aug. 24, 1819, in New Gloucester. In
1871, their great-grandson, Andrew C. Chandler, was living
on Philip Chandler's farm in New Gloucester. Their eleven
children were born in that town, and they have had many
distinguished descendants; among them the Hon. Peleg
W. Chandler, Hon. Theophilus Chandler, and Hon. William
Pitt Fessenden.[*]

    8. Philip [5], b. Aug. 16, 1741, in Duxbury; mar. Christiana
        ———. In 1789, he was chosen selectman of Dux-
        bury, and was reëlected every year until 1801.
        Issue: seven.[†]

    9. A child [5], b. Aug. 16, 1743, in Duxbury.

    10. Mary [5], b. Sept. 25, 1744, in Duxbury; mar. Jan. 15,
        1767, to Joshua Delano 2[d]. She d. Aug. 19, 1824.

    11. Asa [5], b. Sept. 25, 1745, in Duxbury; mar. June 30,
        1763, Martha, daughter to David Delano, of Dux-
        bury. She d. April 21, 1783 (?). His second wife
        was Clarissa ———. There was a large family.

    12. Elijah [5], b. Jan. 4, 1746–47, in Duxbury.

II. Mary [4], b. Aug. 3, 1704, in Duxbury; she was mar. about 1731,
to Jonas Mason, of North Yarmouth.

    Jonas Mason was born in Lexington, Mass., Oct. 21, 1708.
He was of Charlestown, Mass., in 1727; but, before 1731,
he had removed to North Yarmouth, Maine. He was received into the First Church of North Yarmouth, Feb. 27,
1732, from the church in Charlestown. In 1737, he was
chosen Deacon (with Jacob [3] Mitchell, Sr.), continuing in
that office until his death, March 13, 1801, at the age of
ninety-three years. His wife, Mrs. Mary (Chandler) Mason,
became a member of the First Church, July 9, 1732, and d.
Nov. 27, 1787, in North Yarmouth, "aged eighty-five years." [‡]

---

[*] Holton's *Winslow Memorial*, 1888, vol. 2: 705; also, vol. 2, app.: 56.

[†] *Town Records of Duxbury* (original), vol. 5: 235.

[‡] *Records of the First Congregational Church, North Yarmouth*, Maine,
1848.

In 1753, Deacon Jonas Mason purchased of the heirs of Joseph Chandler, his father-in-law, the interest of the latter in the "Hundred & Twenty acre Division," and his pew in the meeting-house. He also conveyed land with his brothers-in-law.* He was a country magistrate, and Judge of the Court of Common Pleas for Cumberland County. He is mentioned as "one of the best of men," a man of sterling integrity and great moral worth. He filled the office of selectman many years.

Issue: 1. Ebenezer Mason, b. Nov. 1, 1732, in North Yarmouth.

2. John Mason, b. Sept. 18, 1734, in North Yarmouth; d. Feb. 3, 1769, in North Yarmouth, aged thirty-four years.

3. Mary Mason, b. Feb. 12, 1735-36; mar. to John Hamilton, of North Yarmouth.

4. Sarah Mason, b. July 20, 1738, in North Yarmouth; mar. Jan. 4, 1760, to Nathaniel Eveleth, of New Gloucester, Maine.

5. Elizabeth Mason, b. March 13, 1740, in North Yarmouth; mar. to Bezaleel Loring.

6. Mercy Mason, b. Nov. 10, 1743, in North Yarmouth.

7. Samuel Mason, b. Aug. 22, 1746, in North Yarmouth. Captain Samuel Mason, a shipmaster, mar., first, Sarah, daughter to Col. Jonathan ⁵ and Sarah (Loring) Mitchell.† She was b. Oct. 24, 1751; d. July 9, 1781, in North Yarmouth. Captain Mason mar., second, Sarah Beals. Issue: Theodosia Mason, bap. Aug. 14, 1791, in North Yarmouth; mar. to Major Daniel Mitchell. There also were other children.

III. Joshua ⁴, b. July 1, 1706,‡ in Duxbury; mar. Nov. 27, 1728,

---

* Vide Appendix LXXXVIII: A, B, C.   † Vide page 415.

‡ William M. Sargent, in *Old Times*, includes Phebe Chandler, b. about 1706, among the children of Joseph and Martha (Hunt) Chandler. Nothing has been found that connects her or her heirs with Joseph Chandler or any of his family. She probably was daughter to Samuel Chandler, one of the early selectmen of North Yarmouth.

Phebe Chandler was the first wife of Andrew ⁸ Gray, b. Sept. 29, 1707, son to

in Duxbury, Mary " Waste," or West.* She d., his widow,
April 28, 1794, in Duxbury.

Joshua Chandler was a shoemaker ; he lived all his life in
Duxbury, and d. there, May 1, 1782, nearly seventy-six years
of age. His will, in which he called himself a " Cordwainer
. . . sick and weak," was dated May 25, 1761.† He named
wife Mary, " only surviving son Ezekiel," who was to be executor, daughter Sarah Chandler, grandson Joseph Chandler,
and granddaughters Esther Chandler and Susanna Chandler. In this will he asked his brother, Philip Chandler, to
buy his salt marsh in Duxbury, and mentioned real estate in
North Yarmouth. This will, made twenty-one years before
his death, was proved June 3, 1782.

Issue : ‡ 1. Joseph[5], b. Sept. 27, 1729, in Duxbury ; mar.
Susanna ——.

John[2] and Susanna (——) Gray, of Harwich, Mass. (John[2] was son to John[1]
and Hannah (——) Gray, of Yarmouth, Mass.) Andrew Gray and Phebe
Chandler were married about 1731 ; she d. Sept. 23, 1744, in North Yarmouth,
aged thirty-eight years. He mar., second, Dec. 19, 1745, Zerviah (Standish)
Ring, widow of Andrew Ring. She was b. in 1706, and d. April 26, 1798, in
North Yarmouth, aged ninety-two years. She was of the fourth generation
from Captain Myles [1] Standish, and was a descendant of John [1] Alden.

Andrew Gray was a farmer of North Yarmouth. He was drowned in crossing Broad Cove, on the evening of Dec. 19, 1757, at the age of fifty years, two
months, and twenty days.

Issue by first wife : I. John[4] Gray, b. Nov. 29, 1732 ; mar. Sarah[5], daughter to Jacob[4] and Rachel (Cushing) Mitchell.

II. Joseph[4] Gray, b. Nov. 19, 1734 ; d. July 17, 1792.

III. Andrew[4] Gray, b. Jan. 12, 1736 ; mar. Elizabeth Bucknam ; he d. Dec.
8, 1810.

IV. Mehitable[4] Gray, b. Dec. 25, 1739 ; mar. to William Cutter. She d.
March 19, 1808.

V. Rhoda[4] Gray, b. Jan. 12, 1741 ; mar. Abraham[4] Mitchell. She d. Aug.
10, 1780.

VI. Joshua[4] Gray, b. Jan. 22, 1743 ; he removed to Barnstable, Mass.

Issue by second wife : VII. Ebenezer[4] Gray, b. Sept. 20, 1746 ; mar. Dorcas
Mitchell. He d. June 19, 1779. No issue.

Vide *Old Times in North Yarmouth :* 1095–1096, 346–347, 115 ; also *Records
of the First Church of North Yarmouth,* 1848 : 52 ; also vide pages 420–421 ; also
vide The Mitchells from Kittery.

* *Town Records of Duxbury* (original), vol. A 1 : 158.

† *Plymouth County Probate,* Book 28 : 395.

‡ *Town Records of Duxbury* (original), vol. 1 : 43 ; vol. 5 : 253.

Joseph Chandler enlisted, April 2, 1759, as seaman, on board " His Majesty's . . . ship Dublin, serving up the St. Lawrence under Vice Admiral Saunders." He was discharged from the ship Oct. 1, 1759, "whole time of service 31 weeks 6 days." * The town records of Duxbury state that Joseph Chandler, Oliver Oldham, Thomas Lucas, and Job Randall, "died on their return from the fleet & Canada expedition of the yellow fever . . . Oct. [ ] 1759." † The age of Joseph Chandler is given as thirty years. His father, Joshua Chandler, on Jan. 7, 1760, prayed that he might be appointed administrator of his son's estate, as he "apprehends the said deceaseds Estate is greatly Insolvᵗ." The widow Susanna's dower was defined, June 9, following; the administrator's final account, by which it appeared that the estate was valued at £21, and the amount owing was £39 : 16 : 5, was rendered Sept. 11, 1760, and division ordered among the creditors.‡

Issue: I. Esther⁶. II. Susanna⁶. III. Joseph⁶, b. Oct. 25, 1759, in Duxbury.

2. Ezekiel⁵, b. Sept. 14, 1733, in Duxbury; mar. Mary——. On May 5, 1756, Ezekiel Chandler appeared in Major Moses Deshon's Co., Col. Joseph Thacher's Regt., "raised for the intended expedition against Crown Point, under John Winslow, Commander-in-Chief." July 26, following, he appeared in the same company and regiment, at Fort Edward; "station, private, age 22, occupation, cordwainer, birthplace Duxborough . . . reported impressed from Col. Bradford's Regt. . . . for Crown Point Expedition." §

As the only surviving son, he was appointed, in 1782, the executor of his father's estate. The four children of Ezekiel and Mary were born in Duxbury, between 1764 and 1772.‖

3. Sarah⁵, b. Oct. 9, 1735, in Duxbury.

---

* *Massachusetts Archives*, Muster Rolls, vol. 97 : 340.
† *Town Records of Duxbury* (copy), vol. 1 : 6.
‡ *Plymouth County Probate*, Book 15: 418, 443, 526, 565, 581.
§ *Massachusetts Archives*, Muster Rolls, vol. 94: 297, 175, 514, 561.
‖ *Town Records of Duxbury* (original), vol. 5 : 248.

IV. Zachariah⁴, b. July 26, 1708, in Duxbury, was mar. Oct. 21, 1736, in Kingston, Mass., by "J Stacey," to Zerviah Holmes, of Kingston.* She was b. in 1715.

Zachariah Chandler was in North Yarmouth with his father before his marriage, and returned there with his bride. As a resident of that town he purchased, Oct. 9, 1731, for £32, of Perez Bradford and his wife Abigail, of Milton, in the County of Suffolk, ten acres of land in North Yarmouth, "part of Lot 82 . . . Together with yᵉ One Halfe of yᵉ Whole of all yᵉ after Divisions and Allotments of Uplands Islands & Meadows within sᵈ Township." † This land adjoined that of his father, in "Lot 81." Zachariah Chandler, "coaster," also purchased, for £55, May 8, 1744, of Jeremiah Powell, thirty-five acres in the same township.‡

On Nov. 20, 1746, "Zachariah Chandler of North Yarmouth . . . coaster," purchased, for £400, a tract of land consisting of six hundred and fifty acres, "lying on the Westermost Side of Great Chebeague Island in Said North-yarmouth . . . in his actual possession Now being." The grantors were "Thomas Waite, Shopkeeper, & Jonathan Williams, wine-Seller," both of Boston, "Deacons of yᵉ first Church in Boston." They conveyed their title to this land by right of a conveyance from Ephraim Savage, gentleman, sole administrator of the estate of Richard Wharton, "Late of Said Boston Esqʳ Decᵈ on the Fifteenth Day of May anno Domⁱ 1713," who sold "unto John Marion Isaiah Tay and John Hubbard then Deacons of the said first Church in Boston their Successors in the Said office and assigns In truth to and for yᵉ use of the poor of sᵈ Church . . . Six hundred & Fifty acres Lying Situate in yᵉ Westermost Side of a Certain Island Called Great Chebeague alias Recompence Island in Casco bay." § This tract of six hundred and fifty acres had been confirmed, by the government of Massachusetts, to Richard Wharton, in 1682. It did not retain the

---

* *The Genealogical Advertiser*, 1898, vol. 2: 57, 126.

† *York County Deeds*, Book 16: 59.

‡ *York County Deeds*, Book 25: 86.

§ *York County Deeds*, Book 28: 39-40.

early name of Recompence Island,* but has been known as Great Chebeague to this day.

This conveyance of Nov. 20, 1746, was "Made to yᵉ sᵈ Zachariah alone as by sᵈ Deed doth fully appear ;" but, eleven days later (Dec. 1), he sold one half to his brothers, and brother-in-law, Jonas Mason, for the sum of £200. Division was then made by which Zachariah's half was "to begin on the westerly Side of the Island at the Boundary or dividing Point, in the Division formerly made between Collᵒ Thomas Westbrook & the first Church in Boston or their Representatives." The deed of partition gave to Jonas Mason, Esq., one sixth of the entire tract ; to Jonathan Chandler yeoman, one sixth ; and to Edmund Chandler and Judah Chandler, yeomen, one sixth, in common between them.†
The first deeds being "Loss'd," and "the said Parties being all Living . . . (having the Original Minits by them)," a new deed was executed Aug. 28, 1775.‡

The two islands in Casco Bay, Great and Little Chebeague, situated about six miles from the mainland, are "famous in their history and ancient proprietors."§ Great Chebeague, the largest island in the Bay, contains over two thousand acres ; Little Chebeague, about one hundred and eighty. The latter was granted, in 1681, to Silvanus Davis, who erected a fort upon it.‖ The larger island suffered, for many years, from conflicting titles on the eastern side. In 1743, Colonel Thomas Westbrook's interest there was " set off on

---

* The General Court, on May 17, 1684, granted to Deputy Governor Thomas Danforth, Esq., and Increase Nowell, Esq., "for there great paynes & good service donn by order of this Court in the expedition & seuerall journeys to Casco, for which no recompense hath binn made them, an island called Chebiscodego [Chebeague], in Casco Bay, in the Province of Mayne." (*Massachusetts Bay Colony Records*, vol. 5 : 309.)

† *York County Deeds*, Book 28 : 39–40.

‡ Vide Appendix LXXXVIII : C, D.

§ Thomas Scottow, in a letter from the garrison at Black Point, dated July 11, 1689, tells of the damage inflicted upon the towns of "Scarborough, ffalmouth and North Yarmoth," and "Severall firings on Chebeeg Island." He requests help from the General Court, as the towns "without your assistance, will be deserted." (*Massachusetts Archives, Revolution*, 1689 : 189.)

‖ *York County Deeds*, Book 13 : 124.

execution to Samuel and Cornelius Waldo, as was Little Chebeague, also belonging to Westbrook and Waldo, and derived by them from the legatees of Silvanus Davis." * Little Chebeague belonged to the town of Falmouth. The fertile island of Great Chebeague, four miles long by three quarters of a mile in breadth, stands high above the water, with a rolling, hilly surface. It was allotted to the plantation at "Swegustagoe" (North Yarmouth), in 1680.† It has two good harbors, that on the southwest being known, to this day, as *Chandler's Cove.*‡ At the time of its purchase by the Chandlers, in 1746, the island was heavily wooded with choice timber that was zealously guarded by the early Proprietors.§ Trees of six to eight feet in diameter were not uncommon, — so large that "a yoke of oxen could be turned around on the butt." To-day, the southerly part of the island is quite destitute of foliage, and is devoted to grazing; but there are a few strips of forest toward the north.

Previous to 1800, the inhabitants attended church in North Yarmouth; but, soon after that date, they built a small church, with a square tower or belfry on the front, which is very quaint. The high pulpit, sounding-board, and ancient pews remain untouched except by the hand of time. The church stands, destitute of paint, in a picturesque spot on the hillside at the northerly end of the island, near the landing of the steamers of the Casco Bay Company. It is surrounded by trees, and attracts many visitors.

How many of the Chandler brothers lived on Chebeague has not been determined; some of their children settled there. About 1800, Judah, David, and Rufus were living on Great Chebeague; in 1821, John, Asa, and Judah paid a poll tax, as "belonging to the west part" of that island.‖

In 1759, Zachariah Chandler paid the third largest tax of

---

* *Maine Historical Society Collections*, vol. 1: 146–147; also *Old Times in North Yarmouth*: 354, 383, 411, 412, 434, 580, 739.

† *Massachusetts Bay Colony Records*, vol. 5: 441–442.

‡ Vide illustration: Martin's Point and Islands of Casco Bay, 1904.

§ Vide page 391.

‖ *Old Times in North Yarmouth*: 589, 981, 982, 580.

the Chandler brothers, — £1 : 8 : 7.* He and his wife, Zerviah, joined the First Church of North Yarmouth, Nov. 25,
1744. He d. in 1782, in North Yarmouth.† March 30, 1790,
Zerviah Chandler, widow, James Pittee, yeoman, and Betty,
his wife, David Barker and Chandler Barker, yeomen, with
John Brown, cordwainer, of Windham (Maine), and Hannah,
his wife, conveyed to David Chandler, land on Great Chebeague, "103½ acres," bounded "northwesterly on the Bay
or Sea shore," it being that part set off to Mary Chandler,
deceased, as a part of the estate of her deceased father,
Zachariah Chandler.‡ The widow, Zerviah Chandler, d.
May 26, 1795, in North Yarmouth, aged eighty years.

Issue : 1. Sarah⁵, b. Aug. 10, 1739, in North Yarmouth ;
mar. Aug. 6, 1761, to David Barker.§ This name is
miscalled "Parker" in a town record of their marriage. She d. before March 30, 1790.

2. Mary⁵, b. Feb. 20, 1741, in North Yarmouth ; d. unmar.,
before March 30, 1790.

3. Hannah⁵, b. Aug. 18, 1745, in North Yarmouth ; mar.
to John Brown, of Windham, Maine.

4. Joshua⁵, b. Oct. 26, 1747, in North Yarmouth ; mar.
Sarah Parker. Their four children, Sally, Enos, Ezekiel, and Sukey, were baptized Oct. 3, 1793, "at a
lecture at Joshua Chandler's house," together with
Enos and Rebecca, children of Edward⁶ and Sarah⁵
(Mitchell) Small.‖ On the same day, Oct. 3, 1793,
Joshua Chandler and his wife Sarah (Parker) Chandler were received, by profession, into the First
Church of North Yarmouth. The church records
add that Mrs. Joshua Chandler d. Oct., 1794, and
that he "Moved Westward." ¶

5. Mercy⁵, b. Feb. 8, 1749, in North Yarmouth. The
marriage intention of David Harvey and Mercy

---

* *Old Times in North Yarmouth :* 71.
† *Records of the First Church of North Yarmouth*, 1848 : 17.
‡ *Cumberland County Deeds*, Book 19 : 486.
§ *Old Times in North Yarmouth :* 658.
‖ Vide pages 226, 228.
¶ *Records of the First Church of North Yarmouth*, 1848 : 26.

Chandler, both of North Yarmouth, was recorded Sept. 4, 1773.

6. Elizabeth[5], b. May 6, 1754; baptized as Betty, July 28, 1754, in the First Church of North Yarmouth. The marriage intention of James "Pittey" and Betty Chandler, both of North Yarmouth, was recorded Sept. 4, 1773; they were married Dec. 23, following.

V. Edmund[4], b. April 9, 1710, in Duxbury. (Vide infra.)

VI. Ebenezer[4], b. Sept. 8, 1712, in Duxbury. "Ebenezer and Anna Chandler," of Kingston, were mar. Feb. 23, 1737, in Kingston, by Joshua Cushing, Justice of the Peace.[*]

Very little is known of Ebenezer Chandler. From the fact that the births of none of his children were recorded in Duxbury, it is surmised that he lived for a number of years in Kingston, or a neighboring town. The record of the deaths [†] of his children in Duxbury indicates his return there before 1770. There is no record of the settlement of his estate in Plymouth County.

Issue: 1. Simeon[5], b. Feb., 1744; d. April 17, 1767, in Duxbury, aged twenty-two years, ten months.

2. Zilpha[5], b. 1749; d. May 7, 1837, in the Duxbury Almshouse, aged eighty-eight years. She was the last survivor of the family.

3. Judah[5], b. Feb., 1751; d. April 24, 1772, in Duxbury, aged twenty-one years, two months.

4. Nathaniel[5], b. April, 1752; d. June 14, 1773, in Duxbury, aged twenty years, nine months.

5. Anna[5], b. ———. An Anna Chandler d. Sept. 1, 1805, in Duxbury; age not given.

6. Sceva[5], b. 1756.

In 1777, "Seva Chandler," of Duxbury, served fifteen days, at Rhode Island, as " private in Lieut. Nathan Sampson's (2d Duxbury) co., Col. Thos. Lothrop's regt." He also "served 33 days on [a] secret expedition to Rhode Island, in Sept. and Oct., 1777, . . . in Capt. Nehemiah Allen's co.,

---

[*] *The Genealogical Advertiser*, vol. 2: 51, 126.
[†] *Town Records of Duxbury*, vol. 1: 251, 252; vol. 5: 243; vol. 2: 50.

Col. Theophilus Cotton's regt.;" "also in Rhode Island service, July 30 to Sept. 13, 1778, under Capt. Calvin Partridge's co., Col. Josiah Whitney's regt.; roll sworn to at Boston." * He mar., first, Edith Sampson. She d. June 2, 1796, in Duxbury; he mar., second, March, 1798, Elizabeth Darling. Sceva Chandler d. March 14, 1832, in Duxbury, aged seventy-six years.

VII. Sarah⁴, b. Oct. 25, 1714, in Duxbury; d. in North Yarmouth, Maine. Her stone in the old graveyard by the "Ledge" bears the following inscription:—

> HERE LYES BURIED
> YE BODY OF MRS SARAH CHANDLER
> WHO DIED APRIL
> 28TH 1737 IN YE 23D YEAR
> OF HER AGE. †

VIII. Martha⁴, b. Nov. 23, 1716, in Duxbury; d. in North Yarmouth. The inscription upon her gravestone, which stands near that of her sister Sarah, is as follows:—

> HERE LIES BURRIED
> YE BODY OF MRS
> MARTHA CHANDLER
> WHO DIED AUGST
> 5TH 1737 IN YE 21ST
> YEAR OF HER AGE. ‡

IX. Jonathan⁴, b. Feb. 18, 1717-18, in Duxbury; mar. Jan. 19, 1749, in North Yarmouth, "Rachael⁵," daughter to Jacob⁴ Mitchell by his second wife, Rachel (Cushing) Mitchell.§

During his earlier years Jonathan Chandler was called a "coaster," later a "yeoman." He purchased, in 1746, with his brothers, Zachariah, Edmund, Judah, and his brother-in-law, Jonas Mason, six hundred and fifty acres of land on the westerly side of the island of Great Chebeague. In the

---

* *Massachusetts Soldiers and Sailors in the War of the Revolution*, vol. 3: 297.

† *Old Times in North Yarmouth*: 656.

‡ *Old Times in North Yarmouth*: 1185.

§ Vide pages 406, 418; also *Old Times in North Yarmouth*: 658.

division that followed, Jonathan retained one sixth;* two of his sons, David and Rufus, remained there.

The name of Jonathan Chandler appears with rank of private in a "list dated North Yarmouth, May 18, 1757, of the 1st Co. of Militia in the town of North Yarmouth, commanded by Capt. Solomon Mitchell, comprising the Train Band and Alarm List . . . as returned to Col. [Ezekiel] Cushing by Capt. Solomon Mitchell." His brothers, Zachariah, "Edmond," and Judah, also were privates in the same company.†

Jonathan was received into the First Church of North Yarmouth, March 31, 1745; his wife, Rachel (Mitchell) Chandler, was received Dec. 30, 1753. The date of his death is recorded in the church manual as July 20, 1786, and that of his wife, Rachel, as Jan. 1, 1814; her age was eighty-three years.‡

Issue: 1. "Tabiatha⁵," b. Sept. 18, 1750, in North Yarmouth; d. Aug. 11, 1756.

2. David⁵, b. June 30, 1752, in North Yarmouth; mar. July 5, 1787, in North Yarmouth, Rebecca Drisco. They lived on Great Chebeague. Issue: I. Lucy⁶, b. March 24, 1789. II. Jacob⁶, b. Sept. 24, 1790. III. Rhoda⁶, bap. Sept. 18, 1793, at Chebeague. IV. John⁶, b. Feb. 26, 1794. V. Rebecca⁶, bap. Sept. 24, 1795, at Chebeague. VI. David⁶, bap. Aug. 23, 1797, at Chebeague; and probably other children.

3. Timothy⁵, b. Oct. 20, 1754, in North Yarmouth; d. Sept. 26, 1757.

4. Jacob⁵, b. June 19, 1757, in North Yarmouth; mar. Huldah ——. She was mar., second, before 1783, to —— Briggs; they removed to Portland.§

5. Rachel⁵, b. May 20, 1761; bap. July 12, 1761, in North Yarmouth. She was mar. to Daniel Waite.

---

* Vide Appendix LXXXVIII: A, B, C, D.
† *Massachusetts Archives*, vol. 95: 383.
‡ *Records of the First Church of North Yarmouth*, 1848: 17.
§ *Records of the First Church of North Yarmouth*, 1848: 22.

6. Lucy⁵, b. Oct. 12, 1763 ; wife of Benjamin Waite.
7. Rufus⁵, b. March 18, 1766; bap. May 4, 1766, in the
First Church of North Yarmouth ; mar., first, Nancy
Cushing. "Mrs. Nancy (Cushing) Chandler . . .
Mrs. Rufus " was received, Oct. 10, 1802, into the
First Church of North Yarmouth.* The date of her
death is not given.

The second wife of Rufus Chandler was Abigail⁵, daughter to David⁵ and Jenny (Haraden) Dennison ; she was b.
Feb. 19, 1777. They lived on Great Chebeague. " Mrs. Abigail (Dennison) Chandler . . . Mrs. Rufus " was received,
Oct. 15, 1810, by public profession, into the First Church
of North Yarmouth. On July 25, 1813, Rufus Chandler and
his wife Abigail were dismissed from the First Church to
the Congregational Church in Freeport;† they were received
into the latter church, Nov. 26, following. He d. Sept. 16,
1844, aged seventy-eight years. His widow, Abigail, was
dismissed Dec. 12, 1850, to a church in Homewood, Mississippi.‡ She was then seventy-three years of age, and probably followed one of her children.

Issue by second wife : § I. Nancy Cushing⁶, b. May 5,
1809. II. Daniel Haraden⁶, b. March 23, 1811 ; d.
July 7, 1812. III. Edward⁶, b. Dec. 21, 1812. IV.
Rufus⁶, b. Jan. 23, 1815. V. David⁶, b. April 12,
1817. VI. Rachel⁶, b. July 7, 1819. VII. William⁶,
b. July 15, 1821 ; d. Nov. 20, 1822.
8. Joel⁵, b. July 21, 1770; bap. July 29, 1770, in the First
Church of North Yarmouth ; mar. Pamelia Lincoln,
of Hingham.
Issue : I. Mary⁶, b. Sept. 18, 1796, in Freeport.
II. Nancy Deering⁶, b. Jan. 19, 1798, in Freeport ; she
was mar. April 18, 1819, to Timothy⁶ Davis, b.
Jan. 10, 1795. ❙

---

* *Records of the First Church of North Yarmouth*, 1848 : 27.
† *Records of the First Church of North Yarmouth*, 1848 : 28.
‡ *Manual of the First Congregational Church, Freeport, Maine* : 25.
§ Dennison's *Genealogy of the Dennison Family*, 1906: 46, 104.
❙ *Old Times in North Yarmouth* : 975-976.

    III. Pamelia⁶, b. June 30, 1799, in Freeport; she was
        mar. Sept. 2, 1824, to Samuel Coleman, of Salem,
        Mass.*

    IV. Charlotte⁶ (twin), b. March 6, 1802, in Freeport.

    V. Jane⁶ (twin), b. March 6, 1802, in Freeport ; she was
       mar. to Timothy⁷, son to David⁶ and Polly (Mann)
       Pratt.†

    VI. Jacob⁶, b. Dec. 30, 1804; d. Jan. 29, 1805.

    VII. Cushing Lincoln⁶, b. March 12, 1806, in Freeport.

    VIII. Julia Ann⁶, b. Aug. 8, 1809, in Freeport.

    9. Reuben⁵, bap. June 6, 1773, in North Yarmouth.

In 1815, Reuben Chandler was taxed $2.75, for "one
farm, bounded S. E. by Broad Cove, containing 45 acres and
buildings thereon." In 1823, he lived in "District No. 2,"
and was taxed $12.30. In the same district, at that time,
lived Joseph Chandler, Joseph, Jr., and Enos Chandler.‡
The homestead of Reuben, according to the deposition of
Rebecca⁶ (Chandler) Pratt, daughter to Edmund⁴ Chandler, in 1833, was the house in which she was born.§ Probably
it was the same house and farm that Joseph² conveyed, in
1734, to his son Edmund⁴.∥

X. Judah⁴, b. Aug. 13, 1720, in Duxbury; mar., first, Martha
    Seabury, of North Yarmouth. "Mrs. Martha (Seabury)
    Chandler . . . wife of Judah," was received April 20, 1742,
    into the First Church of North Yarmouth.¶ His second
    wife was Rebecca Seabury, daughter to Barnabas and Mary
    (——) Seabury, b. Sept. 24, 1723. As the wife of Judah
    Chandler, she was received into the First Church of North
    Yarmouth, "April 5, 1747; moved to Durham."**

According to an ancient deposition found among the
papers of Rev. David Shepley, pastor of the First Church of

---

* *Maine Historical and Genealogical Recorder*, vol. 3 : 33.

† Vide page 814.

‡ *Old Times in North Yarmouth* : 3, 47.

§ Vide page 781.

∥ Vide pages 911–912.

¶ *Records of the First Church of North Yarmouth*, 1848 : 16.

** *Records of the First Church of North Yarmouth*, 1848 : 18.

North Yarmouth, Judah Chandler was nine years of age when he went to North Yarmouth, with his father : —

"Judah Chandler, Oct. 21ˢᵗ, 1796, aged 76 last August, deposes that when he was about nine years old he moved with his father from Duxbury to North Yarmouth. About thirty years ago he (Judah) moved eastward and lived about nine years, then returned to North Yarmouth." *

Early in life he followed the sea ; in 1746 and 1753, he was mentioned as a "coaster." About 1766, he removed to Royalsborough (Durham), where he lived in the "south-westerly part of the town near a small pond from which flowed a small stream called Chandler's River," † — a tributary of Royal River. The first saw-mill was doubtless built by Judah on Chandler's River soon after he removed to the town in 1766. Here he carried on lumbering, sending "ton-timber" to Harrisicket (now Freeport) by the "Old Mast Road." If he "returned to North Yarmouth" after living there "about nine years" (that is, in 1775), he soon went back to Royalsborough ; since, in 1777, he purchased, with others, a tract of land upon which was built another mill. The deed states that "Jonathan Bagley of Almsbury [Amesbury], Essex County, Mass., Esq.," for £30, conveyed to "Judah Chandler, O Israel Bagley,‡ Daniel Bagley, John Randall, Stephen Randall, and John Cushing, all of Royal-borough, Cumberland County, yeomen," three fourths of fifty acres of land in Royalsborough, it "being the south-westerly End or part of Lot number One hundred & Forty Six as laid down in the Plan of said Royalboro'," bordering on the highway, "with the Mill Priviledges and all Appurtenances and Priviledges to the same belonging . . . to hold by severalty & not by survivourship, as followeth, the said Judah Chandler one Eighth part, O Israel Bagley one quarter part, Daniel Bagley one Eighth part, John Randall One Twelfth part, Stephen Randall one Twelfth part, &

---

* *Old Times in North Yarmouth* : 1167.

† Stackpole's *History of Durham, Maine* : vide map on page 41.

‡ This name is never written with a period after the O ; it evidently is from the Biblical phrase, "Hear, O Israel."

John Cushing one Twelfth part." This deed was signed Feb. 24, 1777, by Jonathan Bagley, and recorded May 30, 1788. The witnesses were Mary Bagley and Dorcas Bagley.* It has been conjectured by those most familiar with the locality that the remainder of the fifty acre lot had been occupied previously by Chandler as a homestead. The first mill was located at the head of the falls, near the present bridge. Its successor is now called the "Old Stone Mill." The old road crossed the stream below the present mill, and traces of Chandler's house near by still are visible.

In 1746, Judah Chandler received one sixth of the tract of land on Chebeague, in common with his brother Edmund. With the other heirs, he also conveyed portions of his father's estate.† As a resident of North Yarmouth, he served as private, in 1757, in Captain Solomon Mitchell's Train Band.‡ In 1759, he was taxed £0 : 12 : 1.§ He does not appear to have held any town office in North Yarmouth. In Durham, he was chosen surveyor of lumber. From 1777, he resided in Durham until his death ; he probably died in 1802, at the age of eighty-two years. The date of death of his wife, Rebecca, is unknown.

> Issue (probably) by first wife : ‖ 1. Mary Johnson⁵, b. Oct. 25, 1745 ; bap. Oct. 27, 1745, in the First Church of North Yarmouth.
>
> Issue by second wife : 2. "Edmond,"⁵ b. Jan. 7, 1747 ; bap. Jan. 10, 1747, in the First Church of North Yarmouth.¶
>
> 3. John⁵, b. Feb. 4, 1748, in North Yarmouth.

John Chandler, of Royalsborough (the town also given as Royalston and New Gloucester), appeared in a return of men who enlisted in the Continental Army, for three years. He served as "private, in Capt. Reed's co., Col. John Brooks's (late Alden's) regt. . . . from Feb. 15, 1777, to

---

* *Cumberland County Deeds*, Book 14 : 330.
† Vide Appendix LXXXVIII.   ‡ *Massachusetts Archives*, vol. 95 : 383.
§ *Old Times in North Yarmouth* : 71.
‖ Stackpole's *History of Durham, Maine*, 1900 : 159.
¶ *Old Times in North Yarmouth*, 615.

May 1, 1778; reported died May —, 1778."* He was then thirty years of age, and probably unmarried.

4. Jonathan⁵, b. Dec. 24, 1750, in North Yarmouth.
5. Mercy⁵, b. April 4, 1754, in North Yarmouth.
6. Abigail⁵, b. Sept. 23, 1756, in North Yarmouth.
7. Dorcas⁵, b. Oct. 28, 1758, in North Yarmouth; mar. in Durham, April 1, 1784, to Isaac Davis, of Durham.
8. Huldah⁵, b. Feb. 9, 1761; bap. April 5, 1761, in the First Church of North Yarmouth; mar. (intention Dec. 1, 1787) to Eben Bragdon, of Durham.
9. Ebenezer⁵, b. Sept. 11, 1763, in North Yarmouth.
10. Sarah⁵, b. Aug. 9, 1766, at Pleasant River; bap. June 28, 1767, in First Church of Durham; mar. Nov. 21, 1785, to William Blake. They removed to Ohio.

EDMUND⁴ CHANDLER

Edmund⁴, son to Joseph³ and Martha (Hunt) Chandler, was born April 9, 1710, in Duxbury, Massachusetts. Before he was of age, he accompanied his father from Duxbury to the new settlement at North Yarmouth, Maine. His first wife, to whom he was married, in North Yarmouth, Jan. 1 (13), 1736–37, by the Rev. Nicholas Loring, was Mercy⁴,† daughter to Benoni³ Fogg by his first wife, Abigail (Cass) Fogg.‡ Edmund and Mercy (Fogg) Chandler were received,

---

* *Massachusetts Soldiers and Sailors in the War of the Revolution*, vol. 3: 289.
† *Records of the First Church of North Yarmouth, Maine*, 1848: 16; also *Old Times in North Yarmouth*: 472.

‡ SAMUEL¹ FOGG

There is a tradition in Eliot, Maine (once a part of Kittery), that Samuel¹ Fogg came from Wales. The Kent County, England, family usually spelled the name Fogge, and were of title; some were buried in Canterbury Cathedral.

Samuel¹ Fogg settled in Hampton, N. H. He mar., " 12ᵈ: 10ᵐᵒ: 1652," Anne Shaw, of Hampton, who d. in 1661. He mar., second in 1662, Mary Page; she d. March 8, 1699. He was an early member of the church in Hampton; he d. there, April 16, 1672. Issue by first wife: I. Samuel², b. 1653, in Hampton; mar. " 19ᵈ : 10ᵐᵒ : 1676," Hannah Marston. He was of North Hampton, and d. there æt. " 107 years." He had sons, Joseph³, Samuel³, and Stephen³.

September 13, 1741, by "public profession," into the First
Church of North Yarmouth. She died July 12, 1769, in

II. Joseph[2], b. 1655, in Hampton; d. young.
III. John[2], b. 1656, in Hampton; d. young.
IV. Mary[2], b. 1658, in Hampton.
V. Daniel[2], b. "16ᵈ : 4ᵐᵒ : 1660," in Hampton. He was a blacksmith, and
   settled in Scarborough, Maine. He mar. in 1684, Hannah[2], daughter
   to John[1] Libby, of Scarborough. In 1690, he was driven out by the
   Indians, and lived on an island belonging to Portsmouth, N. H., on
   the Piscataqua River. He removed to Kittery (now Eliot), about
   1700; he d. there, in 1755, æt. 95 years, and was buried on his farm.
   Issue: Daniel[3], and other children.
Issue by second wife: VI. Seth[2], b. 1665, in Hampton.
VII. James[2], b. 1668, in Hampton; mar. Jan. 9, 1695, Mary Barringer
   (Brewer ?). She d. Oct. 14, 1750, æt. 88 years; he d. June 17, 1760,
   "of a slight fever," æt. 92 years. Their children were Mary[3], James[3],
   John[3], Sarah[3], and Enoch[3].

SETH[2] FOGG

Seth[2] Fogg, b. 1665; mar. Sarah Shaw, who d. April 10, 1755, æt. 85 years.
He was admitted to the church in Hampton, Jan. 17, 1697; he d. about 1754,
in Hampton, æt. 89 years.

   Issue: I. Benoni[3], bap. May 2, 1697, with his brother Seth, and sisters,
      Hannah, Sarah, and Esther.
   II. Hannah[3], bap. May 2, 1697; mar. to —— Elkins.
   III. Seth[3], bap. at the same time as his elder brother, Benoni; mar. Meri-
      bah Smith.
   IV. Sarah[3], bap. May 2, 1697; d. July 4, 1701, æt. 4 years.
   V. Esther[3], bap. May 2, 1697; mar. Oct. 24, 1734, to David Fogg; mar.,
      second, to —— Dearborn; mar., third, to —— Wadleigh.
   VI. Samuel[3], bap. March 17, 1700; mar. Nov. 29, 1744, Abigail Fowle.
      He lived in Hampton.
   VII. Simon[3], b. 1702; bap. Dec. 13, 1707; mar. Sarah ——; he d. in 1749,
      at Hampton, æt. 47 years.
   VIII. Abner[3], bap. Feb. 19, 1705; mar. Dec. 10, 1730, Bertha Robie; he d.
      Aug. 27, 1788, at Hampton.
   IX. Abigail[3], bap. Sept. 7, 1707, in Hampton.
   X. Daniel[3], bap. March 9, 1710; mar. Dec. 5, 1734, Esther Elkins; he d.
      Aug. 7, 1757, at Rye, N. H.
   XI. Jeremiah[3], b. May 24, 1712; bap. July 20, 1712.

BENONI[3] FOGG

Benoni[3] Fogg, b. about 1688, in Hampton; bap. May 2, 1797; mar., first,
in Hampton, Abigail Cass. His second wife was Mary Parker; she was re-

North Yarmouth; he married, second, December 25, 1769, Mrs. Sarah Merrill, of North Yarmouth. Their intention of marriage was dated December 9, 1769.

---

ceived, June 3, 1733, into the First Church of North Yarmouth, from the Second Church in Hampton, N. H.

Benoni Fogg was a weaver, also a farmer. He removed, before 1733, from Hampton to North Yarmouth, where he filled several public offices. He was received into the First Church, Dec. 5, 1742, by public profession of faith. His death is recorded in that church, July 5, 1770.

His autograph appears as one of the selectmen of that town: —

Issue by first wife: I. Abigail [4]; mar. Dec. 28, 1737, in North Yarmouth, to Moses Bradbury. Issue: ten. (Vide page 782.)

II. Mercy [4]; mar. Jan. 13, 1736-37, to Edmund [4] Chandler.

III. Sarah [4], mar. Jonathan Thoits. Issue: ten. (Vide page 782.)

IV. Benaiah [4]: mar. Aug. 18, 1746, Esther Parker, b. June 29, 1729, daughter to Capt James Parker, of North Yarmouth.

Issue by second wife: V. Mary [4], b. May 8, 1732, in Hampton; d. June 29, 1738, in North Yarmouth.

VI. Hannah [4], b. May 5, 1734, in North Yarmouth; d. July 20, 1738, in that town.

VII. Jeremiah [4], b. Dec. 29, 1735, in North Yarmouth; d. July 2, 1738. The deaths of these three children, in 1738, were caused by "canker distemper," as Parson Smith calls it in his "Journal;" possibly it was scarlet fever.

VIII. David [4], b. March 17, 1737-38, in North Yarmouth; d. Oct. 10, 1758.

Vide *Old Eliot, Maine*, 1901, vol. 4 : 149-151, 154; also *Old Times in North Yarmouth* : 472, 720, 742, 1062; also *Records of the First Church in North Yarmouth*, 1848 : 15, 17.

Before his marriage, and when he was but twenty-four
years of age, his father, Joseph Chandler, conveyed, "for
£200 old tenor," to Edmund,* then called a blacksmith of
North Yarmouth, his "whole Ten Acre Lot of Upland . . .
the Eighty first ten Acre Lot in Number in North Yarmouth afores^d," also one and a quarter acres of salt marsh,
"with all the House or Housing Fencings that does any
ways belong or accrue unto the Ten Acre Lot above s^d. . .
only excepting & reserving for my self the s^d Joseph Chandler all one half of ye whole of ye above bargained Premises
for my own proper Use & Benefit & Behoof so long as I
shall live & further for my Wife Martha Chandler so long
as I do live & so long as She shall remain my Widow or till
her Time of Marriage after my Decease. . . . And More-
over also I do reserve for my Two Daughters Sarah Chandler & Martha Chandler each of them & both of them a
Priviledge for to Live in the House upon the Lot above s^d
so long as they remain UnMarried." This deed was dated
November 4, 1734, and acknowledged February 14, 1734–35.
In January, 1743–44, Edmund and his younger brother,
Judah, "Blacksmiths of North Yarmouth," for £53, purchased a tract of fifty acres, in the town, from Jonas Rice,
of Worcester, Massachusetts.† April 26, 1755, Edmund
bought, for £40, of Thomas Davee, of Plymouth, Massachusetts, "Seven Acres of the Easterly part of Home Lot
N^o Ten."‡

At that period every man, no matter what his trade or
profession, strove to own a farm, part of which he cultivated for the support of his family. The meadows and salt
marshes were cut to make hay for his cattle, and the wood-
lots furnished his only fuel. Generous fires of wood in the
huge, open fireplaces, often with a back-log "fifteen to four

---

* *York County Deeds*, Book 17 : 249.
† *York County Deeds*, Book 25 : 175.
‡ *York County Deeds*, Book 33 : 74.

and twenty inches in diameter," and six feet in length, were the sole means of beating, and of cooking as well. The brick ovens of later days were then unknown. Edmund Chandler was a thrifty farmer, as well as a blacksmith. In 1759, his tax was £2 : 01 : 01, — a larger tax than that of any of his brothers.*

Edmund Chandler filled a number of town offices. In 1741, 1742, 1745, 1758, and 1764, he was Constable.† He served many years as assessor, and was one of the early selectmen.‡

In 1740, the following record was placed upon the Treasurer's Book : —

"Northyarmouth June 30 day 1740
    then paid to Edmund Chandler the som of two pounds eight shillings and five pence for miking the whipping posts and stones paid by me

                                 Gilbert winslow town treasurer
 02 – 08 – 05." §

In 1665, the town of North Yarmouth, then Wescustogo, had been presented to the Court and fined forty shillings, " for not attending to the Court's order for making a pair of stocks, cage and a ducking stool." It is presumed that the post and stocks erected in the churchyard beside the Ledge, in 1740, by Edmund Chandler, in compliance with the order of the town, were placed there to avoid a similar fine. Winsor says : " Stocks were ordinary appendages to a meeting-house until of late years. They were in Duxbury in 1753." ‖

In response to an order that the assessors make a return of the colored people in the town, the following was entered upon the books, January 17, 1755 : —

---

* *Old Times in North Yarmouth :* 71.
† *First Treasurer's Record Book of North Yarmouth :* 33, etc.
‡ *Records of the First Church of North Yarmouth :* 52.
§ *First Treasurer's Record Book of North Yarmouth :* 18; also vide page 397.
‖ Winsor's *History of Duxbury,* 1849: 834.

" Pursuant to the above order, we certify there are Two Negro Males & one Female. The female belongs to the minister of the Town.

Jonas Mason
Edmund Chandler ⎬ assessors " *
Jno. Lewis

Deacon Jonas Mason thought it of sufficient importance to record in his diary, under date of February 23, 1751, that " Edmund Chandler [was] scalded very bad." † Chandler probably was then living in the same house where his daughter Rebecca was born two years later. Her deposition, in 1833, when she was eighty years of age, stated that she was " born where Reuben Chandler now lives." ‡ In 1763, after the enlargement of the meeting-house, at the sale of the twenty-eight new pews to defray the costs, Edmund Chandler purchased pew " No 25," for "£9:9:4." § In October, 1767, he served in the County Court of Common Pleas, as referee in a plea of ejectment.‖

The name of Edmund Chandler appeared, May 2, 1757, in a list of Captain Solomon Mitchell's company, " comprising the Train Band and Alarm List," in North Yarmouth. It was composed of all males in the town between sixteen years and sixty, and was organized as the First Company of Militia in the town. His brothers, Zachariah, Jonathan, Judah, and his eldest son, Joseph, belonged to the same company.¶

In the division of land at Chebeague in 1746, Edmund Chandler, "blacksmith" or "yeoman," received with his brother Judah, "one third of one half" between them.** It is

---

* *Old Times in North Yarmouth :* 1194. The minister is supposed to have been " Parson Loring."

† *Old Times in North Yarmouth :* 1188.   ‡ Vide page 187.

§ *Old Times in North Yarmouth :* 454, 456.

‖ *Cumberland County Court of Common Pleas,* Book 1 : 644.

¶ *Massachusetts Archives,* vol. 95 : 383.

** Vide Appendix LXXXVIII : C, D.

not probable that Edmund ever occupied it; and, in 1788, he sold his interest, as follows:—

"Edmond Chandler of North Yarmouth . . . yeoman," for £38 : 14, paid by David Chandler, of North Yarmouth, yeoman, conveyed to him forty-three acres on Great Chebeague, it "being a half part of the eighty six acres owned by me and my Brother Judah Chandler . . . in equal halves . . . as set forth in a Deed of partition of three hundred and twenty five acres . . . made by Jonas Mason, Jonathan Chandler & myself & Brother Judah aforesaid." This deed was dated August 28, 1788, and signed:

"Edmond Chandler" [seal] *

His interest in the "one Hundred & Twenty acre Division in North Yarmouth . . . Drawn in the Right of our Hon^d Father Joseph Chandler . . . by virtue of his home Lot N° 81," and the "third Part" of Captain Parker's Island and Seguin Island, in Casco Bay, he sold, together with the other heirs, in 1753 and 1777, respectively.†

Edmund Chandler died March 30, 1793, in North Yarmouth.‡ He may have left a will; but as all the Probate Records of Portland previous to 1866 were destroyed by the fire of that year, there is nothing that shows the distribution of his estate after his decease.

ISSUE BY FIRST WIFE

I. Martha⁵, b. Nov. 10, 1737; bap. Sept. 13, 1741, in the First Church of North Yarmouth. Her marriage intention to Ezekiel Delano was recorded Aug. 2, 1755, in North Yarmouth; they were married Sept. 14, following. Ezekiel, son to Amaziah Delano, of Duxbury, was a prominent citizen of North Yarmouth. In 1759, he was taxed £10 : 10 : 00. He d. in North Yarmouth after 1794; his widow Martha d. March, 1814, in the same town.

---

* *Cumberland County Deeds,* Book 19: 485-486.
† Vide Appendix LXXXVIII: A, B.
‡ *Records of the First Church of North Yarmouth,* 1848: 16.

Issue : * 1. Child, unnamed, b. and d. Nov. 2, 1756, in
North Yarmouth.

2. Amaziah Delano, b. June 16, 1758, in North Yarmouth.
3. Rhoda Delano, b. 1760, in North Yarmouth ; mar. July
   1, 1785, to Amaziah Reed, of North Yarmouth.
4. Sarah Delano, b. 1763, in North Yarmouth ; mar. May
   18, 1786, to Benjamin Merrill, of North Yarmouth.
5. Edmund Chandler Delano, b. 1766, in North Yarmouth.
6. Mercy Delano, b. 1768, in North Yarmouth ; mar. to
   —— Mitchell, of North Yarmouth.
7. Hannah Delano, b. 1770, in North Yarmouth ; d. unmar. in Falmouth.
8. Ezekiel Delano, b. 1773, in North Yarmouth ; was
   drowned at sea, in 1815.
9. Dorcas Delano, b. 1777, in North Yarmouth.

II. Joseph⁵, b. Feb. 11, 1739 ; bap. Sept. 13, 1741, in the First
Church, with his elder sister.

When he was twelve years of age, Joseph Chandler was
captured by the Indians, while driving cows. Solomon
Mitchell, " nigh twelve," and his younger brother, Daniel,
not quite seven, were taken captive at the same time.   Deacon Jonas Mason, in his diary, gives the date as " May 25,
1751," and adds, " King's oxen killed by them." †   Rebecca,
sister to Joseph, in her deposition of 1833, stated that " Joseph Chandler, the boy who was taken by Indians, was my
brother." ‡   The town fathers of North Yarmouth took immediate action, which resulted in the following letter § being
sent, the next day, to the legislature of Massachusetts ; it
was endorsed, on the back — " For Jeremiah Powell Esqʳ in
Boston : " —

" Sr

These follow you with the sorrowfull Actᵗ of the Jndians Carrying of Mʳ Edmond Chandlers Eldest son and Mʳ Benjamin Mich-
ells Eldest and Youngist All which they Took Just by yᵉ Corner

---

* *History and Genealogy of the Delano Family*, by Major Joel Andrew
Delano, New York, 1899: 230.

† *Old Times in North Yarmouth* : 1189.   ‡ Vide page 781.

§ *Massachusetts Archives*, vol. 74 : 12.

of Mr Greeleys Feild yesterday Just before Night they also Kild 2 oxen for Mr King all which J Desire youd Let the Capt Gener!! Know as soon as Possible J need not urge you to use your best Endeavours that Releife may be Jmmediatly Sent Down to ye Frontiers in these Parts their Distres^d Condition is so well known to you that ȷ am perswaded you Can! Possibly omit it — J am Just Come out of your House and am of opinion that Your Family Will soon remove if they Have no Assistance sent Which is in hast from Your Hum!! Serv!   Cornelius Soul

N Y^th May 26 : 1751."

On Sept. 8, 1751, Deacon Jonas Mason recorded : — " News of Joseph Chandler's return from captivity ; " * yet there were further and most distressing delays that called forth the following petition from the father of Joseph. The body of the petition evidently was written by another, but the signature is a genuine autograph of Edmund Chandler : —

" Prov. of the Massachusetts Bay — †

" To the hon. Spencer Phips Esq Lieu! Gov! & Commander in Chief of sd Province to the hon. his majestys Council & house of Representatives in great & genl Court Assembled the Second day of October A D. 1751.

" The Petition of Edmond Chandler of North Yarmouth In ye County of York Humbly Sheweth that on ye 25th day of May last his son Joseph Chandler an Jnfant was taken Prisoner by the Jndians & Carryed to St. Francois & there Sold to a Frenchman who Sold him to mr Cornelius Cuyler of Albany for £25. York Currency & sd Cuyler has been at £3: of sd Currency Expence in Bringin of sd Child from Canada & now detains him for ye paym! of sd Ransom money & Charges as by his letter herewith Exibited will appear —

" Wherefore as your Petitioner is poor & Cannot Raise sufficient to redeem his sd son he humbly prays ye Compassion of your hon! & yt you would be pleased to make him a Grant of Sufficient for Redeeming his sd son or to otherwise order as Jn your hon! Wisdom Shall seem meet & your Pet! as in Duty Bound Shall Ever-pray &.c.

Edmond Chandler "

---

* *Old Times in North Yarmouth :* 1189.
† *Massachusetts Archives,* vol. 74 : 41, 42.

[Endorsed on the Back of the Petition.]

"Jn the House of Repst Octr. 3. 1751 Read and Ordered that the Prayer of the Pet^{tr} be granted. And that the Pet^r be allowed the value of the Sum of twenty eight pounds. York Currency out of the publick Treasury for the purposes within mentioned.

Sent up for concurrence

T Hubbard Spk^r

"In Council Octo^r 4. 1751 Read & Concur'd

Sam Holbrook D^{ty} Secr'y

Consented to = S Phips"

The exact date of Joseph Chandler's return is not known; it is said to have been in November, or December, 1751. The marriage intention of Joseph Chandler to Susanna Brown was published Nov. 23, 1754; they were married Jan. 20, 1755.* He was but sixteen years of age. In 1757, he belonged to the "Train Band" of North Yarmouth, commanded by Captain Solomon Mitchell; because he was under age his father signed for him.† He probably led a seafaring life, as his sister Rebecca stated that he "died in Hispaniola, in 1763."‡

Issue: 1. Joseph⁶. 2. Enos⁶.

III. Enos⁵, b. July 3, 1742, in North Yarmouth; mar. Oct. 21, 1765, Elizabeth⁵, daughter to Barnabas⁴ and Jane (Bradbury) Soule. She was b. Oct. 28, 1747; bap. Nov. 1, 1747, in the First Church of North Yarmouth.§ His family has not been traced.

IV. Abigail⁵, b. Jan. 16, 1744; d. Oct. 24, 1755, in North Yarmouth.

V. Sarah⁵, b. Oct. 25, 1747, in North Yarmouth.

VI. Rhoda⁵, b. June 29, 1750; d. Nov. 4, 1755, in North Yarmouth.

VII. Rebecca⁵, b. April 30, 1753, in North Yarmouth; mar. March 28, 1771, to David⁵ Pratt.‖ Their marriage intention was dated Feb. 23, 1771.

VIII. Mary⁵, bap. June 2, 1754, in North Yarmouth.

---

* *Old Times in North Yarmouth*: 658.
† *Massachusetts Archives*, vol. 95: 383.   ‡ Vide page 781.
§ *Old Times in North Yarmouth*: 865.   ‖ Vide page 777.

IX. Mercy [5], b. Sept. 28, 1755, in North Yarmouth.

X. Edmond [5], b. March 3, 1759; bap. April 30, 1759, in the First Church; d. May 16, 1763.

XI. Submit [5], b. Dec. 31, 1762, in North Yarmouth; mar. (intention May 22, 1784) to "Daniel Mitchell, Jr.," son to Joseph [4] and Susannah (Paul) Mitchell; they were married Sept. 2, following.*

* Vide The Mitchells from Kittery.

EDWARD ALONZO[8] SMALL

MARRIED

MARY CAROLINE ROBERTS

THE ROBERTS FAMILY

THE family of Roberts is of ancient origin. Tradition on this side of the water says it "came from Wales." One encounters this assertion in many distinct lines, where the Planter ancestors may never have heard of one another. It is generally conceded that the family sprang from the original Britons, who were driven, during the many invasions of England by the Normans and other Continental forces, into the mountain fastnesses of Wales. Later, some spread over into County Cornwall, and there remained. While the people of these two sections retained many general characteristics, in the lapse of time they came to speak a different language, and, with local pride, one division came to consider themselves Cornishmen, the other Welshmen. Yet there were not a few intermarriages — for love knows no nationality.

Ancient records in the Archives of the College of Arms,* in London, show that the Roberts family derives its origin from Justin ap Gurgan, Lord of Glanmorganshire, who was forced out of the castle of Cardiff, in Wales, by Sir Robert Fitz Hammond, in the year 1090, during the reign of William I. Justin ap Gurgan, by his second wife, Ankarad, daughter to Elliston Gloderydd, had a son, Cradock ap Justin, who married "Gladys, granddaughter on the paternal side of Rees a Tudor, Prince of South Wales, and maternally of Griffith ap Conan, Prince of North Wales, was by the father of Morgan Argelloyld, father to Morgan ICHAN, Lord of Avon." Several generations later, William Jenkin ap Richard, a descendant of Morgan ICHAN,

---

* *College of Arms Register*, 3. D. fol. 160, etc.

became father to Christopher Roberts, of St. Tathan, the first to use the surname of Roberts. Christopher Roberts, Esq., fifth generation from the first Christopher, was gentleman of the Privy Chamber to King George II. The Coat-of-Arms of this branch of the family bears this motto: "Truth will stand." *

In Cornwall, there was a titled Roberts family living in or near Truro. The first to bear a title was "Richard Robartes," who married, about 1605, Frances, daughter to John Hender, of Botreux Castle. In 1616, Richard Roberts was knighted; in 1621, he was created Baronet, and in 1625, was raised to the peerage as "Baron Robartes of Truro." "His wealth made him a mark for extortion." John Roberts, b. 1606, eldest son to Baron Richard, succeeded to the title and estates of his father. On December 10, 1643, as "J. Roberts," he signed the charter of Roger Williams to Narragansett Bay, in New England; he was known at that time as Lord John Roberts, Earl of Radnor. He was a strong Presbyterian and made himself offensive to the government, with the result that his house at Lanhydrock, in Cornwall, was occupied in September, 1644, by the royalists, and his estates were assigned to Sir Roger Grenville by the king. His children were detained as prisoners, but he himself fled "in a cock-boat to Plymouth." Lord John Roberts married twice; his eldest son, "Robert Robartes, styled Viscount Bodmin," b. about 1633, died March, 1681–82, in England.†

Among those who came early to New England was Simon[1] Roberts. He was married, "18th 5th month, 1654," in Boston, by Richard Bellingham, to Christian Baker. She was born 1634, in England, and came over at the age of one year with her parents, Alexander and Elizabeth Baker.

---

* *New England Historic Genealogical Society*, Boutelle Collection, vol. 7: 53, 54.

† *Dictionary of National Biography*, by Sidney Lee, 1896, London and New York: 339–341; also *New England Historical and Genealogical Register*, vol. 10: 303; vol. 11: 41; vol. 40: 169.

Alexander[1] Baker was at Gloucester, Massachusetts, about 1641, with Rev. Richard Blynman, Obadiah Bruen, Thomas Bray, Hugh Caulkins, and others.* Baker did not remain long in Gloucester, but moved to Boston, where the marriage of his daughter, Christian, and the births of his ten children are recorded.† Simon[1] and Christian Roberts had eight children born in Boston: John[2], Simon[2], Samuel[2], Joseph[2] who died young, Elizabeth[2], Ann[2], Benjamin[2], and Joseph[2]‡ b. Jan. 24, 1673. The obituary notice of Mr. Joseph[3] Roberts, who departed this life February 26, 1774, in Boston, at the age of eighty (son to Joseph[2] and Esther (——) Roberts, and grandson to Simon[1] Roberts, of Boston), states that the father of Simon Roberts was brother to Sir Richard Roberts, of Truro, created Baron of Truro by King James I. It also states that Simon "came over into New England about the year 1649," and that he was cousin to Lady Jane Roberts, and to "Lord John Roberts of Truro . . . created Viscount of Bodwin and Earl of Radnor by King Charles II." § The will of Martin Roberts, of Truro, England, dated 1594, proved 1598, shows that the name Simon was common in the family at that early date. He mentions his wife Joan Roberts, brother John Roberts, brother Richard Roberts (not the later Baron Richard), "sister Philips," and cousins, William, John, and "Simons" Roberts. The will of John Roberts, of Truro, England, dated 1603, proved 1605, mentions wife Mary Roberts, brothers William and "Symon," sister-in-law Jane Roberts, sister Mary, and nephew John.‖

Hugh[1] Roberts, of Gloucester, Massachusetts, was evidently an elder brother to Simon[1] Roberts, of Boston.

---

* Babson's *History of Gloucester*, 1860 : 52–53.
† *New England Historical and Genealogical Register*, vol. 4 : 54; vol. 8 : 3, 349; vol. 9 : 251, 309; vol. 14 : 312.
‡ *Commissioners' Records of Boston*, vol. 9 : 48, 50, 56, 64, 85, 97, 111, 115.
§ *New England Historical and Genealogical Register*, vol. 10 : 303.
‖ *New England Historical and Genealogical Register*, vol. 49 : 239.

"Hugh Robertes," husbandman, was married by Mr. Samuel Symonds, of Ipswich, to "Mary, daughter of Hugh Calkin," of Gloucester, on "the 8th of the 9th month 1649." * In 1650, Hugh Roberts, his father-in-law Hugh Caulkins, Obadiah Bruen, and Rev. Richard Blynman, with a number of others from Ipswich and Gloucester, were in New London, Connecticut.† John Winthrop, Jr., who had opened the settlement at Ipswich, about 1640 turned his energies and his fortune towards New London, of which town he "eminently deserves the title of Founder;" he was afterwards Governor of Connecticut. Hugh Roberts, tanner, left New London and went to Newark, New Jersey. The date does not appear; but a map of the home lots of the first settlers of "Pesayak Towne (Newark)," from 1666 to 1680, shows that Hugh Roberts was allotted the land marked X, in the southeast section.‡ At New London, the following children were recorded: Mary, b. Dec. 9, 1652, Samuel, b. April 25, 1656, and Mehitable, b. April 15, 1658.§ The last will and testament of Hugh Roberts, of Newark, dated February 26, 1670–71, mentions wife Mary, eldest son Samuel, youngest son Hugh, and eldest daughter Priscilla (probably b. 1650), wife of Joseph Osborn. Robert Treat was witness to the will, also one of three executors. Before 1675, Mary Roberts, widow of Hugh, was the wife of Robert Bond, of Newark.‖

Robert[1] Roberts, of Ipswich, whose descendants for several generations will be followed, may have been nearly related to Simon[1] and Hugh[1]. Circumstantial evidence strongly points that way, but there is no absolute proof. Though the descendants of Robert[1] Roberts were numer-

---

* *Gloucester Births, Marriages, and Deaths, 1642–1780*: 234.
† *History of New London, Connecticut*, by Frances M. Caulkins, 1895: 67.
‡ *First Church in Newark, New Jersey*, by Jonathan F. Stearns, D. D., 1853: 316, 318.
§ Savage's *Genealogical Dictionary*, vol. 3: 546.
‖ *New Jersey Archives*, First Series, vol. 21: 31, 20, 40.

ous, the name is not repeated until one "Robert Roberts, a native of Wales," appears in Newbury, about 1745, with a wife Sarah; he had a large family,* and was a man of considerable prominence. He cannot be connected with the family of Robert [1] Roberts. The name of "Vincent Rob-

---

* In September, 1745, "Robert Roberts," who called himself a mariner of Newbury, with his wife, "Sarah Roberts," sold land in Newbury to "Edm^d March." In 1756, Robert Roberts, of Newbury, mariner, and Sarah, his wife, with Thomas Barnard, of Salem, clerk (minister), and Mary, his wife, quitclaimed land in Amesbury, "formerly in possession of John Foot Junr," for £54, to Benjamin Woodbridge, of Newbury.

The will of "Robert Roberts of Newburyport . . . merchant," dated June 9, 1771, proved Aug. 5, 1771, mentions wife Elizabeth Roberts, Elizabeth Starkey widow of William Starkey, "my Wife's Daughter," eldest son Robert, who was to have a double portion, son Thomas, and daughters, Alice Roberts, Ann Roberts, and Sarah Roberts. The inventory of "Capt Robert Roberts," dated Sept., 1771, refers to "Bristol Goods that arrived after Capt Roberts' Decease." The value of merchandise of all sorts was £3605 : 12 : 2¼, to which "Household furniture" was added, making a total of £4628 : 15 : 4. The settlement of the estate shows that the widow received a substantial legacy. On Jan. 12, 1780, the other heirs, whose names appear below, acknowledged the receipt of "our full part" of their father's estate, "also of that part of his estate bequeathed to our Brother Robert Roberts, deceased."

(Their portion)

"Thomas Roberts £914 : 02 : 4¼
John Bromfield £695 : 11 : 10
Allice Roberts £914 : 02 : 05
Ann Bromfield
Sarah Roberts" £695 : 11 : 10¼

ISSUE BY FIRST WIFE

1. Alice, b. May 31, 1747, in Newbury; mar. to Stephen Hooper, Esq.
2. Ann, b. Dec. 19, 1749, in Newbury; mar. to John Bromfield, of Boston.
3. Sarah, b. Dec. 1, 1751, in Newbury.
4. Robert, b. Dec. 28, 1754, in Newbury; died before 1780.
5. Thomas, b. March 3, 1757, in Newbury. The will of Thomas Roberts, of Newburyport, merchant, dated May 17, 1782, was proved May 31, following. He bequeathed to his sisters, Alice Hooper wife of Stephen Hooper, Esq., and Ann Bromfield, £80, each. To his sister, Sarah Roberts, he left the residue of his estate.

Vide *Essex County Deeds*, Book 87: 134; Book 103: 67. *Essex County Probate*, Book 347 : 141; Book 352 : 81; Book 354 : 514, 516, 518 : Book 355 : 297; Book 365 : 436.

erts" appears in Amwell Township, New Jersey, 1714 to 1721; mention is made of his wife Maudlin, and sons Vincent and John.* A little later, the name of Vincent appears in Gloucester among representatives of Robert [1].

The spelling of the name Roberts — Robards, Roberds, Robords, etc. — is probably due to the thick pronunciation of the Welsh and Cornishmen. Those familiar with the Marblehead of fifty to a hundred years ago will recall many such peculiarities. A sample is found in the well-known poem "Skipper Ireson's Ride."

ROBERT [1] ROBERTS

Robert [1] Roberts, of Ipswich, Massachusetts, must have been the emigrant of that name who embarked, May 2, 1635, at London, for the Barbadoes in the ship *Alexander*, Captain Burche and Gilbert Grimes, masters. All the passengers were required to give a "Certificate from the Minister where they late dwelt," and take the "oaths of Allegience and Supremacie." At that time his age was given as eighteen years.† In a deposition, dated September 7, 1659, at Ipswich, he testified that he was then "aged about 40 years," and had "knowne the farm in question above 24 years." ‡ From these statements it is evident that he was born about 1617, in England, and became a settler at Ipswich immediately after his arrival, in 1635, in the Massachusetts-Bay Colony.§

---

* *New Jersey Archives*, First Series, vol. 23 : 387.

† *New England Historical and Genealogical Register*, vol. 14 : 353.

‡ *Essex County Court Papers*, Book 5 : 12, 13.

§ Savage says that Robert Roberts was of Boston, 1640, and of Ipswich, 1648; he also names the first wife of Robert Roberts as Eunice, and his second wife as Susanna. Robert Roberts died in 1663, at Ipswich, and his widow Susanna afterwards was married to Thomas Perrin. To complete the chain, Savage mentions Timothy, b. Aug. 7, 1646, in Boston, as son to Robert and Eunice.

To refute several of these statements, there is no record of Robert Roberts

The first settlement at "Aggawam," incorporated August 5, 1634, as Ipswich, was made in March, 1632-33, at Jeffrey's Neck by John Winthrop, Jr., and twelve associates.* The title to the land at the Neck was obtained by William Jeffrey from the Indians; when Winthrop came there, he called Jeffrey "an old planter." It is supposed that the latter was with the Plymouth company, who went there in 1623-24, and that he remained after the Plymouth men withdrew from the enterprise.† The limits of the town included what are now the towns of Topsfield, Hamilton, and Essex, and parts of Rowley and Boxford. In 1793, "the Hamlet" of Ipswich was set off as Hamilton; "Chebacco" became Essex, in 1819. Ipswich was named for Ipswich, England, "in acknowledgement of the honor and kindness done to our people who took shipping there." The Colonial records state that Masconnomet sold his fee in Ipswich, for £20, on June 28, 1638, to John Winthrop, Jr.; the deed was witnessed by "John Jolyliffe, James Downing, Thomas Coytimore, and Robert Harding." ‡

Felt says, "A large proportion of these inhabitants possessed intelligent minds, virtuous hearts, useful influence

in Boston, either in the First Church, in conveyancing, or as a witness to others. The only Timothy Roberts in Boston was recorded erroneously as son to "Robert and Eunice," in the town books, b. "7ᵗʰ 6 ᵐᵒⁿᵗʰ," 1646; the same Timothy was baptized in the First Church of Boston, "9ᵗʰ 6 ᵐᵒ", 1646, "aged about 1 day," son to "Thomas Robert member of Church in Rocksbury." Eunice, wife of Thomas, in 1647, was a member of the First Church in Boston; after her husband's death, she was mar. "22ᵈ 8ᵗʰ mo, 1656," to Moses Maverick. Her son, Timothy, of Marblehead, was the only Timothy Roberts in Essex County.

Vide Savage's *Genealogical Dictionary*, vol. 3: 547. *Boston Births, Marriages, and Deaths, 1630-1699*: 24, 25. *Records of the First Church of Boston, 1639-1847*: 84, 325. Vide pages 669-670.

* *The Hammatt Papers,* 1633-1700, by Abraham Hammatt, 1854; no. 1: 416.

† Vide page 523; also *Salem Commons and Commoners*, by Herbert B. Adams, 1882: 3.

‡ *History of Ipswich, Massachusetts*, by Joseph B. Felt, 1834: 4, 8. A photograph of the original deed is found in *A Sketch of the Life of John Winthrop the Younger*, by Thomas Franklin Waters, 1899.

and remarkable character. They were careful of their own example, and thereby gave force to their precepts." * Probably no other town outside of Boston could boast of so many representatives in the early affairs of the government of the Massachusetts Bay Colony as Ipswich. A few of the settlers, before 1650, were : —

John Winthrop, Jr., son to the Governor, and himself Governor's Assistant and Deputy Governor.

Thomas Dudley, Governor, Deputy Governor, Assistant, Commissioner of the Colonies, Justice of the Inferior Quarter Court, and influential to the end of his long life.

Simon Bradstreet,† Governor, Deputy Governor, Colonial Secretary, Assistant, Commissioner of the Colonies, and Justice of the Inferior Quarter Court.

Daniel Dennison,‡ Colonial Secretary, Speaker of the House, Commissioner of the Colonies, Assistant, Justice of the Inferior Quarter Court, Deputy to the General Court ten years, with military rank of Major General in eleven years' service.

Samuel Symonds, Town Clerk 1639–1645, Deputy Governor, Assistant, Justice of the Inferior Quarter Court, Registrar of the Court, Deputy six years to the General Court, and Feoffee of the Grammar School.

Samuel Appleton, of the Governor's Council ten years between 1681 and 1692, Assistant, Justice of the Inferior Quarter Court, Deputy to the General Court nine years, and Captain many years, including 1675–76, of the military company of Ipswich and the surrounding towns.

Robert Paine, Deputy to the General Court, County Treasurer, Founder and Feoffee of the Grammar School, and Ruling Elder of the Church.

---

* *History of Ipswich, Massachusetts*, by Joseph B. Felt, 1834: 33.

† His first wife was Ann [2], daughter to Governor [1] Dudley; his second wife was Ann [3], widow of Captain Joseph Gardner, and daughter to Emmanuel [1] Downing.

‡ He married Patience [2], daughter to Governor [1] Dudley.

Richard Saltonstall, Assistant, and Justice of the Inferior Quarter Court.

Robert Lord, Clerk of the Court, and Deputy one year to the General Court.

To these may be added others whose descendants have contributed largely to the growth of the Commonwealth: William Paine, Christopher Osgood, George Carr of Salisbury in 1640, William Bartholomew, Richard Scofield, Reginald Foster, Robert Roberts, William Whitredge, Thomas Whitredge, Thomas Boreman, Jonathan Wade, William Fellows, Edward Harriden, Robert Dutch, Samuel Dudley son to the Governor, Humphrey Bradstreet, and Dudley Bradstreet, the latter son to Governor Simon Bradstreet,* etc.

Johnson, in his *Wonder-working Providence*, published 1654 in London, says of Ipswich : † " The peopling of this Towne is by men of good ranke and quality, many of them having the yearly Revenue of large Lands in England before they came to this Wildernesse. It is a very good Haven Towne, yet a little barr'd up at the Mouth of the River, some merchants are here, (but *Boston*, being the chiefest place of resort of Shipping, carries away all the Trade) they have very good Land for Husbandry, where Rocks hinder not the course of the Plow: . . . their Houses are many of them very faire built with pleasant Gardens and Orchards, consisting of about one hundred and forty families. Their meeting-house is a very good prospect to a great part of the Towne, and beautifully built." Their church, which was the ninth in the Massachusetts-Bay Colony, consisted of about one hundred and sixty souls. Rev. Nathaniel Ward was their second pastor. Johnson describes his people as " being exact in their conversation, and free from the Epidemicall Disease of all Reforming Churches."

---

* *History of Essex County, Massachusetts*, vol. 1² : 627, 628.

† *Wonder-working Providence*, by Captain Edward Johnson, London, 1654; Andover, Massachusetts, 1867 : 66.

Such were the surroundings of Robert Roberts, who, when he took up his abode on New England soil, was not yet of age. In various histories he is credited with having become a citizen of Ipswich in 1643 or 1644. From his deposition in 1659, and another record which will be mentioned later, he was there as early as 1635. The earliest town book is much worn, though it has been preserved from further dilapidation by the "Emery process." The greater part of the writing is faded and almost illegible; many leaves are torn or wholly gone. The copyist states that — "These Records following weare taken out of an old booke, that the most of what was written there is either torne out or much defaced . . . what could be transcribed, is as followeth." * There are few records of births, deaths, or marriages, prior to 1664.

Though John Winthrop, Jr., had obtained title from the Indians of the land upon which Ipswich was built, the general unrest among the neighboring tribes caused organized preparations to be made by the town against a surprise. In the spring of 1642, the General Court, fearing that Passaconaway, a Sagamore of the Merrimac, was involved in a general plot to cut off the English, ordered that upon a public alarm the women and children, the old and infirm, should be hurried to the fort, where the ammunition was guarded. Several times the alarm was given. Early in September, 1642, on a Saturday, a messenger arrived with orders that the militia of Ipswich, Rowley, and Newbury were to march at once against Passaconaway, to disarm him. "On the morning of the Sabbath, in a heavy rain, the twenty Ipswich soldiers started out on their expedition. No blood was shed, and in due time he delivered up his guns." † The town settled with the soldiers, December 4, 1643, paying

---

* *Town Records of Ipswich* (copy), vol. 1 : 24.

† *Ipswich in the Massachusetts Bay*, by Rev. Thomas Franklin Waters, 1905: 126, 127; also *Hammatt Papers, 1633-1700*, by Abraham Hammatt, 1854, no. 1 : 288.

"12ᵈ a day allowing for the Lord's day in respect of the extremity of the wether) and the officers dubble: . . . to Robert Roberts 3ˢ." * On the 25th of the same month, the widow Lumpkin, who kept an ordinary, or tavern, was reimbursed for the provisions she had furnished the soldiers.

That Robert Roberts continued in the military company, for some years at least, is shown by his subscription, at a "generall Towne Meeting held the 19 of December, 1648," when the inhabitants of Ipswich engaged Major Daniel Dennison to "be their Leader." They voted, at the same time, to pay yearly the several sums subscribed against their names, "while he continued to be our Leader." The list, containing the names of one hundred and sixty-three citizens, was headed by "Mr Saltingstall . . . [£]0: 4: 0;" the same amount was to be paid yearly by "Robert Roberds." "Thos. Harris and Robert Roberds" also paid a town rate of £0: 6: 0, that year.†

The traffic in "strong water" early engaged the attention of the town. The first license to sell was granted Robert Roberts, in 1635, by the Court of Assistants.‡ In 1637, the law forbade "sack or strong water" to be sold at any ordinary because the privilege had been abused. March 12, 1638, Mr. Samuel Symonds was appointed to sell "strong water." The price, in 1646, of a license to retail "strong water, wine & beer," at Ipswich, was £2. Men of the highest reputation soon sought like liberty: Mr. Robert Paine, Mr. William Bartholomew, and Jeremy Belcher received licenses in 1652. Deacon Moses Pengry also kept an ordinary, and dispensed spirit.§

On the last day of the 5th month, 1641, a list of the com-

---

* *Town Records of Ipswich* (original), vol. 1; (copy) vol. 1 : 112.

† *Town Records of Ipswich* (copy), vol. 1 : 149, 147.

‡ *Ipswich in the Massachusetts Bay Colony*, by Rev. Thomas Franklin Waters, 1905: 281.

§ *Ipswich in the Massachusetts Bay Colony*, by Rev. Thomas Franklin Waters, 1905: 275, 276, 281.

moners or voters of Ipswich was made out; the first two
names were "Mr Richard Saltonstall" and "Mr Symon
Bradstreet." * As the lower end of the page upon which
these names appear in two columns is torn off, and the name
of Robert Roberts is not among the large number preserved, one is left in doubt as to whether or not he ever
signed it. His name is not in the published lists of freemen
in the Court Records. In view of the fact that he refused
to pay the rate assessed each citizen, in 1647, toward the
expense of building a new meeting-house at Ipswich, it
seems probable that he was not in sympathy with existing conditions in the Church. At that time Church and
State were one; no man could be a freeman, or vote, or
hold office, who did not belong to the Church. "Offences
against the sanctity of the Church and Sabbath were dealt
with summarily." William Bartholomew, in behalf of the
town, brought suit against "Thomas Rolinson" and "Robert
Robards" for refusing to pay the rate; † "Rolingson" was
fined "40^s, and 7^s 6^d more for costs." "The Town was advised to compound with Roberts for 16^s."

The name Robert Roberts appears a number of times
in the Court Papers of Essex County, and always favorably:
— On the " 1mo, 1651," he was a witness at Ipswich in the
case of Mark Symonds; "4mo 1651," he made a deposition
at Ipswich. In 1653, he testified that "the six-acre lot by
Seargent Fowle's had very good corn on it." In 1658,
Richard Shatswell was requested to appear before the Court
at Ipswich, "on complaint of Robert Robarts" for "taking
from him about halfe a load of wood out of his cart."
Judgment was given against Shatswell for " 3^s–6^d damage &
5^s–5^d cost." In March, 1659, Robert Roberts was a witness
in the case of John Baker *vs.* John Andrews, as to the ownership of two heifers which were said to be " very nearly

---

* *Town Records of Ipswich* (original), vol. 1; (copy) vol. 1 : 98, 99.
† *The Essex Antiquarian*, vol. 8 : 9, 10.

alike in appearance." September 7, 1659, "The Testimony of Robart Robarts aged about 40 year — Saith that he hath knowne the farme, granted to the Major Gen[ll] [Denison] & M[r] Dudley from the first & for divers yeares was imployed there to make hay, & looke to cattle in winter, when M[r] Winthrop made use of his farme, in all which time nor sines for more than 25 years he never heard of any crotched or forked tree to be any bounds, nor of any other, than a line from a walnut-tree neere Goodm: fellows house through the glade or hollow on the Eagles nest." There are several copies of this deposition, which vary in some degree. In one it is stated that Robert Roberts had known the bounds of Major General Denison's and Mr. Dudley's land "by the Eagles Nest in the hollow," also the bounds of land at "Labour in Vain Creek." * In March, 1659–60, "Robert Roberts aged 40 yeares" testified about the farm of William Fellows, in Ipswich, which formerly belonged to Mr. Dudley, adding that he had been "imployed vpon the same for divers yeares . . . about fiue yeares," for Mr. Fellows.†

The wife of Robert Roberts was Susan, or Susanna; the date and place of their marriage is unknown. Their eldest son recorded in 1669 was John; his birth appears from his depositions to have been about 1646. Susanna Roberts may have been daughter to Emmanuel Downing.‡ He is said

---

* *Essex County Court Papers*, Book 2 : 88, 96, 154 ; Book 4 : 80, 362 ; Book 5 : 22, 12, 13.

† *Suffolk County Superior Court Files :* 351.

‡ Emmanuel Downing went to Salem, Massachusetts, about 1638, from London, where he was a lawyer of the Inner Temple, and inhabitant of the Parish of St. Michael. He appears to have married twice ; his second wife, whom he married April 10, 1622, was Lucy, daughter to Adam Winthrop, Esq., of Groton, County Suffolk, England, and sister to John Winthrop, Sr., first Governor of the Massachusetts-Bay Colony. On March 14, 1638–39, soon after his arrival in New England, " M[r] Emanuell Downeing " took the oath of freedom before " M[r] Endicot and M[r] John Winthrope, Ju," and was Deputy to the General Court, 1639, 1640, 1641, 1643, 1644, 1648. In 1640, he was

to have had a daughter Susan, but all efforts to obtain proof of her marriage have been unavailing unless the suggestion is accepted that she became the wife of Robert Roberts.

On the "2ᵈ 5ᵐᵒ 1643," which may be considered near the time of his marriage, Robert Roberts bought of Richard Scofield, of Ipswich, for £11 : 17, a house and lot of two acres, with appurtenances, which is described as "having yᵉ house lott of Robert Andrews towards the east, a highwaye leading to yᵉ meeting house towards yᵉ south, a house lott of Mᵣ. Bartlemew [Bartholomew] towards the west, and

---

chosen Register for Salem; in 1641, he was proposed for Magistrate; in 1644 and 1649, he was "associate for Salem Court." In 1639, he "was granted 600 acres of land," which was laid out in 1651, "betwene Hampton and the rivers mouth of Pascataq," in New Hampshire. He also bought large tracts of land "three miles west of Salem;" five hundred acres of which he sold John Porter. This tract is now in Danvers. In 1648, the General Court ordered that "as Mᵣ Downings farm, in the way betwen Linn & Ipswich, is a convenient place for the reliefe of travellers ... Mᵣ Downings tenant shall have liberty to keepe an ordinary;" said tenant "shall live" on the farm. At the same time, Emmanuel Downing was licensed as innkeeper. He went to England a number of times, and was dead before 1656; his widow remained in Salem.

    Issue by first wife: I. James² Downing. He was of Ipswich, Mass., and must have been of age when he signed the deed of "Masconnomet, saggamore of Aggawam," to John Winthrop, Jr., June 28, 1638.

    II. Susan² Downing.

    Issue by second wife: III. George² Downing, b. 1623 or 1624. Sir George Downing, "of East Hatley, in the County of Cambridge," was knighted by Charles the Second. He married, and had children.

    IV. Ann² Downing. She was mar., first, to Captain Joseph Gardner; second, to Governor Simon¹ Bradstreet, after the death of his first wife.

    V. Mary² Downing. She was mar. to Anthony Stoddard, of Boston.

    VI. Lucy² Downing; she became the wife of William Norton.

    VII. John² Downing, bap. March 1, 1640, in Salem; he probably died 1694, at Boston, Mass.

    VIII. Dorcas² Downing, bap. Feb. 7, 1641, in Salem.

    IX. Joshua Downing, Sr., of Kittery, is thought to belong to this family.

    Vide *Massachusetts Bay Colony Records*, vol. 1, 2, 4½ ; Savage's *Genealogical Dictionary*, vol. 2 : 65; also *New England Historical and Genealogical Register*, vols. 13, 15, 38, etc.

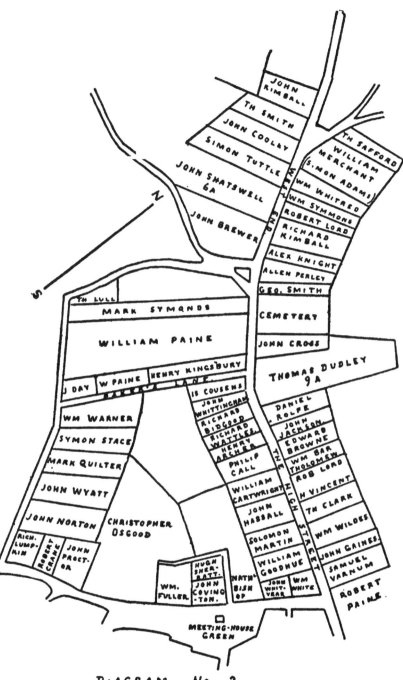

DIAGRAM No. 2

a hous lott of John Perkins the younger, and a piece of land of Thomas Boreman towards the north." * This lot sold to Roberts by Scofield had originally been granted " 10th 4th mo, 1639," to Robert Lord, at which time it was described as a " house lott on the High street, butting upon the same street at the South end, having a house lott of Humphrey Vincent on the East, and a house lott granted to William Bartholomew on the West." † Vincent's land was owned later by Robert Andrews and by Thomas Clark.

In the History of Ipswich, published recently by Rev. Thomas Franklin Waters, President of the Ipswich Historical Society, there is a diagram ‡ which shows the location of this house and land of Robert Roberts — originally the grant to Robert Lord — on " The High Street," a continuation of " West End Street." The diagram also shows the nine acres granted, in 1635, to " Thomas Dudley Esqr," lying between Goodman Cross on the west and " a lott intended to Mr. Bradstreet on the east," upon which the grant says " Mr Dudley hath built an house." §

" The High Street," now called High Street, and many other streets of this picturesque old town are to-day much as they were when the town was first laid out. Central Square, to which five streets converge, is very near the geographical centre. The grassy plot in this Square, which like many New England " Squares " is in reality a triangle, has been given to the Woman's Relief Corps, which has erected there a memorial to THE UNKNOWN DEAD of our Civil War. They have also a flagstaff, a little back of the stone. Following North Main Street up the hill, past the First Church, whose present edifice is on the site of the original building which Captain Johnson thought so " beauti-

---

* *Essex County Deeds, Ipswich Records*, Book 1 : 6.
† *Town Records of Ipswich* (copy), vol. 1 : 55.
‡ Kindly loaned by Rev. T. F. Waters.
§ *Town Records of Ipswich* (original), vol. 1.

fully built," with such "a very good prospect," the visitor turns at the end of the street, to the left, into High Street. This street gradually winds around Town Hill, some distance from the top, which in the early days was densely wooded ; the view to the south and west is extensive. From the top of the hill one can see many miles in every direction. It was this feature probably that caused the first settlement to be made on that spot—it could not easily be surprised by the Indians.

The house of Robert Roberts disappeared long ago, but the ancient dwelling now (1906) numbered 17, on High Street, is said to be very nearly on the site of his original house. It is identical with the Philip Lord place, and still earlier homestead of Robert Lord. Beyond a doubt it is of the eighteenth century.* The lots on the street are narrower than when first laid out, but they all run up the hillside, as in the olden days. In front of the seventh house to the west, on the same side of the street, a tablet has been placed by the Ipswich Historical Society. It is of bronze, about two feet square, set into a granite boulder. The inscription is as follows : —

NEAR THIS SPOT WAS THE HOUSE OF
SIMON BRADSTREET
GOVERNOR
OF
MASSACHUSETTS-BAY
1679–1686 AND 1689–1692
HIS WIFE, ANN, DAUGHTER OF GOVERNOR
DUDLEY, WAS THE FIRST AMERICAN POETESS
THEY LIVED IN IPSWICH 1635–1644

There is also another tablet a short distance beyond, still on the same side of the street, in memory of Governor Dudley. The bronze, about two feet square, is set into a block of hewn granite, and reads : —

---

* *Ipswich in the Massachusetts Bay*, by Rev. Thomas Franklin Waters, 1905 : 382.

ON THIS LOT, ORIGINALLY NINE
ACRES, WAS THE HOUSE
OF
THOMAS DUDLEY
GOVERNOR
OF
MASSACHUSETTS-BAY
1634, 1640, 1645 AND 1650
HE DWELT HERE
1635-1639

The character of the early structures was much the same; they were small, rough houses; many were built of logs and roofed with thatch. The single chimney was constructed chiefly of wood, daubed with clay, or plastered with a sort of lime made of burnt and powdered clam-shells. Repeated accidents from fire caused the town to pass a vote, in 1647, " requiring chimnies to be kept clean . . . also to look to any defect in daubing." The houses were devoid of paint, and most of the windows were provided with oiled paper instead of glass. The use of glass did not become general until more than a hundred years after Robert Roberts bought his house of Scofield. After living there fifteen years, Robert Roberts sold his house and the two acres upon which it stood to Thomas Lord, a shoemaker of Ipswich, for "two bills of fifteen pounds a peece." It was described as on "the north syde of the river," and bounded by land of Thomas Clark on the southeast, "the streete towards ye southwest," and land of William Bartholomew on the northwest. The deed, dated February 22, 1658, was signed:—

Witnesses: " Robert Roberds " [seal]*
" Walter Ropes his mark
   Robert Lord seni^r."

The only reference to the occupation of Robert Roberts is found in the Notarial Records of William Aspinwall, of Boston; he is called a merchant. On July 1, 1650, the

---

* *Essex County Deeds*, Book 2 : 9.

"Notarie" certified that the *Swallow*, of London, William Greene, master, hath here delivered for the account of "Robt Roberts mer.," two bales containing "18 Devon Kersies." * As no other in New England at that time bore the name, this must have meant Robert, of Ipswich. This supposition is strengthened by the fact that William Greene, master of the "shipp *Swallow* of London," who made voyage after voyage between London and the ports of New England, on February 20, 1648–49, made a contract to deliver, for "Wᵐ Bartholomew of Ipswich in New England merchᵗ & Nathaniel Eldred of London Merchᵗ," sixteen hundred quintals of merchantable dry cod-fish, which he should take on "at the port of Cape Anne in New England." The fish was to be delivered to Elias Roberts, of London, Richard Westcome, of London, Richard Ryals and Robert Hamond (no residence given).†

As fishing was the common industry of the town of Ipswich, it is probable that Robert Roberts was more or less engaged in it; but he early became identified with the raising of cattle, an important source of revenue. Johnson wrote, in 1646: "the Lord hath been pleased to increase them in Corne and cattell of late; Insomuch that they have many hundred quarters to spare yearly, and feed, at the latter end of the Summer, the Towne of *Boston* with good Beefe." ‡

The lowlands northeast of Town Hill, rich in herbage then as to-day, were retained by the town as a commonage, or pasture, in which citizens had certain defined rights but no equity. These commons comprised the whole of Jeffrey's Neck and a considerable stretch of land to the westward. At first the children were "sett to keep cattle," but as the herds increased, men were given the task. In 1652,

---

* *Aspinwall Notarial Records*, 1903: 416.

† *Aspinwall Notarial Records*, 1903: 217, 218, 305.

‡ *Wonder-working Providence*, by Captain Edward Johnson, London, 1654; Andover, Massachusetts, 1867: 66.

the General Court ordered every man to fence his land with palings, five-rail fences, or stone walls, conformable to law; yet the herdsmen were retained to keep cattle and sheep from straying, or being assailed by wolves. Bears, too, were not uncommon.

The connection of Robert Roberts with Little Neck, the southeasterly corner of Jeffrey's Neck, and commonly included in it, began in 1651. On February 12, of that year, the town granted to "Robert Roberts, liberty to mowe 2 loades of Hay vpon any part of Jeffreys neck, which he shall solely enjoy during the pleasure of the town, and for wch he shal be ready to serve the towne in taking care that no trespass shall be done vpon s^d neck." Two weeks later it was "Voted and ordered, by the consent of the Towne, that noe Hoggs shall goe at Jeferyes neck vpon the penalty of five shillings for every ofence. Robert Roberts when he pounds them, or brings y^m to the owner shall have halfe the forfitt." * Swine gave the town more trouble than cattle, and the order that they should be allowed to run at large, "yoked and ringed," was repeated year after year in town-meetings; later they were herded the same as sheep and cattle. In 1643, the cows were gathered "over against Mr Robert Paynes house," that is, at the corner of High and North Main Streets. In 1647, all the herdsmen were ordered "to winde a horn before their going out." †

Following the sale, February 22, 1658, of his house on High Street, on June 18, Robert Roberts presented a petition to the town, upon which it was "Voted, to leave the consideration of Robert Roberds, his motion about a little pcell of ground at the great neck [Jeffrey's Neck] to the 7 men, and to report it to the Towne." December 24, "Liberty [was] granted to Robert Roberds to fence in half an acre of Land by the Spring near little Neck, and to build a

---

* *Town Records of Ipswich* (copy), vol. 1: 171, 173.
† *Ipswich in the Massachusetts Bay*, by Rev. Thomas Franklin Waters, 1905: 64, 63.

House on it while he hold the Little Neck. The property still to remain the Townes."* It was probably about this time that he hired Little Neck from William Paine, of Boston, since according to the following deposition, Roberts had his rent reduced from £7 to £6 a year, in 1660 : —

"The deposition of Robert Day.†

"This deponent saith that about 2 years Since, being at Mr. William Paines at Boston, Robert Roberts being alsoe there at the same time, the sayd Roberts desired Mr. Paine to hire the little neck lying heere in Ipswich of him. Mr. Paine consented he should have it of him for one hundred years, upon these conditions : for ten years the said Roberts was to paye the sum of six pound a yeare, and then to returne to the former rent, which was seaven pound a year : and further this deponent saith, that Mr. William Paine did give the full rent of this neck unto the scoole here in Ipswich from that time forward : alsoe to the latter part of this testimony, concerning Mr. William Paine's giving the full rent of this necke to the scoole, Robert Roberts above testifieth. dat : April 17 : 1662.

"Sworne in Court held at Ipswich, the 17th of April : 1662. ℙ me

                                 Robert Lord Cleric."

Robert Roberts remained at Little Neck until his death. To fully understand the conditions of his and his successors' tenure of the land, it is necessary to explain how the rent of Little Neck came to be given for the support of the "scoole."

In 1636, the town records state : "A Grammar School is set up but does not succeed ;" ‡ in 1642 : "It is granted that there shal be a free Schoole." The next year £11 was raised, and it was voted "that there shal be seven free Schollars, or so as the Feffees (to be chosen) from tyme to tyme shall order, soe as the numb. exceed not seven." §

---

* *Town Records of Ipswich* (copy), vol. 1 : 214, 216.
† *Essex County Deeds, Ipswich Records,* Book 2 : 167.
‡ *History of Ipswich, Essex, and Hamilton,* by Joseph B. Felt, 1834 : 83.
§ *Town Records of Ipswich* (copy), vol. 1 : 103, 111.

Lionel Chute was probably the first schoolmaster; he died in 1645. About 1650, " Robert Paine senʳ. of Ipswich . . . after several overtures and Endeavʳˢ among yᵉ Inhabitants of sᵈ Ipswich for settling A Gram̄ar school In yᵗ place," agreed to build a school, if it should be " put into yᵉ hands of Certain Discreet and Faithful persons of the said Town and their successors which Himself should nominate to be Ordered and Managed by them as Feoffes Jn Trust for yᵗ End, & their successors for Ever," provided the town would set apart certain lands in Ipswich " for the yearly maintenance of such a one." * " At a generall Town meeting the 14ᵗʰ (11) 1650," the town voted as follows : " Granted to Mr. Robert Payne and Mr. Willᵐ Payne, and such others as the Towne shall apoynt, for the use of the Schoole, all that neck beyond Chebacco River, and the rest of the Ground (up to Gloster line) adjoyneing to it. Major Denison and Mr. Bartholomew chosen by the Towne and added to the Mr. Paynes." January 26, 1651, nine men, including " Mr. Robert Payne & Mr. Willᵐ Payne," were chosen to receive money towards building and maintaining the " Gram̄ar School and school mʳ [with] full power to regulate all matters concerninge the school mʳˢ and Scholars as in their wisdom they think meet from time to time, who shall also consider the best way to make provision for teaching to write, and to cast accounts." † The Ipswich Grammar School had now become the pride of the town ; it soon fitted students for college under the teachings of Mas·ter Ezekiel Cheever.

Little Neck is now a picturesque and favorite summer resort, yet the land is still held by the town of Ipswich. Each cottager is assessed ten dollars a year for the rent of the land, besides taxes. The report of the " Feoffees of the Grammar School," in 1907, states the value of the land at Little Neck to be $5,000. The land rents and taxes form

---

* *Essex County Deeds, Ipswich Records*, Book 5: 268.
† *Town Records of Ipswich* (copy), vol. 1: 165, 170-171.

a substantial part of the income for the support of that school.* The town has also some claim on the common lands ; just how much is not known. This question has formed the basis of numerous lawsuits in generations past, and others are still pending. Many such curious ancient customs crept into the early settlements of Massachusetts Bay — perhaps a little more noticeably in Ipswich than else-where. Professor Edward A. Freeman alludes to these features in his Introduction to American Institutional History : —

"The most notable thing of all, yet surely the most natural thing of all, is that the New England settlers of the seventeeth century largely reproduced English institutions in an older shape than they bore in the England of the seventeenth century. They gave a new life to many things, which in their older home had well-nigh died out. The necessary smallness of scale in the original settlements was the root of the whole matter. It, so to speak, drove them back several centuries. It caused them to reproduce in not a few points, not the England of their own day, but the England of a far earlier time. It led them to reproduce in many points the state of things in old Greece and in medieval Switzer-land."†

The early settlers of Ipswich were largely men who in-tended to engage in mercantile pursuits, and to make it a port of entry. The condition of the river, which Johnson describes as "a little barr'd up at the mouth," prevented the realization of their plans. Some removed to Boston and other localities ; those who remained turned their attention successfully to the raising of cattle and to husbandry. Prior to 1700, the town had a brilliant history; it was the county seat, and ranked foremost in military affairs. It was dis-tinctively English, and as Freeman says, English of an early type. The setting apart of the commons was a marked

---

* *Ipswich Town Proceedings*, vol. 8 : 270.
† *Johns Hopkins Studies*, Series I : 15-16.

example. On February 25, 1645, the "plot of the cow-common on the north side of the river, containing by estimation " 3244 acres, was "presented unto the freemen of the town ; " the freemen granted the inhabitants, "their heirs & successors for ever, all the aforesaid common to be improved, & the commons were to be managed by 7 men [later called selectmen] & no house should be hereafter built without express leave of the town." * Afterwards land was set apart for "horse-commons," also for the herding of swine and sheep. The ancient terms, cowherd, swineherd, and "sheepherd," are found repeatedly in the records of the town.

The setting apart of a portion of the town's land, at Little Neck, to be managed by Feoffees for the support of the Grammar School, was another custom distinctly English in its origin, though varied, it may be, by conditions peculiar to its new environment. The Puritan founders of the Massachusetts Bay Colony, so ably represented at Ipswich, also brought over with them a modified English form of government, laid out for them in England, which they proceeded to follow ; their wills and deeds (particularly the latter) were written in the elaborate forms then prevailing in the mother country. In this respect they were quite different from the first settlers of Plymouth. The Pilgrims, as they loved to call themselves, had spent many years in Holland. The bitter persecutions which drove them from their native land left few memories of English customs to be perpetuated. Their form of government was expressed in the famous COMPACT, to which the nation to-day is so greatly indebted, though it was not carried out to its fullest intent. Many of their early failures were due to want of concerted action and established government. In 1690, the two colonies were united in the Province of the Massachusetts Bay.

---

* *History of Ipswich, Essex, and Hamilton*, by Joseph B. Felt, 1834: 16.

In April, 1655, Robert Roberts was employed by the town to "look out for" the cattle on Jeffrey's Neck. Three years later it was voted "to haue noe cattle goe on the Neck, but such as [illegible] of the Inhabitants haue liberty to putt on." April 5, 1661, the town engaged Robert Roberts to keep the sheep on Jeffrey's Neck, from "the 8ᵗʰ of this month to the end of October to haue one following them constantly . . . and to haue for his wages thirteen pounds to be payd halfe in merchantable Indian corne, and halfe in English corne at the current price." * Two days later, April 7, Roberts signed an agreement in the Town Records to keep the sheep : —

"Robert Roberds." †

At the same town-meeting it was agreed that Robert Whitman should keep another flock on the north side of the river, at ten shillings a week. The next year there were three shepherds, and the commons on the south side were so burdened that one hundred sheep were transferred to the north side ; ‡ but Robert Roberts was retained as one of the three shepherds. On March 19, 1662–63, he made a similar agreement to that of the year before, the town stipulating also that he should "be always following them by himselfe or to [illegible] a man constantly." This he also signed : —

"Robert Roberds."§

Robert Roberts signed his name in full to the deed conveying his house on High Street, in 1658, to Thomas Lord ;

---

* *Town Records of Ipswich* (copy), vol. 1 : 192–193, 216, 236.
† *Town Records of Ipswich* (original), vol. 2 : 5, 7.
‡ *History of Ipswich, Essex, and Hamilton*, by Joseph B. Felt, 1834 : 45.
§ *Town Records of Ipswich* (original), vol. 2 : 11.

the second time that he made his mark (March 19, 1662–63) his hand was more unsteady than the first, the year before. This indicates that he was in failing health; he may have followed the occupation of a shepherd on that account. He died early in July, 1663,* leaving a widow Susanna and several children. The ten acres of land at Chebacco, mentioned in his inventory, were the "6 acres of vpland and 4 acres of Marsh" granted him by the town, February 27, 1644.† It is notable that while his dwelling-house and barn were valued at £20, there is no mention of the land upon which they stood, for the reason that they were built at Little Neck upon the half acre of land by the spring, leased him by the town in 1658.‡ Of the settlement of the estate of Robert Roberts by the Court, to which allusion is made in connection with the portions of some of his children, the original inventory only remains. This worn and discolored document, which has been reinforced by crossed strips of paper on the back, reads : § —

"July 20, 63 [1663]

"The Jnventorye of Robert Roberts of Jpswich lately deceased of all such goods & Chattells in possession

	li		
"Imp! a dwellinge house and a barne	20	0	0
a Cart & wheeles & plough wᵗʰ the furniture to them	05	5	0
2 oxen. 13–10 : 4 Cowes 16ˡⁱ : 2 steers 8 : 3 Calfes 1ˡⁱ — 16/ . .	39	6	0
10 : acres : of land at Chebacco of vpland and meddow	20	0	0
11 swine and tenn piggs	16	6	8
halfe a mare & half a horse ‖	09	0	0
a sheepe fold	02	10	0
4 Ews 4 lambs : a Ram and a wether	04	6	0
in ground improued	05	0	0

* Savage says (vol. 3 : 547) that Robert Roberts died July 19, 1663. His inventory, signed July 20, 1663, would hardly have been taken the day after his decease, even at that period.

† *Town Records of Ipswich* (copy), vol. 1 : 122.

‡ Vide pages 941–942.

§ *Essex County Court Papers*, Book 9 : 47.

‖ In early days, a half or third interest in an animal was represented as "half a mare," or "one-third of a cow," etc.

3 Canows [canoes]	05	0	0
a bed and Courlett	05	10	0
a bed and Courlets & pillows and bolster	06	12	0
2 blanketts 3 pillows	01	12	6
a bed & Bolster	02	10	0
Indian Corne	6	0	0
Bacon & Porke	1	10	0
his aparall	5	0	0
fethers	0	18	0
wool 1ˡⁱ 2ˢ/ Bedstede 2. 16.	2	16	0
a Cubberd 10ˢ 2 Chest 3 boxes a Case of Bottells	1	16	0
Sheetes & pillow beers	5	2	0
peuter & warminge pan :	2	0	0
pots kettell skillets fiersouell & tonges	2	8	0
a table 5ˢ Charres 5ˢ wheeles 5ˢ a Cradle 5	1	0	0
a Jron pott 6ˢ.	0	6	0
Milke vessells tubbs & other nessessarys	2	0	0
Bottles wedges & [illegible] hows	1	8	0
Instruments for his trade	1	0	0
3 bushells of Malt	0	18	0
	176	10	2
posts & Rayles 7	0	7	0
Powder & shott	0	12	6
2 pair of shoes	0	2	0
Due to me from divers debtors	4	0	0

" This is a true Jnventory of all the goods & Chattells of the late deceased Robert Roberts accordinge to our best aprehension : taken by vs :

Regnald foster Seʳ
Tho : Clarke
Thomas knoult[on]

" The Jnventory red in court held at Jpswich the 29 of Sept : 1663
Ᵽ me Robert Lord Cleric."

Susanna Roberts, who was left with a young child at the time of her husband's death, appears to have been a thrifty widow. On April 9, 1666, the town "Agreed with Good-wife Roberds to keepe the sheepe at the Neck for the year ensueing and to have for hir wages 6ˢ Ᵽ weeke." She was to begin on the 16th of that month, and to be paid by the owners of the sheep "at the end of the time," which would be the middle of November.* In August, of that year, she

---

* *Town Records of Ipswich* (copy), vol. 1 : 271 ; (original) vol. 2 : 21.

bought of John Whipple, of Ipswich, for £12, four and a half acres of marsh at Plum Island. On the "last day of february 1666 [1666-67]," as "Susanna Roberts . . . widow," she bought of Richard Jacob, for £4 : 10, six acres more of marsh land at Plum Island, adjoining her first purchase ; the deed was recorded the same day.*

Later, on that day, she was married to Thomas Perrin, of Ipswich, for it is written that " Thomas Perrin & Sussan Roberds, maryed the 28 of February 1666 [1666-67]." †
Thomas Perrin was a worthy citizen of the town. He had a son Thomas, Jr. (a saddler by trade), whose wife was Margaret; they had several children in Ipswich, including Thomas[8] Perrin. It does not appear whether this Thomas, Jr., was son to Thomas[1] Perrin by a former wife or by Susanna. In 1714, Ephraim Roberts, son to Susanna, called Thomas, Jr., "my Bro!"

On June 6, 1667, Thomas Perrin was allowed to keep the sheep, on much the same terms as his predecessors. He signed the agreement — " Thomas Perrin." ‡ It is probable that he lived at the Neck and cared for the sheep, several years. At a town-meeting, held February 11, 1672, complaints having been made "against Thomas Perin, about the Neck," it was "left to the Selectmen to consider of the complaints . . . and report to the Towne how they find it." On February 27, following, " The Towne declared that the halfe acre of Land, that Rob! Roberds had liberty to fence in, and build upon (while he held the little Neck, the Neck being out of their hands, the lease being out) I say the Towne declared the sᵈ halfe acre to be in the Townes hands." At the same time, " The Feoffees and Towne are willing that Thomas Perrin should hold the Land one yeare more, payeing seaven pounds in mafier as before, he ob-

---

serveing to keepe within those limits the Towne hath tyed other p'sons unto, with reference to Swine, and any other sort of Cattell." In February, 1673, Robert Starkweather desired liberty to "hould the house of Tho: Perrin and little Neck, for seaven years." His request "was granted he agreeing with Thomas Perrin about his interest." *

Thomas Perrin moved up into the town; in 1692, his lot was the second "by yᵉ River side between Samuel Ordway's shop, & yᵉ Towne Bridg . . . 24 foot front." In 1697, he had horses on the common; in 1700, a seat was assigned him in the meeting-house; in 1703, he was chosen Constable.†

Not long after his marriage to the widow Susanna Roberts, Thomas Perrin made over to John Roberts, his stepson, that portion of the estate of his father that was coming to him. That he was the eldest son is proved by his receiving the double portion of £20, while his brother Samuel received but £10. The paper is copied nearly in full : ‡ —

"October the 8ᵗʰ Anno Dom 1669

"Thomas Perrin of Jpswich . . . planter," for £20, "payd, that is to Say as it was a legacie or portion designed & ordered by the Court held at Jpswich in & vpon the eight & twentyeth September last past before the date heerof vnto John Roberts my son in law, as in and by the copie of court Role doth & may more at Large appeare . . . I have and by these presents doe . . . confirme vnto the sᵈ John Roberts, a certaine pcell of land both vpland and meadow or marsh ground being in tyme past the propriaty of Robert Roberts ffather of the sᵈ John now deceased the land conteineing by estimation six acres more or lesse, Scituate lyeing & being beyond Jubaque [Chebacco] Riuer Southward, bounded as followeth to witt the vpland bounded by the land of

---

* *Town Records of Ipswich* (copy), vol. 1 : 345, 346, 356.

† *The Hammatt Papers, 1633–1700,* by Abraham Hammatt, 1854, no. 1 : 261.

‡ *Essex County Records, Ipswich Records,* Book 3: 287.

on [one] John Burnam on the west and the marsh bounded in like manner by the land of yᵉ sayd John Burnam on the south and on the north by a creeke that comes from the Saw mill."

(Signed)

"Sealed & deliuered   "Thomas Perrin & a seale "
in the presence of vs
  Wᵐ White
  James coleman
    and a marke "

The date of death of Thomas Perrin does not appear, nor that of his wife Susanna; but, on September 18, 1713, Ephraim Roberts, of Haverhill, as administrator "att Large" upon the estate of "Susanna Roberds of Ipswich," was required to give bond, and was ordered to bring in an inventory "before yᵉ first Monday In June Next Ensueing." * No inventory was recorded. On May 17, 1714, three months after the decease of his elder brother, John, "Ephraim Roberds of Haverhill . . . yeoman, Surviving hier of my father Robert Roberds Late of Jpswich Decᵈ and administratoʳ to yᵉ Estate of my mother Susannah Roberds of Ipswich aforesᵈ Decᵈ Jntestate," for £15, "paid by my Broʳ Thomas Perrin of Jpswich . . . Sadler," quitclaimed to the said Thomas Perrin, "any right ʝ my Selfe my heires or assigns or any of my Broʳ or Sisters of any of the heires Representative in Law vnder them . . . might Claim Either from Estate of My said Father or Mother . . . in the Township of Jpswich "

Witnesses: "Ephraim Roberds " † [seal]
" Phillip Fowler
  Daniel Rogers"

It is remarkable that this estate should be settled under the name of Susanna Roberts, as her marriage to Thomas Perrin, in 1667, is fully proved. In 1691, question arising

---

* *Essex County Probate*, Book 311 : 40.
† *Essex County Deeds*, Book 28 : 3.

as to the use of the beach at Little Neck, the following depositions were presented in the County Court held at Ipswich : —

"The Deposition of William Hodgkins Senr aged about 69 years

"This Deponent Testifieth that he with Divers other persons hath occupyed vsed & Jmproued, ye beach adjoyneing to the Little neck, Jn Jpswich, as a Towne privelidg, & Common Land for makeing & curing fish, aboue fiftye years more or Less & neuer was demanded, anything for Rent, Either from Mr William Paine, nor Robert Robards said Pains Tennant, nor from Widow Robards, nor from John Robards, nor from old father Stark-weather, nor from John Pengery [Pingree], which persons all did Jn their day Jmproue both ye plow land & pasture Land, apper-taineing to said neck, but none of them, did Either directly, or Jndirectly, demand any thing for rent, Either of me or any person Else that J know of, for vsing & Jmproueing the afforesaid Beach, but did allwayes owne, it to be a priveledged place to make, & Cure fish vpon, nor hinder us, for Erecting & building Stages, and other houses there vpon, untill this present year 1691./

"John Robards aged about 45, years Testifieth that to his knowledg what is aboue written, is Certainly True, for thirty seven years past and further adds, that his father Robards did Tell him this deponant that Mr William Payne, had forbid, him, hindering a fishing Trade vpon, ye Little neck beach, because it was, a Towne priviledg & therefore my father, gaue me this de-ponent, the like Charge that J should not Jntervpt, So beneficiall a designe, which J allways attended

"Sworne Jn Court at Jpswich Sep^t ye 29th 1691 by both par-ties as atteste

Thos Wade. Cler "*

ISSUE

I. John², b. about 1646, in Ipswich. (Vide infra.)
II. Samuel², b. about 1648 or 1649, in Ipswich. He was a mari-ner, and died unmarried, in June, 1670, soon after reaching

---

* *Essex County Deeds, Ipswich Records*, Book 5 : 503.

his majority. The ten pounds he received from the estate of his father is mentioned only in the following inventory : * —

"An Jnventory of the goods & estate of Samuel Roberts late of Jpswich Deceased taken the 21ᵗʰ day of June 1670

	li	s	d
"Jmprimis his wareing Aparrell & linnen with it 3 hatts & 2 p shooes	22	7	00
it in bookes	02	0	00
it 2 Combs 2 Rasors Jnkhorn & Sizars & hoane	00	8	00
it 2 P Compasses 5ˢ	00	5	00
& 2 Chests 10ˢ	00	10	00
it 1 hogshead of feathers 2ˡⁱ	02	00	00
Jn money 6ˡⁱ 8ˢ 7ᵈ	06	08	07½
it his portion giuen him by the Court	10	00	00
	43	15	7½
A fowling peece 30ˢ houlsters brest plate & belt 10ˢ	02	00	00

"This Jnventory was alowed in court at Salem 29 : 4 : 70

atteste Hilliard Veren. Cler :

	li	s	d
"his funerall Charge	2	10	00

"This Jnventory was taken & Apprised by us whose names are underwritten the day & yeare aboue written

Robert Pers
James Chute."

III. Ephraim ², b. about 1650, in Ipswich. "Ephraim Roberts & Dorothie Hendrick" were mar. Aug. 24, 1684, in Haverhill, Mass. She was b. May 31, 1659, in Haverhill, and was the sixth and youngest child to Daniel Hendrick by his first wife, "Dorothie" (Pike) Hendrick.† Dorothy Roberts d. Jan. 9, 1701–02, aged forty-three years. Her husband mar., second (no date given), the widow Hannah How,‡ who survived him.

Daniel Hendrick, on March 13, 1692–93, "for that good Will which I bear to my naturall daughter Dorothy now yᵉ wife of Ephraim Roberts and to my Son in Law Ephraim Roberts," confirmed to them "five acres of land in Haverhill

---

* *Essex County Court Papers*, Book 16 : 29.
† *Haverhill Births, Marriages, and Deaths*, vol. 2 : 57, 21.
‡ *Haverhill Births, Marriages, and Deaths*, vol. 2 : 57.

caled ox comon land which ye Said Ephraim had in his possession Seuen yeares agoe." At the same time, Daniel Hendrick, for £20, confirmed " unto my Son in Law Ephraim
Roberts," land in the third division which he had purchased
of John Ayer, beside " ye Town Brooke of Hauerhill by Old
Spicutt path So caled together with a piece of . . . meadow
by Estimation Twelue acres." Both deeds were signed by
"Daniel Hendrick," and witnessed by " Samuel Dalton and
Deborah Hendrick." *

In 1694, Ephraim Roberts bought of Henry Dow several
parcels of land in Haverhill that belonged to the estate of his
late grandfather, Thomas Dow, also the home lot of Edward
Clarke — " seuen acres with housing," etc. — " On ye South
West End by ye High Way vpon ye Riuer Merrimack," adjoining land " now in ye hands of s^d Ephraim Roberts," which
formerly was John Heath's and after that Samuel Shepard's.†
In these deeds Ephraim Roberts was called a cooper. In
going to Haverhill he simply joined a movement among the
young men from Ipswich to open another new settlement.
Moses Pengry, Jr., Aaron Pengry, John Pengry, and Moses
Burnam asked the town of Haverhill, in 1693–94, to have
land laid out to them in the " 4th division ; " and other
familiar names of Ipswich appear in the early records.

At Haverhill; Ephraim Roberts bore a modest part in
town affairs. In the town-meeting of March 22, 1692–93,
he was chosen a fence-viewer with his brother-in-law, Israel
Hendrick, to view the town "between the Mill brook and
Great Plain ; " March 1, 1694–95, he was chosen to the same
office, " For the Great Plain & Eastwards." In December,
1698, " Eph : Roberds " was one of thirty-four subscribers for
"setting up the new meeting house, as soon as the glass
windows are finished and set up." March 7, 1698–99, he
was chosen surveyor of highways. At the same town-meeting, in answer to a petition from " Eph : Roberds . . . for a
grant of liberty of building a Saw mill upon the place where
the old sawmill was set . . . and to have full liberty of

---

* *Essex County Deeds*, Book 10 : 124, 76.
† *Essex County Deeds*, Book 10 : 123.

that stream," the town refused, as that privilege had been "long since granted to others." In answer to a petition of Ephraim Roberts and several other men, at town-meeting held April 9, 1700, the town refused to allow them to "build a sawmill at Spickett River stream." March 4, 1700–01, he was chosen selectman, and again on March 7, 1709–10.* With rank of Sergeant, Ephraim Roberts "led seven sentinels from the Haverhill garrison," in March, 1706–07.†

As the only surviving heir, and executor of the estates of his father and mother, he sold in 1714, to "my Bro? Thomas Perrin, of Ipswich," all right of the heirs or their children to the real or personal property of Robert and Susanna Roberts, of Ipswich.‡

Ephraim Roberts, of Haverhill, died after October, 1732. His will, dated Oct. 27, 1732, when he was about eighty-two years of age, was as follows: § —

"In the name of God amen This Twenty seventh day of october anno Domini 1732 in the [blank] year of his Majestys Reign: ɟ Ephraim Roberds of Haverhill in the County of Essex in Provence of the Massachusetts Bay in New England yeoman being very sik and apprehensive that my grate and last chang draws near being of perfect mind and memory and sound understanding thanks be given to almighty God. ɟ therefore make and ordain this my Last will and Testament: first ɟ reccomend my soul to almighty God who gave it and my body to the earth to be decently buried att the discretion of my Executor hereafter named hopeing and trusting that By the Power of almighty God through the merits of Christ my redeemer ɟ shall Receve the same again: and as touching such worldly Estate wherewith it hath pleased God to bless me with in this Life: ɟ give demise and dispose thereof in maner and form following: viz

"Imprimis: J give and bequeath unto Hannah my derely beloved wife the one half of my Dwelling House from the botum of the celer to the top of the house ɟ also give her one hors sutable for her to ride on and also three milch Cows and all my sheep and also

* *Town Records of Haverhill*, vol. 2: 307, 323, 345, 348, 349, 363, 370, 413.
† *Massachusetts Province Laws*, 1703–1707, vol. 8: 677.
‡ Vide page 951.
§ *Essex County Probate* (original), No. 23814.

sutable hay and pastering for the s^d cretures ɟ also give her one fatt co[illegible] and also all my swine J also give her thirty bushils of Jndian Corn and ten bushils Jnglish corn J also give her all my Houset stuf: and it is my will and pleasure that all those moveables that my wife shall leave att her decease undisposed of shall be equaly devided among my three daughters namely Hannah Patience & Mary J also give my wife the free and full improvement of that part of my Homstead that lyeth between the highway by my house and the fishing River except four Acres which is for my son Daniel and also convenient pastering by my house on the east side of the highway during her natural life for her three cows and one hors ɟ also let my wife have the whol use of one yoak of my oxen dureing the time she remains my widow and then they are to be my executors ɟ also give her the use of my seed plow

"Secondly: ɟ give and bequeth unto my beloved son Samuels two Children namely Samuel Roberts and Mary Roberts thirty pounds twenty pounds to my grandson Samuel Roberts to be paid to him when he shal come to the age of twenty one years and to my s^d grandaughter Mary ten pounds in or as money on or before her marriage day these somes to be paid by my executor

"Thirdly: ɟ give and bequeth unto my beloved son Ephraim Roberds the sum of thirty pounds in money to be paid by my executor att the end of a full year after my decease ɟ also give him one coat wescoat & brecks which ɟ had last made for me

"Fourthly: ɟ give and bequeth unto my beloved son Jonathan all that land that was my son Davids and also all my land lying on the east side of the way by my dwelling house excepting what was before reserved for my wife and also all my real and personal estate which ɟ have not allredy desposed of in this my last will or shall not depose of herein: and it is my will and pleasure that my s^d son Jonathan pay to such persons as ɟ shall here after name the sums that J shall apoint he being also to be my Executor

"Fifthly: ɟ give and beqeth unto my beloved son Daniel four Acres of land adjoyning to his Dwelling house where he now lives with about four Acres of land on the west side of the fishing River adjoyning to s^d River att my decease and also about Twelve acres of paster land which J bought of m^r James Peker and also all my building that is my dwelling house and barne where ɟ now dwell with about sixteen acres of land lying between the fishing River and the highway it being that part of my Homsted where my s^d buildings now stand this sixteen Acres with my building J reserve for my wife dureing her remaineing my widow: ɟ further order and

ap [worn] my son Daniel to pay unto David felton of Salem
my belove [worn] Grandson fifteen pounds in money or bills of
credit att the end of [worn] year after my decease ɟ also order and
apoint my son Dan [worn] pay unto my wel beloved Daughter
Hannah fifteen pounds in [worn] or bils of credit att or before
the end of two full years after my decease ɟ further will and
order that my sᵈ son Daniel pay to my two beloved Grandaughters
the Daughters of my beloved son David Anne & Sarah fifteen
pounds in money to each att or before their marriage day also J
give my son Daniel one coat wescoat and brecks all well lined

" Sixthly : J give and beqeth unto John Atwood the child that ɟ
have brought up from a child to this day as a reward for his obedi-
ence the time past and to incourage him to be obedient and faithfull to my wife after my decease : all my Right in a medow known
by the name of rubigge [Rubbish] Medow and also fifty pounds
in money at the end of a full year after he shall arive to the
age of Twenty one years provided he live with me or my wife
until he shall come to sᵈ age and if he do not live to the age of
Twenty one years then the sᵈ medow and money is to be my Executors : and if my wife shall not live nor my self til the sᵈ John
Atwood comes to the age of Twenty one so much time as he is
freed from serveing me or my wife before he is Twenty one years
old so much is to be abated of his fifty pounds reconing his time
from the date hereof

" Seventhly : J give and bequeth unto my well beloved Daughter Patience the sum of fifteen pounds in money or bills of credit to be
paid unto her att the end of two full years after my decease to be
paid by my son Jonathan my Executor

" Eighthly : J give and bequeath unto my wel beloved Doughter
mary the some of fifteen pounds in money att the end of two full
years after my decease to be paid to her by my son Jonathan my
Executor

" Lastly it is my will and pleasure and order that my son Jonathan
pay to the sᵈ samuel Roberds and mary Roberds and to my son
Ephraim and to John Atwod and to my daughters Patience and
Mary the several sums allredy named : & at the time before described : ɟ also will and ordain that all those Just debts which in
Duty right or Conscience ɟ owe to any person or persons whatsoever together with my [worn] funeral Expences & Charges be
well and truly paid by my sᵈ son Jonathan in Convenient season
after my decease whom ɟ Constitute sole Executor of this my Last
will and testament Hereby revoking disanulling and disalowing all
former wills Testament Legaces and Executors by me at any time

heretofore willed Constituted and made & Ratifying allowing and Confirming this and no other to be my last will and testament Jn witnes & for Confirmation hereof J have hereto set my hand and seal the day and Year first written

[seal]

" Signed sealed and Delivered by the said
Ephraim Roberds to be his Last will
and Testament before us
Joseph heath
　　　　his
Joseph X Heath jr
　　　mark
Daniel Little "

This will is one of the few originals in the Essex County Probate, and is fairly legible, though much worn at one side. There is nothing in the Probate Records that shows when it was proved, or how the estate was settled.

Hannah Roberts was the widow of John How, of Ipswich, when she became the wife of Ephraim Roberts, of Haverhill, about 1702. On Feb. 8, 1712, Ephraim Roberts was appointed guardian to her son, James How, " a minor upwards of 14 years." * Hannah Roberts died in Methuen ; her will, dated March 22, 1744–45, was proved May 13, 1745. She appointed her " well beloved son James How, to be sole executor ; " he was to have one cow, a yearling and calf, one sheep, and all other real and personal estate. She gave to her " beloved Daughter Martha How, who has been very helpful to Me in my Old age & sickness," a sheep, bedding, and household stuff. To granddaughter, " Susannah Herriman Daughter of my Daught^r Herriman Dec^d," she bequeathed " one of my wearing caps ; " to " Daughter Mary, wife of Moses Stevens . . . two bed blankets and one cap." Her will was signed with a mark, and witnessed by Samuel Parker, Samuel Pingry, and Moses Pingry.†

---

* *Essex County Historical and Genealogical Register*, vol. 1 : 16.
† *Essex County Probate*, Book 326 : 286–287.

Issue* by first wife: 1. Hannah³, b. Sept. 20, 1685, in Haverhill. There is no record of her marriage or death in Haverhill, but she was living in 1732, when her father made his will, wife of Nathaniel Putnam.

2. Samuel³, son to Ephraim², b. Aug. 7, 1687, in Haverhill. He married Abigail Ladd, no date given.

In 1714, with his wife Abigail, Nathaniel Ladd and Jonathan Ladd, both of Norwich, Conn., Samuel Roberts, of Haverhill, conveyed all right in the property of "our Brother Ezekiel Lad Late of Boxford Dec⁴," to John Chadwick, of Boxford. Samuel Roberts lived near the Town Common, in Haverhill, on land adjoining that of his father, which he bought, in March, 1710–11, of Joseph Heath.†

Samuel Roberts d. March 29, 1720, in Haverhill; his widow, Abigail, was married, Jan. 31, 1721–22, to William Johnson, of that town. She d. Aug. 2, 1736, in Haverhill.‡

Issue by first husband: I. Mary⁴, b. June 20, 1718, in Haverhill.

II. Samuel⁴, b. Dec. 6, 1720, in Haverhill. Both these children were mentioned in the will of their grandfather, Ephraim Roberts.

Issue by second husband: III. William Johnson, b. July 21, 1723, in Haverhill.

IV. Abigail Johnson, b. Sept. 25, 1726, in Haverhill.

V. Caleb Johnson, b. Sept. 18, 1730, in Haverhill; d. Sept. 10, 1737.

3. Ephraim³, son to Ephraim², b. Jan. 1, 1689–90, in Haverhill. He mar., Feb. 7, 1714–15, Hannah Smith.§

Issue: I. "Mehetabel"⁴, b. March 9, 1716–17, in Haverhill.

II. Abigail⁴, b. March 3, 1718–19, in Haverhill.

III. Hannah⁴, b. May 10, 1722, in Haverhill; d. May 28, 1722.

IV. Rachel⁴, b. Oct. 30, 1723, in Haverhill.

---

* *Haverhill Births, Marriages, and Deaths*, vol. 2: 57.
† *Essex County Deeds*, Book 29: 87, 116.
‡ *Haverhill Births, Marriages, and Deaths*, vol. 2: 135; vol. 3: 131.
§ *Haverhill Births, Marriages, and Deaths*, vol. 2: 110.

V. "Meriam"[4], b. Aug. 30, 1727, in Haverhill.

VI. Ephraim[4], b. Aug. 9, 1729, in Haverhill; d. Jan. 19, 1730.

VII. David[4], b. June 1, 1732, in Haverhill.

4. "Mehetabel"[3], daughter to Ephraim[2], b. April 10, 1692, in Haverhill. Mehitable Roberts was mar., about 1710, to Ebenezer[3] Felton, of Salem, Mass. He was b. about 1685, son to Nathaniel[2] and Ann (Horn) Felton, of Salem.

This Felton family enjoyed a position of prominence in Salem, and married with other families equally prominent, as the Endicott, Goodale, Pitman, Foot, Waters, and Tompkins. Nathaniel[1] Felton, "the Planter," was b. about 1615, in England. In 1633, he married at Salem, Mary[2] Skelton, daughter to Rev. Samuel[1] Skelton, the first minister of the First Church. Ann[2] Horn, the wife of their son Nathaniel[2], was daughter to Deacon John[1] Horn, of the First Church. Ebenezer[3] Felton was a housewright by trade; his wife Mehitable was baptized Feb. 21, 1713, with her infant son David, and died not long after. Her husband mar., second, Oct., 1716, Jehoadan Ward, b. March, 1690–91, daughter to John and Jehoadan (——) Ward, of Salem, by whom he had nine children. About 1740, Ebenezer Felton went to New Salem, Franklin County, Mass., with his five sons, David[4], Ebenezer[4], Amos[4], Benjamin,[4] and Nathaniel[4]. The father died there, in 1776, aged ninety years. His will, dated Nov. 24, 1762, was proved Sept., 1776. His children were all born in Essex County.*

> Issue by first wife: I. David[4] Felton, b. about 1711, in Salem; mar. 1736, Sarah Houlton, of Salem. He was mentioned in the will of his grandfather, Ephraim Roberts, with a bequest of £15.† In 1740, he went with his father to New Salem.

5. David[3] (twin), son to Ephraim[2], b. Sept. 23, 1696, in Haverhill; mar. March 24, 1718–19, Mary Dow.‡

---

* *The Felton Family*, by Cyrus Felton, 1886: 18–19, 13, 11
† Vide page 957.
‡ *Haverhill Births, Marriages, and Deaths*, vol. 2: 125.

. His death occurred in September, 1722, and administration of his estate was granted Oct. 1, 1722, to his widow, Mary, and father, Ephraim Roberts, who gave bond, etc.* His widow, Mary Roberts, was mar. Nov. 5, 1724, to Nathaniel Marble, of Haverhill.† It is probable that she was the "widow Mary Marble" who was mar. March 17, 1756, in Haverhill, to Obadiah Belknap.‡

Issue by first husband: I. Anna⁴. The date of her birth is not recorded, but she was mentioned in the will of her grandfather, Ephraim Roberts.

II. Sarah⁴, b. April 19, 1722, in Haverhill.

Issue by second husband: III. Rachel Marble, b. July 13, 1727, in Haverhill.

IV. Hannah Marble, b. Oct. 30, 1729, in Haverhill.

V. Abigail Marble, b. Feb. 1, 1731–32, in Haverhill.

VI. Phebe Marble, b. May 12, 1737, in Haverhill.

VII. Nathaniel Marble, b. March 19, 1741–42, in Haverhill.

6. Jonathan³ (twin), son to Ephraim², b. Sept. 23, 1696, in Haverhill; died the same day.

7. Jonathan³, son to Ephraim², b. Jan. 31, 1698–99, in Haverhill. He mar. April 6, 1731, in Haverhill, "Abiah Belknapp." On July 6, 1730, he and his brother Ephraim, yeomen, of Haverhill, sold to Moses Copp, for £40, forty acres in that town, "laid out to the Original Right of Bartholomew Heath." Their signatures were — " Ephraim Roberds" and "Jonathan Roberds." Jonathan Roberts enlisted for the military service at Louisburg, 1744–1745 and "Died at Cape Brittain January 15, 1745/6." §

Issue: I. Hannah⁴, b. Oct. 9, 1731; d. Nov. 26, 1737, in Haverhill.

II. Amos⁴, b. May 25, 1733; d. Nov. 15, 1737, in Haverhill.

---

* *Essex County Probate*, Book 319 : 57.
† *Haverhill Births, Marriages, and Deaths*, vol. 3 : 2.
‡ *The Essex Antiquarian*, vol. 8 : 142.
§ *Haverhill Births, Marriages, and Deaths*, vol. 3 : 26.

III. Mary⁴, b. Sept. 18, 1735; d. Oct. 3, 1737, in Haverhill.

IV. Zilla⁴, b. Jan. 18, 1736–37; d. Nov. 13, 1737, in
Haverhill.

Three of these children are recorded as having died of
the "throat distemper" which caused so many deaths among
the children of Haverhill in November and December, 1737.*
The death of Mary, in October, was probably from the same
disease.

V. Susannah⁴, b. Aug. 16, 1738, in Haverhill.

VI. Meribah⁴, b. May 28, 1741, in Haverhill.

VII. Tamor⁴, b. Sept. 4, 1743, in Haverhill.

8. Daniel³, son to Ephraim², b. April 25, 1701, in Haverhill. He married Martha Heath, of Haverhill (no
date given).† She was b. March 21, 1702, in Haverhill, daughter to Joseph and Hannah (Bradley) Heath,
of that town.

On Nov. 26, 1722, Ephraim Roberts, for "Love & Naturall affection . . . towards my son Daniel Roberts," gave him
four acres, "it being a part of my Homestead," adjoining
land of Joseph Heath and the highway. In 1738, "Danˡ
Roberdes of Haverhill" conveyed land which he bought of
"my Said Father in Law Joseph Heath;" in 1739, Daniel
sold land in Haverhill to his son Daniel Roberts, Jr.;‡ in
1750, father and son were mentioned in Province deeds as
of Hampstead, N. H.

The town of Hampstead, N. H., was set off Jan. 19, 1749,
from Haverhill. The History of Hampstead states that
Daniel and Jonathan Roberts "settled on tracts purchased
in 1742, part of Stephen Kent's 5th division of lands."
"Abiah Roberds," probably wife of Jonathan, " made settlement on a tract north of the Island Pond." §

Daniel Roberts, of Hampstead, N. H., served in the

---

* *The Essex Antiquarian*, vol. 1 : 11.

† *Haverhill Births, Marriages, and Deaths*, vol. 2 : 133.

‡ *Essex County Deeds*, Book 41 : 146; Book 74 : 268; Book 79 : 107.

§ *A Memorial History of Hampstead, New Hampshire*, by Harriette Eliza
Noyes, 1903, vol. 1 : 156, 151.

"Crown Point Expedition" of 1756. He entered service as private, on April 22, and served until Nov. 7, of that year, a period of twenty-eight weeks, four days ; he was in Captain Edmund Mooers' company, Colonel Ichabod Plaisted's regiment. In a roll of that company, dated July 26, 1756, his age was given as fifty-six years, "occupation labourer," birthplace Haverhill, residence Hampstead; in a roll of Oct. 11, he was reported sick in camp at Fort William Henry.[*]

About a year later, Daniel Roberts was dead; his will, dated April 30, 1756, was allowed Oct. 11, 1757. It mentioned his wife Martha, daughters Hannah, Sarah, and Mary Foster, and three children of his deceased son Daniel; daughter Hannah to be executrix. Five children of Daniel and Martha Roberts were recorded in Haverhill, three of whom died of "throat distemper" in the fall of 1737.[†]

Issue: I. Daniel[4], b. March 6, 1721–22, in Haverhill. His wife was Meribah ——— ; they lived in Hampstead near his father. Daniel Roberts enlisted as private April 24, 1755, for the Crown Point expedition. He appears to have served in "Captain Joseph Eastman's co., Col. Joseph Blanchard's regt. . . . time of discharge Oct. 24, 1755."[‡] In an account rendered May 25, 1757, by Meribah Roberts, widow and administratrix of Daniel Roberts, Jr., the date of his death is given Oct. 16, 1755. On Dec. 28, 1768, an additional account was brought in by the widow Meribah.

Issue: 1. Phebe[5], b. "6, 15, 1748," in Hampstead.
2. Meribah[5], b. "8, 23, 1750," in Hampstead. She was mar. Sept. 28, 1769, to John Atwood, Jr., son to John and Abigail (Sanders) Atwood, of Haverhill. John Atwood, Sr., must have been the youth of that name mentioned in the will of

---

[*] *Massachusetts Archives*, Muster Rolls, vol. 95: 112 ; vol. 94: 347, 505.
[†] *The Essex Antiquarian*, vol. I : 11.
[‡] *Report of the Adjutant-General of the State of New Hampshire*, 1866, vol. 2 : 135.

Ephraim² Roberts; he was b. 1714, mar. Jan. 7, 1735, Abigail Sanders, and d. Jan. 1, 1812, in Haverhill, aged ninety-seven years, seven months.

3. Jonathan⁵, b. "10, 15, 1754," in Hampstead; d. four months after his father.

II. Dorothy⁴, b. Feb. 28, 1724-25, in Haverhill.

III. Joseph⁴, b. March 7, 1730, in Haverhill. He probably was one of the children who died of diphtheria, as he never was mentioned afterwards.

IV. Priscilla⁴, b. Aug. 28, 1732, in Haverhill.

V. Martha⁴, b. March 4, 1735, in Haverhill.

VI. Mary⁴, b. "7, 1736," in Hampstead. She was mar. May 10, 1755, in Hampstead, to Ezekiel Foster.

VII. Hannah⁴, b. "4, 19, 1740," in Hampstead. She was executrix of her father's will.

VIII. Sarah⁴, b. "6, 1, 1745," in Hampstead.

IX. Samuel⁴, b. "9, 22, 1748," in Hampstead; he probably died young, as he was not mentioned in his father's will.

Issue by second wife: 9. Patience², daughter to Ephraim² Roberts, b. July 5, 1703, in Haverhill. She was mar. Dec. 25, 1723, in Haverhill, to "Stephen Herriman," or Harriman. She d. Aug. 26, 1742, in Haverhill, aged thirty-nine years.*

Issue: I. Hannah Harriman, b. Oct. 13, 1724, in Haverhill.

II. "Mehetabel" Harriman, b. Jan. 14, 1725-26, in Haverhill.

III. Stephen Harriman, b. March 9, 1727-28, in Haverhill.

IV. Edmund Harriman, b. Oct. 1, 1729, in Haverhill.

V. Susanna Harriman, b. Oct. 12, 1731, in Haverhill.

VI. Ebenezer Harriman, b. Aug. 11, 1733, in Haverhill.

VII. James Harriman, b. Jan. 31, 1734-35, in Haverhill.

VIII. Asa Harriman, b. March 5, 1736-37, in Haverhill.

10. Mary², daughter to Ephraim² Roberts, b. Oct. 17,

---

* *Haverhill Births, Marriages, and Deaths*, vol. 2: 142.

1705, in Haverhill. She was mar. April 23, 1724, to Moses Stevens, of Haverhill.*

Issue: I. Moses Stevens, b. Sept. 29, 1726, in Haverhill.

II. David Stevens, b. Oct. 10, 1728, in Haverhill.

III. Mary Stevens, b. Oct. 29, 1730, in Haverhill.

IV. Hannah Stevens, b. Oct. 3, 1732, in Haverhill.

V. Reuben Stevens, b. Dec. 1, 1734, in Haverhill.

IV. Hannah[2], daughter to Robert[1] and Susanna Roberts, b. about 1656, in Ipswich. "William Whitridge and Hannah Roberts" were mar. March 4, 1684, by William Brown, Esq.†

William[2] Whittredge, b. March 31, 1658, in Ipswich, was son to William[1] Whittredge ‡ by his second wife, Frances, who d. April 26, 1658, in Ipswich.§ The father was from Benindon, County Kent, England. He came to New England in the *Elizabeth*, in 1635; his age was thirty-six years, his wife Elizabeth was thirty, and their son Thomas was ten years of age. His wife Frances having died, William[1] Whittredge mar., third, about 1663, Susanna, widow of Anthony Colby. In April, 1637, "William Whitred" was a Pequod soldier; in 1638, he first was mentioned in the Ipswich records, though he probably was there soon after his arrival in 1635. Under date of 1639, it was mentioned that he had sold to Thomas Smith his house and lot in the street called West End Street.‖ About 1651, he was possessed of ten acres of "Marsh bounded by a creek next to Robert Roberds toward the West." ¶ William[1] Whittredge was a carpenter; his death occurred Dec. 9, 1668, in Ipswich, "his inventory showing estate one third less than his debts." His son Thomas[2] married twice, and had one child by each

---

* *Haverhill Births, Marriages, and Deaths*, vol. 3: 1.

† *Gloucester Births, Marriages, and Deaths, 1642–1780*: 313.

‡ *Ipswich Births, Marriages, and Deaths, 1635–1687*: 2.

§ *Essex County Historical and Genealogical Register*, vol. 1: 42.

‖ *Ipswich in the Massachusetts Bay Colony*, by Rev. Thomas Franklin Waters, 1905: 82, 125, 372, 339.

¶ *Town Records of Ipswich* (copy), vol. 1: 180.

wife.* Their immediate descendants lived in Beverly, occupying positions of wealth and responsibility.

William ³ Whittredge and his wife Hannah probably went to Gloucester soon after their marriage, as all their children were registered there. He was a mariner. In March, 1705–06, he sold to Henry Haskell, of Gloucester, for £5, "One Commonage . . . within yᵉ township of Gloucester," with a right in all the woods, timbers, waters, etc. "July yᵉ 16ᵗʰ 1706," he sold to Isaac Eveleth, for £5, land in Gloucester, "on yᵉ South Side of Squamme river or Ferry contayning One acre . . . with yᵉ dwelling house & housing vpon it together with all other privileges to yᵉ same belonging." His signature in both deeds was the same : —

"William Whitteredge " † [seal]

He does not appear to have left the town, since his death was recorded there : " Wᵐ Whitridge (aged about 70 years) Dyed Aug. 8, 1726." ‡ The date of death of his wife Hannah is not given.

Issue : 1. Hannah ⁸ Whittredge, b. Jan. 4, 1684–85, in Gloucester.

2. Samuel ⁸ Whittredge, b. July 30, 1692, in Gloucester. He was mar. Jan. 20, 1720, by the Rev. John White, pastor of the First Church of Gloucester, to Hannah Whiston (?), of Barnstable. " Mʳ Samuel Whitereg was drowned near the new Barr of the Island of Sable May 10, 1732, in the 42 year of his Eage." His widow appears to have been the Hannah Whittredge who was mar. May 2, 1735, in Gloucester, by Rev. Benjamin Bradstreet, to Joseph Harraden.§

Issue : I. Mary ⁴ Whittredge, b. June 16, 1722, in Gloucester ; d. young.

II. Mary ⁴ Whittredge, b. March 4, 1724, in Gloucester ; d. April 14, 1726, aged two years.

---

* *New England Historical and Genealogical Register*, vol. 14 : 307 ; vol. 8 : 167.

† *Essex County Deeds*, Book 22 : 263 ; Book 20 : 59.

‡ *Gloucester Births, Marriages, and Deaths, 1642–1780* : 313.

§ *Gloucester Births, Marriages, and Deaths, 1642–1780* : 313, 314, 126.

III. Abigail⁴ Whittredge, b. May 18, 1726, in Gloucester.

IV. Sarah⁴ Whittredge, b. May, 1728, in Gloucester.

V. Susanna⁴ Whittredge, b. July 19, 1730, in Gloucester; d. Sept. 3, 1730, aged about six weeks.

VI. William⁴ Whittredge, b. Oct. 17, 1731, in Gloucester; he was mar. Dec. 8, 1755, by Rev. Benjamin
Bradstreet, to Mary Saville. Issue: 1. William⁵.
2. Oliver Saville⁵. 3. Mary⁵.

3. Susanna³ Whittredge, b. Feb. 26, 1697, in Gloucester.
She was mar. Jan. 11, 1722, by the Rev. John White,
to "Nathaniel Soams," or Somes, of Gloucester.*

Issue: I. Nathaniel Somes, b. May 25, 1723, in Gloucester.

II. Susanna Somes, b. Nov. 19, 1725, in Gloucester.
There probably were other children.

V. Abigail², daughter to Robert¹ Roberts, b. March 27, 1658,
in Ipswich.† She does not appear further.

VI. Patience², daughter to Robert¹ Roberts, b. "about 20 Feb.,
1660," in Ipswich.‡ In 1667, when she was seven years
old, she was killed by a log from a fence falling upon her.
The report of the coroner's jury is as follows: § —

"We whose names vnder wrighten being warned By the Con-
stabell to examine the maner of the death of Pacent Roberds:
acording To our best vnderstanding & the best information we
coûd gett is as foloweth: ther was two: children being together on
[one] was this deceased child Pacents Roberds aged about seuen
yeres the other a boy hir Brother between 4 or 5 yeres of age:
the girlle that was found dead was found lying cros two loggs
vpon her Backe & a logge aboute 20 ffeete lying vpon hir . . . this
doth appeare by hir sister that found hir: the littell boye being
caryed with vs to the place wher the decᵈ child had layne showed
vs how his sister satte vpon a small logg vnder a logg ffence he
the littell boy was clambering vpe the fenc a logg ffell vpon his
sister & beate hir Backwarde & this doth apeare to vs to be the
death of pacente Roberds by the lying or maner of lying of the

* *Gloucester Births, Marriages, and Deaths, 1642–1780*: 270.
† *Ipswich Births, Marriages, and Deaths, 1635–1687*: 2.
‡ *Ipswich Births, Marriages, and Deaths, 1635–1687*: 6.
§ *Essex County Court Papers*, Book 13: 26.

logge & by the browses [bruises] that we found vpon hir . . .
arms & hir Back

"Tho Clarke	John Newmarch.
Edward Chapman	John Brown.
Andrew Petters	Nathaniel Treadwell
Roberd Perce	ffreegrace Nortton.
Robert Lord	Robert Duch.
Jacob ffoster.	Joseph Brown:

" The abouenamed appeared before me feb 24 1667: and gaue in
their verdict aboue written   Daniel Denison."

VII. Richard[2], son to Robert[1] Roberts, b. about 1662 or 1663,
        in Ipswich. He probably was the little boy who was
        with his sister Patience, when she was killed.

In 1697, his name was in a list of those citizens of Ipswich
who were entitled to "horse commonage," he having registered, on May 15, "1 black mare, 2 years old, wth 1 white
foot and a starr in her forehead."[*]   In 1700, he had seat
number twelve in the meeting-house.[†]

On May 1, 1712, the name " Richard Roberds " appeared
on a petition for a minister in " The Hamlet." The request
was granted May 22, following, to take effect as soon as the
petitioners should " build a meeting house and call an ortho-
dox minister to preach y[e] Gospel to them."[‡]   Richard Roberts died before 1715, at which time his brother Ephraim, as
sole survivor of the children, administered upon the estate of
their parents.[§]

The wife of Richard evidently was the "Elizabeth Roberts wife to Old Father Roberts" mentioned in a catalogue
of women who belonged to the Third Church of Ipswich, "in
its first formation."[‖]   The number of children born to them
is unknown ; only three can be identified.

Issue: 1. John[3].   "John Roberds" and Mary Abbott

---

[*] *Town Records of Ipswich* (copy), vol. 1 : 268.

[†] *The Hammatt Papers, 1633–1700*, by Abraham Hammatt, 1854; no. 1:
288.

[‡] *Maine Historical and Genealogical Recorder*, vol. 9 : 348.

[§] Vide page 951.

[‖] *Records of the Third Church of Ipswich, now Hamilton* (copy), vol. 1 : 5.

were mar. March 16, 1720–21, in the Third Parish of Ipswich. In 1727, they were members of the Third Church, "in full communion." * After the birth of their fifth child, in 1733, there is no further mention of this family in the town, church, or county records.

Issue : † I. John [4], bap. Dec. 17, 1721, in the Third Church.

    II. Richard [4], bap. Jan. 12, 1723[–24], in the Third Church.

    III. Joseph [4], bap. Aug. 25, 1728, in the Third Church.

    IV. Benjamin [4], bap. June 21, 1730, in the Third Church.

    V. A son [4], bap. Aug. 12, 1733, in the Third Church.

2. Elizabeth [3]. She was admitted to the Third Church, May 27, 1722, as "Elizabeth Roberts." ‡

3. David [3], b. 1704, in Ipswich. David Roberts and Elizabeth [4] Brown, both of Ipswich, were published Jan. 3, 1729[–30] ; they were mar. Feb. 18, 1729–30, in the Third Parish.§ She was b. 1711, daughter to Joseph [3], Jr., and Elizabeth (Abbott) Brown (Joseph [2], Edward [1] Brown, of Ipswich). The name David Roberts is in a list of members who joined the Third Church, Feb. 4, 1727–28 ; "Elizabeth y[e] wife of David Roberts" was admitted to full communion, Aug. 8, 1736.‖ She died, his widow, Dec. 23, 1797, in Ipswich.

"David Roberds" was a mason by trade. The first land that he bought consisted of five acres, in Ipswich, "in the Limits of y[e] Second precincts of s[d] Town called y[e] Hamlet . . . [with] y[e] Homestead of Lands whereon y[e] House & Barn Stands," adjoining land of Samuel Knowlton and "W[m]

---

* *Records of the Third Church of Ipswich, now Hamilton* (original), vol. 1 ; also (copy) vol. 1 : 24, 7.

† *Ipswich Births, Marriages, and Deaths, 1635-1687* : 174 ; also *Records of the Third Church of Ipswich, now Hamilton* (copy), vol. 1 : 14, 15, 17, 19.

‡ *Records of the Third Church of Ipswich* (original), vol. 1 ; also (copy) vol. 1 : 6.

§ *Records of the Third Church of Ipswich, now Hamilton* (copy), vol. 1 : 24.

‖ *Records of the Third Church of Ipswich, now Hamilton* (original), vol. 1 ; also (copy) vol. 1 : 10.

Maxies Land," and another tract "on yᵉ Southerly Side of yᵉ Road passing before sᵈ Dwelling House & Barn." The price paid Robert Holmes, Jr., was £67; the deed was dated Dec. 5, 1729.* To this home, it is supposed, David took his bride, less than three months later. He acquired other land, and prospered.

The death of David Roberts occurred on Dec. 25, 1792, at the age of eighty-eight years. His will, dated Oct. 22, 1782, mentions his wife Elizabeth, to whom he left one third of all his real estate "during her Life," and one third of his personal property. It mentions their sons, Joseph Roberts, Francis Roberts, and Thomas Roberts, who, upon the death of their mother, were to have the land and buildings divided amongst them. David Roberts also left small bequests to his three daughters, Elizabeth Brown, Martha Brown, and Lucy Stone, and to his grandchildren, David Roberts, Jr., and "Hannah Woodberry." This will, proved Feb. 4, 1793, was signed:—

"David Roberts."

In the inventory of his estate, the homestead, consisting of about seventy-eight acres, was valued at £273 : 0 : 0. Four other lots increased the value of his real estate to £404 : 12 : 0; to which was added personal estate — £23 : 19 : 5. The sons Joseph and Francis were executors.†

Issue: I. David⁴, bap. Sept. 27, 1730, in the Third Church. He mar. Jan. 19, 1757, in Hamilton, Sarah Potter; he died early in the year 1761.

Issue: 1. Hannah⁵, b. Sept. 27, 1759, in Hamilton. She was mar. Nov. 4, 1780, to Jacob Brown⁶ Woodbury, b. July 30, 1756, in Hamilton. He was son to Isaac⁵ Woodbury, b. April 14, 1734, in Ipswich, and his first wife, Mary Brown, b. Sept., 1729, daughter to Jacob and Mercy (Quarles) Brown, of Ipswich. Jacob Brown Woodbury went to Winchendon, Mass., where he d. Dec. 25, 1839. He had a distinguished

---

* *Essex County Deeds*, Book 53 : 227.

† *Essex County Probate*, Book 362 : 283, 284, 307.

record as Colonel in the Revolutionary Army.
His widow Hannah d. Feb. 14, 1845, in Winchendon. They had nine children.

   2. David[5], b. 1761, in Hamilton.

II. Joseph[4], bap. Dec. 17, 1732, in the Third Church.
Joseph Roberts mar. Jan. 25, 1760, in Hamilton,
Mercy Clark, b. Dec. 28, 1734, daughter to Israel
and Mercy (Porter) Clark. She d. Feb. 1, 1818,
in Hamilton.

Joseph Roberts was a "bricklayer"; he lived in Hamilton
"back of the cemetery." He d. Feb. 12, 1814; his estate
was settled by his son, "Samuel Roberts of Salem, gentleman," who gave bond with Daniel Roberts and Abraham
Patch as securities.*

   Issue: 1. Joseph[5], b. March 20, 1761, in Hamilton;
       d. unmar., May 15, 1807.

     2. Mercy[5], b. April 27, 1762, in Hamilton; d. unmar.,
       March 27, 1817.

     3. Asa[5], b. Aug. 16, 1763, in Hamilton; d. unmar., at
       sea.

     4. David[5], b. Jan. 3, 1765; he mar. May 21, 1797,
       Polly Lovering, b. May 3, 1773, daughter to John
       Lovering. She d. Nov. 19, 1858, in Hamilton.

David Roberts was a sea-captain. In 1793, with his brothers, Joseph and Samuel Roberts, he bought for £315, land
in Hamilton bounded "by the great road . . . the burying-
yard," and land of George Adams, Joseph Roberts, and the
"reverand Doctor Cutlers land . . . together with all the
buildings thereon also the pew in the Hamlet meeting house
that was formerly owned by John Thompson, late of Ipswich
deceased." † Captain David Roberts died at sea, in 1805;
his widow, Polly, was appointed administratrix, May 7, 1805.
In the settlement of his estate his homestead is mentioned
as one third of the twenty-one acres, with buildings, held in
common with Joseph and Samuel Roberts; his third of the
"pew in the Hamilton meeting house" was valued at $33.

---

* *Essex County Probate*, Book 385: 234.
† *Essex County Deeds*, Book 156: 119.

The widow, Polly Roberts, was appointed June 5, 1805, guardian to her young children — "Sally, aged six years, and Caroline, aged two years." *

> Issue: I. Sarah⁶, b. April 27, 1798, in Hamilton ; she was mar. Dec. 29, 1822, to Ephraim Safford.
> II. Caroline⁶, b. Aug. 16, 1801, in Hamilton ; d. 1813.
> 5. Elizabeth⁵, b. Oct 10, 1766, in Hamilton ; d. 1845.
> 6. Samuel⁵, b. April 15, 1768, in Hamilton. He mar. Nov. 30, 1797, his cousin, Martha Stone, b. 1774, daughter to Benjamin Stone, Jr., and his wife, Lucy⁴ Roberts, daughter to David³ and Elizabeth (Brown) Roberts.

In April, 1793, Samuel Roberts was called a "bricklayer . . . of Ipswich"; later, he appeared as "gentleman . . . of Salem." He died, intestate, March 3, 1835, in Salem ; David Roberts, his son, was appointed administrator March 14, and gave bond May 19, 1835, with Nehemiah Roberts, master-mariner, of Salem, and Patty Roberts, widow of Samuel, as securities.† Martha, or Patty, Roberts d. in 1845.

> Issue: I. Charlotte⁶, b. Dec. 25, 1798, in Hamilton; d. 1873.
> II. Nehemiah⁶, b. Dec. 9, 1800, in Hamilton; he mar. March 12, 1833, Hannah Ward Osborne. He was a master-mariner, and died at sea, March 27, 1840. His widow was left with three children: 1. Caroline Elizabeth⁷, b. Dec. 8, 1833. 2. Henry Osborne⁷, b. March, 1835. 3. David Augustus⁷, b. Oct. 23, 1836.
> III. Samuel⁶, b. March 22, 1802, in Hamilton; d. March 18, 1820, at sea.
> IV. David⁶, b. April 5, 1804, in Hamilton ; d. March 8, 1879.
> V. Martha⁶, b. Feb. 23, 1806, in Hamilton; d. unmar., Aug. 18, 1889.
> VI. Harriet⁶, b. Jan. 2, 1808, in Hamilton; d. unmar., Jan. 2, 1881.

---

* *Essex County Probate*, Book 371: 423.
† *Essex County Probate*, Book 88: 196, 253.

VII. Lucy[6], b. Aug. 12, 1812, in Salem. She was mar. Dec. 8, 1836, to Henry B. Groves; she d. June 8, 1902; he d. in 1876.

VIII. Caroline[6], b. Nov. 18, 1814; d. unmar., March 30, 1893.

IX. Joseph[6], b. 1817. There is no further record.

7. Nehemiah[5], son to Joseph[4] Roberts, b. Jan. 3, 1770; bap. Jan. 21, 1770, in the Third Church; he died at sea.

8. Parker[5], son to Joseph[4] Roberts, b. Dec. 3, 1771; bap. April 26, 1772, in the Third Church. He also was a seafaring man, and lived in Newburyport. He died at sea in January, 1815; on Feb. 15, following, his widow, "Ednah Roberts," was appointed administratrix. June 24, 1817, the widow Edna requested the Court to grant her an allowance out of the estate of her late husband, as she had four children, "the eldest aged 11 years, and the youngest born six months after the decease of its father."[*] She described the children as:—

I. "Parker Roberts, aged 11 years last July"— Parker[6], b. July, 1805. He married, but had no children.

II. "Joseph Roberts, aged 9 years last May"— Joseph[6], b. May, 1808.

III. "Adeline Roberts, aged 5 years last August" —later called "Lucy Adeline[6]," b. Aug., 1811.

IV. "Lydia Ann Roberts, aged 1 year last July"— Lydia Ann[6], b. July, 1815.

9. Sarah[5], daughter to Joseph[4] Roberts, bap. July 3, 1774, in the Third Church.

10. Daniel[5], son to Joseph[4] Roberts, b. March 10, 1776; bap. May 26, 1776, in the Third Church. He mar. Mrs. Abigail (Patch) Stanford, a widow; he d. before 1832.

[*] *Essex County Probate*, Book 386: 517, 605; Book 391: 528.

Issue : I. Daniel [6], b. 1821 ; his wife was Sarah
Story ; they had six children.

III. Thomas [4], son to David [3] Roberts, bap. Aug., 1735,
in the Third Church of Ipswich ; he died in infancy.

IV. Thomas [4], son to David [3] Roberts, bap. Oct., 1736,
in the Third Church. He mar. Feb. 4, 1802,
Sarah (Perkins) Brown, sister to James Perkins,
and widow of —— Brown, by whom she had a
son, Joseph Brown. Sarah Roberts died before
her husband ; there were no children by her second marriage. For many years Thomas Roberts
and his brother Francis possessed their lands in
common.

Thomas Roberts died Oct. 11, 1833, in Hamilton, aged
ninety-seven years. His will, dated May 13, 1833, bequeathed
to "my beloved brother Francis Roberts all my farming
utencils in common with him, and my wearing apparel."
Having no children of his own, he bequeathed to each of the
four daughters of his brother Francis as follows : * —

To "Sally wife of Ezekiel Allen and her children," "one fifth of
all my real estate in common with my brother Francis Roberts,"
one fourth of the household furniture and one fourth of a pew in
the meeting-house, in common.

To "widow Mary Hoyt" one fifth of all real estate, one fourth
of the household furniture, and one fourth of the pew, in common.

To Abigail Roberts, one fifth of the real estate, one fourth of
the furniture, one fourth of the pew, and "one fourth of my dwelling house in common with my brother Francis Roberts."

To Elizabeth Roberts, two fifths of all real estate, "in conse-
quence of her blindness," one fourth of the dwelling house, one
fourth of the furniture, and one fourth of the pew, in common.

To Abigail and Elizabeth Roberts, "a horse for their use in the
family, in common with my brother."

To the "heirs of Benjamin Edwards' wife, Francis, Anna,
Parker, Elizabeth and Harriet Edwards," one dollar each.

To "Jacob B. Woodberry's wife Hannah," two dollars.

To "Samuel, Elizabeth and Daniel Roberts," two dollars each.

---

* *Essex County Probate*, Book 409 : 70.

To "my deceased sister Elizabeth Brown's children," to the children of deceased sisters Martha Brown and Lucy Stone, one dollar each.

To "deceased wife Sarah her heirs, viz. Joseph Brown five dollars, to be divided equally among his children."

To Joseph Brown, Jr., James and Isaac Brown, "one gold necklace, one large silver spoon, and three small ones, to be divided equal among them."

To "my brother James Perkins deceased and family," five dollars; also the same to John Perkins, Robert Perkins, "Jeremiah Western and family," and "Benj. Perkins deceased, to his family."

"If there are any more lawful heirs to my estate, not mentioned herein, I give to each one fifty cents."

Mary Hoyt, of Beverly, widow, was to be sole executrix.

This will, witnessed by O. S. Cressy, Zebulon Burnham, and Samuel Means, was signed: —

"Thomas Roberts." [seal]

On Nov. 5, 1833, Mary Hoyt, of Beverly, widow, was appointed executrix of the estate of "Thomas Roberts, of Hamilton, yeoman, who died Oct. 11, 1833," with Francis Roberts, yeoman, and Oliver S. Cressy, physician, sureties.*

V. Elizabeth⁴, daughter to David³ Roberts, bap. Dec. 11, 1737, in the Third Church. She was mar. Dec. 15, 1758, to Elisha Brown, of Hamilton, known as "Elisha Brown the elder," to distinguish him from "Elisha Brown the younger." The will of "Elisha Brown the elder," dated April 1, 1799, was proved July 1, following. It mentions his wife Elizabeth, sons, Ephraim Brown, Daniel Brown, and daughters, Lydia Brown, Lucy Tibbetts, and Betsey Raymond. Division of his estate was made April 28, 1809.†

VI. Francis⁴, son to David³ Roberts, bap. Nov. 28, 1740, in the Third Church. His first wife was Susanna ——; she did not long survive the birth of triplets. His second wife, whom he mar. Nov. 16, 1783, was Sarah Smith, b. March 5, 1755.

* *Essex County Probate*, Book 75: 221.
† *Essex County Probate*, Book 367: 19; Book 377: 530-534.

Francis Roberts was a Revolutionary soldier. He served in defence of the seacoast of Essex County, in Captain Daniel Giddings' company, Colonel Joseph Foster's regiment, from Jan. 29 to Nov. 18, 1776 — the last eight months with rank of Corporal. "Francis Robards, of Ipswich," also served as private in Captain Richard Dodge's company of volunteers, 3d Essex County regiment ; he enlisted Sept. 30, 1777, marched Oct. 2, 1777, and was discharged Nov. 7, 1777. His service consisted of forty days in a "regiment commanded by Major Charles Smith under General Gates, in the Northern department, and in guarding Lt. Gen. Burgoyne's troops to Prospect Hill," after Burgoyne's surrender. Captain Richard Dodge's company was discharged at Cambridge.*

Francis Roberts, aged ninety-three years, died Dec. 25, 1833, less than three months after the death of his brother Thomas. His widow, Sarah Roberts, on April 1, 1834, recorded in the Essex County Probate that "said Francis, a revolutionary pensioner, died on the twenty-fifth day of December last ; that she is his widow." † On June 30, 1834, the heirs of Francis Roberts, yeoman, of Hamilton, made division of the estate "held in common with the heirs of his brother Thomas." The widow Sarah was to have her third of the real estate, and the "southwestern lower room in the dwelling house, a privilege in the kitchen to wash, bake," etc.‡ She died, his widow, March 14, 1842, aged eighty-seven years.

> Issue : 1. Sarah⁶, b. March 10, 1784, in Hamilton. In 1833, she was the wife of Ezekiel Allen, and had children ; she d. Aug. 5, 1863. Dr. Justin Allen, of Topsfield, was their son.
>
> 2. Francis⁶, b. Dec. 26, 1786, in Hamilton ; d. Dec. 9, 1809, aged twenty-three years.
>
> 3. Susan⁶, b. March 6, 1790, in Hamilton. She was

---

* *Massachusetts Soldiers and Sailors in the War of the Revolution*, vol. 13 : 405, 366.

† *Essex County Probate*, Book 409 : 114.

‡ *Essex County Probate*, Book 409 : 218–220.

the wife of Benjamin Edwards; she d. Aug. 22, 1832. Benjamin Edwards mar., second, Abigail⁵ Roberts, sister to his first wife; she d. June 16, 1885. The children of Benjamin Edwards by his first wife were: I. Francis Edwards. II. Anna Edwards. III. Parker Edwards. IV. Elizabeth Edwards. V. Harriet Edwards.

4. Mary⁶, b. Feb. 14, 1793, in Hamilton. The marriage intention of Isaiah Hoyt, of Beverly, and Mary Roberts, of Hamilton, was published Sept. 3, 1820, in Beverly. Isaiah Hoyt died Aug. 16 (or 14), 1827, in Beverly, aged thirty-three years. In the distribution of his estate among his widow and four children, he was called a "trader." *

Issue: I. Abigail Cressy Hoyt, bap. July 20, 1823, in Beverly.

II. Thomas Hoyt, bap. Aug. 7, 1825, in Beverly.

III. Isaiah Francis Hoyt, bap. Aug. 14, 1831, in Beverly.

IV. Mary Elizabeth Brown Hoyt, bap. Oct. 21, 1831, in Beverly.

5. Abigail⁶, b. July 26, 1796, in Hamilton. She was unmarried in 1833, when her uncle Thomas made his will; later, she became the second wife of Benjamin Edwards.

6. Elizabeth,⁶ b. June 9, 1800, in Hamilton. She was mentioned in the will of her uncle, Thomas Roberts, in 1833, as blind; she d. June 22, 1885, aged eighty-five years.

VII. Martha⁴, daughter to David³ Roberts, b. 1742, in Hamilton. She was mar. March 20, 1762, to Benjamin Brown, b. 1739; she d. March 20, 1786, in Ipswich. Administration upon the estate of Benjamin Brown, of Ipswich, yeoman, was granted in 1818.† Issue mentioned at

---

* *Essex County Probate*, Book 52 : 100.
† *Essex County Probate*, Book 393 : 2, 3.

that time: 1. Benjamin Brown, Jr. 2. Parker
Brown. 3. Martha Brown. 4. Sarah Brown.

VIII. Lucy[4], daughter to David[3] Roberts, b. Nov. 11,
1745, in Hamilton. Benjamin Stone, Jr., and
Lucy Roberts were mar. Jan. 25, 1766. On
Nov. 6, 1781, administration upon the estate of
Benjamin Stone, late of Ipswich, deceased, was
granted to Lucy Stone, who gave bond with
Joseph Roberts and Francis Roberts. His inventory, amounting to £568:13, was dated May
28, 1782.* There probably were several children; the only one traced is Martha Stone, b.
1774, who was mar. Nov. 30, 1797, to Samuel[5]
Roberts.

4. Richard[3]. It is possible that Richard Roberts, of
Kittery, Maine, may have been son to Richard[2] and
Elizabeth (——) Roberts, of Ipswich. The marriage
intention of "Richard Robarts and Lucie Burdeen,
both of Kittery," was recorded July 30, 1737, in Kittery.† No children are recorded there.

VIII. William[2]. There is no absolute proof that William Roberts, of Kittery, was son (possibly the eldest) to Robert[1] Roberts, of Ipswich, yet the circumstantial evidence is so strong that he is mentioned here, with a
few of his descendants. According to his deposition,
William Roberts was born "about 1640," which may
be considered only as approximating the date of his
birth. Robert[1] Roberts was then twenty-three years
of age; the date of his marriage to Susanna (Downing?)
is unknown. William Roberts died between 1708 and
1710; in 1715, Ephraim Roberts was appointed administrator of his parents' estate, as the only surviving
heir.‡

Kittery, with her extensive maritime interests — fishing
and shipbuilding — offered large inducements to the young

---

* *Essex County Probate*, Book 355: 56, 479.
† *Town Records of Kittery*, vol. 1 : 148.
‡ Vide page 951.

men* of that period; many removed there from other coast towns, married, and remained. William Roberts married "Anna (alias Nan)" Crockett, daughter to Thomas[1] and Ann (——) Crockett, who lived at Spruce Creek. In 1634, Thomas Crockett was employed by Captain John Mason, probably at Portsmouth. In 1641, he received a grant of nearly two hundred acres from Thomas Gorges, situated on the east side of Spruce Creek, in Kittery; this was known later as Crockett's Neck. In 1657, Thomas Crockett was Constable of Kittery. He died about 1679; his widow, Ann, was appointed administratrix of his estate. Before 1683, she was married to "Diggory Jeffreys," of Kittery Point; she was living in 1712.† On June 26, 1695, "Anne Jeffry Relict & Admrx of Thomas Crockett, Late of the town of Kittery dec'd, with ffree Consent of my husband, Digory Jeffry & yᵉ more in order to fullfill yᵉ mind of my Late Husband Thomas Crockett afresᵈ . . . granted & confirmed to my Son in Law William Roberts and Anne his Now wife . . . all that Tract of Land Lying & being on that Neck of Land Called Crocketts Neck Near unto yᵉ Homestead of yᵉ sᵈ Crockett & is bounded Southward with a Little Creek . . . it being yᵉ homestead of yᵉ sᵈ Roberts with an adition of Land Six acres." ‡

In 1699, the town of Kittery granted to William Roberts forty acres of land; this land he assigned to "William Pepperrell Esqʳ," June 18, 1702, for a "valluable sum of money to me in hand." The conveyance was witnessed by Joshua Downing and Joseph Hammond, Jr., of Kittery; it was signed: —

William 𝕎 Roberts § [seal]

his mark

---

* Among these was Joshua Downing, b. 1644, supposed by some to be son to Emmanuel[1] Downing, of Ipswich and Salem. It appears more probable, however, that he was son to James[2], one of the children of Emmanuel[1] Downing by his first wife. In 1638, James Downing was of Ipswich, and of age. (Vide page 929.)

† *History of Kittery, Maine,* by Rev. Everett S. Stackpole, 1903: 329.

‡ *York County Deeds,* Book 8: 145.

§ *York County Deeds,* Book 6: 139.

At "Ipswich in ye County of Essex," on Sept. 23, 1706, "William Roberts of Kittery," for £32, "paid me by my Son George Roberts of Ipswich . . . Sold unto s^d George Roberts," his homestead in Kittery, "by Estimation Sixteen Acres . . . on Spruce Creek . . . with all ye houseing on ye s^d land & fences orchard trees," etc., "also one Shallop with all her Appur^ces to her any ways belonging." This deed, which was not recorded until July 11, 1710, probably after the death of William Roberts, was witnessed by Caleb Hobbs and (Colonel) Francis Wainwright, of Ipswich. It bore the signature : —

"William W Roberts "* [seal]

On July 17, 1708 (recorded July 17, 1710), George Roberts, of Ipswich, for £16 : 17, paid by " Wm Pepperrell Esqr of Kittery . . . Set over unto ye s^d Wm Pepperell ye within mentioned deed of Sale or Mortgage," with the condition that if he or his father paid the above mentioned £16 : 17, to Pepperrell, on or before July 17, 1711, "then ye Above to be voyd." The date of the death of William Roberts is not known ; but on Aug. 30, 1715, William Pepperrell levied an execution upon the " Estate of Wm Roberts Late of s^d Kittery dec^d," for the sum of £14 : 13 : 5, and £1 : 08 : 4 for cost of suit. At the same time his " widow Anne Roberts " relinquished her right in " fourteen acres of Land and a Dwelling house . . . Lying in Kittery," and the same was delivered up to " Wm Pepperrell Esqr . . . p me Abraham Preble Sheriff." †

Issue: 1. William³, son to William² and Anne (Crockett) Roberts. The wife of William Roberts was "Sarah Crecy"; they are supposed to have been married about 1700. There is no doubt that she was daughter or granddaughter to "Mighill Cresie," of Ipswich, whose inventory was taken May 2, 1670, by Robert Lord, and presented the next day at Court by his widow, "Mary

---

* *York County Deeds,* Book 7 : 146, 147.
† *York County Deeds,* Book 8 : 127.

Cresie." * This name has passed through innumerable changes to the modern Cressey. The children of Mighill Cressey lived in that part of Ipswich set off, in 1639, as Rowley.

William and Sarah Roberts remained for a time in Kittery, where two sons, William and George, were born. There is no record of them in Kittery after 1704; they appear to be the William and Sarah who had a son Tobias born in Ipswich, in 1711, and a daughter Sarah in 1715. Later, he is credited with being the William Roberds, or Robards, who went to Falmouth, Maine, where the ill luck of his father seemed to follow him.

On July 7, 1730, "William Roberds of s⁴ Falmouth," for "full satisfaction," acquired of William Graves, of Falmouth, one half ·of his title to a thirty acre lot in " Falmouth on the Western Side of Presumpscot River," adjoining land of John Clark, Moses Pearson, and the common land. In 1736, Roberts sold this land to Thomas Westbrook (Colonel Thomas Westbrook), for £40, signing his name : —

his
" William X Robards " †
mark

In 1738, "Thomas Westbrook, Esq.," of Falmouth, for £100, sold to James Doughty and John Clark, husbandmen, William Roberts and George Doughty, laborers, all of Falmouth, his " Part or Proportion of a Certain Island lying in Casco Bay . . . called Sebasco=deggin." This island was within the limits of North Yarmouth, and Roberts removed his family there; afterwards, on Feb. 16, 1740, as a resident of that town, his " one moiety Sixth part of . . . Great Sebascodegon " was attached by Phineas and Stephen Jones for a debt of £15 : 13 : 6. Roberts appears to have compromised with his creditors, and to have raised the money by selling, on Oct. 8, forty acres on the island of Sebascodegan, for £50. Two years later, he sold the " Dwelling-House which I now live in with all my Improvements " on Great Sebascodegan, with all his possessions on the island.‡

---

* *Essex County Probate*, File No. 6540.
† *York County Deeds*, Book 21, 120.
‡ *York County Deeds*, Book 21: 53; Book 22: 153; Book 23: 2; Book 25: 61.

It is not known when or where William and Sarah Roberts died. Besides the four children who are mentioned, others probably went to North Yarmouth with their parents. There is reason to believe that most of those bearing the name of Roberts, in that town, prior to 1800, were descendants of William [3].

Issue: I. William [4], son to William [3] and Sarah (Crecy) Roberts, was b. June 30, 1701, in Kittery. He appears to be the "William Roberts," of Ipswich, who was published Dec. 18, 1725, in Ipswich, to Esther Hodgkins, of the same town.* Mr. Waters states that, in 1726, William Roberts and Nathaniel Newman occupied a house on the original Robert Coles's estate.† On Feb. 7, 1728, "William Robbens Jun[r]" bought for £79, of Robert Cross and his wife Elizabeth, a "Dwelling House and half an Acre of Land . . . in Ipswich . . . on the South Side of the Town River," which said Cross bought of Edward Webber.‡ It is curious that at about this period in Ipswich the name of Roberts appears in the records interchangeable with Robbins and Robbens.

William Roberts, or Robins, died before 1760. On March 6, of that year, his widow, Esther Robins, of Ipswich, William Robins, joiner, and Thomas Robins, cordwainer, both of Gloucester, Esther Robins, Abigail Robins, and Sarah Robins, single women, of Ipswich, sold a small piece of land near the river, in Ipswich, for £3 : 06 : 08, to David Andrews.§ "William Roberts jun[r] and Esther" his wife had but one child recorded in Ipswich.

Issue: 1. William [5], bap. Oct. 27, 1728, in Ipswich.‖ He was a joiner, and lived in Gloucester.
2. Thomas [5], a cordwainer, of Gloucester.

---

* *Ipswich Births, Marriages, and Deaths* (copy), vol. 1 : 166.
† *History of Ipswich, Massachusetts,* by Rev. Thomas Franklin Waters, 1905 : 399.
‡ *Essex County Deeds,* Book 51 : 275.
§ *Essex County Deeds,* Book 160 : 277.
‖ *Ipswich Births, Marriages, and Deaths* (copy), vol. 1.

3. Abigail[6], of age, but unmarried, in 1760.
4. Esther[6], of age, but unmarried, in 1760.
5. Sarah[6]. She became the wife of Nathaniel Rust.
II. George[4], son to William[3] and Sarah (Crecy) Roberts, was b. March 30, 1704, in Kittery. His wife was Catherine[4], b. Feb. 19, 1708, in Kittery, daughter to Samuel[3] and Rhoda (Haley) Skillings, of Kittery.

In 1723, Samuel[3] Skillings lived on Spruce Creek; he was a shipwright.* His grandfather, Thomas[1] Skillings, was settled as early as 1651 in Falmouth, Maine, where he had a farm at Back Cove. He died in 1666. John[2], son to Thomas[1] Skillings, had a grant of land upon the Neck, in 1680; he also possessed a farm near Long Creek, where he lived in 1688. Tradition says that he died before he was forty years old; his widow Elizabeth with her children fled, during the Indian War of 1690, to Kittery. Before 1730, Samuel returned and established himself on his father's land at Long Creek.†

George Roberts went to Falmouth with his father-in-law. On July 1, 1731, he and his wife "Katherine" acknowledged the covenant, in the First Church of Falmouth; she was admitted to full communion Aug. 20, 1732.‡

In 1734, George Roberts bought of "Phinehas Jones," for £42, thirty-two acres of land in Falmouth, "about twenty Rods Southerly from the now dwelling House of the said Roberts." Two years later, Samuel Skillings, for £20, "paid by my Son in Law George Roberts of Falm? Labourer," sold him fifty-four acres, "the same being so much of the Right in Common Lands in Falm? allowed to the Heirs or assigns of my Father John Skillings late of Falm° . . . Carpenter Dec^d by the Proprietors of Falm°." July 23, 1745, "George Roberts of Falmouth . . . yeoman," for £172, paid by Thomas Cummings, sold him thirty acres

---

* *York County Deeds*, Book 8 : 43.
† *Collections of the Maine Historical Society*, vol. 1 : 121, 141, 314; vol. 3 : 223.
‡ *Records of the First Church of Falmouth, Maine*, 1898 : 9.

"near Long Creek by a place called the Indian Spring."
The deed was signed:—

"George Robbards   [seal]

Catteren Robbyads " *   [seal]

George Roberts later acquired from the other heirs fifty-eight acres, "which was part of the Estate of said Samuel Skellen our Honour^d Father," situated "on the Banks by the South West Side of Long Creek, & down to land of Wm Westcoat." Before 1781, George Roberts and his wife had passed away. On Sept. 12, of that year, their sons, George Copson Roberts and Joseph Roberts, both of Cape Elizabeth, sold to Richard Crockett, Jr., for £20, "Our whole Right & Title to the real estate that belonged to our late Honoured Father & Mother, George Roberts yeoman Deceased & Katharine Roberts late of Cape Elizabeth either in s^d Cape Elizabeth or other where Excepting their Dwelling House & Right in a Corn Mill & mill Privilege & s^d Georges share in a Thatch Bed & a certain Tract of Land commonly called the Corn Field." Their signatures were " George Copson Roberts . . . Joseph Roberts." †

Eight children of George[4] and Catherine Roberts have been traced; there may have been others.

Issue: 1. Rhoda[5], bap. Aug., 1731, in Falmouth.‡

2. William[5], b. Sept. 19, 1733, in Falmouth.

3. Elizabeth[5], b. March 5, 1736, in Falmouth. She was published Nov. 14, 1755, to Richard Crockett, Jr., of Cape Elizabeth. He was a " chairmaker." §

4. "George Copson " [5], also called "George, Jr." (twin), b. June 1, 1738, in Falmouth.

On October 29, 1759, "George Roberts" appeared as " centinel " on a Muster Roll of Captain James Cargill's company, in service on the Penobscot River. Roberts entered service March 31, and served until July 23, 1759, length of

---

* *York County Deeds*, Book 16: 195; Book 18 : 126; Book 26 : 54.

† *Cumberland County Deeds*, Book 1 : 69, 101 ; Book 11 : 408.

‡ *Records of the First Church of Falmouth, Maine*, 1898 : 95.

§ *Cumberland County Deeds*, Book 15 : 99.

service sixteen weeks and three days; "reported — Son of George Roberts."[*] The detachment of "24 men from Falmouth," under command of Captain Cargill, rendered signal service in the Penobscot Expedition. They first went to Pemaquid to collect whale-boats, by order of Brigadier-General Preble,[†] and had them on the Penobscot River when Governor Pownall arrived. The boats, with their crews, were sent out with surveying parties, and were retained at the Fort some time after the departure of the troops for Boston.[‡]

On Oct. 20, 1759, George Roberts published his intention of marriage with Deborah York, daughter to Samuel and Joanna[4] (Skillings) York, of Cape Elizabeth. Susanna, sister to Deborah York, became the wife of Vincent[5] Roberts, of Cape Elizabeth, later of Durham, Maine.[§] George Roberts lived all his life at Long Creek, in Cape Elizabeth; the following inscription is on his headstone in an old cemetery there: "M[r]. George Roberts died August 28, 1824 . . . Ae. 86." But three of his children have been identified.

> I. Deborah[6]. Nathaniel Skillings and Deborah Roberts were mar. April 28, 1796, in Cape Elizabeth.
>
> II. Richard[6], mentioned as "my son" in a deed from his father, in 1803.[‖]
>
> III. George[6]. "Mr. George Roberts of Cape Elizabeth," was mar. Dec. 16, 1805, in Portland, by Rev. Elijah Kellogg, to "Miss Susan Woodbury, of Portland."[¶]

5. Joseph[5] (twin), b. June 1, 1738, in Falmouth.

In 1758, when he was but twenty years of age, Joseph Roberts served as private, six months and nineteen days, in Captain John Libby's company, Colonel Jedidiah Preble's

---

[*] *Massachusetts Archives*, Muster Rolls, vol. 97 : 244.
[†] *Massachusetts Archives*, Muster Rolls, vol. 97 : 244, 244 a.
[‡] Vide pages 187–189.
[§] *Maine Historical and Genealogical Recorder*, vol. 3 : 19.
[‖] *Cumberland County Deeds*, Book 48 : 216.
[¶] *Records of Portland*, Marriages, vol. 3 : 166.

regiment. This was the same command under which Lieutenant John Small, afterwards Captain, went through that mem-
orable campaign.* Joseph Roberts enlisted April 8, in the
town of Falmouth; because he was under age, his "Father
. . . George Roberts" signed for him. The service of Joseph Roberts expired Oct. 11, 1758, though he was "reported
discharged Sept. 20," probably through disability. The
irregularity of his leaving the service may be responsible for
his being "charged £3, for arms not returned." † The company of Captain Libby delivered up their "Province arms"
at Albany, before starting homeward.‡

On Feb. 8, 1776, Joseph Roberts, of Cape Elizabeth, married Anna⁶ Fogg, of Scarborough. She was b. Nov. 29, 1755,
daughter to Samuel⁴ and Rachel⁵ (Mariner) Fogg.§ At
the time of his marriage, Joseph Roberts was thirty-eight
years old. Perhaps some of his descendants now living in
Portland may be able to trace his late marriage to shattered
health, or to wounds received in 1758.

As early as 1769, Joseph Roberts bought land, in Gorham, of Thomas Pote; it was described as twenty-five acres
of the "Easterly End of the 100 acre Lot numbered 9 in the

---

* Vide pages 172–185.

† *Massachusetts Archives*, Muster Rolls, vol. 96: 533.

‡ This Joseph Roberts was not in the Revolutionary service; nor was the
Joseph Roberts who married Hannah Freeman, and later moved to Gorham.
The only one of the name enlisting from Cape Elizabeth was the Joseph Roberts who married Hannah Young; they went to Windham, in the winter of
1775-76.
He enlisted May 15, 1775, at Cape Elizabeth, in "Capt. Samuel Dunn's
co., Col. Edmund Phinney's (31st) regt.;" he appeared in a return of that
company in Oct., 1775, and on an order for a bounty coat, Nov., 1775. He
was in "service at Dorchester Heights, Aug. 31, 1776; was reported sick
in barracks at Fort George, Dec. 8, 1776; residence, Windham, Maine." In
1777, he was at Bennington, Vermont, and at Fort Edward, New York. In
the summer of 1779, he was at "Major Biguaduce," with Colonel Jonathan
Mitchell, and left the service Nov. 3, 1779. He appears in a list of men who
moved from Cape Elizabeth about 1776, list dated Jan. 17, 1782, at Cape
Elizabeth.
Vide *The Roberts Family*, by Mrs. Amorena Grant: 7, 8, 9; also *Massachusetts Soldiers and Sailors in the War of the Revolution*, vol. 13: 408, 409.

§ Vide The Mariner Family.

second Division of land in Gorham." * Soon after the close of the Revolutionary War, in which he did not participate, Roberts removed his family to Gorham. He was all his life a farmer, and died on his farm in Gorham, Oct. 12, 1798. His widow, Rachel, made her home, after the death of her husband, in Gardiner, Maine, where she died.

Issue : † I. Joseph *, b. March 5, 1777, in Cape Elizabeth. He married, and settled in Gardiner, Maine.

II. Samuel *, b. June 2, 1779, in Cape Elizabeth. He mar., first (intention Sept. 30, 1809), Elizabeth Staples; his second wife was Betsey Houston. Samuel remained in the homestead of his father, in the south part of the town.

III. Rhoda *, b. Nov. 22, 1782, in Cape Elizabeth; she was mar. June 27, 1802, to Daniel Merrill, Jr.

IV. Rachel *, b. July 23, 1785, in Gorham. In 1816, Rachel Roberts, of Gorham, single woman, quitclaimed to Joseph Roberts, of Gardiner, and Samuel Roberts, of Gorham, her share in the estate of her father, "Joseph Roberts, Jr., late of Gorham, deceased." ‡ "Joseph Roberts, Jr.," was so called because there was another and older Joseph Roberts (said to have " come from Cape Cod," wife Hannah Freeman) in the town. Rachel never married.

V. Anna *, b. March 17, 1789, in Gorham; she was mar., about 1805, to Elkanah McLellan.

6. Benjamin *, b. 1741, in Falmouth. He was a ship-carpenter by trade. His wife was Mary Weeks, whom he mar. March 7, 1765, in Cape Elizabeth.§ After their marriage, they lived a few years at Falmouth, now Portland.

---

* *Cumberland County Deeds*, Book 12 : 371.
† *History of Gorham, Maine,* by Hugh D. McLellan, 1903 : 742.
‡ *Cumberland County Deeds*, Book 73 : 316.
§ *Maine Historical and Genealogical Recorder*, vol. 3: 102.

Benjamin Roberts, in 1759, though but eighteen years of age, served as "centinel" in Captain James Cargill's company, at the Penobscot. Benjamin enlisted at the same time as his brother, George Copson, on March 31 ; he was mustered out July 15, one week earlier than George. Benjamin, too, was signed for by his "father, George Roberts."* On Feb. 25, 1760, Benjamin Roberts was enlisted by Nathaniel Ingersoll, "for the total reduction of Canada." His age was then given as nineteen years, and his birthplace, as well as present residence, Falmouth. "Reported Son to George Roberts." Benjamin's service was in Colonel Waldo's regiment, probably under Captain Benjamin Waite.†

Before 1776, Benjamin Roberts took his family to Gorham, where they lived on the "south part of the 100 acre Lot No. 9;" this was the same lot to which his brother Joseph removed later. Benjamin Roberts died before Oct. 26, 1805, on which date his widow, Mary Roberts, and her son Benjamin, with his wife Rebecca, conveyed land in Gorham, adjoining that purchased, in 1769, by Joseph Roberts from Thomas Pote.‡

Issue : § I. Mary⁶ b. April 30, 1767, in Falmouth ; she was mar. Dec. 14, 1794, to James Sturgis.

II. Benjamin⁶, b. Aug. 29, 1768, in Falmouth ; mar. Rebecca, daughter to Joshua Dyer, of Cape Elizabeth.

III. John⁶, b. May 17, 1770, in Falmouth, mar. July 30, 1794, Lucy Libby.

IV. Jane⁶, b. Nov. 13, 1771, in Falmouth ; she was mar. Oct. 4, 1792, to John Whitmore.

V. William⁶, b. Oct. 23, 1774, in Cape Elizabeth. He mar., first, Betsey, daughter to Rev. Nathaniel Hatch, of Westbrook ; he mar., second, Dorcas, daughter to John Johnson, of Falmouth. William Roberts lived and died in Westbrook.

---

* *Massachusetts Archives*, Muster Rolls, vol. 97 : 243.
† *Massachusetts Archives*, Muster Rolls, vol. 98 : 110.
‡ *Cumberland County Deeds*, Book 65 : 139.
§ *History of Gorham, Maine*, by Hugh D. McLellan, 1903 : 740.

VI. Susanna⁶, b. Oct. 5, 1776, in Gorham; she was
      mar. Jan. 10, 1799, to Nathaniel Knight.

VII. Stephen⁶, b. Aug. 20, 1778, in Gorham, mar.
      Abigail Tibbetts. He died about 1830.

VIII. Dorcas⁶, b. Aug. 27, 1781, in Gorham; she was
      mar. July 29, 1802, to John Libby, of Scar-
      borough.

7. Joshua⁶, b. about 1743, in Falmouth.

As "Jos'h Roberts," of Falmouth, he enlisted as private,
June 13, 1761, in a company under the command of Captain Simon Jefferds. Roberts appears in continued service
in the same company, until July 15, 1762. As he was under
age, in 1761, when he enlisted, his "Father . . . George
Roberts" signed for him.* Joshua Roberts has not been
traced further.

8. Lydia⁶, b. about 1745, or 1746, in Falmouth; she
      was mar. Dec. 18, 1766, in Cape Elizabeth, to
      her cousin, Thomas Millett, Jr.,† son to Thomas
      and Susanna⁴ (Skillings) Millett.

Thomas Millett, Jr., bought part of the "100 acre Lot No.
46," in Gorham, in 1774, and soon removed there. He enlisted as private, in 1775, in Captain David Strout's company, Colonel Enoch Freeman's regiment, and was called
out to work on the fort at Falmouth Neck, in Nov., 1775.
He also enlisted Jan. 1, 1777, as private in "Lieut. Colonel's
company, Colonel Vose's regiment," for the three years' service of the Continental Army. Aug. 15, 1777, his name appeared on a "return of men who were in camp;" on Oct.
19, following, he was "reported deceased." ‡ Not long after
his death, his widow, Lydia, returned to Cape Elizabeth.

On Jan. 30, 1786, Benjamin Roberts, of Gorham, and
Lydia Millett, widow, of Cape Elizabeth, for £6, sold to
George Copson Roberts a small tract of land in Cape Eliza-
beth, also two fifths of a "piece of land called the Barnfield

---

* *Massachusetts Archives*, Muster Rolls, vol. 99 : 135, 177, 244.
† *Maine Historical and Genealogical Recorder*, vol. 3 : 103.
‡ *Massachusetts Soldiers and Sailors in the War of the Revolution*, vol. 10 :
781, 780.

in said Cape Elizabeth on the Eastern Side of the County Road, which formerly belonged to M[r] George Roberts late of Falmouth, deceased." This deed was signed "Lydia Millett . . . Benjamin Roberts." [*]

The children of Thomas Millett, Jr., and his wife Lydia have not been traced.

> III. Tobias[4], "son of William Roberds," b. "19–6–1711," in Ipswich.[†]

> IV. Sarah[4], "daughter to William and Sarah Roberts," b. July 17, 1715, in Ipswich.[‡]

> 2. Mary[3], daughter to William[2] and Anne (Crockett) Roberts, was "mentioned in 1702." [§]

> 3. Elizabeth[3], daughter to William[2] and Anne (Crockett) Roberts. She was married, first, to John Surplus; after his death, she became the wife of William[2] Godsoe, b. March 4, 1680–81, in Salem, Mass., son to William[1] and Elizabeth (Lord) Godsoe, of Salem.

> Issue by first husband: I. Catherine Surplus; she was mar. July 16, 1719, to John Marr, a mariner, of Kittery.

> Issue by second husband: II. John[3] Godsoe. III. Elizabeth[3] Godsoe; died young. IV. Alice[3] Godsoe. V. Joseph[3] Godsoe. VI. James[3] Godsoe. VII. Dorothy[3] Godsoe. VIII. Elizabeth[3] Godsoe. IX. Hannah[3] Godsoe. X. William[3] Godsoe.[‖]

> 4. George[3], son to William[2] and Anne (Crockett) Roberts, of Kittery, was a fisherman, of Ipswich. The publishment of "George Roberds," of Ipswich, to "Hannah Pettee of Haverhill," was recorded Oct. 25, 1712, in Ipswich.[¶]

On Nov. 8, 1706, Benjamin Dutch, of Ipswich, for £65, sold to "George Robbins of Ipswich, mariner . . . all that

---

[*] *Cumberland County Deeds*, Book 14 : 150.

[†] *Ipswich Births, Marriages, and Deaths* (copy), vol. 1 : 53.

[‡] *Ipswich Births, Marriages, and Deaths* (copy), vol. 1 : 63.

[§] *History of Kittery, Maine*, by Rev. Everett S. Stackpole, 1903 : 701.

[‖] *History of Kittery, Maine*, by Rev. Everett S. Stackpole, 1903 : 449, 450, 604.

[¶] *Ipswich Births, Marriages, and Deaths* (copy), vol. 1 : 145.

my Mansion house and homestead that was My father John
Dutch late of Ipswich Deceased" — about one and a half
acres — "on the Street or towne highway." Three years
later, "George Roberds of Ipswich * . . . fisherman," conveyed to John Dennis, of Ipswich, for £37, about an acre
of land on "the upper part of My homestead which I bought
of Benjamin Dutch in Ipswich," the boundary "to begin
within one rod and an halfe of the End of My Dwelling
house running from the high way or road on the northerly
End of said House on a Streight line to Coll⁰ ffrancis Wainwright['s] Stone wall." The deed was signed with the mark
of "George Robbins." On Jan. 18, 1713–14, a few months
after his marriage, he and his wife Hannah sold to John
Staniford, for £40 : 6, one fourth of an acre "on the highway," adjoining land of John Dennis. Their signatures
were : —

ye mark of

"George   X   Robins   [seal]

Hannah Robins" †   [seal]

They probably removed, soon after 1726, to some distant
town. Two children were recorded, in Ipswich, to "George
and Hannah Roberds." ‡

Issue : I. Jeremy⁴, b. " 1–12–1718," in Ipswich.
II. Hannah⁴, bap. May 22, 1726, in Ipswich.

JOHN² ROBERTS

John² Roberts, of Ipswich, son to Robert¹ and Susanna
(——) Roberts, was born about 1646, in Ipswich. His age
is stated in three depositions, sworn to at Ipswich ; in the
first, "John Roberds aged about 24 yeres" testified, in
March, 1670, as to the exchange of horses between John
Burnam, Jr., and John Andrews, Jr. On March 31, 1674,
"The deposition of John Roberts aged about eight and

---

* Vide page 980.
† *Essex County Deeds*, Book 18 : 212 ; Book 22 : 37 ; Book 29 : 156.
‡ *Ipswich Births, Marriages, and Deaths* (copy), vol. 1 : 74, 99.

twenty years testifieth and Saith that henery bennett did lett a parsell of grass for tenn Shillings to the said deponent, for his use, that lay next to John kimball, and I went to mowe the grass and Deacon pengrys Sons did hinder me, and Saith that Good : bennett [Goodman Bennett] had noe meddow there, for it was theires." Also, in 1681, "John Roberts : aged 34 yeares" deposed that "at the house of John Wainwright, he heard Robert Haines : demand of Joseph Lee : possession of a house . . . sittuated upŏ the Iles of Shoales," and further, he "heard Joseph Lee say that he Gaue Robert Haines : order to pay Jnᵒ Wainwright Ten pounds for the house now sued for By Robt Haines." *

In September, 1666, "John Robards & Susan Robards, his mother," of Ipswich, were presented at Court by John Leigh, Sr., of the same town, "for trespass in mowing, disposing, & carrying away his grass, or hay from his marsh at Hogg island." † His mother probably was haled into Court because her son John was still under age; but that did not prevent his adding his signature to the Loyalists' petition, which was presented to the General Court, September 11, 1666.‡ Similar petitions were presented at the same time by other towns : Boston, with twenty-six names ; Salem, with thirty-five names ; Newbury, with thirty-nine names ; and Ipswich, with seventy-three, far exceeding her neighbors.

In a list of Commoners of Ipswich who had the privilege of the ballot at the meetings of the Commoners, in 1677 and 1678, appear the names of John Roberts and Thomas Bray. This list seems to include "all the youth and men from the Topsfield line to Gloucester, who lived in scattered hamlets, and were members of large families." §

---

* *Essex County Court Papers*, Book 15 : 94; Book 21 : 29; Book 35 : 7.
† *Essex County Court Papers*, Book 11 : 141.
‡ *Ipswich in the Massachusetts Bay Colony*, by Rev. Thomas Franklin Waters, 1905 : 135-138.
§ *Ipswich in the Massachusetts Bay Colony*, by Rev. Thomas Franklin Waters, 1905 : 98, 104, 99.

On the "4 of 12ᵐᵒ 1677 [Feb. 4, 1677–78]," John Roberts and Hannah Bray were married by Mr. Samuel Symonds, of Ipswich.* Hannah ² Bray, born March 21, 1661–62, in Gloucester, was the seventh child of Thomas¹ and Marie (Wilson) Bray; who were married "3ᵈ of 3ᵈ mo 1646," in Gloucester. He was one of the first settlers of the town. On the "7ᵐᵒ: 47 [1647]," the town granted to Thomas Bray three acres of marsh "lying on the South Side of Little River and Between a cove of marsh of obadiah Brven y [Bruen] and william Euens." † Thomas Bray was by trade a carpenter; he always lived at the head of Little River, in West Gloucester, and died there November 30, 1691. His widow, "Mary Bray the aged d. March 21, 1707." ‡ On May 12, 1712, "John Roberts who married with Hannah Daughter of said Thomas Bray Decᵈ," Mary Ring, widow of John Ring, deceased, Sarah Sawyer, widow of James Sawyer, deceased,§ Thomas Bray, Sr., yeoman, and Philip Stanwood who married Esther, daughter of said Thomas Bray, deceased — all of Gloucester, quitclaimed to "our brothers John Bray & Nathaniel Bray both of Said Gloucester . . . the two Eldest Sons," all right that they might have in the "housing lands or other Estate," in Gloucester, "wᶜʰ our father yᵉ Said Thomas Bray Deceas'd Dyed Seized or Possessed off." This deed was signed by the above heirs including —

	ye mark of	
Witnesses :	" John **I R** Roberts	[seal]
"John Newman	Hannah **H** Roberts " ‖	[seal]
John Ring		
Abraham Sawyer."		

"Jnᵒ Roberts" was made freeman, May 19, 1669, with a number of other Ipswich men; ¶ he was a commoner

---

* *Gloucester Births, Marriages, and Deaths, 1642–1780* : 234.
† *Suffolk County Court Files,* No. 133.
‡ *Gloucester Births, Marriages, and Deaths, 1642–1780* : 26.
§ Vide The Mariner Family.
‖ *Essex County Deeds,* Book 25 : 3.
¶ *Massachusetts Bay Colony Records,* vol. 3 : 583.

or voter of that town in 1677 and 1678. The date of his
removal to Gloucester is fixed as early in 1679 by the sale,
in September of that year, of the land derived from the
"propriaty of Robert Roberts ffather of the said John now
deceased :" * —

"I John Roberts of Cape Ann alias Gloster † . . .
planter," for £18, paid by John Burnam of Chebacho . . .
carpenter viz John Burnam Senʳ . . . twelue pounds of
the Sayᵈ Some in money and six pounds in Sheepe or cattle
or both . . . Sell . . . vnto the afore sayᵈ John Burnam
Senior . . . A certaine pcell of Land both vpland & meadows or marsh ground, conteineing by estimation Six acres
more or less, Scituate lying and being in the South Syd of
Chebcho riuer, bounded . . . round by the land of the sᵈ
John Burnam Senior and the meadow or marsh on the South
& the north bounded upon a creeke, coming from the Saw
mill . . . I the sayᵈ John Roberts haue sett my hand &
seale the thirtieth day of September," 1679.

> Witnesses: "John Roberts & a mark   [seal]
> "William White   Hanah Roberts & a Marke"   [seal]
>   Thomas Bray"

"John Roberts and Hanah his wife acknowledged the
aboue written to be there act & deed before me March 25
1680   Daniell Denison "

On May 10, 1705, the town committee of Gloucester,
consisting of nine men, laid out to " John Roberts Seor . . .
about six acres being situate and lying on the southeasterly side of a lott which the said Roberts formaly had of
the town for goeing out a solder near Nathanaell Hadlocks
dwelling house." ‡ As Hadlock's land bordered on the
Ipswich line, Babson suggests that the lot alluded to, as a
grant for military service, might have been given to John

---

* Vide page 950.
† *Essex County Records, Ipswich Records,* Book 4 : 311.
‡ *Transcript of Commoners' Records, 1707-1820,* vol. I : 234-235.

Roberts by the adjoining town of Ipswich ; * but the phrase
— "formaly had of the town" — can only be construed as
a Gloucester grant of which there is now no record. The
service appears to have been in King Philip's War, when
John Roberts and Nathaniel Hadlock were credited with
£3 : 01 : 08, each, on January 25, 1675–76, at the Lancaster
Garrison.†

At a town-meeting held in Gloucester, June 16, 1707, six
acres more were granted to John Roberts, "Beginning [at]
Benjamin Haskells Seor corner . . . with a stripe of land
lying between his own land he had his house upon."

"John Roberts, se," died January 10, 1714, in Gloucester,
leaving no will. The only record of the settlement of his
estate appears in the two following documents : ‡—

On February 5, 1714–15, "Nathan¹ Robards Late of Gloster
now of Beverly . . . Bricklayer Eldest son of Mʳ John Robards
Late of sᵈ Gloster Decᵈ," for the "consideration of Twenty pounds
to him in hand payᵈ by & received of his father yᵉ Said John
Robards decᵈ, in yᵉ time of his Life," acknowledged himself
"to be full content, . . . & for Ever quitt Claime unto my Honʳᵈ
Mother Hannah Robards & to my Broʳ William Robards both
of Gloster," all interest in the estate of his father.

(Signed)

Witnesses :   "Nathan¹ Robards" [seal]
" John Herrick
  Richard Hascall junʳ"

On January 21, 1714–15, "John Robards, housewright, David
Downing Cordwʳ who married with Susannah Daughter to John
Robards Senʳ Late of Gloster Decᵈ Thomas Robards Ebene-
zerʳ Robards & Mary Robards all of Gloster . . . all Children
foresᵈ John Robards Decᵈ . . . for yᵉ sum of ten pounds " each,
their share of "yᵉ whole of yᵉ som of fifty pounds," quitclaimed
to their mother, "Hannah Robards, and brother, William Rob-

---

* Babson's *History of Gloucester*, 1860 : 133.
† *King Philip's War*, by George M. Bodge, 1906 : 355.
‡ *Essex County Probate*, Book 311 : 255, 256.

ards . . . All yᵉ Right . . . Title," etc., to their father's estate, with all the "personall or moveables our Honʳᵈ ffather Jnᵒ Robards Dyed seized or possessed off." (Signed)

Witnesses: "Thomᵉ Robards [seal] John Robards [seal] "Thomas Bray Ebenᵗ Robards [seal] David Downing [seal] John Ring" Mary Robards [seal] Susanna Downing[seal]"

Sworn to before "John Newman Just Peace" Jan. 21, 1714, at Gloucester.

Hannah Roberts, widow of John Roberts, died March 23, 1717, in Gloucester, "aged about 55 years." *

ISSUE †

I. Nathaniel⁸, b. March 26, 1679, probably in Gloucester.

The marriage intention of Nathaniel Roberts to Mary Biles was published "April 22, 170–," in Gloucester; they were married July 1, 1707, in Beverly, Mass.‡ Mary Biles (or Boyles), b. March 27, 1681, in Beverly, was daughter to Jonathan and Elizabeth (Patch) Biles, of that town.

On Feb. 19, 1710–11, the Commoners of Gloucester laid out to Nathaniel Roberts, "two acres . . . bounded southerly by the land which the said Roberts bought lately of Aaron Davis." § In 1714, "Nathaniel Roberts of Gloucester . . . bricklayer," sold to his brother "John Roberts . . . carpenter," for £16,‖ eleven acres "on the southwesterly Side of Anna Squam river . . . Near unto yᵉ Land which is Joseph Prides," together with the five acres which he bought of Aaron Davis. This deed was signed : —

"Nathaniel Robberts   [seal]
The mark Mary Robberts"   [seal]
of

Nathaniel Roberts moved soon afterward to Beverly, where he purchased a farm and called himself husbandman.

---

* *Gloucester Births, Marriages, and Deaths, 1642–1780*: 234.
† *Gloucester Births, Marriages, and Deaths, 1642–1780*: 234.
‡ *Vital Records of Beverly*, 1907: vol. 2 : 265.
§ *Transcript of Commoners' Records of Gloucester, 1707–1820*, vol. 1 : 236.
‖ *Essex County Deeds*, Book 66 : 174.

In 1733, he sold his home, described as "an old House & Ten acres" of land, bounded "Northerly with the High Way That leads to Manchester at the Crook Gate (So Called) . . . & a little distance from the late Dwelling house of Jnᵒ. Woodbery & now of John Lee Junᵗ."* Nathaniel Roberts died in 1751, at Beverly, aged seventy-one years. The widow of Nathaniel Roberts (no name given) died Jan. 30, 1761, in Beverly, aged eighty-two years. There may have been a number of children, though but one was recorded in Gloucester or Beverly.

Issue : 1. Jonathan⁴, b. March 28, 1708, in Gloucester.†

The marriage intention of Jonathan Roberts, of Beverly, and Hannah Badcock, of Manchester, was published Oct. 27, 1734, in Beverly. He d. Feb. 25, 1786, in Manchester, aged "seventy odd" years.

> Issue: ‡ I. Mary⁵, b. 1735 ; bap. Nov. 29, 1741, in Manchester ; d. Jan. 15, 1748-49, "of yᵉ throat distemper."
>
> II. Joanna⁵, bap. Nov. 29, 1741, in Manchester.
>
> III. Miriam⁵, bap. Nov. 29, 1741, in Manchester.
>
> IV. Jonathan⁵, bap. Oct. 7, 1744, in Manchester ; d. Jan. 29, 1748-49, aged four years.
>
> V. William⁵, bap. April 5, 1747, in Manchester ; d. March 21, 1749, aged two years.
>
> VI. William⁵, bap. Sept. 3, 1749, in Manchester.
>
> VII. Mary⁵, bap. Nov. 17, 1751, in Manchester.
>
> VIII. Anna⁵, bap. April 28, 1754, in Manchester.

2. Nathaniel⁴. Nathaniel Roberts, who had a wife, Hannah, in Manchester, was probably another son of Nathaniel Roberts.

> Issue : § I. Nathaniel⁵, bap. Jan. 20, 1741, in Manchester. He mar. March 17, 1764, Mary Presson, of Beverly. Their children recorded in Beverly were John⁶, Nathaniel⁶, and David Presson⁶ Roberts.

---

* *Essex County Deeds*, Book 60 : 121 ; Book 72 : 263.
† *Gloucester Births, Marriages, and Deaths, 1642-1780* : 234.
‡ *Vital Records of Manchester*, 1903, vol. 1 : 108, 210, 286.
§ *Vital Records of Beverly*, 1907, vol. 2 : 544, 264 ; vol. 1 : 282-283.

II. John[2], b. Dec. 12, 1680, in Gloucester.   He was mar. March 17, 1702–03, in Beverly, to Patience[3] Haskell, by Rev. Robert Hale, of Beverly.* She was daughter to Benjamin[2] Haskell (William[1] Haskell), of Gloucester; she d. Oct. 13, 1749, in Gloucester, in her "69th year."

John Roberts, Jr., was a carpenter by trade.   He was granted, June 16, 1707, seven acres in Gloucester, adjoining "his owne land and near the dwelling house westerly from his house . . . also two acres near Jones bridge," near land he had recently bought of Aaron Davis.   In 1708, he was granted ten acres "on Chebacco Side," and about six acres more which "fell out to be the seventy-first lot in number." On Jan. 14, 1722–23, he drew a wood lot "between Kittle Cove and Little River by virtue of a comõn right given to Jacob Elwell by the town."   Twelve acres were laid out to him, in 1726, "beginning at the way that leads from the precinct meeting house to Thomas Haskells."   On Aug. 4, 1729, there were laid out to John Roberts nine acres "near the road that leads from the head of Little River to Haskell's sawmill," adjoining land of John Mariner.   This lot was receipted for April 21, 1730 —

"As witness my hand

John Roberts."

In Jan., 1731–32, a tract of fifty acres, "in the westerly Precinct in s^d Gloaster," was granted to "Capt. Isaac Eveleth, Lieut. Samuel Herrick, Mr John Roberts, Ensign Thomas Bray," and seventeen others, to be laid out in lots for them, on condition that the owners fence the land and make several ways (roads) as defined in the grant.   In 1760, the town sold to "John Roberts Es.^r" about two acres "near the precinct meeting house adjoining the parsonage land."†

Babson says of this "John Roberts, Esq.," that he "spent his whole life near the place of his birth, in the West Parish, esteemed by neighbors and friends as a just and upright man.   He was selectman of the town several years.   He d.

---

* *Vital Records of Beverly, Massachusetts*, 1907, vol. 2 : 264.

† *Transcript of Commoners' Records, 1707–1820* : 235, 237, 396, 513, 616, 685.

May 3, 1767, in Gloucester," aged eighty-six years, four months.* His descendants were numerous in the town, as late as 1850, most of them living in the West Parish.

Issue : † 1. Benjamin⁴, b. Dec. 11, 1703, in Gloucester. "Benjamin Robards & Ruth Marston" were mar. Dec. 14, 1728, in Gloucester, by Rev. Richard Jaques. They were members of the Second Church, in which several of their children were baptized. Benjamin Roberts d. April 4, 1777, in Gloucester, aged seventy-three years.

Issue : I. William ⁵, b. Sept. 22, 1729 ; d. Nov. 21, 1729, in Gloucester.

II. Mary ⁵, b. Aug. 1, 1731 ; bap. Aug. 15, 1731, in the Second Church ; d. Nov. 24, 1731, in Gloucester.

III. "Judeah" ⁵, b. Jan. 13, 1733, in Gloucester. Although this name is distinctly written Judeah in the Gloucester records, she must have been the Judith Roberts who was mar. Nov. 30, 1752, to Benjamin Averill, Jr., by Rev. Richard Jaques. Benjamin Averill, Jr., was son to Benjamin and Sarah (Blye) Averill, of Ipswich.

Issue : ‡ 1. Ruth Averill, bap. Dec. 2, 1754, in Gloucester.

2. Samuel Averill, bap. May 18, 1755, in Gloucester. He married, and lived in Gloucester.

3. Joshua Averill, bap. Sept. 18, 1757, in Gloucester ; d. Dec., 1778, on a Privateer.

4. Benjamin Averill, bap. July 21, 1760, in Gloucester.

5. John Averill, bap. Oct. 10, 1762, in Gloucester ; he was drowned Oct. 1, 1784, near the bar of Chebacco River.

IV. Samuel ⁵, b. Aug. 28, 1735 ; bap. Aug. 31, 1735, in the Second Church.

V. Joshua ⁵, b. Jan. 8, 1738 [1737–38] ; bap. Jan. 8, 1737–38, in the Second Church.

---

* *Babson's History of Gloucester*, 1860: 133.
† *Gloucester Births, Marriages, and Deaths, 1642–1780:* 235.
‡ *The Essex Antiquarian*, vol. 6: 88.

VI. Ruth[5], b. Sept. 11, 1740; bap. Sept. 14, 1740, in the Second Church.

VII. William[5], b. July 15, 1744, in Gloucester.

2. Patience[4], b. March 9, 1707; d. Dec. 24, 1713, in Gloucester.

3. Samuel[4], b. Feb. 25, 1710; d. Aug. 2, 1727, in Gloucester.

4. John[4], b. April 20, 1714, in Gloucester. John Roberts and Mary Lane, dau. to John Lane, Jr., were mar. Nov. 13, 1735, in Gloucester. He was deacon of the Second Church of Gloucester, many years. Mary Roberts d. in 1787, at Gloucester, aged about seventy-two years. Deacon John Roberts died, "much lamented," Dec. 27, 1793, aged seventy-nine. His will, dated March 18, 1788, was proved Jan. 6, 1794.[*]

Issue: [†] I. David[5], b. Aug. 8, 1736, in Gloucester; d. next day.

II. Comfort[5], b. Aug. 8, 1737, in Gloucester; d. same day.

III. Sarah[5], b. Nov. 22, 1740, in Gloucester; d. young.

IV. Eliphalet[5], b. Oct. 20, 1743, in Gloucester, mar. March 21, 1765, in Gloucester, to Abigail Lufkin, by Rev. John Rogers. One child was recorded in Gloucester: Adam[6], b. Jan. 29, 1766.

V. Levi[5], b. July 10, 1746, in Gloucester; mar. Oct. 25, 1774, in Gloucester, to Susanna Lincoln (widow), by Rev. Samuel Chandler. Only child recorded in Gloucester: 1. Mary[6], b. May 2, 1776.

VI. Hannah[5], b. May 8, 1748, in Gloucester. She was mar. (intention, Dec. 26, 1772) to her cousin, Josiah[5] Choate, Jr., of Gloucester.[‡]

VII. John[5], b. Dec. 30, 1750, in Gloucester.

VIII. Sarah[5], b. Oct. 17, 1753, in Gloucester. She was mar. (intention, Jan. 1, 1774) to Elias Haskell, of Gloucester. They had sons, Epes, Eli, and William Haskell, who were mentioned in her father's will.

---

[*] *Essex County Probate*, Book 363: 78–80.
[†] *Gloucester Births, Marriages, and Deaths, 1642–1780*: 235.
[‡] *Gloucester Births, Marriages, and Deaths, 1642–1780*: 43.

5. Patience[4], daughter to John[3], b. Dec. 2, 1715, in Gloucester. Patience Roberts was mar. Nov. 11, 1736, in Gloucester, to Josiah[4] Choate, by Rev. Richard Jaques.* Josiah[4] Choate, b. Sept. 16, 1715, was son to John[3] and Miriam (——) Choate, of Ipswich (Thomas[2], John[1] Choate).† Josiah[4] and Patience (Roberts) Choate were members of the Second Church of Gloucester.

Issue: I. Ephraim[5] Choate, b. Jan. 8, 1738, in Gloucester; d. young.

II. Elizabeth[5] Choate, b. Sept. 20, 1740, in Gloucester.

III. Ephraim[5] Choate, b. Feb. 2, 1743, in Gloucester.

IV. Sarah[5] Choate, b. July 28, 1745, in Gloucester.

V. Josiah[5] Choate, b. Oct. 20, 1747, in Gloucester; he mar. (intention, Dec. 26, 1772) Hannah[5] Roberts, daughter to Deacon John[4] and Mary (Lane) Roberts.

VI. Thomas[5] Choate, b. Feb. 26, 1749–50, in Gloucester.

VII. Patience[5] Choate, b. Nov. 28, 1752, in Gloucester.

VIII. William[5] Choate, b. Jan. 22, 1756, in Gloucester.

IX. Judith[5] Choate, b. Aug. 10, 1758, in Gloucester.

6. Ephraim[4], b. Nov. 5, 1721, in Gloucester. "Ephraim Robberts and Dolly Francis, of Medford," were mar. June 13, 1751, in Gloucester, by Rev. Mr. Jaques.‡

Several members of the Francis family removed from Medford to Beverly, among them Colonel Ebenezer Francis, who fell at Hubbardton, Vt., July 7, 1777. He married, 1766, in Beverly, Judith Wood, by whom he had four daughters and one son. Dolly Francis appears to have been daughter to John Francis (younger brother to Colonel Ebenezer) and his wife Dorothy.§

Four children of Ephraim[4] and Dolly (Francis) Roberts were recorded in Gloucester.

* *Gloucester Births, Marriages, and Deaths, 1642–1780*: 42.
† *The Hammatt Papers, 1633–1700*, by Abraham Hammatt, 1854, No. 1 : 52.
‡ *Gloucester Births, Marriages, and Deaths, 1642–1780*: 235.
§ *History of Medford, Massachusetts*, by Charles Brooks, 1886 · 179–180, 534.

Issue: I. Patience[5], b. May 18, 1758, in Gloucester; d. Nov. 28, 1759.

II. Ephraim[5], b. April 13, 1759, in Gloucester.

III. Nathan[5], b. March 8, 1766, in Gloucester.

IV. Dolly[5], b. June 11, 1769, in Gloucester.

III. Susanna[3], daughter to John[2], b. about 1682, in Gloucester, was mar. Nov. 5, 1701, in Ipswich, to David Downing.* He was b. about 1677, in Ipswich, son to John[3] and Mehitable (Braybrook) Downing, of that town.

On June 12, 1699, soon after David became of age, his father, "John Downing Sen[r]," and Mehitable, wife of John, both of Ipswich, for "love & natural afection," conveyed to "David Downing our Sonne . . . the full halfe part of that halfe of y[e] farm Wee now liue vpon . . . in Chebacco in Ipswich . . . formerly called Richard Braybrooks farme from whom we derived our right." In 1701, "Thomas Luskin [Lufkin?] Jun[r]" and David Downing, both of Ipswich, husbandmen, took measures to establish the bounds between their lands "w[ch] they had By gift and purchase from their father John Downing Sen[r] of Ipswich." Jan. 19, 1704–05, David Downing and "Susanna my now wife," of Ipswich, sold to Thomas Butler, of that town, for £118, sixty acres of the westerly end of "Braybrooks farme . . . Chebacco," adjoining land of "John Burnam, Mr Adams Coggswell," and the "widow Varney's two acres." That same month, he also sold "half of that comoñage" belonging to Braybrook's farm.†

David Downing went to Gloucester, soon after the sale of his holdings in Ipswich. On Jan. 25, 1708–09, the Commoners of Gloucester granted to William Coggswell and David Downing, ten acres on "Chebacco Side . . . & the lot they drew . . . fell out to be the 65th;" at the same time they "drew the lot on the Cape No. 112." Later in the year, a lot that "buts on Jonesses riuer att the north end" was granted to the heirs of "M[r] William Cogswell deceased of Chebacco in Ipswich & David Downing." Jan.

---

* *Ipswich Births, Marriages, and Deaths*, vol. 1: 203.
† *Essex County Deeds*, Book 15: 287, 62; Book 17: 70; Book 33: 256.

20, 1710–11, the town also laid out to David Downing, "by virtue of half a common right," land on the southerly side of his own land.*

"David Downing, of Gloucester, . . . yeoman," for £24, sold to Daniel Ring, of Gloucester, half of ten acres of salt marsh "on Brewin's Island," near Jones's River. This deed was signed Dec. 16, 1709, by

Witnesses :

"John Roberds jun*r*
Will*m* Ring
John Ring."

"David Downing [seal]

Susan*h* S Downing [seal]
    mark

her

"John Roberts, aged 79 years," made oath Sept. 26, 1760, that he signed the deed as "John Roberds jun*r* altho y*e* seal now appears to be torn of." The deed was recorded Feb. 26, 1761, nearly fifty-two years after it was made.†

On Feb. 14, 1710–11, David and Susanna Downing, of Gloucester, sold to Daniel Riggs, of the same town, for £127, their "now dwelling house & about fourteen Acres of vpland Lying most parte of it on y*e* Northwardly Side of y*e* high way or road leading along towards y*e* ferry." This farm he bought of Colonel John Wainwright, of Ipswich, in 1704. When he sold it to Riggs, he also added five acres of marsh, half an island, and half of ten acres of salt marsh, — the latter presumably what was remaining "on Brewin's Island." ‡

The sale of his farm looks as though he contemplated removal elsewhere, yet there is no record of it. "Susanna, wife of David Downing (aged about 39 years) dyed Dec*r* 22, 1719," in Gloucester; "David Downing (aged about 46 years) Dyed Sept. 20, 1723." § It is probable that there were other children ; the following appear in the Town and Church records : —

---

* *Transcript of Commoners' Records, 1707–1820*, vol. 1 : 343, 633, 717, 169.
† *Essex County Deeds*, Book 109 : 111.
‡ *Essex County Deeds*, Book 16 : 161 ; Book 35 : 161.
§ *Gloucester Births, Marriages, and Deaths, 1642–1780* : 79.

Issue : * 1. Hannah⁴ Downing, bap. September, 1703, in
the First Church of Gloucester, was mar. Dec. 3,
1719, in the Second Church, to Ebenezer Day, by
Rev. Samuel Tompson. Issue: I. Jonathan Day.
II. Lucy Day. III. Hannah Day. IV. Job Day.
V. Jerusha Day. VI. David Day. VII. James
Day. †

2. David⁴ Downing, b. about 1704 or 1705 in Gloucester ;
was mar. Dec. 14, 1722, to Mary Joslin, of Gloucester, by Rev. Samuel Tompson. Issue: I. Jonathan⁵
Downing, bap. Oct. 26, 1729, in the Second Church.

3. Lucy⁴ Downing, b. Nov. 29, 1706 ; bap. Dec. 10, 1706,
in the First Church of Gloucester.

4. Jonathan⁴ Downing, b. about 1708 in Gloucester, was
mar. Jan. 30, 1728–29, to Sarah Day, by Rev.
R. Jaques, in the Second Church. Issue: I. Sarah⁵
Downing, b. Dec. 11, 1729, in Gloucester ; bap. Dec.
14, in the Second Church.

IV. Samuel³, b. March 25, 1685, in Gloucester. "Samuel Roberts & ———— ——, mar. Feb. 27, 17—, by Mr White." ‡ The
record of this marriage was partially erased in the original town book ; it has been impossible to trace him
further.

V. Thomas³, b. Aug. 2, 1687, in Gloucester. It seems probable that this Thomas Roberts was the one who later
appeared in Newbury, Mass. His wife was Elizabeth
Richardson ; she had, in 1743, brothers Thomas and Caleb
Richardson, and "brother William late deceased." §

In August, 1746, Samuel Roberts, of Dover, N. H., was
appointed executor of the estate of his father, "Thomas
Roberts late of Newbury in the County of Essex." The
appraisement of the estate, taken Sept. 30, 1746, gave the
house and land as £9 : 7 : 6, cash, £9 : 3 : 6, total valuation,

* *Gloucester Births, Marriages, and Deaths, 1642–1780 : 79* ; also *Church Records of Gloucester, 1703–1835.*
† *Gloucester Births, Marriages, and Deaths, 1642–1780 : 71.*
‡ *Gloucester Births, Marriages, and Deaths, 1642–1780 : 234.*
§ *Essex County Deeds, Book 114 : 53.*

£30 : 19 : 1. The following account was sworn to by " Sam^{ll} Roberts," the executor, Oct. 6, 1746 : "The Ballance of the Personal Estate Clear of All Charges amounts To £13 : 14 :2½ which proportion Among ye Children gives 34/3½ New Tenor." * Two children of "Thomas and Elizabeth Roberts" were recorded in Newbury ; there must have been several others.

> Issue : † I. Elizabeth⁴, b. Nov. 13, 1715, in Newbury.
>
> II. Samuel⁴, b. Jan. 21, 1716, in Newbury. In 1746, he was of Dover, N. H.

VI. Ebenezer³, b. Jan. 22, 1690, in Gloucester. (Vide infra.)

VII. William³, b. about 1693, in Gloucester. There is no record of his birth, but he must have been of age in 1718, when he signed the petition of the Proprietors of Falmouth, Maine, with Job Harris, James Mariner, Adam Mariner, and others, for the reëstablishment of their ancient rights.‡

In the winter of 1719–20, "William Robards " was granted sixty acres of land in Falmouth, on condition that he settle there within a year, § — a condition which he fulfilled. He served in Captain Francis Baker's company, from Feb. 28 to Nov. 6, 1722, in Colonel Thomas Westbrook's expedition against the Indians.|

The wife of William Roberts was Sarah ——— ; they probably were married at Falmouth. He died in the spring of 1723. At Ipswich, May 6, 1723, a "Letter att Large of Administration " on the "estate of William Roberds . . . Late of Casco Bay . . . having Estate Jn ye Town of Gloster Jn the County of Essex," was "granted unto Sarah Roberds Widow and Relict of said William Roberds." The inventory of his estate included the homestead which he and his mother bought, Jan. 21, 1714–15, of the other heirs.¶

---

* *Essex County Probate*, Book 323 : 225 ; Book 327 : 113.
† *Town Records of Newbury*, vol. 1 : 170, 176.
‡ Vide The Mariner Family.
§ *Records of the Proprietors of Falmouth, Maine*, vol. 1 : 12.
| *New England Historical and Genealogical Register*, vol. 48 : 437.
¶ Vide pages 995–996.

"A True Jnventory * of all and singular both Reall and Passonall estate Jn Gloster of William Roberds Late of Casco Bay Dec.ᵈ wᵗʰ was show.ᵈ to us who are Desired by yᵉ Administratrix &c.ᵉ viz.ᵗ

"Jmpᵐ To his House and Homestead about six acres £50	0	0
To his Wareing Apparrill of all Sorts 100/: table Linnen of all sorts 32/ 6	12	0
To an old Suit Curtains 30/ to yarn 8/ Earthen ware 4/6 . . . 2	2	6
To Puter 12/ wooden ware 6/ glass bottles 2/ Sword & Catutch box 8/ 1	8	0
To Gunn 12/ Chest Draws 25/ 2 other D.ᵒ 12/ Bedsteed &c.ᵉ 15/ 3	4	0

her

Sarah X Roberds admˣ

mark

"This was Pìuᵈ: by: us under Oath as Wittness our hands May 16ᵗʰ: 1723 Before yᵉ: Honbˡᵉ John Appleton Esqʳ Judge of yᵉ Prob.ᵗ &c.ᵉ: this 16ᵗʰ May 1723 Sarah Roberds made oath yᵉ above was a true Jnventory to yᵉ best of her [illegible] and jf more come to hand to give an acco.ᵗ thereof sworne

attestt Dan.ᵘ Appleton Reg.ᵗ "

In a further account of the estate, May 17, 1725, Sarah Roberts brought in a bill of £15, for "Bringing up young child."

Issue: 1. Job⁴, b. March 14, 1721, in Falmouth, Maine.†

He settled in Biddeford, where he mar. July 25, 1745, Sarah⁴ Tarbox, b. 1720, daughter to Nathaniel³ Tarbox, of Biddeford.‡ On Jan. 1, 1748, Job Roberts, of Biddeford, yeoman, sold to Daniel Sawyer, of Falmouth, for £74, seventy-four acres, it being his portion of the hundred and four acres of common land granted by the town of Falmouth to "William Roberds," § his father. Before 1750, Job Roberts had removed with his family to Buxton.

VIII. Mary³, b. Oct. 28, 1696, in Gloucester; d. Aug. 16, 1717, "near 21 year."

IX. Job³, b. March 19, 1701, in Gloucester; d. June 16, 1725, in Gloucester, "aged 24 years."

---

* *Essex County Probate*, Book 313: 624; Book 315: 234.

† *Willis's Manuscript*, New England Historic Genealogical Society, Boston: 80.

‡ *New England Historical and Genealogical Register*, vol. 42: 32.

§ *York County Deeds*, Book 30: 54.

EBENEZER[3] ROBERTS

Ebenezer[3] Roberts, son to John[2] and Hannah[2] (Bray) Roberts, was born January 22, 1690, in Gloucester. He was married January 13, 1715, by Rev. John White, to Sarah[4] Elwell, of Gloucester.* Ebenezer Roberts probably never made a wiser move than his marriage. His wife Sarah, b. February 8, 1692, was daughter to Jacob[3] and Abigail[2] (Vincent) Elwell, of Gloucester, descendants of two of the earliest and most prominent families of the town. Jacob[3] Elwell was son to Samuel[2], and grandson to Robert[1] Elwell. The latter was not only a pioneer, but was prominent in no small measure in building up the town. To understand the value of his services, it is necessary to note conditions at that period.

The attention of the colonists was first attracted to Cape Ann by its natural advantages as a fishing station. On January 24, 1623–24, Robert Cushman, acting for the Pilgrims at Plymouth who already had erected fishing-stages on Stage Neck (now Stage Fort Park), wrote to Governor Bradford from England : "We have tooke a patente for Cap Anne." † At about the same time, the Rev. John White, of Dorchester, England, sent over a company equipped for fishing, who took possession of all the improvements there. For a time it was disputed territory, but in less than three years it was abandoned by both parties.‡ A permanent settlement was begun in 1631 ; in 1639, special privileges were granted by the General Court to such as shall "inhabit there." § In February, 1642, the Rev. Richard Blynman, who had been accompanied to New England by several Welsh gentlemen of note, went to Gloucester from

---

* *Gloucester Births, Marriages, and Deaths, 1642–1780:* 234, 235.

† The original patent may be seen at the Essex Institute, Salem, Massachusetts.

‡ Vide pages 523, 524.

§ *New England Historical and Genealogical Register,* vol. 23 : 396.

Plymouth, Massachusetts. This "Welch party," as it was termed, included among others Hugh Caulkin, Obadiah Bruen, Hugh Pritchard, Walter Tybbot (now Tibbets or Tebbets), John Sadler, and Mr. Fryer. All these men except the last had been propounded for freemen, March 2, 1640–41, at Plymouth.* Others joined them at Gloucester, including Hugh Roberts, who married a daughter to Hugh Caulkin.

The first church was organized at once by Mr. Blynman, who became their pastor. William Stevens, Mr. Sadler, Obadiah Bruen, George Norton, William Addes, Thomas Milward, Mr. Fryer, and Walter Tybbot were appointed by the Massachusetts Commissioners "to manage the affairs of the plantation," which was incorporated in May of that year (1642) as the town of Gloucester. On May 14, 1645, "Hugh Caulkin, Thomas Smyth & Obedia Brewen" were "chosen to end small controversies at Gloucester." †

Robert Elwell‡ was first at Dorchester, Massachusetts,

---

* *Plymouth Colony Records*, Court Orders, vol. 2 : 8.

† *Massachusetts Bay Colony Records*, vol. 2 : 98.

‡ Robert [1] Elwell mar., first, Joane or Jane; she d. March 31, 1675, at Gloucester. His second wife was Alice, widow of —— Leach, who survived him. She d. April 10, 1691. Her will, dated March 24, 1690–91, was proved June 30, 1691; it referred to an agreement made with her sons, Samuel and Robert Leach, and daughter, Alice Bennett.

ISSUE BY FIRST WIFE

I. Samuel [2] Elwell, b. about 1636, in Dorchester, Mass.

II. "Second Child," bap. Aug. 28, 1639, in Salem; d. aged six months.

III. John [2] Elwell, bap. "23 (11) 1639–40," in Salem.

IV. Isaac [2] Elwell, bap. " 27 (12) 1641–2," in Salem; he mar. Mehitable Millet.

V. Mary [2] Elwell. She became the second wife of Samuel [1] Dolliver, son to Robert Dolliver, of Stoke Abbot, Dorset, England. Samuel [1] Dolliver was of Marblehead, Mass.; in 1652, he bought a farm at Freshwater Cove, in Gloucester; he d. there in 1683. Issue by first wife: 1. Joseph [2] Dolliver. 2. William [2] Dolliver. Issue by second wife : 3. Samuel [2] Dolliver, b. July 9, 1658. 4. Mary [2] Dolliver, b. March 26, 1662. 5. Richard [2] Dolliver, b. April 18, 1665. 6. Sarah [2] Dolliver, b. Dec. 10, 1667. 7. John [2] Dolliver, b. " 2 (7) 1671 [Sept.

in 1634, perhaps earlier; he afterwards went to Salem. In 1642, he bought land at Gloucester, but did not at once

---

2, 1671]." He mar. Nov. 1, 1700, Susanna [2] Mariner, daughter to John [1] and Elizabeth (——) Mariner, of Gloucester.

 VI. Josiah [2] Elwell, who d. before his father, leaving a son William [3].

 VII. Joseph [2] Elwell, mentioned in his father's will.

 VIII. Sara [2] Elwell, b. 1651; d. same year in Gloucester.

 IX. Sarah [2] Elwell, b. May 12, 1652; d. Aug. 26, 1655, in Gloucester.

 X. Thomas [2] Elwell, b. Nov. 12, 1654, in Gloucester.

 XI. Jacob [2] Elwell, b. June 10, 1657, in Gloucester; d. May 21, 1658.

 XII. Richard [2] Elwell, bap. April 11, 1658, in Gloucester.

SAMUEL [2] ELWELL

Samuel [2] Elwell mar. Esther or Hester Dutch, daughter to Osman and Grace (——) Dutch, of Gloucester. Samuel Elwell had land at Little Good Harbor, Gloucester; he d. about 1697, in that town. His widow d. Sept. 6, 1721, in Gloucester, aged about eighty-two years.

ISSUE

 I. Samuel [3] Elwell, b. March 14, 1659, in Gloucester.

 II. Jacob [3] Elwell, b. Aug. 10, 1662, in Gloucester.

 III. Robert [3] Elwell, b. Dec. 13, 1664, in Gloucester.

 IV. Esther [3] Elwell, b. Aug. 25, 1667, in Gloucester.

 V. Sarah [3] Elwell, b. 1670; d. the same year in Gloucester.

 VI. Ebenezer [3] Elwell, b. Feb. 29, 1670–71, in Gloucester.

 VII. Hannah [3] Elwell, b. Aug. 11, 1674, in Gloucester.

 VIII. Elizabeth [3] Elwell, b. July 30, 1678, in Gloucester.

 IX. Thomas [3] Elwell, b. in Gloucester.

JACOB [3] ELWELL

Jacob [3] Elwell mar. July 5, 1686, in Gloucester, Abigail, daughter to William and Rachel (Cook) Vincent. Abigail Elwell was b. May 8, 1668, in Gloucester. Jacob Elwell was killed in the French and Indian War, at Cape Sable, May 2, 1710. His widow sold land in 1714 and 1728.

ISSUE

 I. Benjamin [4] Elwell, d. Sept. 11, 1694, in Gloucester, aged about seven years.

 II. Rachel [4] Elwell, b. Feb. 21, 1688, in Gloucester; mar., first, Peter Lurvey; mar., second, John Day, of Gloucester, who d. before Nov., 1743. In Jan., 1743–44, she was the wife of John Scott, of Rowley.

 III. Abigail [4] Elwell, b. Jan. 30, 1690, in Gloucester; mar. Joseph Foster.

 IV. Sarah [4] Elwell, b. Feb. 8, 1692, in Gloucester; mar. Ebenezer [3] Roberts.

 V. Jacob [4] Elwell, b. March 26, 1695, in Gloucester; d. Sept. 20, 1713.

remove his family.   They were established in 1649 at Gloucester, when he was chosen selectman, an office he filled
several other terms.   He had a grant of land at Stage Neck,
in 1651, but finally settled at Eastern Point.   On the "27ᵗʰ
of 7ᵐ 1652," William Stevens, Robert Tucker, and Robert
Elwell were "Commissioners of Gloster apoynted to end
small causes."*   In February, 1652–53, and March, 1654(-
55), Robert Elwell was again appointed Commissioner; in
1658, he was chosen Magistrate,† and "did considerable
business in this judicial position."   March 5, 1657–58, he
was chosen Constable, and served for one year.‡   The title
"Goodman" was often prefixed to his name.   In September, 1660, Goodman Elwell and William Vincent were sureties for John Jackson; in March, 1663, Goodman Elwell was
"master of the voyage."§   Robert Elwell died May 18,
1683, in Gloucester.   The day before his death, "being
caste upon my Bed of sicknesse and weaknesse," he signed
his will with a mark.   He bequeathed to his eldest son,
Samuel, the "House I now dwel in together with all the
Barnes & buildings neare adjoyning . . . also all the Neck
of Land whereupon my sayd House standeth," on condition that Samuel maintain "my selfe and his mother my
wife . . . while we live."   Mention was made of sons John,
Joseph, Isaac, Thomas, "Josiah deceased," and "Daughter

VI. Hannah⁴ Elwell, b. May 6, 1697, in Gloucester; mar. John Brown, of
    Falmouth, Maine.

VII. Vinson⁴ (Vincent) Elwell, b. July 15, 1700, in Gloucester.

VIII. Lydia⁴ Elwell, b. Dec. 10, 1702, in Gloucester; mar. Jonathan Brown.

IX. William⁴ Elwell, b. April 6, 1705, in Gloucester; mar. Elizabeth ——.
   Before 1727, they were in Falmouth, Maine, where he became the possessor
of large tracts of land.

X. Mary⁴ Elwell, b. Jan. 29, 1708, in Gloucester; mar. Joseph Brown.

   Vide *The Elwell Family in America*, by Rev. Jacob Thomas Elwell, 1899:
3, 7, 12.

* *Essex County Probate* (copy), Book I: 143.

† *Essex County Court Papers*, Book 2: 115, 120, 155; Book 4: 359.

‡ *Essex County Court Papers*, Book 5: 287, 325.

§ *Essex County Court Papers*, Book 6: 71; Book 8: 271.

Deleber [Dolliver]." His will was proved June 26, 1683, at Salem; the original paper is preserved.* His inventory valued houses and lands at £182; total amount £290 : 10 : 0. "William Vinson, William Sargent [and] Steven Glover" were the appraisers.†

Abigail[2], wife of Jacob[3] Elwell, was daughter to William[1] Vinson, or Vincent,‡ by his second wife, Rachel. William[1]

---

* *Essex County Court Papers*, Book 39 : 145-146.

† *Essex County Probate* (copy), Book II : 701-708.

‡ The first wife of William[1] Vincent was Sarah; she d. Feb. 4, 1660-61. He was mar., second, June 10, 1661, by Mr. Samuel Symonds, to Rachel Cooke, daughter to Bridget Verney, of Gloucester. In the will of Bridget Verney, dated Nov. 10, 1671, proved "27 : 9 : 72," she mentioned "daughter Rachel Vinson (the wife of William Vinson) . . . my sonne in law," and appointed him executor of her estate. Rachel Vinson, widow of William, d. Feb. 15, 1707, in Gloucester.

ISSUE BY FIRST WIFE

I. Sarah[2] Vincent, b. about 1639-40, in Salem, Mass. She was mar., "11th : 9mo : 57 [1657]," by Major Hathorne to Jeffrey[1] Parsons, of Gloucester.

Issue: 1. James[2] Parsons, b. "18 : 10m : 58," in Gloucester.

2. "Jeffery"[2] Parsons, b. "25 : 11mo : 1660," in Gloucester.

3. Sara[2] Parsons, b. "April 19, '63," in Gloucester.

4. John[2] Parsons, b. "24 : 3 : 1666," in Gloucester.

5. Elizabeth[2] Parsons, b. "22 : 1 : '69," in Gloucester.

6. Nathaniel[2] Parsons, b. "16 : 1mo : 7⅜ [1674-75]," in Gloucester.

7. Abigail[2] Parsons, b. "25 : 1 : '78," in Gloucester.

8. Ebenezer[2] Parsons, b. "28 : 11 : '81," in Gloucester.

II. Hannah[2] Vincent, b. about 1642, in Salem.

III. Elizabeth[2] Vincent, b. May 16, 1644, probably in Gloucester.

IV. Richard[2] Vincent, b. "1 : 7 : ——;" d. July 24, 1652.

V. John[2] Vincent, b. May 15, 1648, in Gloucester.

VI. William[2] Vincent, b. Sept. 9, 1651, in Gloucester; d. Dec. 9, 1675.

VII. Richard[2] Vincent, b. Sept. 1, 1658, in Gloucester · d. Dec. 26, 1675.

ISSUE BY SECOND WIFE

VIII. Thomas[2] Vincent, b. April 1, 1662, in Gloucester; d. Dec. 31, 1675.

IX. Abigail[2] Vincent, b. May 28, 1668, in Gloucester; mar. July 5, 1686, Jacob[3] Elwell.

Vide *Essex County Probate* (copy), vol. 1 : 745, 747; *Gloucester Births, Marriages, and Deaths, 1642-1780* : 301; *Salem Births, Marriages, and Deaths*, vol. 1 : 195, 196.

Vincent, born about 1610, in England, was son to Francis
Vincent, who married Sarah, daughter to Sir Francis Paulet;
Sarah Paulet was maid of honor to Queen Anne, wife of
James I.*   About 1635, William Vincent, a potter by trade,
appeared in Salem, Massachusetts ; in 1636, he had a grant
of land.   On the "12th 5mo, 1637," he sent in "his request
for acomodation;" the "7th 6th ^{mo} 1637," he "desireth 5
acres and it is granted him."   On the "30th 1mo, 1640," there
was granted by the town of Salem to William Vincent, two
acres, to "Vincents mother," two acres, and to "Vincents
Cozen Antho: Buckstone," two acres.†

   William Vincent did not long remain at Salem.   In 1643,
he was made freeman;‡ in 1646, and several years afterwards, he was selectman of Gloucester.   He built three
houses near Vincent's Spring; and, though the name became extinct in the town after the second generation, it is
perpetuated in Vincent's Spring and Vincent's Cove, and
in the baptismal name of many of his descendants, to the
present day.   From a deposition of 1663, we learn that he
was then about fifty-three years of age, and from another
deposition that his wife Sarah, in 1660, was about forty.§
They both were devout members of the First Church of
Gloucester.   In June, 1652, "William Vincent, goodwife
Vincent, Sarah Vincent & Grace Dutch," testified in Court
at Salem that Mrs. Holgreave, of Gloucester, had said that
"the Teacher [minister] was more fitted to be a Ladies
chamberman than to be in the pulpit."   In September,
1653, William Vincent was witness that "reproachful
speeches" had been made "against their teacher in town
meeting."   At the same session of Court, Vincent brought
suit against Edmond Marshall, of Ipswich, "for defaming
his wife saying She was a witch."   In "The free offer for

---

* *History of Gloucester*, by James R. Pringle, 1892: 52.
† *Essex Institute Collections*, vol. 9: 24, 51; vol. 4: 116; vol. 9: 102.
‡ *Massachusetts Bay Colony Records*, vol. 2: 293.
§ *Essex County Court Papers*, vol. 8: 271; vol. 6: 73.

the present maintenance of Brother Millet being faithfull to gitt an Elder" for the church, March, 1658, William Vincent subscribed £2, Samuel Dolliver, £1, Thomas Bray £0 : 7, and Robert Elwell £0 : 0.*

In 1646, William Vincent, who was "chosen by the town to keep an ordinary and to sell wine, petitioned for confirmation" from the Court. March, 1657, "Sylvester Everleth" and William Vincent were appointed Commissioners to end small causes in Gloucester; in 1658, William Vincent was Constable.† His numerous depositions, scattered through the Court Papers, show that his judgment was sought in many different directions. He does not appear to have been related to Humphrey Vincent, of Ipswich, who died about 1664, childless and alone.‡ William Vincent died September 17, 1690, in Gloucester, aged about eighty years.§ His will, dated March 19, 1684, was proved November 25, 1690. It left to his "loving wife Rachel Vinson" all his houses and lands "during her natural life." Upon her death, the property was to revert to "John Vinson," his son, "in case he be living and return home again." Said son was to "have my house and barn and all the upland upon the western side of the Cartway," also all the saltmarsh at Little Good Harbor; but "if my sone John comes no more then my daughter abigail shall have all the Estate given to him, to her own propper use and behoofe." The will was signed with his mark. The dwelling-house and lands mentioned in the inventory were valued at £125 : 00 : 03 ; total amount, £180 : 03 : 08. The widow *Sarah* takes oath to the truth of the inventory, November 25, 1690; ‖ she must have been a third wife.

Before 1725, Ebenezer Roberts joined in the movement

---

* *Essex County Court Papers*, vol. 1 : 104; vol. 2 : 138, 134; vol. 4 : 287, 288.
† *Essex County Court Papers*, vol. 1 : 43; vol. 3 : 254, 255; vol. 4 : 243, 259.
‡ *Essex County Court Papers*, vol. 10 : 161, 163, 164.
§ *Gloucester Births, Marriages, and Deaths, 1642-1780* : 301.
‖ *Essex County Probate*, Book 303 : 4-7.

for the re-settlement of Falmouth, Maine. As a resident of Falmouth, with his wife Sarah, he joined the other heirs in conveying, for £10, to William[4] Elwell, son to Jacob[3] and Abigail[2] (Vincent) Elwell, of Falmouth, all title to "any Estate of one kind or other Real or Personal of William Vincent alias Vinson late of Glocester . . . Potter Deceased our Grandfather and any Estate of Iacob Elwell late of said Glocester yeoman Deceased or in any Estate of Abigail Elwell widow of said Iacob Elwell Deceased & Daughter of said William Vinson Dec^d our Mother . . . with all Priviledges," etc. This deed was signed November 15, 1743.

Witnesses :

"Andrew Riggs Peter ✗ Lovery
his
mark

Benj^a Allen Christ^o Strout

Orlando Bagley Thomas Bagley

John Corny Daniel Brown

Daniel Brown Mary 𝑚 Elwell
her
mark

(Signed)

"Rachel ℛ Day [seal]
her
mark

Joseph Foster [seal]

Abigail ⚡ Foster [seal]

Ebenezer Roberds [seal]

Sarah ✝ Roberds [seal]
her
mark

Jon^a Brown [seal]

Lydia ⊃ Brown [seal]
her
mark

Joseph Brown [seal]

Mary Brown " * [seal]

Ebenezer Roberts received his first grant of land in Falmouth, May 29, 1727, consisting of thirty-four acres on the south side of Fore River. On August 27, 1728, "John Brown & Joshua Woodbery of Falmouth," granted to "Joseph Cobb Ebenezer Robords Robert Thorndike & John White all of the Town . . . aboves^d to each of them . . . a

---

* *Essex County Deeds*, Book 87 : 20.

sixth Part or an equal Priviledge with us in the Stream & Falls granted to us by the aboves^d Town at Barberry Creek."[*] In 1736, Joshua Woodbery, yeoman, Joseph Cobb, glazier, and Ebenezer Roberds (no occupation given), all of Falmouth, sold to Phinehas Jones, for £24, their "half parte" of the mill-stream, at Barberry Creek, on the southerly side of Fore River, with all the "land on both sides for building mills Dams & Laying loggs & the priviledge of flowing," also half of the "Remains of the former mill that was built on s^d stream." The original deed is in the Willis Collections, at the Portland Public Library; from it the following signatures have been copied : —

Witnesses :
"Sam^{ll} Moody
Robert Bayley
   witnesses for Roberts
John Sawyer Jun
Robert Bayley "

Joshua Woodbery [seal]

Joseph Cobb [seal]

Ebnoezer roberds [seal]
                   †

The condition imposed by the Falmouth Proprietors was that the lots should be built upon "within twelue months."

---

[*] *York County Deeds*, Book 25 : 90; Book 13 : pt. 1 : 162.
† *Willis Collections*, Portland Public Library, Book T : 206; also *York County Deeds*, Book 20 : 265.

On May 11, 1730, among those who had "fulfilled the conditions of settlement" were Joshua Woodbury, Samuel Cobb, John White, William White, Ebenezer Roberts, John Mariner, and Adam Mariner.* In "minutes of grants," without date, showing a list of Ancient Proprietors and their lands as laid out, is the following: "Eber Roberts—90 [acres]—parte of his prors Rit [proprietor's right]."† This does not appear to include his other grants: sixty acres, laid out September 30, 1731, "beginning at a Birch tre the northeast Corner of sd Roberts his ten acre lott;" thirty-four acres, on February 13, 1739-40, lying in Falmouth "on the South Side the fore River it being so made in the Room of 34 acres which was laid out to him the 29th of Ma[y] 1727 and now Improved by Robert Elder," adjoining "Joseph Wessons [Weston's] Sixty Acre lott;" thirty acres, March 10, 1739-40, on the south side of Fore River, "bounded Northerly on the head of wm Elwells Sixty acre lott thirty rods in Breadth . . . until thirty acres be made up."‡

On December 12, 1741, "Ebenezer Robards of Falmouth . . . Husbandman," for "Love & good will and affections," conveyed to his son Ebenezer, forty acres on the south side of Fore River, adjoining land of Joseph Parker, William Elwell and —— Wesson. Two years later, father and son bought, for £50, of William Elwell and his wife Elizabeth, forty acres adjoining "land of Joseph Parker and Ebenezer Roberts Forty and Two Rods," also joining land of Elisha Parker, William Dyer, Joseph Parker, "Halls Land and Reuben Dyers." It was described in the deed as "neigh to my [Elwell's] now Dwelling House, it being all the Lands that I have to the Southward of the Highway." In March, 1746-47, Ebenezer Roberts, Jr., bought the half owned by

---

* *Collections of the Maine Historical Society*, Documentary History, Second Series, vol. 11: 13–14; also *Proprietors' Records of Falmouth* (copy), vol. 1: 12; vol. 2: 433–434.

† *Willis Collections*, Portland Public Library, Book T: 82.

‡ *Records of the Proprietors of Falmouth* (original), vol. 1: 124, 238, 239.

his father, for £50.* These tracts of land will be mentioned later in connection with the son.

During the period 1729-1735, Ebenezer Roberts was a fence-viewer, hogreeve, fish-culler, constable, and tithing-man, of the town of Falmouth. In a list of tax-payers of the Second Parish of Falmouth, in 1735, Ebenezer Roberts was taxed £0 : 11 : 8 for polls, £0 : 2 : 0 real estate, and £0 : 0 : 10 personal. No one paid more, many paid less.

He was all his life a farmer. On October 30, 1764, when he was seventy-four years of age, "Ebenezer Roberts of Falmouth . . . yeoman . . . in Consideration of Love Good-will and Affection which I have and do bear towards my loving Grandson Ephraim Roberts Son of my Son Vincent Rob-erts Deceased," conveyed to Ephraim by deed, "after my Decease and the Decease of my now Wife . . . all my House where I now dwell with all the Lands whereon the House stands & all the Upland that belongs to me near the said House it being eighteen Acres and three quarters & eleven square Rods," with the barn, orchard, cattle, and "Implements for the carrying on my Husbandry," with all the timber and wood standing on the said land. He gave to Ephraim his sheep, horses, and all his cattle, all the "Goods and Chattels now being in my present Dwelling House," and four acres of fresh marsh joining the homestead ; also twenty-one acres, it being part of two thirty acre lots, the other part of which had already been given "to my son Ebenezer Roberts." The deed was signed : —

Witnesses :

"George Dyer   "Ebenezer Roberts [seal]

                                                            her
Daniel Merritt "   Sarah + Robers " [seal]
                                                            ma rk

"The condition of this Instrument is" that the "within named Ephraim Roberts is to maintain & to provide . . . for the comfortable Support . . . of the within named

---

* *York County Deeds*, Book 24 : 90 ; Book 26 : 114.

Ebenezer Roberts & wife during their natural Life." Acknowledged November 19, 1764, by : —

Witnesses :

"George Dyer

Daniel Merrit"

"Ebenezer ┿ Roberts [seal]
his / mark

Sarah ≥ Roberts   [seal]
her / mark

Ephraim Roberts " * [seal]

This deed, in lieu of a will, disposed of his estate.   There
is no record of his death; he was living in 1767, and died
before 1773, when his son Ebenezer had dropped the "Jr."
The date of death of his wife Sarah is not known.   The births
of their first three children are recorded in Gloucester ; †
two more are recorded in Falmouth.   There probably were
a number of others, but they cannot be identified.

ISSUE

I. Samuel⁴, b. Nov. 9, 1715, in Gloucester ; d. April 6, 1717.

II. Ebenezer⁴, b. Sept. 13, 1717, in Gloucester. (Vide infra.)

III. Sarah⁴, b. April 11, 1720, in Gloucester.   She was mar. (intention, June 19, 1737) at Falmouth, to John³ Mariner,
son to John² and Sarah (Sawyer) Mariner.‡

IV. William⁴, b. March 18, 1725, in Falmouth,§ Maine.   There
appears to be no further trace of him.

V. Vincent⁴, b. June 8, 1727, in Falmouth.   This date is given
as a correction in the city records, from July 25, 1727 ;
his name is there spelled "Vinson Robards." ‖   He was
baptized as "Vincent Robards," July 9, 1727, in the First
Church of Falmouth.¶   "Vincent Robards and Isabella
Dyer, both of Falmouth," were published March 16, 1744–
45, in that town.**   Isabella⁴ Dyer, b. July 10, 1729, was

---

* *Cumberland County Deeds*, Book 4 : 273.

† *Gloucester Births, Marriages, and Deaths, 1642–1780 : 235.*

‡ Vide The Mariner Family.

§ *Records of Portland*, Births, vol. 1 : 356, 358.

‖ *Records of Portland*, Births, vol. 1 : 360.

¶ *Records of First Parish of Falmouth*, 1898 : 95.

** *Falmouth Intentions and Marriages*, vol. 1 : 592.

daughter to William [2] and Hannah (Strout) Dyer, of Cape Elizabeth, formerly of Truro, Mass.[*]

Family tradition says that Vincent Roberts was killed at Pemaquid by the Indians, but it appears more probable that his death occurred at Annapolis, Nova Scotia. The Rev. Thomas Smith, in his diary, wrote under date of Feb. 25, 1747: "We hear father Hall and Roberts of this place lately died at Annapolis."[†] Little is known of Vincent Roberts; he was seventeen years of age at the time of his marriage, and but twenty when he died — not yet of age. His widow, Isabella Roberts, was mar. (intention, Dec. 13, 1749) to John Fickett, of Cape Elizabeth.[‡] John and Isabella (Roberts) Fickett were the parents of a number of children, but their births are not recorded in Falmouth nor Cape Elizabeth. Benjamin, b. 1750, John, Jr., b. 1752, and Vincent Fickett have been proved their sons; Nathaniel, Abner, and Zebulon Fickett may also belong to the same family. These six young men served in the Revolution, from Cape Elizabeth.[§]

> Issue by first husband: 1. Ephraim [5], b. about 1745, in Falmouth. Ephraim Roberts and Joanna Dyer, both of Cape Elizabeth, were mar. July 2, 1766, by Rev. Ephraim Clark.[‖]

At a town-meeting, held March 15, 1768, in Cape Elizabeth, "Sargent Ephraim Roberts" was chosen one of twelve hogreeves; in 1774, he was tithing-man and surveyor of highways; in 1781, "Lieut. Robards" was assisting Captain Benjamin Fickett in enlisting soldiers. He was also collector of taxes and Constable; the latter office he again filled, in 1783.[¶] It is not often that a man appears locally with such rank as Sergeant or Lieutenant, without official recognition in the Archives; in this case, "Ephrain Robards, of Cape

---

[*] Vide The Dyer Family.
[†] *Smith and Deane's Journal*, 1849: 127.
[‡] *Falmouth Intentions and Marriages*, vol. 1 : 448.
[§] *Massachusetts Soldiers and Sailors in the War of the Revolution*, vol. 13: 642, 643, 643, 644, 643, 642.
[‖] *Maine Historical and Genealogical Recorder*, vol. 3 : 101.
[¶] *Cape Elizabeth Town Proceedings*, vol. 1 : 18, 58, 127, 128.

Elizabeth," is mentioned only as private, in Nov., 1775, in Captain Daniel Strout's company, Colonel Enoch Freeman's regiment, assisting in building the fort at Falmouth Neck.*

On Oct. 30, 1764, Ephraim Roberts received by deed of gift from his grandparents, Ebenezer and Sarah Roberts, the homestead on which they lived and other land, amounting to forty-three acres.† There is no record of the death of Ephraim Roberts; on April 27, 1808, his heirs sold, to Rishworth Jordan, for $1,000, fifty-six acres of land in Cape Elizabeth, it "being the estate of the late Ephraim Roberts & whereon he lately dwelt."‡

Issue:§ I. Sarah⁶, b. April 20, 1767, in Cape Elizabeth. She was mar. March 31, 1783, to Josiah Wallace, or Wallis, a mariner of Cape Elizabeth. In 1808, they were living in Harrington, Washington County, Maine.

II. Vincent⁶, b. May 27, 1769, in Cape Elizabeth. Vincent Roberts and Abigail⁵ Jordan were mar. July 12, 1806, by Rev. William Gregg, pastor of the Church in Cape Elizabeth. Abigail Jordan, b. 1777, in Cape Elizabeth, was daughter to John⁴ and Elizabeth⁴ (Jordan) Jordan, of that town.

Vincent Roberts settled on the Jordan farm, situated on what is now Sawyer Street, between Cottage Street and South Portland Heights. He and his sons built boats and carried them to Portland to sell. Sometimes he was obliged to exchange them for goods; when he had no use for the goods, he sold them at his house to his neighbors. On April 14, 1838, he conveyed, for $900, to his sons, Jordan Roberts and Ebenezer Roberts, all the real estate he owned in Cape Elizabeth, including buildings; the deed was signed, "Vincent Roberts." ‖

---

* *Massachusetts Soldiers and Sailors in the War of the Revolution*, vol. 13: 365.

† Vide page 1017.

‡ *Cumberland County Deeds*, Book 55 : 243.

§ *Cape Elizabeth Records*, vol. 1 : 355.

‖ *Cumberland County Deeds*, Book 191 : 206.

Abigail, wife of Vincent Roberts, died Dec. 30, 1837; she was buried in Mt. Pleasant Cemetery, on Meeting-House Hill. He died, about 1847, on the homestead, "a very old man," and was buried beside his wife. His age was about seventy-eight years.

Issue: 1. Betsey[7]; she was mar. Jan. 8, 1829, in Cape Elizabeth, to Ephraim Dyer.

2. Jordan[7], b. 1814, in Cape Elizabeth; he mar., about 1842, Martha G. Boynton. He was a boatbuilder and farmer at Cape Elizabeth, and lived on a part of the homestead of his father, "near Great Meadow, at the head of Mill Creek Brook." Jordan Roberts d. April 8, 1861, aged forty-seven years. He was buried in Mt. Pleasant Cemetery, where his widow, Martha, was placed later beside him.

Issue: I. Sarah A.[8], b. March 20, 1843, in Cape Elizabeth.

II. Emily C.[8], b. July 15, 1845, in Cape Elizabeth.

3. Ebenezer[7]; he mar., about 1847, Mary ——. She was of the Society of Friends.

4. A daughter, who went to Baldwin, Maine.

III. Ephraim[6], b. Aug. 12, 1774, in Cape Elizabeth. He probably was not living in 1808, when all the other children signed the deed of sale of their father's homestead.

IV. Asa[6], b. June 27, 1776, in Cape Elizabeth. He was a boatbuilder of Cape Elizabeth; his wife was Miriam Dyer; their marriage intention was published Jan. 25, 1800, in Cape Elizabeth.

Issue: 1. Mary[7], b. Nov. 13, 1800, in Cape Elizabeth; d. Nov., 1801.

2. Joseph[7], b. Sept. 20, 1802, in Cape Elizabeth.

3. Mary[7], b. Sept. 10, 1804, in Cape Elizabeth.

4. Joanna[7], b. Oct. 8, 1806, in Cape Elizabeth.

V. Ebenezer[6], b. Dec. 10, 1779, in Cape Elizabeth. In 1808, he was a coppersmith, of Portland; later he removed to Buxton. His wife was Sally Thorn-

dike, of Buxton (mar. intention, Feb. 8, 1801, in
Cape Elizabeth); they had a large family.

VI. Joseph[6], b. Jan. 11, 1783, in Cape Elizabeth. Joseph Roberts and Achsah Dyer were mar. Aug.
8, 1802, by Rev. William Gregg.* Achsah Dyer,
b. July 22, 1783, in Cape Elizabeth, was daughter
to Robert[5] and Miriam[5] (Jordan) Dyer, of that
town. Soon after his marriage, Joseph Roberts
removed to Portland, where he was engaged in
building boats. In September, 1835, he bought
of William, Edward, and John Oxnard, grandsons
to General Jedidiah Preble, a lot of land on Oxford Street, Portland, which his executors sold
on Oct. 25, 1836.† Achsah, widow of Joseph
Roberts, d. Oct. 21, 1845, in Portland, aged
sixty-two years.

Issue:‡ 1. Zilpah[7], b. Aug. 15, 1803, in Portland;
d. April 19, 1821.

2. Sarah D.[7], b. Dec. 28, 1804, in Portland; d. Feb.
13, 1805.

3. Sarah D.[7], b. Jan. 13, 1806, in Portland. She became the second wife of William Briggs, of Portland, a "rigger" by occupation.

William Briggs mar., first, Elizabeth ——, who d. July 31,
1827, aged twenty-nine years. His second wife was Sarah
D. Roberts; she d. "Jan. 5, 1838, in Portland (parents unknown)." His third wife was Mary ——.

Issue by first wife: I. Abner Briggs, b. June 22,
1822, in Portland; d. April 5, 1839.

II. William Briggs, b. Sept. 13, 1824, in Portland.

III. Elizabeth Ann Briggs, b. Jan. 27, 1827, in Portland; d. Jan. 7, 1828.

Issue by second wife: IV. Joseph R. [Roberts?]
Briggs, b. June 9, 1829, in Portland.

V. Sarah Elizabeth Briggs, b. April 3, 1831, in
Portland; d. Jan. 7, 1832.

---

* *Cape Elizabeth Records*, vol. 1: 474.
† *Cumberland County Deeds*, Book 145: 384; Book 150: 129.
‡ *Records of Portland*, Births, vol. 5: 5.

VI. Sarah Elizabeth Briggs, b. March 8, 1833, in Portland; d. Aug. 8, 1833.

VII. Mary Frances Briggs, b. May 9, 1834, in Portland.

Issue by third wife: VIII. Elizabeth Briggs, b. April 24, 1839, in Portland.

IX. Sarah Augusta Briggs, b. Dec. 8, 1840, in Portland.

X. Catharine G. Briggs, b. Nov. 16, 1843, in Portland.

4. Joseph G.[7], b. Dec. 30, 1808, in Portland.

5. Enos D.[7], b. Jan. 7, 1810, in Portland. He was a sailor; he d. at sea, May 15, 1827.

6. Thomas F.[7], b. June 22, 1813, in Portland. He was a boatbuilder in Portland. In 1836, he was administrator, with his mother, of the estate of his father. Adaline, wife of Thomas F. Roberts, d. Aug. 7, 1850, aged thirty-one years; he d. Oct. 1, 1861, in Portland, aged forty-eight years.

7. Harriet N.[7], b. Nov. 26, 1814, in Portland.

8. Thomas U.[7], b. June 22, 1817, in Portland.

9. Nathan D.[7], b. Jan. 24, 1821, in Portland. His wife was Louisa[7] Jordan, b. 1820, daughter to Rufus[6] and Mary (Waterhouse) Jordan, of Cape Elizabeth. Nathan D. Roberts kept a store in Portland. He d. Nov. 10, 1907, in Portland, aged eighty-six years.

Issue: I. Harriet Louisa[8]. II. Mary Augusta[8]. III. Georgianna[8]. IV. Minnie[8].

10. Eunice D.[7], b. April 14, 1823, in Portland; d. Dec. 11, 1824.

VII. Joanna[6], daughter to Ephraim[5] Roberts, b. Feb. 13, 1786, in Cape Elizabeth; she was mar. to Benjamin Strout. In 1808, they were living in Harrington, Washington County, Maine.

VIII. Betsey[6], daughter to Ephraim[5] Roberts, b. June 19, 1791, in Cape Elizabeth; she was mar.

Dec. 30, 1807, in Cape Elizabeth, to Benjamin
Fickett, a farmer of that town.

VI. A son[4]. There must have been one or more sons to Ebene-
zer[3] and Sarah[4] (Elwell) Roberts, in Cape Elizabeth, who
have not been accounted for; yet it is impossible to prove
relationship. There was another Vincent Roberts in Cape
Elizabeth, who without doubt was grandson to Ebenezer[3]
Roberts. Vincent[5] Roberts and Sarah Sawyer were mar.
Nov. 21, 1790, in Cape Elizabeth, by Rev. Ephraim Clark.[*]
"Sarah, wife of s[d] Vincent Robarts Departed this Life
March the 3[d] A D 1806, in the 36th year of her age."
Nothing further is known of Vincent Roberts.

Issue: [†] 1. Daniel[6], b. Jan. 16, 1793, in Falmouth.
2. Joanna[6], b. Jan. 6, 1795, in Falmouth.
3. Mary[6], b. March 21, 1797, in Falmouth.
4. William[6], b. Sept. 14, 1800, in Falmouth.
5. Ephraim[6], b. —— 30, 1802, in Cape Elizabeth.
6. Sarah[6], b. Sept. 11, 1804, in Cape Elizabeth.

EBENEZER[4] ROBERTS

Ebenezer[4] Roberts, son to Ebenezer[3] and Sarah (Elwell)
Roberts, was born September 13, 1717, in Gloucester.[‡] His
brother Samuel died several months before the birth of
Ebenezer, consequently the latter occupied through life the
position of the eldest son. He was ten years old when his
father went to Falmouth. In his youth he probably followed
the sea, more or less; for many years he was a fisherman,
and lived at Purpooduck in Cape Elizabeth. Purpooduck
was a local term borrowed from the Indians. In the first
settlement, the Purpooduck side of Fore River, from Simonton's Cove to Stroudwater, "was fringed with farms and
settlers;" there was a fort as early as 1689 at Purpooduck
Point, where Fort Preble now stands.

---

[*] *Cape Elizabeth Records*, vol. 1 : 469.
[†] *Cape Elizabeth Records*, vol. 1 : 369.
[‡] *Gloucester Births, Marriages, and Deaths, 1642–1780*: 235.

Spring Point received its name from a spring of water just above high-water mark; it was enclosed by the outworks of Fort Preble, when that fort was constructed. In an attempt to improve the ancient boiling spring by blasting, seams were opened in the ledge which let in the sea and greatly damaged its pure waters. There is no trace of the spring to-day. The Point formerly belonged to John [3] and William [3] White, sons to Rev. John [2] White, of Gloucester, Massachusetts. Jerusha, widow of John [3] White, was married before 1741 to Benjamin Thrasher,[*] who occupied the property. In 1808, the Thrasher family sold the site to the government for a fort. It was on this lot that the first log meeting-house stood. The burying-ground connected with it adjoined the shore; the encroachment of the sea has washed much of it away, but a few headstones remain. Occasionally the Rev. John White sailed along the coast from Gloucester, to hold services. Parson Smith, of Falmouth, wrote in his Journal, under date of Sunday, July 24, 1725: "M[r] White preached over to Purpooduck A. M. . . . Sept. 21, 1741: Rev. M[r] White, of Gloucester, and his son dined here [at Rev. Thomas Smith's]. . . . Sept. 24: M[r] White preached an evening lecture at my house: it was very full. . . . Sept. 27: M[r] White preached; a very full meeting; people were pleased with the meeting. . . . Sept. 29: M[r] White went away." [†]

On April 13, 1737, Ebenezer Roberts, Jr., of Falmouth, was published to "Mary Kinnecum, of Gloucester;" [‡] they were married June 7, following, by Rev. John White, of Gloucester.[§] The groom was not quite twenty, and the bride lacked a month of being seventeen. She was born July 6, 1720, in Gloucester, daughter to Benjamin and Margaret

---

[*] *York County Probate*, Book 5: 136, 176.
[†] *Smith and Deane's Journal*, 1849: 47, 101, 102.
[‡] *Falmouth Intentions and Marriages*, vol. 1 : 567.
[§] *Gloucester Births, Marriages, and Deaths, 1642-1780*: 235.

(Josline) Kinnecum, of Gloucester.* The name Kinnecum is a corruption of Cunningham; through various transitions of "Kinningham," in Cape Elizabeth, "Chinecum" and "Kennecum," in Durham, etc., it has resolved itself correctly as Cunningham, in the Roberts family. There is little doubt that those who early bore the name of Cunningham, in Massachusetts, were of Scotch descent. The first mentioned was one Andrew Cunningham, of Boston; neither the "date of his arrival nor from whence he came" has been learned.† On October 25, 1684, he signed the records of the Scots Charitable Society, of Boston, commencing: "Wee are this day convined being Scottsmen and the sons of Scottsmen Inhabitants of Boston." ‡ It is possible that Benjamin "Kinnecum" was related to Andrew Cunningham, of Boston, but the records do not show it.

On February 1, 1738–39, about a year after his marriage, Ebenezer Roberts, Jr., yeoman, bought of Joseph Cobb, of Falmouth, three acres and twenty-four rods of land adjoining land of his father.§ Later, he acquired land from his

---

* Benjamin Kinnecum and Margaret Josline were married Feb. 8, 1711, by Rev. John White, of Gloucester.

ISSUE

I. John Kinnecum, b. Nov. 23, 1711, in Gloucester; d. 29th of the same month.

II. Joseph Kinnecum, b. April 6, 1717, in Gloucester; d. July 14, 1717.

III. Mary Kinnecum, b. July 6, 1720, in Gloucester; she was married to Ebenezer Roberts, Jr.

IV. Hannah Kinnecum, b. Aug. 29, 1722, in Gloucester.

V. Ann Kinnecum, b. Aug. 11, 1725, in Gloucester. She was mar. Feb. 8, 1743, to Joseph Davis, Jr., of Gloucester; their eldest son was called "Cunningham Davis."

VI. Sarah Kinnecum, b. Dec. 11, 1727, in Gloucester.

VII. Lydia Kinnecum, b. Sept. 19, 1732, in Gloucester.

Vide *Gloucester Births, Marriages, and Deaths, 1642–1780*: 161.

† *Andrew Cunningham of Boston, and Some of his Descendants*, by Henry Winchester Cunningham, 1901 : 3.

‡ *The Constitution and By-Laws of the Scots' Charitable Society of Boston*, 1878: 28.

§ *York County Deeds*, Book 21 : 144.

father and from William Elwell, eighty acres in all, on "Purpooduck side," as it was commonly called.* Though for a
time Ebenezer Roberts, Jr., called himself a yeoman, or
farmer, he soon returned to the fishing — probably because
most of his neighbors were engaged in it, and it brought
better financial returns. As a fisherman of Falmouth, he
sold for £13 : 06, in 1754, to Jonathan Fairbanks, fisherman,
the three acres he bought in March, 1738–39, of Joseph
Cobb. It was "agreed between the Parties that the said
Fairbanks is to allow Mr Ebenezer Robards a Road from
the s^d Mr Robards House across the head of the said Land
to the Main Road said Road is to be one Rod Wide." This
deed he signed : —

"Ebenezer Robard Ju^r/" [seal] †

By some means he became possessed with the idea that
there were coals and minerals on his land. This was not
strange, as the peculiar geological formation of many sections of Maine has given rise to a similar belief. Roberts
first appears to have interested one Archelaus Stone, a shoemaker of Cape Elizabeth, to whom he sold, March 8, 1748–
49, for £4, an acre and a quarter of this land, "with all
Whatsoever is thereon Growing Standing Lying & being." ‡
On June 7, 1756, he proceeded to organize a company among
his near neighbors to develop the mines, each binding himself to "the termes of partnership . . . in the sum of £200,"
as expressed in the following document : § —

"Ebenezer Roberts Junr Joseph Weston Elisha Parker and
Archelaus Stone all of Falmouth in the County of Cumberland
yeomen send Greeting *Whereas* we have reason to Believe that
there are Coals or Mines in Lands belonging to us lying and
Being in Falmouth afores^d being a Certain Ledge Bounded Northeasterly by the Line Between said Ebenezer Roberds and William

---

* Vide page 1016.
† *York County Deeds*, Book 32 : 218.
‡ *York County Deeds*, Book 27 : 230.
§ *York County Deeds*, Book 32 : 274.

Dyers Land as it Runs over Said Ledge to the Road that Leads to Black Point thence as Said Ledge Runs Southwesterly thro said Ebenezer Roberds Elisha Parkers Archelaus Stones and Joseph Westons Lands and being by ourselves alone unable and unwilling to be at the Expense of Sinking Pits and other Charges Nessessary for fully Discovering the same *Now Know* yᵉ that we the said Ebenezer Roberds Joseph Weston Elisha Parker and Archelaus Stone for the Consideration herein after mentioned Have and by these Presents do freely fully and absolutely . . . Sell unto Walter Simonton Esqʳ William Cotton Tanner Edmond Weston and Thomas Anderson Labourers all of Falmouth, each . . . an Equall Share and Proportion of all Coals and Mines that now are or hereafter may be opened and Discovered in sᵈ Ledge or any Part of our Lands."

	(Signed)	"Joseph Weston	[seal]
Witnesses:		Ebenezer Robards Junʳ	[seal]
"Enoch Freeman		Archeus Stone	[seal]
		ʰⁱˢ	
Stephen Longfellow "		Thomas T A Anderson	[seal]
		ᵐᵃʳᵏ	
		Walter Simonton	[seal]
		Edmund Weston	[seal]
		Elisha Parker	[seal]
		William Cotton "	[seal]

It is evident that in starting so momentous an undertaking these parties had sought advice from two leading men of Falmouth Neck, "Squires" Freeman and Longfellow, who appeared as witnesses. There is no further record of the development of these mines, which to-day would be known as worthless; there is no local tradition about them; no one living ever heard of them.

Upon the death, in 1754, of the Rev. Benjamin Allen, for twenty years pastor of the Second Parish, it was discovered that the church had become divided on the subject of Presbyterianism, through the teachings of Rev. William McClanathan, who had made himself and his religious tenets popular. On Oct. 4, 1754, certain of the inhabitants and freeholders petitioned the legislature of Massachusetts, for permission to divide the parish into "two Distinct Parishes or Districts." The petition, headed by William Wentworth, was signed by sixty-six citizens, including Christopher Mitchell, Robert Mitchell, and fourteen by the name of Jordan.* The attempted division was unsuccessful, but local feeling was intense, and "the parish was in a sad situation, dismally divided and quarreling." In the "midst of the confusion Rev. Ephraim Clark came among them to preach, and so great was the interest taken in the neighboring parish that many persons went from Portland to hear him." There was, however, a distinct opposition from the disaffected parties. They objected so strongly to his settlement that the "council first called" did not think proper to recommend him for installation; but the installation was finally held "in Mr. Simonton's orchard, at Purpooduck, May 21, 1756." Twenty-four members of the parish, refusing to pay their rates, were committed to jail. The religious warfare finally subsided, and Mr. Clark remained strongly intrenched in his parish until his death, in 1797.†

Ebenezer Roberts did not sign the petition; further evidence of his attitude in the matter is shown by the baptism of his son William, in the First Congregational Church of the neighboring town of Scarborough, on December 15, 1754, when the dissension was at its height.

As "Ebenez^r Robards," private, his name appears in the Train Band and Alarm List of the town of Falmouth, under command of Captain Loring Cushing. The roll was "sworn to at Falmouth, Second Parish, April 29, 1757." ‡ He also appeared as private, September 18, 1758, in Captain John Robinson's Falmouth company, which was "provided with

---

* *Collections of the Maine Historical Society*, Documentary History, Second Series, vol. 12 : 310.

† *History of Cumberland County, Maine*, Everts and Peck, 1880 : 254.

‡ *Massachusetts Archives*, vol. 95 : 330.

Bayonets." *   Although the "Jr." was not used by Ebenezer Roberts in either of these rolls, it is obvious that the
son, not the elderly father, was "training."

In the town affairs of Cape Elizabeth, Ebenezer Roberts
bore an inconspicuous part.   This section of the town of
Falmouth, early called the Second Parish, was set off as
Cape Elizabeth in 1765; the first town-meeting was held
December 2, of that year.   Captain John Robinson, Jr., was
moderator, Mr. Thomas Simonton, clerk, Mr. Peter Woodbury, constable.†   On March 10, 1767, Jonathan Sawyer,
William Mitchell, Levi Strout, William Webster, Jeremiah
Jordan Junr, James Leach, and Ebenez^r Roberts Junr" were
chosen field-drivers and fence-viewers.   March 13, 1773, it
was voted that Patrick Maxwell, "Ebenezer Robards," Benjamin Jordan, Dominicus Jordan, Daniel Strout, Peter Woodbury, Samuel Skillings, Noah Jordan, Zebulon Trickey, and
William Ray be surveyors of highways.‡   It is notable that
Ebenezer Roberts had this year, 1773, dropped the "Jr."
from his name, because of the death of his father.

There is no mention of the death of Ebenezer[4] Roberts in
Cape Elizabeth.   The oldest cemetery, near the site of the
first log meeting-house at Purpooduck, is nearly obliterated;
here naturally would be his last resting-place.   His name
does not appear in deeds nor in the records of Cape Elizabeth,
after the town-meeting of March 13, 1773, when he was but
fifty-six years of age; yet it is not probable that he went to
Royalsborough (now Durham), with his sons, as suggested.§
Had he gone, his son Ebenezer would have been designated
as Ebenezer, Jr., and he as Ebenezer, Sr., but the records
there have only "Ebenezer Roberds," "Robbarts," etc.

---

* Original Muster Roll, in possession of a descendant at Cape Elizabeth
(South Portland).

† *Cape Elizabeth Town Proceedings,* vol. I : 1.

‡ *Cape Elizabeth Town Proceedings,* vol. I : 13, 50.

§ *History of Durham, Maine,* by Rev. Everett S. Stackpole, 1903 : 243.

ISSUE

I. William⁵, b. March 15, 1737-38, in Falmouth;* d. before
1754.

II. Ebenezer⁵, b. about 1740, in Falmouth. He appears to be
the " Ebenezer Roberts and —— ——," whose marriage
was recorded March 15, 1764, in the Second Parish of Falmouth. They were married by Rev. Ephraim Clark.† The
name of his wife was torn out when the three following
records were mutilated. About 1774, he removed to Royalsborough, with others of the family. The hundred acres
upon which he settled consisted of the northeasterly half
parts of lots thirty and thirty-two.

The first recorded religious service in Royalsborough was
held on Feb. 23, 1774, by " Mr. Prince." On July 30, 1776,
it was voted at town-meeting that " Major Charles Gerrish &
Mʳ Ebenezer Robards be a commity and to hire a preacher,
voted that the minister preach at the House of Mʳ Ellot
Frost." Sept. 15, 1777, it was " Voted Messˢ Josiah Dunn,
Benjamin vining, Ebenezer Robbarts and Charles Hill Esqʳ
[be] a Commity of Correspondance, Inspection & Safety,"
and they were "sworn;" at the same time, it was voted " to
Purch[ase] some Corn to Suply the women whose Husbands
are gon in the army." ‡ In the History of Androscoggin
County the name of " Ebenezer Robbins " is erroneously
given on this committee.§

Previous to 1795, the church had been furnished with
various supplies. In the summer of that year, it was voted
to settle Rev. Jacob Herrick as their minister; Ebenezer
Roberts, Nathaniel Osgood, and William True were chosen
a committee to send for the new minister. Ordination services were held Feb. 22, 1796, — parsons Eaton, Lancaster,
Gilman, Johnson, Coffin, and Keylock, assisting. Among

---

* *Records of Portland*, Births, vol. 1 : 395.
† *Maine Historical and Genealogical Recorder*, vol. 3: 101.
‡ *Records of the Plantation of Royalsborough, 1774-1789.*
§ *History of Androscoggin County, Maine*, edited by Georgia Drew Merrill,
1891 : 792.

the thirty-five pew-owners, prior to 1804, were Ebenezer
Roberts, Nathaniel Osgood, Simeon Sanborn, Benjamin Vining, Jacob Sawyer, David Dyer, and Micah Dyer. In 1796,
Ebenezer Roberts was chosen surveyor of highways; in 1796
and 1797, he and Jabez Dyer formed the school committee.
In 1802, "Ebenezer Roberds" served on "petty jury," and
as tithing-man.*

There was a Train Band in Royalsborough, in 1778. In
1787, O Israel Bagley was captain of a military company, of
which John Randall and Joshua Snow were sergeants. The
company consisted of eleven officers, fifty-seven privates, and
sixteen men on the Alarm List. Among the privates were
Stephen Randall; Benjamin, Vincent, and William Roberts;
Nathan[iel] Osgood; James, John, and Joseph Parker; on
the Alarm List were John Cushing, Esq., Ebenezer Roberts,
and Benjamin Vining.†

The house of Ebenezer Roberts, on "lot 32," was burned
in 1805; he lost his life in the fire. An elderly lady, a descendant now living in Durham, remembers hearing it talked
about. It was said that her great-grandfather (whose name
she did not recollect, but which she felt sure was not Benjamin), at the time of the fire, went back into the house in
an effort to save something; he fell through into the cellar,
and could not get out. She also said that the children she
knew, "of the Roberts burned in his house," were Susanna,
wife of Joseph B. Allen, Benjamin her grandfather, Deborah
who married a Cross, and Stillman, whose wife's name she
did not know.

Benjamin⁶, son to Ebenezer⁵, afterwards built a house
upon the same lot, and nearly on the same site, which is still
standing. It is on the right side of the road leading from
Freeport to South West Bend, about a mile beyond the old
burying-ground where Rev. Jacob Herrick is buried. In the
settlement of the estate of Ebenezer Roberts by his son
Joseph, the following deed, dated May 17, 1806, was made

---

* *Town Records of Durham*, vol. I : 90, 91, 94, 95, 104, 143, 147.
† *History of Durham, Maine*, by Rev. Everett S. Stackpole, 1899 : 96, 97.

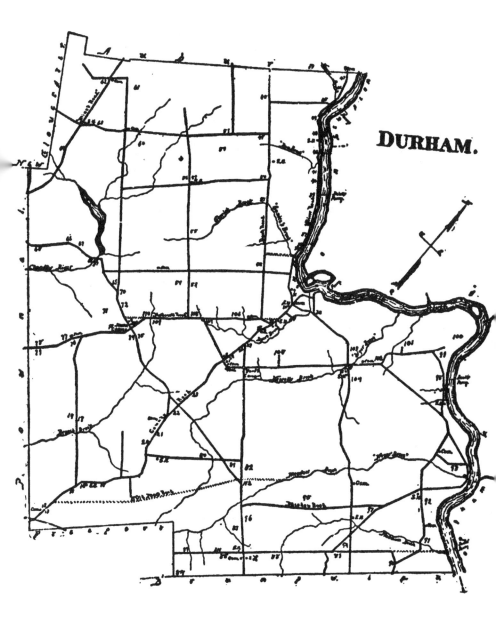

DURHAM.

LOCATIONS (IN PART) OF THE EARLY SETTLERS OF DURHAM, MAINE, AS SHOWN BY STACKPOLE'S MAP

1. North Meeting House
2. Friends' Meeting House
3. Methodist Episcopal Church
4. Union Church
5. Freewill Baptist Church
6. Congregational Church
7. Old Stone Mill
8. Gerrish's or Plummer's Mill
11. Steam Mill
14. Nathaniel Osgood
15. John Sydleman
17. Aaron Osgood
19. Major Charles Gerrish
20. Reuben Dyer, Francis Harmon
22. O Israel Bagley
24. Parson Herrick
26. Joshua Strout
28. Benjamin Vining
29. David Dyer (?), Barnabas Strout
30. Universalist Church
32. Micah Dyer
33. John Cushing, Abel Curtis
34. Dr. John Converse
35. Joseph Proctor's Tavern
36. Proprietor's House, built by Little
37. Jonathan Bagley, James Strout
38. Rev. Elijah Macomber, later Rev. Joseph Roberts
39. Jonathan Strout
41. Samuel Merrill, William Stoddard
44. William Webster
45. John Stackpole
46. Samuel Mitchell
52. Joseph Weeman
66. Samuel Roberts
68. Judah Chandler, Isaac Turner
69. Samuel York
70. Zebulon York
71. William Roberts
72. John Randall, Ezekiel Turner (?)
73. William True
74. Abel True, William Miller
79. Joseph Paul, Matthew Duran
80. Ezekiel Jones, Thomas Pierce
81. Ebenezer Roberts
97. Job Blethen, Josiah Day
99. James Blethen
101. Ebenezer Woodbury
102. John Vining
103. William Gerrish
105. Bela Vining
106. Peter Mitchell
108. Nathan Lewis, Benjamin Osgood
109. John Cushing
112. Israel Estes, Amos Knight

out by Josiah Little, representative of the Pejepscot Proprietors : * —

"Whereas Ebenezer Roberts, Late of Durham, in the County of Cumberland, Deceased, had a deed from the Pejepscot Proprietors, of the northeasterly half part of Lot numbered thirty, in said Town of Durham — which deed was burnt with his Dwelling House and all his other papers, which deed not being upon record — Now therefore Know ye, That I Josiah Little of Newbury . . . by Virtue of a Vote of the Pejepscot Proprietors . . . In Consideration of one Dollar paid me by Joseph Roberts of Durham aforesaid, Administrator upon the estate of said Deceased, and one of the Heirs to the same, for himself, and in behalf of the other heirs to the said deceased . . . do hereby . . . absolutely grant . . . unto the said Joseph Roberts and the other lawfull heirs . . . fifty acres of land in said Durham, being the Northeasterly half part of lot n? thirty."

On Oct. 9, 1807, the other heirs, Benjamin Roberts, yeoman, of Durham, Moses Roberts, merchant, of Portland, Susanna Roberts, "singlewoman," of Durham, Cunningham Roberts, yeoman, of Monmouth, Kennebec County, Joseph Paul, yeoman, of Monmouth, and Hannah Paul, wife of said Joseph, quitclaimed, for $500, to Joseph Roberts "all our right . . . in and to, two certain half lots of land " in Durham, " said lots being numbers thirty & thirty two, on which the said Joseph Roberts now lives . . . and formerly owned and possessed by Ebenezer Roberts late of said Durham deceased . . . also their right & interest to and in the Pew in the congregational Meeting house in said Durham which was the property and estate of the said Ebenezer Roberts together with all the buildings on said premises standing."
This deed was signed : —

"in presence of	"Benjamin Robarts	[seal]
test Joshua Snow	Moses Robards	[seal]
Peter sanborn	Susanna Robards	[seal]
kennecum Robards	Joseph Paul	[seal]
test Zebulon Harmon."	Hannah Paul	[seal]
	Kennecum Robards " †	[seal]

---

* *Cumberland County Deeds*, Book 49 : 403.
† *Cumberland County Deeds*, Book 57 : 385.

Joseph Roberts, "administrator upon the estate of Ebenezer Roberts late of Durham," by an order of Court holden at Portland, on the third Tuesday of November, 1807, sold to Elijah Macumber, of Durham, for $323, seventy-five acres of the "northeasterly end of lot N.° thirty two and the northeasterly end of the lot next adjoining . . . the remainder being set off to the widow for her dower in said farm and contains 26 acres, with one third of the barn and one third of the shed thereon standing." This deed was dated March 22, 1810; on the same date, Elijah Macumber re-conveyed the same land to Joseph Roberts, for $1,000. In both deeds Joseph Roberts is called "of Pejepscot . . . blacksmith;" the witnesses were John Cushing and Dorothy Cushing.*
He was called " Rev.ᵈ Joseph Roberts, of Pejepscot," in December, 1810, when Benning Wentworth, of Freeport, sold him land "in the town of Pejepscot . . . part of the Great lot N.° 5, on the Bank of the Great river Androscoggin," near Maxwell's claim.†

It is singular that the name of the wife of Ebenezer Roberts did not appear in the notice of their marriage, in Cape Elizabeth, or the name of his widow in the settlement of his estate or elsewhere. His widow probably was a second wife — Deborah Sawyer, of Freeport, whom he mar. Sept. 8, 1798, in Durham.‡ The records of Durham do not mention the date of the first wife's death, so she must remain nameless until some descendant, at present unknown, shall furnish it.

Issue by first wife: 1. Hannah⁶. She was mar. Oct. 26, 1789, to Joseph Paul, of Durham.§ In 1807, when they conveyed to Joseph Roberts their interest in the estate of her father, they were living on a farm in Monmouth, Maine.

2. Benjamin⁶, b. Oct. 24, 1769, at Cape Elizabeth. He

---

* *Cumberland County Deeds*, Book 59: 133; Book 60: 189.

† *Cumberland County Deeds*, Book 66: 95, 44; Book 65: 262; Book 63: 257; Book 67 : 340.

‡ *Durham Births, Marriages, and Deaths*, vol. 1 : 23.

§ *Durham Births, Marriages, and Deaths*, vol. 1.

mar. July 12, 1791, Sarah Paul, b. June 28, 1769, in Berwick, Maine.

Benjamin Roberts was a farmer of Durham. His house was on the right side of the road leading from Freeport to South West Bend, on "lot 32," which was originally sold by the Pejepscot Proprietors to his father. He and his wife were buried on his farm in the family lot; seven of their eight children were buried there. A stranger would have difficulty in finding the lot, it is so covered with low shrubbery; yet within the high stone wall surrounding the enclosure, on the opposite side of the road and a little nearer South West Bend than the house, there were once many gravestones, now crumbled away. "Grandma Sarah," shortly before her death, placed two memorial stones of granite in the lot, one for herself and husband, the other for their children; the stones are now well hidden among the bushes. Benjamin Roberts died in 1849, aged eighty years; his widow, Sarah, died in 1852, at the age of eighty-three.

Issue:* I. Elizabeth[7], b. April 26, 1793, in Durham; d. 1857.

II. Sarah[7], b. March 9, 1795, in Durham; d. unmar., 1823.

III. Abigail[7], b. July 14, 1797, in Durham; d. 1820.

IV. Benjamin[7], b. July 14, 1799, in Durham; d. April 29, 1805.

V. Patience[7], b. May 4, 1802, in Durham; d. 1805.

VI. Hiram[7], b. March 16, 1804, in Durham; d. unmar., 1856.

VII. Benjamin Paul[7], b. May 28, 1807, in Durham. He mar. Lucy Tyler, b. Aug. 22, 1811, in Pownal;† they lived at Durham in the house occupied (1906) by Mr. Fred. D. Miller. Captain Benjamin P. Roberts d. June 11, 1888, aged eighty-one years, fourteen days; his widow, Lucy, died May 4, 1896, aged eighty-four years, nine months. White marble stones mark their graves in the cemetery at

---

* *Durham Births, Marriages, and Deaths*, vol. 1 : 72.
† *Durham Births, Marriages, and Deaths*, vol. 2.

Durham, near the Freeport line, on the left side
of the road leading to South West Bend.

Issue: 1. Nahum[9], b. 1831. 2. John T.[9], b. 1832.
3. Harriet[9], b. 1834. 4. Sarah[9], b. 1836. 5. William H.[9], b. 1840. 6. Lucy E.[9], b. 1844. 7. Benjamin F.[9], b. 1846; d. July 9, 1865, in a hospital in
Virginia, aged eighteen years, eight months. He
was a member of Co. C, 32d Maine Regiment.
8. Mary E.[9], b. 1851.

VIII. Nahum[7], b. 1809; d. 1826, aged seventeen years.

3. Moses[6]. He mar. Jan. 18, 1798, Susanna Harmon, of
Durham.[*] In 1807, he was a "merchant of Portland," when he sold his interest in the estate of his
father to his brother Joseph;[†] in 1815, he lived in
Paris, Maine; in 1823, he was a citizen of Portsmouth, N. H.[‡] One of his sons appears to have returned to Portland; he probably had other children.

Issue: I. Moses[7]. The marriage intention of Moses
Roberts and Susan M. Knight, both of Portland, was
published June 16, 1838, in Portland; she d. Dec. 25,
1851, aged thirty-five years.[§] Moses Roberts must
have married again, as a daughter was born to him,
in Dec., 1853.

Issue by first wife:[‖] 1. Mary Caroline[8], b. Oct. 29,
1840, in Portland; d. there March 20, 1845.

2. William H.[8], b. Nov. 3, 1842, in Portland.

3. Harriet M.[8], b. Dec. 28, 1843, in Portland; d.
"1848, in Boston, aged 2 years, four months
... interred in Portland." (Obviously an error.)

4. Mary Ella[8], b. March 24, 1845, in Portland; d.
May 1, 1848, in Boston, aged three years; "interred in Portland."

---

[*] *Durham Births, Marriages, and Deaths*, vol. 1.

[†] Vide page 1033.

[‡] *Oxford County Deeds*, Book 11 : 187; Book 13 : 307; Book 25 : 14.

[§] *Records of Portland*, Marriages, vol. 5 : 15; Deaths, vol. 5 : 44.

[‖] *Records of Portland*, Births, vol. 5 : 35, 163; Deaths, vol. 4 : 204, 249; vol.
5 : 7, 32, 104.

5. Moses [8], b. April 25, 1846, in Portland. He probably was the "Moses, son of Moses," who d.
Nov. 29, 1847, in Boston, "aged five and a half
months . . . interred in Portland;" his age,
however, is given incorrectly.

6. Clarissa [8]. She d. Sept. 27, 1847, in Boston, "aged
fourteen months." There is something wrong
about these dates, also.

7. Evelyn L. [8]; d. May 26, 1850, in Boston, aged one
year.

8. Ellen Mora [8]; d. Sept. 25, 1855, in Boston, aged
four years.

Issue by second wife: 9. Mary Angeline [8] [b. Dec.,
1853]; d. Dec. 2, 1855, "aged two years."

4. Ebenezer [6]. The marriage intention of "M[r] Ebenezer
Roberds Ju[r] & Miss Lydia Merrill of Lewiston " was
recorded July 13, 1801, in Durham.* Although he
did not convey his interest in the estate of his father,
with the other heirs, it is evident that he belonged to
this family.

5. Joseph [6], b. April 10, 1781, in Durham. He mar. Nov.
25, 1802, in Brunswick, Susanna Dunning,† b. March
14, 1780, in Brunswick, daughter to Captain William
and Jean [5] (Stanwood) Dunning. Jean [5] Stanwood,
b. July 26, 1757, was daughter to Samuel [4] Stanwood
and Jean (Lithgow) McFarland, his first wife, whom
he married "soon after 1742." Lieutenant Ebenezer [8] Stanwood (father to Samuel [4]), b. July 20, 1695,
in Gloucester, Mass., went to Brunswick, Maine,
about 1719; he is recognized as the "founder of the
Brunswick branch" of this family. He settled on
the shores of Maquoit Bay on land adjoining that
of James Dunning.‡

In October, 1806, Arthur Given and his wife Elizabeth, of
Wales, Lincoln County, David Stanwood and his wife Sarah,

---

* *Durham Births, Marriages, and Deaths,* vol. 1: 30.
† *Records of the Inhabitants of the Town of Pejepscot, in their Families*: 126.
‡ *The Stanwood Family,* by Ethel Stanwood Bolton, 1899: 66, 46.

of Brunswick, Nathan Bucklin, Jr., and his wife Mary, of Warren, Lincoln County, with Joseph Roberts and his wife Susanna, of Durham, sold to Joseph Dustin, of Brunswick, for $1,073, land on the "east side of a twelve rod road that leads from Brunswick falls to Maquoit shore," also marsh "at the end of pump Log point . . . a reduction out of the above land of one third for the Widows dower." In 1808, "Joseph Roberts of Durham . . . blacksmith," for $675, paid by Samuel Patten, of Brunswick, sold him land in Brunswick near Maquoit Landing, on the county road. The deed was signed : —

" Joseph Roberts " *   [seal]

Joseph Roberts lived in Brunswick for a short time after his marriage. After the death of his father, whose estate he settled,† he went to Durham, where he remained until he moved, in 1808, to " Pejepscot Gore," a new settlement on an irregular tract of land adjoining Durham on the northwest; it was incorporated March 6, 1802, under the Indian name of Pejepscot. In 1817, the name of the town was changed to Danville ; it is now annexed to the city of Auburn. Probably no man of that region was wider or more favorably known than Elder Joseph Roberts. Early in life a blacksmith, as shown by the records, he commenced preaching, as many others did, with little preparation ; it was the fashion of the time. As a Baptist licentiate he preached with marked success in the town; "extensive revivals followed, a church of fifty-six members was formed, and he was ordained its pastor in December, 1808. This position he held nearly a score of years, and was an honored and influential citizen." ‡

He was the only Representative sent from Pejepscot to the General Court of Massachusetts before the State of Maine was set off in 1820. He was present at sessions beginning June 12, 1812, Feb. 10, 1813, and through those years ;§ in

---

* *Cumberland County Deeds*, Book 65: 262; Book 66: 95.

† Vide pages 1032–1034.

‡ *History of Androscoggin County, Maine*, edited by Georgia Drew Merrill, 1891 : 700.

§ *Journal of the House of Representatives*, vol. 33.

other years no one was sent to represent that district. At a legal town-meeting " convened at the barn of William Stinch-field of said town [of Danville], on Monday the twentieth day of September A. D. 1819 . . . Elder Joseph Roberts " was elected " Delegate to the Convention to be holden at the Courthouse in Portland, on the Second Monday of October next." At this meeting, " Elder Joseph Roberts " received forty-three votes, " Mr Nathaniel Sturgis " received forty votes, and the former was declared elected. The object of the convention was to frame a constitution for the new State of Maine. On Monday, April 10, 1820, the town-meeting was held "at the school house near Elder Joseph Roberts." The " Roberts place so called " was in the fifth School District.*

In 1820, it was written : " Mr. Joseph Roberts, the present minister of the Predestinarian Baptists, was the first and only ordained minister in the town. He has no stated salary. He supports himself as others do by the cultivation of the land — assisted now and then by small contributions of a voluntary nature from his brethren." † The " Revd Elder Joseph Roberts " officiated in a large proportion of the marriages in the town, between 1815 and 1827. The church, after his retirement in the latter year, remained for several years without a pastor.

Elder Roberts and his wife probably did not finish their days in Danville, since there are no records of their deaths in the town. It is remembered by some of the descendants of his brother Benjamin, now living in Durham, that Rev. Joseph Roberts, a cousin, was living many years ago near Bangor, Maine ; he may have been the son, Joseph Parker Roberts. The names of Elder Roberts's sons — Parker and Joseph Parker — appear as conclusive evidence that the Elder had visited Joseph Roberts, of Ipswich and Newbury-port, who also had a son Parker,‡ and that the Elder knew much of the early beginnings of the family. It is probable

---

* *Town Records of Danville, Maine, 1818-1847*: 28, 38, 64.
† *Maine Historical and Genealogical Recorder*, vol. 5: 15.
‡ Vide page 973.

that Elder Roberts was the only one of his generation, in Durham, who travelled as far as Boston.

Issue:[*] I. Parker[7], b. May 20, 1804, in Brunswick; d. June 4, 1806.

II. Sally[7], b. July 14, 1806, in Brunswick; d. Aug. 2, 1808.

III. Mary[7], b. March 12, 1808, in Durham.. Mr. James Mitchell and Mary Roberts, both of Pejepscot, were mar. Oct. 2, 1826, in Pejepscot, by "Elder Joseph Roberts."

IV. Sally[7], b. June 3, 1810, in Pejepscot.

V. Susannah[7], b. Oct. 1, 1812, in Pejepscot; d. Feb. 10, 1813.

VI. Susannah[7], b. April 16, 1815, in Pejepscot.

VII. Joseph Parker[7], b. June 11, 1817, in Pejepscot.

6. "Cunningham"[6]. He mar. June 20, 1806, in Durham, his cousin, Sally[6] Roberts, b. March 31, 1784, daughter to William[5] and Susanna (Randall) Roberts, of Durham. The year following their marriage, they were living in Monmouth, Maine.

7. Susanna[6]. She was unmarried in October, 1807, when she signed the deed conveying her interest in the estate of her father to her brother Joseph. On Sept. 12, 1807, the marriage intention of Joseph B. Allen, of Monmouth, to Susanna Roberts, of Durham, was recorded; they were mar. Nov. 14, 1807,[†] and lived in Monmouth.

8. Samuel[6]. There was a Samuel Roberts in Monmouth, who appears to belong to this family. In the Pejepscot records is the following: Anna Roberts, daughter to "Sam[l] Roberts, b. Nov. 1, 1801, at Monmouth, d. Oct. 29, 1815." This was written below the record of Elder Joseph's children.[‡]

Issue by second wife: 9. Deborah[6], daughter to Ebenezer[5] Roberts. She was mar. to —— Cross.

---

* *Record of the Inhabitants of the Town of Pejepscot, in their Families* : 126.
† *Durham Births, Marriages, and Deaths,* vol. i.
‡ *Record of the Inhabitants of the Town of Pejepscot, in their Families* : 126.

10. Stillman [6], son to Ebenezer [5] Roberts. He married, but the name of his wife is not remembered.

III. Joseph [5], son to Ebenezer [4] Roberts. (Vide infra.)

IV. Vincent [5], son to Ebenezer [4], b. about 1745, in Cape Elizabeth. He mar. Nov. 24, 1772, in Cape Elizabeth, Susanna, daughter to Samuel [5] and Joanna [5] (Skillings) York.*

Vincent Roberts moved to Royalsborough, about 1774 or 1775, with his brother Ebenezer and brothers-in-law, Samuel and Joseph York. Dec. 10, 1776, as a resident of Royalsborough, he bought of Belcher Noyes, Esq., of Boston, representative of the Pejepscot Proprietors, half of lot thirty-two in the "intended Township of Royalsborough." His lot contained fifty acres, and cost him £26 : 13 : 04; in 1782, he sold it to Matthew Duran, of Cape Elizabeth, for £91 : 06. It was described in the deed of sale as the southwest half of lot thirty-two, adjoining to Charles Gerrish's land and the road, " it being the lot whereon Ebenezer Robards now lives on vizt the northeast fifty acres of said hundred acre lot."† Three years later, he bought of Moses Little and Josiah Little, of Newbury, Mass., Pejepscot Proprietors, for £105, the whole of " Lot Nº. 128." He removed to this hundred acre lot near Chandler's mill ; in 1803, he sold forty acres of it to his eldest son, Samuel York Roberts.‡

On Sept. 15, 1777, " Mr Vinson Robbarts " was chosen the first constable of Royalsborough; in 1779, he was chosen surveyor of highways.§ In 1793, he was surveyor of highways and surveyor of lumber for the town of Durham ; in 1801, surveyor of highways.‖

There is no record of the birth or death of Vincent Roberts ; he is supposed to have died before 1805. The births of the first three children only are recorded.

Issue : ¶ 1. Joanna [6], b. Oct. 1, 1773, in Royalsborough.

---

* *Maine Historical and Genealogical Recorder*, vol. 3 : 19.

† *Cumberland County Deeds*, Book 47 : 458 ; Book 21 : 252.

‡ *Cumberland County Deeds*, Book 41 : 474; Book 44 : 494.

§ *Records of the Plantation of Royalsborough, 1774-1789.*

‖ *Town Records of Durham*, vol. 1 : 67, 130.

¶ *Records of the Plantation of Royalsborough, 1774-1789.*

She was mar., first, Jan. 12, 1792, to Ezekiel Turner, of Freeport ; she was mar., second, to Samuel Sawyer. She d. March 27, 1858.

2. Samuel York⁶, b. May 3, 1776, in Royalsborough. He mar. (intention, Jan. 5, 1799) Betsey Plummer, of Durham, and lived on the homestead of his father.

3. James⁶, b. Dec. 10, 1779, in Royalsborough ; he mar. (intention, Jan. 23, 1802) Sally Turner, of Freeport.

4. Thomas⁶. There is no record of his birth ; he mar. Dec. 4, 1806, in Durham, Submit York, of that town. Four children are recorded in Durham : I. Samuel⁷. II. Rebecca⁷. III. True Glidden⁷. IV. Susannah⁷.

5. Ebenezer⁶ ; he mar. (intention, Jan. 14, 1809) Sally Plummer, of Durham.

6. Susanna⁶. She was mar. Oct. 16, 1811, to Robert Hunnewell, of Durham.

7. Daniel⁶, b. July 16, 1790, in Durham. In 1812, he married Abigail, daughter to George Goodwin, of Durham. Five years after his marriage, he went to Ohio. At Cincinnati, he united with the Christian Church, and was ordained to preach the Gospel. He settled in Dearborn County, Indiana, where he spent the remainder of his life. He preached over sixty years "without compensation in money, relying upon the products of his small farm for a living." In the course of his ministry he organized upwards of two hundred churches. He died June 24, 1882, in Sparta, Indiana, aged ninety-two years ; his wife died fifteen years before. They had twelve children, only two of whom survived their father. Judge Omar F. Roberts, of Aurora, Indiana, son to Rev. Daniel Roberts, has furnished a Memorial to his father.*

8. Reuben⁶ ; he mar. (intention, Jan. 1, 1817) Sally Goodwin, of Durham.

9. Hannah⁶. She is supposed to be the "Hannah Roberts, of Cape Elizabeth," who was published, Feb. 24,

---

* *History of Durham, Maine,* by Rev. Everett S. Stackpole, 1899: 66.

1798, to Jacob Sawyer, of Durham,* and was married March 12, following.

  10. Sally⁶, b. in Durham.

  11. Lemuel⁶, b. in Durham.

V. Anna⁵, daughter to Ebenezer⁴, b. March, 1749, in Falmouth. Anna Roberts was mar. Nov. 24, 1769, in Cape Elizabeth, to John Randall,† b. July 16, 1747, in Falmouth. He probably was brother to Stephen Randall, Jr., who married Anna's sister Lydia.

In 1774, John and Stephen Randall went with Ebenezer and Vincent Roberts to Royalsborough; in 1777, the Randalls became interested in Judah Chandler's mill, with O Israel Bagley, Daniel Bagley, and John Cushing.‡ In 1813, Joseph Spaulding sold the southwesterly half of "lot 126" to John Randall.§ "His house stood near where James Hascall lived in 1898; he and his wife were buried on that lot." The road from South West Bend came over the hill near his house; close by were the schoolhouse and church. This was the original "Methodist Corner," which was shifted eastward by a change in the road. Besides running a farm of fifty acres, John Randall kept a store.‖

John Randall's name appears first in the records of Royalsborough, June 20, 1776, in connection with his "creatures [cattle] mark." In 1791 and 1794, he was fence-viewer, field-driver, and hogreeve; in 1796, he was surveyor of highways; in 1805, on the school committee. He was living in 1815; there is no record of his death.

  Issue: ¶ 1. Jacob Randall, b. Oct. 24, 1770, in Cape Elizabeth. He settled in Pownal.

  2. Anna Randall, b. Dec. 19, 1772, in Cape Elizabeth. She was mar. (intention, April 27, 1794) to Simeon Sanborn. Anna appears to have been a second wife, as three children of Simeon Sanborn were previously

---

* *Durham Births, Marriages, and Deaths*, vol. 1 : 21.

† *Maine Historical and Genealogical Recorder*, vol. 3 : 104.

‡ Vide page 907.

§ *Cumberland County Deeds*, Book 72 : 349.

‖ *History of Durham, Maine*, by Rev. Everett S. Stackpole, 1899 : 240.

¶ *Durham Births, Marriages, and Deaths*, vol. 1 : 79.

recorded: I. Peter Sanborn, b. April 5, 1779, in North Salisbury, N. H. II. Susanna Sanborn, b. July 1, 1781, in Royalsborough. III. Molly Sanborn, b. Oct. 18, 1783, in Royalsborough.

3. Molly Randall, b. April 18, 1775, in Royalsborough.
4. Sarah Randall, b. Jan. 6, 1777, in Royalsborough.
5. Benjamin Randall, b. April 12, 1781, in Royalsborough.
6. Margaret Randall, b. March 1, 1783, in Royalsborough.
7. John Randall, b. March 13, 1785, in Royalsborough.
8. Isaac Randall, b. April 18, 1787, in Royalsborough.
9. Hannah Randall, b. March 9, 1789; d. June 24, 1790, in Durham.
10. Ebenezer Randall, b. Nov. 27, 1791, in Durham.
11. Samuel Randall, b. Jan. 5, 1794, in Durham.

VI. Lydia[5], daughter to Ebenezer[4], b. in Falmouth, was mar. Oct. 20, 1774, in Cape Elizabeth, to Stephen Randall, Jr., of Cape Elizabeth.* Stephen Randall, Sr., was one of the most prominent citizens of Cape Elizabeth. He was sealer of wood and surveyor of lumber, 1765, 1769, 1774; warden, 1770; collector of taxes, 1772; constable, 1774; selectman, 1780–1783; moderator at town-meetings, 1780, 1782, and later. He d. Jan. 16, 1797; his widow, Mercy, d. Nov. 18, 1803; they were buried in the Meeting-House Hill Cemetery.

Stephen Randall, Jr., the third of the name in Cape Elizabeth, went to Royalsborough (Durham) at about the time of his marriage, perhaps before, and settled on "lot 125." In 1777, he purchased one twelfth interest in Chandler's mill. In 1790, he sold seventy acres of his hundred acre farm to Joshua Strout, of Durham, and returned to Cape Elizabeth; he and his wife Lydia were living there in 1815.†

Issue: 1. Joseph Randall, b. March 9, 1775, in Royalsborough.
2. Deborah Randall, b. Feb. 12, 1777, in Royalsborough.
3. Stephen Randall, b. June 7, 1779, in Royalsborough.
4. Nathaniel Randall, b. May 12, 1781, in Royalsborough.

---

* *Maine Historical and Genealogical Recorder*, vol. 3: 106.
† *Cumberland County Deeds*, Book 14: 330, 508; Book 74: 241.

5. "Chinecum [Cunningham]" Randall, b. Oct. 12, 178. in Royalsborough.

6. Hannah Randall, b. Dec. 22, 1789, in Durham.*

7. Dolly Randall, b. April 27, 1791, in Cape Elizabeth.

8. Sally Randall, b. May 13, 1793, in Cape Elizabeth.

9. Benjamin Randall, b. Nov., 1795, in Cape Elizabeth.†

VII. William⁶, son to Ebenezer⁴, bap. Dec. 15, 1754, in th First Church of Scarborough;‡ He was mar. Oct. 1(1777, in Cape Elizabeth, by Rev. Ephraim Clark, to S(sanna Randall.§ He probably soon followed his br(thers to Royalsborough (Durham), and later settled o the farm which he bought, in 1784, of Isaac Randall, (Amesbury, Mass., for £45. It was known as "lot N? on hundred and forty seven," and was originally a part (Colonel Jonathan Bagley's estate.‖ William Roberts too no part in town affairs; he is said to have died in Du ham, about 1804. His widow removed with some of h(children to Genesee County, New York, before 1815; i November of that year, Ebenezer Roberts, blacksmit of Durham, as administrator of the estate, sold land ("William Roberts, deceased," in Durham.¶

Issue:** 1. Catherine⁶, b. Nov. 10, 1778, in Royalsbo ough; she was mar. (intention, Oct. 7, 1797) to Thom; Wharff, Jr. (?), of New Gloucester.

2. Mercy⁶, b. Aug. 7, 1780, in Royalsborough; d. young

3. Susanna⁶, b. Jan. 15, 1782, in Royalsborough; she w; mar. Nov. 26, 1801, to James Gerrish, of Freeport.

4. Sally⁶, b. March 31, 1784, in Royalsborough; she w; mar. June 20, 1806, to "Mʳ Cunningham Roberds .. of Durham." His name appears as Kennecum Rober in other records. They moved to Monmouth, Main

---

* *Durham Births, Marriages, and Deaths*, vol. 1 : 87.
† *Town Records of Cape Elizabeth*, vol. 1 : 354.
‡ *Maine Historical and Genealogical Recorder*, vol. 2 : 29, 34.
§ *Maine Historical and Genealogical Recorder*, vol. 3 : 185.
‖ *Cumberland County Deeds*, Book 32 : 245.
¶ *Cumberland County Deeds*, Book 75 : 22.
** *Durham Births, Marriages, and Deaths*, vol. 1 : 53.

5. William⁶, b. Dec. 29, 1787, in Royalsborough.

6. Mary⁶, b. Feb. 20, 1791, in Durham; she was married to Robert Jones.

7. Hannah Chapman⁶, b. May 20, 1793, in Durham; she was mar. to Eldrick Smith.*

8. Benjamin⁶, b. Feb. 21, 1795, in Durham.

9. Michael⁶ (Micah), b. June 24, 1797, in Durham.

10. Catherine⁶, b. Dec. 12, 1799, in Durham. She probably was named after the death of the first Catherine.

[VIII.] Samuel⁵, b. in Falmouth. He appears to be one of the sons to Ebenezer⁴ Roberts, but it cannot be proved. In 1775, he was in Revolutionary service as "Sam! Robards of Cape Elizabeth." In 1777, he enlisted in the Continental Army, for three years, and remained until his term expired. During the year 1778, he was private in Captain Daniel Strout's company from Cape Elizabeth.†

Samuel Roberts and Hannah Small, both of Cape Elizabeth, were mar. Aug. 24, 1780, by Rev. Ephraim Clark, pastor of the Second Parish. In 1787, Jonah Dyer, for £72 : 13 : 04, sold to "Samuel Robards," of Cape Elizabeth, half a sixty acre lot "adjoining to Beriah Westons land whereon he [Samuel] now dwells." In 1791, Hannah Roberts, widow and administratrix of the estate of Samuel Roberts, mariner, late deceased, sold "two acres and 17 rods" to Joshua Elder, for £5 : 09 : 03; it was described as "adjoining Beriah Westons and the road." ‡

Issue: § 7. "Micah"⁶, b. Feb. 9, 1781, in Cape Elizabeth.

2. Mary⁶, b. Oct. 18, 1782, in Cape Elizabeth; d. Nov. 5, 1786.

3. Hannah⁶, b. Nov. 21, 1784, in Cape Elizabeth.

4. Samuel⁶, b. Oct. 3, 1786, in Cape Elizabeth. In 1807, as a housewright, of Cape Elizabeth, he sold

---

* *History of Durham, Maine*, by Rev. Everett S. Stackpole, 1899: 244.

† *Massachusetts Soldiers and Sailors in the War of the Revolution*, vol. 13: 366, 411, 365, 412.

‡ *Cumberland County Deeds*, Book 18: 375; Book 28: 231.

§ *Town Records of Cape Elizabeth*, vol. 1 : 348.

for $230 to Micah Higgins, his half of the thirty acres "that my Hon? Father Samuel Roberts, Late of said Cape Elizabeth Deceased, purchased of Jonah Dyer, by deed dated February 3ᵈ 1787."*

[IX.] Thomas⁶. There are many reasons for thinking that this Thomas was son to Ebenezer⁴ Roberts. As "Thomas Roberts, of Falmouth," he enlisted July 19, 1776, in Captain Samuel Knights's company, stationed on the seacoast. In an abstract of pay, due to Nov. 1, 1776, he was allowed £1 : 18 : 9. †

Thomas Roberts and Hannah Wormwell were married April 21, 1777, by Rev. Ebenezer Williams, "Minister of the Gospel in Falmouth." ‡ In 1784, Thomas Roberts, of Falmouth, yeoman, bought for £12, of George Knight, of Falmouth, twenty acres of the common and undivided lands in that town. In April, 1797, "Thomas Roberts, of Falmouth," and his wife, "Hannah Roberts," sold for $500, a tract of thirty-four acres, and another of twenty-five acres, near their "homestead." In 1802, they bought of Othniel and William Merrill, a small lot of land adjoining that of Dr. Stephen Cummings, which is described as on Main Street, near Vaughn Street. A part of this lot they exchanged, the next year, for a strip of land belonging to Dr. Cummings. In Sept., 1805, they sold, for $900, the land and buildings on Main Street.§ There is no further record of Thomas Roberts, in Portland, except his death, Sept. 20, 1831, at the age of seventy-seven years. That would make him b. in 1754, the year William⁵ Roberts was baptized in Scarborough. The Portland records are compilations; discrepancies of several years often have been proved. No children were recorded there; a strong probability exists, however, that Nathaniel, born 1796, was their son, and they may have had other children.

---

* *Cumberland County Deeds*, Book 54: 60.
† *Maine Historical and Genealogical Recorder*, vol. 4: 21.
‡ *Cumberland County Commissioners' Records*, vol. 2: 251.
§ *Cumberland County Deeds*, Book 12: 397; Book 29: 88; Book 39: 169; Book 40: 220; Book 46: 355.

Issue : 1. Nathaniel[6], b. April 5, 1796, probably in Portland. He was a ship-carpenter ; he lived all his life in
Portland, and died there July 17, 1869.

Nathaniel Roberts was mar., first, June 13, 1816, by " Samuel Rand," to Miriam Adams. She was b. July 28, 1796,
and is supposed to have been daughter to Jacob Adams ; she
d. July 23, 1840, in Portland. The second wife of Nathaniel
Roberts, to whom he was mar. Sept. 3, 1843, by Rev. A. K.
Moulton, was Susan P. Townsend, of Portland; she d. Dec.
22, 1846, in Portland, aged forty-four years. She left no
children. Nathaniel Roberts was mar., third, Feb. 21, 1848,
by Rev. William T. Dwight, to Eliza West, of Portland.[*]
In 1846, Nathaniel Roberts was living on the corner of York
and Brackett Streets. He d. August 17, 1869, in Portland,
aged seventy-three years.[†]

Issue by first wife : [‡] I. Thomas Adams[7], b. July 7, 1817, in
Portland ; he married and had a family. It is well
known among the descendants of Colonel Thomas A.
Roberts that he was " second cousin to Moses Roberts, of Portland, who spent some years in Boston
prior to 1860." Thomas A. Roberts was captain in
the State Militia from 1854 to 1861, commanding
during that time the " Mechanic Blues," of Portland.
He served as colonel in the Seventeenth Regiment
of Maine Volunteers, from July 15, 1862, until discharged July 3, 1863 ; he died in 1888, at Portland.
His son, Charles W. Roberts, known as Colonel
though he disclaims any title to that rank, was Adju-
tant of the Seventeenth Regiment of Maine Volunteers, in 1862 and 1863. He is well known in Portland
from his long service in the Custom-House.

II. Dorcas[7], b. Jan. 16, 1819, in Portland; d. Oct. 5,
1820.

III. Dorcas Adams[7], b. Sept. 25, 1820, in Portland.

IV. James Stetson[7], b. Nov. 5, 1822, in Portland. He

---

[*] *Records of Portland*, Marriages, vol. 3 : 7, 89, 112.
[†] *Records of Portland*, Deaths, vol. 6 : 174.
[‡] *Records of Portland*, Births, vol. 5 : 7.

married, and died young, leaving a son and a daughter.

V. George Washington[7], b. Oct. 22, 1824, in Portland. He went to Albany, New York, about 1861, married, and had two daughters, also a son William. George W. Roberts and his wife both died in Albany.

VI. William Henry[7], b. Nov. 11, 1826, in Portland. He married, and died in Portland.

VII. Frances Ellen[7], b. Sept. 22, 1828, in Portland. She became the second wife of Thomas[7] F. Roberts, a boatbuilder of Portland, son to Joseph[6] and Achsah (Dyer) Roberts. Thomas F. Roberts had two daughters by his first wife, Adaline.*

VIII. Margaret Stetson[7], b. June 20, 1830, in Portland. She was married to —— Rackliffe; she died, of consumption, in Portland.

IX. Mary M.[7], b. Aug. 23, 1832, in Portland. She was married to —— Bridges; she d. about 1861. Mr. Bridges "moved West;" they had one son.

X. Sarah Watrus[7], b. Sept. 2, 1834, in Portland. She was married to George Merry; she is now (1907) a widow, living at Cape.Elizabeth.

XI. Harriet Eliza[7], b. Jan. 29, 1838, in Portland. She was married to James R. Gray; they reside in Haverhill, Mass.

Issue by third wife: XII. Ella E.[7]; she died at the age of eighteen years.

XIII. Edith[7], "probably died young."

[X.] James[6].† James Roberts and Abigail Pierce were mar. Feb. 6, 1783, in Portland, by Rev. Ebenezer Williams.‡

James Roberts and his wife soon removed to Freeport, where, as a resident of that town, he bought, in 1790, thirty acres of land at "Little River Point," on the southeasterly

---

* Vide page 1023.

† There is no doubt that James was brother to Thomas Roberts. If any one can prove that they (or Samuel) were not sons to Ebenezer[4] Roberts, the writer would be glad to learn their parentage.

‡ *Cumberland County Commissioners' Records*, vol. 2: 252.

side of Little River, "with one half of the Mill Privilege, supposed to be on the above land." The next year, with his wife, Abigail, he sold the same to Hezekiah Merrill, of Freeport; he and his wife also conveyed land in the town, in 1797.[*]

> Issue:[†] 1. Moses[6], b. Jan. 6, 1784, probably in Freeport.
> 2. Samuel Pierce[6], b. March 26, 1786, probably in Freeport.
> 3. Benjamin[6], b. May 2, 1788, probably in Freeport.
> 4. Daniel[6], b. Feb. 5, 1791, in Freeport.
> 5. James[6], b. Nov. 11, 1793, in Freeport.
> 6. Merrill[6], b. July 7, 1796, in Freeport.
> 7. Abigail[6], b. May 12, 1799, in Freeport.

JOSEPH[5] ROBERTS

Joseph[5] Roberts, son to Ebenezer[4] and Mary (Kinnecum) Roberts, appears to have been their second or third child. There is no record of the date of his birth; probably it was about 1741 or 1742. His marriage is in the Commissioners' Records of Portland, in a "List of Persons Joined in Marriage by the Rev[d] M[r] Thomas Smith Minister of the Gospel in Falmouth as ꝑ Return of Certificates on File . . . Joseph Roberts and Ruth White . . . April 12, 1767. Recorded by Stephen Longfellow Town Clerk."[‡] Ruth White probably was daughter to William[3] and Christina[2] (Simonton) White, of Cape Elizabeth, and granddaughter to Rev. John[2] White, of Gloucester, Massachusetts.

John[3] and William[3] White went to Falmouth, where, on April 22, 1728, they were admitted inhabitants upon payment of £10, each; two years later, they were mentioned among those who had fulfilled the conditions of settlement.[§] That they were sons to the Rev. John White, of

---

[*] *Cumberland County Deeds*, Book 18: 249, 250; Book 27: 15.

[†] *Freeport Births, Marriages, and Deaths*, vol. 1: 41.

[‡] *Cumberland County Commissioners' Records*, Book 1: 148; also *New England Historical and Genealogical Register*, vol. 17: 33.

[§] Vide page 1016.

Gloucester, Massachusetts, is proved by the following deed, dated March 14, 1736–37 : —

John White and his wife Abigail, of Gloucester, in the County of Essex, "for love & parental affection," conveyed " to my Sons John & William White of Falmouth . . . Tanner & Carpenter . . . fifty acres in Falmouth . . . adjoining to Maiden Cove it being the Fifty acres bought of the Heirs of Josiah White formerly of Falmouth and which were granted to him by said Town under Govern.ᵗ Danforths Settlement as by the Town Grant may farther appear or by living evidences of sᵈ Grant viz of an Hundred Acres between Maiden Cove Brook & Little Brook so called which Fifty acres William White has given to him Twenty acres Adjoining to the Fifty formerly given to him & to John White Thirty acres adjoining to said Williams Land & between that & Maiden Cove Brook."

Witnesses:	(Signed)	
" Samuel Stevens Junʳ	" John White	[seal]
Abigail White Junʳ "	Abigail White "*	[seal]

There appears to be no occasion to doubt (though it has been questioned) that the Rev. John White, of Gloucester, was son to Josiah White, one of the grantees of Falmouth in its first settlement. Josiah and his brother Nathaniel went there early, had grants at Maiden Cove, and remained until they were obliged to flee from the Indians. Nathaniel was killed later by the Indians; he left two daughters, Mary and Dorcas, who were married respectively to Nathaniel and John Danford, of Newbury. Josiah White, before 1703, had returned to Purpooduck with Michael Webber, Joseph Morgan, Thomas Loveitt, Joel Madford, and Benjamin, Joseph, James, and Josiah Wallis, sons to John Wallis. They built houses, brought their families there, and " engaged heartily in establishing of the Settlement;" but they were again driven away by the savages. Josiah White had two sons, John and Samuel;† his daughter Miriam was

---

* *York County Deeds*, Book 21 : 17.
† *York County Deeds*, Book 11 : 212.

married to Richard Suntay or Sontag.* The Rev. John White, in the desire that his sons should profit by the land that had cost his father so dear, purchased, as he says, of the other heirs their interests at Maiden Cove. On February 16, 1724–25, he bought of "Hannah White, Relict of Samuel White in the Town of Boston," for £10, one half of the grant of fifty acres formerly "laid out to and possessed by Josiah White of Falmouth . . . in Casco Bay . . . Situate on Papooduck;" it is evident that the other half already belonged to Rev. John White, as an heir.

On April 18, 1727, "ye Reverd John White of ye Town of Gloucester in ye County of Essex Pastour," bought of Nathaniel Danford, of Newbury, for £25, fifty acres "joining to little Brook near Maiden Cove . . . in Falmouth . . . Casco Bay." † This was the land formerly granted to Nathaniel White, as deposed by one John Lane, in August, 1727. The said John Lane, aged seventy-three years, testified that about forty-two years ago, "while I lived there the Town of Falmouth did grant unto Josiah White & Nathanael White one hundred Acres of Land lying between Little Brook so called & a Brook called Maiden Cove Brook," which they divided equally and lived, "each on his Part," several years. "Josiah died possessed of his Part of sd Land, and Nathanael White possessed his . . . until he was driven away from the same by the Indian War & he was afterward slain by the Indians." ‡ Besides these hundred acres, Rev. John White bought, for £40, on January 26, 1724–25, of James Wallis, of Gloucester, his tract of land "in papooduck, which he drew by lot near his brother Benjamin." §

Rev. John White assisted substantially the new settlement at Cape Elizabeth; he also organized the town of New

---

* *Smith and Deane's Journal,* 1849 : 47.
† *York County Deeds,* Book 11 : 212; Book 12 : pt. 1 : 137.
‡ *York County Deeds,* Book 12 : pt. 1 : 170, 177.
§ *York County Deeds,* Book 11 : 212.

Gloucester, Maine, and was moderator at the first meeting of the Proprietors of the new town, held in Gloucester, Massachusetts. In March, 1736–37, when the first division of lots at New Gloucester was made, " The Rev. John White " had "lot Nº 20 " set off to him ; "lot Nº 21 " was given to him for his son Thomas, who removed there.

Probably no divine of his day was more sincerely revered for his learning and piety than Rev. John White. He was graduated from Harvard College in 1698, and was ordained April 21, 1703.* The following notice of his death is in the Gloucester records : —

"The Rev⁴. M⁵ John White who had been settled a minister in this town from the 21 day of October 1702 as appears by Votes of the Town on Record deceased in his chair about eleven of the clock in the forenoon on the 16 day of January 1760 being the 59 year after his beginning his ministry here and the eighty third year of his age." †

The will of the Rev. John White,‡ of Gloucester, " clerk

---

* *History of Gloucester, Massachusetts*, by John J. Babson, 1860: 224.

† *Gloucester Births, Marriages, and Deaths, 1642–1780*: 312.

‡ Rev. John ² White, of Gloucester, was born about 1677. His first wife, whom he married about 1703, was Lucy Wise, daughter to "the excellent John Wise." " Mʳˢ Lucy (wife of our Rev. pastʳ aged about 46 years) Dyed March 5, 1727," in Gloucester. She was the mother of all his children. The marriage intention of " Rev. Mʳ John White & Miss Abigail Blague of Boston " was dated Aug. 26, 1727 ; there is no record of her death. His third wife was " Mrs. Alice Norwood," to whom he was married June 1, 1749, by " Mʳ Bradstreet." She survived her husband.

Issue by first wife: I. John ⁸ White, b. June 10, 1704, in Gloucester. He was a tanner, and lived at Cape Elizabeth on the present site of Fort Preble. He died in 1738 ; on Oct. 17, of that year, his widow, Jerusha (said to be daughter to Joshua Woodbury, though not mentioned in his will), was appointed administratrix of his estate. His inventory, presented June 25, 1739, amounted to £1275 : 9 : 6. On Nov. 17, 1740, Jerusha White was published to Benjamin Thrasher, a tanner of Cape Elizabeth.

Issue by first husband: 1. Lucy ⁴ White, b. Feb. 1, 1731–32, at Falmouth ; she was mar. (intention April 13, 1751) to Aaron Chamberlain.

[minister]," dated Aug. 4, 1758, was admitted to probate, at Ipswich, February 4, 1760.* His wife Alice was to receive

---

    2. Hannah⁴ White; she was mar. (intention Sept. 22, 1752) to Peter⁵ Woodbury, b. April 18, 1724, in Beverly, Mass., son to Joshua⁴ and Sarah⁴ (Woodbury) Woodbury, of Cape Elizabeth. Peter Woodbury was one of the most prominent citizens, and occupied the position of legal adviser in many affairs of the town, as well as of private individuals. In this capacity, he was interested in the Ossipee claim. (Vide page 49.)

It is known that Peter and Hannah Woodbury had children, Joshua and Jerusha; there may have been others.

    3. Jerusha⁴ White; she was mar. (intention Oct. 5, 1758) to Isaac⁴ Dyer.

    4. Abigail⁴ White; she was mar. (intention June 30, 1756) to Josiah Wallis, or Wallace.

  II. Lucy³ White, b. March 27, 1706, in Gloucester. She became the wife of Joseph Moody; they had four children, of whom Samuel, Joseph, and Thomas, in 1760, were living at York, Maine. Hannah Moody, the daughter, was married to Doctor Samuel Plummer, of Gloucester; in 1760, she was mentioned as dead, leaving a son Samuel.

  III. Joseph³ White, b. Feb. 21, 1708, in Gloucester; d. Nov. 4, 1708.

  IV. William³ White, b. Nov. 11, 1709, in Gloucester. Before he was of age, he went to Cape Elizabeth, with his brother John. He mar. (intention Jan. 19, 1735–36) Christina, or Christian, Simonton, daughter to Andrew Simonton. The latter, with sons William, Andrew, and Walter Simonton, were of a party from Scotland that landed at Cape Elizabeth in 1718; ten years later, they had grants of land at Simonton's Cove, now called Willard's Beach.

William White died in 1758; his widow, "Christian White," was appointed administratrix of her husband's estate, on Oct. 2, 1758; his inventory was brought in the same day. The names of her children were not mentioned in the settlement. "Mʳ Jacob Sawyer & Mʳˢ Christian White," both of Cape Elizabeth, were published Nov. 21, 1772, in that town. The births of her seven children by her first husband are not recorded, but there is good evidence to prove that the following list is correct.

    Issue by first husband: 1. Abigail⁴ White; she was mar. to Andrew Crockett.

    2. Mary⁴ White; she was mar. (intention Nov. 27, 1762) to Ebenezer Robinson.

    3. Ruth⁴ White. There appears to be little doubt that Ruth White, b. 1744, was daughter to William and Christina White. Joseph

---

* *Essex County Probate* (original), No. 29590.

such part of his real and personal estate "as is proscribed in the Law of this Province." The "four Daughters of my Son John [to] have each of them ten shillings. He having in his Life time received a double portion." Following mention of his son Samuel, the Rev. John ordered, that after payment of debts, legacies, and funeral charges, "the whole of what remains both real & personal . . . be equally divided by the Heirs of my Son William and to my daughter Moodyes Heirs & to Abigail Allin, Hannah Haskel & Mary Allin . . . Sons in Law Deacon Haskell & Deacon Allin in conjuction with Doctor Samuel Plumer . . . to be

---

Roberts and Ruth White were mar. April 12, 1767, in Falmouth; she d. May 12, 1784, aged forty years.

4. Anna [4] White, b. 1745. She was mar. (intention Sept. 26, 1765) to Israel [5] Woodbury, b. 1745, son to Hugh [4] and Jane (Green) Woodbury, of Cape Elizabeth. Israel Woodbury d. Feb. 10, 1831; his widow d. Dec. 27, 1837, in Cape Elizabeth, aged ninety-two years. They had ten children.

5. William [4] White. He mar. (intention Nov. 30, 1775) Mary Simonton, of Cape Elizabeth.

6. Christian [4]. Joseph Cobb, 3d, mar. (intention July 1, 1774) "Miss Christian White;" both were of Cape Elizabeth.

7. Matthew [4]; known to be son to William [3] White.

V. Thomas [3] White, b. Jan. 27, 1712, in Gloucester; he went to New Gloucester, Maine.

VI. Joseph [3] White, b. Feb. 2, 1716, in Gloucester; d. Feb. 17, 1718.

VII. Benjamin [3] White, b. Jan. 18, 1718, in Gloucester.

VIII. Abigail [3] White, b. April 17, 1720, in Gloucester. When her father made his will, in 1758, she was the widow of Isaac Allen; in August, 1760, she was dead, leaving three children.

IX. Hannah [3] White, b. Oct. 10, 1721, in Gloucester. She was the wife of Deacon Nathaniel Haskell, one of the executors of her father's estate.

X. Mary [3] White, b. March 20, 1723, in Gloucester. She was married to Deacon David Allen, another executor.

XI. Samuel [3] White, b. May 20, 1725, in Gloucester. His father mentioned this son in his will as follows: "My will is that the Heir of my Son Samuel if he leaves any to receive ten Shillings J having paid him his portion in his Lifetime."

Vide *Gloucester Births, Marriages, and Deaths, 1642–1780*: 311, 312; *York County Probate*, Book 5: 136, 176; Book 10: 18, 38; *Essex County Probate* (original), No. 29590; *Massachusetts Archives*, vol. 19: 708.

Exequitors." This will, which is a model of brevity was signed: —

Witnesses:
"Thomas Allen   *John White*   [seal]
Susanah Haskell
Jemima Allen "

The inventory of his estate, dated March 8, 1760, was presented three days later in Court. The first item is "Books . . . £21 : 5s." His "House Barn & Land adjoyning" were valued at £240, "Orchard & Land adjoyning . . . £52," and "A piece of Salt Marsh in Jones's River . . . £13 : 6 : 8;" total valuation of real estate, £305 : 6 : 8. To this was added £271 : 14 : 3, in personal estate, "dues," etc. On August 13, 1760, a petition * was presented to the Governor, Council, and House of Representatives, by Thomas Allen, Nathaniel Haskell, David Allen, Samuel Plummer, and Christian White, stating that the real estate of the " Revd John White of Gloucester deceased " was valued at £305 : 6 : 8, and that "one Third Part " has been set off to the "Widow of the said Testator as her Dower." As the remaining two-thirds will be "very much preduced . . . by Division," they pray as guardians of the minor heirs, for permission to sell it as it stands. The petition cites the heirs who were living in 1758, when his will was made, and those who were then (1760) living. "The Names of those of Testators Children that were deceased when his will was made are William White who left seven Children to whom your said Petitionor Christian White is appointed Guardian ; and Lucy who married m^r Joseph Moodey by whom she had four Children," etc. This is the only reference to the number of William White's children ; their names are nowhere given.

It is claimed by many, though no attempt is made here to prove it, that the Rev. John White, of Gloucester, Massachusetts, was a descendant of Rev. John White, of Dorches-

---

ter, England, whose autograph appears in this volume on a bill of Isaac Allerton's, in 1640.* This branch of the White family certainly was superior, and had more money than was common in that day.

Besides the lands at Maiden Cove and other locations given by their father to John and William White, they received several grants of land from the Proprietors of Falmouth.† They also bought and sold land on the south side of Fore River. John built a house of white oak logs, "squared," which is still standing close by Fort Preble; it is the ell of a more modern house. William lived at Deep Brook, towards the present Casino, on the Purpooduck side of Mountain View Park, near the dividing line (1906) between South Portland and Cape Elizabeth.

The Rev. Thomas Smith was pastor of the First Church of Falmouth from January 23, 1727, until his death, "aged and feeble," on May 25, 1795. There is no mention of Joseph or Ruth Roberts in the records of this First Congregational Church (now Unitarian); but in 1768, the year following his marriage, Joseph Roberts was taxed for the first time in St. Paul's (Episcopal) Church, his tax being seven shillings a year. He was the only person bearing the name of Roberts mentioned in the records of St. Paul's during the first fifty years of its existence, yet it is difficult to determine whether he belonged to that church through his employment by Jedidiah Preble, or because his early education tended toward that faith.

The history of this First Episcopal Church in Portland is unique. It was founded by a few of the prominent and wealthy men of that town; ‡ but within a few years of its

---

* Vide page 635.

† *Records of the Proprietors of Falmouth*, vol. 1 : 75, 175, 206, 179, 180.

‡ The following is the first entry in "The Oldest Book" of records of St. Paul's Church, Portland, Maine : —

"FALMOUTH, Nov. 4, 1763.

"Whereas the Inhabitants on the Neck are become so numerous as to render it inconvenient to meet together in one House for publick Worship — for the

establishment, it had members from North Yarmouth, Brunswick, Georgetown, Scarborough, and other settlements along

better accommodation of all the Inhabitants it is proposed to build another House for divine Service between Major Freemans and the House improved as a School house, we therefore the underwritten oblige our selves our Heirs & Assigns to pay the respective Sums affixed to our Names to the Person or Persons appointed to receive the Monies toward building a convenient meeting-House provided —

" First. said Meeting House be made fitt to meet in at or before the last Lords Day in June 1764

" 2ly That the Subscribers have the first Choice of Pews in this Order — The Largest subscriber choosing first &c —

" 3ly That if the Rev^nd John Wiswall Pastor of the third Parish of this Town should leave his people he be invited to settle as a Minister in said Meeting House.

	£ s d		£ s d
John Waite Junr	26: 13: 4	Joseph Pollow	5: – –
Daniel Ilsley	13: 6: 8	Stephen Waite	13: 6: 8
Benjamin Waite	40: – –	Benjamin Weeks	1: 10 –
Ebenezer Hilton	13: 6: 8	Jon^a Ilsley in Work	13: 10 –
Jedidiah Preble Junr	20: – –	John Wildridge	2: 8 –
David Wyer	5: – –	Joshua Boynton	5: – –
Jonathan Craft	2: 8 –	Jeremiah Webber	5: – –
William Waterhouse	2: 8 –	Joshua Eldridge	6: – –
John Burnam	2: 8 –	Jedidiah Preble	30: – –
William McLellan	2: 8 –	John Minott Junr	13: 6: 8
Isaac Ilsley in Work	20: – –	Samuel Moody	13: 6: 8
Henry Wallis	2: 8 –	Jacob Stickney	5: 10 –
John Lowther	4: 4 –	William Pike	6: – –
John Preble	3: 0: 0	Edward Watts	10: – –
Abraham Osgood	3: – –	Isaac Waite	6: 13: 4
James Hope	5: – –	Andrew Patterson	6: 13: 4
James Ross	3: – –	David Woodman	2: 8: –
Thomas Bradbury	13: 6: 8	Joseph McLellan	10: – –
Joseph Bean Barber	13: 6: 8	Robert McLellan	13: 6: 8
John Motley in Work	10: – –	Wheeler Briggs	13: 6: 8
Daniel Pettingail	10: – –		

" A true Coppy of the original Minit
Atts^r Jon^a Craft Cler "

" Falm^o Febry 6th 1764

" At a meeting of the Subscribers for building a new Meeting House it was voted viz —

" 1st That Jedidiah Preble Esqr be Moderator

the coast, for it was the only church of that denomination, at that period, in the territory now comprising the State of Maine. The first house of worship was a wooden building on Middle Street, near what is now Pearl Street; when Captain Mowatt burned the greater part of the town, October 18, 1775, this "Church," as well as the "Meeting House" of Parson Smith, was destroyed.* In 1839, the name of the Society was changed from St. Paul's to St. Stephen's. Fire again visited Portland in 1866, and again the church was burned. The present home of St. Stephen's Church is the fine stone edifice on Congress Street, near the public library.

It is evident that Jedidiah Preble, Sr., was one of the most active founders of this church. He was the first moderator; and, together with his sons, Jedidiah, Jr., and John, he contributed more than any other toward the building of the first meeting-house. He was "confirmed one of the Vestry, March 31, 1766," and again was chosen to that office, April 20, 1767.† In 1772, he was the wealthiest man in Falmouth, his property being valued at £311 : 08. Enoch Ilsley's estate was valued at £300, and but two others exceeded £150 each. In the church, Jedidiah Preble paid his tax rate of two or three pounds annually, with liberal contributions toward extra expenses, up to and including the year 1773. It is said

---

"2ly That William Pike be Clerk

"3ly That James Hope John Waite Junr & Daniel Ilsley be a Committee to agree with William Waterhouse, or some other Person for a Place to sett said House upon."

------◆◆------

" Falmo May 6th 1765

" James Hope } Wardens . . .
  Geo Tate }

"3ly That Mr Wheeler Riggs warn the subscribers to attend at the Church at 3 o'clock to draw the Pews."

Vide *First Book of Records, St. Paul's Church, Portland, Maine, 1763* : 1, 2, 6.

---

* Willis's *History of Portland, Maine*, 1865: 520–521.
† *First Book of Records, St. Paul's Church, 1763* : 7½, 8.

that he abandoned the Episcopal form of worship about this time, "because the Episcopal clergyman had offended him by continuing to pray for the King and royal family." It is a curious coincidence that the eldest son of Joseph Roberts was baptized in that church in 1769, that Joseph paid his tax rate of seven shillings a year from 1768 to 1773, inclusive,* and that he dropped out of the church at precisely the same time as Jedidiah Preble and his sons. The Preble family returned to the First Congregational Church, and "took seats under the droppings of Pastor Smith's eloquence." It also is significant that George Roberts, b. March 1, 1773, in Falmouth, second son to Joseph and Ruth Roberts, was not baptized in St. Paul's; at least, there is no record there of his baptism. But the church records became fragmentary during the following year, 1774; they were discontinued altogether while the Revolutionary War was in progress, and for some years afterward.

In 1780, several families of Falmouth united in an effort to secure the services of an Episcopal clergyman. The Rev. Stephen Lewis, pastor of Christ Church in Boston, responded by going to Falmouth, where he baptized fifteen children, between October 18 and 31 ; among them, " Polly daughter to Joseph and Ruth Roberts," who was "baptised Oct. 31, 1780." † In August, 1783, Bishop Bass, of Massachusetts, held services in a new three-story building which stood where the passenger station of the Grand Trunk Railway is now. At that time he baptized thirteen children, and, on September 29, " Cato, adult negroe of Brigadier Preble." ‡

---

* *First Book of Records, St. Paul's Church, 1763* : 1, 2, 4; also *Second Book, 1765 : 2.*

† *Records of Christ Church, Boston, 1723–1851 :* 132.

‡ *Records of Christ Church, Boston, 1723–1851 :* 138. This negro servant of Brigadier-General Preble is described as "quite a character," and somewhat imposing when dressed, as was usual during his later years, in the General's cast-off military clothing and wig. Vide *The Preble Family,* by Captain George H. Preble, U. S. N., 1868: 265.

The records of Christ Church state, under date of April 11, 1775: "The Church shut from this Time till August 1778." * It is remarkable that, with the prevailing public sentiment during the Revolutionary period, it should have opened its doors so soon. Christ Church was the second Episcopal Church in Boston.† From its situation at the North End, it is perhaps more widely known as the Old North Church. The corner-stone was laid in April, 1723. Rev. Timothy Cutler, the first rector, was settled December 29, 1739, and remained until his death, August 17, 1765. On April 22, 1768, Rev. Mather Byles, Jr., became the second incumbent. He was a Royalist, and left in April, 1775; he died March 12, 1814, in St. John, New Brunswick. The church was reopened in August, 1778, by Rev. Stephen Lewis, who remained until September, 1784.‡ Christ Church, though somewhat changed by various repairs, has been greatly admired for its architecture. The old steeple, blown down in 1804 during a violent gale, was rebuilt as far as possible on the original lines. The "Peal of eight Bells," set up in 1744, is still in the tower. As one of the few Episcopal churches of New England that always has remained in that faith, Christ Church stands preëminent.

At the time of his marriage, Joseph Roberts must have been living at Cape Elizabeth, for on March 10, of that year (1767), he was chosen "Hog Reve," with Jeremiah Sawyer, Daniel Sawyer, Barzillai Delano, Ebenezer Sawyer, Richard Jordan, Joshua Jordan, and Christopher Dyer. In 1766, and a number of years afterward, it was annually "voted that the Hoggs Go at Large well Yoked and Ringed under ye Care of ye hogg Reves." This ancient custom was brought to the Cape by the settlers from Ipswich and Gloucester. Captain Nathaniel Jordan and Captain Samuel

---

* *Records of Christ Church, Boston, Mass., 1723-1851* : 128.
† King's Chapel was the First Episcopal Church in Boston.
‡ Drake's *History of Boston, Mass.*, 1856: 567.

Skillings frequently served the town as "Dere Reves [deer reeves]." *

In 1768, Joseph Roberts was at Falmouth. The lack of any record to show that he owned land in Falmouth indicates that he may have followed the sea or been engaged in the construction of ships. At that period, ship-builders and men who worked for them drifted from one town to another on the coast, wherever work could be obtained. Sometimes they took their families with them, and were gone a year or two. Since Joseph Roberts had children born at Falmouth in 1769, 1773, and 1784, and a daughter baptized there in 1780, it is probable that Falmouth was his permanent home. It is probable, too, that his family was there at the time of the burning by Captain Mowatt, October 18, 1775 ; yet the name of Joseph Roberts does not appear among the sufferers by that fire,† nor in a list, dated February 26, 1777, of tax-payers who resided at Falmouth the preceding year — 1776.‡ March 9, 1791, on petition of Enoch Ilsley and two others, "in behalf of themselves and the other sufferers by the destruction of the town of *Falmouth* (now Portland) by the British forces, in the year 1775," there was granted "two townships of land, of six miles square, each . . . in the counties of *Cumberland* or *Lincoln* . . . to be apportioned among the sufferers according to their present respective circumstances and wants."§ The towns finally set off were New Portland and Freeman, in Lincoln County. Further divisions of counties have brought New Portland into Somerset County, and Freeman into Franklin County. Neither town nor county records show that Joseph Roberts lived at any time in Freeman or New Portland.

It is probable that Joseph Roberts, like his brother Eben-

---

* *Town Proceedings, Cape Elizabeth,* vol. 1 : 13, 6, 13.
† *History of Portland, Maine,* by William Willis, 1865: 900-902.
‡ *Maine Genealogist and Biographer,* vol. 1 : 116.
§ *Report of the Committees on Eastern Lands, 1781-1803,* Boston, 1803 : 106.

ezer, was a blacksmith. In those days, all iron-work (even nails) was hand-wrought; such iron as entered into the construction and rigging of ships was laboriously forged by the local blacksmith. There is a tradition among the descendants of George Roberts, son to Joseph, that the father of George (whose name they did not know) was a man of marvellous strength and tact. They tell this story: The "father of George" was working in the fields when two Indians came along; they told him they meant to kill him. He replied — "Wait a minute," which so astonished the natives that they hesitated. He grabbed them and knocked their heads together — killing them instantly.

In his Manuscript Records of Portland, Willis writes of the deaths there: "Roberts wife, of childbed," died May 12, 1784, aged forty years.* There is no doubt that this was Ruth, wife of Joseph Roberts. The birth of their last child, Priscilla, is everywhere given as in the month of May, though no one can give the day; Priscilla died May 26, 1806, in Portland, aged twenty-two years. This appears to be conclusive evidence that the death record of 1784 was of the wife of Joseph. The date and place of death of Joseph Roberts cannot be found, nor where he lies buried. Four children have been identified as belonging to Joseph and Ruth; there may have been others.

ISSUE

I. John⁹, b. Oct. 26, 1769, son to "Joseph⁴ & Ruth Roberts of Falmouth," was baptized Oct. 29, 1769, in St. Paul's Church.† Of his boyhood nothing is known; in mature life he followed the occupation of a caulker of vessels, and probably went more or less to sea. When about thirty years of age, John Roberts was married,‡ April 21, 1799, in Portland, to Mary

---

* *Willis's Manuscript*, New England Historic Genealogical Society : 122.
† *Second Book of Records of St. Paul's Church, Portland, Maine, 1765* : 11.
‡ *Records of Portland*, Marriages, vol. 3 : 61.

Snow, by Rev. Samuel Deane, pastor of the First Congregational Church, now Unitarian.

About a year later, John Roberts and his brother George
bought a small lot of land on the northerly side of Fore
Street, near Hancock Street, with the evident intention of
building upon it. They sold it, Sept. 28, 1805, to Samuel
Stephenson, later known as General, and on the same day
bought of William Moulton, Jr., land situated "one hundred
feet from Hancock Street by the Southerly side of Waite
Street." Later, they divided this equally; in 1808, George
Roberts and his wife Hannah conveyed their half of the lot
to their "brother John," and bought other land in the neighborhood, upon which they built a double house.* On Dec.
16, 1813, "John Roberts of Portland . . . Caulker" and his
wife Mary sold to Dudley Cammett, of Portland, for $600,
all right, title, and interest in a lot of land in Portland, it
"being the same lot I together with George Roberts purchased of William Moulton Jun.ᵣ Sept. 28, A. D. 1805 . . .
Excepting however out of the above described premises all
to satisfy Execution in favor of the Executors to the estate
of Enoch Ilsley late of said Portland deceased against me
. . . and all the right I have to redeem the part set off as
aforesaid is hereby conveyed."

(Signed)

"John Roberts   [seal]

Recorded Dec. 16, 1818.   Mary Roberts" †   [seal]

In 1821, Mary Cammett, widow, William Haynes, block-
maker, his wife Ann Haynes, and Anthony Fernald, cooper,
quitclaimed to "Mary Roberts of said Portland Caulker,"
for $350, all interest in "a certain lot of land in said Port-
land . . . Beginning at a Stake standing on the Southwesterly side of Mountfort Street seventy feet distant from fore
street, thence Northwesterly on said Mountfort St. about
fifty feet to a lot James Alden purchased of the Executors of
the late Enoch Ilsley's estate . . . to land of Samuel Freeman Esqᵣ, and is the same Dudley Cammett Junᵣ purchased

---

* Vide George ⁶ Roberts.
† *Cumberland County Deeds*, Book 70: 26.

of Benjamin Rolfe [Book 76 : Page 71] . . . Reserving however liberty for the Proprietors of the Acqueduct the use of
the fountain therein and of the Acqueduct running from the
same." This deed was recorded May 20, 1824.*

On this land John and Mary Roberts built a medium-sized,
single house, on Mountfort Street, which stands to-day in
good condition. It was number 10 Mountfort Street in the
Portland Directory of 1847, and still retains that number.
The gable end faces the street. There are four rooms on
the first floor and probably as many on the second. The
adjoining corner lot, on Mountfort and Fore Streets, has no
building on it, and looks as though it never had been built
upon.

There is no record of John Roberts's death; it is remembered by residents in the vicinity that Mary Roberts was
many years a widow, and that a grandson, George Carr,
made his home with her. She also had a grandson in California who frequently sent her long letters. She is described
as a "little woman," whom her many friends called "Polly
Roberts;" she was fond of children, especially little girls.
Mary Roberts died at her home on Mountfort Street, July 12,
1849, aged seventy-seven years.†

Two years before her death, probably to perfect the title,
Edwin Fernald, Henry B. Fernald, and Mary C. Gay, widow,
all of Portland, for $1, quitclaimed to Mary Roberts, of
Portland, "widow of the late John Roberts," ‡ the land upon
which she dwelt "on the southwesterly side of Mountfort
Street . . . bought of Dudley Cammett Senior, May 21, 1817,"
referring for a fuller description to "Book 78 : Page 191."
Her surviving daughters, Mary Ann Noyes, of Somerville,
Mass., and Catherine Carr, of Boston, Mass., both widows,
conveyed, Aug. 17, 1857, to John Cammett, of Portland, for
$666.66, "two undivided third parts" of the lot of land on
Mountfort Street, "seventy feet distant from Fore Street . . .
with the buildings thereon," reference being given to "Book

---

* *Cumberland County Deeds*, Book 97 : 502.
† *Records of Portland*, Deaths, vol. 5 : 14.
‡ *Cumberland County Deeds*, Book 207 : 9.

76 : Page 71 " and " Book 97 : Page 502," Cumberland County Deeds.

(Signed)

Witnesses :   " Mary Ann Noyes   [seal]
" Joshua Magoun   Catharine Carr "   [seal]
Lucia Magoun "
Recorded Oct. 12, 1857.[*]

Mr. John Cammett sold the house and land, some years ago, to a Mr. O'Flaherty, who built an addition to the house in the rear, larger than the original building. This once aristocratic neighborhood is now filled with tenements, while on the opposite side of Fore Street are the tracks and elevators of the Grand Trunk Railway.

Issue : [†] 1. Mary A.[7], b. Dec. 12, 1802 ; d. Dec. 23, 1802, in Portland, aged eleven days.

2. Mary Ann[7], b. May 6, 1804, in Portland ; she was mar. June 7, 1824, in Portland, by Rev. Joshua Taylor, to Osgood[7] Noyes, of Portland.[‡]

Osgood[7] Noyes, son to David[6] and Sarah (Sawyer) Noyes, was born, 1803, in Portland, Maine ; [§] he was a shoemaker by trade. Previous to 1845, he moved his family to Boston, for that year they were living on Lowell Street. In 1849, they removed to 4 Auburn Court, [‖] where he died, on July 16, of heart disease, aged forty-six years. He was buried in King's Chapel burying-ground, near the corner of School and Tremont Streets ; the official record says — number " 21 west side." [¶] His widow removed, the following year, to 44 Myrtle Street ; in 1852, she was living with her son, John O. Noyes, at 26 Minot Street.[**]

On Aug. 17, 1852, Mary A. Noyes, of Boston, Mass., widow,

---

* *Cumberland County Deeds*, Book 281 : 453.
† *Records of Portland*, Births, vol. 4 : 172–173.
‡ *Records of Portland*, Marriages, vol. 4 : 26.
§ *Descendants of Nicholas Noyes*, by Brigadier-General Henry E. Noyes, U. S. N., 1904 : 215.
‖ Boston Directories, 1845–1849.
¶ *Records of Boston*, Deaths, 1849 : no. 2438.
** Boston Directories, 1850, 1852.

mortgaged " an undivided third " of land on the southwesterly side of Mountfort Street, Portland, with buildings, for $93.37, to Charles H. Parker, of Boston. This deed was accompanied by a promissory note signed by Mary A. Noyes and John O. Noyes. The mortgage was discharged Oct. 20, 1857,* two months after the sale of the homestead by Mary Ann Noyes and her sister, Catharine Carr. Mrs. Noyes was then living in Somerville. The date of her death has not been learned.

Issue: I. William H.[6] Noyes, b. Oct. 17, 1825, in Portland, Maine.

II. John Osgood [6] Noyes, b. 1828, in Portland, Maine. In his youth he learned the trade of a printer, and followed it. In 1852, he was living with his mother at 26 Minot Street, Boston.† This was the year when he and his mother signed the mortgage note. At the time of his marriage, he was a resident of Charlestown. The record in Somerville states that John O. Noyes, of Charlestown, aged twenty-eight years, was married Nov. 27, 1856, by the Rev. B. Judkins, Jr., of Somerville, to Harriet J. Wild, of Somerville, aged twenty, born in Boston, daughter to Charles D. and Rebecca Wild.‡ The young people probably lived in Somerville during the few years of their married life. In 1859, their home was at East Somerville, on the old turnpike road leading from Boston to Medford. John O. Noyes died Dec. 5, 1861, in Somerville, of consumption, aged thirty-three years ; he was buried in Woodlawn Cemetery. §

Issue: | 1. Henry Q.[6] Noyes, b. Sept. 10, 1857, in Somerville.

2. Almira F.[6] Noyes, b. March 28, 1859, in East Somerville, on "Turnpike St." She was mar. June 8, 1881, in Somerville, by Rev. Daniel T. Noyes, to Frank E. Barnes, of Somerville, son to

---

* *Cumberland County Deeds*, Book 238 : 499; Book 282 : 253.
† Boston Directories, 1850, 1852, 1857.
‡ *Records of Somerville*, Marriages, vol. 3 : p. 5, no. 20.
§ *Records of Somerville*, Deaths, vol. 3 : p. 22, no. 172.
‖ *Records of Somerville*, Births, vol. 3 : p. 36, no. 200; p. 52, no. 168.

John and Hannah E. Barnes.* Frank E. Barnes, born in Chelsea, Mass., was twenty-six years of age at the time of his marriage. He was a bank-teller. No children have been recorded in Somerville or Boston.

III. Frances E.⁸ Noyes, b. April 11, 1831, in Portland. At the age of twenty-two, she was married, April 11, 1853, in Boston, by Rev. Horatio Southgate, to Henry C. Quimby, b. 1832, in Westbrook, Maine, son to Moses Quimby. Henry C. Quimby was at that time a watchmaker, residing in Somerville.† No children are recorded in Boston or Somerville.

IV. Charles Holden⁸ Noyes, b. Feb. 13, 1834, in Portland; d. Jan. 27, 1836,‡ and was buried in the Eastern Cemetery. The small gravestone, beside that of Moses N. Carr, is inscribed: "Charles Holden | son of | Osgood & Mary Ann | Noyes | died Jan. 27, 1836 | aged 2 years."

3. Catharine⁷, daughter to John⁶ Roberts, b. Jan. 7, 1806, in Portland; she was married (intention dated May 10, 1828) to Moses Nowell Carr, of Portland.§

Moses Nowell Carr, b. Sept. 22, 1805, in Hampden, Penobscot County, Maine, was third son to John and Avis Binney⁶ (Preble) Carr.‖ Avis was daughter to Jedidiah⁴ Preble, Jr., eldest son to Brigadier-General Jedidiah⁵ Preble, of Colonial and Revolutionary fame, and his first wife, Martha Junkins. The wife of Jedidiah, Jr., was Avis Phillips, of Boston. Soon after their marriage, about 1761, Jedidiah, Jr., was placed in command of Fort Pownal, which had been completed after his father's notable possession, in May, 1759.¶ Although Fort Pownal was destroyed by Captain Mowatt, in 1775,

---

* *Records of Somerville*, Marriages, vol. 1 : 110, no. 85.
† *Records of Boston*, Marriages, 1853: no. 697.
‡ *Records of Portland*, Deaths, vol. 4 : 30.
§ *Records of Portland*, Marriage Intentions, vol. 5 : 143.
‖ *Records of Portland*, Births, vol. 5 : 36.
¶ Vide pages 186–191.

Jedidiah remained at Castine; he died there in 1782 or 1783. His widow married again, and removed to Portland. She was a devout member of the Episcopal Church, and though most of her married life was spent far from the services of that church, she "often discoursed with her children concerning religion and taught them the Catechism and Hymns." *

John and Avis Carr lived several years at Hampden, Maine, then moved to Warren. One or both of them probably ended their days in Portland, since the births of their eight children were recorded, in 1844, at Portland. Moses N. Carr lived in Portland, and died there May 2, 1839.† He was buried in the Eastern Cemetery, which was begun in 1668; a small gravestone, on the right side of the central path near the middle of the ground, bears this inscription : —

MOSES N. CARR

DIED MAY 2, 1839

AGED 33 YEARS

In 1848, "Catherine Carr, widow," was living with Osgood Noyes and his family at 2 Lowell Street, Boston; from 1857 to 1859, she was again in Boston.‡ As her death is not recorded in that city, she probably spent her last years elsewhere, with some of her children.

Issue:§ I. Charles Henry Carr, b. March 19, 1829, in Portland.

II. George W. Carr, b. April 5, 1832, in Portland.

III. Ellen Maria Carr, b. Dec. 20, 1833, in Portland; her gravestone, beside her father's, is inscribed : "Ellen W. Carr | died March 6, 1836 | aged 2 yrs."

IV. "Ellen Maria Carr 2ᵈ," b. Aug. 31, 1836, in Portland.

---

* *The Preble Family*, by Captain George H. Preble, U. S. N., 1868: 130–137.

† *Records of Portland*, Deaths, vol. 4: 149.

‡ Boston Directories, 1848, 1857–1859.

§ *Records of Portland*, Births, vol. 4: 42.

V. Moses Carr, b. April 16, 1838; d. July 29, 1839,*
aged fifteen months.

4. Franklin[7], son to John[6] Roberts, b. Dec. 27, 1808,
in Portland. He did not remain long in Portland after he became of age, neither did he go
to Boston with his sisters. From the fact that
his sisters, in 1857, conveyed to John Cammett
but "two undivided third parts" of the homestead on Mountfort Street,† it is judged that
Franklin Roberts was then living; the deaths of
the three other children are on record at Portland.

5. Francis[7], son to John[6] Roberts, b. July 18, 1810, in
Portland; d. Dec. 4, 1828, in Portland,‡ aged eighteen
years, four months.

6. George[7], son to John[6] Roberts, b. Sept. 12, 1814, in
Portland; d. Aug. 3, 1834, in Portland,‡ aged nineteen years, eleven months.

II. George[6], son to Joseph[5] Roberts, b. March 1, 1773, in
Falmouth, now Portland. (Vide infra.)

III. "Polly"[6], daughter to Joseph[5] Roberts, bap. Oct. 31, 1780,
in Falmouth, by Rev. Stephen Lewis, pastor of Christ
Church, Boston.§

Henry McKenney and Polly Roberts, both of Portland,
were published Oct. 2, 1803.‖ He was a mariner, of Portland; on Sept. 1, 1803, he conveyed to "Lord and Thomas,"
of Portland, merchants, for $50, a lot of land in Portland,
"adjoining land formerly owned by William Waterhouse &
on the westerly side of Washington Street . . . carrying the
same wedth of Four rods to high water mark." This deed,
recorded the same day, was signed: —

"Henery McKinney"   [seal] ¶

---

* *Records of Portland*, Deaths, vol. 4 : 26.
† Vide page 1065.
‡ *Records of Portland*, Deaths, vol. 4 : 66.
§ *Records of Christ Church, Boston*, Baptisms, 1723–1851 : 132.
‖ *Records of Portland*, Marriages, vol. 3 : 93.
¶ *Cumberland County Deeds*, Book 40 : 544.

There is no other record of this family in Portland; it is impossible to trace it further.

IV. Priscilla[6], daughter to Joseph[5] Roberts, b. May, 1784, in Falmouth.*

The date of Priscilla's birth appears as "May, 1783," in the old Family Bible of Captain James[1] Slater, her husband; neither church nor city records show it. There is good reason, however, to believe that she was born early in May, 1784.† Priscilla Roberts was married Sept. 23, 1804, in Falmouth, to James Slater, by Rev. Samuel Deane,‡ pastor of the First Congregational Church of Falmouth (now Unitarian). She died May 26, 1806, in Portland,§ leaving an infant daughter; her age then was given correctly as twenty-two years. She was buried in the Eastern Cemetery, in "section F., no. 174." James Slater mar., second, June 19, 1812, in Portland, Betsey Davis, b. July, 1792, in Portland, daughter to Samuel and Hannah[5] (Dyer) Davis.‖

James Slater, b. Jan. 18, 1776, in the Shetland Isles, off the coast of Scotland, came to New England at the age of twelve years. The name of his father is not known; his mother, whose maiden name was Catharine Fullington, was then a widow. She either came with him, or was brought over soon afterward. James had sisters Catharine and Isabella. From his boyhood he followed the sea; until past middle life he sailed as shipmaster to foreign ports, — principally to the West Indies. During the War of 1812, when merchantmen did not dare to leave port for fear of seizure, he made a number of short voyages on the Privateer *Dash*. On her last voyage before she was lost, with all on board, Captain Slater was one of the prize-masters.¶ Late in life he kept a store, down near the wharves, where he sold West

---

* Falmouth Neck was organized as the town of Portland, Aug. 9, 1786; it became a city in 1832.

† Vide page 1063.

‡ *Records of Portland*, Marriages, vol. 3 : 174.

§ *Records of Portland*, Eastern Cemetery Records.

‖ Vide The Dyer Family.

¶ Vide page 1084.

India goods and ship supplies; to-day he probably would be called a ship-chandler. He was licensed as a retailer of spirits, July 21, 1821, and renewed his license every year until 1835.*

The second wife of Captain Slater, Betsey Davis, was sister to Hannah, wife of Captain George Roberts, his brother-in-law. A few months before his second marriage, Captain Slater bought of George and Hannah Roberts "one undivided moiety," or the westerly half, of the double house in which they lived, with the land about it. The deed was dated Feb. 13, 1812, and recorded five days later.† The house, which was built originally for two families, in 1847 was number 12 Mountfort Street. On March 13, 1837, "James Slater, of Portland . . . marriner," for $160, paid by Hannah Roberts, widow of George, conveyed to her a strip of land consisting of "about 14 sq. rods, which I bought of James Alden by deed dated April 29, 1816."

(Signed)

"James Slater"‡   [seal]

On Dec. 26, 1844, Hannah Roberts, widow, of Portland, for $150, conveyed to James M. Slater, son to Captain James Slater, the same " 14 sq. rods . . . on the southwest side of Mountfort Street," which had been sold to her, March 13, 1837, by Captain Slater.

(Signed)

" Hannah Roberts "§   [seal]

The old Family Bible of Captain Slater, to which reference has been made, was printed in 1825 ; the early records transferred to its pages are invaluable. The Captain gave it to his daughter, Mary Caroline Dyer, who died Jan. 26, 1907, in Portland ; she, in turn, has left it to her daughter, Elizabeth Wallace Smith. Captain Slater died April 10, 1853, in Portland, aged seventy-seven years, three months. He was buried in the Eastern Cemetery, " section A, Range 13, no.

---

* *Willis Collections*, Portland Public Library, Book I : 3–80.
† *Cumberland County Deeds*, Book 64 : 445.
‡ *Cumberland County Deeds*, Book 74 : 399.
§ *Cumberland County Deeds*, Book 151 : 140.

6." His gravestone, which stands beside that of George and Hannah Roberts, is of white marble, and measures forty-two inches in height by twenty-one and a half inches in breadth. The inscription is as follows : —

JAMES SLATER

Born on the Shetland I's
Jan. 18, 1776
Died
Apr. 10, 1853

" God's noblest work an honest man."

His widow Betsey died March 8, 1863, aged sixty-nine years, eight months. Her white marble stone, the same size as her husband's beside it, is inscribed : —

BETSEY

wife of
James Slater
died Mar. 8, 1863
Aet. 70

" God giveth his beloved rest."

Issue by first wife: 1. Priscilla Knight[2] Slater, b. May 1, 1806, in Portland; she was mar. Dec. 10, 1826, in Portland, to John White. The names of his parents have not been ascertained ; he had a sister Ann, and brothers, Horatio, Joseph, and Henry White. Priscilla White d. Dec. 9, 1834, in Portland, aged twenty-eight years, seven months. John White d. Sept. 11, 1843, in Portland.*

    Issue: I. James Slater White, b. Dec. 10, 1828, in Portland.

---

* *Records of Portland,* Deaths, vol. 5: 82, 112.

II. Ann Maria White, b. May 7, 1831, in Portland.

Issue by second wife: 2. James [2] Slater, b. Dec. 10, 1813, in Portland; d. Sept. 1, 1825, in Portland; aged eleven years, nine months.

3. Catharine Fullington [2] Slater, b. Jan. 20, 1817, in Portland; she was mar. May 15, 1837, in Portland, to Joseph W. Dyer, son to Lemuel and Betsey (Wallace) Dyer.

Issue: I. Joseph Franklin Dyer, b. June 28, 1838, in Portland; lives, unmarried (1907), in Portland.

II. Isabella Slater Dyer, b. 1840, in Portland; she was mar., first, to Samuel Hudson, of Portland, second, to Major John Craig, of Portland.

Issue by first husband: 1. Marion B. Hudson; she resides in Washington, D. C.

Issue by second husband: 2. Harry Craig. 3. John Craig. 4. Winifred Craig. 5. Joseph Craig.

III. Eunice Churchill Dyer, b. 1842, in Portland; she was mar. in Portland, to Henry Inman; resides in Ellsworth, Kansas. Issue: four.

IV. Ansel Dyer, b. 1844, in Portland; d. young.

V. Ansel Lewis Dyer, b. Aug., 1846, in Portland; he was lost on the steamer *Portland*, when she went down with all on board, November 29, 1898. His age was fifty-two years. He married about a year before he was lost; his widow resides in Portland.

VI. Gertrude Dyer, b. 1849, in Portland; d. unmar., Oct., 1879, in Deering, now Portland, aged thirty years.

VII. Mildred Dyer, b. 1851, in Portland; she was mar. in Portland, to John Goddard; resides in Portland.

Issue: two.

VIII. Kate Fullington Dyer, b. Dec. 6, 1860, in Portland; she was mar., in Portland, to Henry P. Wood. They reside in San Rafael, California.

Issue: 1. Parker Wood. 2. Mildred Wood.

4. John Mountfort[2] Slater, b. Feb. 25, 1819, in Portland;
d. unmar., March 31, 1871, in Portland, aged fifty-
two years. He was a sea-captain. The date of his
death is inscribed on the gravestone of his brother,
Daniel Mountfort Slater.

5. Mary Caroline[2] Slater, b. May 6, 1821, in Portland;
she was mar. May 22, 1844, in Portland, to Augustus
A. Dyer.

Augustus A. Dyer, b. June 23, 1820, in Portland, was son
to Lemuel and Betsey (Wallace) Dyer. He d. June, 1885,
in Portland, aged sixty-five years. His widow, Mary Caroline
Dyer, d. Jan. 26, 1907, in Portland, aged eighty-five years,
eight months. She cherished the ancient Bible that was
given to her by her father, from which nearly all the family
records have been copied.

Issue: I. Augustus Fuller Dyer, b. Dec. 16, 1845, in
Portland; d. Dec., 1846, aged one year.

II. Elizabeth Wallace Dyer, b. Feb. 21, 1847, in Port-
land; mar. Oct. 2, 1879, in Portland, to Abiel
Manley Smith, b. Oct. 23, 1837, in Boothbay,
Maine, son to Stevens and Harriet Newell (Knight)
Smith. They have always lived in Portland.

Issue: 1. Elizabeth Manley Smith, b. July 26, 1880,
in Portland. She has been a teacher in the
Cathedral School (Episcopal), at Washington,
D. C.; she is now (1907) at Albany, N. Y., interested in library work.

2. Margaret Slater Smith, b. Oct. 24, 1883, in Portland; d. June 5, 1892, in Portland, aged eight
years.

6. Hannah Elizabeth[2] Slater, daughter to Captain James[1]
Slater, b. Nov. 17, 1823, in Portland; she was married in Portland to Daniel Hall. He d. 1852, in Portland; his widow d. April 18, 1855, aged thirty-one
years.

Issue: I. Thomas Hall, b. 1845; d. in South America.

II. Mary E. Hall, b. 1847, in Portland; she was
mar. June 4, 1874, in Portland, to William S.
Lowell. They reside in Portland.

7. James F.² Slater, b. Jan. 23, 1826, in Portland; mar. Nov. 14, 1858, in Portland, Eliza B. Parsons, of Portland. She d. about 1880, and was buried in Portland. James F. Slater d. about 1898.

8. Isabella² Slater, b. Feb. 10, 1829, in Portland; d. May 26, 1832, in Portland, aged three years, three months.

9. Daniel Mountfort² Slater, b. Jan. 12, 1832, in Portland; d. Aug. 11, 1855, of yellow fever, in New Orleans. The gravestone of white marble, thirty-nine inches in height by nineteen and a half inches in width, erected in his memory beside the stone of his mother, has this inscription : —

DANIEL MOUNTFORT
son of
James & Betsey Slater
died in New Orleans
of yellow fever
Aug. 11, 1855
Aet. 23 yrs. 7 mos.
A token of mother love.

CAPT. JOHN M.
Died Mar. 31, 1871
Aet. 52 yrs.

10. Isabella² Slater, b. Feb. 8, 1834, in Portland; d. Nov. 6, 1836, in Portland, aged two years, nine months. Many years after her death, a stone of white marble, twenty-nine inches in height by sixteen in width, was placed beside that of Daniel M. and Captain John M. Slater, in memory of the three children who had died young : —

JAMES
died Sept. 1, 1825,
aged 11 yrs. 9 mos.

ISABELLA
died May 26, 1832,
aged 3 yrs. 3 mos.

ISABELLA
died Nov. 6, 1836,
aged 2 yrs. 9 mos.
children of
James & Betsey Slater.

GEORGE [6] ROBERTS

George [6] Roberts, second son to Joseph [5] and Ruth (White) Roberts, was "born March 1, 1773, in Falmouth," Maine. The date of his birth appears in the Bible of his son Benjamin, and in the "Family Bible" of Captain James Slater, his brother-in-law. No church or city records show it; yet it is probable that he was baptized in St. Paul's Church, since his father paid his tax in the church that year. "George Roberts entered his name & intention of marriage with Hannah Davis, both of Portland, May 13, 1794;" they were married October 25, 1797, in Portland, by "Rev. Samuel Dean, Minister of the Gospel," [*] and pastor of the First Congregational Church (now Unitarian). The lapse of three and a half years between the publishment of their intention of marriage and their marriage was very unusual; the law required three weeks, the period seldom exceeded three months. As George Roberts was a mariner, from his youth, it is probable that he spent much of the intervening time at sea.

---

[*] *Records of Portland*, Marriages, vol. 3 : 40, 51.

Hannah Davis, b. November 10, 1774, in Falmouth, was daughter to Samuel and Hannah[5] (Dyer) Davis, of Falmouth. It has been impossible to trace the parentage of Samuel Davis, yet without doubt he was a descendant of Isaac Davis, one of the earliest settlers of Falmouth. The marriage intention of "Samuel Davis of Falmouth & Hannah Dyer of Cape Elizabeth" was dated November 24, 1773; * they were married December 13, 1773, in Falmouth, by Rev. Ephraim Clark. Before 1809, Hannah[6] (Dyer) Davis was a widow.† She died August 18, 1844, in Portland, aged eighty-nine years.‡

Soon after their marriage, George and Hannah Roberts had silhouettes § made; these pictures, time-worn and yellowed by age, are now in the possession of their only surviving granddaughter, Mrs. Mary Caroline Small.‖ George, with the fashionable cue and forelock of the period, is evidently gotten up with great care; while Hannah, "with comely carriage of her countenance trim" and matronly cap, is the personification of daintiness.¶ At this time they were living on what locally has been known in Cape Elizabeth (now South Portland) as the "Chris Dyer estate," at the foot of Meeting-House Hill, on the right. Originally there were two houses on the place, besides the barn; none of the buildings appear to have been painted. One of the houses was taken down some years ago; the house now remaining is thought to be the one in which they lived. Here their eldest son, Reuben Davis Roberts, was born — for he himself so told his son. Not far from the house a small

---

* *Records of Cape Elizabeth, Maine,* Births, Deaths, and Marriages, vol. 4 : 6.
† *Cumberland County Deeds,* Book 56 : 501.
‡ Vide The Dyer Family.
§ Profiles were traced by an instrument with a black pencil on the shadow cast by a candle on white paper — an inexpensive fashion at that time styled "à la Silhouette." In this case, the white paper was cut and placed upon the black, the reverse of such efforts to-day.
‖ Vide page 284.   ¶ Vide page 1088.

MR. GEORGE ROBERTS, 1797.

MRS. GEORGE ROBERTS, 1797.

creek flows into Fore River, and by it stands an ancient tide-mill once belonging to the estate. Its crumbling and windowless frame, standing on piles, looms up in the perspective like a shadowy ghost of the past. Between the tide-mill and the rear of the house is the main road over Meeting-House Hill, upon which passes the trolley-line to the Casino. Facing the house and the main road, the view, as seen in the illustration, is most attractive. It embraces the large, old house and barn, overtopped by trees of more than a century's growth, while beyond, Fore River, a salt water indent, ebbs and flows with the waters of Casco Bay; in the distance lies the city of Portland. Portland then (1797), with its green and wooded hills, was a somewhat rural town rising out of the ashes of Revolutionary fires. There is no record that accurately fixes the date of George Roberts's removal to Portland. In 1800, he was mentioned in a deed as of Cape Elizabeth, and his son Benjamin was born there, August 2, 1803; but in 1805, he was a citizen of Portland.

The earliest conveyance to George Roberts was of a tract of land in Portland, as follows: "Joseph Plumer of Portland . . . Trader," for $450, paid by "John Roberts of said Portland . . . Mariner and George Roberts of Cape Elizabeth . . . Mariner," sold to them a "certain parcel of Land in Said Portland . . . beginning at a stake standing by the northerly side of Fore Street three rods & a half northeasterly from the corner where said side is intersected by the easterly side of Hancock Street, thence from said stake northwesterly on a course parallel with said Hancock Street to John Dole's land, thence by said Dole's land northeasterly to Land belonging to Stephen Longfellow Esq. thence southeasterly by said Longfellow's Land to Fore Street." This deed was dated May 29, 1800, and signed and acknowledged on the same day by Joseph Plummer and his wife, Mary Plummer; it was recorded June 14, following. At the same time, the above land was mortgaged back to Plummer, for $450, by John and George Roberts, "Mary wife of John & Hannah wife of George" relinquishing their right of dower; May 24, 1804, the mortgage was discharged.* This lot of land, "situated on Fore & Hancock Streets," in Portland, was sold, September 28, 1805, by "John Roberts of Portland . . . caulker" and "George Roberts of Portland . . . yeoman," for $450, to Samuel Stephenson, a merchant of Portland. The deed was signed :—

"John Roberts

George Roberts

Hannah Roberts

Recorded: Oct. 8, 1805.   Mary Roberts"†

On September 28, 1805, John and George Roberts bought of William Moulton, Jr., shipwright, of Portland, for $500, a lot of land "100 feet from Hancock Street by the Southerly side of Waite street." This land they divided, July 10, 1807, George taking the southwesterly half. The next year, April 25, 1808, "George Roberts of Portland . . . yeoman," and his wife Hannah, conveyed, for $230, to John Roberts, of Portland, "all my right title interest that I have to a certain lot of land that I and my brother John bought of William Moulton," on Wait and Hancock Streets.

(Signed)

"George Roberts   [seal]

Recorded: April 26, 1808.   Hannah Roberts"‡ [seal]

The latter deed contains the only positive reference to the relationship of the brothers, John and George Roberts, that has been found after a search extended through several years. It is singular that from this year, 1808, their ways gradually diverged, until their grandchildren had no knowledge of each other.

In the fall of that year (October 3, 1808), George Rob-

---

* *Cumberland County Deeds*, Book 33: 61, 62, 63.

† *Cumberland County Deeds*, Book 46: 580.

‡ *Cumberland County Deeds*, Book 46: 618; Book 53: 111; Book 55: 55.

BIRTHPLACE OF REUBEN D. AND

LD BENJAMIN ROBERTS, CAPE ELIZABETH,
ME.

erts bought of Enoch Ilsley and his wife Abigail, for $276, "a certain small Lot of land in Portland bounded as follows, viz! Beginning at a Stake Standing in the Southwest side of Mountfort Street, sixty two feet Northwesterly from the North Corner of the house lately built by Joseph Stilson, then northwesterly by said Street forty feet to a Stake,"* etc. Five hundred and fifty dollars of the amount used to build the house upon this lot was advanced by "Hannah Davis of Portland . . . widow," mother-in-law to George Roberts, to whom he mortgaged the land with the "Dwelling house thereon standing." The mortgage was signed, acknowledged, and recorded February 8, 1809, by "George Roberts"; it was discharged February 13, 1812, by

"Hannah $\overset{\text{her}}{\underset{\text{mark}}{\times}}$ Davis"† [seal]

On the day of discharge, George and Hannah Roberts sold "to James Slater of s^d Portland Marriner . . . One undivided moiety" of the estate on Mountfort Street, with the "westerly half of the house thereon."‡ The first wife of Captain James Slater was sister to George Roberts; his second wife was sister to Hannah, wife of George Roberts. These ties, strengthened by marriages of Captain Slater's children to Dyers (relatives to both), kept the descendants of James Slater and George Roberts near together. When the house was first built, there was but one house on Munjoy Hill beyond Mountfort Street; for a long time afterward, there was an uninterrupted view of the harbor, with the water not more than four hundred feet away. Later, on the opposite side of the street, lived the Chases, the Potes, and the Mountforts. The latter lived on the corner of Fore and Mountfort Streets in the house built about 1800–1804 by Daniel Mountfort, who went there from Boston. Mrs. Chase

---

* *Cumberland County Deeds*, Book 56: 281.
† *Cumberland County Deeds*, Book 56: 501.
‡ *Cumberland County Deeds*, Book 64: 445.

and Mrs. Pote were daughters to James Mountfort, son to Daniel. The Mountfort house is now (1906) occupied by Mrs. Sarah T. (Moulton) Carleton, a widow, daughter to Edward and Mary Ann (Mountfort) Moulton. Mary Ann Mountfort was daughter to Daniel Mountfort, who built the house. In 1847, the Roberts house was number 12 Mountfort Street.* Within a few years, the old house has been torn down, and a brick house arranged for two families has been erected on the same site; it is numbered 12 and 12½ Mountfort Street.

During his earlier years, and until the War of 1812 made it unsafe for merchantmen to venture out, Captain George Roberts sailed in command of ships to foreign ports. On one of these voyages he brought home a complete set of china that had been made for him in Liverpool. The design represents a full-rigged ship, in black, upon a sea of green. Eleven of the original dozen dinner plates are in the possession of descendants. The accompanying illustration shows a mahogany "light stand," with leaves outspread, that belonged to George and Hannah Roberts; it has the original brass rings.† On the table at the left is one of the dinner plates, scalloped edged, the ship in the centre; its diameter is nine and a half inches. The bowl near this plate was owned by Hannah, also the *Staffordshire* plate, an early English ware something like the ancient "flowing-blue." The plate, cup, and saucer, at the right, belonged to Clarissa Roberts, daughter-in-law to George and Hannah. The decoration on these consists of bands of "pink lustre" with gilt edges.

The pitcher,‡ eleven inches in height, was a part of the original set with the ship design. On one side is the ship; on the opposite side is *The Shipwright's Arms.* Under the

---

* Portland Directory, 1847.
† Vide illustration, page 1046.
‡ Vide illustration, page 1096.

lip, surrounded by a wreath, *George and Hannah Roberts*, and below, *Success to America.* The design under the handle, which shows very little in the illustration, is a copy of the first "Great Seal of the United States of America," adopted June 20, 1782.* It greatly enhances the value of the pitcher. Though made in Liverpool, it is almost an exact copy; the chief variation being in the number and arrangement of the stars.† On the pitcher is an eagle with wings outspread, a shield covering his body. The right talon holds an olive branch, the left a bundle of arrows. On a streamer, held in the beak, is *E Pluribus Unum.* There is a star above the head of the eagle and one on each side of the neck, while a curved row of stars overarches the whole from the tip of one wing to the tip of the other. This pitcher is in the possession of a great-granddaughter to Hannah Roberts; the "light stand" and china belong to her sister, while a third sister has the brass andirons, shovel, and tongs which were used by Hannah Roberts in her room on Mountfort Street.

George Roberts was lost at sea, in the *Dash*, January 23, 1815; the city records of Portland add, "son of Joseph." ‡ The circumstances surrounding his tragic death have long been a matter of history. The brig *Dash* had been one of the most efficient and successful of the armed privateers

---

* *U. S. Curious Facts, Historical, Geographical, and Political*, by Malcolm Townsend, 1890 · 392, 393.

† "The Great Seal" is thus described by the chairman (1907) of the committee of Heraldry of the New-England Historic Genealogical Society, Boston: "ARMS: Argent six pallets gules, a chief azure, the shield borne on the breast of an American eagle displayed, holding in his dexter talon an olive branch, and in his sinister talon a bunch of thirteen arrows, all proper. In his beak a scroll bearing the motto *E Pluribus Unum.* Above the eagle appears a semi-circular band of clouds bounded by the scroll held in the eagle's beak, irradiated on the outer side, the field enclosed being semi of thirteen stars."

There are thirteen leaves on the olive branch, thirteen arrows in the bunch, thirteen tail-feathers, and thirteen edge-feathers on each wing of the eagle.

‡ *Records of Portland*, Deaths, vol. 4: 155.

during the War of 1812. She was not designed originally for a privateer, but when war was declared, she was fitted out to operate much like our blockade-runners in the Civil War. The *Dash* was of 222 tons, was pierced for sixteen guns, and carried forty men. She was launched early in 1813 at Porter's Landing, in Freeport, where she was built for her owners, William Porter, Seward Porter, and Samuel Porter, merchants of Portland. She was clipper built, and rigged at first as a top-sail schooner, a style now obsolete, but she outsailed everything she came across. Her first voyage as a blockade-runner was under the command of Captain Edward Kelleran, to Santo Domingo ; Henry Cobb was Lieutenant.* She skipped south unobserved, and disposed of her cargo at good prices ; on her return voyage, laden with coffee, etc., she was chased by a British man-of-war, and came near being captured. An accident to her foremast, which occurred during the exciting pursuit, made it necessary to refit her on her return, so her whole rig was changed to that of a "hermaphrodite brig." She made three successful voyages under Captain Kelleran.

Captain Cammett next commanded the *Dash*. Hitherto she had not been aggressive, but had sailed in the regular Santo Domingo trade and "wasted no ammunition except in self defence." Under her new commander, she made several sorties on British shipping, capturing between August, 1814, and January 4, 1815, several valuable prizes. Captain James Slater, of Portland, was one of the prize-masters.† Soon after her arrival, it was known that the *Dash* was making ready for another cruise as a privateer, under the command of Captain John Porter, a younger brother of her owners. They were totally unaware that a treaty of peace had been signed, December 24, between Great Britain and the United States. The Porter brothers chose their own

---

* *Manuscript Records of Portland, Maine*, by William Willis, 1850.
† *Portland in the Past*, by William Goold, 1886: 457.

ship's company "from the best families* of Portland and the sea-board towns;" many of the men previously had commanded their own ships. "No vessel ever sailed from the port which had the prayers of such a multitude for her safety." The privateer schooner *Champlain* had been built and fitted out in Portsmouth, and by arrangement was ready to sail with the *Dash*, to test her speed. Copper sheathing was then unknown, but, just before she sailed, the *Dash* was given a coating of soap and tallow, which was good while it lasted.

On January 21, the two ships passed the lighthouse in company, and not till then did the crowd leave the hill overlooking the harbor. "For what more is known of the *Dash* we are indebted to the *Champlain*." The *Dash* led the way for more than twenty-four hours; at dark, on the second day, she was a long distance ahead, steering nearly south; but the *Champlain* kept her light in sight. A gale sprang up, the captain sounded and found the water shoaling; fearing the Georges Banks, he changed his course. When last seen, "the light of the *Dash* bore the same by the compass." It was the opinion of nautical men that Captain Porter underrated his speed and foundered on Georges Banks. The records of the *Dash* are among the ancient files of the Custom-House at Portland. That they are records to be proud of is shown by references to her prowess in nearly every history of the city of Portland and the State of Maine, as well as the Cumberland County History.†

It was years before the bereaved families of those who sailed in the *Dash* would believe that their loved ones were

---

* Among those who were lost on the *Dash* were Edward and Enoch Oxnard, sons to Thomas and Martha (Preble) Oxnard, of Portland, and grandsons to Brigadier General Jedidiah Preble. Vide *The Preble Family*, by Captain George H. Preble, U. S. N., 1868: 143, 146, 148.

† *Portland in the Past*, by William Goold, 1886: 449–466; also *Stories of Maine*, by Sophie Swett, 1899: 262–268; also *History of Cumberland County, Maine*, 1880: 284.

lost. Cruel reports that some of the ship's company had been heard of on desolate islands came to them; then again it was feared that they had been captured and held as slaves in some of the Barbary States.* But at last all hope died out, and many wives were compelled to feel that they indeed were widows. Hannah Roberts was inconsolable; from the time of the return of the *Champlain* without her consort, the *Dash*, she dressed in black. Later, she added a white stomacher and a white cap, but she dressed as a widow to the end of her days. She was a dainty little woman, with black eyes and black hair, whom everybody respected and loved. She was "aunt Hannah" to her relatives, and was called "aunt Hannah" by her many friends. That her husband *might* return was her daily thought, and her many suitors were made to feel that her kindly refusals to marry again were final.

Hannah Roberts was a "very religious woman," and regularly attended the Chestnut Street Methodist Church, in Portland. Each day, at twelve o'clock, she went into her closet to pray; a well-worn copy of Baxter's "Saint's Rest," bound in calfskin, was her constant companion. There are those living who remember the beauty of her daily life; how cheerful she was, how her ever ready sympathy helped others. She had a store of old-fashioned "maxims" that were brought forth to fit every emergency. Many of these

---

* For many years the United States, as well as nearly every European government, had been annoyed by the outrages of the Algerine corsairs against commerce. Officers and crews of vessels were captured and held prisoners for the purpose of extorting ransoms from their respective governments. These prisoners were not only kept in slavery, but were subjected to every indignity; in addition, they were decimated by the plague. Stories of their sufferings had reached the shores of Maine, and when the American government, on March 3, 1815 (six weeks after the loss of the *Dash*), declared war against Algiers, it must have appeared to the bereaved ones that their worst fears would be realized. The war was of but a few months' duration, and the United States was the first nation to free herself from Algerine piracy.

Vide *The Old Shipmasters of Salem, Mass.*, by Charles E. Trow, 1905: 76–81.

have been forgotten, but there are a few that have been passed on to her great-granddaughters:—

"Take time in time while time lasts,
For time's no time when time's past."

"Never seem to mind it, nor count your fate a curse,
For however bad you find it, there's somebody's worse."

She was able to keep the homestead on Mountfort Street; but in 1818, with two minor children to maintain, she felt obliged to apply for a pension. The eldest son, Reuben, was self-supporting. A copy of her pension-paper states that the application for a pension was dated "June 11, 1818," and "her claim was allowed." The "statement of the military history of George Roberts, a sailor of-the War of 1812," shows that he had the rank of "Carpenter," that is, ship's-carpenter, under "Captain John Porter, on the Private armed Brig 'The Dash,'" which "sailed from Portland, Jan. 21, 1815, and was lost in a gale about Jan. 23, 1815." His "residence . . . at enlistment, Portland." "Sailor married Hannah ——, Oct. —, 1797;" her "residence at date of application, Portland, Cumberland County, Massachusetts." Their children were "Mary Caroline, born Feb. 26, 1801 — and Benjamin, born Aug. 2, 1803." *

The declining years of Hannah Roberts were cheered by the loving care of her son Benjamin and his wife. Her sunny "front room," immaculate as herself, was the Mecca of all her friends and relatives. Some of her grand-nephews, now gray-haired men, remember the pleasure they had, as little boys, visiting "aunt Hannah" on certain Sunday afternoons. "Hannah, widow of the late George Roberts," died August 4, 1855, in Portland.† Her age, as given in the city records of Portland, was eighty-three years; from the date

---

* Department of the Interior, Bureau of Pensions, Washington, D. C., "Wid. File No. 119, Privateer."
† *City Records of Portland*, Deaths, vol. 5: 104.

of her birth in the family Bible, it was eighty years and nine months. Her grave is in the old Eastern Cemetery,* whose southeastern boundary was then, as now, Mountfort Street. Over the gateway on Congress Street is this inscription — "Eastern Cemetery, 1668." Following the central path and soon turning to the left, one reaches the graves of the Roberts family, near the Cushing monument which is enclosed with an iron fence. The second stone, of white marble and measuring thirty-eight inches in height by twenty and a half inches in breadth, bears this inscription : —

HANNAH

widow of

George Roberts

died Aug. 4, 1855

Æt. 83.

GEORGE ROBERTS

was lost in the Dash

Feb. 1815. Æt. 42.

A small stone, marked " H R " stands at the foot of her grave. In 1906, the Memorial Association of the Grand Army of the Republic placed before the headstone one of its markers, with a flag and wreath of evergreens, which is to remain *in perpetuam rei memoriam.*

ISSUE†

I. Reuben Davis⁷, b. Nov. 4, 1798, in Cape Elizabeth. Reuben Davis Roberts and Mary Ann Flagg⁶ Baker were married April 10, 1822, in Portland, by Rev. David Kilburn. She was b. May 20, 1803, probably in Portland, Maine, daughter to Thomas⁵ and Mary (Cullis) Baker.

---

* Records of Eastern Cemetery (City Hall, Portland) : "Section A, Range 13, no. 5."

† *City Records of Portland,* Births, vol. 5 : 53.

Thomas[5] Baker was b. Dec. 30, 1780, in Springfield, Mass.; his wife, Mary Cullis, was b. April 23, 1782, in Norwich, Conn. They had nine children. Lieutenant-Colonel Thomas Baker belonged to the Maine Militia, and served in the War of 1812. He was Coroner and Constable of Portland, Deputy Sheriff and Crier of the Courts nearly twenty years, and for thirteen years Messenger of the Maine House of Representatives. "He was a man beloved and respected by the leading citizens of Portland, as well as by all who knew him in Augusta." He d. in Portland, Sept. 5, 1838, twenty years after the death of his wife, Mary, who passed away June 18, 1818.

Thomas[5] Baker and his father, John[4] Baker, established a bakery in Portland; their business later passed into the hands of Reuben D. Roberts. John[4] Baker (Thomas[3], Thomas[2]) was descended from Edward[1] Baker, of Lynn, Mass. The wife of John[4] Baker was Mary Flagg Tappan, daughter to Rev. Benjamin Tappan, of Manchester, Mass. A son of Reuben D. Roberts was named Benjamin Tappan Roberts, for that reverend gentleman.[*]

Reuben D. Roberts mar., second, about 1839, Rachel Webster, b. Aug. 1, 1812, in Freeport, daughter to Captain Benjamin Webster by his second wife, Mary (Waite) Webster. Mary Waite was daughter to Daniel and Rachel[5] (Chandler) Waite, the latter daughter to Jonathan[4] and Rachel[5] (Mitchell) Chandler, of North Yarmouth. Lucy[5], sister to Rachel[5] Chandler, mar. Benjamin Waite.[†] Rachel Roberts d. Jan. 9, 1841, in Portland, leaving an infant son, now (1906) the sole survivor of the family. The third wife of Reuben D. Roberts, to whom he was mar. Oct. 24, 1841, in Portland, by Rev. William S. Dwight, was Julia Ann Webster, b. Aug. 9, 1807, in Freeport, daughter to Captain Benjamin Webster by his first wife, Lydia (Soule) Webster. Mrs. Julia Ann Roberts d. May 20, 1893, in South Paris, Maine; she had no children.

The birthplace[‡] of Mr. Roberts was the "old Chris Dyer" estate in Cape Elizabeth. Not long before his death, while

---

[*] *Maine Historical and Genealogical Recorder*, vol. 8 : 159–163.
[†] Vide pages 904, 905.   [‡] Vide illustration, page 1078.

driving by the old house with his youngest son, he pointed
it out as the place where he was born. In his youth, he
learned from Thomas Baker, later his father-in-law, the trade
of a baker, which he continued to follow. In addition, he
was licensed, in 1823 and 1824, as a retailer of spirits.*
Every shopkeeper of standing at that time had to sell wine,
beer, and spirits, if he wanted to keep his trade. Dram-
drinking was the universal custom; many of the oldest inhabitants of Portland can remember that, in their youth, the
bell of the First Church was rung at eleven in the forenoon
and four in the afternoon, for the men to take their "toddy."
The excesses arising from this custom led to the formation
of the Washingtonian Society — akin to the modern Total
Abstinence Society. This organization was of slow growth,
but it effected, by public opinion, a much-needed reform. As
Reuben Davis was licensed for that trade but two years,
while his neighbors carried it on much longer, it appears
that he was somewhat ahead of his time in the movement;
for that reason he probably died a poorer man.

The small shop where he sold his wares is entered by the
door to the left; in the rear were the oven, the mixing-table,
the moulding-table, etc. A door to the right led upstairs to
the family living-rooms. Little is changed except at the foot
of the stairs, where the door once leading to the bake-shop is
now boarded up. In 1847, the shop was 94 Federal Street, the
house number 96;† in 1906, the numbers were 204 and 204½
Federal Street, near Temple Street.

Reuben D. Roberts was a member of the Chestnut Street
Methodist Church, in Portland, which he regularly attended
with his family. He died Oct. 27, 1851, in Portland, aged
fifty-three years.‡

Issue § by first wife: 1. Amanda M.³, b. Dec. 24, 1825, in
          Portland; d. Aug. 28, 1827, aged one year, eight
          months.

---

* *Willis Collections*, Portland Public Library, Book I: 20, 23.
† Portland Directory, 1847.
‡ *Records of Portland*, Deaths, vol. 5: 44.
§ *Records of Portland*, Births, vol. 5: 16.

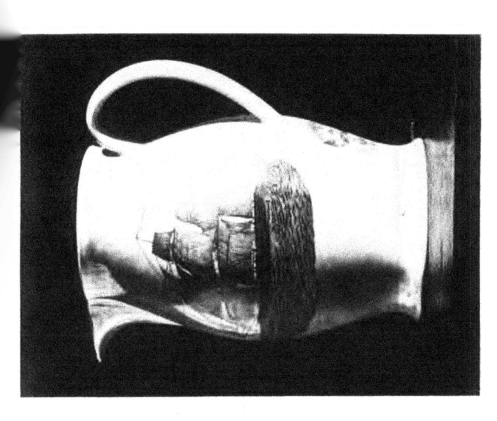

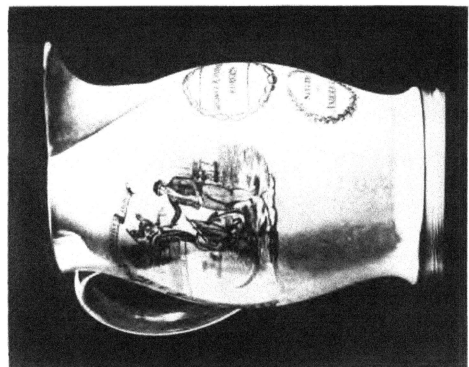

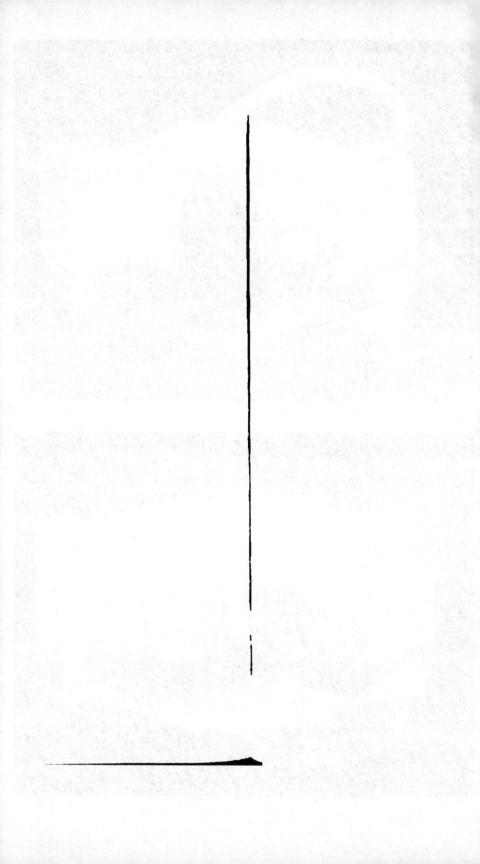

2. Amanda[8], b. July 9, 1828, in Portland; she was mar., in Portland, to Lorenzo De M. Ling. She d. March 10, 1851, in Portland, aged twenty-two years, eight months.* Her husband married again and "went West."

    Issue: I. Inez Ling, b. Aug. 1, 1850; she was seven months old when her mother died; she was married in the West.

3. Benjamin Tappan[8], b. Aug. 16, 1830, in Portland. He enlisted early in the Civil War, and was killed Nov. 9, 1862, at the Battle of Fredericksburg, while serving under General Burnside.

4. Ezra Kellogg[8], b. Dec. 13, 1832, in Portland. He was accidentally killed, about 1878, in Chicago, by a moving train; he was a sea-captain; he never married.

Issue by second wife: 5. William Webster[8], b. Nov. 14, 1840, in Portland.

He mar. Sept. 3, 1862, in Medford, Mass., Arabella Waterman, b. June 3, 1840, in Medford. She was daughter to Eben Waterman, born in Pembroke, Mass., and his wife, Sarah (Rogers) Waterman, who was born in Marshfield, Mass. Mrs. Waterman d. April 7, 1884, in Medford; her husband removed to Portland, where he d. Jan. 22, 1885, at the home of his daughter, Mrs. Arabella Roberts.

For a while after his marriage, Mr. Roberts resided in Ohio; returning East, he was in Portland with Hall L. Davis (books, stationery, etc.) for about eight years. In May, 1900, he formed the corporation of "William W. Roberts Co.," stationers, at Portland. Mr. Roberts is a member of the Maine Lodge of Odd Fellows, of the Knights of Pythias, the Elks, and a "32° Mason." With his family, he attends the Congress Square Universalist Church of Portland; his residence is in Westbrook.

    Issue: I. Lora Josephine[9], b. Oct. 24, 1867, in Cincinnati, Ohio; d. Sept. 14, 1886, in New Gloucester, Maine, aged eighteen years, ten months.

---

* *Records of Portland, Deaths, vol. 5: 31.*

II. George Clinton[9], b. Jan. 23, 1871, in Portland,
    Maine; mar. Nov. 27, 1895, in Portland, Nancy
    Day Kimball. He learned the business of a
    druggist, but failing health obliged him to re-
    linquish it. He has a small farm in Westbrook,
    a suburb of Portland.
    Issue: 1. Pauline Alice, b. Oct. 1, 1896, in Portland.
    2. Marian, b. Jan. 4, 1900, in Portland.
III. Alice McLellan[9], b. July 10, 1876, in Portland;
    mar. April 24, 1901, in Portland, to Alan O.
    Goold. They reside in Westbrook.
    Issue: 1. Gilbert Goold, b. Feb. 28, 1904, in Port-
    land.

II. Mary Caroline[7], daughter to George[6] Roberts, b. Feb. 26,
1801, in Cape Elizabeth.

At the time her father was lost at sea, she was fourteen
years of age. Within the next two years, she developed a
delicacy of constitution that caused her family great anxiety.
Her condition probably was the direct result of the shock
of her father's death; she never fully recovered. Debarred
from much that other young girls enjoyed, she turned her
attention to books. She studied and read; and, when she
grew a little stronger, she opened a private school in her
home. This school she kept for years, and employed her
spare time in writing both verse and prose, which were published in the local papers. For a long time she was secretary
of the Martha Washington Society, of Portland, — a temperance organization throughout the state; her beautiful handwriting in the Society's books has been greatly admired.

Flowers were her children; she planted, tended, encouraged,
and petted them until her summer garden was a wonder. In
the winter her windows were filled with blossoms. Knowing
how fond she was of plants, neighbors and friends sent her
slips of their rarest blooms, seeds, or pots of growing flowers.
She always lived with her mother in the Mountfort Street
home. From 1834 to 1846, they lived there by themselves.
She died April 16, 1848, in Portland, aged forty-seven years;[*]

---

* *Records of Portland*, Deaths, vol. 5 : 7.

the memory of her beautiful life is still green. Her grave in the Eastern Cemetery is beside that of her mother. The headstone * of white marble is twenty-three inches in height by sixteen inches in width. The inscription is as follows: —

MARY CAROLINE
daughter of
George & Hannah
Roberts
Died
April 16, 1848

III. Benjamin[7], son to George[6] Roberts, born Aug. 2, 1803, in Cape Elizabeth. (Vide infra.)

BENJAMIN[7] ROBERTS

Benjamin[7] Roberts, younger son to George[6] and Hannah (Davis) Roberts, was born August 2, 1803, in Cape Elizabeth (South Portland), Maine, as is shown by the record in his Bible. That his birth and the births of his brother and sister are found recorded in Portland† is accounted for by the fact that a large proportion of the present vital statistics of that city is a compilation of records secured by a house-to-house canvass, and collected from other sources, both before and since the fire of 1866.

Benjamin Roberts and his brother Reuben looked very much alike; their mother always said they strongly resembled their father, whom they but dimly remembered. Benjamin, described as a little above medium height, with black eyes and black hair, "as a young man was considered very handsome, and his manners unusually polished for those days." His education was obtained in the public schools of Portland. Among his schoolmates was Henry Wadsworth

---

* Records of Eastern Cemetery: "Section A, range 13, no. 4."
† *Records of Portland*, Births, vol. 5: 53.

Longfellow (son to Stephen and Zilpha (Wadsworth) Longfellow), who was to establish a world-wide reputation as
scholar and poet.   Longfellow was born in the house of his
uncle, General Samuel Stevenson, at the corner of Fore and
Hancock Streets.   The latter street was next parallel to
Mountfort Street, on the west; and the land of General
Stevenson originally joined that of Hannah Roberts, in the
rear.   Later, his parents moved into the so-called Longfellow
House, on Congress Street, but Henry W. remained in the
same school district.   His first poetic attempt is said to have
been a few "verses" that he brought, when quite young, to
his school-teacher : —

> "*Mrs. Phinney had a turnip, and it grew and it grew.*"

A tablet has been placed on the front of the ancient Stevenson mansion, at the corner of Hancock Street, facing
Fore Street : —

AMERICA'S GREATEST POET
HENRY W. LONGFELLOW
WAS BORN IN THIS HOUSE
FEBRUARY 27ᵀᴴ 1807

While Longfellow went to college, the exigencies of the
home demanded that Benjamin Roberts should learn a trade
and become self-supporting as soon as possible.   He chose
the trade of a cabinet-maker, probably serving an apprenticeship, as was then customary.   He became a superior
workman in every line of light wood-working, and is mentioned in deeds first as a "chair maker," and then as "chaise
maker;" in 1838, he first was called a "carriage maker," or
builder.   The reputation which he established in Portland
for good workmanship, fidelity, and thorough honesty lasted
throughout his fourscore years.

On April 24, 1825, Benjamin Roberts was married by
"Rev. Phineas Crandall, minister of the Gospell," in Falmouth, to Clarissa Mitchell;* their marriage intention was

---

* *Records of Portland*, Marriages, vol. 5 : 29.

dated a month before — "March 26 . . . both of Portland." *
Their wedded life extended over a period of nearly fifty-nine
years. Clarissa[6] Mitchell, born September 23, 1800, in Freeport, Maine, was the youngest child to John Hayes[6] and
Hannah (Bowdoin) Mitchell, of Freeport. † Her father was
lost at sea when she was but one year old ; the death of her
mother, "widow Hannah Mitchell," in 1804, left six children quite unprovided for. Clarissa was adopted into the
family of Nathaniel and Sarah (Bradbury) Osgood, who
lived in Durham on the west side of the "County Road"
near the Freeport line.

Nathaniel Osgood and his brothers, William and David,
moved about 1780 from Deerfield, New Hampshire, to Durham, where they possessed a large farm of three hundred and
forty-two acres, in common, for nearly twenty years ; then it
was amicably divided. Nathaniel spent his early life in Salisbury, Massachusetts, where he was born, August 12, 1747.
He served in the Revolutionary War, and treasured a gun
taken by him from one of the British in 1777, at the surrender of Burgoyne. Both he and his wife were persons of more
than ordinary education and refinement. They had three
sons, Benjamin, David, and Joseph, all born before September, 1779, in Deerfield, New Hampshire ; but there were no
daughters. A young woman, who had been taken into the
family, begged to be allowed to bring the "pretty little girl,"
then four years old, into the home and care for her. Clarissa
remained with the Osgood family until she was about twenty-
one ; she then left to take care of her mother's mother, who
was aged and feeble. It was at the Osgoods that Clarissa
Mitchell developed the strong character, remarkable executive ability, and clear, logical brain that served her well. Up
to the time of her death, at the age of eighty-eight years, she
was mentally very active. She was small of stature — not

---

* *Records of Portland*, Marriage Intentions, vol. 4 : 99.
† Vide The Mitchells from Kittery.

much over five feet, and of dark complexion. Though gifted with a keen sense of humor, she was ever ready to sympathize with those in trouble and to help them.

The year following his marriage, Benjamin Roberts, "Chaise Maker," bought of James Deering a small lot of land in Portland, which he mortgaged July 23, 1829, to his mother for $415. It was described as having "a small dwelling house thereon standing . . . on Newbury Street" near Theophilus Bradbury's dwelling-house, it "being the same land I purchased of James Deering as per his deed Dated June 1, 1826 . . . Clarisa Roberts wife of the said Benjamin hereby relinquishing her dower."

Witnesses: (Signed)
" Elliot G. Vaughan   " Benjamin Roberts [seal]
   Reuben D. Roberts."   Clarisa Roberts "   [seal]
This mortgage was discharged September 11, 1833, by

Hannah Roberts * [seal]

On December 17, 1830, Reuben D. Roberts, "baker," Benjamin Roberts, "chaisemaker," and Mary C. Roberts, "singlewoman," all of Portland, for $500, conveyed to Hannah Roberts, their mother, all right and title to the half of the house and land where she lived on Mountfort Street. Elliot G. Vaughan and William C. Vaughan were the witnesses to this deed." †

About 1836, Benjamin Roberts removed his family to Boston. In the Boston Directory of 1837, his occupation is given as chaise-maker; his home, 4 Stillman Place. The following year, they were living at 6 Province Street, which was a short street running from 30 School Street to Brom-

---

* *Cumberland County Deeds*, Book 119 : 36; Book 118 : 400.

The signatures of Benjamin and Clarissa Roberts in this deed are copies, but the signature of Hannah Roberts, written on the margin after the deeds were copied and bound, is an autograph.

† *Cumberland County Deeds*, Book 125 : 14.

MAHOGANY TABLE, WITH A PLATE OF A SET OF CHINA BROUGHT FROM
LIVERPOOL, ABOUT 1800, BY CAPT. GEORGE ROBERTS

field Street. From 1840 to 1843, inclusive, he was called a wheelwright; but in 1847, 1848, and 1849, he appears as a "carriage maker," * or manufacturer of carriages. Early in 1848, his family was called back to Portland by the illness and death of his sister, Mary Caroline, which left the mother unprotected and alone; Mr. Roberts followed them the next year.

On June 29, 1850, Hannah Roberts conveyed to her son Benjamin "an undivided half" of the estate on Mountfort Street, for $1,000, stipulating that the said Benjamin "shall well & truly support and maintain the said Hannah Roberts who is my mother in sickness and health during her natural life, in my family, & shall in all things treat her, and conduct towards her as a son should, then this, as also a Bond [for $1,000] this day given to support and maintain my mother, given by the said Benjamin Roberts to the said Hannah Roberts . . . shall be void, otherwise remain in full force." The two instruments of the same date were witnessed by Mary C. Roberts, daughter to Benjamin, and by Samuel Fessenden.†

In 1852, this daughter, Mary Caroline⁸ Roberts, was married to Edward A.⁸ Small, and removed to Illinois,‡ but Benjamin Roberts and his wife remained in the old home until after the death of his mother on August 4, 1855, at the advanced age of eighty years. They also had the stone placed upon her grave.§ On September 12, following, they sold to Bethuel Sweetser, of Portland, an "undivided half part" of the lot "with that half of the buildings thereon standing which fronts upon Mountfort Street, said half part being the part which has been occupied by my late Mother Hannah Roberts for more than forty years."

---

* Boston Directories, 1837–1849.
† *Cumberland County Deeds*, Book 225: 59; Book 224: 318.
‡ Vide page 284.
§ Vide page 1088.

1855, was signed:—

Witnesses: "Benjamin Roberts [seal]
"Lucy A. Hartshorn Clarissa Roberts"* [seal]
Jere. Mitchell"

Not long afterward, they removed to Winona, Minnesota, with their eldest son, George, where they remained for a time. The closing years of their lives were spent in the home of their only daughter, Mrs. Mary C. Small, at Geneva, Illinois. Benjamin Roberts died there in February, 1886, aged eighty-two years and six months; his wife Clarissa died in the same place, four years later, in April, 1888, aged eighty-seven years and seven months. They were buried in the family lot of Edward A. Small, at Oakwood Cemetery, Chicago.

ISSUE

I. George Henry[9], b. Oct. 7, 1827, in Portland, Maine; mar. July 27, 1856, in Portland, Maine, Sarah Melvina[9] Small, b. Sept. 2, 1833, in Readfield, Maine, daughter to Dr. Joseph P.[8] and Pamelia (Dolly) Small.† Immediately after their marriage, they removed to Winona, Minnesota, where he engaged in farming. About 1859, he went to Utica, in the same state, but later moved to Minneapolis, where he died Aug. 8, 1905, aged seventy-seven years, ten months. His widow still remains (1908) in Minneapolis.

Issue: 1. Benjamin Edward[9], b. March 21, 1858, in Winona, Minnesota; mar. Aug. 28, 1879, in Minneapolis, Sarah Elizabeth Rutledge, b. April 19, 1858, at Fish Lake, Scott County, Minnesota. Her parents were John Rutledge, b. Jan. 6, 1828, in Mercer County, Ohio, and Belinda (Whipps) Rutledge, b. Dec. 16, 1832, in the same county. In 1906, they were living at Edina Mills, Minnesota. Mr. Benjamin E. Rob-

---

* *Cumberland County Deeds*, Book 266: 266.
† Vide pages 258–260.

erts is a "sheet metal worker;" he resides in Minneapolis.

Issue: I. Sarah Mabel [10], b. May 8, 1881, in Minneapolis; she was mar. Oct. 17, 1900, in Minneapolis, to Hugh Robinson Campbell, b. Aug. 1, 1879, in Pembroke, Maine. He was son to John Colby Campbell, b. April 25, 1848, in Pembroke, Maine, and Eva S. (Clark) Campbell, b. Nov. 26, 1856, in the same town.

Issue: 1. Lora Louise Campbell, b. Dec. 4, 1902, in Minneapolis.

2. Sarah Inez Campbell, b. March 15, 1904, in Minneapolis.

3. Hugh Roberts Campbell, b. Nov. 14, 1905, in Minneapolis.

II. Ralph Benjamin [10], b. June 12, 1884, in Minneapolis; d. Jan. 7, 1890, in Seattle, Washington, aged five years, seven months.

2. George Henry [9], son to George Henry [8] Roberts, b. March 24, 1860, in Utica, Minnesota; mar. April 11, 1889, in Minneapolis, Margaret Florence Butler, born in Finnsville, New Jersey. Her parents, William and Hannah (Strong) Butler, were both born at Upper Black Eddy, Bucks County, Pennsylvania. They live in Minneapolis. No issue.

II. Mary Caroline [8], b. Aug. 7, 1829, in Portland; she was mar. Aug. 10, 1852, in Portland, to Edward Alonzo [8] Small.*

III. Andrew Rose [8], b. Aug. 27, 1835, in Portland. About 1854, he went to the far West, and has never been heard from since. It has been supposed that he was killed by the Indians.

---

* Vide page 284.